T0230331

Lecture Notes in Computer Science 594

Edited by G. Goos and J. Hartmanis

Advisory Board: W. Brauer   D. Gries   J. Stoer

B. Monien   Th. Ottmann (Eds.)

Data Structures and Efficient Algorithms

Final Report on the
DFG Special Joint Initiative

Springer-Verlag

Berlin Heidelberg New York
London Paris Tokyo
Hong Kong Barcelona
Budapest

Series Editors

Gerhard Goos
Universität Karlsruhe
Postfach 69 80
Vincenz-Priessnitz-Straße 1
W-7500 Karlsruhe, FRG

Juris Hartmanis
Department of Computer Science
Cornell University
5149 Upson Hall
Ithaca, NY 14853, USA

Volume Editors

Burkhard Monien
Fachbereich Mathematik/Informatik, Universität-Gesamthochschule Paderborn
Postfach 1621, W-4790 Paderborn, FRG

Thomas Ottmann
Institut für Informatik, Universität Freiburg
Rheinstr. 10–12, W-7800 Freiburg i. Br., FRG

CR Subject Classification (1991): F.2.2, I.3.5, E.5, G.1.0, H.2.8, I.2.1, G.2.2, C.2.1

ISBN 3-540-55488-2 Springer-Verlag Berlin Heidelberg New York
ISBN 0-387-55488-2 Springer-Verlag New York Berlin Heidelberg

Typesetting: Camera ready by author/editor
Printing and binding: Druckhaus Beltz, Hemsbach/Bergstr.
45/3140-543210 - Printed on acid-free paper

Preface

The German Science Foundation (Deutsche Forschungsgemeinschaft, DFG) started a special joint intiative (Schwerpunktprogramm) entitled "Datenstrukturen und effiziente Algorithmen" in 1986. The aim of the initiative was to encourage collaborative research on *algorithms*, a central concept in computer science. For a period of five years about a dozen projects were funded with an emphasis on algorithms and data structures for *geometric problems*, on the one hand, and *parallel and distributed algorithms*, on the other.

The first group of projects addressed research on fundamental data structures, computational geometry, graph algorithms, computer graphics, and spatial databases. The second group of projects centered around the following problems: the design of parallel architectures and routing strategies, simulation of parallel machines, and the design of distributed algorithms for solving difficult problems.

The initiative has proven to be very successful. Within the last five years numerous results were obtained by the research groups taking part in the initiative. The results were presented at national and international conferences as well as at the annual DFG symposium organized by the iniative participants. Most of the papers in this volume were presented during the final symposium held at the Freie Universität Berlin, Sept. 23–26, 1991, organized by H. Alt and E. Welzl.

The 18 papers contained in this volume are intended to give an impression of the achievements of this joint research initiative. They either survey some of the results obtained by a research group or present single results falling into the scope of the initiative.

As coordinators of this joint initiative we would like to thank all who contributed to this volume. We would, in particular, also like to thank the referees for their help in evaluating the projects. Finally, we greatly acknowledge the financial support of the DFG.

Paderborn and Freiburg, March 1992 B. Monien, Th. Ottmann

Contents

Parallel and Distributed Algorithms

Resemblance and Symmetries of Geometric Patterns

Helmut Alt   Johannes Blömer *

Abstract

· This article is a survey on research done in recent years at FU Berlin applying methods from Computational Geometry to problems in pattern and shape analysis. In particular, algorithms are described for determining the exact and approximate *congruence* of finite sets of points in the plane. This problem is generalized to polygonal curves in the plane, where variuos cases are considered depending on the set of rigid motions (translations, rotations) allowed to match the given curves. Furthermore, algorithms are given for *approximating* convex polygons by "simpler" curves. In addition, the problem of finding all *symmetries* of a finite set of points is considered, the approximate version of which turns out to be NP-complete in general.

1   Introduction

A standard problem occurring in areas such as Computer Vision or Pattern and Shape Analysis and Recognition can informally be stated as follows:

Given two figures or shapes, how much do they 'resemble each other'?

Up to now this problem has mostly been solved quite successfully by numerical methods using, for example, the discrete Fourier transform. These methods not only work for black-and-white objects, but also for images consisting of many different gray-levels. For objects with a more geometric structure, however, it should be useful to design algorithms analyzing that structure and possibly using methods and paradigms from the field of Computational Geometry. In this article we will give a survey on research in this direction done at Freie Universität Berlin within the past few years. We will state the most important results and give a few sketches of their proofs in order to show the underlying ideas and techniques. For more details, we refer the reader to the original papers [ABB, ABGW, AMWW, G1, G2, I].

If, in the problem stated above, a perfect resemblance of the two objects is wanted, this means geometrically *congruence*. We will describe congruence finding algorithms for finite sets of points in arbitrary dimensions in section 2. But these results only have a theoretical significance, since in order to solve nontrivial instances of the congruence problem, it must be assumed that there are no round-off errors in the data and that our

---

*Fachbereich Mathematik, FU Berlin, Arnimallee 2-6, W-1000 Berlin 33, Germany

model of computation can represent and process arbitrary real numbers exactly. So a more realistic formulation of the problem is to ask for *approximate congruence*, i.e. congruence with a certain tolerable error bound. We developed various algorithms for this problem in the case of point sets, depending on what kind of motions are allowed to 'match' the two sets and whether an assignment of the points to each other is known in advance or not.

Closely related to the congruence problem is the problem of determining all *symmetries* of a geometric object, i.e. its symmetry group. We address this problem for finite point sets in section 2. Again it is easy to solve for the exact case with a model of computation capable of exact real arithmetc. The approximate version of the problem, however, turned out to be NP-complete. Nevertheless, polynomial time algorithms can be found, if the points are not too close together compared to the given tolerance bound.

For more sophisticated geometric objects than point sets, like, for example, *curves*, even the exact formulation of our question stated in the beginning becomes problematic. What is the 'distance' between two curves P, Q? We considered three different distance measures:

What seems most natural, is the *Hausdorff-metric*, $\delta_H(P, Q)$ and in most cases, it is an appropriate measure. However, there are examples of curves looking completely different and, nevertheless, having a small Hausdorff-distance. Therefore, we also consider the so-called *Fréchet-metric* $\delta_F(P, Q)$ which is compatible with parametrizations of the curves. In addition, for closed simple curves P, Q the *symmetric difference* $\delta_S(P, Q)$ between the two areas encircled by the curves is a possible distance measure.

Here we will consider *polygonal* curves. In section 3 algorithms will be given for *computing* $\delta_F(P, Q)$ and $\delta_H(P, Q)$ for polygonal chains P, Q. For the Hausdorff-metric we will also give algorithms for the *matching problem*, which means finding a rigid motion to match P and Q as good as possible, i.e. to minimize their distance. Again, algorithms will be designed for the general problem and for special cases, for example, that only translations are allowed as motions. These algorithms, although polynomial, are quite slow. Much more efficient ones can be found, if not necessarily the optimal match is sought, but a *pseudo-optimal* one, i.e. one which is only by a constant factor worse than the optimum.

Another problem we address, is the *approximation* of polygonal chains by ones with a smaller number of edges or by simpler curves. For the δ_S-metric a very efficient algorithm can be found for optimally approximating convex polygons by axes-parallel rectangles. δ_H and δ_F can be shown to be essentially identical in the case of convex curves. Efficient algorithms will be given for approximating pseudo-optimally convex n-gons by convex k-gons ($k < n$).

2 Congruence, Similarity and Symmetry

In this section we consider the following problems which occur for example in Computer Vision and Pattern Recognition:

(i) Given two finite point sets A, B in $\mathbf{R}^d$, decide whether these sets are congruent or similar.

(ii) Given a finite point set A in $\mathbf{R}^d$, determine its symmetry group.

Here a *congruence* is any mapping μ that preserves distances, therefore μ can be represented as

$$\mu(x) = Ax + t,$$

where A is an orthogonal matrix, i.e., $A^T = A^{-1}$, and t is some vector in $\mathbf{R}^d$. From $A^T = A^{-1}$ it follows $|\det A| = 1$. We say that μ is of the first (second) kind if $\det A = 1 (\det A = -1)$. Any congruence of the second kind can be written as $x \mapsto AJx$, where $Jx = J(x_1, \ldots, x_d) = (-x_1, x_2, \ldots, x_d)$ and A is of the first kind. Furthermore a mapping $x \mapsto \lambda x$, for some $\lambda \in \mathbf{R}, \lambda \neq 0$, is called a *dilation* (or stretching). A *similarity* is a congruence followed by a dilation.

Observe that the exact congruence, similarity and symmetry problem as stated above are not realistic in practice and, strictly speaking, they are ill-posed. In fact, small perturbations in the input data will destroy congruences, similarities, and symmetries. In order to allow inaccuracies in the input data in [AMWW] the notion of ϵ-approximate congruence, and symmetry has been introduced which we are now going to define. We will not give the original definition of [AMWW] but the equivalent definition of [I]. We start with

Definition 1 *Let $A = \{a_1, \ldots, a_n\}$ be a set of n points in $\mathbf{R}^d$. $A' = \{a'_1, \ldots, a'_n\}$ is in the ϵ-neighborhood of A if there is a one-to-one correspondence between the points of A and A' (w.l.o.g. let a'_i correspond to a_i) such that a'_i lies in the ϵ-neighborhood of a_i.*

Now we define ϵ-approximate congruence and ϵ-approximate symmetry groups.

Definition 2 *Two point sets $A, B \subset \mathbf{R}^d$ of n points each are called ϵ-approximately congruent if and only if there exist point sets A' and B' in the respective neighborhoods of A and B that are exactly congruent.*

Definition 3 *S is called an ϵ-approximate symmetry group of A if S is a symmetry group of some point set A' in the ϵ-neighborhood of A.*

With respect to ϵ-approximate congruence and ϵ-approximate symmetry we may ask two different kinds of questions. First there are the so-called *decision problems*. That is, given ϵ, A, and B, decide whether A and B are ϵ-approximately congruent or, given ϵ, A and a symmetry group S, decide whether S is an ϵ-approximate symmetry group of A. Second there are the so-called *optimization problems*. That is, given point sets A and B, find the smallest ϵ such that A and B are ϵ-approximate congruent. Or, given a point set A and a symmetry group S, find the smallest ϵ such that S is an ϵ-approximate symmetry group of A.

Before we can actually investigate these problems we have to say a word about the model of computation. For the exact congruence and the exact symmetry group problem (for this problem see also below) in [AMWW] a RAM has been assumed that can perform exact real arithmetic. For the approximate congruence a RAM has been assumed that can represent integers of length at most L, for some constant L. Furthermore additions and multiplications can be performed in constant time. The input data are given in the form p/q, where p and q integers of length at most L. Note that the time bounds derived under this model of computation are not equivalent to the bit-complexity of the problem. This is because L does not show up in the running time bounds. The bit-complexity of the ϵ-approximate congruence has been considered in [S]. The bit-complexity of the ϵ-approximate symmetry problem in the plane has been investigated in [I], where a model of computation has been used that is polynomially related to the Turing machine. We remark that assuming rational coordinates makes the exact symmetry problem trivial because then only finitely many symmetry groups are possible for any finite point set A.

With these definitions and remarks we can start to state the results in [AMWW] and [I] and sketch their proofs. Let us begin with the exact congruence and exact symmetry problem.

Theorem 4 ([AMWW]) a) For any $d \geq 3$ the congruence of two n-points sets in $\mathbf{R}^d$ can be decided in $\mathcal{O}\left(n^{d-2}\log n\right)$ time.

b) The symmetry group of an n-point set in $\mathbf{R}^3$ can be determined in $\mathcal{O}(n\log n)$ time.

Sketch of Proof:

a) We describe an algorithm that decides whether there exists a congruence of the first kind between A and B. Applying this algorithm to the point sets A and $J(B)$ tests whether there exists a congruence of the second kind. For a point set A denote by c_A the centroid (center of mass) of A, i.e., $c_A = \left(\sum_{a \in A} a_i / |A|\right)$. We observe that any congruence (or similarity) between point sets A and B must map c_A onto c_B.

For $d = 3$ the following algorithm is applied:

Algorithm 1:

Step 1: Determine the centroids c_A, c_B. If $c_A \in A$, then check if $c_B \in B$. If not give a negative answer, otherwise remove c_A, c_B from A, B, respectively.

Step 2: Project all points of $A(B)$ onto the unit sphere using $c_A(c_B)$ as an origin. Mark the points in the sets $A'(B')$ obtained this way with the distances of the original points from $c_A(c_B)$. Observe, that one point of the sphere can be the image of several points of $A(B)$ and, thus, be marked with several distances. In this case, sort these distances.

Step 3: Construct the convex hulls of A', B'. Observe that all points in A', B' are extreme and therefore vertices of the convex hulls. Let v be any such vertex, and let $v_0, v_1, \ldots, v_{k-1}$ be the vertices adjacent to v listed in clockwise fashion about v. For $0 \leq i \leq k-1$ let l_i be the length of the arc from v to v_i and φ_i the angle on the sphere between v_i, v and $v_{(i+1)\bmod k}$. In addition to the information attached in Step 2 mark v with the lexicographically smallest cyclic shift of the sequence $(\varphi_0, l_0), \ldots, (\varphi_{k-1}, l_{k-1})$.

Step 4: The convex hulls together with the labels attached in Step 2 and Step 3 can be considered as planar graphs [PS]. Now the two input sets are congruent if the two labeled graphs are isomorphic. Whether the labeled graphs are isomorphic is decided by a variant of the partitioning algorithm of Section 4.13 in [AHU]. For the details the reader is referred to [AMWW].

Analysis: Step 1 as well as the construction of the sets A', B' take linear time. The sorting in Step 2 may take $\mathcal{O}(n \log n)$ time. Also in $\mathcal{O}(n \log n)$ time the convex hulls can be constructed. For proofs that the smallest cyclic shifts can be computed in time $\mathcal{O}(n \log n)$ and that the graph isomorphism algorithm works in $\mathcal{O}(n \log n)$ time, we refer to [AMWW] and [AHU].

For arbitrary dimension d the following algorithm is applied:

Algorithm 2:

If $d \leq 3$ Algorithm 1 is applied, otherwise the d-dimensional problem is reduced to n problems of dimension $(d-1)$ in the following way:

Step 1: Construct the labeled sets A', B' as in Step 2 of Algorithm 1.

Step 2: For some point $a \in A'$ intersect the d-dimensional unit sphere S_A around c_A with some hyperplane which orthogonally bisects the line segment $\overline{c_A a}$. The intersection will be some $(d-1)$-dimensional sphere S on the surface of S_A. Project each point $x \in A' - \{a\}$ onto S along the arc from x to a on the surface of S_A. This yields a new set A''. To each $x'' \in A''$ attach the following information: from each $x' \in A'$, which was projected onto x'', the label obtained in previous steps of the algorithm and, additionally, the length of the arc from a to x'. If there are several points in A' which are projected onto x'', list their labels sorted with respect to the lengths of the arcs. A'' still contains all the geometric information necessary to identify the original set A.

Step 3: Do the same construction as in Step 2 for all points of B, yielding labeled point sets $B_1'', \ldots, B_n''$.

Step 4: The sets $A'', B_i''(i = 1, \ldots, n)$ are subsets of $(d-1)$-dimensional hyperplanes. Transform them by an isometric mapping into subsets $A''', B_i'''(i = 1, \ldots, n)$ of $\mathbf{R}^{d-1}$ and apply this algorithm recursively to each pair $A''', B_i'''(i = 1, \ldots, n)$. It is easy to see that the original sets A, B are exactly congruent if there is a label preserving congruence from A''' into at least one of the sets $B_1''', \ldots, B_n'''$.

Analysis: Steps 1 and 2 may take $\mathcal{O}(n \log n)$ time because of the sorting of labels. Step 3 takes time $\mathcal{O}(n \log n)$ for each $B_i''(i = 1, \ldots, n)$, i.e., $\mathcal{O}(n^2 \log n)$ altogether. The transformations in Step 4 take linear time, the recursive calls take n times the run time of the $(d-1)$-dimensional problem. This is, certainly for $d \geq 4$, the most significant term and, since Algorithm 1 runs in time $\mathcal{O}(n \log n)$ for $d = 3$, we get a total run time of $\mathcal{O}(n^{d-2} \log n)$.

b) The proof of part b) is based on the following theorem (cf. [M]):

Theorem 5 (Hessel's Theorem) *Any finite symmetry group for a subset of* $\mathbf{R}^3$ *is one of the following groups:*

(a) *The rotation groups* $T, \ C, \ I$ *of the platonic solids tetrahedron, cube, and icosahedron, respectively.*

(b) *The cyclic groups* C_n, $n = 1, 2, \ldots$, *and the dihedral groups* D_n, $n = 2, 3, \ldots$.

(c) *The groups* $\overline{T}$, $\overline{C}$, $\overline{I}$, $\overline{C_1}$, $\overline{C_2}, \ldots, \overline{D_2}$, $\overline{D_3}, \ldots$, *where* $\overline{G}$ *denotes the group generated by G and a reflection at a point (inversion).*

(d) *The groups* CT, $C_{2n}C_n$, $D_{2n}D_n$, D_nC_n, $n = 2, 3, \ldots$, *where* GH *denotes the group* $H \cup (G - H) \circ i$ *where i is an inversion.*

Now the algorithm that computes the symmetry group of a point set A applies Algorithm 1 to the input pairs (A, A) and $(A, J(A))$ to compute the orbits of all points in A under the symmetry group. Once these orbits are known using Theorem 5 the symmetry group can be determined. For details see [AMWW]. □

Finally we remark that the question whether two point sets are *similar* can be reduced to the question whether two point sets are congruent. In fact, if A and B are given, and $m_A(m_B)$ denotes the maximum distance of a point in $A(B)$ to the centroid $C_A(C_B)$. Then A and B are similar if and only if A and B' are congruent, where B' is obtained by stretching B around C_B by a factor of m_A/m_B.

Let us now turn to the version of the problem, which is more realistic in practice, namely determining whether two point sets in the plane are *approximately* congruent. As we mentioned above here we have to consider two different kinds of problems, decision and optimization problems. Furthermore, in both cases we may consider various restrictions. For example, we may consider translations or rotations only, we may consider different metrics (the notion of neighborhood assumes some kind of metric in $\mathbf{R}^d$), we may be guaranteed that there is some lower bound on the distances between points in A and B, we may know a labeling in advance, that is, we know which points in A and B are to be mapped into each others neighborhood.

In [AMWW] polynomial time algorithms have been derived for various combinations of these restrictions. The most general version that has been solved in polynomial time in [AMWW] is the above mentioned decision problem with no restrictions at all on the allowed congruences, the point sets and the labeling. It applies to both the euclidean metric and the maximum metric and its running-time is $\mathcal{O}(n^8)$. For a complete overview of the results in [AMWW] we refer to Theorem 3 in that article. As an example of the methods used we show how to decide for given point sets A, B and an $\epsilon > 0$ whether there is an ϵ-approximate translation between A and B.

Theorem 6 ([AMWW]) *Let A, B be point sets of n points in the plane. For given $\epsilon > 0$ it can be decided in time $\mathcal{O}(n^6)$ whether there exists a translation that maps some point set B' in the $\epsilon-neighborhood$ of B into the $\epsilon-neighborhood$ of A.*

Proof:

Algorithm 3: It is not hard to see that if there is any ϵ-approximate translation at all then there is one that maps some point b_j on a circle C_i of radius 2ϵ around some point a_i $(1 \leq i, j \leq n)$. The algorithm checks this property for all pairs. For a fixed pair (i, j) the algorithm works as follows:

Assume a_i is the origin. Describe any position of b_j on C_i by polar coordinates. If we consider all possible translations mapping b_j onto C_i, the set of possible images of each point b_l, $l \neq j$, is some circle K_l. For $m \neq i$, we determine the set $I_{m,l}$ of angles $\varphi \in [0, 2\pi[$ such that if the image of b_j has polar coordinate φ then the image of b_l is contained in the 2ϵ-neighborhood of a_m. $I_{m,l}$ is an interval of $[0, 2\pi[$. We compute all endpoints of intervals $I_{m,l}, m \neq i, l \neq j$, and sort them. These endpoints determine a partition of $[0, 2\pi[$ into subintervals such that any subinterval I is contained in some $I_{m,l}$. For each I we build a graph

$$G_I = (V, E_I), \quad V = \{a_i, \ldots, a_{i-1}, a_{i+1}, \ldots, a_n\} \cup \{b_i, \ldots, b_{j-1}, b_{j+1}, \ldots, b_n\},$$

$$E_I = \{(a_m, b_l)|I \subseteq I_{m,l}\}.$$

G_I is a bipartite graph. Now there is a translation mapping b_j on the circle around a_i if and only if for some I G_I has a perfect matching. Therefore in the last step of the algorithm known algorithms are used to determine whether some G_I has a perfect matching.

Analysis. A straightforward analysis shows that the running-time of the algorithm for a fixed pair (i, j) is $\mathcal{O}(n^4)$. Therefore the overall running-time is $\mathcal{O}(n^6)$.

$\square$

In [I] based on a generalization of Megiddo's Linear Programming algorithm to convex functions several other special cases of the approximate congruence problem were shown to be solvable in polynomial time. In some cases these algorithms are even asymptotically optimal.

An efficient "approximate" decision algorithm for the general case assuming that the ϵ-neighborhoods of the points are disjoint can be found in [B]. "Approximate" means that the algorithm does not have to find the correct answer, if the given tolerance bound is close to the optimal ϵ_{opt}, as long as it works correctly for, say, $\epsilon < (1/\alpha)\epsilon_{opt}$ or $\epsilon > \alpha\epsilon_{opt}$ for some constant $\alpha > 1$.

Meanwhile, new results on point pattern matching have been obtained by researchers outside of our group: In [ISI] more efficient algorithms are given for the case that the assignment of the points in the set B to the ones in A is already given. In [HS] approximate decision algorithms are studied in detail and efficient methods are found using network flow algorithms. In [AKMSW] the notion of ϵ-neighborhoods is generalized to arbitrary convex "noise regions".

The main contribution of [I] was to show that the approximate *symmetry* problem in the plane is in general NP-complete. To give a more precise statement of the result we need the following well-known theorem (see [M]):

Theorem 7 *Any symmetry group of a finite point set in the plane is either C_k, $k = 1, 2, \ldots$, or $D_k, k = 1, 2, \ldots$. Here C_k is the cyclic group generated by a rotation with angle $2\pi/k$ and D_k is the group generated by C_k and a reflection at a line.*

We now can state the NP-completeness result in its correct form:

Theorem 8 ([I]) *The following decision problems are NP-complete: Given a finite point set A in the plane, some $\epsilon > 0$ and a fixed symmetry group S of the form $C_k, k \geq 3$, or $D_k, k \geq 2$.*
Decide whether there is a set A' in the ϵ-neighborhood of A with symmetry group S.

Below we will sketch a proof that the decision problem for the groups C_k is NP-hard. But first let us state the results for the symmetry groups C_1, C_2, D_1.

Theorem 9 ([I]) *The above mentioned decision problems for the groups C_1, C_2, D_1 are solvable in polynomial time.*

Moreover in [I] it has been shown that under certain restrictions all decision problems are in P. In fact, if we call the point set A δ-*disjoint*, if any two points in A have distance more than δ then the following theorem holds.

Theorem 10 ([I]) *Suppose that the point set A is 8ϵ-disjoint then the ϵ-approximate symmetry decision problem can be solved for any symmetry group C_k, D_k in polynomial time.* $\square$

We now outline the reduction that shows that the decision problem for the groups $C_k, k \geq 3$, is NP-hard. For the details and proofs we refer to Section 4 of [I].

To describe the reduction we need some notations. By a *grid* we understand a rectangle divided by equidistant parallel line segments in both directions. The *width* of a grid is the distance between two adjacent parallel line segments, its *size* the total number of intersection points of the line segments. Next we describe a well-known NP-complete problem:

Problem Planar 3-SAT:
Instance: A Boolean formula $\Phi = c_1 \wedge c_2 \wedge \ldots \wedge c_m$. Each c_i is a clause of the form $c_i = l_{i_1} \vee l_{i_2} \vee l_{i_3}$. Each l_{i_k} is a variable u_j or its negation $\overline{u_j}$ from a set $U = \{u_1, \ldots, u_n\}$. The set of clauses is denoted by $C = \{c_1, \ldots, c_m\}$. Formula Φ is planar, i.e., the bipartite graph $G = (U \cup C, E)$ is planar, where E contains exactly those pairs $\{u, c\} \in U \times C$ such that literal u or $\overline{u}$ belongs to clause c.
Question: Is there a truth assignment for U that satisfies Φ?

The symmetry group problem will not be reduced directly to Planar 3-SAT but we need an intermediate problem, the so-called kD-Disc-Matching.

Problem kD-Disc-Matching:
Instance: A set D of n closed discs in the plane each assigned with one of k colors, where k divides n.
Question: Does there exist a partitioning of D into $\frac{n}{k}$ disjoint sets D_i, such that each D_i consists of k differently colored discs that have a common intersection?

In Step 1 of the reduction it is shown how to construct for a planar formula Φ a k-colored set $D(\Phi, \epsilon, k)$ of $\mathcal{O}(k(n + m)^2)$ discs with radius ϵ and centers on a grid in the plane of width $\frac{\epsilon}{4}$ and size $\mathcal{O}(n + m) \times \mathcal{O}(n + m)$[1] such that Φ is satisfiable if and only if $D(\Phi, \epsilon, k)$ has a kd-disc-matching.

Step 2 of the reduction almost establishes an equivalence between kd-disc-matching and finding an approximate symmetry group. It is shown that, given instance $D(\epsilon, k)$ of

---

[1] Actually there are more restrictions that $D(\Phi, \epsilon, k)$ has to obey, but these are of purely technical nature so we may disregard them here.

the kd-disc-matching problem consisting of discs with equal radius ϵ and centers on an appropriate grid in the euclidean plane, a set $A_{(0,0)}(\epsilon, C_k)$ of n points can be constructed such that the following conditions are equivalent:

a) The disc set $D(\epsilon, k)$ has a kd-disc-matching.

b) In the ϵ-neighborhood of $A_{(0,0)}(\epsilon, C_k)$ there is a set $A'_{(0,0)}(\epsilon, C_k)$ with centroid exactly $(0,0)$ and symmetry group C_k.

c) In the ϵ-neighborhood of the point set $A_{(0,0)}(\epsilon, C_k)$ there is a set $A'_{(0,0)}(\epsilon, C_k)$ with centroid in the $\frac{c}{4}$-neighborhood of $(0,0)$ and symmetry group C_k.

This reduction only almost establishes the desired equivalence because of the restriction on the centroid of $A'_{(0,0)}(\epsilon, C_k)$. So far we cannot guarantee that any solution to the symmetry group problem will lead to a solution of the kd-disc-matching. This is true only if the set A' in the neighborhood of A has almost the same centroid as A, which need not be true in general. In the last step of the algorithm it is shown how to fix the centroid by adding $2k$ points. In more detail, for the output set $A_{(0,0)}(\epsilon, C_k)$ of Step 2 a set $F(\epsilon, C_k)$ of $2k$ points is constructed such that for $F(\epsilon, C_k)$ and $A(\epsilon, C_k) = A_{(0,0)}(\epsilon, C_k) \cup F(\epsilon, C_k)$ the following is true:

(1) There is a set in the ϵ-neighborhood of $F(\epsilon, C_k)$ with centroid $(0,0)$ and symmetry group C_k.

(2) Any set in the ϵ-neighborhood of $F(\epsilon, C_k)$ with symmetry group C_k has its centroid in the $\frac{c}{4}\epsilon$-neighborhood of $(0,0)$ for some constant $c > 0$.

(3) If there exists a set $A'(\epsilon, C_k)$ in the ϵ-neighborhood of $A(\epsilon, C_k)$ with symmetry group C_k then each orbit of $A'(\epsilon, C_k)$ consists either of elements of $A'_{(0,0)}(\epsilon, C_k)$ (corresponding to the subset $A_{(0,0)}(\epsilon, C_k)$) only or of elements of $F'(\epsilon, C_k)$ (corresponding to the other subset $F(\epsilon, C_k)$) only.

By property (3) $A'_{(0,0)}(\epsilon, C_k)$ and $F'(\epsilon, C_k)$ separately have symmetry group C_k. Furthermore, (2) forces the centroid of any set $A'(\epsilon, C_k)$ in the ϵ-neighborhood of $A(\epsilon, C_k)$ to be contained in the $\frac{c}{4}\epsilon$-neighborhood of $(0,0)$. Using these observations the following lemma that establishes the equivalence of approximate symmetry group and kd-disc-matching is not hard to prove:

Lemma 11 ([I]) *The point set $A(\epsilon, C_k)$ has C_k as an ϵ-approximate symmetry group if and only if the disc set $D(\epsilon, k)$ has a kd-disc-matching. Further, we know that if these conditions are satisfied, then there is a set $A'(\epsilon, C_k)$ in the ϵ-neighborhood of $A(\epsilon, C_k)$ with symmetry group C_k and centroid exactly $(0,0)$.*

Furthermore it is shown in [I] that the three steps of the reduction from Planar 3-SAT to approximate symmetry group can be performed in polynomial time on a deterministic Turing machine. Therefore we have

Theorem 12 ([I]) *The following problem is NP-hard: Given a finite point set $A \subset \mathbf{R}^2, \epsilon > 0$, and a fixed group of the form $C_k, k \geq 3$. Decide whether A has ϵ-approximate symmetry group C_k.* □

As was mentioned above this result can be extended to the groups D_k, $k \geq 2$. It is also shown that the approximate symmetry group problem can be solved in polynomial time on a non-deterministic Turing machine. The algorithm guesses the orbit of any point of A under the symmetry in question. This algorithm together with the previous theorem shows that in general the approximate symmetry group problem is NP-complete. This is a rather surprising result if we compare it with the corresponding results on the approximate congruence problem. There almost everything can be solved in polynomial time, here almost everything is NP-hard.

We conclude this section by a summary of the results we mentioned:

The exact congruence problem can be solved in $\mathcal{O}(n^{d-2} \log n)$ time in dimension d. The exact symmetry group problem can be solved in $\mathcal{O}(n \log n)$ time in $\mathbf{R}^3$. For the plane several restricted versions of the approximate congruence problem can be solved in polynomial time. On the other hand the approximate symmetry group problem in general is NP-complete. Only if some restrictions (8ϵ-disjointness) are imposed on the point set A can the symmetry group be determined in polynomial-time.

3 Computing the Distance for Geometric Objects, Matching and Approximation Algorithms

In the first section we compared geometric objects (point sets in $\mathbf{R}^d$) by considering their inner geometric structure. In this section we generalize that approach to the problem of measuring the resemblance of other geometric objects. More specifically assume that a certain class $\mathcal{C}$ of geometric objects is given, for example convex polygons, simple polygons or parametrized curves (see below). Furthermore suppose that some metric is defined between objects in this class. Then the problem is to compute the distance of two given objects in $\mathcal{C}$. Moreover, one can try to approximate a given element in $\mathcal{C}$ by elements of a subclass of $\mathcal{C}$. For example one can try to approximate a simple n-gon by a simple k-gon for $k < n$. In [ABB], [ABGW], [G1], [G2] both problems have been considered for various metrics. In this section we will first define these metrics and then present some theoretical results and algorithms for the problems described above.

3.1 The Metrics

The first metric is defined for convex polygons P_1, P_2. It is the area of the *symmetric difference* of P_1 and P_2 and is denoted by $\delta_S(P_1, P_2)$. The second metric, the well-known *Hausdorff-distance*, is defined for arbitrary point sets P_1 and P_2. We will use this metric for simple polygons, or, more generally, for sets of line segments. To define this metric denote by $d(.,.)$ the euclidean distance in the plane. Then

$$\delta_H(P_1, P_2) := \max \left(\sup_{a \in P_1} \inf_{b \in P_2} d(a, b), \sup_{b \in P_2} \inf_{a \in P_1} d(a, b) \right).$$

Unfortunately, there are cases where the Hausdorff-distance may give a totally wrong picture of the resemblance between simple polygons as can be seen from the Figure 1.

This is due to the fact that the Hausdorff-metric ignores the course of the polygonal chain. To take care of this course the so-called *Fréchet-metric* δ_F has been introduced.

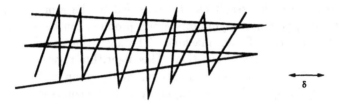

Figure 1: Two curves with Hausdorff-distance δ

This metric applies to pairs of parametrized curves in $\mathbf{R}^d$, d arbitrary. We recall the definition of a parametrized curve:

Two continuous mappings $C_1 : [a, b] \rightarrow \mathbf{R}^d, a, b \in \mathbf{R}$ and $C_2 : [a', b'] \rightarrow \mathbf{R}^d, a', b' \in \mathbf{R}$ are called equivalent iff there exists a continuous, surjective, strictly increasing mapping $\alpha : [a, b] \mapsto [a', b']$ such that $C_1(t) = C_2(\alpha(t))$ for all $t \in [a, b]$. Now a curve is an equivalence class of mappings.

For any curve there exist representatives that are defined on the interval $[0, 1]$. In the sequel we specify an equivalence always by such a representative.

The Fréchet-metric δ_F is defined as follows.

Definition 13 *Let $C_1 : [0, 1] \rightarrow \mathbf{R}^d$ and $C_2 : [0, 1] \rightarrow \mathbf{R}^d$ be curves. Then the Fréchet-metric*

$$\delta_F(C_1, C_2) := \inf_{\alpha, \beta} \max_{t \in [0,1]} d(C_1(\alpha(t)), C_2(\beta(t))$$

where $\alpha : [0, 1] \rightarrow [0, 1], \beta : [0, 1] \rightarrow [0, 1]$ are continuous, surjective and increasing.

Due to the fact that α, β need not be strictly increasing it can be shown that the infimum will be assumed. Furthermore, it should be mentioned that for closed curves a more general definition may be applied in which no points on C_1 and C_2 are fixed as start- and endpoint like $C_i(0)$ and $C_i(1)$ in the definition above, but in this survey we restrict ourselves to Definition 14.

One can illustrate the Fréchet-metric as follows: Suppose a woman is walking her dog. The woman walking on C_1, the dog on C_2. $\delta_F(C_1, C_2)$ is the minimal length of a leash that is possible.

3.2 δ_S-Approximation Algorithms for Convex Polygons

In this subsection we consider the following problem: Given a convex polygon in the plane, approximate it by a much simpler object, for example a circle or a rectangle using δ_S as distance measure. The following definition and lemma proved to be very useful.

Definition 14 *Let F be a figure, C a curve whose arc-length is well defined. Let ℓ_0, ℓ_i, ℓ_b be the total arc-lengths of the portions of C lying outside, inside, and on the boundary of F, respectively. Then C is called <u>balanced</u> with respect to F, iff $|\ell_0 - \ell_i| \leq \ell_b$.*

Lemma 15 ([ABGW]) *Let F be some arbitrary figure. Let $\mathcal{A}$ be a set of figures, $A \in \mathcal{A}$, and C some curve segment of A's boundary. Then for the cases described below, A approximates F optimally, only if C is balanced with respect to F.*

(a) $\mathcal{A}$ the set of simple polygons or convex polygons, C any edge of A.

(b) $\mathcal{A}$ the set of disks or disks around some fixed center M, C the circle bounding A.

(c) $\mathcal{A}$ the set of rectangles or axes-parallel rectangles, C any edge of A.

Based on Lemma 15 the following results have been obtained in [ABGW].

Theorem 16 ([ABGW])   *a) For a convex polygon with n vertices given in clockwise order the optimally approximating axes-parallel rectangle can be found in time $\mathcal{O}(\log^3 n)$.*

b) Given a convex polygon P and a point $M \in \mathbf{R}^2$ that circle C with center M which optimally approximates P can be found with a precision of L bits in time $\mathcal{O}(n \log np(L))$ bit operations where p is some polynomial. It is assumed that input coordinates can be represented by $\leq L$ bits.

c) Given a convex polygon P, radius and center of the optimally approximating circle C can be found in time $\mathcal{O}(n^5 \log np(L))$, where p and L have the same meaning as in part b).

We do not want to present the rather complicated proof of this theorem here, instead the reader is referred to [ABGW].

3.3 δ_H and δ_F-Approximations for convex polygons

We begin by analyzing the relation between the Hausdorff- and the Fréchet-metric. In [ABGW] it has been shown that for convex polygons the Hausdorff-metric and the Fréchet-metric are basically the same. To justify this statement observe first that the Hausdorff-distance between two convex polygons will be assumed at two boundary points. So we may consider a convex polygon as the set of its boundary points only. Now the following theorem has been proved in [ABGW].

Theorem 17 ([ABGW]) *Let P_1, P_2 be convex polygons with $\delta_H(P_1, P_2) = \epsilon$. Suppose $\alpha : [0, 1] \to \mathbf{R}^2$ is a parametrization of the boundary of P_1. Then a parametrization $\beta : [0, 1] \longmapsto \mathbf{R}^2$ of the boundary of P_2 exists such that $d(\alpha(t), \beta(t)) \leq \epsilon$ for all $t \in [0, 1]$.* $\square$

This theorem does not necessarily say $\delta_F = \delta_H$ (obviously $\delta_H \leq \delta_F$) because it assumes that no specific starting point for the parametrization β of C_2 bas been fixed in advance, while for δ_F it is assumed that parametrizations of P_1 and P_2 and, therefore, that starting points have been specified [2]. But on the other hand the theorem does say that in a way

---

[2]As was mentioned above, in [G1] a definition of δ_F for polygons has been given that takes into account any parametrization of the boundary regardless of the start- and endpoints. With respect to this definition the above theorem says $\delta_F = \delta_H$.

for convex polygons δ_H also reflects the course of the boundaries. Justified by this result, in the sequel we will only consider the δ_H-metric for convex polygons, however, the results apply to δ_F as well.

In [ABGW] the concept of a *pseudo-optimal algorithm* for approximation problems with respect to the Hausdorff-metric has been introduced, which proved to be very useful. The idea is not to compute the best possible approximation with a rather inefficient algorithm but to compute an approximation that is almost as good as the optimal approximation. In a sense an approximation to an optimal approximation is computed [3]. More specifically:

Suppose we want to approximate an element P of a class $\mathcal{C}$ of geometric objects by an element of a subclass $\mathcal{S}$ of $\mathcal{C}$, where some metric δ is given between objects in $\mathcal{C}$. Furthermore suppose that Q_{opt} is some element in $\mathcal{S}$ that optimally approximates P and that $\delta(P, Q_{\mathrm{opt}}) = \epsilon_{\mathrm{opt}}$. Then

Definition 18 *An algorithm is said to be pseudo-optimal or to produce a pseudo-optimal solution (approximation) if it finds an element $Q \in \mathcal{S}$ such that $\delta(P, Q) \le c\epsilon_{opt}$, where $c \ge 1$ is some constant, i.e. does not depend on P.*

As a first example for a pseudo-optimal algorithm we have:

Theorem 19 ([ABGW]) *Let P be a convex polygon with n vertices and let $\epsilon_{opt} = \min\limits_{R\ rectangle} \{\delta_H(P, R)\}$. A rectangle R_0 with $\delta_H(P, R_0) \le \sqrt{2}\epsilon_{opt}$ can be computed in time $\mathcal{O}(n)$.*

Proof: Let ϵ_0 be the minimal Hausdorff-distance between P and an *enclosing* rectangle of P. It is easily seen that:

$$\epsilon_0 \le (1 + \sqrt{2})\epsilon_{\mathrm{opt}}$$

Now we claim that given an optimal enclosing rectangle of P we can easily find a rectangle R_0 with $\delta_H(R_0, P) \le (2 - \sqrt{2})\epsilon_0$. Since $\epsilon_0 \le (1 + \sqrt{2})\epsilon_{\mathrm{opt}}$, we obtain: $\delta_H(P, R_0) \le \sqrt{2}\epsilon_{\mathrm{opt}}$, so R_0 is the desired rectangle. To prove our claim let R be an optimal enclosing rectangle. We move each side of R parallel inwards by $(\sqrt{2} - 1)\epsilon_0$. As is shown in Figure 2 there are three cases to consider. In cases I, II we only have to consider the distance between a point p on ∂P and its nearest neighbor $\omega(p)$ on R. In case III we have to determine the distance between a point p on R and its nearest neighbor $\omega(p)$ on ∂P. It is easily seen that in all three cases

$$\|p - \omega(p)\| \le (2 - \sqrt{2})\epsilon_0,$$

which proves the claim. The optimal enclosing rectangle can be computed in linear time using rotating calipers. ▢

---

[3]Because 'approximation to an approximation' sounds rather weird we chose to call these algorithms pseudo-optimal.

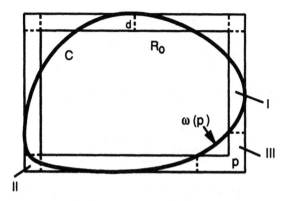

Figure 2: A convex closed curve, the optimal enclosing rectangle and the adjusted rectangle.

Another way to get pseudo-optimal approximation algorithms is indicated by the following theorem which we will prove in detail.

Theorem 20 ([ABGW]) *Let P be a convex n-gon and $k < n$ fixed. Furthermore assume that ϵ is the minimal Hausdorff-distance of a convex k-gon to P. Then there exists a convex k-gon Q whose set of vertices is a subset of the vertices of P with $\delta_H(P,Q) \leq 4\epsilon$.*

Proof: We first need a definition.

Definition 21 *Let P be a polygon. Regard P as an oriented contour. Let $u, v \in P$. Then define P_{uv} as the segment of P from u to v. Define (for this proof) the **error** of the line segment $\overline{uv}$ as the maximum distance of any $x \in P_{uv}$ to $\overline{uv}$.*

With this definition we first prove

Lemma 22 ([ABGW]) *There exists a k-gon Q' whose vertices lie on P such that the error of any edge in Q' is $\leq 2\epsilon$.*

Proof: Let O be a k-gon with $\delta_H(O, P) = \epsilon$. For any vertex of O fix a point on P in its ϵ-neighborhood. Let these points be the vertices of Q'. The distance of the vertices of O to the corresponding vertices of Q' and thereby of the entire O to Q' is $\leq \epsilon$ and vice versa. Therefore we get $\delta_H(Q', P) \leq \delta_H(Q', P) + \delta_H(O, P) \leq \epsilon + \delta_H(O, P) = 2\epsilon$. Because of convexity this is an upper bound for the error of any edge in Q', too. ꛱

We proceed with the proof of the theorem.

Let Q' as in Lemma 22. Regard Q' as oriented contour with the same orientation as P. Construct Q by moving each vertex v of Q' to the closest vertex v'' of P *on the same edge of P*. Let $\overline{u''v''}$ be any edge of Q. Suppose that u and v do not lie on the same edge of P, otherwise u'' and v'' will do so too and the error of $\overline{u''v''}$ will be zero. Let $u' := u$ if $u'' \in P_{uv}$ and $:= u''$ otherwise. Let $\hat{u}$ be the mirror image of u' by u. Define v' and $\hat{v}$ analogously.

Let U be the 2ϵ-neighborhood of $\overline{uv}$. It follows $\hat{u}, \hat{v} \in P_{uv} \subseteq U$.

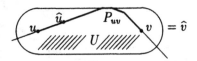

Let U_u, U_v be the mirror image of U by u, v resp. Because $\hat{u}, \hat{v} \in U$ it is $u' \in U_u$ and $v' \in U_v$. Consider the orthonormal system in which u is the origin and v has the coordinates $(w, 0)$ with $w := d(u, v)$.

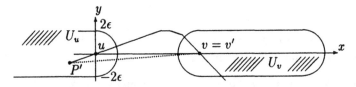

Claim: The distance of u, v and thereby of the entire $\overline{uv}$ to $\overline{u'v'}$ is $\leq 2\epsilon$.

Proof: (We show this only for u.) If $d(u, u')$ or $d(u, v')$ is $\leq 2\epsilon$, there is nothing to show. Otherwise the x-coordinate of u' will be negative and the one of v' will be positive. Then there exists a point $(0, y) \in \overline{u'v'}$. It will be $y \in [-2\epsilon, 2\epsilon]$ and therefore $d(u, (0, y)) = |y| \leq 2\epsilon$. $\qquad\qquad$ ⊡

The distance of P_{uv} to $\overline{uv}$ was $\leq 2\epsilon$. Now the distance of $\overline{uv}$ to $\overline{u'v'}$ is $\leq 2\epsilon$, too. It follows that the distance of any vertex of P_{uv} to $\overline{u'v'}$ is $\leq 4\epsilon$. The only possible new vertices of $P_{u'v'}$ are u' and v'. So the error of $\overline{u'v'}$ is $\leq 4\epsilon$, too. Since $\overline{u''v''}$ is moved inward of conv $P_{u'v'}$ the error of $\overline{u''v''}$ is not greater than the one of $\overline{u'v'}$ and therefore $\leq 4\epsilon$.

$\qquad\qquad$ ⊡

Together with an algorithm of Imai, Iri [II] that computes for a convex n-gon P the optimally approximating k-gon whose vertices are vertices of P, Theorem 20 yields:

Theorem 23 ([ABGW]) *Let P be a convex n-gon. Let ϵ be the minimal $\delta_H(P, Q)$ for any k-gon Q. Then a k-gon Q' with $\delta_H(P, Q') \leq 4\epsilon$ can be constructed in time $\mathcal{O}(n^3 \log^2 n)$.*

As will be seen in the next subsection a similar approach applies to the Fréchet-metric and polygonal chains.

Finally we remark that by a result of Atallah the Hausdorff-distance between two convex polygons can be computed in linear time. We will show later that for non-convex polygons this can be done in time $\mathcal{O}(n \log n)$ where n is the total number of vertices.

3.4 Computing δ_F for polygonal chains

We consider the Fréchet-metric (see Definition 13). In what follows we always assume that the curves are in $\mathbf{R}^2$, however, the results hold for any d-dimensional euclidean vector space.

We describe an algorithm that computes the Fréchet-distance of two given polygonal chains C_1, C_2. Mostly due to the fact that a curve is a class of geometric objects rather than a single object this problem is quite difficult already. Therefore we first restrict ourselves to the following *decision problem:*

Given two parametrized polygonal chains P, Q with p and q edges, respectively, and $\epsilon \geq 0$, decide whether $\delta_F(P, Q) \leq \epsilon$.

First we consider polygonal chains P, Q each consisting of one line segment only, which are given by linear parametrizations α, β, respectively. We consider the set of *allowed* points $(t, s) \in [0, 1]^2$ with $d(\alpha(t), \beta(s)) \leq \epsilon$. This set is convex (in fact it is part of an ellipse) and clearly $\delta_F(P, Q) \leq \epsilon$ if and only if there exists a path from $(0, 0)$ to $(1, 1)$ within the set of allowed points. Since this set is convex the path, if it exists, may be chosen as a line segment. In Figure 3 line segments P, Q are shown and the set of allowed points are the grey shaded regions.

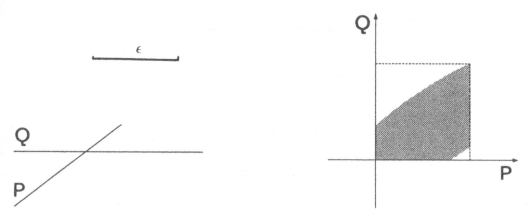

Figure 3: Line segments P, Q and the corresponding set of allowed points

To extend this idea to the case of arbitrary polygonal chains we compute the set of allowed points $(s, t) \in [0, 1]^2$ for all pq pairs of edges of P and Q and combine them to a diagram as shown in Figure 4. Then we check whether a monotone path from from the lower left corner of the diagram to the upper right corner of the diagram can be found lying completely in the set of allowed points. Since for each pair the set of allowed points is convex, it follows that if there exists any monotone path then a monotone polygonal chain from $(0,0)$ to $(1,1)$ exists, too. The running-time of this algorithm is $\mathcal{O}(pq)$ (two polygonal chains, the set of allowed points, a monotone path and the corresponding assignment of points are shown in Figure 4 and Figure 5).

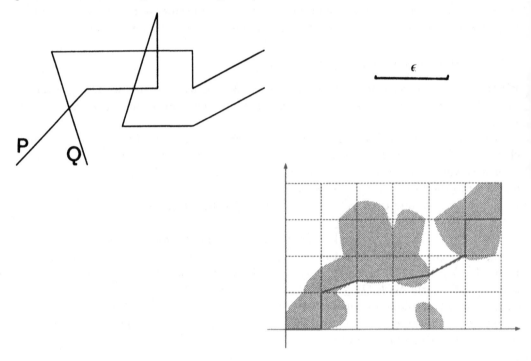

Figure 4: Diagram for polygonal chains P, Q

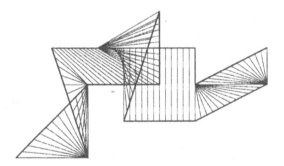

Figure 5: Assignment between the points on the curves.

The problem of *computing* the Fréchet-distance between two polygonal chains is solved by Megiddo's parametric search technique (see [Me]), which we will not describe here. We only mention that this technique applies the above decision algorithm at certain stages. The running-time of this algorithm can be analyzed as $\mathcal{O}(pq \log^3(pq))$ (see [G2]).

Next we consider approximation algorithms for the Fréchet-metric. We distinguish two different kinds of approximation problems:

1. min $-\epsilon$-*approximation:* Given a polygonal chain P and an integer $k > 0$, find a polygonal chain Q_{opt} with at most k edges minimizing $\delta_F(P, Q_{\mathrm{opt}})$.

2. min $-\sharp$-*approximation:* Given a polygonal chain P and a number $\epsilon \leq 0$, find the polygonal chain Q_{opt} with a minimal number of edges satisfying $\delta_F(P, Q_{\mathrm{opt}}) \leq \epsilon$.

As in the case of δ_H-approximation it turns out that optimal solutions are hard to find. On the other hand there are efficient algorithms that determine pseudo-optimal solutions. In case of the min $-\epsilon$-approximation it is clear what is meant by a pseudo-optimal solution: *For the* min $-\epsilon$-*approximation a polygonal chain Q with k edges satisfying $\delta_F(P, Q) \leq c\epsilon_{opt}$, where ϵ_{opt} is the smallest distance between P and a polygonal chain having k edges is called a c-pseudo-optimal solution.*

However, for the min $-\sharp$-approximation the pseudo-optimality does not refer directly to the number of edges of the chain found, instead we define: *A polygonal chain Q with k edges and $\delta_F(P, Q) \leq \epsilon$ is said to be a c-pseudo-optimal solution for the* min $-\sharp$-*approximation if any polygonal chain Q' satisfying $\delta_F(P, Q') \leq \frac{1}{c}\epsilon$ has at least k edges.*

The algorithms for the pseudo-optimal solutions follow the same lines as the ones for the pseudo-optimal solutions for approximating convex n-gons by convex k-gons. Instead of allowing arbitrary polygonal chains only those chains are considered whose vertices are vertices of P. In fact in [G1] the following theorem has been shown.

Theorem 24 ([G1]) *If we restrict ourselves in the* min $-\epsilon$- *and* min $-\sharp$-*approximations to polygonal chains whose vertices are vertices of the chain to be approximated the optimal solution under this constraint is a pseudo-optimal solution for the unconstrained approximation problems. In both cases the constant c is ≤ 7.*

To find the optimal solution in the constrained case again the techniques of Imai and Iri are applied. The running-times are as follows:

Theorem 25 ([G1]) *Given a polygonal chain P with n edges. A pseudo-optimal solution for the* min $-\sharp$-*approximation can be found in time $\mathcal{O}(n^3)$. A pseudo-optimal solution for the* min $-\epsilon$-*approximation can be found in time $\mathcal{O}(n^3 \log^2 n)$.*

3.5 Matching Algorithms for δ_H

Finally we discuss algorithms that solve the following fundamental problem in pattern recognition: Given two simple polygons P and Q, find the best possible match between P and an isometric copy of Q, that is, find the isometry I_{opt} that minimizes the Hausdorff-distance between P and any isometric copy $I(Q)$ of Q (An example is given in Figure 6.).

Also special cases of this general matching problem have been considered in [ABB], which are obtained by restricting the set of admissible isometries.
Let **A3** denote the case were we allow all isometries. The special cases are defined as follows:

A2: Only translations are allowed.

A1: Only translations along a fixed direction $\vec{t_0}$ are allowed.

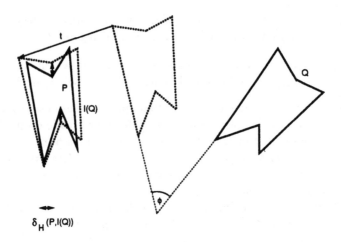

Figure 6: An example for the matching problem

A0: No isometries are allowed, i.e., determine the Hausdorff-distance between two simple polygons P, Q.

For all problems polynomial time algorithms have been found that compute the optimal isometry and the optimal distance. But for **A3** and **A2** the polynomials are of degree 9 and 7, respectively, which is not efficient anymore. Therefore we consider again algorithms that compute only a pseudo-optimal solution, that is an isometry I, or a translation in the restricted case, such that $\delta_H(P, I(Q))$ differs from $\delta_H(P, I_{\text{opt}}(Q))$ only by a constant factor that is independent of P. The results are summarized in the following theorem:

Theorem 26 ([ABB]) *The different versions of the problem of measuring the resemblance between polygons P, Q with p, q vertices respectively, can be solved within the following time bounds:*

	Optimal	Pseudooptimal
A0	$O((p+q)\log(p+q))$	—
A1	$O(\lambda_{66}(pq)\log(pq))$	$O((p+q)\log(p+q))$
A2	$O((pq)^3(p+q)\log(p+q))$	$O((p+q)\log(p+q))$
A3	$O((pq)^4(p+q)\log(p+q))$	$O(\lambda_{66}(pq)\log(pq))$

Here $\lambda_s(n)$ denotes the length of the longest Davenport-Schinzel-sequence (see [ASS]) of type s on n symbols. As is well-known $\lambda_s(n) = \mathcal{O}(n \log^* n)$ for all s. In the rest of this section we partially prove two of the results, namely, the result for **A0** and the pseudo-optimal solution for **A3**.

An algorithm for A0 To compute the Hausdorff-distance between two polygons P, Q with p, q vertices, respectively, we only need to show how to compute the maximal distance of a point of P to Q, that is the distance $\tilde{\delta}_H(P, Q)$ from P to Q. The distance $\tilde{\delta}_H(Q, P)$

from Q to P can be computed in the same way. In order to compute $\tilde{\delta}_H(P, Q)$ we consider the Voronoi-diagram $\text{Vor}(Q)$ of Q, which consists of $\mathcal{O}(q)$ edges and vertices. The edges are either line segments or parabolic segments. $\text{Vor}(Q)$ can be constructed in time $\mathcal{O}(q \log q)$ (see [F], [Y]). Furthermore we assume that if a parabolic segment has a vertical tangent at some point, then the segment is cut into two pieces at the point where this tangent occurs. With this assumption it is not too difficult to prove the following lemma.

Lemma 27 ([ABB]) *The distance of P to Q, $\tilde{\delta}_H(P, Q)$ is assumed either at some vertex of P or at some intersection point of P with some Voronoi-edge e having smallest or largest x-coordinate.*

It remains to show how to find the critical points of Lemma 27 and their nearest neighbors on Q, that is we have to determine the cells of $\text{Vor}(Q)$ containing the vertices of P and the elements of Q closest to the critical intersection points.

We do this by a plane sweep across the arrangement obtained by $\text{Vor}(Q)$ and P. In order to obtain only the extreme intersection points of each edge e of $\text{Vor}(Q)$, we delete e from the data structure (e.g. 2-3-tree) as soon as the first intersection point with P has been found. Two such sweeps, one from left to right and one from right to left are necessary. Since there are $O(p + q)$ event points we obtain an $O((p + q) \log(p + q))$-algorithm for determining all candidates in the sense of Lemma 27. By determining their distance to Q and taking their maximum we get $\tilde{\delta}_H(P, Q)$. Analogously, $\tilde{\delta}_H(Q, P)$ and thus $\delta_H(P, Q)$ can be determined.

A Pseudo-Optimal Solution for A3 We describe an algorithm that, given two simple polygons P, Q, computes an isometry I such $\delta_H(P, I(Q))$ differs from the Hausdorff-distance determined by the optimal isometry between P and Q only by a constant factor.

The algorithm is based on the fact that the optimal isometry I_{opt} between P and Q almost maps the centroids of the edges of the convex hulls of P and Q onto each other. To give a more precise statement of this fact and to prove it, we need some notations and definitions. The convex hull of a simple polygon P is always denoted by $\tilde{P}$. By a *natural parametrization* of a curve C we understand a parametrization $\alpha : [0, L_C] \longrightarrow C$ which satisfies the following condition: For all $t \in [0, 1]$ the arc-length from point $\alpha(0)$ to point $\alpha(t)$ equals t. Here L_C denotes the total arc-length of C.

For a convex polygon P let S_P be the centroid of the edges of P. S_P can be determined in linear time by assigning to each edge e of P the length of e as a weight to its midpoint and to compute the weighted arithmetic mean of these midpoints. Another way to define the centroid is via the following integral representation

$$S_P = \frac{1}{L_P} \int_0^{L_P} \alpha(t)\, dt,$$

where $\alpha(t)$ is some ($\alpha(0)$ is chosen arbitrary) natural parametrization of the boundary of P and L_P the total arc length of P. We will not use this formula to compute the centroid of the edges of the convex hull of a simple polygon. But we will use it to prove the fact mentioned above.

Theorem 28 ([ABB]) *For a simple polygon P let S_P be the centroid of the edges of the convex hull of P. If P, Q are simple polygons and I_{opt} is the optimal isometry between P and Q then*

$$d\left(S_P, I_{opt}(S_Q)\right) \leq (4\pi + 3)\delta,$$

where $\delta = \delta_H(P, I_{opt}(Q))$.

Sketch of a Proof: W.l.o.g. we assume that $I_{opt}(Q)$ contains the origin, denoted by o. To prove the theorem we need several lemmata. The first one relating δ_H and δ_F has already been mentioned in the section on approximation algorithms for δ_H. We restate it here in precisely the form we need for the proof.

Lemma 29 *Let C_1, C_2 be closed convex curves. To any natural parametrization α of C_1 there exists a parametrization β of C_2 with $d(\alpha(t), \beta(t)) \leq \delta_H(C_1, C_2)$ for all $t \in [0, L_{C_1}]$.*

Furthermore we need the following elementary geometric lemma:

Lemma 30   *a) Let C_1 and C_2 be convex closed curves, L_{C_1}, L_{C_2} their lengths and $\delta = \delta_H(C_1, C_2)$. Then $|L_{C_1} - L_{C_2}| \leq 2\pi\delta$.*

b) Let P, Q be polygons, then for the convex hulls $\delta_H(\tilde{P}, \tilde{Q}) \leq \delta_H(P, Q)$.

We are now in the position to prove Theorem 28. Let $R := \tilde{P}$, $T := \widetilde{I_{opt}(Q)} \left(= I_{opt}(\tilde{Q})\right)$, α a natural parametrization of R, and $\tilde{\beta}$ a parametrization of T such that according to Lemma 29

$$\begin{aligned} d\left(\alpha(t), \tilde{\beta}(t)\right) &\leq \delta_H(R, T) \quad \text{for all } t \in [0, L_R] \\ &\leq \delta \quad \text{by Lemma 30 b).} \end{aligned}$$

Let $\beta : [0, L_T] \to \mathbf{R}^2$ be the natural parametrization of T, with $\beta(0) = \tilde{\beta}(0)$, and the orientation in which β traverses T is the same as the one of $\tilde{\beta}$. Now,

$$\begin{aligned} d(S_P, S_{I_{opt}(Q)}) &= \left\| \frac{1}{L_R} \int_0^{L_R} \alpha(t)dt - \frac{1}{L_T} \int_0^{L_T} \beta(t)dt \right\| \\ &\leq \frac{1}{L_R} \int_0^{L_R} \|\alpha(t) - \beta(t)\| dt \\ &\quad + \left\| \left(\frac{1}{L_R} - \frac{1}{L_T} \right) \cdot \int_0^{L_R} \beta(t)dt \right\| \\ &\quad + \frac{1}{L_T} \left\| \int_{L_R}^{L_T} \beta(t)dt \right\| \end{aligned}$$

assuming wlog., that $L_T \geq L_R$. Let us denote the three terms in the last expression by J_1, J_2, J_3, respectively. By Lemma 30 the difference between L_R and L_T is at most $2\pi\delta$. This fact together with the observation that the assumption $o \in I(Q)$ implies $\|\beta(t)\| \leq \frac{L_T}{2}$ can be used to show that

$$J_2 \leq \pi\delta \text{ and } J_3 \leq \pi\delta. \tag{1}$$

In order to get an upper bound for J_1, we show

Claim: $\|\alpha(t) - \beta(t)\| \leq (2\pi + 3) \cdot \delta$ for all $t \in [0, L_R]$

Proof: For a fixed $t \in [0, L_R]$ consider the curve segments from $\alpha(0)$ to $\alpha(t)$ of R and from $\tilde\beta(0)$ to $\tilde\beta(t)$ of T and close them by line segments ℓ_R and ℓ_T (see Figure 7).

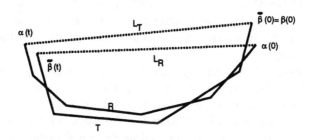

Figure 7: Two curves with Hausdorff-distance δ

The resulting curves R', T' have Hausdorff-distance $\leq \delta$, therefore by Lemma 30 a)

$$|L_{R'} - L_{T'}| \leq 2\pi\delta \tag{2}$$

Now, if b is the arc-length of T from $\tilde\beta(0)$ to $\tilde\beta(t)$, then

$$\begin{aligned} |L_{R'} - L_{T'}| &= |t + \ell_R - b - \ell_T| \\ &\geq |t - b| - |\ell_R - \ell_T| \end{aligned} \tag{3}$$

Since $|\ell_R - \ell_T| \leq 2\delta$, we have by (2) and (3):

$$|t - b| \leq (2\pi + 2)\delta$$

On the other hand since b is the arc-length of T between $\tilde\beta(0)$ and $\tilde\beta(t)$ and t the arc-length of T between $\beta(0)$ $\left(= \tilde\beta(0)\right)$ and $\beta(t)$, we have

$$\begin{aligned} \|\tilde\beta(t) - \beta(t)\| &\leq |t - b| \\ \text{So} \quad \|\beta(t) - \alpha(t)\| &\leq \|\beta(t) - \tilde\beta(t)\| + \|\tilde\beta(t) - \alpha(t)\| \\ &\leq (2\pi + 2)\delta + \delta \end{aligned}$$

and the claim follows. □

Clearly, the claim implies that $J_1 \leq (2\pi + 3)\delta$, so altogether we have

$$d(S_P, S_{I(Q)}) \leq (4\pi + 3)\delta$$

which finishes the proof of the theorem. □

Using this theorem we can describe an algorithm that produces a pseudo-optimal solution for **A3**. Given P and Q we first apply to Q the translation that maps S_Q onto S_P. Let Q' be the image of Q. Second we find the rotation ρ_{opt} around S_P that minimizes the Hausdorff-distance between P and any copy of Q' one can get by rotating Q' around

S_P. This problem (like **A1**) can be solved using results on Davenport-Schinzel-sequences (for details see [ASS]). We get a time bound of $\mathcal{O}(\lambda_{66}(pq)\log(pq))$.

Obviously $\delta_H(P, \rho_{\text{opt}}(Q')) \leq (4\pi + 4)\delta$, where δ is the minimal distance between P and an isometric copy of Q. The algorithm therefore produces a pseudo-optimal solution. The running-time of the algorithm is dominated by the time needed to determine ρ_{opt}, therefore it is $\mathcal{O}(\lambda_{66}(pq) \lg pq)$. The constant $4\pi + 4 \approx 17$ may seem quite large, but with the following idea (cf. [S]) it can be reduced to any fixed constant without increasing the asymptotic running-time:

We know by Theorem 28 that the optimal isometry I maps S_Q into the $(4\pi + 3)\delta$-neighborhood U of S_P. For some fixed $c \geq 1$ we place onto U a sufficiently small grid so that no point in U has distance greater than $(c-1)\delta$ from a gridpoint. Since c is fixed, there are constantly many gridpoints within U. We place S_Q instead of onto S_P only, onto each one of these gridpoints and proceed as described before. It follows from the previous discussion that for the solution $\tilde{I}$ found this way it holds:

$$\delta_H(P, \tilde{I}(Q)) \leq c\delta.$$

References

[ASS] P. K. AGARWAL, M. SHARIR, P. SHOR, Sharp Upper and Lower Bounds on the Length of General Davenport-Schinzel Sequences, *J. Comb. Theory*, Ser. A 52, 1989, pp. 228-274.

[AHU] A. V. AHO, J. E. HOPCRAFT, J. D. ULLMAN, *The Design and Analysis of Computer Algorithms*, Addison-Wesley, Reading, MA, 1974.

[ABB] H. ALT, B. BEHRENDS, J. BLÖMER, Approximate Matching of Polygonal Shapes, *Proccedings of the 7th ACM Symposium on Computational Geometry*, 1991, pp. 186-193.

[ABGW] H. ALT, J. BLÖMER, M. GODAU, H. WAGENER Approximation of Convex Polygons, *Proceedings ICALP, International Colloquium on Automata, Languages and Programming*, Warwick, England, 1990, pp. 703-716.

[AKMSW] E. M. ARKIN, K. KEDEM, J. S. B. MITCHELL, J. SPRINZAK, M. WERMAN Matching Points into Noise Regions: Combinatorial Bounds and Algorithms, in *Proceedings SODA, 2nd Symposium on Discrete Algorithms*, 1991.

[AMWW] H. ALT, K. MEHLHORN, H. WAGENER, E. WELZL, Congruence, Similarity and Symmetries of Geometric Objects, *Discrete Comp. Geom.* 3, 1988, pp. 237-256.

[At1] M. J. ATALLAH, A Linear Time Algorithm for the Hausdorff-distance between Convex Polygons, *Information Processing Letters* 17, 1983, pp. 207-209.

[B] B. BEHRENDS, Algorithmen zur Erkennung der ϵ-Kongruenz von Punktmengen und Polygonen, Diplomarbeit, Freie Universität Berlin, 1990.

[F]   S. FORTUNE, A Sweepline - Algorithm for Voronoi-Diagrams, *Algorithmica 2*, 1987, pp. 153-174.

[Fr]   M. FRÉCHET, Sur quelques points du calcul fonctionnel, *Rendiconti del Circolo Mathematico di Palermo*, Vol. 22, 1906, pp. 1-74.

[G1]   M. GODAU, A Natural Metric for Curves-Computing the Distance for Polygonal Chains and Approximation Algorithms, *Proceedings Symposium on Theoretical Aspects of Computer Science*, STACS'91, Springer Lecture Notes in Computer Science, Vol. 480, pp. 127-136.

[G2]   M. GODAU, Die Fréchet-Metrik für Polygonzüge — Algorithmen zur Abstandsmessung und Approximation, Diplomarbeit, Fachbereich Mathematik, FU Berlin 1991.

[HS]   P. J. HEFFERNAN, S. SCHIRRA, Approximate Decision Algorithms for Point Set Congruence, Report MPI-I-91-110, Max-Planck-Institut für Informatik, Saarbrücken, 1991.

[II]   H. IMAI, M. IRI, Polygonal Approximations of a Curve – Formulations and Algorithms. *Computational Morphology*, G. T. Toussaint (ed)., Elsevier Science Publ., 1988, pp. 71-86.

[ISI]   K. IMAI, S. SUMINO, H. IMAI, Minimax Geometric Fitting of two Corresponding Sets of Points, in *Proceedings of 5th ACM Symp. on Computational Geometry*, 1989, pp. 276-282.

[I]   S. IWANOWSKI, *Approximate Congruence and Symmetry Detection in the Plane*, Ph.D. Thesis, Fachbereich Mathematik, FU Berlin, 1990.

[M]   G. E. MARTIN, *Transformation Geometry*, Springer-Verlag, New York, Heidelberg, Berlin, 1982.

[Me]   N. MEGIDDO, Applying Parallel Computation Algorithms in the Design of Serial Algorithms, *J. of the Assoc. for Comp. Machinery* 30, 1983, pp. 852-866.

[PS]   F. P. PREPARATA, M. I. SHAMOS, *Computational Geometry*, Springer-Verlag, New York, 1985.

[S]   S. SCHIRRA, *Über die Bitkomplexität der ε-Kongruenz*, Diplomarbeit, Fachbereich Informatik, Universität des Saarlandes, 1988.

[Y]   C. K. YAP, An $O(n \log n)$ Algorithm for the Voronoi Diagram of a Set of Simple Curve Segments, *Discrete Comp. Geom.* 2, 1987, pp. 365-393.

Selected Topics from Computational Geometry, Data Structures and Motion Planning

Rudolf Fleischer*   Otfried Fries[†]   Kurt Mehlhorn*   Stefan Meiser*
Stefan Näher*   Hans Rohnert[†]   Stefan Schirra*   Klaus Simon[‡]
Athanasios Tsakalidis[§]   Christian Uhrig*

1   Introduction

This paper is intended to give a survey over the work done at the University of Saarbrücken in the project "data structures and efficient algorithms" of the "Deutsche Forschungsgemeinschaft". Within this project research at Saarbrücken covered the fields *motion planning, computational geometry* and *data structures*. In this paper we present selected work from these fields. In particular, Section 2.1 discusses motion planning for a point- or disk-shaped robot, whereas Section 2.2 deals with approximate motion planning for arbitrary robots and configurations. Sections 3 to 5 are devoted to problems of computational geometry, namely dynamic planar point location (Section 3), the construction of Voronoi diagrams (Section 4) and hidden line elimination (Section 5). Section 6 addresses the union-split-find problem.

The discussion of the problems is very short. This paper is only meant to give a survey and references to related and new work. Wherever the reader is interested in details of the algorithms, he or she is referred to the full version papers as listed in the bibliography.

The above list of authors includes all people engaged in the project during the last 4 years. Two PhD-theses were completed by H. Rohnert and O. Fries, see Sections 2.1 and 3.1, respectively. They now both work for SIEMENS. Klaus Simon is now at the ETH Zürich and Athanasios Tsakalidis is now Associate Professor at the University of Patras in Greece.

2   Motion Planning

Motion planning is a fundamental problem in robotics and has gained attention in several research disciplines. To get insight into the intrinsic mathematics of the problem the purely geometric motion planning problem has been studied in computer science: given a geometric description of the robot and its environment, and an initial placement Z_{in} and

---

*Max Planck Institut für Informatik and Universität des Saarlandes, D-6600 Saarbrücken, Germany
[†]SIEMENS AG, D-8000 München, Germany
[‡]Institut für Informatik, ETH Zürich, CH-8092 Zürich, Switzerland
[§]Department of Computer Engineering and Informatics, School of Engineering, University of Patras, 26500 Patras, Greece

a final placement Z_{fi}, find a path for the robot from Z_{in} to Z_{fi} which avoids the obstacles in the environment. Dynamic constraints are not considered.

The first solutions to such find path problems were heuristics. Starting with several research papers of Schwartz and Sharir exact algorithms were developed for various find path problems in two dimensions, e.g. moving a disc, a line segment (often called rod or ladder), a convex polygon amidst obstacle polygons (cf. [SS90]), or an "L-shaped" object amidst point obstacles [HO89].

Section 2.1 deals with such point- and disc-robots. We discuss algorithms for computing a (somehow) optimal path. Section 2.2 addresses approximate motion planning. In particular, we introduce a new parameter for the difficulty of a motion planning problem (Section 2.2.1) and study the problem of approximating a more complex robot by a convex k-gon (Section 2.2.2).

2.1 Motion Planning for Points and Disks

We are given a robot R and a set of obstacles $\mathcal{O}$. In an abstract setting, R and the obstacles in $\mathcal{O}$ are usually modelled by simple geometric objects. In the sequel we always assume $\mathcal{O} = \{P_i \mid 1 \leq i \leq f\}$ to consist of f simple polygons with a total number of n vertices; sometimes intersections between the polygons are allowed. The robot R is modelled as a disk or simpler as a point. In most cases the smallest enclosing disk is a good approximation for a robot. Modelling a robot through a point is reasonable when the robot is very small compared to the arrangement and the size of the obstacles. See Section 2.2.2 for an approximation by k-gons. For the motion planning aspect however approximations by polygons introduce an additional difficulty: rotations of the robot are no longer negligible.

2.1.1 Point robots

In the following the robot R is assumed to be a point; its start and endpoints are denoted by a and b, respectively. Before we address the computation of a (shortest) path, we want to decide whether there is a path from a to b at all.

Clearly, such a path exists if and only if a and b lie in the same region of the decomposition of $\mathbb{R}^2$ induced by the polygonal obstacles. In a preprocessing step, this decomposition can be computed in time $O((n + s) \log n)$, where s is the number of intersection points between the polygons, see for example [OW84]. For any pair of points a and b, a point location query then answers the question in time $O(\log n)$, see for example [EGS86]. If the obstacles are disjoint, the same question can be answered in time $O(n)$ without the need for preprocessing: Simply ask whether a and b both lie outside each polygon.

The rest of this section is devoted to the problem of computing a shortest path between a and b. Depending on the complexity of the scene we discuss three different cases: shortest paths between disjoint simple polygons, between convex polygons with intersections, and between polygons whose convex hulls are disjoint. We need some more terminology.

The *visibility graph* for f disjoint simple polygons has the n vertices of the polygons as nodes. An edge in the visibility graph joins two nodes that *see* each other, i.e. whose connecting line segment does not intersect the interior of a polygon. See [Wel85, AAG+86, GM87, OW88, AW88] for various algorithms. An edge is called *locally tangent* if at its two endpoints its extension does not intersect the interior of the polygons. In particular all polygon edges are visibility edges.

It is a well known fact that the shortest path (for a point robot from point a to point b) between disjoint simple polygons consists only of locally tangent edges of the visibility graph for the polygons, where a and b are considered as additional trivial polygons. This fact suggests to compute in a preprocessing step the graph formed by these edges and then to use Dijkstra's algorithm (for the computation of a shortest path in a graph) for answering the query. In general there can be as many as $\Omega(n^2)$ locally tangent edges of the visibility graph. We therefore turn to special cases with a lower number of such edges.

Disjoint convex polygons

First observe that for disjoint convex polygons any locally tangent edge of the visibility graph is a tangent edge of two polygons. On the other hand, only those tangents are visibility edges, that do not intersect other polygons. Such tangents are called *useful* in the sequel. In [Roh89, Roh86] we prove that all $O(f^2)$ tangents between pairs of polygons in $\mathcal{O}$ can be computed in time $O(f^2 \log \frac{n}{f})$ and space $O(n + f^2)$. Moreover, the useless tangents can be distinguished from the useful tangents in time $O(n + f^2 \log f)$ and space $O(n + f^2)$. Dijkstra's algorithm applied to the resulting graph with n vertices and the at most $O(f^2)$ edges then yields a shortest path in time $O(n \log n + f^2)$.

Kapoor and Maheshwari in [KM88] give an algorithm with the same running time that also handles non-convex polygons. However their preprocessing time is in $O(n \log n + f^2 \log n)$.

We can reduce the space bound for our algorithm from $O(n + f^2)$ to $O(n)$ if we do not store the whole graph. Instead, during a run of Dijkstra's algorithm, we compute at the currently visited node the useful edges at that node; after updating the values of their endpoints we forget about them again. The drawback is that the running time increases to $O(f \cdot n \log n)$, see [Roh89, Roh88] for details and [AAG+86] for similar results.

Convex polygons with intersections

Intersecting polygons may partition the plane into one unbounded and several bounded regions. We therefore first compute the so-called contour. This is possible in time $O((n + s) \log n)$ by an algorithm of Ottmann and Wood [OW84], where s is the number of intersection points. In which region start and endpoint lie can be determined with the help of a point location structure, cf. [EGS86].

In case any two polygons intersect in at most 2 points, the size of the contour is in $O(n)$, otherwise it may be as large as $\Omega(f \cdot n)$, cf. [LS85]. This leads to different approaches for the two cases. In the first case a small modification of the algorithm of the last section can be applied with the same running time and space complexity. Only the preprocessing time increases to $O(n \log n + f^3)$. In the second case we construct the complete visibility graph inside the particular polygonal region containing a and b and run Dijkstra's algorithm on this graph.

Polygons with disjoint convex hulls

Obstacles whose convex hulls do not enclose point a or b can be replaced by their convex hulls, since the shortest path between a and b always runs outside these regions;

this can be done in time $O(n \log n)$. For the at most two remaining obstacles the portion of the shortest path inside their convex hulls corresponds to a path in the dual graph of a triangulation of the difference between the convex hull and the polygon; this strategy follows the ideas of Lee and Preparata for constructing a shortest path inside a simple polygon, cf. [LP84]. Thus only with a little more preprocessing, namely time $O(n \log n + f^2 \cdot \log n)$, we achieve the same time and space bounds as above.

2.1.2 Disk shaped robots

We address the same problems as with point robots: is there a path, and if so, compute an optimal path. Note, however, that this time the answer depends on the radius of the robot. For a large robot there may be "bottlenecks" that small robots pass easily. As an additional restriction we assume the scene to be enclosed by some large triangle; this triangle models the 'natural' borders of the scene. We shall show that we can preprocess the scene such that queries of the above form can be answered in time $O(\log n)$ and O(length of the path), respectively.

The path we compute maximizes the bottleneck among all possible paths. In this way we choose the most secure way for our robot. Moreover, we can within the same time bound compute the location of the bottleneck and its width. An algorithm for computing the path of minimum Euclidean length in $O(n^2 \log n)$ time has been given by P. Chew [Che85].

Our algorithm is based on an algorithm by Yap and Ó' Dúnlaing, cf. [OY85]. They propose to move the center of the robot on the *Voronoi diagram VD* defined by the edges and vertices of the polygons, compare Section 4. They show that if the center of R can be placed on startpoint a and endpoint b without hitting an obstacle, then there is a feasible path for R from a to b amidst the obstacles if and only if there is a feasible path from *image*(a) to *image*(b) restricted on *VD*. *image*(a) and *image*(b) are two points on *VD* close to a and b, respectively, that are easily computable and reachable without collisions. Thus searching in *VD* for a path yields a linear time algorithm for the problems stated above.

As said above we aim for a path of maximum security. Therefore we restrict ourselves to a subgraph B of *VD*; B is a spanning tree for the vertices of *VD* with the property that the sum over all edge widths is maximal over all spanning trees of *VD*. The *edge width* measures the size of the largest disk that can be moved on this edge. The *bottleneck* of a path is then the smallest edge width on that path. The above property of B ensures that for any pair of Voronoi nodes the path that maximizes the bottleneck among all paths between these nodes is also a path in B.

B is computed using Kruskal's algorithm for computing minimum spanning trees, see [AHU74]. With some small modifications, this algorithm produces a representation of B in form of a binary tree with the Voronoi nodes as leaves and the edges of B as nodes, such that the nearest common ancestor of the two Voronoi nodes is the Voronoi edge on the path in B that establishes the bottleneck. As shown in [Roh89, Roh91] the construction of the Voronoi diagram and the representation of B can be accomplished in time $O(n \log n)$ in a preprocessing step. The answers on the reachability and the find-path problem can then be given in time $O(\log n)$ and O(length of the path), respectively.

2.2 Approximate Motion Planning

2.2.1 Introducing Tightness

In the area of motion planning usually the worst case behaviour of the exact algorithms is studied and time and space bounds are measured in the complexity of the robot and its environment. For a convex object moving amidst a set P of polygons the complexity is given as a function of the number of corners of the robot-polygon and the total number of corners of the obstacle-polygons.

However, the complexity of the environment captures only part of our intuition on the difficulty of a motion planning problem. Another crucial parameter for the difficulty is the thightness of a find path problem, i.e. how much can we enlarge (diminish) the robot without changing the state of the problem from solvable to unsolvable (or vice versa). Let us consider a simple example: moving a rectangle R with sides of length a and b, $a \geq b$, amidst polygons with n corners. Let Z_{in} and Z_{fi} be the initial and final placement of R. We propose the following definition of tightness: Let $\mathcal{P} = (P, R, Z_{in}, Z_{fi})$ be a motion planning problem. For real number $\alpha > 0$ we use αR to denote the rectangle with sides αa and αb and $\mathcal{P}_{\alpha}$ to denote the problem $(P, \alpha R, Z_{in}, Z_{fi})$. The *tightness* ε_{crit} of $\mathcal{P}$ is given as follows:

a) If $\mathcal{P}$ is solvable then $\varepsilon_{crit} = \inf\{\varepsilon; \mathcal{P}_{1+\varepsilon}$ is unsolvable$\}$.

b) If $\mathcal{P}$ is unsolvable then $\varepsilon_{crit} = \inf\{\varepsilon; \mathcal{P}_{1/(1+\varepsilon)}$ is solvable$\}$.

Exploring an old idea used in some heuristics we have developed an algorithm with tightness-dependent running time for the problem above in [AFK+90]. Whilst the bounds of the best known algorithms measured in n are $\Omega(n^2)$ [KS88, CK90], the algorithm of [AFK+90] has running time $O((\frac{a}{b}\frac{1}{\varepsilon_{crit}} + 1)n\log^2 n)$. The running time has been improved to $O((\frac{a}{b}\frac{1}{\varepsilon_{crit}} + 1)n\log n)$ in [Sch]. For easy problems with $\frac{a}{b}\frac{1}{\varepsilon_{crit}} = O(1)$, these algorithms are practical even for environments with a large complexity. For non-convex objects scaling is not the appropriate way to define the tightness. In [Sch] hulls are used to define the tightness of more general motion planning problems and algorithms with tightness-dependent running time are given for several polyhedral motion planning problems. E.g. an arbitrary s-gon can be moved amidst polygons with n sides in time $O((sn)^2(1/\varepsilon_{crit}+1))$, an arbitrary convex polyhedron with n faces can be moved amidst convex polyhedra with n faces in time $O((sn)^3(1/\varepsilon_{crit} + 1))$. Two rectangles with a common corner can be moved in time $O(n^2((1/\varepsilon_{crit})^2 + 1))$ between polygons with n corners. For easy problems with $1/\varepsilon_{crit} = O(1)$, the time bounds are better than the bounds for the best known algorithms for these problems.

2.2.2 Simultaneous Inner and Outer Approximation of Shapes

In [FMR+90] we study a different approach. Remember that a large value ε_{crit} should reflect the property of a problem instance to have an "easy-to-see" solution. This is true because for a solvable problem a large ε_{crit} means that the room is rather empty, and it is usually quite easy to move (even complicated shaped) small objects through large nearly empty rooms.

But in this case we can reduce the time complexity of a motion planning algorithm considerably by using the following strategy: First we try to find a simple figure Q (e.g. a disk or a k-gon with small k) circumscribing the robot P, and then we run a fast algorithm for Q instead of P; since the running time usually depends on the complexity of the robot (e.g. the number of corners if it is a polygon) we thus obtain the desired speedup. And we still find a solution of our problem as long as Q is contained in $(1 + \varepsilon_{\text{crit}}) \cdot P$.

Hence we can design an algorithm whose running time degrades gracefully as the tightness parameter $\varepsilon_{\text{crit}}$ approaches zero by starting with an approximating 3-gon and then continuing with 4,5,6,...-gons; if we also run a standard algorithm in parallel, this will not increase the usual time bound. To handle non-solvable problems we also have to find enclosed k-gons Q instead of circumscribed ones.

The preceding discussion motivates the following concept of approximation: For any two compact subsets Q, P of Euclidean space, let $\lambda(Q, P)$ be the infimum of the ratio $\frac{r}{s}$ where $r, s > 0$ satisfy $sQ' \subseteq P \subseteq rQ''$ and Q', Q'' are some translates of Q. We call (sQ', rQ'') an *approximating pair* for P.

With this notion, our shape approximation problem can be formulated as follows : Given a convex figure P in the plane, find a "simple" polygon Q which minimizes $\lambda(Q, P)$.

The distance measure $\lambda(Q, P)$ only depends on the *shape* of P and Q (the *shape* of a body P is the class of bodies equivalent to P under translation and positive scaling, i.e. the homothets of P). If homothetic bodies are identified, the logarithm of the function $\lambda(Q, P)$ turns out to be a metric. But in contrast to other classical distance measures like Hausdorff distance, symmetric difference metric or perimeter deviation metric (see [Gru83] for an overview), this metric is invariant under all affine transformations. We note that it has also been used by [KLS90] under the name of Banach-Mazur metric.

The above algorithm depends on the ability to find good approximations efficiently. In our paper [FMR+90] we study approximation by triangles and give asymptotic bounds for k-gons. The case of approximation by rectangles can be found in [FRSW90]. Thus, define $\lambda_k(P) := \inf\{\lambda(Q, P) | Q \text{ convex } k\text{-gon}\}$ and $\lambda_k := \sup\{\lambda_k(P) | P \text{ convex body}\}$.

A natural candidate for a good approximation seems to be the maximum area k-gon contained in P. We show that for any convex body P, any maximum triangle t contained in P has the property that $\lambda(t, P) \leq \frac{9}{4}$. Moreover, for any convex n-gon P, we can find in $O(n)$ time a triangular approximating pair (t, T) with $\lambda(t, P) \leq \frac{9}{4}$. The proof of this theorem is very long and technical and is based on finding a worst-case example among hexagons P. [DS79] showed how to find the maximum area triangle in $O(n)$ time.

But the maximum area strategy is, in general, suboptimal. A short calculation shows that the regular pentagon can be approximated by a triangle with $\lambda = 1 + \frac{\sqrt{5}}{2} = 2.118...$, but this is not the maximum area enclosed triangle. We conjecture that the regular pentagon is a worst case example for triangle approximation, i.e. $\lambda_3 \leq 2.118....$

At least for Polygons P we can do better than the maximum area heuristic: Given an n-gon P one can compute an optimal triangular approximating pair (t, T) and the value $\lambda_3(P)$ in time $O(n^2 \log^2 n)$. This algorithm uses the fact that there is always an optimal approximating triangle with some specific properties such as having a vertex in common with the polygon or an edge being parallel to one of the polygon edges. Thus the search can be restricted to a finite set of triangles of size $O(n^3)$; and since the function λ is unimodular on some subsets of this set, we can use Fibonacci search to achieve a better running time than $O(n^3)$.

For k-gon approximations with $k > 3$ we can only give an asymptotic bound on λ_k, namely $\lambda_k = \Theta(\frac{1}{k^2})$. The lower bound is achieved by approximating a disk, whereas the proof of the upper bound uses some well-known results of approximations with respect to the Hausdorff metric.

2.2.3 The Complexity of the Union of Simple Plane Figures

The complexity of the union of simple plane figures is a combinatorial problem related to purely translational motion planning in the plane amidst point obstacles. Let B be a robot in the plane with reference point at the origin. If only translations are allowed a placement of B can be fully described by the position of the reference point. It is easy to see that the set of positions leading to a collision with an obstacle point p is $\{p\} - B = \{p - b; b \in B\}$, i.e. $-B = \{-b; b \in B\}$ translated by p. Hence the set of forbidden positions is the union of translates of $-B$ placed at the point obstacles.

It is known that the complexity, i.e. the number of intersection points on the boundary, of the union of n translates of a convex polygon is $O(n)$. This follows from the topological result that the complexity of the union of n Jordan regions is $O(n)$, if the boundaries of each pair of regions intersect in at most 2 points [KLPS86]. On the other hand it is not hard to find examples of n translates of an "L-shaped" polygon, whose union has complexity $\Omega(n^2)$. In [AFK+90] we study rotation figures of rectangles. The set of positions where a rotation figure can be placed without collision is clearly the set of positions where the rectangle can be rotated without collisions between the extreme orientations contained in the rotation figure. Although such rotation figures are not convex and two rotation figures may have 6 intersection points, the union of n translates of such a figure is $O(n)$ if the rotation angle is small.

3 Dynamic Point Location in Planar Subdivisions

The *dynamic planar point location problem* is the task of maintaining a dynamic set S of n non-intersecting, except possibly at endpoints, line segments in the plane under the following operations:

- Locate(q point): Report the segment immediately above q, i.e. the first segment intersected by an upward vertical ray starting at q;

- Insert(s segment): Add segment s to the collection S of segments;

- Delete(s segment): Remove segment s from the collection S of segments.

Call a set S a *connected subdivision* of the plane if the graph defined by S (vertices $\hat{=}$ endpoints, edges $\hat{=}$ segments) is connected. Connected subdivisions include the *monotone subdivisions* of [PT89] as a special case. For connected subdivisions, the *locate* operation is usually required to return the name of the region containing the query point (and not only the segment immediately above the query point), and some papers reserve the term dynamic planar point location problem for the searching problem in connected subdivisions. Overmars [Ove85] has shown how to reduce the point location problem in connected subdivisions to the dynamic planar point location problem (as defined above) with only

Subdivision	Space	Locate	Insert	Delete	Reference
horizontal segments	$n \log n$	$\log n \log \log n$	$\log n \log \log n$	$\log n \log \log n$	[MN90]
monotone	n	$\log^2 n$	$\log^2 n$	$\log^2 n$	[PT89]
monotone	$n \log n$	$\log n$	$\log^2 n$	$\log^2 n$	[CT91]
monotone	n	$\log^2 n$	$\log n$	$\log n$	[GT91]
connected	n	$\log^2 n$	$\log^2 n$	-	[Meh84]
connected	n	$\log^2 n$	$\log^4$	$\log^4$	[Fri89]
general	$n \log n$	$\log^2 n$	$\log^2 n$	$\log^2 n$	[Ben77]
general	n	$\log^2 n$	$\log n$	$\log n$	[CJ90]
general	n	$\log n \log \log n$	$\log n \log \log n$	$\log^2 n$	[BJM92]

Figure 1: Running Times of Dynamic Point Location Structures

$O(\log n)$ additional cost per operation. On the other hand, there are applications of the dynamic point location problem, e.g. space sweep, where the connectedness assumption is unnatural.

We present two solutions. In Section 3.1 we describe the results of O. Fries for connected subdivisions [Fri89]; in Section 3.2 we present a very new algorithm for general subdivisions that for the first time allows linear space and query time below $O(\log^2 n)$ [BJM92].

Table 1 summarizes our results and compares them to previous work.

3.1   Dynamic Point Location in Connected Planar Subdivisions

In [Fri89] we present a new dynamic technique for locating a point in a connected planar subdivision. The supported updates are insertion and deletion of vertices and edges in S. The method achieves query time $O(\log^2 n)$, space $O(n)$ and update time $O(\log^2 |P| \log^2 n)$; P is the current region of S where the updates are realised.

Our method combines the methods of Lee and Preparata [LP77] for the static case (i.e. S is fixed) and of Preparata and Tamassia [PT88] for monotone subdivisions. First we describe shortly the so-called chain method of Lee and Preparata.

A *chain* c is a sequence of edges; it is *simple* if non-selfintersecting; it is *monotone* if any line parallel to the x-axis intersects c in either a point or a segment. A simple polygon P is a *region* of the plane delimited by a simple closed chain called the boundary of P. A polygon P is *monotone* if its boundary can be partitioned into two monotone chains c_1 and c_2 called the left chain and right chain of P, respectively. A subdivision S is called *monotone* if each region of S is monotone. Let $High(S)$ and $Low(S)$ be the highest and lowest vertex of S, respectively. We call a family F of chains *complete* for S if

1. each chain consists of edges in S only, starts in $High(S)$ and ends in $Low(S)$,

2. each edge of S belongs to at least one chain in F,

3. no two chains in F cross each other, and

4. each chain in F is monotone.

Condition 4 induces a natural left-right total order on F, i.e. a chain c_1 is said to be to the left (right) of another chain c_2, if no point of c_1 is to the right (left) of c_2. For any monotone subdivision S there exists a complete family F of chains.

The significance of complete families of chains is their usefulness in locating a query point q. The strategy is to determine those two chains adjacent in the left-right order which lie to the left and right of q. The edges of these two chains that intersect the horizontal line through q then determine the region of S which contains q.

Not every planar subdivision S is monotone. A node v of S is called *extreme* if there is no vertex connected to v with smaller (larger) y-value. $High(S)$ and $Low(S)$ are extreme nodes. If there exists any extreme node v other than $High(S)$ or $Low(S)$, then S is not monotone. If S is not monotone we can construct a monotone subdivision S' by adding supporting edges to S. We call S' a *regularization* of S. Lee and Preparata [LP77] show how to construct a regularization S' in time $O(n \log n)$. For S' they construct the static data structures with query time $O(\log^2 n)$ and space $O(n)$.

Let S' be the regularization of S. If we want to insert a new edge e in S we have to rebuild S'. In the worst case e intersects $O(n)$ supporting edges in S'. These edges have to be replaced by new edges in time at least $O(n)$. In [Fri89] we show that there exists a regularization S'_1 of S with the following properties:

1. Any new edge e inserted in S can intersect at most $O(\log |P|)$ supporting edges in S'_1 where P is the region of S in which e is inserted.

2. After insertion or deletion of an edge in S we can construct a new regularization by replacing $O(\log^2 |P|)$ supporting edges in S'_1.

We call a regularization with the two properties above a well-behaved regularization of S. A well-behaved regularization S'_1 has another useful property: After insertion or deletion of an edge e in S we construct the new regularization S''_1 step by step with $O(\log^2 |P|)$ updates. Each of the intermediate $O(\log^2 |P|)$ planar graphs is monotone. Thus we can rebuild our search structures by using the results of Preparata and Tamassia [PT88], which yields query time $O(\log^2 n)$ and space $O(n)$. An update can be done in time $O(\log^2 |P| \cdot \log n)$ and a new regularization can be built in time $O(\log^4 |P|)$.

3.2 Dynamic Point Location in General Planar Subdivisions

In this section we turn to general planar subdivisions as described in the introduction to Section 3. In [BJM92] we present two algorithms that achieve $O(\log n \log\log n)$ location and insertion time and $O(\log^2 n)$ deletion time, the bounds for insertions and deletions being amortized. The space bound is $O(n \log n)$ for our first solution, and $O(n)$ for our second solution. The second solution is a refinement of the first solution. Previously, a query time below $O(\log^2 n)$ was known only for the special cases of monotone subdivisions [CT91] and horizontal line segments [MN90], respectively. In both cases non-linear space was needed.

In our first solution we combine segment trees and fractional cascading, in the second solution we combine interval trees, segment trees, fractional cascading and the data structure of Cheng and Janardan [CJ90]. The following two difficulties arose.

(1) Fractional cascading [CG86] was developed to speed up (binary) search for the same key in many lists. The search algorithm in the Cheng-Janardan data structure is more complex than binary search and hence the searches in several such data structures interact in a more complex way than binary searches do.

(2) Fractional cascading copies elements from lists to neighboring lists, i.e. it creates bridges between lists. In this way an element may have copies in several lists. Suppose now that a segment with many copies is deleted from the collection S of segments. In standard dynamic fractional cascading ([MN90]), it is possible to leave the copies as *ghost elements* in the data structure. In the case of segments, the difficulty arises that ghost segments may intersect with segments inserted later. We allow intersections, but in a carefully controlled way, e.g. we guarantee that bridges never intersect and that no segment intersects more than one bridge.

4   On-line Construction of Abstract Voronoi Diagrams

The *Voronoi diagram* of a set of sites in the plane partitions the plane into regions, called *Voronoi regions*, one to a site. The Voronoi region of a site s is the set of points in the plane for which s is the closest site among all the sites.

The Voronoi diagram has many applications in diverse fields, cf. Leven and Sharir [LS86] or Aurenhammer [Aur90] for a list of applications and a history of Voronoi diagrams. Different types of diagrams result from considering different notions of distance, e.g. Euclidean or L_p-norm or convex distance functions, and different sorts of sites, e.g. points, line segments, or circles. For many types of diagrams efficient construction algorithms have been found; these are either based on the divide-and-conquer technique due to Shamos and Hoey [SH75], the sweepline technique due to Fortune [For87], or geometric transforms due to Brown [Bro79] and Edelsbrunner and Seidel [ES86].

A unifying approach to Voronoi diagrams was proposed by Klein [Kle88a, Kle88b, Kle89a, Kle89b], cf. [ES86] for a related approach. Klein does not use the concept of distance as the basic notion but rather the concept of *bisecting curve*, i.e. he assumes for each pair $\{p, q\}$ of sites the existence of a bisector $J(p, q)$ which is homeomorphic to a line and divides the plane into a p-region and a q-region. The intersection of all p-regions for different q's is then the Voronoi-region of site p. He also postulates that Voronoi-regions are simply-connected and partition the plane. He shows that these so-called *abstract Voronoi diagrams* have already many of the properties of concrete Voronoi diagrams.

In [MMO91] and the refinement [KMM91] we present a randomized incremental algorithm that can handle abstract Voronoi diagrams in (almost) their full generality. When n denotes the number of sites, the algorithm runs in $O(n \log n)$ expected time, the average being taken over all permutations of the input. The algorithm is simple enough to be of great practical importance. It is uniform in the sense that only a single operation, namely the construction of a Voronoi diagram for 5 sites, depends on the specific type of Voronoi diagram and has to be newly programmed in order to adapt the algorithm to the type of the diagram. Moreover, this operation is the only geometric operation in our algorithm, and using this operation, abstract Voronoi diagrams can be constructed in a purely combinatorial manner.

Our algorithm is based on Clarkson and Shor's randomized incremental construction technique [CS89]. We make use of the refinement proposed in [GKS90, BD89, BDT90, BDS+90]; in particular, we use the notion of history graph instead of the original conflict graph. Thus our algorithm is on-line in the sense that the input sites need not be known in advance.

The idea is to construct the abstract Voronoi diagram of a set S of sites incrementally by adding site after site in random order. When adding a new site to an existing Voronoi diagram some of its edges are (at least partially) deleted. We say that the new site is in *conflict* with these edges. We show that a conflict between an edge e and a site s can be checked by computing the Voronoi diagram of 5 sites, namely s and the 4 sites 'defining' e. This diagram also supplies the type of conflict, i.e. whether e disappears completely or only partially, and if so what parts disappear.

The algorithm starts with set $R_3 = \{p, q, r\}$, where p, q and r are chosen uniformly at random from S, and then adds the remaining sites in random order, i.e. $R_{k+1} = R_k \cup \{s\}$, where s is chosen uniformly at random from $S - R_k$. For the current set $R = R_k$ of sites the Voronoi diagram $V(R)$ and a history graph $\mathcal{H}(R)$ are maintained. The history graph is a directed acyclic graph with a single source. Its node set is given by $\{source\} \cup \bigcup_{3 \leq i \leq k} \{e \mid e$ is an edge of $V(R_i)\}$. Thus $\mathcal{H}(R)$ stores the edges of all intermediate Voronoi diagrams. The following history-graph invariants are maintained:

1. Every node of $\mathcal{H}(R)$ has outdegree at most 5 and the nodes corresponding to the edges of $V(R)$ have outdegree 0.

2. For every site $s \in S - R$ and every edge e of $V(R)$, such that s conflicts with e, there is a path from *source* to e that visits only nodes ($\hat{=}$ edges of some intermediate Voronoi diagram) in conflict with s.

We now sketch the insertion process for a new site $s \in S - R$, i.e. the construction of $V(R \cup \{s\})$ and $\mathcal{H}(R \cup \{s\})$ from $V(R)$ and $\mathcal{H}(R)$. By the history graph invariants, a graph traversal of $\mathcal{H}(R)$ that visits only nodes in conflict with s yields all edges of $V(R)$ in conflict with s. When we assume the finite part of $V(R)$ to be enclosed by an appropriate closed curve Γ, then the set of conflicting edges forms a connected subset of $V(R)$. We then remove these edges and construct the new ones. A new edge e always splits some old region $VR(p, R)$ and can thus be computed by walking along the removed part $\mathcal{P}$ of the boundary of $VR(p, R)$. Also a site $t \in S - R - \{s\}$ in conflict with the new edge e must be in conflict with some edge on $\mathcal{P}$ and therefore e is made child of all nodes in $\mathcal{H}(R)$ representing edges of $\mathcal{P}$. It is readily seen that the history graph invariants are maintained in this way. This completes the construction of $V(R \cup \{s\})$ and $\mathcal{H}(R \cup \{s\})$ from $V(R)$ and $\mathcal{H}(R)$.

We now apply the results of [BDS+90] on the running time and space complexity of the randomized incremental construction to our algorithm. To do so, we claim that the time for adding site s to R is proportional to the number of nodes in $\mathcal{H}(R)$ in conflict with s. The update of $V(R)$ and $\mathcal{H}(R)$ can even be accomplished in time proportional to the number of edges of $V(R)$ in conflict with s. For the traversal of $\mathcal{H}(R)$ the claim is obvious. It then follows from the framework given in [BDS+90] that the expected time for inserting the n-th site is $O(\log n)$, the expected overall time is $O(n \log n)$, and the expected space is $O(n)$.

5 Hidden Line Elimination for Isooriented Rectangles

In [MNU90] we consider the following problem:

> Given n isooriented rectangles in $\mathbb{R}^3$, i.e. rectangles which are parallel to the xy–plane and whose edges are parallel to the x– and y–axis, compute and report all parts of the edges that are visible to an observer at $z = +\infty$.

The hidden line elimination problem is of considerable interest. The running time of former hidden line elimination algorithms usually depends on the complexity of the projected scene, i.e. on the number of intersections between the edges projected into the xy–plane. Of course, in general, many of these intersections are invisible to the observer. The first output–sensitive algorithm for the hidden line elimination problem of isooriented rectangles was described by Güting and Ottmann ([GO87]). They achieved running time $O((n + k)(\log n)^2)$, where k is the number of the visible parts of the edges. Preparata, Vitter and Yvinec [PVY88] have improved the running time to $O(n(\log n)^2 + k \log n))$. They also mentioned that one can reach running time $O((n + k) \log n \log \log n)$ using dynamic fractional cascading ([MN90]). Bern ([Ber88]) presented an algorithm with running time $O(n \log n \log \log n + k \log n)$. Later on he improved the running time of his algorithm to $O((n + k) \log n)$ ([Ber89]). Another $O((n + k) \log n)$ algorithm was given by Atallah, Goodrich and Overmars ([AGO89]).

The algorithm described in our paper is almost identical to Bern's improved algorithm, although the analysis is slightly sharper at one point. It was found independently from his work. It runs on a random access machine in time $O(n \log n + k \log \frac{n^2}{k})$ and uses $O(n \log n)$ space. Note that for small and great k the running time is optimal.

As many researchers before, we use plane–sweep to solve the problem. First we sweep a plane parallel to the xz–plane along the y–axis and compute the visible parts of the edges being parallel to the x–axis. Afterwards we sweep a plane parallel to the yz–plane along the x–axis to compute the visible parts being parallel to the y–axis. We maintain the intersection of the sweep–plane with the scene in a static segment tree ([Ben77]). Whenever a rectangle starts (ends), an appropriate segment is inserted into (deleted from) the segment tree and its visible parts are computed.

Using standard results about segment trees, the approach outlined so far yields a running time of $O((n + k)(\log n)^2)$. We introduce two techniques to improve upon this.

1) We augment the segment tree with additional information which allows us to identify visible parts in time $O(\log \frac{n^2}{k})$ per part. The additional information records for each node of the tree the highest and lowest visible part stored in its subtree. Thus, when we check the visibility of a segment, we are able to decide in each node if it is necessary to visit some nodes in its subtree. This type of augmented segment tree was already used in [Ber88]; our running time analysis is slightly sharper than his.

For the computation of the mentioned lowest and highest visible part in a subtree we need the maximal z–coordinate of the segments actually stored in each node list. Instead of using a balanced binary tree we use the following technique to get a better time bound.

2) We show how to solve a two–dimensional hidden line problem for a set of q horizontal line segments in the xy–plane with an observer at $y = \infty$ in linear time $O(q)$. This assumes

that the endpoints of the line segments have distinct integer coordinates in $\{1, \ldots, 2q\}$ and that the line segments are given in order of decreasing z–coordinate. We use this algorithm to solve the hidden line problem for the node lists of all nodes of the segment tree in total time $O(n \log n)$. This technique is also used in [Ber89].

To fulfill the mentioned conditions for the coordinates we do some preprocessing steps where we replace the occurring coordinates by leading integer numbers and use bucket-sort to get the line segments in the wanted order.

6 A Lower Bound for the Complexity of the Union-Split-Find Problem

We consider the following three operations on a linear list $x_1, x_2, \ldots, x_n$ of items, some of which are marked.

- Union(x_i): given a pointer to the marked item x_i unmark this item

- Split(x_i): given a pointer to the unmarked item x_i mark this item

- Find(x_i): given a pointer to the item x_i return a pointer to x_j
  where $j = \min\{\ell | \ell \geq i$ and x_ℓ is marked $\}$

Note that the marked items partition the linear list $x_1, \ldots, x_n$ into intervals of unmarked items. Then Find(x_i) returns (a pointer to) the right endpoint of the interval containing x_i, Split(x_i) splits the interval containing x_i, and Union(x_i) joins the two intervals having x_i as a common endpoint. We call the problem above the *Union-Split-Find Problem*; P. van Emde Boas [EKZ77] called it a priority queue problem. He referred to the three operations as Insert, Delete and Successor, and exhibited a $O(\log \log n)$ solution for it. We will also consider the *Split-Find Problem* and the *Union-Find Problem* (only operations split, find and union, find, respectively). Note that our Union-Find problem is a restriction of the usual Union-Find problem (here called the general Union-Find problem) because we allow only adjacent intervals to be joined. The Union-Split-Find problem is important for a number of applications, e.g. dynamic fractional cascading and computing shortest paths.

In [MNA88] we study the complexity of the Union-Split-Find problem in the pointer machine model of computation (Kolmogorov [Kol53], Schönhage [Sch80], Tarjan [Tar79]). A pointer machine captures the list processing capabilities of computers; its storage consists of records connected by pointers. Previously, lower bounds in a restricted pointer machine model (the term "restricted" is explained below) were obtained by Tarjan [Tar79] and Blum [Blu86]. Tarjan proved a $\Theta(\alpha(n))$ bound on the amortized cost of the general Union-Find problem and Blum proved a $\Theta(\log n / \log \log n)$ bound on the worst-case cost. Tarjan's and Blum's lower bounds rely heavily on the following *separation assumption* (quoted from Tarjan [Tar79]):

> "At any time during the computation, the contents of the memory can be partitioned into collections of records such that each collection corresponds to a currently existing set, . . . and no record in one collection contains a pointer to a record in another collection."

Because of this assumption we call their model *restricted*. If one views pointers as undirected edges in a graph then the separation assumption states that every currently existing set corresponds to a component of the graph.

Our main results are:

- The complexity of the Union-Split-Find problem in the pointer machine model is $\Theta(\log \log n)$. Here, the upper bound is on the worst-case cost of the three operations and the lower bound is on the amortized cost of the three operations, i.e. there are arbitrarily large m and sequences of m Split, Find and Union operations having a total cost of $\Omega(m \log \log n)$.

- In the restricted pointer machine model the worst-case complexity of the Split-Find problem is $\Theta(\log n)$ and the amortized complexity of the Union-Split-Find problem is $\Theta(\log n)$.

7 Acknowledgements

The work presented in this paper has many parents, not all working at our institute in Saarbrücken. We would like to thank all of them, especially Helmut Alt, Hanna Baumgarten, Rolf Klein, Hermann Jung, Colm Ó Dúnlaing, Günther Rote, Emo Welzl and Chee Yap.

References

[AAG+86] Ta. Asano, Te. Asano, L.J. Guibas, J. Hershberger, and H. Imai. Visibility-polygon search and euclidean shortest paths. *Algorithmica*, 1(1):49–64, 1986.

[AFK+90] H. Alt, R. Fleischer, M. Kaufmann, K. Mehlhorn, S. Näher, S. Schirra, and C. Uhrig. Approximate motion planning and the complexity of the boundary of the union of simple plane figures. In *Proc. of the 6th ACM Symposium on Computational Geometry*, pages 281–289, 1990.

[AGO89] M.J. Atallah, M.G. Goodrich, and M.H. Overmars. New output–sensitive methods for rectilinear hidden surface removal. Presented on a Workshop on Computational Geometry in Princeton, Oct. 1989.

[AHU74] A.V. Aho, J.E. Hopcroft, and J.D. Ullman. *The Design and Analysis of Computer Algorithms*. Addison-Wesley Publishing Company, 1974.

[Aur90] F. Aurenhammer. Voronoi diagrams — a survey of a fundamental geometric data structure. Technical Report B 90-09, Freie Universität Berlin, 1990. To appear in ACM Computing Surveys.

[AW88] H. Alt and E. Welzl. Visibility graphs and obstacle-avoiding shortest paths. *Zeitschrift für Operations Research*, 32:145–164, 1988.

[BD89] J.D. Boissonnat and M. Devillers-Teillaud. On the randomized construction of the delaunay tree. Technical Report 1140, INRIA Sophia-Antipolis, 1989.

[BDS+90] J.D. Boissonnat, O. Devillers, R. Schott, M. Teillaud, and M. Yvinec. Applications of random sampling to on-line algorithms in computational geometry. Technical Report 1285, INRIA Sophia-Antipolis, 1990.

[BDT90] J.D. Boissonnat, O. Devillers, and M. Teillaud. A dynamic construction of higher order voronoi diagrams and its randomized analysis. Technical Report 1207, INRIA Sophia-Antipolis, 1990.

[Ben77] J.L. Bentley. Solutions to klee's rectangle problems. Unpublished manuscript, Carnegie–Mellon University, Department of Computer Science, 1977.

[Ber88] M. Bern. Hidden surface removal for rectangles. In *Proc. of the 4th ACM Symposium on Computational Geometry*, pages 183–192, 1988.

[Ber89] M. Bern. Hidden surface removal for rectangles. Personal Communication, Oct. 1989.

[BJM92] H. Baumgarten, H. Jung, and K. Mehlhorn. Dynamic point location in general subdivisions. To be presented at the ACM-SIAM Symposium on Discrete Algorithms, 1992.

[Blu86] N. Blum. On the single-operation worst-case time complexity of the disjoint set union problem. *SIAM Journal on Computing*, 15(4):1021–1024, 1986.

[Bro79] K.Q. Brown. Voronoi diagrams from convex hulls. *Information Processing Letters*, 9:223–228, 1979.

[CG86] B. Chazelle and L.J. Guibas. Fractional cascading. *Algorithmica*, 1:133–196, 1986.

[Che85] L.P. Chew. Planning the shortest path for a disc in $o(n^2 \log n)$ time. In *Proc. of the 1st ACM Symposium on Computational Geometry*, pages 214–220, 1985.

[CJ90] S.W. Cheng and R. Janardan. New results on dynamic planar point location. In *Proc. of the 31th Annual IEEE Symposium on Foundations of Computer Science*, volume 1, pages 96–105, 1990.

[CK90] L.P. Chew and K. Kedem. High-clearance motion planning for a convex polygon among polygonal obstacles. Technical Report 184/90, Tel Aviv University, 1990.

[CS89] K.L. Clarkson and P.W. Shor. Applications of random sampling in computational geometry, ii. *Discrete and Computational Geometry*, 4:387–421, 1989.

[CT91] Y.J. Ching and R. Tamassia. Dynamization of the trapezoid method for planar point location. *Proc. of the 7th ACM Symposium on Computational Geometry*, 1991.

[DS79] D. Dobkin and L. Snyder. On a general method for maximizing and minimizing among certain geometric problems. In *Proc. of the 20th Annual IEEE Symposium on Foundations of Computer Science*, pages 9–17, 1979.

[EGS86]   H. Edelsbrunner, L.J. Guibas, and J. Stolfi. Optimal point location in a monotone subdivision. *SIAM Journal on Computing*, 15(2):317–340, 1986.

[EKZ77]   P. van Emde Boas, R. Kaas, and E. Zijlstra. Design and implementation of an efficient priority queue. *Math. Systems Theory*, 10:99–127, 1977.

[ES86]   H. Edelsbrunner and R. Seidel. Voronoi diagrams and arrangements. *Discrete and Computational Geometry*, 1:25–44, 1986.

[FMR+90] R. Fleischer, K. Mehlhorn, G. Rote, E. Welzl, and C. Yap. On simultaneous inner and outer approximation of shapes. In *Proc. of the 6th ACM Symposium on Computational Geometry*, pages 216–224, 1990. Also available as "Technical Report B 91-08, FU Berlin".

[For87]   S. Fortune. A sweepline algorithm for voronoi diagrams. *Algorithmica*, 2:153–174, 1987.

[Fri89]   O. Fries. *Suche in dynamischen planaren Unterteilungen der Ebene*. PhD thesis, Universität des Saarlandes, 1989.

[FRSW90] U. Fuchs, G. Rote, O. Schwarzkopf, and E. Welzl. Approximation of convex figures by pairs of rectangles. In *Proc. of the 7th Annual Symposium on Theoretical Aspects of Computer Science*, pages 240–249, 1990.

[GKS90]   L.J. Guibas, D.E. Knuth, and M. Sharir. Randomized incremental construction of delaunay and voronoi diagrams. In *Proc. of the 17th International Colloqium on Automata, Languages and Programming*, pages 414–431, Warwick, 1990. LNCS 443.

[GM87]   S.K. Ghosh and D.M. Mount. An output sensitive algorithm for computing visibility graphs. Technical Report CS-TR-1874, University of Maryland, 1987.

[GO87]   R.H. Güting and T.H. Ottmann. New algorithms for special cases of the hidden line elimination problem. *Computer Vision, Graphics and Image Processing*, 40, 1987.

[Gru83]   P.M. Gruber. Approximation of convex bodies. In *Convexity and its Applications*, pages 131–162. Birkhäuser Verlag, 1983.

[GT91]   M.T. Goodrich and R. Tamassia. Dynamic trees and dynamic point location. In *Proc. of the ACM Symposium on Theory of Computing*, 1991.

[HO89]   D. Halperin and M. Overmars. Efficient motion planning for an l-shaped object. In *Proc. of the 5th ACM Symposium on Computational Geometry*, pages 156–166, 1989.

[Kle88a] R. Klein. Abstract voronoi diagrams and their applications (extended abstract). In H. Noltemeier, editor, *Proc. of the Workshop on Computational Geometry and its Applications*, pages 148–157, Würzburg, 1988. LNCS 333.

[Kle88b]   R. Klein. Voronoi diagrams in the moscow metric (extended abstract). In J. van Leeuwen, editor, *Proc. of the Workshop on Graphtheoretic Concepts in Computer Science*, pages 434–441, Amsterdam, 1988. LNCS 344.

[Kle89a]   R. Klein. Combinatorial properties of abstract voronoi diagrams. In M. Nagl, editor, *Proc. of the Workshop on Graphtheoretic Concepts in Computer Science*, pages 356–369, Rolduc, 1989. LNCS 411.

[Kle89b]   R. Klein. *Concrete and Abstract Voronoi Diagrams*. Springer Verlag, 1989. LNCS 400.

[KLPS86]   K. Kedem, R. Livne, J. Pach, and M. Sharir. On the union of jordan regions and collision-free motion amidst polygonal obstacles. *Discrete and Computational Geometry*, 1:59–71, 1986.

[KLS90]   R. Kannan, L. Lovász, and H.E. Scarf. The shapes of polyhedra. *Mathematics of Operations Research*, 15:364–380, 1990.

[KM88]   S. Kapoor and S.N. Maheshwari. Efficient algorithms for euclidean shortest path and visibility problems with polygonal obstacles. In *Proc. of the 4th ACM Symposium on Computational Geometry*, pages 172–182, 1988.

[KMM91]   R. Klein, K. Mehlhorn, and St. Meiser. Randomized incremental construction of abstract voronoi diagrams. Unpublished manuscript, 1991.

[Kol53]   A.N. Kolmogorov. On the notion of algorithm. *Uspehi Mat. Nauk.*, 8:175–176, 1953.

[KS88]   K. Kedem and M. Sharir. An automatic motion planning system for a convex polygonal mobile robot in 2-d polygonal space. In *Proc. of the 4th ACM Symposium on Computational Geometry*, pages 329–340, 1988.

[LP77]   D.T. Lee and F.P. Preparata. Location of a point in a planar subdivision and its applications. *SIAM Journal on Computing*, 6(3):594–606, 1977.

[LP84]   D.T. Lee and F.P. Preparata. Euclidean shortest paths in the presence of rectilinear barriers. *Networks*, 14:393–410, 1984.

[LS85]   R. Livne and M. Sharir. On intersection of planar jordan curves. Technical Report TR 153, N.Y. University, Courant Institute, 1985.

[LS86]   D. Leven and M. Sharir. Intersection and proximity problems and voronoi diagrams. In J. Schwartz and C.K. Yap, editors, *Advances in Robotics, Volume 1*, pages 187–228. Lawrence Erlbaum, 1986.

[Meh84]   K. Mehlhorn. *Data Structures and Algorithms*. Springer Verlag, 1984.

[MMO91]   K. Mehlhorn, St. Meiser, and C. Ó'Dúnlaing. On the construction of abstract voronoi diagrams. *Discrete and Computational Geometry*, 6:211–224, 1991.

[MN90]   K. Mehlhorn and S. Näher. Dynamic fractional cascading. *Algorithmica*, 5:215–241, 1990.

[MNA88]   K. Mehlhorn, St. Näher, and H. Alt. A lower bound on the complexity of the union-split-find problem. *SIAM Journal on Computing*, 17(6):1093–1102, 1988.

[MNU90]   K. Mehlhorn, S. Näher, and C. Uhrig. Hidden line elimination for isooriented rectangles. *Information Processing Letters*, 35:137–143, 1990.

[Ove85]   M.H. Overmars. Range searching in a set of line segments. In *Proc. of the 1st ACM Symposium on Computational Geometry*, pages 177–185, 1985.

[OW84]   T. Ottmann and D. Wood. The contour problem for polygons. Technical Report CS-84-33, University of Waterloo, 1984.

[OW88]   M.H. Overmars and E. Welzl. New methods for computing visibility graphs. In *Proc. of the 4th ACM Symposium on Computational Geometry*, pages 164–171, 1988.

[OY85]   C. Ó'Dúnlaing and C.K. Yap. A 'retraction' method for planning the motion of a disc. *Journal of Algorithms*, 6:104–111, 1985.

[PT88]   F.P. Preparata and R. Tamassia. Fully dynamic techniques fo point location and transitive closure in planar structures (ea). In *Proc. of the 29th Annual IEEE Symposium on Foundations of Computer Science*, pages 558–567, 1988.

[PT89]   F.P. Preparata and R. Tamassia. Fully dynamic point location in a monotone subdivision. *SIAM Journal on Computing*, 18:811–830, 1989.

[PVY88]   F.P. Preparata, J.S. Vitter, and M. Yvinec. Computation of the axial view of a set of isothetic parallelepipeds. Technical Report LIENS–88–1, Laboratoire d'Informatique, Ecole Normale Superieure, Paris, 1988.

[Roh86]   H. Rohnert. Shortest paths in the plane with convex polygonal obstacles. *Information Processing Letters*, 23:71–76, 1986.

[Roh88]   H. Rohnert. Time and space efficient algorithms for shortest paths between convex polygons. *Information Processing Letters*, 27:175–179, 1988.

[Roh89]   H. Rohnert. *Bewegungsplanung in der Ebene*. PhD thesis, Universität des Saarlandes, 1989.

[Roh91]   H. Rohnert. Moving a disk between polygons. *Algorithmica*, 6(2):182–191, 1991.

[Sch]   S. Schirra. *Approximative Bewegungsplanungsverfahren*. PhD thesis, Universität des Saarlandes. In preparation.

[Sch80]   A. Schönhage. Storage modification machines. *SIAM Journal on Computing*, 9:490–508, 1980.

[SH75] M.I. Shamos and D. Hoey. Closest point problems. In *Proc. of the 16th Annual IEEE Symposium on Foundations of Computer Science*, pages 151–162, 1975.

[SS90] J.T. Schwartz and M. Sharir. Algorithmic motion planning in robotics. In *Handbook of Theoretical Computer Science, Volume A: Algorithms and Complexity*. Elsevier, 1990.

[Tar79] R.E. Tarjan. A class of algorithms which require nonlinear time to maintain disjoint sets. *Journal of Computer and System Sciences*, 18:110–127, 1979.

[Wel85] E. Welzl. Constructing the visibility graph for n line segments in $o(n^2)$ time. *Information Processing Letters*, 20:167–171, 1985.

Processing of Hierarchically Defined Graphs and Graph Families

Franz Höfting*   Thomas Lengauer*   Egon Wanke*

1 Introduction

Hierarchical definitions of graphs play an increasingly important role in computer science and engineering. The progress in many fabrication technologies affords us with levels of design complexity that can only be handled in an economical manner if powerful mechanisms of parameterization and duplication can be employed to describe the designs.

This phenomenon is most prominent in *integrated circuit design* where the level of complexity has risen from a few hundred transistors to over a million transistors per chip in less than twenty years. At the same time, the amount of human resources that is available for the design of microelectronic systems has remained the same. Thus, today, it is not even possible to develop a design that taxes the possibilities of the fabrication technology unless we employ hierarchical design methods.

Other fabrication technologies show the same trend, even though the levels of complexity are not growing as explosively. In *mechanical engineering*, for instance, hierarchical design methods become more and more essential.

Another important example of hierarchical design is an *iterative* or *recursive program*. Here, we are not linked to a fabrication technology; the final expanded design is the flow graph of a program. However, since the program text is always a highly folded version of the flow graph, hierarchical graph issues come into play when one wants to reason about program flow on the basis of the program text. Many research contributions in the area of the automatic parallelization of sequential programs in software and hardware have exploited this fact.

The present paper gives an overview of most of the results obtained in a five-year research project on *Hierarchical Graph Processing* that was conducted within the research program *Efficient Algorithms* which is the topic of this volume. Most of the results that we report on have appeared in international conferences or refereed journals. However, some of the newer results are still unpublished and, of course, there are open problems still under investigation and concrete plans for future research. This paper will discuss all of these aspects of the project.

---

*Department of Mathematics and Computer Science, University of Paderborn, W-4790 Paderborn, Germany

2   The hierarchical graph models

A hierarchical graph description consists of a collection of *special graphs* which are conventional graphs with some additional so-called *nonterminal* parts. Each nonterminal part provides two kinds of information. The first kind of information specifies a certain *locus* or *region* of the usual graph. The second kind of information specifies a special graph from the collection of all special graphs which is to replace the nonterminal part. One of the special graphs is the *axiom* of the system.

The graph represented by a hierarchical description is obtained by successive substitutions of the nonterminal parts by copies of their replacements. The substitution starts with the axiom and terminates when there are no further nonterminal parts. In general, a substitution is performed in three steps.

1. Add a copy of the special graph defined by the nonterminal part.

2. Embed the inserted copy at the place defined by the nonterminal part.

3. Delete the nonterminal part and its information.

Hierarchical graph models differ by their embedding methods. The two most common embedding methods are based on the identification of vertices and the addition of new edges, respectively. To make this intuitive concept precise, we will give two definitions of hierarchical graph models. The first is from [LW88b] and the second from [Wan89b].

Definition 1: A *hierarchical cellular graph* Γ is a system $(G_1, \ldots, G_k)$ of *pin-graphs*. Each *pin-graph* G_i is a system $(V_i, E_i, P_i, N_i, vert_i, num_i)$, where (V_i, E_i) is the *underlying graph* of G_i, $P_i \subseteq V_i^*$ is a sequence of pairwise distinct vertices from V_i, called the *pin-list* of G_i, N_i is a finite set of abstract objects called *nonterminals*, $vert_i : V_i \rightarrow V_i^*$ is a mapping that associates with each nonterminal a list of pairwise distinct vertices from V_i, and $num : N \rightarrow \mathbb{N}$ is a mapping that associates with each nonterminal an integer that specifies a pin-graph from Γ. A pin-graph with a pin-list of length h is called a h-graph. The vertices in the pin-list are called *pins*.

Figure 1 shows a hierarchical cellular graph.

Let G and H be two pin-graphs and let n be a nonterminal of G such that the size of $vert_G(n)$ is equal to the size of the pin-list P_H of H. The pin-graph $G[H/n]$ is defined by the following procedure:

1. Take the disjoint union of G and a copy $\hat{H}$ of H.

2. Identify the ith vertex from the pin-list of $\hat{H}$ with the ith vertex from $vert_G(n)$.

3. Delete the nonterminal n.

The pin-list of $G[H/n]$ is the pin-list of G. Figure 2 shows a substitution step used in the cellular graph model. The substitution in the cellular graph model is *associative* and *confluent*. That is, if G, H, and J are three pin-graphs then:

1. If n is a nonterminal from G and m is a nonterminal from J such that $|vert_G(n)| = |P_H|$ and $|vert_H(m)| = |P_J|$, then

$$G[H/n][J/m] = G[H[J/m]/n].\qquad\text{(Associativity)}$$

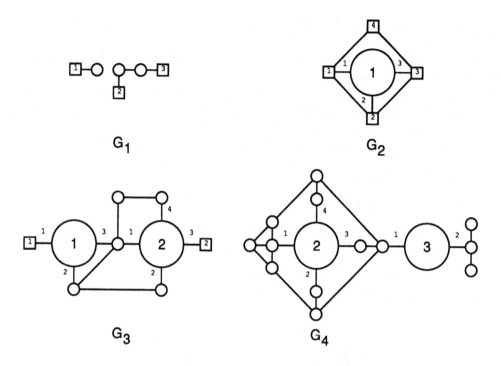

Figure 1: A hierarchical cellular graph with four pin-graphs. Pins are represented by squares containing a number that identifies the position of the pin in the pin-list. Non-terminals are represented by large circles. Inside the circle for nonterminal n, the integer $num(n)$ is written. There are lines between the big circle of a nonterminal n and all vertices from $vert(n)$. The integers on the line denote the position of the vertices in $vert(n)$.

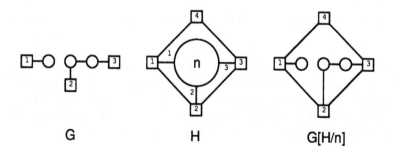

Figure 2: A substitution step in the cellular graph model.

2. If n and m are two nonterminals from G such that $|vert_G(n)| = |P_H|$ and $|vert_G(m)| = |P_J|$, then

$$G[H/n][J/m] = G[J/m][H/n].$$ (Confluence)

Since the substitution is confluent we will write $G[H/n, J/m]$ instead of $G[H/n][J/m]$ or $G[J/m][H/n]$.

Let $\Gamma = (G_1, \ldots, G_k)$ be a hierarchical cellular graph such that for each pin-graph G_i and each nonterminal $n \in N_i$ we have $1 \leq num_i(n) < i$ and $|vert_i(n)| = |P_{num_i(n)}|$. The following *expansion procedure* computes a pin-graph $\tilde{G}_i$ that represents the *expansion* of the *hierarchical cellular subgraph* $\Gamma_i := (G_1, \ldots, G_i)$. The expansion $E(\Gamma)$ of Γ is the underlying graph of the pin-graph $\tilde{G}_k$, where G_k is the axiom of Γ.

Figure 3 shows the expansion of the hierarchical cellular graph of Figure 1.

The expansion procedure:

> FOR $i := 1, \ldots, k$ DO
>
> > LET $n_1, \ldots, n_m$ be the nonterminals of G_i;
> > IF $m > 0$
> > > THEN $\tilde{G}_i := G_i[\tilde{G}_{num_i(n_1)}/n_1, \ldots, \tilde{G}_{num_i(n_m)}/n_m]$;
> > > ELSE $\tilde{G}_i := G_i$;

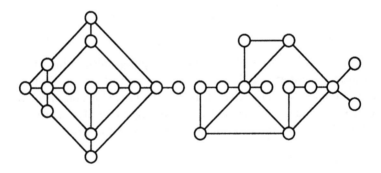

Figure 3: The expansion of the hierarchical graph depicted in Figure 1.

The *parse-tree* of $\tilde{G}_i$ is a directed rooted tree. Let $n_1, \ldots, n_m$ be the nonterminals of G_i and $T_1, \ldots, T_m$ be copies of the parse-trees of $\tilde{G}_{num_i(n_1)}, \ldots, \tilde{G}_{num_i(n_m)}$. The parse-tree of G_i is defined by the disjoint union of $T_1, \ldots, T_m$ with an additional vertex u and all edges from u to the roots of the joined parse-trees. If $m = 0$, then there is only the vertex u. Vertex u becomes the root of the parse tree of $\tilde{G}_i$.

We have also analyzed a second embedding mechanism that is based on the addition of new edges. The hierarchical graph model that uses this embedding is called the *hierarchical BNLC graph model*, see [Wan89b].

Definition 2: Let Σ be a finite set of symbols. Each labeled graph G over Σ is a system (V, E, lab, Σ), where (V, E) is the underlying graph of G and $lab : V \to \Sigma$ is a mapping that labels each vertex with a symbol from Σ. Let G and H be two labeled graphs over Σ, u be a vertex of G, and $C \subseteq \Sigma \times \Sigma$ be a so-called *connection relation*. The labeled graph $G[H/_C u]$ over Σ is defined by the following procedure:

48

1. Take the disjoint union of G and a copy $\hat{H}$ of H.

2. Add all edges between all vertices v incident with u and all vertices w from $\hat{H}$ with $(lab_G(v), lab_{\hat{H}}(w)) \in C$.

3. Delete the nonterminal vertex u.

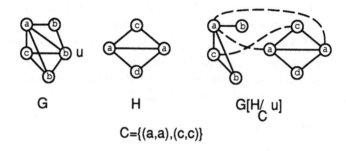

$$C=\{(a,a),(c,c)\}$$

Figure 4: A substitution step in the BNLC graph model.

Figure 4 shows a substitution step used in the BNLC graph model. The substitution in the BNLC model is also confluent but not associative. Note that it is possible to add edges between vertices that can be substituted in a subsequent step. However, in the hierarchical BNLC graph model, we can only substitute special *nonterminal vertices*, which will be never adjacent. Then the associativity can be enforced by a simple additional labeling trick, see [Wan89b].

The hierarchical BNLC graph, its expansions, and the parse-trees of the expansion are defined analogously to the hierarchical cellular graph model, where some nonterminal vertices u will be substituted by other labeled graphs.

3   Analysis of hierarchical graphs

For certain graph problems Π, the solution of Π on the expansion $E(\Gamma)$ can be obtained by certain solutions of Π on the sub-expansions $\widetilde{G}_i$ for $1 \leq i < k$. Our solution method for graph problems on hierarchical cellular and hierarchical BNLC graphs is based on the following definition of *replaceability*.

Definition 3: Let Π be any graph problem.

1. Two h-graphs H and J are called *replaceable* with respect to Π, denoted by $H \sim_\Pi J$, if and only if for all pin-graphs G with a nonterminal n and $|vert_G(n)| = h$:

$$\Pi(G[H/n]) = \Pi(G[J/n]).$$

2. Two labeled graphs H and J over some alphabet Σ are replaceable with respect to Π, denoted by $H \sim_\Pi J$, if and only if for all labeled graphs G over Σ with a vertex u and all connection relations $C \subseteq \Sigma \times \Sigma$:

$$\Pi(G[H/_C n]) = \Pi(G[J/_C n]).$$

Replaceability is always an equivalence relation that will be preserved by a confluent and associative substitution, see Lemma 1 in [Wan89b] and [LW88a]. The graph problem Π need not be a graph property. For instance, G could have weighted edges and $\Pi(G)$ could be the size of a minimum spanning forest of G [Len87, FBW89].

Our method of solving graph problems on the expansion of a hierarchical graph is called the *bottom-up* method. We analyze each pin-graph G_i for $i = 1, \ldots, k$. The result of the analysis of pin-graph G_i is a small graph G_i^b that is *replaceable* with the expansion $\widetilde{G}_i$ of pin-graph G_i. We construct G_i^b by replacing each nonterminal n_j in G_i with the (already constructed) small graphs $G_{num_i(n_j)}^b$ that are replaceable with the expanded graph $\widetilde{G}_{num_i(n_j)}$. The result is then transformed into a small replaceable graph by a procedure $burn_\Pi()$ that is particular to the graph property Π. This procedure is called *burning procedure*, and its result G_i^b is called the *burnt* graph.

The bottom-up procedure:

> FOR $i := 1, \ldots, k$ DO {
>
> > LET $n_1, \ldots, n_m$ be the nonterminals of G_i;
> > IF $m > 0$
> > > THEN $G_i^b := burn_\Pi(G_i[G_{num_i(n_1)}^b/n_1, \ldots, G_{num_i(n_m)}^b/n_m])$;
> > > ELSE $G_i^b := burn_\Pi(G_i)$; }

The bottom-up procedure is just an extended expansion procedure. The whole process can be organized in a tabular fashion. This so-called *bottom-up table* has three columns, and one row for each pin-graph of the cellular graph definition. Initially, the pin-graphs of the cellular graph definition are entered in column 1 of the table in the order in which they are defined in the input. The rest of the table is filled rowwise from top to bottom, each row is filled from left to right. Let G_i be the cell in table entry $(i, 1)$. Then table entry $(i, 2)$ contains the graph $\widetilde{G}_i$ in that all nonterminals are replaced by burnt graphs, and table entry $(i, 3)$ contains the burned graph G_i^b. Finally we test the graph property on the graph in the bottom right corner of the table.

The correctness of this procedure is ensured if the burning procedure produces replaceable graphs. Its efficiency is determined by two performance measures of the burning procedure, namely the *size* of the graphs it produces and the *time* it needs to produce them. Graph properties that have linear time and linear size burners—*linear* burners, for short—can be decided in linear time in the size of the cellular description of the graph.

The connectivity property has an especially simple burner. In addition to the pins this burner provides a vertex for each connected component that contains a pin, and a vertex representing all other connected components. Each pin is connected to the vertex that represents the connected component containing the pin. It is not hard to see that this burner is linear. For practical implementation the burner can be further optimized by collapsing the vertices representing connected components that have one or two pins. Figure 5 shows a bottom-up processing for connectivity of the hierarchical cellular graph from Figure 1.

Many graph properties have efficient burners, however, not all of them are linear. The table in Figure 6 gives a short overview about the time and space complexity of some burning procedures for the cellular and BNLC graph model.

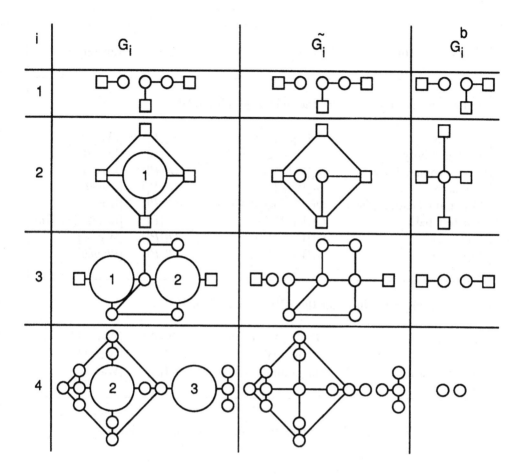

Figure 5: A bottom-up processing for connectivity.

In general, a burner does not depend on a special method for the nonhierarchical solution of the graph property. This observation is very important for practical purposes. In practice, it is often preferable to implement a robust nonhierarchical algorithm that may not be optimal asymptotically. This is, because such an algorithm runs better on small graphs (such as we expect single pin-graphs to be), and it is easier to implement.

Deciding a graph property is only one step of a graph processing. Often we have to construct graphs from other graphs, label graphs, or provide data structures for answering queries on graphs. Further problems related to graph connectivity may be:

1. Construct the connected component given by a vertex v in the graph

2. Label each vertex in the graph with the number of its connected component

3. Answer queries of the following type: Given two vertices v, w in the graph, are they connected?

The construction of the bottom-up table provides a data structure for solving all these problems very efficiently in the cellular model. Its contents can be used to restructure

Graph problem	Time	Space	Reference
Some burning procedures for the cellular graph model			
Connectivity	$O(|V| + |E|)$	$O(|P|)$	[LW88b]
Biconnectivity	$O(|V| + |E|)$	$O(|P|)$	[LW88b]
Strong-connectivity	$O(|V|^{2.39\cdots})$	$O(|P|^2)$	[LW88b]
Planarity	$O(|V| + |E|)$	$O(|P|)$	[Len89]
Minimum spanning forest	$O(|E| \cdot \log(\beta(|V|, |E|)))$	$O(|P|)$	[Len87]
Shortest path	$O(|V|^{2.39\cdots})$	$O(|P|^2)$	[Len82, LW87b]
Euler path	$O(|V| + |E|)$	$O(|P|)$	[Wan86]
Bipartite	$O(|V| + |E|)$	$O(|P|)$	[Wan86]
Some burning procedures for the BNLC graph model			
Bipartite	$O(|V| \cdot |\Sigma|^2 + |E| \cdot |\Sigma|)$	$O(|\Sigma|^2)$	[Wan89b]
Cycle	polynomial	$O(|\Sigma|^2)$	[Wan89b]
Shortest path	polynomial	$O(|\Sigma|^2)$	[Wan89b]

Figure 6: The complexity of some burning procedures.

the hierarchical description of the graph such that it is completely compatible with the connectivity structure, i.e., each connected component can be identified with a subset of the hierarchical graph definition, see Figure 7. The two connected components of the expansion in Figure 3 are hierarchically represented by the hierarchical cellular graph in Figure 7 with the axioms G_6 and G_7, respectively. The modified hierarchical description is a basis for efficiently solving a whole host of graph problems related to connectivity. Similar modifications of the cellular description are known for biconnectivity problems, but not for strong connectivity problems and not for the BNLC graph model.

4 The complexity of graph problems on hierarchical graphs

Not all graph properties have efficient burners. Furthermore, the classical complexity of a graph problem does not correlate with its complexity in the hierarchical model (as opposed to the small circuit model [PY86]). Lengauer and Wagner [LW87a] discuss the complexity of several graph problems in the classical and the cellular graph model.

Figure 8 shows a number of graph problems, their classical complexities, and their

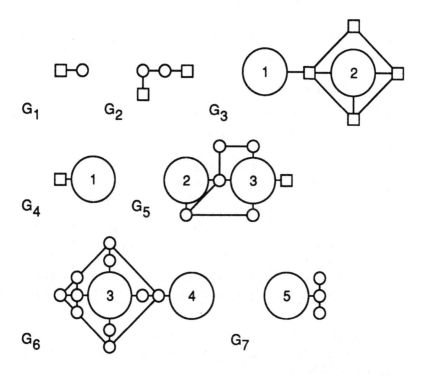

Figure 7: The cellular definition modified to reflect the connectivity structure of the expansion.

hierarchical complexities in the cellular model. The rows and columns in the table are labeled with the complexity classes L, NL, P, NP, and PSPACE. A graph problem is put in the table entry (X,Y) if its nonhierarchical version is log-space complete for Y, and its cellular hierarchical version is log-space for X. Note that the upper right region of the table cannot contain any graph problem, since the hierarchical graph model properly contains the classical nonhierarchical graph model. In the BNLC graph model, there is also no correlation between the complexities of the two versions of a graph problem, see [Wan89c, Wan89a] for some examples.

5   Families of graphs

If one extends the hierarchical models such as to allow for alternatives of replacing non-terminals with special graphs, and if one also allows for nonterminals representing special graphs that have not been defined previously in the hierarchy—thus providing for recursive definitions—one obtains families of graph grammars that are known as *hyperedge replacement systems* (or *cellular graph grammars* [LW88a]) and *BNLC graph grammars* [RW86].

Definition 4: A *cellular graph grammar* Γ is a hierarchical cellular graph $(G_1, \ldots, G_k)$, where the mappings num_i of the pin-graphs G_i associate each nonterminal $n \in N_i$ with a

nonhier. → hier. ↓	L	NL	P	NP
L	VERTEX			
NL	EDGE	GAP (ordered)		
P	AGAP	GAP (log depth, bounded degree, ordered)	AGAP (ordered)	
NP	CLIQUE (log degree)	CGAP	ACGAP (ordered)	CLIQUE
PSPACE	MONOTONE CIRCUIT VALUE (log depth)	3-COLORABILITY (log bandwidth)	NETWORK FLOW	HAMILTONIAN CIRCUIT

Figure 8: Some graph problems and their complexity classes in the hierarchical and nonhierarchical version. (AGAP and CGAP stand for the alternating and chromatic graph accessibility problem, respectively.)

set of integers between 1 and k.

A pin-graph H *directly derives* (in Γ) a pin-graph J, denoted by $H \Rightarrow_\Gamma J$, if G has a nonterminal n and there is an integer $i \in num_G(n)$ such that $|vert_G(n)| = |P_i|$ and $J = G[G_i/n]$. By $\Rightarrow_\Gamma^*$ we denote the reflexive and transitive closure of $\Rightarrow_\Gamma$. The *language* of Γ is the set of all graphs underlying the pin-graphs that have no nonterminals and are derivable from the axiom of Γ.

BNLC graph grammars are defined analogously by an extension of hierarchical BNLC graphs.

The graph grammars we use here are succinct versions of the grammars defined in [HK87] and [RW86]. Both types of graph grammars are context-free, i.e., there are no specific side constraints that control the applicability of a derivation step.

6   Analysis of graph families

The hierarchical methods discussed in Section 3 carry over directly to the analysis of graphs generated by graph grammars. We will first consider the decision of graph properties. *Deciding a graph property on a graph grammar* means deciding whether the language generated by the grammar containers at least one graph that has the property. Replaceability plays again a central role in deciding graph properties on context-free graph grammars.

Definition 5: Let Π be a decidable graph property. Replaceability with respect to Π is an equivalence relation on pin-graphs with k pins in the cellular model and on labeled graphs with k labels in the BNLC model.

1. The equivalence classes of the equivalence relation $\sim_\Pi$ are called *glue types*.

2. Π is called *k-finite* for the cellular model or the BNLC model if there are only finitely many glue types for all pin-graphs with k pins or all labeled graphs with at most k labels, respectively. The number of such glue types is called the *k-size*.

3. Π is called finite if Π is k-finite for all k.

Many interesting graph properties are finite for the cellular and BNLC graph models. Figure 9 shows that there are six glue types for 3-graphs and the connectivity property. In particular, a graph property is finite if it has a burner producing burnt graphs whose size only depends on the number of pins or the number of labels, respectively. It does not matter how efficient the burner is. But we can even ensure that properties are finite for which no finite burner is known. For instance, Hamiltonicity is a finite graph property for the cellular graph model. We can bound the number of glue types for k-graphs from above by $2^{(k/2+2)^k}$. On the other hand, it does not seem to be simple to develop a burner for Hamiltonicity. Also, Hamiltonicity is not finite for the BNLC graph model [Wan89b].

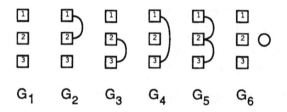

Figure 9: Each 3-graph is replaceable with exactly one of the six depicted 3-graphs with respect to connectivity.

Courcelle has shown in [Cou90] that each graph property definable in *counting second monadic logic* is finite for the cellular graph model. This logic uses quantifications over vertices, edges, sets of vertices, and sets of edges and allows to count the cardinalities of sets modulo positive integers. In [Cou87], Courcelle has shown that this logic with quantifications only over vertices and sets of vertices defines finite graph properties for the BNLC graph model.

Deciding a graph property Π on a graph grammar is possible if, given k, one can compute an upper bound U_k on the k-size of Π. The way to go about this is to process graphs in the language defined by Γ according to increasing size of their smallest parse tree. For $i = 1, \ldots, k$, let $A^j[i]$ be the set of terminal pin-graphs that can be derived starting with pin-graph G_i, and that have parse trees of height at most j. We compute $A^j[i]$ for, $i = 1, \ldots, r$ and increasing j. The set $A^{j+1}[i]$ is computable simply by performing the appropriate substitutions out of the $A^j[i']$, $i' = 1, \ldots, k$ in G_i. The key observation is that, as soon as, for all i, $A^{j+1}[i]$ does not contain graphs from more glue types than

$A^j[i]$, the set of glue types covered by $A^j[i]$ never changes again, for all i. As soon as this happens, we can stop the process and just test Π on all graphs generated so far. If we do not find a graph among them that satisfies Π none such graph can be produced by the grammar. This stabilization is sure to happen before j exceeds the value $\sum_{i=1}^{r} U_{p_i}$, where p_i is the number of pins or labels of G_i.

Deciding the graph property Π is also possible if, given k, one can decide replaceability of two pin-graphs or labeled graphs. Then, instead of collecting all graphs generated so far, one need only keep track of one graph per glue type, and one can detect stabilization as soon as it happens. Figure 10 shows a bottom-up analysis of a cellular graph grammar with respect to the connectivity property. The entry in row j and column i contains the graphs of $A[i]$ after the jth iteration of step 2. After 4 iterations the bottom-up process stabilizes. All pin-graphs generated in further steps will be replaceable with one of the pin-graphs already generated.

The bottom-up analysis:

1 FOR $i := 1, \ldots, k$ DO $A[i] := \emptyset$;

2 FOR $i := 1, \ldots, k$ DO

      LET $n_1, \ldots, n_m$ be the nonterminals of G_i;

      IF $m > 0$ THEN

          FOR ALL $j_1 \in num_i(n_1), \ldots, j_m \in num_i(n_m)$

          FOR ALL $H_1 \in A[j_1], \ldots, H_m \in A[j_m]$ DO

             $A[i] := A[i] \cup \{G_i[H_1/n_1, \ldots, H_m/n_m]\}$);

          ELSE $A[i] := A[i] \cup \{G_i\}$;

3 REPEAT STEP 2 UNTIL STABILIZATION

7 Efficient analysis of graph families

The bottom-up algorithms for deciding graph properties on graph grammars do not require a burner. However, these algorithms become much more efficient if an efficient burner is available. For certain special cases, such as the restriction to grammars with a specified maximum size, such algorithms can even run in polynomial time, see [LW88a]. However, the constants involved are large, since they contain the k-size, which is usually exponential in k or larger.

Making this decision algorithm more efficient in various settings starts out with investigating the involved performance parameters. To this end we define the k-domination graph $D_{\Pi,k}$ for property Π. The vertices of $D_{\Pi,k}$ are the glue types of k-graphs for Π. There is a directed edge from glue type G to glue type J in $D_{\Pi,k}$ if in all graph neighborhoods in which G satisfies property Π also J satisfies property Π. Thus $D_{\Pi,k}$ is a dag, see Figure 11.

The significance of $D_{\Pi,k}$ is that, for each $A^j[i]$, we need only keep track of the glue types for p_i from which no other glue types in $A^j[i]$ are reachable. Hence, the number of glue types to be considered for each $A^j[i]$ does not exceed the *width* of D_{Π,p_i}, i.e., the

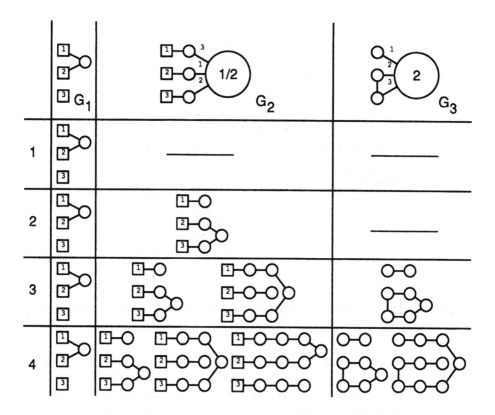

Figure 10: A bottom-up processing of a cellular graph grammar.

largest size of a set of mutually non-adjacent vertices in D_{Π,p_i}. Unfortunately, the width of $D_{\Pi,k}$ can still be very large. For instance, for connectivity, the width is exponential in k. But by restricting the graph grammars further, one can make sure that at most a small number c of glue types have to be considered for each $A^j[i]$. As j increases, the sizes of the graphs in $A^j[i]$ increase and the glue types covered by these graphs show a movement from the sources of D_{Π,p_i} to its sinks. Thus, the maximum number j of passes over the grammar depends on the *depth* $d_{\Pi,k}$ of $D_{\Pi,k}$. If only c glue types need be considered for each $A^j[i]$ then j need only increase to $c\sum_{i=1}^r d_{\Pi,p_i}$.

Thus, the width and depth of the domination graph for Π have a strong influence on the efficiency of testing Π on cellular graph grammars. If one carries the ideas outlined here further one achieves quadratic time algorithms for deciding connectivity and biconnectivity on ϵ-deterministic cellular graph grammars. (These are grammars where only an alternative between one nonempty and one empty derivation is allowed for each nonterminal.) Similar arguments show that deciding connectivity (biconnectivity) on cellular graph grammars is in P if the grammars are restricted to have cells of size $O(1)$, or if the number of connected (biconnected) components in the graph obtained if one deletes all nonterminals in a cell is $O(1)$ for all cells in the grammar. The development of efficient decision algorithms for other special cases is currently under way.

In general, practical applications do not tend to comply with the restrictions put

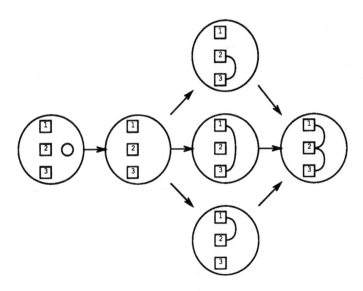

Figure 11: The transitive reduction of the 3-domination graph for connectivity.

on graph grammars to achieve polynomial time decision algorithms. Thus, currently, there are investigations under way how to make the decision algorithms faster in practice. This can be done by merging glue types for nonterminals that cannot be distinguished in the set of neighborhood the grammar can provide for the nonterminal. In order to achieve this goal one uses state reduction methods known from the area of finite automata. Furthermore, the framework is being extended to other kinds of graph problems, i.e., construction, labeling, and query problems. Details on the results covered in this section are given in [LW88a].

8 The Complexity of connectivity problems

The connectivity problem can be solved in linear time on hierarchical cellular graphs [LW88b] and is NP-complete on hierarchical BNLC graph [Wan89b]. This fact raises the question whether the connectivity problem is also more complex if we consider cellular and BNLC graph grammars. In [Wan89c, Wan89a] we have analyzed the complexity of connectivity problems on several graph languages generated by cellular and BNLC graph grammars under various restrictions:

1. The language of Γ has at most one graph. This is the case if Γ is a hierarchical cellular or BNLC graphs.

2. The language of Γ is finite. Here we do not allow loops in derivations. In such graph grammars the derivation height is less than or equal to the number of graphs in Γ.

3. The graph grammar is *linear*. In a linear graph grammar each special graph has at most one nonterminal object.

For all combinations of these restrictions we have proved the complexity classes for the questions: "Given a cellular graph grammar or a BNLC graph grammar Γ, does the language $L(\Gamma)$ of Γ contain a disconnected graph?" The results are summarized in the table of Figure 12. All results are proved using log-space reductions.

restriction		complexity of disconnectivity	
$L(\Gamma)$	Γ	cellular	BNLC
single	not linear	P-complete	NP-complete
finite	linear	NP-complete	NP-complete
	not linear	PSPACE-complete	PSPACE-complete
infinite	linear	PSPACE-complete	PSPACE-complete
	not linear	DEXPTIME-complete	DEXPTIME-complete

Figure 12: The complexity classes of the disconnectivity problem for graph grammars.

The table shows that connectivity problems are not more complex on BNLC graph grammars than on cellular graph grammars. This is only the case if both systems are deterministic, i.e., the grammars are hierarchical graphs. The problem, whether a given graph grammar can generate a *connected* graph is of the same complexity class a the problem whether the grammar can generate a *disconnected* graph. (If Γ is a hierarchical BNLC graph, then the connectivity problem is in co-NP.) Some of the membership results are also shown in [LW88b, LW88a, Wan89b].

9 Deciding integer subgraph problems

Our decidability results from Section 6 can be extended to graph properties defined by comparing certain integer values associated with graphs. These are the so-called *integer subgraph problems* (ISPs) which, in general, cannot be solved with the methods for deciding graph properties from [Cou90, LW88a, Hab89].

Definition 6: For a graph G and a subgraph J of G the pair (G, J) is called a *graph×subgraph pair*. An *integer subgraph problem* (ISP) $\Pi =< s_\Pi, f_\Pi >$ consists of a *subgraph property* s_Π and an *integer subgraph mapping* f_Π. The integer subgraph mapping f_Π associates with each graph×subgraph pair (G, J) an integer.

Decidability results of ISPs on cellular graph grammars are considered in [Wan91a], where a characterization of certain ISPs is given that guarantees their decidability on cellular graph languages.

Definition 7: A pin-graph J is a *pin-subgraph* of a pin-graph G if it can be obtained by removing some edges and some vertices from G. If a vertex u_i is removed that belongs to a vertex list $(u_1, \ldots, u_n)$, then the resulting list is $(u_1, \ldots, u_{i-1}, u_{i+1}, u_n)$. The pair (G, J) is called a *pin-graph×subgraph pair* or a *h, h'-graph×subgraph pair*, if G is a h-graph and J a h'-subgraph of G.

1. Two h, h'-graph×subgraph pairs (H, H') and (J, J') are replaceable with respect to a graph×subgraph property s_Π, if for all pin-graph×subgraph pairs (G, G') that have a common nonterminal n with $|vert_G(n)| = h$ and $|vert_{G'}| = h'$:

$$s_\Pi(G[H/n], G'[H'/n]) = s_\Pi(G[J/n], G'[J'/n]).$$

s_Π is called *finite* if the equivalence relation *replaceability* has a finite number of equivalence classes. (We assume that the vertices of P_H missing in P'_H always occupy the same positions as the vertices of P_J missing in $P_{J'}$.)

2. An integer graph×subgraph mapping f_Π is called *additive* if for all pin-graph×subgraph pairs (G, G') and (H, H'), where G and G' have a common nonterminal n with $|vert_G(n)| = |P_H|$ and $|vert_{G'}| = |P'_H|$:

$$f_\Pi(G[H/n], G'[H'/n]) = f_\Pi(G, G') + f_\Pi(H, H').$$

3. An ISP $\Pi =< s_\Pi, f_\Pi >$ is called *finite* and *additive* if s_Π is *finite* and f_Π is additive. Π is called *effectively finite* and additive if, in addition, procedures for computing f_Π and procedures for deciding replaceability with respect to $\sim_{s_\Pi}$ are given.

Finite and additive ISPs are, for instance, defined by the set of all graph×subgraph-pairs (G, J) where J is a *spanning tree*, a *Hamiltonian circuit*, a *feedback vertex set*, or a *path of G*. In these examples, the mappings f_Π merely return the number of vertices or edges of the subgraph or compute for each graph×subgraph pair (G, J), the number of edges from G that have exactly one end vertex belonging to the subgraph J.

To explain the decidability results from [Wan91a], we need the notion of a *semilinear* set of integers. A set $T \subseteq \mathbf{Z}^n$ of n-tuples is called *linear* if there is an integer $k \geq 0$ and n-tuples $R_0, \ldots, R_k \in \mathbf{Z}^n$ such that T consists of all n-tuples defined by $R_0 + \sum_{i=1}^{k} r_i R_i$, where the r's are nonnegative integers. The system $\mathcal{R}(T) = (R_0, \ldots, R_k)$ is called a *representation* for T. A set of n-tuples T is called *semilinear* if it is a finite union of linear sets $T_1, \ldots, T_l$. The system $(\mathcal{R}(T_1), \ldots, \mathcal{R}(T_l))$ is called a *representation* for the semilinear set T. A semilinear set T of integers is called *effectively semilinear* if a representation for T is computable.

We have shown the following result:

Fact 1: Let Γ be a cellular graph grammar and let $\Pi_1, \ldots, \Pi_n$ be n effectively finite and additive ISPs. Then the set of all n-tuples

$$(f_{\Pi_1}(G, J_1), \ldots, f_{\Pi_n}(G, J_n)),$$

where $G \in L(\Gamma)$, $J_i \subseteq G$, $1 \leq i \leq n$, and $s_{\Pi_i}(G, J_i)$ holds true is effectively semilinear.

Fact 1 is an extension of Parikh's theorem from [Par62]. If we consider only subgraphs without edges, then Fact 1 holds also true for BNLC graph grammars. Using linear programming methods, we can solve many further graph problems on context-free graph languages. For instance, let Γ be any cellular graph grammar and Π_1, Π_2 be two ISPs with

1. $s_{\Pi_1}(G, J)$ holds true if J is a simple cycle,

2. $s_{\Pi_2}(G, J)$ holds true if J is an independent set of G,

3. $f_{\Pi_1}(G, J)$ and $f_{\Pi_2}(G, J)$ return the number of vertices in J.

Then by Fact 1 the set of all triple

$$(f_{\Pi_1}(G, J_1), f_{\Pi_1}(G, J_1'), f_{\Pi_2}(G, J_2))$$

with $G \in L(\Gamma)$, $J_1, J_1', J_2 \subseteq G$, and $s_{\Pi_1}(G, J_1)$, $s_{\Pi_1}(G, J_1')$, $s_{\Pi_2}(G, J_2)$ hold true is an effectively semilinear set of integers for each cellular graph grammar Γ, because both ISPs are effectively finite and additive for cellular graph grammars. The problem whether there is a graph $G \in L(\Gamma)$ that has two simple cicles J_1, J_1' and an independent set J_2 such that $|J_1| \leq |G_2| \leq |J_1'|$ can be solved by using linear integer programming.

However, the time complexity for constructing a realization for the semilinear set of integers may be exponential in the size of the graph grammar. But, for practically interesting ISPs, e.g., for connectivity or path problems, there could be efficient algorithms on special classes of graph grammars.

For finite and additive ISPs, *boundedness* problems are also decidable. That is, it is decidable whether there is a *bound* $k \in \mathbf{Z}$ such that $f_\Pi(G, J) \leq k$ for all $G \in L(\Gamma)$ and $J \subseteq G$ with $s_\Pi(G, J)$. If such a bound k exists, then the minimum bound k is also computable.

Boundedness problems on cellular graph grammars are also considered in [HKV89, CM90b]. Habel, Kreowski, and Vogler [HKV89] showed that there are some integer functions on graphs whose boundedness problems are decidable on sets of graphs defined by cellular graph grammars. The integer functions have to be composed by maxima, sums, and products in a certain way. Courcelle and Mosbah [CM90b] used monadic second-order logic and semiring homomorphisms to describe a large class of functions on graphs. They claim that boundedness problems for cellular graph grammars are decidable for expressions using maxima (or minima) and sums of integers specified by the size of subgraphs defined by monadic second-order formulas.

10   Controlled derivation

In applications in engineering design, one often wants to construct families of balanced graph structures such as, for instance, complete binary trees. Typically, such graph families are not context-free. They can be produced by graph grammars that result from adding to cellular graph grammars a controlling mechanism that establishes the balance. In [LW88a] we have also analyzed such controlling mechanism, and shown that our decidability results generalize to graph grammars using this mechanism.

In our controlled cellular graph grammar, each controlled pin-graph G_i has, in addition, two positive integers a_i and b_i, where b_i may also be infinite. The set $L(\Gamma, i, j)$ is the set of all cells obtained by a substitution that is controlled by j. That is, the nonterminals in G_i are substituted by cells from $L(\Gamma, t, h)$, where $t \in num_i(x)$ and h is an integer from $\{j - c, ..., j - 1\}$ with $a_t \leq h \leq b_t$. The substitution is carried out in the same way as with cellular graph grammars. The integer j is used as a general *parameter*—which may differ from the height of the parse tree that controls the substitutions. Note that if Γ is controlled, then $L(\Gamma, i, j)$ need not contain all pin-graphs from $L(\Gamma, i, j - 1)$.

Each cellular graph language is also a controlled cellular graph language. In fact, if we set $c = 1$, $a_i = 1$, and $b_i = \infty$ for all $1 \leq i \leq k$, we do not change the language of the corresponding cellular graph grammar, and obtain a controlled cellular graph grammar. Many balanced graph families are controlled cellular graph languages. Figure 13 shows a controlled cellular graph grammar that generates all complete binary trees.

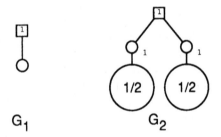

G_1 $\qquad$ G_2

Figure 13: A controlled cellular graph grammar $\Gamma = (G_1, G_2)$, where $a_1 = 1$, $b_1 = 1$, $a_2 = 1$, and $b_2 = \infty$.

Let Γ be a controlled cellular graph grammar and $cgg(\Gamma)$ be the cellular graph grammar obtained by ignoring the controlling mechanism, or equivalently, by setting $c = 1$, $a_i = 1$, and $b_i = \infty$ for all $1 \leq i \leq k$. It is easy to see that $L(\Gamma, i) \subseteq L(cgg(\Gamma), i)$ and $E(\Gamma, i) \subseteq E(cgg(\Gamma), i)$.

The problem in analyzing controlled cellular graph grammars is that the sets $L(\Gamma, i, j)$ lose their monotonicity properties, i.e., $L(\Gamma, i, j)$ need not be a subset of $L(\Gamma, i, j + 1)$ if Γ is controlled. Nevertheless, in [LW88a] we have shown the decidability of finite graph properties on controlled cellular graph grammar.

Similarly as for uncontrolled graph grammars, we can analyze controlled graph grammars more efficiently if we can test replaceability and if we have efficient burning procedures. However, the algorithm loses its monotonicity properties and there is one more level of exponentiation in the time complexity.

11 Undecidability results

If the language $L(\Gamma)$ of a cellular or BNLC graph grammar Γ is infinite, then the decidability of a graph property Π does not imply its decidability on $L(\Gamma)$. An example for a decidable graph property that becomes undecidable on cellular graph grammars and BNLC graph grammars is the *bandwidth property*. An undirected graph $G = (V, E)$ has *bandwidth k* if and only if there is a bijective *layout mapping b* from the vertices V of G to the integers $1, \ldots, |V|$ such that for each edge $\{u, v\} \in E$: $|b(u) - b(v)| \leq k$.

In [WW89] it is shown that the bandwidth k property for $k \geq 3$ is undecidable for linear cellular graph grammars in that all pin-graphs have two pins. This shows also that the bandwidth k property is not finite for 2-graphs and all $k \geq 3$ Thus, the bandwidth k property is not definable in counting monadic second order logic. However, on conventional graphs, the bandwidth k property can be decided in polynomial time. Saxe [Sax80] introduced an algorithm that decides the bandwidth k property in time $O(|V|^{k+1})$. This time bound was improved by Guari and Sudborough [GS84] to $O(|V|^k)$.

Another undecidability result shows that our solution method for integer subgraph problems cannot be extended to quantifications over all graphs in $L(\Gamma)$. In [Wan89b] it is shown that there are very simple finite and additive integer subgraph problems $\Pi_1, \ldots, \Pi_n$ and a set of pairs $S \subseteq \{1, \ldots, n\}^2$ such that the following problem is undecidable.

Given a cellular graph grammar Γ. Does *each* graph G in $L(\Gamma)$ have n subgraphs $J_1, \ldots, J_n$ such that

(a) $s_{\Pi_i}(G, J_i)$ holds true for $i = 1, \ldots, n$ and

(b) $f_{\Pi_i}(G, J'_i) \leq f_{\Pi_j}(G, J'_j)$ holds true for each $(i, j) \in S$?

This undecidability result was proved by reduction from the bandwidth property.

Kalbers [Kal91] has extended our controlled cellular graph grammar to so-called *multiply controlled cellular graph grammars*. The approach in [Kal91] allows for controlling the derivation using a finite list of $m > 1$ integer parameters $(p_1, \ldots, p_m)$ instead of a single one. The *m-controlled cellular graph grammar* is a cellular graph grammar in which each pin graph G_i is associated with a set of *conditions*

$$C(G_i) \subseteq \{1, \ldots, m\} \times \{<, \leq, >, \geq, =, \neq\} \times \{1, \ldots, m\}.$$

In each pin graph each nonterminal n is associated with a list of m integers $l(n) \in \mathbf{Z}^m$. The derivation starts with the axiom G_k and a parameter-list $p = (p_1, \ldots, p_m) \in \mathbf{Z}^m$. Initially the parameter-lists $l(n_1), \ldots, l(n_l)$ associated with the nonterminals of the axiom are set to $l(n_i) := p + l(n_i)$, where the addition of m-tuples are carried out componentwise. In a *controlled derivation step*, a nonterminal n can only be substituted by a pin-graph G_t if $t \in num(n)$ and for each condition $(l_1, \circ, l_2) \in C(G_t)$: $l(n)_{l_1} \circ l(n)_{l_2}$. After the substitution of the nonterminal n by the pin-graph G_t, the parameter-lists of the nonterminals n_i from G_t are updated by executing $l(n_i) := l(n) + l(n_i)$.

In [Kal91] it is shown that the emptiness problem for multiply controlled cellular graph grammars, with more than 3 parameters, is undecidable. This implies that each nontrivial graph property is undecidable on such multiply controlled cellular graph grammars.

12 Implementations

During the past five years, our theoretical work was accompanied with the development of a software system called PLEXUS, see [Wan88, Wan91c]. The PLEXUS system was developed for implementing graph algorithms. It consists of a library system, a graph editor, and some tools to animate algorithms. Its strength is the support of the development of graph algorithms that process hierarchically defined graphs and context-free graph grammars.

The PLEXUS library [Wan91b] supports the implementation of algorithms by providing the necessary basic data structures and functions. The PLEXUS graph editor allows the manipulation of graphs on a graphic screen. During the interactive generation of new terminal and nonterminal objects, the editor assigns to each new object screen coordinates. Several commands within the editor can change these screen coordinates and thus modify the image of the graph on the screen. Other commands execute procedures that generate expansions and draw the result of the derivation step on the screen or store it into files (if the result does not fit into memory).

The PLEXUS system has been implemented in the programming language C under the UNIX system on a SUN-3 workstation. All graphics routines are implemented with the SUN-VIEW and the X11 system.

13 Current work and open problems

The previous sections reflect a state of the knowledge of hierarchical graphs that we consider as quite mature. In comparison, there are other areas of hierarchical graph processing that we know comparatively little about.

The most prominent example is the concept of grid-structured hierarchical graphs. A grid-structured hierarchical graph is defined by giving what is called a *static graph*. The static graph defines the contents of one cell, that is replicated infinitely often in a fixed number d of dimension. In addition, labels on the edges of the static graph determine how the different replicas are connected. Specifically, a *d-dimensional static graph* is a system $S = (V, E, f)$, where $S \backslash f := (V, E)$ is a directed graph and $f : E \rightarrow \mathbf{Z}^d$ is a *transit function* mapping a d-dimensional integer vector to each edge of E. The *dynamic graph* S^x, $x \in \mathbf{N}^d$, is a (directed) graph (V', E'), where

$$V' := \{u^z | u \in V \wedge \overline{0} \leq z < x\} \text{ and}$$

$$E' := \{(u^z, v^{z+f(u,v)}) | (u, v) \in E \wedge \overline{0} \leq z, z + f(u, v) < x\}.$$

If we set some component in x or more to infinity, the dynamic graph becomes infinite. In Figure 14 an example of a 2-dimensional static graph together with a small dynamic graph is given.

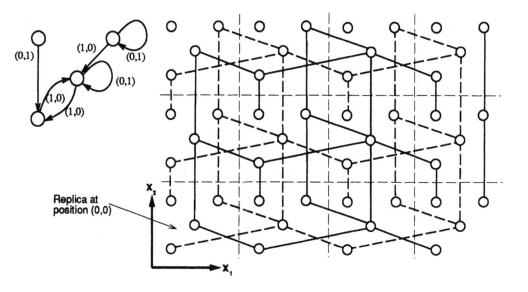

Figure 14: Example of a 2-dimensional static graph S together with the dynamic graph $S^{(4,3)}$. It contains seven components, while $S^{(\infty,\infty)}$ contains only two components. For any $x \in \mathbf{N}^2$ S^x is planar, but $S^{(\infty,\infty)}$ is not planar. One of the components is drawn with dashed edges in order to make the figure clearer.

Grid-structured graphs play in important role in parallel programming where they are the natural model of flow graphs of uniform iterative or recursive programs (Uniform programs are programs that have simple index dependencies which are based on translations by a constant term). In addition, mesh-like chip architectures naturally translate into grid-structured hierarchical graphs.

Grid-structured hierarchical graphs have been invented by Karp et al. [KMW67] as a model for systems of uniform recurrence equations and were redefined independently by Orlin [Orl81] as a model for long range scheduling tasks. A lot of research on such graphs has been conducted in the 80s [Orl84, Rao85, IS87, KS88, CM89, QS90, CM90a, KO91]. Practically all of the known results are concerned with the infinite version $S^{(\infty,\dots,\infty)}$ of the dynamic graph. However, in all practical cases, when time or space constraints come into account, the finite dynamic graphs are the ones that are really of interest.

In the context of our approach to hierarchical graph design, the following questions are of interest. Given a graph property Π, a static graph S, and $x \in \mathbf{N}^d$, does $\Pi(S^x)$ hold? Does $\Pi(S^{x'})$ hold for any or for all $x' \le x$ ($x' \ge x$)? Examples of interesting graph properties are, for instance, connectivity, planarity, bipartiteness or the question whether a graph is acyclic.

Although most of the results in the literature are on infinite graphs $S^{(\infty,\dots,\infty)}$, the results and algorithms are useful in the finite case, as the table in Figure 15 shows. Thus we may, for instance, use the polynomial algorithms of Cohen and Megiddo [CM90a] to derive sufficient criteria for a finite graph to be acyclic or bipartite. However, if the infinite graph $S^{(\infty,\dots,\infty)}$ contains a cycle (an odd length cycle, in the case of bipartiteness), a finite dynamic graph S^x may be small enough such that it does not contain an (odd length) cycle.

Property Π	Relationship $\Pi(S^\infty)$ versus $\Pi(S^{<\infty})$
Connectivity Planarity	$\exists x \in \mathbf{N}^d, x \geq \overline{2}: \ \Pi(S^x) \Rightarrow \Pi(S^\infty)$ $\Pi(S^\infty) \Rightarrow \forall x \in \mathbf{N}^d : \Pi(S^x)$ but $\forall x \in \mathbf{N}^d : \Pi(S^x) \not\Rightarrow \Pi(S^\infty)$
Bipartiteness Contains no cycle	$\Pi(S^\infty) \Leftrightarrow \forall x \in \mathbf{N}^d : \Pi(S^x)$ $\Pi(S^\infty) \Leftrightarrow \forall x \in \mathbf{N}^d : \Pi(S^x)$

Figure 15: The relationship of graph properties on infinite and finite grid-structured graphs.

While cycle-properties depend on merely the size of the finite dynamic graph, as previously mentioned, planarity problems depend on the entire structure of the graph. Here every finite dynamic graph S^x may be planar, even if the infinite graph $S^{(\infty,\ldots,\infty)}$ is not planar. An example for this situation is given in Figure 14. Again we can construct a polynomial time algorithm to solve the problem.

In the case of connectivity the situation is even more difficult. The connectivity of the infinite graph is just a necessary condition for any S^x, $x \in \mathbf{N}^d$, to be connected. Here totally different methods have to be developed. Furthermore, we are not only interested in the connectivity property, but also in the number of connected components of a dynamic graph and their structure. First results on this problem show that the number of connected components of dynamic graphs $S^{x'}, x' \geq x$, for some $x \in \mathbf{N}^d$, is a polynomial with degree at most d. The coefficients and the degree of the polynomial as well as the size of the bound x are dependent on the static graph. For $x' \leq x$ the number of components does not necessarily follow this function. An example of a function of the number of connected components is given in Figure 16 for the 2-dimensional dynamic graph in Figure 14. Our current interest is in determining the size of the bound x, from where the function sets in, and the coefficients and degree of the function. The general method is to identify the structure of the connected components of the dynamic graph, which can again be represented as static graphs of dimension smaller than d. For these static graphs the number of components is recursively analyzed.

Grid-structured hierarchical graphs can only represent simple programs or architectures, where all cells are identical and locally connected. In programs this restriction corresponds to the absence of if-then-else constructs and to the translation of indices by constants, respectively. We are also interested in allowing conditional constructs and a more sophisticated arithmetic on parameters. Currently we are working on a graph model that incorporates these possibilities.

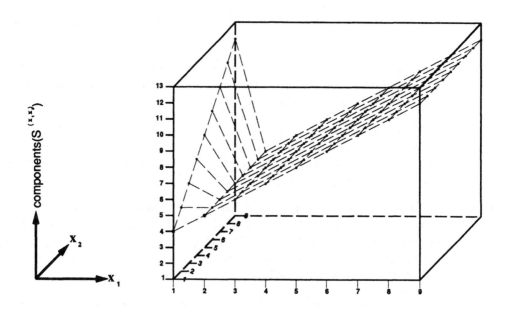

Figure 16: The figure shows the number of the connected components of S^x for the static graph S that is given in Figure 14 as a function of the x_i. The function in this case is $components(S^{(x_1,x_2)}) = 3 + x_1$ for all $(x_1, x_2) \geq \overline{3}$.

References

[CM89]   E. Cohen and N. Megiddo. Strongly polynomial-time and NC algorithms for detecting cycles in dynamic graphs. In *Proceedings of Annual ACM Symposium on Theory of Computing '89*, pages 523–534, 1989. Preliminary Version.

[CM90a]   E. Cohen and N. Megiddo. Recognizing properties of periodic graphs. to appear in: "The Victor Klee Festschrift", Honorary Volume of "Applied Geometry and Discrete Mathematics", 1990.

[CM90b]   B. Courcelle and M. Mosbah. Monadic second-order evaluations on tree-decomposable graphs. Technical Report 90-110, Laboratoire Bordelais de Recherche en Informatique, Université de Bordeaux I, Talence, France, November 1990.

[Cou87]   B. Courcelle. An axiomatic definition of context-free rewriting and its application to NLC graph grammars. *Theoretical Computer Science*, 55:141–181, 1987.

[Cou90]   B. Courcelle. The monadic second-order logic of graphs I: Recognizable sets of finite graphs. *Information and Computation*, 85:12–75, 1990.

[FBW89]   D. Fernandez-Baca and M.A. Williams. Augmentation problems on hierarchically defined graphs. In F. Dehne, J.R. Sack, and N. Santoro, editors,

Proceedings of WADS '89, volume 382 of *Lecture Notes in Computer Scienece*, pages 563–576. Springer-Verlag, Berlin/New York, 1989.

[GS84]   E.T. Gurari and I.H. Sudborough. Improved dynamic programming algorithms for bandwidth minimization and the mincut linear arrangement problem. *Journal of Algorithms*, 5:531–546, 1984.

[Hab89]   A. Habel. Graph-theoretic properties compatible with graph derivations. In J. van Leeuwen, editor, *Proceedings of Graph-Theoretical Concepts in Computer Science, WG '88*, volume 344 of *Lecture Notes in Computer Scienece*, pages 11–29. Springer-Verlag, Berlin/New York, 1989.

[HK87]   A. Habel and H.J. Kreowski. May we introduce to you: Hyperedge replacement. In H. Ehrig, M. Nagl, A. Rosenfeld, and G. Rozenberg, editors, *Proceedings of Graph-Grammars and Their Application to Computer Science '86*, volume 291 of *Lecture Notes in Computer Scienece*, pages 15–26. Springer-Verlag, Berlin/New York, 1987.

[HKV89]   A. Habel, H.J. Kreowski, and W. Vogler. Decidable boundedness problems for hyperedge-replacement graph grammars. In *Proceedings of TAPSOFT '89*, volume 351 of *Lecture Notes in Computer Scienece*, pages 275–289. Springer-Verlag, Berlin/New York, 1989.

[IS87]   K. Iwano and K. Steiglitz. Testing for cycles in infinite graphs with periodic structure. In *Proceedings of Annual ACM Symposium on Theory of Computing '87*, pages 46–55, 1987.

[Kal91]   B. Kalbers. Parameterisierte zellulare Graphgrammatiken. Diplomarbeit, Universität-Gesamthochschule-Paderborn, Paderborn, FRG, Oktober 1991.

[KMW67]   R.M. Karp, R.E. Miller, and A. Winograd. The organization of computations for uniform recurrence equations. *Journal of the ACM*, 14(3):563–590, July 1967.

[KO91]   M. Kodialam and J.B. Orlin. Recognizing strong connectivity in (dynamic) periodic graphs and its relation to integer programming. *Proceedings of the second annual ACM-SIAM Symposium on Discrete Algorithms*, pages 131–135, 1991.

[KS88]   S.R. Kosaraju and G.F. Sullivan. Detecting cycles in dynamic graphs in polynomial time. In *Proceedings of Annual ACM Symposium on Theory of Computing '88*, pages 398–406, 1988. Preliminary Version.

[Len82]   T. Lengauer. The complexity of hierarchically specified layouts of integrated circuits. In *Ann. ACM Symp. on Foundations of Computer Science*, pages 358–368. IEEE, 1982.

[Len87]   T. Lengauer. Efficient algorithms for finding minimum spanning forests of hierarchically defined graphs. *Journal of Algorithms*, 8:260–284, 1987.

[Len89]   T. Lengauer. Hierarchical planarity testing algorithms. *Journal of the ACM*, 36(3):474–509, 1989.

[LW87a]   T. Lengauer and K. Wagner. The correlation between the complexities of the non-hierarchical and hierarchical version of graph problems. In F. J. Branden-burg, G. Vidal-Naquet, and M. Wirsing, editors, *Proceedings of STACS '87*, volume 247 of *Lecture Notes in Computer Scienece*, pages 100–113. Springer-Verlag, Berlin/New York, 1987. To appear in JCSS.

[LW87b]   T. Lengauer and C. Wieners. Efficient solutions of hierarchical systems of linear equations. *Computing*, 39:111–132, 1987.

[LW88a]   T. Lengauer and E. Wanke. Efficient analysis of graph properties on context-free graph languages. In T. Lepistö and A. Salomaa, editors, *Proceedings of International Colloquium on Automata, Languages and Programming*, volume 317 of *Lecture Notes in Computer Scienece*, pages 379–393. Springer-Verlag, Berlin/New York, 1988. To appear in Journal of the ACM.

[LW88b]   T. Lengauer and E. Wanke. Efficient solution of connectivity problems on hierarchically defined graphs. *SIAM Journal of Computing*, 17(6):1063–1080, December 1988.

[Orl81]   J.B. Orlin. The complexity of dynamic languages and dynamic optimization problems. In *Proceedings of Annual ACM Symposium on Theory of Computing '81*, pages 273–293, 1981.

[Orl84]   J.B. Orlin. Some problems on dynamic/periodic graphs. In W.R. Pulley-blank, editor, *Progress in Combinatorial Optimization*, pages 273–293. Academic Press, Orlando, Florida, 1984.

[Par62]   R.J. Parikh. Language generating devices. Technical Report 60, M.I.T. Res. Lab. Electron. Quart. Prog. , 1962.

[PY86]   C. Papadimitriou and M. Yannakakis. A note on succinct representation of graphs. *Information and Control*, 71:181–185, 1986.

[QS90]   P. Quinton and Y. Saouter. Computability of recurrence equations. Technical Report 1203, Institute Nationale de Recherche en Informatique et en Automatique, Domaine de Voluceau, Rocquencourt B.P.105, 78153 Le Chesnáy Cedex, France, 1990.

[Rao85]   S.K. Rao. *Regular iterative algorithms and their implementations on processor arrays*. PhD thesis, Stanford University, 1985.

[RW86]   G. Rozenberg and E. Welzl. Boundary NLC graph grammars—basic defini-tions, normal forms, and complexity. *Information and Control*, 69(1–3):136–167, April/May/June 1986.

[Sax80]   J.B. Saxe. Dynamic programming algorithms for recognizing small bandwidth graphs in polynomial time. *SIAM Journal of Algebraic and Discrete Methods*, 1:363–369, 1980.

[Wan86] E. Wanke. Resultate und Implementierungen hierarchischer Graphenalghorith-men.   Diplomarbeit, Universität-Gesamthochschule-Paderborn, Paderborn, FRG, Januar 1986.

[Wan88] E. Wanke. PLEXUS: A system for implementing hierarchical graph algo-rithms. In R. Cori and M. Wirsing, editors, *Proceedings of STACS '88*, volume 294 of *Lecture Notes in Computer Scienece*, pages 401–402. Springer-Verlag, Berlin/New York, 1988. System demonstration.

[Wan89a] E. Wanke. *Algorithmen und Komplexitätsanalyse für die Verarbeitung hi-erarchisch definierter Graphen und hierarchisch definierter Graphfamilien.* PhD thesis, Universität-Gesamthochschule-Paderborn, 4790 Paderborn, FRG, November 1989.

[Wan89b] E. Wanke. Algorithms for graph problems on BNLC structured graphs. *Infor-mation and Computation*, 94(1):93–122, September 1989.

[Wan89c] E. Wanke. The complexity of connectivity problems on context-free graph lan-guages. In J. Csirik, J. Demetrovics, and F. Gécseg, editors, *Proceedings of Fundamentals of Computation Theory*, volume 380 of *Lecture Notes in Com-puter Scienece*, pages 470–479. Springer-Verlag, Berlin/New York, 1989.

[Wan91a] E. Wanke. On the decidability of certain integer subgraph problems on context-free graph languages. In L. Budach, editor, *Proceedings of Fundamentals of Computation Theory*, number 529 in Lecture Notes in Computer Scienece, pages 415–426. Springer-Verlag, Berlin/New York, 1991.

[Wan91b] E. Wanke. The PLEXUS 4.0 library system programmer's guide. Technical report, Universität-Gesamthochschule-Paderborn, 1991.

[Wan91c] E. Wanke. PLEXUS: Tools for analyzing graph grammars. In *Proceedings of Graph-Grammars and Their Application to Computer Science '90*, Lecture Notes in Computer Scienece. Springer-Verlag, Berlin/New York, 1991. System demonstration, to appear.

[WW89] E. Wanke and M. Wiegers. Undecidability of the bandwidth problem on cer-tain linear graph languages. *Information Processing Letters*, 4(33):193–197, December 1989.

The Combination of Spatial Access Methods and Computational Geometry in Geographic Database Systems[+]

Hans-Peter Kriegel, Thomas Brinkhoff, Ralf Schneider

Institut für Informatik, Universität München, Leopoldstr. 11b, D-8000 München 40, Germany

Abstract

Geographic database systems, known as geographic information systems (GISs) particularly among non-computer scientists, are one of the most important applications of the very active research area named spatial database systems. Consequently following the database approach, a GIS has to be seamless, i.e. store the complete area of interest (e.g. the whole world) in one database map. For exhibiting acceptable performance a seamless GIS has to use spatial access methods. Due to the complexity of query and analysis operations on geographic objects, state-of-the-art computational geometry concepts have to be used in implementing these operations. In this paper, we present GIS operations based on the computational geometry technique plane sweep. Specifically, we show how the two ingredients spatial access methods and computational geometry concepts can be combined for improving the performance of GIS operations. The fruitfulness of this combination is based on the fact that spatial access methods efficiently provide the data at the time when computational geometry algorithms need it for processing. Additionally, this combination avoids page faults and facilitates the parallelization of the algorithms.

1 Introduction

Geographic database systems, also known as geographic information systems (GISs), are one of the most important applications of spatial database systems. Basically, they consist of two parts: First, components to query and manipulate geographical data and second, components to manage and store the data. However, the main purpose of a GIS is to analyze geographical data.

GIS algorithms presented in the past assume that the maps are kept in main memory or in sequential files on secondary storage. The following two important requirements of future GISs demand for new approaches: First, the database system of a GIS must be able to manage very large volumes of data. The large amount of data (in the order of Giga- and Terabytes) is additionally increased by pursuing the goal to manage scaleless and seamless databases [Oos 90]. Second, the database system has to support spatial access to parts of the database, such as maps, and to the objects of a map. Such access is a necessary condition for efficient query and manipulation processing.

Pursuing these goals we want to take advantage of spatial access methods (SAMs). In the past few years many access methods were developed which allow to organize large sets of spatial objects on secondary storage. There are three basic techniques which extend multidimensional point access methods (PAMs) to multidimensional spatial access methods [SK

[+] This work was supported by grant no. Kr 670/4-3 from the Deutsche Forschungsgemeinschaft (German Research Society) and by the Ministry of Environmental and Urban Planning of Bremen

88]: clipping, overlapping regions, and transformation. Point access methods such as the grid file [NHS 84], PLOP-hashing [KS 88], the BANG file [Fre 87] and the buddy tree [SK 90] can be extended by these techniques. Additionally, there are access methods which are designed for managing simple spatial objects directly. They use one of the above techniques inherently, e.g. the R-tree [Gut 84] and the R*-tree [BKSS 90] use overlapping regions, or the cell tree [Gün 89] uses clipping. An excellent survey of such access methods is given in [Sam 89].

The use of SAMs as an ingredient in GISs is absolutely necessary to guarantee good retrieval and manipulation performance, in particular for large maps. The use of SAMs enables us to perform operations only on relevant parts of seamless databases. GIS operations on maps modelled by a vector based representation are often very time intensive. Therefore the use of state-of-the-art computational geometry algorithms as a second step of performance improvement is straightforward [Nie 89]. In [KBS 91] we have shown in detail that the performance of the operation map overlay -an important and often used analysis operation in a GIS- can be considerably improved by applying the computational geometry technique 'plane sweep'.

The basic approach of this paper is to partition the seamless databases using SAMs according to the requirements of the GIS operations. Then state-of-the-art computational geometry algorithms are performed on these partitions and the results are combined in order to increase the overall performance of the GIS operations. Thus we combine spatial access methods and computational geometry in order to improve the efficiency of GISs. The combination of these two areas is based on the fact that both use spatial order relations.

The next section describes seamless, vector based databases in GISs. How the efficiency of a GIS is increased by using computational geometry algorithms is shown in section 3. The coupling of spatial access methods and the plane-sweep technique is presented in section 4. An approach to parallelize plane-sweep algorithms follows in section 5. The paper concludes with a summary and an outlook to future work.

2   Seamless vector-based databases in GISs

One important requirement to future GISs is the efficient management of so-called *seamless spatial databases* [Oos 90]. A database is seamless if it does not store sets of map sheets describing only particular small parts of the database, but the whole area managed by the GIS (e.g. the whole world) is stored in one database map. For analysis the user can select any area of interest by a window query. An example is shown in figure 1. This window contains the map which is of further interest to the user. Queries to and manipulations of objects of this map need access to the whole database which is in the order of Giga- and Terabytes. Therefore, the database system of the GIS must be able to support efficient access to any parts of the data on secondary storage.

A GIS is based on two types of data [Bur 86]: spatial and thematic data. *Thematic data* is alphanumeric data related to geographic objects, e.g. the degree of soil pollution. *Spatial data* has two different properties: (1) geometric properties such as spatial location, size, and shape of spatial objects, and (2) topological properties such as connectivity, adjacency, and inclusion.

Topological data can be stored explicitly or can be derived from geometric data.

Figure 1: Window query selecting a part of the spatial database

There exist two models for spatial data: vector and raster representations. We consider in this paper only maps modelled by a *vector representation* because there are two main disadvantages of raster representations [Oos 90]: (1) Raster data depends on a specific projection. Therefore, there are problems when combining raster maps from different sources. A scaleless database cannot be realized using a raster representation. (2) Objects in raster maps generally are not handled individually. Thus, a support by access methods is more difficult. Additionally, raster data are more voluminous.

In this paper the term map is used for *thematic maps*. Those emphasize one or more selected topics, e.g. land utilization, population density etc. Thematic maps are generally represented by *choropleth maps* which separate areas of different properties by boundaries [Bur 86], e.g. forests, lakes, roads, or agriculturally used areas (see figure 2).

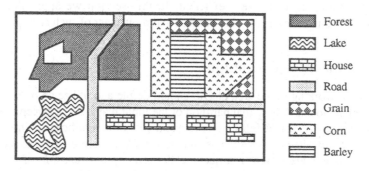

Figure 2: Example of a thematic map

We assume that the connected areas with the same property are described by *simple polygons with holes*, and that the used data structures are able to handle such polygons explicitly [KHHSS 91a]. A polygon is simple if there is no pair of nonconsecutive edges sharing a point. A simple polygon with holes is a simple polygon where simple polygonal holes may be cut out (see figure 3). There may be other areas in such a hole. The areas of a map are disjoint but they do not need to cover the map completely. Each area refers to exactly one thematic attribute. In figure 2 these characteristics of a thematic map are depicted by an example which visualizes the land utilization of a part of a map.

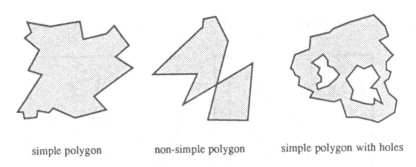

simple polygon   non-simple polygon   simple polygon with holes

Figure 3: Different polygons

Below, a formal definition of a thematic map is presented where $\cap_r$ denotes the regularized intersection [Til 80] and T is the set of values of the thematic attributes of M:

$$M := \{\, t = (t.P, t.A) \mid t.P \text{ is a simple polygon with holes, } t.A \in T \,\} ,$$
$$\text{where } t_1 \in M, t_2 \in M, t_1 \neq t_2 \;\Rightarrow\; t_1.P \cap_r t_2.P = \varnothing$$

Maps of different topics describing the same part of the world are called *map layers*.

3 Increasing the performance of a GIS using computational geometry

Efficient algorithms typically use general techniques such as divide-and-conquer or recursion. For algorithms solving computational geometry problems the algorithmic technique called *plane sweep* has proven to be very efficient. In this section we apply this technique to operations in GISs and examine the performance and robustness of such an approach.

3.1 The plane-sweep technique

An algorithm working in the area of GIS should define and utilize an order relation on the objects in the plane to enable a spatial partition of the input maps. Plane sweep is a technique of computational geometry which fulfills this demand [PS 88]: significant points of the objects *(event points)* are projected onto the x-axis and are processed according to the order relation on this axis. Event points are stored in a queue called *event point schedule*. If event points are computed during processing, the event point schedule must be able to insert event points after initialization. A vertical line sweeps the plane according to the event points from left to right. This line is called *sweep line*. The state of the plane at the sweep line position is recorded in vertical order in a table called *sweep line status*. The sweep line status is updated when the sweep line reaches an event point. Event points which are passed by the sweep line are deleted from the event point schedule. Figure 4 depicts an example of the event point schedule and the sweep line status.

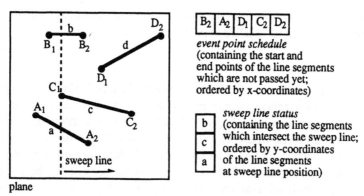

Figure 4: Example of a plane sweep

3.2 Applications of plane-sweep algorithms in a GIS

The map overlay

One of the most important operations in a GIS is the *map overlay*. It combines two or more input maps of different topics into a single new output map. The combination of the thematic attributes or of geometric or topological properties of the input areas is controlled by an *overlay function* f, where f is defined or selected by the user of the GIS. The goals are to derive new maps, to find correlations between the information encoded in maps, and to process complex queries. C.D. Tomlin's map analysis package (MAP) [Tom90] is completely based on the map overlay operation.

We want to illustrate the overlay operation by an example. Figure 5 depicts two input maps 'land utilization' and 'soil pollution'. In the output map all areas should be reported, which are forests or agriculturally used land and where the degree of soil pollution is greater than 2.

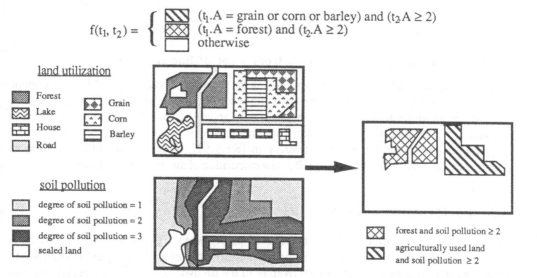

Figure 5: Example of a map overlay and an overlay function

In [KBS 91] we presented an overlay algorithm in detail which was based on the plane-sweep technique. This algorithm is called *plane-sweep overlay*.

The merge algorithm

Plane-sweep algorithms can be used for further problems in a GIS. The *merge operation* is one of them which is closely related to the map overlay [Fra 87]: Its purpose is to merge neighboring areas in one map representing the same thematic attribute (see figure 6). For example, such maps may result from a classification of the attributes or from an overlay with a non-injective overlay function. The neighboring areas with identical attributes can be merged by an plane-sweep algorithm similar to the plane-sweep overlay algorithm. The merge algorithm does not insert edges which separate areas with identical attributes into the sweep line status. Thus the resulting polygons describe the merged areas.

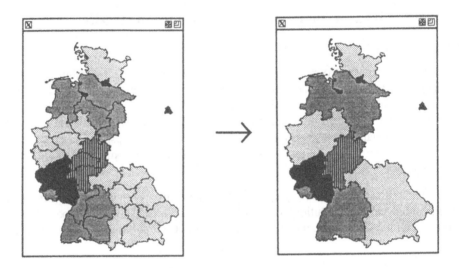

Figure 6: Merging neighbored areas with identical thematic attributes

Geometric computation of polygons from a set of line segments

Another application of plane-sweep algorithms is the following operation: Given a planar graph by a set of line segments, generate the areas limited by these line segments. This operation is needed for example to perform a geometric conversion of spatial data between different geographic information systems. Our implementation of this operation is based on the implementation of the plane-sweep overlay in [KBS 91]. Necessary modifications are an adaption of the intersection treatment and a new calculation of the thematic attributes.

3.3 Performance analysis

In this section we examine the performance of plane-sweep algorithms in an experimental framework. Because the map overlay is the most costly operation of the algorithms mentioned above, we investigated the plane-sweep overlay in the following. The principle results are also valid for the other operations if we consider that those algorithms need not to compute intersections.

Let n be the total number of edges of all polygons and k be the total number of intersection points of all edges. In [KBS 91] we showed that the worst case performance of the plane-sweep overlay is $t(n,k) = O((n+k) * \log(n))$ (under the assumption that the number of edges attached to one event point is limited by a constant).

We implemented the plane-sweep overlay algorithm in Modula-2. To examine the performance experimentally, we ran tests on a SUN workstation 3/60 under UNIX. We used a 8 Byte floating point representation which was supported by the hardware and system software. The implementation was developed to demonstrate the properties of the plane-sweep algorithm but it was not tuned for speed. Consequently, there is scope to speed up the overlay.

We performed four test series between two input maps. The maps consist of (1) a regular net of areas to get a constant proportion p of k / n, (2) areas covering the map completely which are generated by a tool, (3) tool-generated areas covering only 50 per cent of the map, and (4) real data. Test series 1 was performed with different proportions p. In test series 4a two maps of administrative divisions of Italy were overlaid where one was translated by an offset. In test series 4b the state frontier of Uganda and lakes near by were overlaid. Typical input maps of the series are depicted in figure 7:

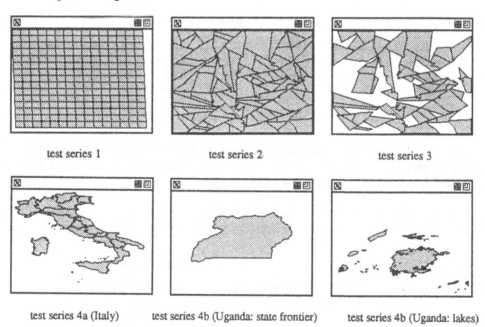

| test series 1 | test series 2 | test series 3 |

| test series 4a (Italy) | test series 4b (Uganda: state frontier) | test series 4b (Uganda: lakes) |

Figure 7: Input maps of the test series

The results of the test series 1 are shown in table 1. t is the used CPU time in sec which is needed to perform the overlay. Additionally, we want to determine the constant c of the map overlay algorithm hidden by the O-notation ($c = t / (n * \ln n)$).

series 1a (p = 0.25):

n	t [sec]	c [msec]
2048	25	1.61
4608	59	1.52
8192	112	1.51
10368	142	1.48
15488	227	1.52
21632	313	1.45
25088	363	1.43

series 1b (p = 0.1):

n	t [sec]	c [msec]
2880	29	1.26
5120	53	1.22
8000	86	1.20
11520	130	1.21
15680	183	1.21
20480	246	1.21
25920	307	1.17

series 1c (p = 0.033):

n	t [sec]	c [msec]
2160	18	1.11
4860	44	1.06
8640	83	1.06
11760	113	1.03
15360	147	0.99
19440	190	0.99
24000	246	1.02

Table 1: Results of the test series 1

The test series of table 1 demonstrate how the constant depends on the number of intersection points. An analysis of these tests results in the following function:

$$t(n,k) = c' * (n + 1.75 * k) * \ln(n)$$

The value of c' in the test series 1a to 1c is approximately 1.05 msec. We would like to emphazise that this constant is very small with respect to performance criteria.

In table 2 the test series 2 and 3 are depicted where c' is calculated additionally.

series 2:

n	p	t [sec]	c [msec]	c'[msec]
13176	0.240	188	1.50	1.02
28837	0.154	372	1.26	0.97
30285	0.161	413	1.32	1.01

series 3:

n	p	t [sec]	c[msec]	c'[msec]
6251	0.262	101	1.85	1.21
14179	0.184	221	1.63	1.20
15260	0.188	245	1.66	1.22

Table 2: Results of the test series 2 and 3

Series 2 and 3 demonstrate another dependency of the running time: If a large number of edges of the polygons coincide (see figure 7), the running time decreases. The reason is that the algorithm detects such edges and combines them.

Table 3 depicts the results of test series 4 with files of real data. In series 4a (Italy) varying administrative divisions and in series 4b (Uganda) varying resolutions are considered.

series 4a (Italy):

division	n	p	t [sec]	c [msec]	c'[msec]
state	6666	0.012	67	1.14	1.12
groups of regions	9622	0.015	94	1.07	1.04
regions	11542	0.014	110	1.02	0.99
provinces	20378	0.023	194	0.96	0.92

series 4b (Uganda, p < 0.004):

n	t [sec]	c[msec]
1852	16	1.16
8973	86	1.05
17829	180	1.03

Table 3: Results of the test series 4

The results of test series 4 demonstrate the validity of the previous results for real data.

3.4   A suitable coordinate representation for plane-sweep algorithms

The instability of plane-sweep algorithms against numerical errors is an objection being raised. This reproach may be justified if a floating point representation is used to compute the intersection points. However rational coordinates are a more suitable representation because they form a vector space. For example, a rational representation of coordinates is used in an implementation of a map overlay in [FW 87].

A more detailed analysis of such a representation leads to the following statements:

1.   The coordinates in maps recorded by a GIS can be represented by pairs of integers. This assumption is realistic because both, the described part of the world and the resolution are limited.

2.   To compute intersection points, integer coordinates are insufficient [Fra 84]. But the computation of the intersection of line segments described by integer coordinates, needs only a limited number of digits to represent the intersection points by rational numbers. Let n the number of digits of the integers of the input map then the number of digits of the nominator of the intersection points is smaller than $2*n+4$ and the number of digits of the denominator is smaller than $3*n+4$ (see [Bri 90]).

3.   If the input maps of an overlay or of another operation producing intersections, result from an analysis operation (thus containing rational coordinates), the same number of digits as in statement 2 is sufficient for the representation of the intersection points. This is due to the fact that no line segments connecting intersection points are introduced.

Under realistic assumptions rational coordinates of finite precision are an easy, relative efficient, and numerical exact coordinate representation for geographic information systems. Plane-sweep algorithms are absolutely robust by this approach. For an efficient use of rational coordinates an adequate support by hardware and system software is desirable but lacking today.

4   Coupling spatial access methods and plane-sweep algorithms

The database system of a GIS must support efficient query processing as well as efficient manipulation and combination of maps. To fulfill these requirements we assume that the database system uses suitable *spatial access methods (SAMs)* for the management of the database. In particular, this allows to extract the relevant parts from the seamless database (maps). In the following we assume that each map layer is organized and supported by its own SAM because in GISs an efficient access to a map of one topic is desirable, e.g. land utilization or soil pollution.

An often used technique to store areas with SAMs is to approximate them by *minimal bounding boxes (MBBs)*. MBBs preserve the most essential geometric properties of geometric objects, i.e. the location of the object and the extension of the object in each axis. The query processing is carried out in two (or more) steps. MBBs are used as a first *filter* to reduce the set of candidates. The second step *(refinement)* examines those candidate polygons by decomposing them into simple spatial objects such as convex polygons, triangles, or trapezoids ([KHHSS 91a], [KS 91]). To test the polygons for intersection with a sweep line or query rectangle, MBBs are a sufficient first filter.

In the following we assume that the SAM organizes the access to the objects of a database using a tree-like *directory*. Such access methods are adequate in handling non-uniform spatial data [KSSS 89]. The inner nodes are called *directory pages*, the leaves of the tree are *data pages*. The data and directory pages of a SAM define a partition of the data space. In our case a record in a data page consists at least (a) of a MBB, (b) of the value of the thematic attribute, and (c) of a polygon description or of a pointer to such a description depending on the size of the polygon, see [KHHSS 91b].

As mentioned in the introduction, the database and the maps in a GIS may be very large. Therefore it is not useful to keep all maps in main memory, especially not in multi user systems. In systems with a virtual storage manager the efficiency could decline by a large number of page faults.

Instead of processing the maps completely, it is more efficient to partition the maps and to carry out the plane sweep algorithms on these partitions. One approach is to partition the map using a uniform grid like in [Fra 89]. Obviously, this is not the best way because a non-uniform data distribution is not adequately handled by this approach. We will partition the map by using SAMs and the plane-sweep technique.

Another important reason to partition the maps is the running time of plane-sweep algorithms which is often more than linear. By partitioning we reduce the number of polygons and edges which have to reside in main memory performing the plane sweep. This speeds up the running time for the complete plane sweep.

4.1 Sweep-line partition

For a plane-sweep algorithm only those polygons are relevant which intersect the sweep line. Thus we have a criterion for partitioning by the algorithm itself: Only polygons intersecting the sweep line or close to the sweep line, are kept in main memory. In terms of SAMs this means to read data pages from secondary storage as soon as the sweep line intersects them. We call this approach *sweep-line partition*.

Sweep-line partition and transformation

For example, the sweep-line partition can be realized by the *transformation technique* [SK 88]. This technique transforms the coordinates of a 2-dimensional MBB into a 4-dimensional point. There are two representations of such points:
(1)   The *center representation* consists of the center of the rectangle (c_x, c_y) and the distance of the center to the sides of the rectangle (e_x, e_y).
(2)   The *corner representation* stores the lower left (x_1, y_1) and the upper right corner (x_2, y_2) of the box.
The 4-dimensional points are stored by a suitable *multidimensional point access method*, e.g. the grid file [NHS 84], PLOP-hashing [KS 88], the BANG file [Fre 87], or the buddy tree [SK 90] .

In the following we use the transformation technique with corner representation. The SAM uses its own sweep line. These sweep line is driven by the partition of the SAM. Performing a plane-sweep algorithm, we must synchronize the sweep line of the algorithm and the sweep line of the SAM. When the sweep line of the algorithm overtakes the sweep line of the SAM, new data pages must be read from secondary storage by the SAM. An example is depicted in fig. 8.

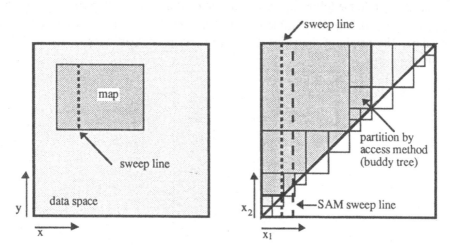

Figure 8: Sweep-line partition and realization by transformation (x-dimensions are shown only)

The sweep-line partition is also applicable to the other techniques (i.e. *clipping* and *overlapping regions* [SK 88]) and to access methods inherently using these techniques, e.g. the R-tree [Gut 84] and the R*-tree [BKSS 90] (overlapping regions), or the cell tree [Gün 89] (clipping).

Performance

Using the sweep line partition reduces the number of page faults considerably because only those parts of the maps intersecting the sweep line reside in main memory. Minimizing the number of page faults during the algorithm improves the overall performance.

This gain of efficiency is only slightly reduced by the following effect: Without partition every required page is accessed exactly once. The pass through the tree of the SAM according to the sweep line may cause several accesses to the same directory page. However, the number of accessed directory pages is, compared to the total number of read pages, generally very small. In table 4, the space requirements of real maps are listed (assuming an R*-tree with pages of 2 KB):

map	data	directory	directory share
Africa (countries)	4679348 byte	3924 byte	0.084 %
Africa (topography)	5528816 byte	46332 byte	0.831 %
Latin America (countries)	5178440 byte	10332 byte	0.199 %
Latin America (topography)	3785440 byte	51480 byte	1.342 %
EC (regions)	1126360 byte	29916 byte	2.587 %

Table 4: Space requirements of data and directory

4.2 Strip Partition

Contrary to a partition driven by the sweep line, an orthogonal partition is possible. To support the plane sweep, it is sensible to divide the map into strips S_i which extend over the whole map *(strip plane sweep)*. In the following we assume proceeding from the top strip S_1 to the bottom strip S_M (see figure 9). The strip partition shortens the length of the sweep line which decreases running time. The height of the strips may vary to adapt the partitions to non-uniform data distributions.

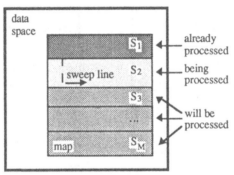

Figure 9: Strip partition

Some areas of a map may intersect more than one strip. One solution is to read all necessary areas for each strip. The consequence is that many data pages are accessed several times. Therefore, this procedure is too costly. Another way is to store such areas temporarily in a buffer. Those areas are an additional input to the next strip plane sweep. Thus, every area of an map can be assigned to exactly one strip S_i and needs to be read from secondary storage only once.

As in section 4.1 we assume that each accessed data page is completely read. Areas not intersecting the actual strip are buffered. The access to the areas of one strip corresponds to standard region queries which supply all polygons intersecting the strip. There is only one exception: Data pages accessed by previous strips are not read again. We call this kind of query *modified region query*. Such queries are performed very efficiently by the R*-tree [BKSS 90], a variant of the well-known R-tree [Gut 84]. This is caused by the minimization of area, margin, and overlap of directory rectangles in the R*-tree.

Generating an optimal strip partition

In the following, we want to describe how an optimal strip partition of the map is generated. An optimal strip partition adapts the strips to the distribution of the areas of the map, exploits the size of main memory, and avoids page faults. The strip partition is best supported by using an efficient SAM, such as the R*-tree.

As mentioned, the areas of each map which are simple polygons with holes, are approximated by minimal bounding boxes, which preserve the location and the extension of the areas. The number of bytes representing an area is assigned to the MBB. This is necessary because we cannot expect in GIS applications that each area is described by the same number of bytes. Each data page represents a set of areas. Thus, for each data page the number of bytes can be calculated which is necessary to store the data of this page in main memory. This information is stored in lowest level of the directory.

In a preprocessing step of a plane-sweep algorithm, we determine the data pages which intersect the map. Each data page of the SAM corresponds to a region of the data space, e.g. the regions of the R*-tree are rectangles. These regions are sorted in descending order according to the highest y-coordinate of the region. Initially, the buffer is empty which stores areas which are not performed completely by a strip sweep line. According to the order mentioned above the first k regions are determined where the sum of bytes which are represented by these k regions is smaller than the size of main memory minus the size of the buffer. Thus, the first strip S_1 is limited by the highest y-coordinate of the (k+1)st data page. The areas which are not handled completely in the first strip sweep line will be stored in the buffer. The above procedure is iterated.

To illustrate this approach we present the following example where the size of main memory is restricted to 8 mega bytes (see figure 10).

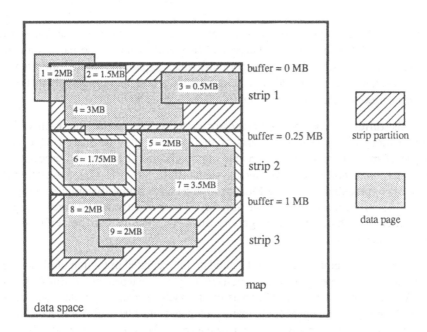

Figure 10: Example of generating an optimal strip partition

The numbers 1 to 9 of the data pages indicate the order mentioned above. The size of the data pages 1 to 4 amounts to 7 MB. With the next data page the size of main memory would be exceeded (7MB+2 MB ≥ 8MB) and page faults could occur. Therefore, the first strip ends at the highest y-coordinate of the data page 5. Let us assume that after the first strip plane sweep 0.25 MB are stored in the buffer. Then the second strip can be extended until 7.75 MB are not exceeded. Thus, the data pages 5 to 7 are associated to the second strip. Finally, the data pages

8 and 9 and the regions stored in the buffer are accomodated in the third strip.

Generating the optimal strip partition is not time intensive because only directory pages are read to get the necessary information, such as the size of the data pages and bytes represented by the data pages. Data pages are only read from secondary storage when the plane-sweep algorithm is performed actually. The ratio of read directory pages to read data pages is very small when performing a plane-sweep algorithm (compare section 4.1).

5   Parallel processing of plane sweeps

In the last years there are many efforts to design, to manufacture, and to utilize computer architectures of multiple, parallel central processing units (CPUs). Computers using such architectures are called *multiprocessor systems* or *parallel computers*. Their main objective is to increase the performance compared to one-processor systems. Future database systems and particularly spatial database systems of GISs have to pursue using such architectures. This is important especially for time-consuming operations such as the map overlay or related GIS operations.

The use of parallel architectures necessitates the development of spatial access methods which support parallel access to the database and (if possible) utilize the parallel architecture. The second goal is the design of parallel algorithms which exploit the parallelism offered by the architectures and the parallelism hidden in the problem in a best possible way. In this section we demonstrate such exploitation of parallelism for plane-sweep algorithms.

There exist different types of multiprocessor systems. We assume that each CPU has its own main memory *(local memory)*. Parts of the memory may be shared. One important characteristic of multiprocessor systems is the communication between the processors. There exist many *interconnection networks* in such systems ([GM 89], [SH 87]), e.g. static networks as rings, trees, hypercubes, or grids. Modern architectures allow dynamic routing between arbitrary processors. In the following, we assume a linear arrangement where each processor can communicate with its direct neighbor. Such a structure can be realized by most interconnection networks.

The strip partition seems to be the best candidate for a parallel execution of plane sweeps. A natural approach is to process the strips simultaneously and independently. But there are some problems: As mentioned in section 4.2, areas exist which intersect more than one strip. If we perform the plane sweeps independently, many data pages must be read from secondary storage several times. This effect decreases the performance of the approach considerably. Another problem is that we may need the results of strip S_{i-1} for processing strip S_i which is e.g. necessary for the plane-sweep overlay of thematic maps without complete cover by the areas.

Therefore, we have to synchronize the strip processing. We introduce a second sweep line for each strip indicating the part of the map which is already processed completely. The first sweep line of strip S_{i+1} is not allowed to overtake the second sweep line of S_i. The process of S_{i+1} is suspended if necessary. An example of parallel strip processing is shown in figure 11:

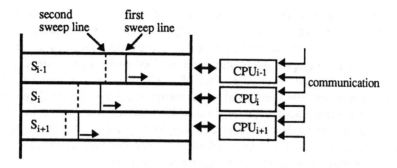

Figure 11: Parallel strip processing

Parallel plane-sweep overlay

This approach can be realized for the plane-sweep overlay [KBS 91] with little extensions to the original algorithm: For maintaining the second sweep line, we need a new data structure L. The actual x-position P of the first sweep line and an identification number of the region are inserted into L when a new region is starting. L is ordered by P and can be implemented using a balanced tree. The position P and the region ID are also stored additionally to the edges in the sweep line status. If the algorithm detects that two regions with different region IDs are identical, the entry with P starting further to the right is deleted from L. When a region is closed, the associated entry is deleted from P. If this entry was the minimum entry, the second sweep line is allocated at the position of the new minimum entry of L. This processing is illustrated in figure 12. Other plane-sweep algorithms can be modified in a similar way.

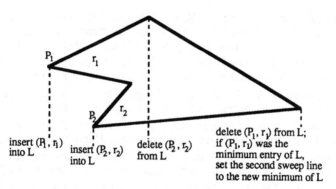

Figure 12: Update of the data structure L

6 Conclusions

In this paper, we demonstrated the fruitfulness of combining spatial access methods and computational geometry concepts, in particular for the plane-sweep paradigm, in order to increase the efficiency of geographic database systems. The marriage of these two areas was enabled by the property that the spatial access method supports the plane-sweep paradigm.

Since plane-sweep processing generates results in sorted order, the spatial access method must be robust with respect to sorted insertions for storing these results. As an example of providing good performance we presented the plane-sweep map overlay which is a very important analysis operation in a geographic information system. Good analysis and retrieval performance are important factors for good user acceptance of a GIS. Thus, in our future work, we will design efficient algorithms based on spatial access methods and computational geometry for all retrieval operations. Performance improvements which exceed those realized in this paper by coupling spatial access methods and computational geometry, are feasible by using processors suitable for rational numbers and by implementing parallel GIS algorithms on parallel multiprocessor systems. These issues are important goals in future work.

Acknowledgement

We thankfully acknowledge receiving real data representing national administrative divisions of the European countries by the Statistical Office of the European Communities. Further real data are taken from the World Data Bank II. Additionally, we would like to thank Holger Horn for making his map generator available to us.

References

[BKSS 90]   Beckmann, N., Kriegel, H.-P., Schneider, R., Seeger, B.: The R*-tree: An Efficient and Robust Access Method for Points and Rectangles. Proc. ACM SIGMOD Int. Conf. on Management of Data, 322-331, 1990

[Bri 90]   Brinkhoff, T.: Map Overlay of Thematic Maps Supported by Spatial Access Methods. Master thesis (in German), University of Bremen, 1990

[Bur 86]   Burrough, P.A.: Principles of Geographical Information Systems for Land Resources Assessment. Oxford University Press, 1986

[Fra 84]   Franklin, W.R.: Cartographic Errors Symtomatic of Underlying Algebra Problems. Proc. Int. Symp. on Spatial Data Handling, Vol. I, 190-208, 1984

[Fra 87]   Frank, A.U.: Overlay Processing in Spatial Information Systems. Proc. 8th Int. Symp. on Computer-Assisted Cartography (Auto-Carto 8), 16-31, 1987

[Fra 89]   Franklin, W.R. et al.: Uniform Grids: A Technique for Intersection Detection on Serial and Parallel Machines. Proc. 9th Int. Symp. on Computer-Assisted Cartography (Auto-Carto 9), 100-109, 1989

[Fre 87]   Freeston, M.: The BANG file: a new kind of grid file. Proc. ACM SIGMOD Int. Conf. on Management of Data, 260-269, 1987

[FW 87]   Franklin, W.R., Wu, P.Y.F.: A Polygon Overlay System in Prolog. Proc. 8th Int. Symp. on Computer-Assisted Cartography (Auto-Carto 8), 97-106, 1987

[GM 89]   Gonauser, M., Mrva, M. (eds.): Multiprozessor-Systeme: Architektur und Leistungsbewertung. Springer, 1989

[Gün 89]   Günther, O.: The Design of the Cell Tree: An Object-Oriented Index Structure for Geometric Databases. Proc. IEEE 5th Int. Conf. on Data Engineering, 598-605, 1989

[Gut 84]   Guttman, A.: R-Trees: A Dynamic Index Structure for Spatial Searching. Proc. ACM SIGMOD Int. Conf. on Management of Data, 47-57, 1984

[KBS 91]   Kriegel, H.-P., Brinkhoff, T., Schneider, R.: An Efficient Map Overlay Algorithm based on Spatial Access Methods and Computational Geometry. Proc. Int. Workshop on DBMS's for geographical applications, Capri, May 16-17, 1991

[KHHSS 91a] Kriegel, H.-P., Heep, P., Heep, S., Schiwietz, M., Schneider, R.: An Access Method Based Query Processor for Spatial Database Systems. Proc. Int. Workshop on DBMS's for geographical applications, Capri, May 16-17, 1991

[KHHSS 91b] Kriegel, H.-P., Heep, P., Heep, S., Schiwietz, M., Schneider, R.: A Flexible and Extensible Index Manager for Spatial Database Systems. Proc. 2nd Int. Conf. on Database and Expert Systems Applications (DEXA '91), Springer, 179-184, 1991

[KS 88]   Kriegel, H.-P., Seeger, B.: PLOP-Hashing: A Grid File without Directory. Proc. 4th Int. Conf. on Data Engineering, 369-376, 1988

[KS 91]   Kriegel, H.-P., Schneider, R.: The TR*-tree: A New Representation of Polygonal Objects Supporting Spatial Queries and Operations. Proc. 7th Workshop on Computational Geometry, 1991. In: Lecture Notes in Computer Science 553, Springer, 1991

[KSSS 89]   Kriegel, H.P., Schiwietz, M., Schneider, R., Seeger, B.: Performance Comparison of Point and Spatial Access Methods. Proc. 1st Symp. on the Design of Large Spatial Databases, 1989. In: Lecture Notes in Computer Science 409, Springer, 89-114, 1990

[NHS 84]   Nievergelt, J., Hinterberger, H., Sevcik, K.C.: The Grid File: An Adaptable, Symmetric Multikey File Structure. ACM Trans. on Database Systems, Vol. 9, No. 1, 38-71, 1984

[Nie 89]   Nievergelt, J.: 7±2 Criteria for Assessing and Comparing Spatial Data Structures. Proc. 1st Symp. on the Design of Large Spatial Databases, 1989. In: Lecture Notes in Computer Science 409, Springer, 3-28, 1990

[Oos 90]   Oosterom, P.J.M.: Reactive Data Structures for Geographic Information Systems. PhD-thesis, Department of Computer Science at Leiden University, 1990

[PS 88]   Preparata, F.P., Shamos, M.I.: Computational Geometry. Springer, 1988

[Sam 89]   Samet, H.: The Design and Analysis of Spatial Data Structures. Addison-Wesley, 1989

[SH 87]   Siegel, H.J., Hsu, W.T.: Interconnection Networks. In: Milutinovic (ed.): Computer Architecture: Concepts and Systems. North-Holland, 225-264, 1987

[SK 88]   Seeger, B., Kriegel, H.-P.: Techniques for Design and Implementation of Efficient Spatial Access Methods. Proc. 14th Int. Conf. on Very Large Data Bases, 360-371, 1988

[SK 90]   Seeger, B., Kriegel, H.-P.: The Buddy-Tree: An Efficient and Robust Access Method for Spatial Database Systems. Proc. 16th Int. Conf. on Very Large Data Bases, 590-601, 1990

[Til 80]   Tilove, R.B.: Set Membership Classification: A Unified Approach To Geometric Intersection Problems. IEEE Trans. on Computers, Vol. C-29, No. 10, 874-883, 1980

[Tom 90]   Tomlin, C.D.: Geographic Information Systems and Cartographic Modeling. Prentice-Hall, 1990

A Flexible and Extensible Index Manager
for Spatial Database Systems*

Hans-Peter Kriegel[1], Peter Heep[2], Stephan Heep[3], Michael Schiwietz[1], Ralf Schneider[1]

1 Institut für Informatik, Universität München, Leopoldstraße 11B, D-8000 München 40

2 NANU NANA GmbH, Lange Straße 48, D-2900 Oldenburg

3 Praktische Informatik, Universität Bremen, Bibliothekstraße, D-2800 Bremen 33

Abstract: The management of spatial data in applications such as graphics and image processing, geography as well as computer aided design (CAD) imposes stringent new requirements on socalled spatial database systems. In this paper we propose a flexible and extensible index manager for efficient query processing in spatial database systems by integrating spatial access methods. An essential ingredient for efficient query processing is spatial clustering of objects using common clustering properties, such as spatial location. In our approach an extensible set of alternative access paths is provided, in order to accelerate queries on properties which are not supported by clustering. Clustering and alternative access paths are organized in such a way that redundant storage of objects as well as time consuming reorganizations are avoided. This guarantees flexibility with respect to storage and access of the objects as well as efficient query processing. To support the index manager, we propose a storage method for handling arbitrary long objects, which is suitable in an environment that demands for clustering and multiple indexing.

1 Introduction

The demand for using database systems in application areas such as graphics and image processing, computer aided design (CAD) as well as geography and cartography is considerably increasing. The important characteristic of these applications is the occurance of spatial objects. The management of spatial objects imposes stringent new requirements on socalled spatial database systems.

One characteristic of spatial databases is that the description of spatial objects is a combination of nonspatial, atomic attributes (as supported by standard database systems) and additional spatial attributes. Spatial attributes may contain an arbitrary long description as well as a spatial location and spatial relations to other spatial objects which have to be supported for query processing. Efficient query processing can only be achieved by integrating spatial access methods and index methods into spatial database systems.

For example, in a geographical database system a spatial object could be a lot. The description of the spatial object lot consists of the nonspatial attribute 'owner' as well as the spatial attributes 'boundary polygon' and 'MBB' the minimum bounding box of the lot. The boundary polygon is an example of a spatial attribute of arbitrary length.

* This work was supported by grant no. Kr 670/4-3 from the Deutsche Forschungsgemeinschaft (German Research Society)

Additionally, the boundary polygon gives an exact specification of the spatial location and it implies the neighbour relationship as a spatial relation. Because no available query processing concept is able to support polygons directly, minimum bounding boxes are used as a spatial attribute approximating size, location and spatial relationship of polygons. For efficient query processing, the lots should be clustered according to their spatial location using available spatial access methods (SAMs) for multidimensional rectilinear boxes (see [KSSS 89], [KS 88]). Assume, in our example we want to retrieve lots according to their owner. Obviously, we need an alternative access path which organizes lots according to the nonspatial attribute owner. In order to handle the combination of clustering by spatial access methods and additional alternative access paths, an index manager is needed. In particular the index manager should avoid redundant storage of objects as well as time consuming reorganizations.

In the next chapter we specify some modeling concepts which are essential to spatial database systems. Such concepts impose requirements for our underlying flexible and extensible index manager and are therefore described here. Next we present the conceptual features of our proposal. In this context we derive what kind of metadata has to be provided for the index manager. In chapter 4 we describe the realization of this index manager. In chapter 5 we propose a storage method for handling arbitrary long objects supporting the index manager. The paper concluds with a summary that points out the main contributions of our proposal and gives an outlook to future possibilities of applications, as for example in a Bioindication database system [KS 90].

2 Conceptual requirements in spatial databases

The support of applications which use spatial data, such as CAD or geographic applications, asks for modeling capabilities that exceed those of relational database systems. There exist a lot of proposals for data models and data modeling capabilities for this reason. Some of them are concerned with general capabilities, e.g. the functional data model [Ship 81], POSTGRES [SR 86] or the EXODUS proposal [CDRS 86] and others are directly concerned with the modeling of spatial data like [Guet 89]. In the following we do not propose a new data model but we would like to describe those modeling capabilities which every spatial database system should support in our oppinion in any case. Furthermore, we will emphasize that our index manager may be integrated in a straightforward way into systems which provide those modeling capabilities.

On the conceptual level we consider a (structured) object as a record consisting of a set of attributes that are referenced by their names. In the following we describe the set of available attribute types, the internal structure of a record and of a database.

2.1 The attribute types

This section deals with the description of the six attribute classes (see figure 1) which should be included in a spatial database system.

First of all such a spatial database system should include the attribute types of the traditional relational model with relations of normalized form. Attribute types are only system given atomic types. Generally, they are fixed length types such as INTEGER, REAL, CARDINAL and STRINGS of fixed length. These types, called atomic attribute types, are system supported by a set of type dependent operations such as comparison operations, identity checking and others.

For spatial databases, the available attribute types should be augmented by types for simple spatial objects as proposed in [Guet 89]. In order to support geometric queries which are typical in geographical or CAD database systems, we introduce a class of atomic geoattribute types for point objects as well as 2 and 3-dimensional rectangular objects. This class consists of the types Point_2D, Point_3D, INTERVALL, RECTANGLE and RECTANGULAR SOLID. These types are considered as atomic types even though they are composed. As a consequence type dependent operations on these objects are supported. An example for such an operation is the predicate Intersects (R, S) which is defined on two rectangles R and S. In case of an intersection of R and S this predicate returns TRUE.

An essential feature of new data models is the representation of arbitrary and variable length objects or attributes as described for example in [CDRS 86]. This feature is used to accommodate objects which are difficult to decompose in atomic types, e.g. unstructured objects such as text. Our approach provides an attribute type called *complex*. Due to the hidden structure information of an attribute of type complex only special read and write operations (see chapter 5), but no additional operations such as comparison operations, are assigned to this type.

An additional feature which we require are user defined types in order to support extensibility of the database system. Their internal representation may be based on the type complex. For an efficient handling the user may define special operations to gain more type specific accuracy, e.g. more sophisticated read and write operations. These operations are strictly bound to their special types. Their description is given in a procedural manner and is declared to the system at the time of type definition. As an example we consider the type POLYGON. An instance of this type can on the logical level be described by the number of points and an ordered point list. User defined type definitions may contain procedures for reading and writing an arbitrary point of a point list.

Attribut Type	sytem supported operators	user defined operators
atomic attr.	<, = , type dependent operators	no
atomic geo attr.	operators like lower, equal, intersects, ...	no
complex attr.	-	no
user-defined attr.	-	yes
derived attr.	<, =	yes
object identifier	=	no

Figure 1: Table of data types and operators

The values of all attributes described until now are explicitly given. Derived attributes are handled differently. A special derivation procedure defines the type of such an attribute. An example is given by a procedure computing the minimum bounding box (MBB), which is of type rectangle, from a user-defined attribute of the type polygon. The existance of a derivation procedure automatically extends the record by the derived attribute. For simplicity we assume that the type of a derived attribute is atomic, such that its value can be stored in the attribute directly. If the procedure evaluates to more complex types, a procedural (uninterpreted) or object identifier based representation is necessary. A detailed discussion of such representations for complex objects can be found in [JS 90] and [KC 86].

As shown in figure 1, user-defined and derived attributes are supported by user-defined operations. We distinguish between operations which provide a change of data such as write operations and those that generally leave data unchanged such as comparison operations do. Because 'changing' operations need additional activities, they must be separately handled.

A helpful feature which should be included is object identity which allows identification of a record by its own system given unique identifier (surrogate). This surrogate is represented by an additional atomic data type called object identifier (type OID) which remains hidden to the user. Every single record internally is supplemented by an attribute of type OID which itself has a central significance for indexing purposes (see chapter 3).

2.2 The record structure

For the index manager to be proposed some kind of metadata which describes the structure of records has to be included. This metadata can be provided by specifying a record descriptor shown in example 1 (see figure 2). Thus a fixed structure defined by the record descriptor is attached to each record. For each single attribute this record descriptor contains the name and the type of the attribute and the update mode which propagates object changes. Derived attributes are locked for direct manipulation which is denoted by a '*' within the update mode field (see attribute 'MBB' in example 1). A trigger is attached to each attribute which contains related derived attributes. This trigger is defined by an update mode pointer representing derivation procedures which are called in the case of changes of the attribute. In example 1 the entry within the update mode of the attribute 'boundary' refers to a procedure computing the minimum bounding box of the polygon and adding the value to the attribute 'MBB'. For the rest of the attributes no special update mode information is necessary. For simplification and internal purposes every single attribute obtains a system given attribute number.

AttrNo	AttrName	Type	Update Mode
1	boundary	polygon	pointer
2	name	STRING	-
3	population	INTEGER	-
4	MBB	RECTANGLE	*

Figure 2: Example 1: Description of a record

2.3 Relations and cluster

All data models provide the possibility to aggregate collections of records of the same type which are known as sets or relations. The concept of combining sets of those relations to one cluster seems to be suitable for spatial databases. A cluster defines an area within secondary storage where all data belonging to the corresponding relations is accumulated. Then, a database consists of a set of such clusters. The idea of combining different relations and thus differently typed objects to the same cluster is based on a possible common connection between objects belonging to different structures. For example, in a geographic database, objects describing cities and agricultural areas are to be stored, where the attribute 'population' which is relevant for cities is meaningless for agricultural areas. City and agricultural objects are therefore differently structured and thus assigned to different relations. Yet, a common reference is given by the spatial location. This relationship should be used within geographical queries, such as, 'what agricultural areas and what cities are included in a given region?'. An efficient query support by access paths is only possible by introducing a component which we call an index manager.

3 The concepts of the index manager

As outlined before, any single object is assigned to an unique relation within a cluster. With respect to application demands atomic attributes as well as combinations of atomic attributes are candidates for indexing. The index manager facilitates the support of any number and combination of attributes. In the following we assume m attributes, according to application demands, should be supported.

As a first attempt a single m-dimensional ($m \geq 1$) (super-)index may be formed over all the m attributes. Such an index defines object organization and localization on secondary storage. Additional to information managing problems in the case of a high number of attributes the main problem due to this approach is the performance of any m-dimensional access method degenerates in the case of partial match queries specifying $n \ll m$ attributes. Thus, the number of attributes managed by one index has to be limited for the sake of efficiency. Because every query relevant attribute should be supported by indexing, more than one index turns out to be necessary. In our approach, arbitrary one- or multidimensional access methods may be assigned in arbitrary combination on the attributes of any object type. This index manager, introducing the concept of cluster and inverted indexes, is described in the following sections. A lot of index structures have been proposed in literature for different purposes([BM 72], [NHS 84], [SK 90]). Some of them excellently manage point data but are not suitable for spatial data, whereas others are exclusively proposed for spatial data management ([Gutt 84], [RL 85], [GB 88], [BKSS 90], see also [Same 90]). Thus an additional advantage arises when using more than one single index. Contrary to using one single index, any attribute as well as any combination of attributes may be organized using a tailorcut access method. Spatial data should be supported by spatial access methods whereas point data should be organized by efficient point access methods. Special superimposed coding structures, e.g. known for text representation, may be included as well (see [Ston 83]). This kind of open architecture is most adequate to face the requirements mentioned above.

3.1 The different types of indexes and their interaction

In this section, we describe the meaning of the concepts *cluster index*, *inverted index* and *relation index*. The interaction of these different types of indexes is additionally visualized in figure 3.

The clustering of records and relations is a central design goal of our approach. Objects belonging to different relations and therefore consisting of different internal structures may be grouped to a cluster with respect to a common relationship, e.g. their spatial location. Because different relations may be accommodated in one cluster, such a cluster is called heterogenous. A heterogenous cluster generally makes sense in an environment of many different object classes consisting of only a few objects, which are similar to each other with respect to some essential semantic property.

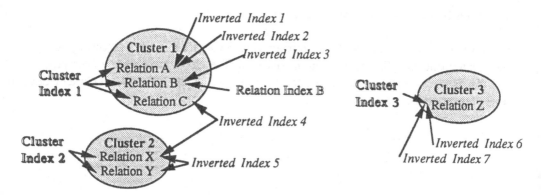

Figure 3: Interaction of the indexes

The clustering of records and relations is a central design goal of our approach. Objects belonging to different relations and therefore consisting of different internal structures may be grouped to a cluster with respect to a common relationship, e.g. their spatial location. Because different relations may be accommodated in one cluster, such a cluster is called heterogenous. A heterogenous cluster generally makes sense in an environment of many different object classes consisting of only a few objects, which are similar to each other with respect to some essential semantic property.

The cluster property is defined by those attributes contributing to that common relationship. The position of a record on secondary storage is (uniquely) defined by the *cluster index* which also provides an access path to the objects. Choosing the cluster index on attributes of high selectivity and considering an application dependent semantic suitability of the attributes will lead to good query performance. High selectivity is characterized by a low number of duplicates. Another criterion is the number of attributes handled by the cluster index. For the sake of efficiency too many cluster attributes should be avoided to prevent deterioration of partial match query performance. The cluster index itself consists of a suitable index structure augmented by the management of arbitrary length records (see chapter 5).

Because a set of records cannot be clustered by different cluster indexes without object redundancy and on the other hand one index may not support an arbitrary number of key attributes for performance issues, we use a second type of indexes. Due to the indexing based on a given clustering of the objects, those indexes are called *inverted indexes*. These indexes perform no clustering on the objects themselves but on pointers to the objects. They describe alternative access paths to the object instances organized under the given clustering by the cluster index. For the cluster index any arbitrary but suited one- or multidimensional access method may be applied. For inverted indexes a variety of different index structures can be applied for different indexes. Therefore any particular query can be supported by an index meeting application specific requirements. As different applications may use the same attributes for selections, the attribute sets of different indexes are not restricted to be disjoint.

The notion of a relation corresponds to a semantic clustering of equally typed objects. The explicit clustering is performed by a cluster index which may be unified for several different relations. To support an efficient access to a single relation within a cluster, a special inverted index, called *relation index*, may be defined over the primary key or the surrogate of that relation. That relation index provides a partial indexing on those records of the cluster index belonging to the relation.

3.2 Architecture of the index manager

Our objective is a superimposed system optimizing the access to a set of objects by adapting to the requirements of a flexible internal management. The global architecture of our proposal of an index manger is shown in figure 4. A central aspect is the interaction of one cluster index and a set of inverted indexes.

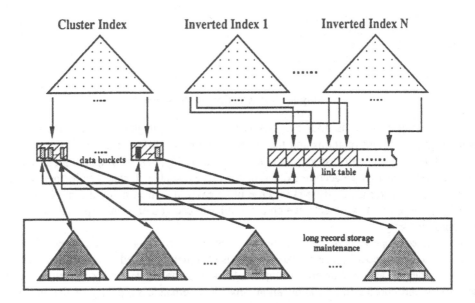

Figure 4: Architecture of the index manager

As described before, objects of the same type and structure may be combined to relations and sets of relations to a cluster. The cluster index provides the location of the data objects on secondary storage data pages. However, inverted indexes organize only references to such clustered objects. Special access paths can be modeled using suitable inverted indexes on single relations or multirelational indexes over different clusters. As mentioned before, an inverted index is called a relation index if it is defined over the primary key or surrogate of a single relation. In addition, an arbitrary number of different set oriented access paths may be modeled within one or many clusters. As the data objects and their clustering is dynamic an additional structure that enables a dynamic referencing to the clustered objects is necessary. We will call this structure, which will be described in more detail in chapter 4, a link table.

3.3 Metadata for the index manager

The following three structures are used as metadata for the index manager: the index list, the record descriptor and the index descriptor.

The necessary information on the set of indexes used within one database is managed in the form of an index list. The index list consists of the following entries:

- index Id
- access method description
- pointer to that access method
- type of the index: (cluster index, inverted index or relation index)
- key dimension (number of key attributes)
- key types of every dimension
- relation counter: number of relations managed by the index
- key attributes: key names within each relation

Note: A relation index is built on the surrogates or primary keys of one single relation,

therefore: key dimension = 1; key type = OID or primary key; relation counter = 1; key attribute = NULL

or primary key attribute

As mentioned before three types of indexes may be assigned to each single relation. The association between the relation attributes and the attributes used for indexing is given by assignments within a relation descriptor. The relation descriptor consists of:

- name of the relation
- pointer to the corresponding record descriptor
- one cluster index
- one or none relation index
- set of inverted indexes

where the relation index and the inverted indexes are optional. Every single index is represented by an index description, that consists of:

- the number of the index within the actual list of indexes (see Chapter 4)
- the array of key attributes used for indexing

A compatibility checking of the relation descriptor attribute types and the indexed attributes, described by the corresponding entry within the index list, is performed by the system.

3.4 Creation and deletion of indexes

As applications are subject to continuous development, an index management has to adapt dynamically. Therefore creating new and deleting old indexes has to be supported. This dynamic is different for cluster and inverted indexes.

A cluster index is created when the objects are inserted and physically clustered on secondary storage. Defining the internal secondary storage location of the objects, a deletion of the cluster index involves a global reorganization of all data. Although not explicitly excluded, this possibility will lead to a complete reorganization of both the cluster index and the link table. An adaption of the inverted indexes however is not necessary. Creation of an additional cluster index is not provided, because of redundant object storage. Contrarily, inverted indexes may be created in parallel to the cluster index at object insertion time, but additional inverted indexes may be constructed at any time for supporting new access paths. Creating a new inverted index, all relations or, more exactly, all clusters affected by the new index require an explicit examination. The index is build on the surrogates of the objects depending on the new query criterion. The datapage location does not change for any object. As the deletion of an inverted index neither affects the cluster index nor the objects themselves it can be performed in constant time.

4 Realisation of a dynamic index manager

In the last section the static architecture of a global index management system is described on conceptual level. The aspect of dynamic behaviour was considered only for creating and deleting a whole (inverted) index and therefore on query support level, but not for the dynamic behaviour of the objects itself. In spatial database applications objects are not static. New objects appear whereas old ones should be deleted or updated. Thus an object management must be provided in a dynamic way just as for the index management. The used index structures themselves are dynamic by definition, i.e. efficiently support insertions, deletions and updates. The global index management, however, has to be made dynamic explicitely.

As the references to the objects used for inverted indexing depend on the explicit clustering of those objects, any object change affecting the clustering location must be taken into account within the inverted indexes in form of new reference assignments. Therefore, in order to avoid a global scan of all inverted indexes, the objects themselves are referenced by a dynamic assignment structure called linktable. This linktable provides the correspondance between the datapage addresses in inverted index and cluster index. References managed by inverted indexes represent no explicit pointers to cluster index data page locations but to locations within the linktable, where the actual object position is stored.

The linktable concept

The function of the linktable is to link the object surrogates or references organized by the inverted indexes to the object instances positioned within the datapages of the cluster index. The linktable organizes a direct reference between the object surrogates and the cluster index datapages. Every object of all object clusters in the database is represented by exactly one specific entry within that linktable, whereas any of the inverted indexes generally is a partial index, i.e. not every object of the linktable and therefore of the database is organized.

Maintainance of the linktable: The dynamic behaviour of the cluster index in case of insertions and deletions is propagated to the location of the records which are never fixed to a specific datapage. In case of a datapage split the locations of all records transmitted to the new datapage are changed. Therefore all pointers to those objects within the inverted indexes have to be adapted to the new position in order to maintain a valid reference. As the reference between the object surrogates and the datapages containing the records is provided by the global linktable only the corresponding object entries within the linktable have to be adjusted. Most important, a particular treatment of every single inverted index, which would highly decrease in performance with an increasing number of such indexes, is avoided by introducing the global architecture of a linktable. Therefore the update performance does not depend on the number of inverted indexes.

As a datapage split will typically affect more than one object, an immediate adjustment of all entries affected by that update seems to be inefficient. Notice, that there is no demand for an actual linktable entry of an object in the time between two inverted index accesses to that object. Just in the case of an access to an object the corresponding linktable entry has to be actual. For supporting a delayed adjustment we use a reorganization protocol. If an object is not placed at the location given by its linktable entry, there exists a unique protocol entry containing the actual position of that record. By copying the object address to the corresponding linktable entry, the object reference is actualized and the protocol entry removed. Though, in the case of a not actual link table entry, the search for an object leads to at least one additional page access. For that reason, the linktable adjustment in the case of an access should be the exception. Using a background process the linktable is adjusted in parallel while queries and other database operations are performed.

The protocol file is organized as a search structure using the object surrogates as primary keys. We employ an AVL tree, a well known type of balanced primary key search structure storing the triples (surrogate, datapage, offset) using the surrogate as search key, see figure 5. Multiple updates of one and the same object are protocolled only once. Only the last object position is stored, whereas all previous positions are neglected by deleting the old entry in the case of an entry inserted, bound to the same unique surrogate. Therefore any object may only be represented once within the protocol file.

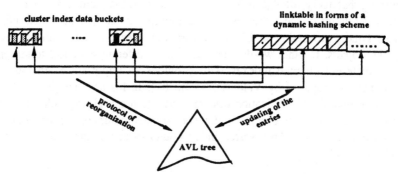

Figure 5: Reorganization and update of the linktable

Implementation aspects: As every object is uniquely represented within the linktable and the set of objects is not static, the linktable provides a dynamic organization. The management of one-dimensional pairwise disjoint and static entries is the objective of the linktable. A one-dimensional hashing scheme seems to be best suitable guaranteeing a one-access exact match query, randomly distributed key values provided. If object surrogates with no semantic meaning in clustering are organized, an exact match query is the only relevant type of query in the linktable. We suggest using of the following hashing scheme: Let the surrogates be instanciated by cardinal values assigned randomly to the objects. Taking their bitstrings, interpreting them as a binary number between zero and one, and inverting that bitstring, we receive uniformly distributed values within the range (0,1]. An efficient management of such values is provided by the onedimensional orderpreserving linear hashing scheme (see [Lars 80], [KS 86]).

A linktable entry consists of a key part and an info part. The key part contains the surrogate as search key for accessing purposes, whereas the info part contains a pointer to the object position in terms of an address within the cluster index data file consisting of a page address and an offset value, see figure 6. Changing the location of an object causes an actualization of the corresponding linktable entry pointer part. Notice the important property that the key part, and therefore the access to that entry, remains unchanged for the time of existence of that object.

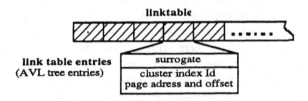

Figure 6: Structure of the linktable entries

Query management: The access to objects using an inverted index consists of a three level query. The first is a query to the index returning a set of object surrogates fullfilling the application query condition, followed by an access to the linktable for every single object surrogate, and finally reading the objects from their locations within the datapages of the cluster index. Accessing an object using the linktable requires the evaluation of a hash function and generally exactly one additional page access. To avoid multiple access to the same datapage, range queries to inverted indexes are treated in a breadth first manner. The set of object pointers is collected before running a set oriented access to the objects themselves. Notice, if there is no index supporting that query, all objects have to be scanned in a sequential manner.

An additional feature of the linktable and the multiple index scheme is the possibility of surrogate based query processing on different inverted indexes in parallel, minimizing the set of accesses to the objects. In other words, one query with different selection conditions may be distributed to different inverted indexes. This provides an important extension of join and selection indexes as proposed by Valduriez [Vald 87]. In his scheme [Vald 87] neither the concept of multidimensional application oriented indexes nor a global, delayed updated, link structure is included. His notion of a join index corresponds to our concept of a multi-cluster or multi-relation inverted index. An inverted index bound to one single relation of a cluster is known as selection index.

5 A storage method supporting the index manager

In chapter 2 we described which objects have to be supported in spatial database systems and in chapter 3 and 4 we introduced a flexible index manager for those objects. Some types of indexes and global object clustering are basic to support an efficient access to objects.

Permitting an arbitrary object length we cannot assume that each object fits in a single datapage of the cluster index. In such cases the storage of objects is twofold: some more essential attributes, e.g. attributes used for indexing, reside in the datapages of the cluster index whereas others, e.g. variable length attributes, are evacuated. Just as an access to attributes not being evacuated is efficient an access to evacuated ones should never increase excessivly.

At a logical level each object occurance (a record) may be stored within a datapage of a cluster index introduced in chapter 4. However due to efficiency limitations for index structures the number of entries within such a datapage may not be arbitrary small and thus there is a restriction to the length of records at this level. A solution for such is to evacuate records or portions of them by adding an external storage layer which handles long objects (long fields). In this context we have to take into account an efficient access to all types of fixed length attributes as well as to any portions of variable length attributes. How can this be done? The first idea is using one of the well known storage systems which support long objects. We describe some of them in the next section including their problems with respect to the requirements of storing and accessing records in our sense. Then we introduce a new storage method derived from the EXODUS storage manager [CDRS 86] combined with storage management at the level of a cluster index. This storage method utilizes efficient access and update to indexed and atomic attributes as well as to variable length attributes, portions of those and also to sequences of attributes.

5.1 Previous work in storage management

Well known storage systems which support the storage of objects of (virtually) any length are the Wisconsin Storage System (WiSS) [CDKK 85], the Starburst Long Field Manager [LL 89] and the EXODUS Storage Manager [CDRS 86].

In WiSS so called "long data items" are proposed. A long data item consists of two parts, a number of data segments and a directory to those segments where a segment is considered to be at most one page long. Therefore WiSS supports pageoriented access within long objects. However, there is no semantic access at page level, i.e. interpreting data is up to the user.

The Starburst Long Field Manager stores long objects by a long field descriptor which is a tuple in a relation with maximum size of 255 Bytes. The descriptor consists of pointers to "buddy segments" which are portions of storage in a socalled Buddy-System. In Starburst long fields are handled, in the case of reading and writing, as entities and therefore no partial updates are allowed.

In EXODUS the basic unit of data is a storage object which is virtually unlimited in size. A storage object is internally represented by a B^+-tree indexed on byte positions within the object, with the B^+-tree leaves as data blocks (this is derived from the storage management in INGRES [Ston 83]). Small storage objects may span a maximum of one page (a degenerated B^+-tree). For storage objects any amount of data may be read or written.

Taking one of these storage managers the global problem of storing and accessing long objects or attributes can be solved. However for objects in our sense none of the above storage mangers is adequate. Using WiSS allows no semantic access to long attributes at page level which is basicly the same in Starburst. Storing objects in our sense in Starburst leads to another problem: at the level of the cluster index a record may completely fill a datapage or exceed the page capacity if there are some long attributes with descriptors of maximum length in additon to the other attributes. EXODUS seems to be suitable for the requirement of individual access to any portion of data. However EXODUS is guided by the idea that a long object covers a relation structure (or something similar), which is similarly handled in WiSS.

5.2 A storage method depending on global object structure

Storing records we distinguish between short and long ones at the level of the cluster index where short ones are completely stored in the datapages. A record is called short, if a given maximum record length defined for the datapage entries of the cluster index is not exceeded. Long records are split in such a way that some attributes are stored in the datapages of the cluster index and the remaining ones are stored as an interpretable byte string in a B^+-tree which is derived from the B+-tree introduced for use in EXODUS [CDRS 86]. Remaining of attributes at the level of the cluster index is handled by the following three rules:

1. An attribute for which a cluster index is defined has to reside there.
2. Attributes supported by an inverted index should reside there, because high access frequency is assumed.
3. Access to atomic attributes (typically a few bytes) should be considerably faster than access to long attributes.

Setting these concepts into action, some additional information is needed: Each object in our system is therefore preceeded by a predefined structured header, see figure 7. The first entry in the header is the object identifier which is inter alia needed for clustering purposes. The next entry points to the record description where information about attribute types and indexing is stored. These are the basic facts which influence the evacuation decision, as discussed before. For evacuation purposes we store entry pairs (evacuation flag, attribute length) for each attribute containing the information whether an attribute is evacuated or not and containing its actual length. The entry pairs are stored in the sequence given by the record descriptor. The structure of such an entry pair may physically be modeled in different ways, e.g. by integer values where the plus/minus sign indicates the evacuation flag (plus = evacuated, minus = not evacuated) and the absolute value indicates the attribute length.

RECORD WITHIN THE CLUSTERINDEX

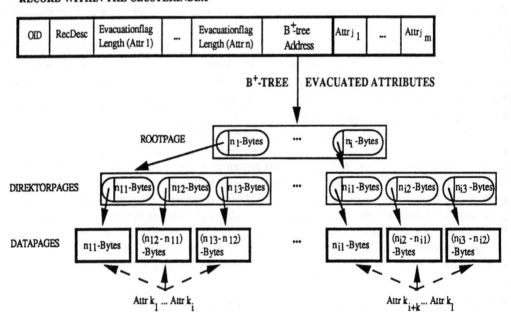

Figure 7: The record storage structure

Generally, the attributes which are not evacuated can be named $\text{Attr}_{j_1},...,\text{Attr}_{j_m}, j_i \in \{1..n\}, i \in \{1..m\}$. Those attributes are stored directly in the datapages of the cluster index. The remaining attributes $\text{Attr}_{k_1},...,\text{Attr}_{k_l}, k_i \in \{1..n\}; k_i \neq j_i, i \in \{1..m\}$, are stored in a B⁺-tree, which can be accessed by a pointer. There are many strategies for evacuation, each having application specific advantages. A simple strategy is given when the complete record with all attributes is stored in a B⁺-tree. In this case an access to an atomic attribute leads always to multiple page accesses. Another strategy is to place a maximum number of attributes in the datapages of the cluster index with no regard to the structure of the attributes, e.g. take the first n attributes. If queries rarely refer to these attributes, query performance will degenerate. Our approach is to apply a heuristic strategy which first tries to store all indexed attributes and then all atomic attributes in the datapages of the cluster index. With this strategy the access to indexed or atomic attributes is sped up to the greatest possible extent. On the other hand for some kind of attributes it is sensible or necessary to evacuate them, e.g. because of their length or low query frequency. In particular attributes of type complex are candidates for evacuation.

The strategies mentioned above do not guarantee for indexed or atomic attributes not to be evacuated, except for attributes defining clustering. Furthermore, no statement with respect to the number of accesses to evacuated attributes is possible. Due to these facts we introduce a specific storage strategy for evacuated attributes by taking the record structure and the length information into account in the operations of the B⁺-tree. The B⁺-tree introduced in EXODUS [CDRS 86] manipulates an arbitrary number of bytes not considering the structure which is inherent to the byte string, i.e. the interpretation of the byte string is left to a higher level in the system. Our variant of this B⁺-tree is able to store attributes in such a way that no attribute covers multiple datapages of the B⁺-tree if it spans less than the page capacity. Attributes that span multiple pages are stored in the smallest possible number of datapages, as defined later. This can be done by using the header information, more precisely by using the length information of the attributes. The following fundamental properties of the B⁺-tree are retained:

- Datapages are allowed to vary from being half full to completely full (50% full convention)
- An entry of a directory page consists of a byte counter and a pointer to a page on the next level
- The root page has a minimum of two entries and the other directory pages have a minimum of n and a maximum of 2n + 1 (for a short time overfilled) entries.

In general we have an ordered subset of attributes $\text{Attr}_i, i \in \{1..k\}, k \in \{2..n\}$, of the record $R = \text{Attr}_1,..., \text{Attr}_n$. A subsequence $\text{Attr}_i,..., \text{Attr}_j, j \geq i$, will be inserted into a datapage, if this page is, as a consequence, minimally filled and the next attribute Attr_{j+1} would overfill this page. For i = 1 the attribute Attr_i is stored in the first datapage, and the attributes $\text{Attr}_{j+1},...,$ Attr_k are distributed to the following datapages in the same way. If for a sequence $\text{Attr}_i,...,$ Attr_j the 50 % full convention is not fullfilled, the attribute Attr_{j+1} is split. By this strategy one page is filled completely and the next right page can be handled in the usual way. In the worst case only the first attribute is covered by a single page and all other attributes are covered by at least two pages even if most of the attributes could be covered by a single page. To avoid a disadvantageous storage in such a case, a datapage is allowed to be underfilled if it fullfills the 50 % full convention together with its right neighbour page. The rightmost page is allowed to be underfilled if the left neighbour page fulfills the 50 % full convention and the last attributes cannot be stored there. Thus the 50 % full convention can be guaranteed in the whole B⁺-tree. For attributes that span multiple pages, a number of pages is filled completely, lets say p. The remaining bytes, which span less than a page, will be stored on the current page (the first bytes of the attribute) or on the page that follows the p pages (the last bytes of the attribute).

The algorithms introduced in EXODUS can be used in our approach with little modifications. These are the operations to search for, to insert, to update and to delete arbitrary sequences of bytes. As an additional feature each attribute of a record can be handled as a null value, which is modeled by the length information in the record header. Therefore a null value is known at the level of datapages in the cluster index. As a conclusion we give an overview of the main operations of our B⁺-tree, in MODULA-2 notion.

```
PROCEDURE  ExpandAttribut (info:ARRAY OF BYTE; no:AttrNo; pos:CARDINAL; item:ARRAY OF BYTE)
PROCEDURE  ShortenAttribut (info:ARRAY OF BYTE; no:AttrNo; pos, offset:CARDINAL)
PROCEDURE  UpdateAttribut  (info:ARRAY OF BYTE; no:AttrNo; item:ARRAY OF BYTE)
PROCEDURE  ModifyAttribut  (info:ARRAY OF BYTE; no:AttrNo; pos, offset:CARDINAL; item:ARRAY OF BYTE)
PROCEDURE  DeleteAttribut  (info:ARRAY OF BYTE; no:AttrNo)
```

The variable "info" is passed to each operator representing the record header. The operator ExpandAttribute allows to insert a byte sequence "item" at an arbitrary point into an attribute of type complex. ShortenAttribute is the inversion of ExpandAttribute. The operator UpdateAttribute allows to substitute the byte sequence "item" and the operator ModifyAttribute allows to substitute portions of an attribute of type complex. Deleting attribute values can be done by DeleteAttribute. As operations for special purposes reading and writing of sequences of attributes from the B⁺-tree is possible. This is done by applying a "concatenation read" or "concatenation write", i. e. the length information in the header is used to form a single read or write operation.

6 Conclusions

The index manager we proposed is suitable for efficient query processing in spatial database systems. As pointed out in the paper efficient query processing is achieved by supporting an extensible set of access paths. The index manager organizes cluster and inverted indexes facilitating these access paths and fullfilling two essential demands: non-redundant storage as well as avoidance of time consuming reorganizations within a dynamic environment. For additionally supporting the index manager, we proposed a specific storage method for handling arbitrary long objects.

Starting point for our concept was the problem to design and implement a Bioindication database system [KS 90] in an interdisciplinary project in which lichen were used as a biological indicator for environmental pollution. This project lead to the design of a multi-level query processor for structured spatial objects [Krie 91]. Another application area for our concept is the storage management in object oriented database systems. This concept can be used to instantiate a class hierarchy index, see [KKD 89].

The goal for our future work is to implement the extensible index management presented in this paper as well as the above mentioned query processor in an object oriented geographical database system in order to verify efficiency and flexibility with respect to query processing of structured spatial objects. The efficiency will be particularly determined by the physical implementation of the presented logical concept. One particular problem is the implementation of such a concept onto an operating system such as UNIX because physical clustering may only be implemented by detouring the operating system. One possible approach in that respect was taken in the Wisconsin Storage Manager [CDKK 85].

References

[BM 72]   Bayer, R. & E. McCreight, 'Organization and Maintenance of Large Ordered Indexes', Acta Informatica, Vol.1, No.3, 173-189, 1972.

[BKSS 90]   Beckmann, N., H.P. Kriegel, R. Schneider & B. Seeger, 'The R*-tree: An efficient and robust access method for points and rectangles', in Proc. 1990 ACM SIGMOD International Conference on Management of Data , 322-331, Atlantic City, USA, May 1990.

[CDKK 85]   Chou, H.-T., D.J. DeWitt, R.H. Katz & A.C. Klug, 'Design and Implementation of the Wisconsin Storage System', Software Practice and Experience, Vol. 15(10), 943-962, October 1985.

[CDRS 86]   Carey, M. J., D.J. DeWitt, J.E. Richardson & E.J. Shekita, 'Object and File Management in the EXODUS Extensible Database System', Proc. 12 th Int. Conf. on Very Large Data Bases, Kyoto, Japan, August 1986.

[GB 88]   Günther, O. & J. Bilmes, 'The Implementation of the Cell-tree: Design alternatives and performance evaluation', Technical Report TRCS88-23, University of California, Santa Barbara, October 1988.

[Guet 89]   Güting, R.H., 'Gral: an extensible relational database system for geografic applications', Proc. 15th Int. Conf. on Very Large Data Bases, 33-44, Amsterdam, The Netherlands, August 1989.

[Gutt 84]   Guttman A.: 'R-trees: a dynamic index structure for spatial searching', Proc. ACM SIGMOD Int. Conf. on Management of Data, 47-57, June 1984.

[JS 90]   Jhingran, A. & M. Stonebraker, 'Alternatives in Complex Object Representation: A Performance Perspective', Proc. 6th Int. Conf. on Data Engineering, 94-102, Los Angeles, February 1990.

[KC 86]   Khoshafian, S.N. & G.P. Copeland, 'Object Identity', Proc. of OOPSLA, 1986.

[KKD 89]   Kim, W., K.-C. Kim & A. Dale, 'Indexing Techniques for Object-Oriented Databases', in Kim W. & F. Lochovsky, (Eds.), 'Object-Oriented Concepts, Databases, and Applications', Addison-Wesley Publishing Company, Inc., 371-394, 1989.

[Krie 91]   Kriegel, H.P., P. Heep, S. Heep, M. Schiwietz & R. Schneider, 'An Access Method Based Query Processor for Spatial Database Systems', Proc. Int. Workshop on DBMS's for geographical applications, Capri, May 16-17, 1991.

[KS 86]   Kriegel, H.P. & B. Seeger, 'Multidimensional order preserving linear hashing with partial expansions', Proc. Int. Conf. on Database Theory, Lecture Notes in Computer Science 243, 203-220, 1986.

[KS 88]   Kriegel, H.P. & B. Seeger, 'PLOP-Hashing: a grid file without directory', Proc. 4th Int. Conf. on Data Engineering, 369-376, Los Angeles, February 1988.

[KS 90]   Kriegel, H.P. & R. Schneider, 'Entwurf eines Bioindikations-Datenbanksystems', in Proc. 5.Symposium 'Informatik für den Umweltschutz', Wien, September 1990.

[KSSS 89]   Kriegel, H.P., M. Schiwietz, R. Schneider & B.Seeger, 'Performance Comparison of Point and Spatial Access Methods', in Proceedings "Symposium on the Design and Implementation of Large Spatial Databases", 89-114, Santa Barbara, USA, July 1989.

[Lars 80]   Larson, P.-A., 'Linear Hashing with partial expansions', Proc. 6th Int. Conf. on Very Large Data Bases, 212-223, 1980.

[LL 89]   Lehman, T.J. & B.G. Lindsay,'The Starburst Long Field Manager', Proc. 15th Int. Conf. on Very Large Data Bases, Amsterdam, The Netherlands, August 1989.

[NHS 84]   Nievergelt J., H. Hinterberger & K.C. Sevcik: 'The grid file: an adaptable, symmetric multikey file structure', ACM Trans. on Database Systems, Vol. 9, 1, 38-71, 1984.

[RL 85]   Roussopoulos N. & D. Leifker: 'Direct spatial search on pictorial databases using packed R-trees', Proc. ACM SIGMOD Int. Conf. on Managment of Data, 17-31, May 1985.

[Same 90]   Samet, H., 'The Design and Analysis of Spatial Structures', Addison-Wesley Publishing Company Inc., 1990.

[Ship 81]   Shipman, D., 'The functional data model and the data language DAPLEX', ACM Transactions on Database Systems, Vol. 6, No. 1, March 1981.

[Ston 83]   Stonebraker, M., H. Stettner, N. Lynn, J. Kalash & A. Guttman, 'Document Processing in a Relational Database System', ACM Transactions on Office Information Systems, Vol. 1, No. 2, April 1983.

[SK 90]   Seeger, B. & H.P. Kriegel, 'The Buddy Tree: An Efficient and Robust Access Method for Spatial Databases', Proc. 16th Int. Conf. on Very Large Data Bases, Brisbane, Australia, August 1990.

[SR 86]   Stonebraker, M. & L. Rowe, 'The Design of POSTGRES', Proc. 1986 ACM SIGMOD Conf. on Management of Data, Washington DC, May 1986.

[Vald 87]   Valduriez, P., 'Join Indices, ACM Transactions on Database Systems', Vol. 12, No. 2, June 1987.

The Performance of Object Decomposition Techniques for Spatial Query Processing

Hans-Peter Kriegel, Holger Horn and Michael Schiwietz

Institut für Informatik, Universität München, Leopoldstr. 11, D-8000 München 40, Germany

Abstract:

The management of spatial data in applications such as graphics and image processing, geography as well as computer aided design (CAD) imposes stringent new requirements on spatial database systems, in particular on efficient query processing of complex spatial objects. In this paper, we propose a two-level, multi-representation query processing technique which consists of a filter and a refinement level. The efficiency of spatial query processing is improved considerably using the following two design paradigms: first, divide and conquer, i.e. decomposition of complex spatial objects into more simple spatial components such as convex polygons, triangles or trapezoids, and second, application of efficient and robust spatial access methods for simple spatial objects. The most powerful ingredient in our approach is the concept of object decomposition. Applied to the refinement level of spatial query processing, it substitutes complex computational geometry algorithms by simple and fast algorithms for simple components. In this paper, we present four different decomposition techniques for polygonal shaped objects. The second part of the paper consists of an empirical performance comparison of those techniques using real and synthetic data sets. The four types of decomposition techniques are compared to each other and to the traditional approach with respect to the performance of spatial query processing. This comparison points out that our approach using object decomposition is superior to traditional query processing strategies.

1 Introduction

The demand for using database systems in application areas such as graphics and image processing, computer aided design (CAD), as well as geography and cartography is considerably increasing. An important characteristic of these applications is the occurance of spatial objects. The management of spatial objects imposes stringent new requirements on socalled spatial database systems. One of the most challanging requirements is efficient query processing of complex spatial objects.

The typical type of objects occuring in those applications are two- or three-dimensional spatial objects. Points, lines, or rectangles are known as simple spatial objects, because their complete description is given by only a small number of parameters. Semantically complex objects with an application specific complexity, such as contour lines, limits of lots, and contours of CAD objects have the shape of simple polygons. Complexity properties of such polygonal objects, such as the shape, the number of vertices, or the smoothness of the contour are difficult to predict. Additionally, as a general property of polygons, holes have to be taken into account for a general handling of objects occurring in geographic information systems, e.g. to model an area of land containing lakes. In order to support the above type of spatial applications, the ability for managing simple polygons is fundamental to a spatial database system. In this paper, we present and evaluate a spatial query processing system based on spatial access methods (see for example [NHS 84], [See 90]) and computational geometry techniques [PS 85].

In the next chapter we introduce a spatial query processing system using filter techniques based on spatial access methods. The basic ingredient for achieving performance improvements is the introduction of redundancy [Ore 89]. This is the subject of chapter 3. A special approach of introducing redundancy to object representations are the socalled *structural object decompositions*. Chapter 4 presents four different structural decomposition techniques for SPHs. In chapter 5 we describe the processing of spatial queries based on object decompositions in more algorithmic detail. Chapter 6 contains a comparison of the different structural decomposition techniques with respect to their performance gain for spatial query processing. The paper concludes with a summary pointing out the main contributions and giving an outlook to future activities.

2 Query processing using filter techniques

In this chapter, we will introduce a special type of polygonal objects and a query processing mechanism for managing large sets of such objects.

2.1 Spatial objects and spatial queries

The types of spatial objects we consider in this paper is the class of *simple polygons with holes* (SPH for short). A polygon is called simple if there is no pair of nonconsecutive edges sharing a point. An SPH is a simple polygon where simple polygonal holes may be cut out. From our experience, the class of SPH´s is adequate for GIS applications (see [Bur 87]) and most other spatial applications such as 2D CAD/CAM applications.

Figure 1:   simple polygon   simple polygon with holes

Queries in spatial applications generally refer to spatial and nonspatial data. Spatial data can be classified into geometrical and topological aspects whereas nonspatial data is given by alphanumerical data related to spatial entities. Geometric data describes properties such as the spatial location, size, and shape of spatial objects. Topological data specifies properties such as connectivity, adjacency, and inclusion modelling relationships between geometric data. By the way, it is not necessary to store topological data explicitly, because it can be derived from geometric data by spatial queries formulating suitable query conditions. Most spatial query conditions however, describe such topological aspects between stored objects and the query object. Additionally, spatial queries are not only restricted to retrieving data, but also may construct new objects. Usually these objects are displayed but not necessarily stored in the database.

From literature no standard set of spatial queries fulfilling all requirements of spatial applications is known [SV 89]. Thus it is necessary to provide a small set of basic spatial queries which are efficiently supported by the database query facilities. Application specific queries, e.g. presented in [Oos 90], typically using more complex query conditions, can be decomposed into a sequence of such basic spatial queries. We propose the following set of basic spatial queries:

- **PointQuery:** Given a point $p \in E^2$, find all SPHs in the database where $p \in$ SPH.
- **WindowQuery:** Given a rectilinear window $w \subseteq E^2$, find all SPHs in the database where $w \cap$ SPH $\neq \emptyset$.
- **RegionQuery:** Given an SPH* $\subseteq E^2$, find all SPHs in the database where SPH* $\cap$ SPH $\neq \emptyset$.
- **EnclosureQuery:** Given an SPH* $\subseteq E^2$, find all SPHs in the database where SPH* $\supseteq$ SPH.
- **ContainmentQuery:** Given an SPH* $\subseteq E^2$, find all SPHs in the database where SPH* $\subseteq$ SPH.
- **IntersectionQuery:** Given an SPH* $\subseteq E^2$, compute the intersection of it with all SPHs in the database.

As a further example consider the following query: Given an area bounded by two latitudes and two meridians. Find the most populated city within this area and the state, this city belongs to. This query can be evaluated by initially enforcing a window query yielding the set of all cities lying within the specified area. After computationally determining the most populated one, a point/enclosure query finds out the unique state this city belongs to.

2.2 Query processing supported by access methods and computational geometry

A typical property of spatial queries is their restriction to a specific spatial location in data space. Only that location and some limited neighbouring area is essential for the evaluation of most spatial queries. The window query is a typical example for such a query (see figure 2).

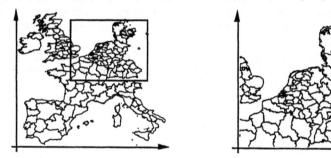

Figure 2: Zooming into a query window

Obviously, objects (SPHs) lying close together in dataspace are often accessed jointly by a window query. The same holds for the other basic queries defined above. Therefore, a physical clustering of spatial objects with respect to their spatial location is essential for providing efficient locality based query processing. This type of spatial clustering is supported by spatial access methods (SAMs), introduced below. In the absence of such spatial clustering no spatial locality can be exploited by the query processing algorithm. In that case, every single stored object has to be evaluated against the query condition leading to poor performance that is further decreasing with an increasing number of stored objects and an increasing object complexity. Therefore, one essential ingredient of efficient query processing within a spatial database system is spatial clustering of the objects.

In the past few years many spatial access methods were developed which provide the clustered organization of large sets of simple spatial objects on secondary storage. The most simple class of spatial objects managed by such access methods is given by (multidimensional) point objects. The grid file [NHS 84], PLOP-hashing [KS 88], the BANG file [Fre 87], and the buddy tree [SK 90] are well known representatives of this class of access methods. A survey can be found in [SK 90]. There are three basic techniques for extending multidimensional point access methods (PAMs) to multidimensional spatial access methods (SAMs) for rectangles [SK 88]: clipping, overlapping regions and transformation.

An important characteristic of a SAM is the type of spatial objects handled directly, i.e. the type of objects which are exactly represented. All spatial access methods proposed up to now, are restricted to the storage of simply shaped objects such as cells of a fixed grid (grid cells for short) [OM 86], rectilinear rectangles (with their sides parallel to the axis, rectangles for short) [Gut 84], [NHS 84], [SK 88], [SK 90], [BKSS 90], spheres [Oos 90], or convex cells (convex polygons) [Gue 89].

However, no spatial access method is available for handling more complex spatial objects and particularly is not for the class of SPH. In order to provide an efficient access method for complex spatial objects, a 'brute force' approach was applied up to now. Any spatial object is placed within a rectilinear rectangle or convex polygon of minimum shape forming a *container* for that object, yielding a socalled conservative approximation. A simple spatial object is called a container iff any point inside the contour of the complex spatial object is also contained in the container object. The type of those containers is selected according to the suitability to be handled by one of the spatial access methods mentioned above.

As simple containers just provide approximations of the objects, query processing of complex spatial objects has to procede in a two-step manner. The first step, the socalled *filter step*, reduces the entire set of objects to a subset of candidates using their spatial location. This filter step is based on spatial access methods managing container objects using the following property: if the container does not fulfill the query condition, so does not the object itself. However, because container objects provide no exact object representation, the filter step does not exactly evaluate the query, but only yields a set of candidates which may fulfill the query condition. Therefore, these candidates have to be examined in a second step, called *refinement step*. This step applies complex algorithms known from the field of computational geometry to the original spatial objects and thus detects exactly those objects finally fulfilling the query condition.

Consider the following Point Query as an example for this concept of spatial query processing. Two objects remain to be examined in the refinement step, but only one of them fulfills the query condition (figure 3).

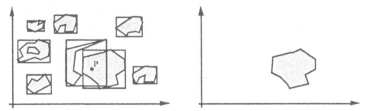

Figure 3: Example for the Point Query

At first glance, this brute force approach of coupling a spatial access method and computational geometry algorithms seems to be a good approach for spatial query processing. However, more detailed considerations reveal the main disadvantages of this approach: in the case of a bad approximation of an object by its container, a large number of 'false drop' candidates, i.e. objects not fulfilling the query condition, have to be refined. On the other hand, the refinement of one single object is very costly particularly if the object complexity is high, because complex and time-consuming computational geometry algorithms have to be applied. We have to consider these two aspects when tuning the performance of spatial query processing.

In the next section we will examine both steps of spatial query processing in more detail to show possible ways of performance improvements.

2.3 Improving the performance of spatial query processing

The filter step
The performance of the filter step considerably depends on the quality of the spatial object approximation by the container used for filtering issues. The approximation quality is defined as the amount of area covered by the container but not by the object itself. As containers, e.g.

minimal bounding boxes, are simple spatial objects, they cannot exactly represent complex spatial objects without introducing additionally covered area. Minimizing the amount of that area will directly and proportionally improve the filter step. Additionally more complex containers may yield a better approximation. The only requirement to the container type is the ability to be efficiently managed by a SAM. Particularly for rectangles there are very efficient access methods, e.g. the R*- tree [BKSS 90]. Therefore, we propose rectilinear polygons as a particular type of container. They can be formed by a set of rectilinear boxes, at the expense of introducing redundancy in object representation. Using a number of containers to represent one single object is the basic idea of any redundant object representation. For SAMs some limited amount of redundancy will lead to better query performance, as we will see in chapter 6.

The refinement step
The performance of the refinement step depends on the number of refined objects as well as on their complexity. Minimizing the number of objects to be refined is the task of the filter step. Therefore, object complexity is the issue to be examined here. The more complex the spatial objects are, the more time consuming are the computational geometry algorithms needed for query evaluation. A simplification of the refined objects with respect to their complexity may lead to a better overall performance of the refinement step even if a limited amount of redundancy has to be handled.

Summarizing, the two main goals for improving the performance of filter based query processing are:
1. Improvement of the accuracy of the filter step to minimize the number of candidates.
2. Improvement of the refinement step by using objects considerably simpler than the original SPHs in order to speed up computational geometry algorithms.

The above considerations show, that for improving the performance of spatial query processing, we have to give up using one single container for every complex spatial object. Therefore, our objective is to represent SPHs within spatial access methods using a number of containers inducing redundancy in object representation.

3. Object representation based on redundancy

The basic idea of any redundancy based object representation is to improve query performance by shifting time requirements from query processing to update and restructuring operations. Retrieval operations typically occur considerably more often than update operations, e.g. insertions. Thus it is worth to invest more time in preprocessing which is saved in a manyfold way in query processing. Specifically, we will generate a new type of object representation in preprocessing which is time saving in query processing. In more detail, the preprocessing step calculates a redundant object representation given by a decomposition into less complex components. This leads to a better filter approximation and more efficient computational geometry algorithms within the refinement step.

In the following, we will present different types of redundant object representations for the class of SPHs known from the literature [Ore 89].

Minimum bounding boxes (no redundancy):
The object management using one object container in the filter step coupled with a refinement step on the original complex object representation is a widely used traditional method (see [Gut 84]). This approach is called 'identity' representation from now on. Without introducing redundancy this is the only approach managing complex spatial objects by SAMs preserving spatial locality and exploiting spatial clustering. The disadvantages of this approach, leading to a bad query performance, have been outlined before.

Redundancy induced by cells of a fixed grid:
In the quad tree / z-value ([Sam 84], [Ore 89]) approach the container of a spatial object is formed by exactly those cells of a fixed grid which have a common intersection with the object. As a cell of a fixed grid can be efficiently represented by a bitstring, i.e. a z-value, representing the recursive grid partitioning of the dataspace, those cells can be efficiently stored using an one-dimensional access method, e.g. a B-tree. Inducing redundancy is intended by forming a smaller and more complex container and therefore increasing the performance of the filter step. As the object complexity is not generally decreased using this approach, the refinement step is not improved.

Redundancy induced by grid and object structure:
A further approach is taken by grid based methods which are not restricted to a predefined grid resolution, but taking account of the object location and structure. Similiar to the edge-quadtree [Sam 84], an object is partitioned into grid cells, socalled base grid cells. A base cell is the largest cell formed by recursive grid partitioning containing parts of the object which fulfill a predefinable complexity condition. Therefore, no overall minimum cell resolution can be guaranteed. The resolution depends on the shape of the object. Thus, the partitioning process can typically produce a high amount of cells of very small area. The refinement step, however, contrary to original grid cell methods using a fixed grid resolution, is tuned by the occurrence of very simple objects represented by each grid cell. The amount of redundancy, however, essentially depends on the object structure and can arbitrarily grow.

Redundancy induced by structural object decomposition:
The usage of grid cells representing spatial objects has its origin in the lack of suitable spatial access methods for higher dimensional dataspace. Grid cells represented by bit strings form a transformation to a one-dimensional linearly ordered dataspace. However, grid cells are bound to a fixed partitioning scheme and therefore provide no location independent object approximation as minimum bounding boxes do. Therefore a more promising approach introducing redundancy to object representation methods is a *structural decomposition* of complex spatial objects into simpler components. The term 'structural' expresses that the decomposition is oriented on the boundary of the polygonal object. Similar to the original bounding box approach, object components are managed by a SAM by placing them into containers, e.g. minimum bounding boxes. Structural decompositions provide a high degree of choices for component types and decomposition algorithms. Typical types of decomposition components are convex polygons, trapezoids, triangles and rectangles. Choosing a proper decomposition algorithm will improve both, the filter step and the refinement step. The filter step performance will benefit from a better overall object approximation by container approximation of each single component. However, the problem of multiple representation of one and the same object induced by redundancy has to be considered. Additionally to the object approximation the refinement step will be improved by simpler objects which can be processed faster by computational geometry algorithms.
In the next chapter, we present four different decomposition techniques for SPHs.

4. Structural decomposition techniques

The goal of the following sections is to examine different structural decomposition techniques with respect to their performance within a spatial query processing system. Primarily, a catalogue of important properties is given which provides a classification of different decomposition algorithms for polygonal objects. Then, we will describe four particular algorithms in more detail.

4.1 Properties of structural decomposition techniques

The basic properties of a structural decomposition method can be divided into qualitative and those describing quantitative aspects of that method. Qualitative aspects are the type of generated object components and the distinction between a partitioning and a covering of spatial objects. A decomposition is called a partition iff all components are pairwise disjoint. Otherwise, it is called a covering. The application of specific techniques from the field of computational geometry (plane sweep, divide and conquer, etc.) is another qualitative aspect of a decomposition technique.

Quantitative aspects are the number of generated components with respect to the complexity of the original object and the quality of container approximation of these components. The time needed to decompose one object and to apply computational geometry algorithms to the decomposition components is a further quantitative aspect of a decomposition technique.

Abstracting from the specific properties mentioned above, decomposition techniques can be classified with respect to the complexity and the number of generated components. It is important to realize that decomposing into very simple components will lead to a high number of components and vice versa.

The basic idea of comparing different decomposition techniques (see chapter 6) is to experimentally evaluate which degree of object decomposition, i.e. which degree of component complexity, leads to best performance in spatial query processing. What is an adequate type of object components with respect to complexity of components and the amount of redundancy?

To answer that question we selected and implemented four different decomposition algorithms which will be explained in detail in the next chapter.

Most decomposition techniques known from the field of computational geometry were developed under requirements different from those arising in spatial query processing. In order to achieve best query performance, it is necessary to take into account a number of requirements concerning object representation. The algorithms proposed in computational geometry ([CD 85], [KeSa 85]) mostly are optimal with respect to one of those properties, e.g. minimal number of components, but totally ignore other aspects such as run time. Therefore, it was necessary to develop special decomposition methods supporting query processing of complex spatial objects. The most important requirements are:

- **Low number of components**
  Increasing redundancy induced by a high number of components affects the performance of the filter step which has to manage a significantly larger number of container objects. Therefore, an important goal is to limit the number of generated components.

- **Good run time performance**
  Whenever a new object is inserted into the database, a decomposition of that object must be perfromed. An algorithm producing an optimal number of components but requiring an exponential run time, e.g. proposed in [PS 85] or other papers, is quite unacceptable. Thus, decomposition algorithms with a run time of low order have to be provided.

- **Good container approximation**
  As outlined in chapter 2, the evaluation of a spatial query consists of the filter and the refinement step. The filter step, based on a object container representation, yields the set of candidates to be examined in the refinement step. It is of crucial importance to minimize the 'dead space' between a spatial object and its container and thus to reduce the number of components passing the filter step. So object decomposition techniques must supply components that can be well approximated by containers, e.g. minimum bounding boxes.

- **Small amount of storage**
  Until now, we only focussed on efficient processing of spatial queries. Nevertheless, limiting the amount of additional storage required for the redundant object representation is an important issue.

- **Ease of implementation**
  The integration of object decomposition techniques into a real spatial database system demands in the developement of robust algorithms, easy to implement and maintain.

Obviously, there are many different criteria influencing the quality of a given decomposition method. Without further examination the importance of any of these criteria is not foreseeable. Therfore, we performed an empirical comparison (chapter 6) to evaluate which method achieves actually best query performance.

In the next sections, we will introduce four selected decomposition methods. We will give a brief algorithmic description and try to depict their particular properties with respect to the criteria outlined above. One important premise for the developement of the algorithms was to use minimum bounding boxes as containers for the components.

4.2   Decomposition into convex polygons

As geometric algorithms for the type of convex polygons are more efficient than those for arbitrary SPHs, we consider as a first approach the decomposition of an SPH into a set of convex polygons. The basic idea is to transform the original SPH into a simpler but equivalent spatial object and then to decompose this new object applying an appropriate algorithm. This idea leads to the following two step algorithm [DHH 90]:

Step 1: Transform the original SPH P into a polygon P´ describing the same infinite set of points as P but containing no holes. This polygon P´ is simple with the exception that edges may overlap. From now on, those polygons are called simple*.

Step 2: Decompose the simple* polygon P´ into a set of convex polygons.

Within the following algorithm the two techniques, *transformation* (step 1) and *divide and conquer* (step 2), from the field of computational geometry are applied (see [PS 85]).

Step 1: Hole integration
The objective of the first step is to integrate all holes of the given SPH *P* into the enclosure polygon of *P* without changing the infinite set of points described by the object. This will be achieved by sending out *hole integration rays* from the holes of the SPH towards the enclosure polygon until all holes are removed from the original SPH. For a successful termination of the hole integration step it is necessary to define an integration order on the holes. This will be achieved by building up the *convex hull* over all the holes of the polygon and sending out integration rays from those holes edging to that hull towards the enclosure polygon. Thus, a subset of the holes are integrated into the enclosure polygon and the algorithm continues with building up the convex hull of the remaining holes and so on. It stops, if no more holes are left. At the end of step 1 a simple* polygon is produced describing the same (infinite) set of points as the original SPH.

An important feature of the algorithm is that the integration rays, i.e. all new segments, should be parallel to one axis of the coordinate system whenever possible. This is due to the fact that all decomposition components generated by step 2 of the algorithm will be approximated by rectilinear rectangles. Figure 4 gives an example of the effect of step 1.

Figure 4: Example for the hole integration step

Step 2: Decomposition of the simple* Polygon

After removing the holes using step 1, the task of step 2 is to perform the actual decomposition of the object P' into convex components. As mentioned before, the only difference between simple polygons and simple* polygons is the existence of overlapping edges. Therefore, most algorithms for the decomposition of simple polygons into convex parts (see [CD 85]) can also be applied to simple* polygons with only slight modifications. The vertices of a given simple polygon which display a reflex angle, called *notches*, will play the crucial role in the following, because the result objects (convex polygons) must not contain such vertices. So the basic idea of step 2 is to remove each notch by means of simple line segments drawn from the notch. As in step 1, line segments should be parallel to one axis whenever possible. The algorithm uses the technique of *divide and conquer* because after removing one notch from the original polygon it will be applied to both produced result components in the same way until no more notches remain and a set of convex components is achieved. Applying step 1 and 2 to the original SPH gives the result set of convex components. Figure 5 shows the effect of step 2.

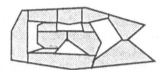

Figure 5: Example for the convex decomposition of the simple* polygon

We can summarize the properties of the above decomposition algorithm: it is easy to implement, has a good run time performance ($O(n \log^2 n)$, where n is the number of vertices), and the number of produced components in the worst case is twice the optimum number of convex components (see [DHH 90]).

4.3 Decomposition into trapezoids

The second partitioning method we take into consideration is the decomposition of an SPH into a set of trapezoids introduced by Asano/Asano [AA 83]. The components produced by this algorithm are formed as trapezoids containing two horizontal sides. This property provides a good container approximation by means of rectilinear rectangles. The algorithm uses the plane sweep technique known from the field of computational geometry. The basic idea is for each vertex to send out one or two horizontal rays into the interior of the polygon to the first edge encountered. In the following we give a brief description.

As mentioned before the algorithm uses the plane sweep technique, i.e. the vertices will be passed and handled with increasing y-coordinates, for example. Thus, the entire algorithm consists of two steps:

Step 1: Sorting the vertices of the given SPH builds up the *event point list*, i.e. a sorted list of all the points which have to be treated by the algorithm.

Step 2: Processing the event point list by switching from one event point (vertex) to the next sending out partition rays (*event point scheduling*). Within this process, each ray and its successor form one trapezoid.

Applying step 1 and step 2 to the original SPH produces the resulting set of trapezoids. Figure 6 shows an example of the effect of the algorithm.

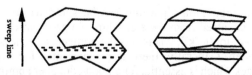

Figure 6: Decomposition of an SPH into a set of trapezoids

Summarizing, the main properties of the presented decomposition technique are: it is very easy to implement and has a good run time performance of O(n log n) (where n is the number of vertices). The number of produced components is three times the optimum number of components in the worst case, but it is quite better for most SPHs [AA 83].

4.4 Triangulation

The basic concept of any decomposition of arbitrary SPHs is generating a possibly low number of simple components which support fast query processing. Triangles are very simple spatial objects with a fixed length description, and are easy to handle by computational geometry algorithms. The triangulation algorithm introduced here guarantees the generation of a minimum number of triangles for a given SPH where the triangles introduce no new vertices. The algorithm works in a three step manner:

Step 1:
Triangulate the SPH using the Delaunay triangulation [Del 34]. The Delaunay triangulation works on the set of vertices of the SPH and generates a triangulation of its convex hull, see figure 7a/b. It fulfills the socalled Lawson criterion which guarantees homogenous triangles in the sense that the deviation of the angles of a triangle is small. Thus, the degeneration of the shape of the triangles is restricted. The resulting component triangles may be completely inside the SPH, completely outside of the SPH, or may have intersection with edges of the SPH. Figure 7a/7b illustrates that the Delaunay triangulation does not necessary represent the original SPH. This is only happens if the SPH is convex and has no holes.

Figure 7: a) Sample SPH   b) Delaunay   c) Provisional   d) Final
          (19 vertices)   Triangulation   Triangulation   Triangulation
                              (27 Triangles)   (50 Triangles)   (17 Triangles)

Step 2:
In the second step a plane sweep algorithm is applied which detects all intersections of the set of triangles with the edges of the SPH. The intersections are removed by decomposing a triangle with intersection points into a set of subtriangles where no more intersections occur, see figure 7c. The number of the additionally generated triangles depends on the number of intersections. At this point, the algorithm does not restrict to the vertices of the SPH but introduces new vertices, socalled 'Steiner points'.

Step 3:
In the third step all Steiner points are completely by examining each set of Steiner points lying on the same edge of the SPH and merging all triangles belonging to these Steiner points into a single triangle. Figure 7d depicts the final triangulation of the original SPH.

The properties of this triangulation algorithm can be summarized as follows: a minimum number of triangles is guaranteed from the algorithm. No new vertices are generated. The run time complexity is O((n+k) log(n+k)), where n is the number of vertices and k is the number of intersections found in step. Generally, there is no guarantee for triangles to contain only horizontal or vertical edges which is essential for a good container approximation.

4.5   Heterogeneous decomposition

The idea of this decomposition technique is to represent an SPH by components even more simple than arbitrary triangles or trapezoids. With respect to a container approximation by its bounding box, the most simple type of component are (rectilinear) rectangles. As this object type is insufficient for the representation of arbitrary SPHs, i.e. an arbitrary SPH can not be exactly represented by a set of rectangles, it is necessary to use further types. Therefore, the decomposition technique is called *heterogeneous*. With respect to a good approximation of the components by bounding boxes, we choose rectilinear rectangles and rectilinear triangles, i.e. triangles with two edges parallel to the axes, as decomposition components. To provide a unique representation of the area covered by an arbitrary SPH, an additional type of components managing notches, a particular shape property of polygonal objects described before, is necessary. This type of component is called a peak. Particularly for real applications this type of component turns out to occur only in exceptional cases. Therefore, a more detailed description of peaks is ignored in this paper. Figure 8 shows an example for a heterogeneous decomposition of a polygonal object.

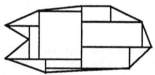

Figure 8: Decomposition of an object into a set of rectilinear triangles and rectangles

The complete algorithm for decomposing an SPH into the three types of components mentioned above consists of 3 steps:

step 1:   Remove the peaks representing them by means of peak components. This step builds up a new SPH without peaks.

step 2:   Remove all non rectilinear edges of the resulting SPH by using rectilinear triangles. Thus, a set of rectilinear polygons is generated.

step 3:   Decompose each rectilinear polygon into a set of rectilinear rectangles.

Figure 9 depicts snapshots of the result of the algorithm (step 1-3) for a sample polygon. Let us mention that the decomposition process can as well be performed by a plane sweep type algorithm. However, this algorithm is considerably more complex, and therefore not presented here.

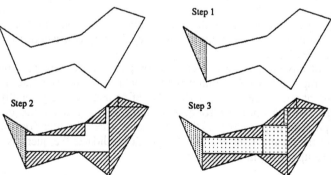

Figure 9: Heterogeneous decomposition in a 3 step algorithm

One important property of the heterogeneous decomposition technique is that the generated components are very simple. Therefore, we expect them to be processed very fast by geometric algorithms. However, this is enforced by a larger number of components than in other decomposition methods (twice the number of vertices in practice). As the algorithmic complexity strongly depends on the structure and on the shape of the decomposed object, an exact run time investigation of the above algorithm cannot be performed analytically.

5. Query processing based on object decomposition

The objective of this chapter is to describe in more algorithmic detail the processing of different spatial queries based on decomposed object representations. Particularly, we will take a closer look at the insert operation, the point query and the window query. These operations will be analyzed with respect to their performance in chapter 6. The algorithms described below are not restricted to a specific decomposition technique, but hold for any redundant spatial object representation.

5.1 Insert operation

The task of the insert operation is to add a new spatial object, i.e. an SPH, to an existing set of spatial objects, managed by a given access method. This operation consists of three steps.

Within the first step, the new object is decomposed into a set of simpler components (e.g. convex polygons, triangles) by applying one of the decomposition algorithms introduced in the previous section. Then, in step two, the minimum bounding box, i.e. the container object, for each of those components is generated. Furthermore, a unique identifier (a surrogate) for the original SPH is determined and assigned to all of its components. This identifier represents the correspondence between the original spatial object and its decomposition components. Thus, the records describing the components consist of three parts: the minimum bounding box of the component, the representation of the decomposition component, and the object identifier. In a last step, all these records belonging to the original SPH are inserted into the database using the insert algorithm of the SAM.

The result of the insertion operation is a new data file which now contains the components of the inserted SPH. The components refering to the original SPH are labeled by their unique identifier.

5.2 Point query

The result of a point query consists of all stored spatial objects containing a given query point. As described in chapter 1 the processing of any spatial query consists of two steps: The filter step and the refinement step.

The filter step of a point query asked on a decomposed object representation using a SAM yields all those components whose bounding box contains the query point. They are supplied by evaluating a point query against the SAM. The refinement step sequentially examines these candidates performing a computational geometry algorithm on the exact component representation ('point-in-object' test). If this test yields 'true', the identifier of the component record is added to the result. After examination of all candidates the query is finished. The set of found ids makes up the result of the query.

5.3 Window query

The window query yields all the spatial objects intersecting a given query window. Similarily to the point query the filter step of a window query is based on the SAM: a window query is performed on the file of components yielding all those components whose bounding box intersects the query window. Within the refinement step the exact representation of all these candidates is tested against the query window, i.e. a computational geometry algorithm is performed on the exact representation of each component. If there is an intersection, the object identifier of the component record is added to the result. Contrary to the point query the described algorithm of query processing has to deal with object redundancy. In general, there may be a number of different components labeled with the same identifier and therefore refering to the same spatial object intersecting the query window (see figure 10).

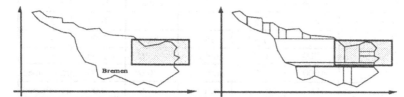

Figure 10: A query window intersecting different components of the same SPH

In such a case, the same identifier, i.e. the same spatial object, is handled more than once by the refinement algorithm. To avoid a multiple refinement of the same object and a duplicated output of objects we propose the following strategy. We use a one dimensional main memory search structure, e.g. an AVL-tree, to manage the resulting object identifiers. Whenever the identifier of an object is added to the result, it is also inserted into this structure. Then, before applying the refinement step to a filtered object, the corresponding object identifier is retrieved in the search structure. If it occurs in it, an unnecessary refinement step is prevented. Using this technique we avoid duplicates in the result and do not perform redundant refinement operations.

6. Performance comparison of object decomposition techniques

After presenting different structural object decomposition techniques as well as adequate query processing algorithms, the main goal of this chapter is to compare the different techniques to each other and to the original, undecomposed representation. Thus, we will determine whether it is worth decomposing complex spatial objects and which decomposition technique is best suitable. We will present a series of test results which we ran with Modula-2 implementations on SUN 3/60 workstations under UNIX. The main question we consider is whether decomposition techniques lead to better query performance and which technique achieves best performance improvements in spatial query processing. The comparison consists of two parts: Part one (section 6.2) compares the different decompositions to each other with respect to their number of components, their quality of container approximation, and their amount of additional storage. Then, in part two of the test (section 6.3) the different decomposition techniques are investigated with respect to query processing time.

6.1 Selection of test data

One basic problem of any empirical performance comparison is the selection of an appropriate standardized set of test data. The best choice is to examine data files used daily in real applications. We provided large sets of real spatial data, e.g. digitized maps used in existing geographic information systems. Additionally, large sets of synthetic data, i.e. polygons, were generated in order to facilitate testing the query processing system under a wide range of varying data. To describe the test files used for the comparison, we provided a set of parameters characterizing single polygons and sets of polygons. For single polygons we choose the number of vertices, the number of holes, the size and the shape complexity as parameters. The shape complexity is characterized by the class the polygon belongs to, i.e. convex, starshaped, simple polygons and simple polygons with holes (SPH) (see [PS 85]). For sets of polygons, the number of polygons, their cover, and their distribution in data space are additional parameters to be investigated. The cover of a set of objects is the sum of the size of the objects in relation to the size of the data space. In particular, the following files were selected for the performance comparison.

Name	Num. of Objects	Cover	Distrib.	Num. of Vertices	Num. of Holes	Shape
europe	471	0.27	real	95.1	0.02	SPH
sph_85_1	1000	1.00	uniform	85.0	2.00	SPH
sph_85_10	1000	10.00	uniform	85.0	2.00	SPH
star_20_1	1000	1.00	uniform	20.0	0.00	starshaped
star_20_10	1000	10.00	uniform	20.0	0.00	starshaped

Table 1: The test files

The first file consists of 471 polygons representing the counties of the European Community[1]. In addition to the examination of this real data file we generated two pairs of test files, each of them consisting of 1000 polygons. The 'sph_85' files contain SPHs, whereas the 'star_20' files contain simple starshaped polygons without holes. We selected different covers for the files, cover 1 and cover 10, to simulate different degrees of object overlap, e.g. occurring in multi attribute maps. The objects of the four synthetic files are distributed uniformly in dataspace due to the fact that the performance of the R*-tree which is used as a SAM for handling the bounding boxes is practically independent of the data distribution [BKSS 90].

6.2 Comparing decomposition techniques with respect to structural properties

Within the first part of the comparison we examined the different decomposition techniques of chapter 4 with respect to the number of generated components, the quality of container approximation and the amount of storage. Table 2 contains the test results for the files presented in section 6.1.

europe	ident	convex	trapezoids	triangles	heterogen
Num. of Components	471	22296	44332	44218	81338
Approximation	2.15	1.31	1.20	3.13	1.25
Amount of storage	1.00	2.15	2.77	2.63	3.73

sph_85_1/10	ident	convex	trapezoids	triangles	heterogen
Num. of Components	1000	51149	83998	85004	198305
Approximation	1.72	1.31	1.10	3.13	1.15
Amount of storage	1.00	2.99	3.00	3.03	5.19

star_20_1/10	ident	convex	trapezoids	triangles	heterogen
Num. of Components	1000	7764	18958	17958	34429
Approximation	1.41	1.21	1.11	3.06	1.19
Amount of storage	1.00	2.06	2.79	2.64	3.67

Table 2: Test results for the structural properties of the decomposition techniques

[1] We thankfully acknowledge receiving this file from the 'Statistical Office of the European Communities'

For the interpretation of the results presented in table 2, we start with the real data file 'europe'.

Considering the degree of redundancy, i.e. the number of components introduced by decomposition, shows that the number of generated components essentially depends on the type of objects stored in the file. For the trapezoid and the triangle decomposition the number of components is approximately the same as the number of vertices in the original object (see section 4.3 and 4.4). The convex decomposition generates about half, the heterogeneous decomposition about twice the number of components compared to the trapezoid and triangle decomposition. The number of convex components essentially depends on the shape, i.e. the number of notches, of the SPHs, whereas the heterogeneous decomposition generates one triangle and one rectangle for each vertex of the SPH in most cases. The influence of the number of components and the quality of container approximation on the performance of spatial query procesing is evaluated in the next section.

Considering the quality of container approximation, the bad value of 2.15 for the identity (undecomposed) representation is conspicuous. Within query processing, such a bad value leads to a frequent application of the refinement step, which is particularly time consuming due to the undecomposed representation. The application of decomposition techniques results in much better approximation values within the range of 1.2 - 1.3 for the convex, the trapezoids, and the heterogeneous decomposition. This is caused by the generation of partition rays parallel to one axis of the coordinate system. Using the triangle decomposition leads to values between 2 and larger than 3, because rectangles are no adequate type of container for triangles.

The reason for the introduction of redundancy introduced by structural decomposition techniques was to speed up spatial query processing. However, this type of object representation requires a higher amount of (secondary) storage than the identity representation. For real data, the convex representation needs twice as much, the trapezoid and triangle representation requires almost three times as much, and the heterogeneous representation needs almost four times as much storage compared to the identity representation.

Within the next section we will evaluate the performance of spatial query processing based on different decomposition techniques and compare it to the identity representation.

6.3 Comparing decomposition techniques with respect to query processing

In this part of the comparison, we empirically evaluate which object representation technique (undecomposed, convex polygons, etc.) leads to best performance in spatial query processing.

As described in section 1 and in more detail in section 5, spatial query processing consists of two steps, the filter step and the refinement step. According to this two phases, we evaluated the query performance of different types of spatial object decompositions comparing their results to the undecomposed object representation.

The performance of the filter step is considerably determined by the performance of the SAM handling bounding boxes of the components. We used the best performing access method handling bounding boxes known to us, the R*-tree [BKSS 90] with page capacity (directory and data) bound to 2K. The most time consuming operations during queries in the R*-tree are accesses to secondary storage and comparisons within the directory and the data pages. Thus, we counted the number of page accesses and the number of comparisons in directory as well as data pages and then multiplied them by typical time constants.

The refinement step performes computational geometry algorithms for those candidate objects supplied by the filter step. In our bookkeeping of query time we include the time spent with the main memory search structure for the found object identifiers in the time for the refinement step. This is due to the fact that decomposition techniques simplify complex computational geometry algorithms by using a set of object components. Therefore, we assign the task of handling this redundant object representation to the refinement step. Consequently, the refinement performance is determined by the time spent for computational geometry algorithms and, in case of redundancy in object representations, the time needed for performing insertions and search operations in the main memory search structure managing the identifieres of found objects. As these performance parameters strongly depend on the particular set of data, we explicitly measured them using implementations of the different decomposition techniques. Finally, we added the performance parameters of the filter and the refinement step to obtain a measure for the overall query performance for different spatial queries.

The queries that we performed are classified into point queries (window query with zero extension) and window queries with different window sizes referring to a varying selectivity of spatial queries. The size of the query window was fixed to the values of 0.01%, 0.1%, 1%, and 10% of the data space size (which we consider for typical within real applications). More complex queries, e.g. region queries, were not considered in this test series. Those queries typically are evaluated by performing a window query with a minimum bounding box of the query region followed by more complex computational geometry algorithms on the objects supplied by the filter step of a window query. Therefore, those algorithms are even more crucial in overall query processing and, in fact, additionally favour object decomposition techniques.

The query results are presented in three figures for each of the data files introduced in the last section. The figures depict the following information: the horizontal axis represents the size of the query window. The number below the window size is the percentage of answers with respect to the total number of objects. Let us mention that a low percentage of answers corresponds to a high query selectivity and vice versa. The vertical axis gives the time requirements for performing queries of varying window sizes. The time is given in microseconds per found object. Every decomposition technique is characterized by its own curve carrying an abbreviation of the name of the technique. The first figure corresponds to the time spent for the filter step. The next one depicts the time spent for performing the computational geometry algorithms on the object/component representations and, in case of redundant object representations, the time spent for the main memory search structure avoiding duplicate refinement operations. Finally, the rightmost figure represents the complete result adding the results of the first two figures and therefore corresponds to the overall query time of spatial query processing.

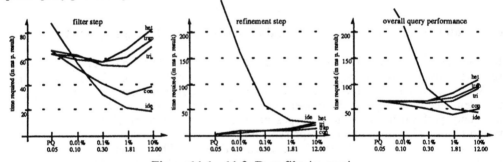

Figure 11.1 - 11.3: Data file: 'europe'

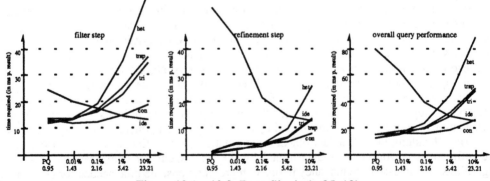

Figure 12.1 - 12.3: Data file: 'sph_85_10'

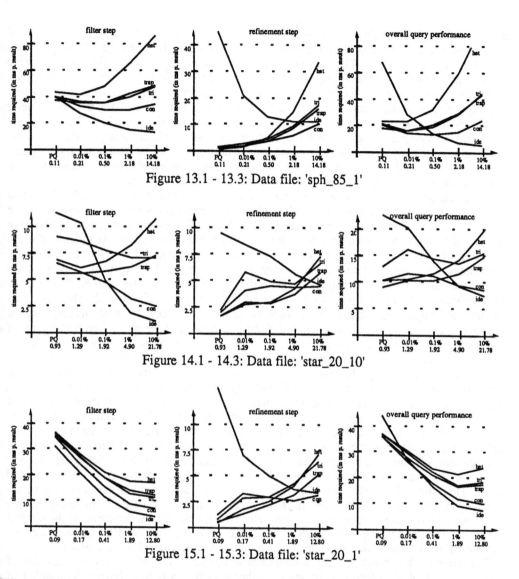

Figure 13.1 - 13.3: Data file: 'sph_85_1'

Figure 14.1 - 14.3: Data file: 'star_20_10'

Figure 15.1 - 15.3: Data file: 'star_20_1'

The overall query time clearly shows a strong dependance on the size of the query window. Further important criteria which influence the performance of different object representations are the object complexity, i.e. the number of vertices, and the cover of the objects. The main results are:

- decomposition techniques clearly outperform (up to an order of magnitude) the undecomposed representation for point queries and window queries with small query windows, i.e. high selectivity
- with decreasing query selectivity the performance of the undecomposed representation improves relative to the performance of decomposition techniques with a break-even point for a rather low selectivity
- the performance of decomposition techniques for window queries of low selectivity strongly depends on the amount of redundancy
- the more complex the objects are, the more clearly appear the trends outlined above

Independent of the data file, point queries and high selectivity window queries are performed more efficiently by any of the decomposed object representations than by the undecomposed representation. Particularly, the real data file 'europe' (fig. 11) shows a significant gain of decomposed representations up to the factor 5 in overall query time. As the first two figures, e.g. of the 'europe'-file (fig. 11.1 and 11.2), show, this behaviour is due to the very expensive refinement operations for the undecomposed objects and to the fact, that small query windows will profit from the selectivity of the spatial access method, limiting the number of disk accesses and supplying a small amount of redundant components. Particularly, for the point query, caused by the good container approximation of most decomposition methods, frequently no redundant components are accessed at all. This trend obviously holds for any of the data files. The gain in efficiency of object decompositions depends on the complexity of the data objects. The higher the complexity of the objects with respect to the number of vertices, the better is the performance of object decompositions relative to the identity representation.

Regarding low selectivity window queries, i.e. query windows covering 5-10 % of the data space, this trend turns around. Redundant object representations perform worse for large window queries depending on the amount of redundancy. This is strongly caused by the large amount of components which have to be managed by the access method. As queries of small selectivity relate to large portions of the data, the total amount of stored data essentially determines the number of disk accesses necessary to answer those queries. Typically, the amount of stored data for object decompositions is significantly higher than for an undecomposed object representation, as we see from section 6.2, table 2. Therefore, for decomposed object representations the time spent with the access method increases with a growing size of the query window, i.e. a shrinking selectivity of the query (see first figures of the performance results). The amount of redundancy that has to be handled within the refinement step obviously increases at the same time. Therefore, eliminating redundancy strongly determines the performance of the refinement step of decomposed representations. Contrarily, the average time spent for one explicite object test of the undecomposed representation decreases, as the number of cheap object tests increases (i.e. the bounding box of an object is fully included in the query window and therefore no further action is necessary).

The influence of an increasing object complexity is reflected in an intensification of the basic trends. On one hand, complex objects require complex geometry algorithms in the case of undecomposed representation (see fig. 11.2, 12.2, and 13.2), on the other hand, decompositions of complex objects lack in a further increase of redundancy (fig. 11.1, 12.1, and 13.1). Therefore, the performance of high selectivity queries which strongly depend on efficient refinement operations will decrease with an increasing object complexity for the undecomposed object representation. As low selectivity queries basically depend on the number of disk accesses and the amount of redundancy, object decompositions will degenerate for very complex objects which enlarge the degree of redundancy. (see fig. 11.3, 12.3, and 13.3)

The cover of the objects directly corresponds to the selectivity of a query of fixed size. If only the cover of the objects increases (all other parameters remain fixed), the number of answers will grow. Therefore, the undecomposed representation needs a higher number of expensive refinement operations which can be considered as a penalty for the performance. However, object decompositions suffer in handling a large amount of redundancy in the case of low selectivity queries. (see fig. 12 and 14)

Summarizing over all shapes of objects, decomposition techniques gain by performing cheap computational geometry algorithms in the refinement step. This advantage is strongly valid for high selectivity queries where secondary storage accesses are not dominant. Low selectivity queries, however, supply a high amount of redundancy which must be accessed on secondary storage and handled in main memory. These efforts rise with an increasing size of query windows, i.e. a decreasing query selectivity. The degree of redundancy of a decomposition method, i.e. the number of components for originally one single spatial object, is strongly reflected in the performance of low selectivity queries. The performance of the different decomposition techniques is similar for high selectivity queries. This is due to the fact, that computational geometry algorithms perform very similiar for all decomposition techniques considered here. The undecomposed representation performes worse for high selectivity queries. Depending on the decomposition technique and the particular type of objects, a specific size of query window exists, where the performance curves of the undecomposed representation and object decompositions intersect in a break-even point. Queries with higher selectivity are more efficiently performed by the decomposed representations, queries with lower selectivity are handled faster by the undecomposed representation.

Among the decomposition techniques considered here the convex object decomposition turns out to be the best performing technique. It gains from a relatively small amount of redundancy (see section 6.2, table 2) and cheap computational geometry algorithms. The break-even point of the performance curve, particularly for complex data (fig. 12.3) and real data (fig. 11.3), corresponds to a considerable large query size, i.e. a considerably low query selectivity. For most queries and arbitrary types of objects, the convex decomposition technique outperforms the undecomposed representation.

From our tests we learned, that an optimal decomposition technique is not obtained by minimizing the complexity of the components due to the penalty of a very large amount of redundancy (see the heterogeneous decomposition). It is desirable to find a decomposition method which restricts the computational effort for its components and as well reduces the number of components. The performance of such an ideal decomposition method within our test bed will correspond to a parallel to the axis representing query sizes, i.e. its relative performance will be the same for small and for large query windows.

7 Conclusions

In this paper, we presented a two-level, multi-representation query processing technique for polygonal objects consisting of a filter and a refinement step. The efficiency of the spatial query processor is gained by decomposition of complex spatial objects into simple components and the application of efficient and robust spatial access methods for simple spatial objects. We introduced three new decomposition techniques for simple polygons with holes. Within an extensive performance comparison, we compared these techniques to each other, to another technique known from the literature and to the undecomposed representation with respect to their performance in spatial query processing. The main results are:

- Decomposition techniques generally perform extremely good for high selectivity spatial queries and they outperform the traditional object representation up to one order of magnitude.
- Decomposition is a proper representation scheme especially for complex objects, i.e. polygonal objects with an average vertex number larger than 80.
- Decomposed representations lead to a very good query performance particularly for files with high object cover (e.g. multi-layer maps).
- The convex decomposition turns out to be the best compromise between simple computational geometry algorithms and a moderate degree of redundancy and is the winner of all decomposition techniques.

Summarizing, we showed that query processing based on object decomposition is a promising approach worth to be further researched. In our future work, we will extend the query processor to more complex queries and we plan to integrate additional decomposition techniques and other spatial access methods, e.g. the cell tree [Gue 88] and the P-tree [KS 91].

Acknowledgement

We thankfully acknowledge receiving real data representing the countries of the European Community by the 'Statistical Office of the European Communities'. In particular, we would like to thank Thomas Brinkhoff for preprocessing the above data.

References

[AA 83] Asano, Ta. & Te. Asano, 'Minimum Partition of Polygonal Regions into Trapezoids', in Proc. 24th IEEE Annual Symposium on Foundations of Computer Science, 233-241, 1983.

[BKSS 90] Beckmann, N., H.P. Kriegel, R. Schneider & B. Seeger, 'The R*-tree: An efficient and robust access method for points and rectangles', in Proc. 1990 ACM SIGMOD International Conference on Management of Data, 322-331, Atlantic City, USA, May 1990.

[Bur 87] Burrough, P.A., Principles of Geographical Information Systems for Land Resource Assessment', Clarendon Press, Oxford, 1987

[CD 85] Chazelle, B. & D.P. Dobkin, 'Optimal Convex Decompositions', Computational Geometry, G.T. Toissant (Ed.), Amsterdam, The Netherlands: North Holland, 63-134, 1985

[Del 34] Delaunay, B.,'Sur la sphere vide', Izvestiya Akademii Nauk SSSR, VII Seria, Otdeline Matematicheskii i Estestvennyka Nauk, 7, 6, 793-800, 1934.

[DHH 90] Droste, U., H.-G. Harms, H. Horn, 'Decomposition Based Representation and Query Processing of Polygonal Object in Database Systems', Master Thesis (in German), University of Bremen, 1990

[Fre 87] Freeston, M., 'The BANG file: a new kind of grid file', Proc. ACM SIGMOD Int. Conf. on Management of Data, 260-269, 1987

[Gue 89] Günther, O., 'The design of the cell tree: an object-oriented index structure for geometric databases', in Proc. IEEE 5th Int. Conf. on Data Engineering, 598-605, Los Angeles, 1989.

[Gut 84] Guttman A., 'R-trees: a dynamic index structure for spatial searching', in Proc. ACM SIGMOD Int. Conf. on Management of Data, 47-57, June 1984.

[KBS 91] Kriegel, H.-P., Brinkhoff, T., Schneider, R.: An Efficient Map Overlay Algorithm based on Spatial Access Methods and Computational Geometry. Proc. Int. Workshop on DBMS's for geographical applications, Capri, May 16-17, 1991

[KHHSS 91a] Kriegel, H.-P., Heep, P., Heep, S., Schiwietz, M., Schneider, R.: An Access Method Based Query Processor for Spatial Database Systems. Proc. Int. Workshop on DBMS's for geographical applications, Capri, May 16-17, 1991

[KHHSS 91b] Kriegel, H.-P., Heep, P., Heep, S., Schiwietz, M., Schneider, R.: A Flexible and Extensible Index Manager for Spatial Database Systems. Proc. 2nd Int. Conf. on Database and Expert Systems Applications (DEXA '91), Berlin, August 21-23, 1991

[KS 85] Keil, J.M. & J.R. Sack, 'Minimum decomposition of polygonal objects', Computational Geometry, G.T. Toissant (Ed.), Amsterdam, The Netherlands: North Holland, 197-216, 1985

[KS 88] Kriegel, H.P. & B. Seeger., 'PLOP-Hashing: A Grid File without directory', Proc. 4th Int. Conf. on Data Engeneering, 369-376, 1988

[KS 91] Kriegel, H.P.& M. Schiwietz, 'The P-tree: an efficient access method for complex spatial objects', University of Munich, Germany, 1991, in preparation.

[KSSS 89] Kriegel, H.P., M. Schiwietz, R. Schneider & B.Seeger, 'Performance Comparison of Point and Spatial Access Methods', in Proc. "Symposium on the Design and Implementation of Large Spatial Databases", 89-114, Santa Barbara, USA, July 1989.

[NHS 84] Nievergelt J., H. Hinterberger & K.C. Sevcik: 'The grid file: an adaptable, symmetric multikey file structure', ACM Trans. on Database Systems, Vol. 9, 1, 38-71, 1984.

[OM 86] Orenstein, J.A. & F.A. Manola, 'Spatial Data Modeling and Query Processing in PROBE', Technical Report CCA-86-05, Xerox Advanced Information Technology Devision, 1986.

[Oos 90] Oosterom, P.J.M., 'Reactive Data Structures for Geographic Information Systems', PhD-thesis, Department of Computer Science at Leiden University, The Netherlands, 1990.

[Oren 89] Orenstein, J.A., 'Redundancy in Spatial Databases', in Proc. 1989 ACM SIGMOD International Conference on Management of Data, 294-305, Portland, USA, June 1989.

[PS 85] Preparata, F.P. & M.I. Shamos, 'Computational Geometry: An Introduction', Springer-Verlag, New York, 1985

[Sam 84] Samet, H., 'The Quadtree and Related Hierarchical Data Structures', ACM Computing Surveys, Vol. 16, No. 2, 187-260, 1984

[See 90] Seeger, B., 'Design and Implementation of multidimensional access methods' (in German), PhD-thesis, University of Bremen, Germany, 1990.

[SK 88] Seeger, B. & H.P. Kriegel, 'Techniques for design and implementation of efficient spatial access methods', in Proc. 14th Int. Conf. on Very Large Databases, 360-371, Los Angeles, USA, 1988.

[SK 90] Seeger, B. & H.P. Kriegel, 'The Buddy Tree: An Efficient and Robust Access Method for Spatial Databases', in Proc. 16th Int. Conf. on Very Large Data Bases, Brisbane, Australia, August 1990.

[SV 89] Scholl, M. & A. Voisard, 'Thematic Map Modelling', in Proc. "Symposium on the Design and Implementation of Large Spatial Databases", 167-190, Santa Barbara, USA, July 1989.

Distributed Image Synthesis with Breadth-First Ray Tracing and the Ray-Z-Buffer*

Heinrich Müller, Jörg Winckler[‡]

Abstract

Breadth-first ray tracing for realistic image synthesis differs from usual pixel-by-pixel rendering in tracing whole generations of rays together. This means that first all rays of view are treated, next the set of reflection and refraction rays, then the reflection and refraction rays caused by them, and so on. The calculation of intersections for a generation of rays uses the ray-z-buffer algorithm. Like the original z-buffer algorithm, the ray-z-buffer algorithm allows to render scenes with an unlimited number of primitives within a working space dependent only on the resolution of the picture. A distributed implementation of breadth-first raytracing in a network of workstations is presented and analyzed.

1 Introduction

The main task of realistic image synthesis by ray tracing is the detection of the intersection point of a ray with a given spatial scene, closest to the origin of the ray. A spatial scene usually consists of a number of primitives, like triangles, spheres, and patches.

Many algorithms were developed for speeding up this calculation [Müller, 1988, Schmitt, Müller, Leister, 1988, Glassner, 1989]. Nearly all of them first preprocess the scene into a data structure before rendering. The data structure reduces the number of primitives to be tested against a ray. A well-known approach uses regular grids. The min-max bounding box of the scene is subdivided into congruent cells. For each cell a list is held collecting all its intersecting primitives. Once these lists are established in the preprocessing phase, the algorithm detects for each ray those grid cells the ray is passing through. The ray is intersected with the primitives referred to in the traversed cells until the closest intersection point is found, or the bounding box is left. Thus the number of intersection tests is reduced on the number of primitives along the ray. The rays are treated pixel-wise, including all reflecting and refracting rays induced by the pixel, according to a *depth-first strategy*. The storage requirements for rays are neglectable, since only one ray is treated once a time.

A disadvantage of depth-first ray tracing is the dependency of the memory required by the data structure on the number of primitives in the scene. This dependency is one

---

*supported by Deutsche Forschungsgemeinschaft (DFG), Mu 744/1

[†]Institut für Informatik, Universität Freiburg, Rheinstr. 10–12, W-7800 Freiburg/i.Br. Email: mueller@informatik.uni-freiburg.de

[‡]Email: winckler@informatik.uni-freiburg.de

difference between todays ray tracing and the classical z-buffer algorithm. The main data structure of the z-buffer algorithm is the z-buffer holding for each pixel the distance of the primitive closest to the observer. The primitives are processed sequentially. Coming up with a new primitive, its distance from the observer at each relevant pixel is calculated and compared against the value in the z-buffer. If the primitive is closer, the z-buffer is updated with the new distance and the primitive is registered visible at this pixel.

Evidently, the memory requirements of the z-buffer algorithm depend on the size of the z-buffer which in turn depends on the resolution of the image. The scene may be stored on secondary memory. The possibility to handle a practically unlimited number of primitives within an predictable bound of memory makes the z-buffer algorithm particularly suitable for implementation in hardware.

In [Müller, 1988], also cf. [Schmitt, Müller, Leister, 1988], this property of the z-buffer algorithm is transferred to ray tracing. The main idea is to replace depth-first ray tracing by *breadth-first ray tracing*. Breadth-first ray tracing opens by first treating all rays of view. Because of their special orientation they can be handled by the z-buffer algorithm. Once their first intersection points are determined, calculation continues with the rays of shadow starting at the intersection points and ending at the point light sources in the scene. The rays of shadows may be treated by the z-buffer algorithm too. The result of the algorithm up to now is the portion of color contributed by the the first generation of rays, i.e. the rays of view, to the image. Beyond the color the z-buffer algorithm has to calculate the rays of reflection and refraction for the first generation of rays. They make up the second generation of rays. For the second generation, again the first intersections have to be found out. Their calculation (and that for all following generations) is done by the *ray-z-buffer algorithm*.

Although breadth-first ray tracing based on the ray-z-buffer algorithm has the advantage of a main memory size dependent only on the resolution of the picture and not on the size of the scene, the considerable time requirements inherent in the ray tracing approach must also be expected here. One way to cope with this problem is parallelization. In [Müller, 1989] a parallelized version of the ray-z-buffer algorithm was developed based on the abstract model of a CREW-PRAM. The purpose now is to present and analyze an implementation of parallel breadth-first ray tracing in a distributed computing environment.

The distributed environment focused on consists of a network of workstations. The workstations are operating under a multi-process operating system, specifically Unix. The communication is based on the *Remote Procedure Call (RPC)* mechanism [Birrell, Nelson, 1984] and the *Network File System (NFS)* [Apollo Comp. Inc., 1987]. This type of configuration was successfully used in the past for the rendering of ray traced computer animations [Peterson, 1987, Leister, Müller, Neidecker, Stößer, 1988]. Rendering was performed frame by frame, thus leading to independent processes with nearly no communication among them. The processes performing the distributed ray-z-buffer calculation, however, have to communicate data. Hence the typical questions of parallel computing for the communication overhead with a growing number of nodes in the network do arise now.

In order to analyze the behavior of the distributed ray tracing based on the breath-first approach a more general environment for the implementation of distributed computations named CARTOON based on RPC was designed and implemented. It generalizes the ideas of the Network Computing System (NCS). The environment consists of two interacting tools, the *Resource Information System (RIS)* and the *Application Distributor (AD)*. The AD carries out a distribution strategy for the remote procedure calls. RIS collects the informations about the network environment necessary for the distribution strategy. If an application process intends a remote procedure call, first the AD is called. The AD in turn calls the RIS to get information about the current state. Based on the information the AD finds the most favorable server for the remote procedure call of the application which then is directed to this server. A special property of RIS/AD is that no modification of the source code of the application is required when changing the load distribution strategy.

Objectives of the analysis of CARTOON are the time of computation dependent on the number of nodes in the network, the influence of local disks, and several other parameters characteristic for CARTOON. The interpretation of the specific results requires some knowledge about CARTOON and thus is postponed to a later section.

The remainder of the paper is organized as follows. In section 2, some details of the ray-z-buffer algorithm are outlined. Section 3 describes the distributed version of breadth-first ray tracing, its implementation CARTOON, and RIS/AD. Section 4 is to devoted the analysis of the distributed ray-z-buffer approach. Measurements and their interpretations are the contents of section 5.

2   The ray-z-buffer algorithm

Basic for the distributed image synthesis algorithm described here is the ray-z-buffer algorithm. The ray-z-buffer algorithm solves the following problem:

Ray-Scene-Intersection.

Input. A set R of rays in 3-space.

Output. Those rays in R intersected by any primitive in the scene, as well as the first point of intersection.

The algorithm is split in two phases, the preprocessing and the query phase. In the *preprocessing phase*, the set of rays, R, is preprocessed into a data structure called *ray-z-buffer*. The ray-z-buffer generalizes the z-buffer. However, it is more complex since it has to take into account the origin and the direction of the rays.

A ray not orthogonal to the z-axis may be described by two equations,

$$x = a \cdot z + b,$$

$$y = c \cdot z + d,$$

and two z-values,

$$z_o, \; z_e$$

for the origin respectively the current end point of the ray. The ray-z-buffer contains tuples $(a, b, c, d, z_o, z_e, prim)$ describing the set of rays R currently stored and information *prim* about the currently visible primitive.

In the *query phase*, the ray-z-buffer is used to answer queries for the rays intersecting a given primitive. The task of this phase is similar to the main phase of the z-buffer algorithm in which the pixels covered by a projected polygon are found out.

Suppose the primitives of the scene are given implicitly by

$$F_0(c_0, x, y, z) = 0,$$

$$F_i(c_i, x, y, z) \geq 0, \ i = 1, \ldots, p.$$

The first equation defines a surface in 3-space from which a part is cut off by the additional inequalities. The $c_i \in \mathbb{R}^d$, $d \geq 1$, are parameters controlling the shape of the surface. For example, rectangles perpendicular to the z-axis can be described by

$$z = c_0,$$

$$c_{11} \leq x \leq c_{12}, \ c_{21} \leq y \leq c_{22}, \ c_0, c_{ij} \in \mathbb{R}, \ i, j = 1, 2.$$

A ray intersects a primitive if a solution z of

$$F_0(c_0, a \cdot z + b, c \cdot z + d, z) = 0$$

exists which satisfies the constraints

$$F_i(c_i, a \cdot z + b, c \cdot z + d, z) \geq 0, \ i = 1, \ldots, p.$$

Among the solutions, only that one between z_o and z_e closest to z_o is of interest. It defines the new z_e of the ray $(a, b, c, d, z_0, z_e, prim)$.

If $z = z(c_0, a, b, c, d)$ can be isolated in the equation it can be put into the constraints leading to z-free inequalities

$$\overline{F_i}(c_i, c_0, a, b, c, d) \geq 0, \ i = 1, \ldots, p,$$

for the rays intersecting the primitive. For iso-oriented rectangles, the inequalities are

$$c_{11} \leq a \cdot c_0 + b \leq c_{12},$$

$$c_{21} \leq c \cdot c_0 + d \leq c_{22},$$

$$c_0, c_{ij} \in \mathbb{R}, \ i, j = 1, 2.$$

The ray-z-buffer has to be organized into a data structure so that the rays $(a, b, c, d, z_0, z_e, prim)$ satisfying the inequalities can be found quickly for arbitrary parameters c_i.

The difference in computational complexity between the classical z-buffer algorithm and the ray-z-buffer can now be quantified. While the search space in the first case is two-dimensional (the indices of the pixels covered by the primitive have to be found) here it is the four-dimensional a-b-c-d-space. The space and time required depends on the shape of the query range given by the constraints. In [Yao, 1982, Yao, Yao, 1985] it was shown that for constraints given by polynomials, n rays can be preprocessed into a data structure of size $O(n)$ so that a query can answered in time $O(n^\beta)$, with a constant $0 < \beta < 1$. If the query range consists of only one bi-linear inequality, $\beta = (\log 15)/4$

was obtained which is very close to 1. Better query times are achieved by investing more than linear storage. However, the amount of storage required for a significant speed up of query time is considerable [Chazelle, 1985].

These worst-case complexity results are not very promising. However, like for the usual approaches of ray tracing, data structures with a good practical behavior, though bad in the worst case, may still exist. In the implementation described here the special case of scenes of iso-oriented rectangles was chosen. They are of particular significance since other geometric primitives can easily be approximated by them, for example by using the min-max bounding boxes or better approximating rectangular polytopes. Rays intersecting the bounding box are then additionally to be tested against the enveloped primitive.

In the case of iso-oriented rectangles the inequalities of intersection simplify to

$$-a \cdot c_0 + c_{11} \leq b \leq -a \cdot c_0 + c_{12},$$

$$-c \cdot c_0 + c_{21} \leq d \leq -c \cdot c_0 + c_{22},$$

$$c_0, c_{ij} \in \mathbb{R}, \ i,j = 1,2.$$

An important observation is that the first line only concerns a and b, and the second line only c and d. This means that the four-dimensional query problem is reduced to two two-dimensional coupled query-problems, one for the a-b-projection and one for the c-d-projection of the given rays. For both problems, the query ranges are stripes. The projected rays are points. Those of them falling in the stripe have to be found.

In this situation, the solution of the planar stripe query problem by an *hierarchical subdivision* shows favorable. The given set of points is subdivided by lines into a constant number of subsets which are in turn divided recursively. Coming up with a stripe, the query for the points within the stripe can be solved by descending down the tree of subdivision along the subsets intersected by the stripe. The number of inspected subsets is small if the subdivision is balanced, or, in other words, if the subsets of a subdivision contain nearly the same number of points.

There are several known strategies of subdivision which may be applied, the *polygon trees* [Willard, 1982], the *conjugation trees* or *ham sandwich tree* [Edelsbrunner, Welzl, 1986], the *ϵ-nets* [Haussler, Welzl, 1986], and the *partition trees* [Welzl, 1988]. All of them were developed to minimize the asymptotic worst case complexity in time and space. For example, the ham sandwich tree requires $O(n)$ space, $O(n \log n)$ preprocessing time, and $O(n^\beta)$ query time for n points, $\beta = \log 0.695$. The query times of the later structures are better, however the preprocessing times known yet seem considerably worse.

The application of these data structures require considerable amount of arithmetic operations, in particular multiplications and divisions. Further, since the line of division can be arbitrary, some amount of memory is necessary to store the subdivision. This is less severe when allowing horizontal and vertical lines for partition only. One data structure thus obtained is the well known *quadtree* [Samet, 1990]. A quadtree carries out a subdivision of a rectangular region in the plane into rectangles by recursively dividing each region by a pair of horizontal and vertical line segments into four subregions called *quads*.

Different from the data structures mentioned above a balanced partition is not always possible. For example, it is not if all the points lie on a straight line. However, it is possible to guarantee a partition of a set of n points by a pair of a horizontal and a vertical line so that a quad contains $n/3$ points at most [Overmars, 1983]. A quadtree of this sort can be constructed in time $P(n) = O(n \log n)$ [Overmars, 1983, Lamparter, Müller, Winckler, 1990].

A stripe query asks for all points lying in a stripe defined by two parallel lines (g_1 : $b = s \cdot a + t_1$ and $g_2 : b = s \cdot a + t_2$). Using a quadtree it is answered by visiting recursively the maximal quads intersecting the stripe and listing the points found in these quads. The time necessary for answering a query can be estimated by an expression $Q(n) = O(q(n) + I)$. I is the number of points found in the stripe, $q(n)$ is the overhead for traversing the tree. In the worst case, $q(n) = O(n)$. However, there are many special nontrivial subclasses of point sets having $q(n) = O(n^\beta)$ for some constant β, $0.5 \leq \beta < 1$ [Lamparter, Müller, Winckler, 1990].

For the 4d case to be solved here a coupling between the projections is now carried out as follows. To each member Q in the hierarchy of quads in the a-b-projection, a secondary quadtree in the c-d-projection is assigned. The set of points over which the secondary quadtree is constructed is the c-d-projection of those rays whose a-b-projections fall in Q. The time for preprocessing this nested quadtree is bounded by $P(n) = O(n \log^2 n)$.

A query in the 3d-case is answered by first searching for the maximal quads of the a-b-projection contained in the a-b-stripe. For each quad found, the secondary quadtree is searched for cells with the same property, but now for the c-d-projection and the c-d-stripe. The lists of rays belonging to these cells are concatenated and reported as solution. Evidently, they satisfy the inequalities in both projections simultaneously, thus intersecting the query rectangle. The query time is a factor of $\log n$ worse than for the two-dimensional case, hence $q(n) = O(n^\beta \log n)$, $0 \leq \beta \leq 1$, β dependent on the subclass of rectangles involved.

This algorithm was implemented in the programming language C++. In order to get an impression of the behavior of the query times of the quadtree two experiments were carried out. In the first experiment, an image was computed with five different resolutions. The resolution varied from 60×60 to 300×300. The results are presented graphically in the left part of Fig. 1. Both axes have a logarithmic scale. All points approximately lie on a straight line with slope 0.54. Hence the query time increases sublinearly ($O(n^{0.54})$) in the size of the image. Thus the quadtree seems to behave quite favorable in practice, compared with the worst case efficient data structures mentioned above.

In the second experiment, images of the same fixed resolution were calculated from scenes with increasing numbers of primitives. The graphical presentation of the results in the right part of Fig. 1 shows an expected linear behavior.

In summary, the relative behavior of the ray-z-buffer looks quite promising. The absolute times, however, are poor when compared with efficient implementations of usual depth-first ray tracing strategies. Partly, inefficiencies of the implementation are responsible for that. Examples are superfluous procedure calls in the most busy loops caused by to the strict application of the class concept of $C++$. On the other hand there are still too many multiplications for the stripe queries. Probably, regular quadtrees dividing strictly in the middle may be better, although balancing is worse then.

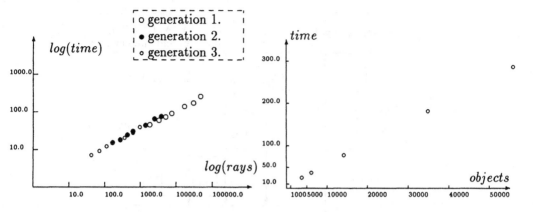

Figure 1: Number of rays versus time for the ray-z-buffer algorithm using a logarithmic scale (left side), and number of primitives versus time (right side).

3 Distributed computing

For distributed computing, the set of rays to be processed is partitioned into groups of a given fixed size (Fig. 2). For the rays of view partitioning corresponds to splitting the picture into sub-pictures. Each group is preprocessed by the z-buffer algorithm respectively the ray-z-buffer algorithm, dependent on the class of rays. Parallelization is achieved by preprocessing the groups by independent processes. Each process also performs the queries with the scene primitives on its preprocessed data structure.

This approach is a compromise between the under worst case considerations asymptotically more efficient parallelization in [Müller, 1989], and ease of implementation. It avoids the strong time dependency of the different processes as it is characteristic for the worst-case efficient solution. Thus the system architecture is more simple and more flexible to control.

The strategy was implemented in the distributed image synthesis system CARTOON. CARTOON is written in C++ and runs in a network of Unix workstations. Fig. 2 gives a survey of the architecture of CARTOON. CARTOON consists of the components SHADER, CPMS, CALLSHELL, HERA, RIS, and AD. These components run as processes in the distributed system. The communication is based on the *remote procedure call (RPC)* mechanism, in the current implementation supported by the product RPCGEN [SUN Microsystems, Inc., Mountain View, CA, 1990]. The idea of RPC is to distribute the call and the execution of a procedure on separate processes. The caller usually is denoted as *client*, the executing instance is the *server*. Distributed computing becomes possible when client and server run on different nodes in the network.

When running CARTOON, usually one SHADER process and several HERA processes are active. In the HERA processes, the rays are processed by the simple z-buffer algorithm or the ray-z-buffer algorithm. The SHADER process carries out the calculation of the color

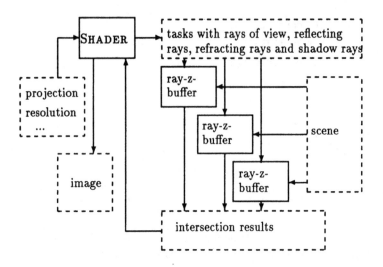

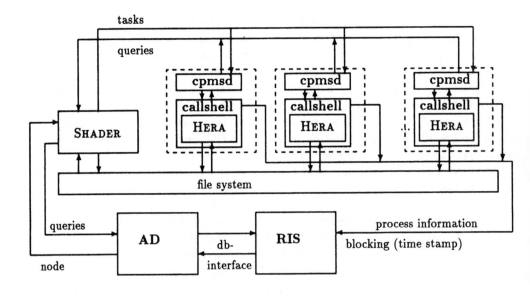

Figure 2: The drawing above shows distributed breadth-first ray tracing, the drawing below its implementation in CARTOON.

and the preparation of the next generation of rays. It also partitions the rays into groups which are to be transferred to the CPMS. CPMS in turn initiates the corresponding HERA processes using the CALLSHELL. The destination of a group of rays depends on the information delivered by RIS/AD. The details are as follows.

3.1 Tasks

The calculation of CARTOON is directed by *tasks*. Tasks are composed of two parts, the *task description* and the *task data*. The task description is transferred to the CPMS when starting the task. It consists of a program name, a parameter list, a working directory, a list of environment variables and the class of the task. The program name localizes the program to be executed in the file system of the destination node. The parameter list contains the parameters required for the execution of the program. The environment variables contain information about access paths and other items typical for them. The class of a task allows processing of the tasks according to priorities.

The data for a task are stored in several files:

myfile-task: contains global information about the picture, like projection, scene diameter, and ray tracing depth.

myfile-query-i: contains the query rays of the i-th task.

myfile-result-i: contains the resulting rays of the i-th task after processing it.

myfile-obj: contains the scene primitives.

A common file system accessible by NFS avoids replicated data. However, reasons of efficiency may make copies necessary in order to avoid a bottleneck in the file system.

3.2 Shader

The central control instance of the image synthesis process is the SHADER process. The shader process reads the rays of result of a HERA process from the corresponding myfile-result. A ray of result is made up by its point of origin, point of destination, type, generation, its source pixel, and intensity. If the point of destination is the intersection point with a scene primitive found, the normal vector, the local coordinates of the intersection point, and the material of the intersected primitive are reported too. The SHADER uses this information to calculate the contribution of this ray to its pixel. It further calculates the rays of the next generation induced at the intersection point, this means a possible ray of reflection, a possible ray of refraction, and a ray of shadow for each light source. Finally the rays are composed into tasks and transferred to HERA processes.

The internal task control of the SHADER works as follows. At the start of the program, the SHADER process partitions the rays of view into groups and defines the corresponding tasks. The tasks are held in three lists, one for the rays of view, one for the rays of reflection and refraction, and one for the rays of shadow. The rays of shadow have the least priority since they do not induce new rays. The running tasks and the terminated tasks are held in additional lists.

The tasks are administrated in a central loop. The first action in this loop is to look for tasks waiting for processing. If any, the AD is consulted for the node best suited for the task. Criteria are

CPMS server: On the node, a CPMS server must be available.

CPMS job: No Hera process is running on this node.

MFLOPS: The processor performance is beyond a given bound.

LOAD: The load of the machine is below a given bound.

If the AD reports a node, the task is sent by a remote procedure call to the CPMS demon of this node. The task is also registered in the list of running tasks, and the SHADER re-iterates the loop.

If the AD does not find a node for the task or if no task is ready for execution, the SHADER checks the list of running tasks. If any, the CPMS demon of the corresponding nodes are asked whether the task has terminated. This continues until either a finished task is found or all tasks are recognized still running. In the first case the SHADER reads the results of the terminated tasks, processes them, and establishes new tasks. The terminated task is moved to the list of terminated tasks, and SHADER re-iterates the loop after some suspension.

If none of the running tasks has finished yet or if there are no running tasks, but still tasks waiting for processing, the loop is re-iterated.

3.3   CPMS and Hera

The tasks distributed by the SHADER are processed by HERA processes. The HERA processes are started and controlled by a CPMS (*Cartoon Process Managing Service*) server running on each node.

The CPMS server registers the task into its internal task table and forks into a new process, the CALLSHELL. The CALLSHELL notifies RIS that a new task is started by this CPMS demon, starts the program and waits for its termination. After termination, the CALLSHELL informs RIS about this event, reports by RPC the exit status and the resources used by the program to the CPMS server, and terminates. The CALLSHELL allows to run the program completely independent of the RIS/AD environment. The exit status code is reported by a **wait** call to the CALLSHELL. The resources are got by a **getrusage** call.

On request by the SHADER, the CPMS server reports whether a dedicated process has terminated, and, if so, its status and its resources used.

The services of the CPMS server are offered by the following procedural interface:

int do_task(JobData): starts the task on the destination node. The structure **JobData** contains the command for starting the process and the necessary parameters. The function returns the process-id to the caller.

int `signal_task(SigData)`: allows to send a signal to the process. If, for example, the SHADER process has to be aborted under control, it can send signals to all its running tasks to kill them as well (*Softkill*).

int `set_usage(TaskResources)`: returns information about the resources used by the task.

`TaskRes check_task(int)`: checks whether a task with the given process-id int is already finished. The structure `TaskRes` contains information, whether and in which status the program was terminated, as well as whether it was terminated by errors occurring during run time.

`TaskRes delete_task(int)`: deletes all information about a task.

3.4 Application Distributor (AD)

The Application Distributor (AD) as well as the Resource Information System (RIS) are tools of value independent of the image synthesis application. Both are installed as RPC servers. AD carries out a strategy of distribution of remote procedure calls in the network. The strategy collects and evaluates the possible alternatives of servers and assigns one of them to the call. The quality of the distribution strategy depends on the evaluation of the information available about the network environment. The source for this information is RIS which is accessed from AD by RPC.

Distribution strategies can be found in the literature under the terms *Load Balancing* and *Load Sharing* [Wang, Morris, 1985]. They may be classified into static/dynamic, deterministic/stochastic, centralized/non-centralized, sender-initiated/receiver-initiated strategies. AD/RIS is designed to allow practically the whole spectrum of these strategies. An exception is process migration i.e. the migration of an already running process from one machine to an other [Eager, Lazowska, Zahorjan, 1988].

Internally, the AD consists of four modules. A *query module* collects the alternatives using the RIS interface. An *evaluation module* calculates the rank of the alternative. The *selection module* selects the best alternative. The result is either returned to the AD client or reported to the *execution module* for processing.

The interface of AD consists of the following functions accessible by RPC:

`ad_get_best_server(QueryList)`: evaluates the alternatives and returns the address of the best server for the given request.

`ad_get_server(QueryList)`: returns a list of servers satisfying the request.

`ad_get_sorted_server(QueryList)`: returns a list of servers satisfying the request, sorted according to their quality.

`ad_rpc(QueryList,Service,Parameter)`: selects the best server for the given requests, carries out the remote procedure call of the request, and reports the result to the client.

`ad_get_best_client()`: transfers the request to an available server which matches the requirements of the request best.

`ad_get_client()`: reports a list of requests, sorted according to requirements.

3.5 Resource Information System (RIS)

During a distributed computation with RIS/AD, a RIS server is running on one of the participating machines. On each machine in the network a process, the RIS *demon*, is running permanently. The RIS demon collects the static and dynamic parameters of the machine and reports them periodically to the RIS server. The periodical update of the information has the advantage that the RIS server has not to collect the necessary data when a request is coming up, but can them report immediately.

By the RIS demon a basic set of information is transferred to the data base of the RIS server. Four types of information are distinguished in the basic set:

node_data: machine related data like machine type, operating system, cpu-type, performance (MIPS, MFLOPS, benchmark results), main memory size, disk capacity, and disk access time. They give a static description of the machine.

load_data: dynamic data like the number of active processes, short- and mid-term load factors, page faults, and process swaps. These data describe the dynamic behavior of the machine.

server_data: information about servers available on this node. A newly started server notifies RIS about its existence. When terminating, a server announces this at RIS. The data about servers stored by RIS are the program name, version number, performance numbers, socket address, and interfaces. These informations correspond to that of the NCS location broker [Apollo Computer, Inc., 1987].

client_data: information about jobs to be processed, like a request identifier, an interface identifier, a function identifier, the parameters, the requests, the date of termination, and the path of reply. These data characterizing client requests allow client initiated distribution strategies. A request is identified by its request identifier. The interface identifier and the function identifier describe the service requested. The date of termination gives a limit for the time interval within the request has to be answered. The path of reply describes the destination the results have to be reported too.

Internally, a RIS server has a table for each registered node in which the entries described above are collected. A symbol table contains all the keys used. From the keys in the symbol table, references are set to those tables having at least one entry with this key.

The interface to RIS consists of the following functions accessible by RPC:

`int ris_set(Data)`: an entry is inserted, modified or removed.

`LoadData ris_get(Data)`: the value of an entry is asked for.

`int ris_clear_host(HostName)`: the table of the indicated host is initialized. This action is performed by the local RIS demon during booting.

`HostList ris_get_host_list(Keyword)`: the symbol table is searched for those nodes having an entry under `Keyword`. If `Keyword` is the empty string, all registered nodes are reported.

`int ris_dump_host_tab(FileName)`: the data base is textually saved on the file `FileName`.

`int ris_init_tab(Name)`: all tables are re-initialized.

4   Performance analysis

The following idealized worst case performance analysis is based on the CREW-PRAM model, cf. e.g. [Borodin, Hopcroft, 1985].

Proposition.
Suppose the access to the scene and the tasks is by concurrent read, the access to the results by exclusive write. Let further be n the number of primitives of the scene, m_i the number of rays of the generation i, $i = 1, \ldots, r$, m the total number of rays processed, s the number of rays in a task, p the number of processors, γ_1 the weight of the preprocessing time for rays, γ_2 the weight of the query time, γ_3 the weight for the time of reporting the results, reading the results by the SHADER, and composing the tasks of the next generation. Then, using the time bounds of section 2, the total time of computation, $T(n,m,p)$, of the distributed ray-z-buffer algorithm is bounded by

$$T(n,m,p) \leq \gamma_3 \cdot m_0 + \sum_{i=1}^{r}(\lceil \frac{m_i}{s \cdot p} \rceil \cdot (\gamma_1 \cdot P(s) + \gamma_2 \cdot n \cdot Q(s)) + \gamma_3 \cdot m_{i+1})$$

$$\leq \tilde{\gamma}_3 \cdot m + (\frac{m}{s \cdot p} + r) \cdot (\tilde{\gamma}_1 \cdot s \cdot \log^2 s + \tilde{\gamma}_2 \cdot n \cdot s^\alpha \log s).$$

The first term in the first line of the formula, $\gamma_3 \cdot m_0$, estimates the time requirements for partitioning the rays of views in jobs. The sum is over a term bounding the time requirements of the rendering processes and the partitioning of the next generation rays into tasks. The expression $\lceil m_i/(s \cdot p) \rceil$ gives the maximum number of rendering processes that must be executed sequentially. The time requirements for one process consists of the preprocessing time, bounded by $\gamma_1 \cdot P(s)$, and the query time, estimated by $\gamma_2 \cdot n \cdot Q(s)$. The resulting m_{i+1} new rays are partitioned into new jobs within $\gamma_3 \cdot m_{i+1}$ time. The formula shows a limit in the speed-up obtainable which is expressed in the term $\lceil m_i/(s \cdot p) \rceil \geq 1$. In the second line of the formula, $P(s)$ and $Q(s)$ are replaced by the bounds of section 2.

A higher degree of parallelism is possible if the ray-z-buffer algorithm itself is parallelized [Müller, 1989]. The reason is that the partioning of the rays performed by the quadtree is more adapted to the expected queries than the partioning proposed for the distributed version here. On the other hand, it can be expected for our distributed version that the arrangement of the rays resulting from a line-wise processing of the image induces some coherence favorable for query processing too. Furthermore, our version avoids the strong dependency in time of the more sophisticated approach and lets some degree of freedom in the arrangement of the jobs on the processors. Finally, the structure of the system is less complicated, thus easier implementable, and the distribution can be controlled more flexible.

The distributed version has two bottlenecks, the sequential calculation of new jobs by the SHADER and the concurrent access by several processes to the same data, like the given scene and the results of intersection. The time requirements at this bottleneck are estimated by the term $\tilde{\gamma}_3 \cdot m$ in the analysis above. The value of $\tilde{\gamma}_3$ depends on the access behavior of the processes which can be hardly predicted for asynchronous processes. For example, reporting and reading of the results may not be totally sequential since the rendering processes may have different running times so that the accesses may occur overlapped. The analysis of the bottlenecks are subject of the experimental analysis carried out in the next section.

5 Measurements

The computing environment of the measurements consisted of Sun 4 workstations (Fig. 3, left). The performance of most of them was approximately 12 MIPS, except of the workstation orion which had approximately 15 MIPS. The workstations were connected by a LAN in thin-Ethernet-technology. There were additional 25 workstations in the network not used for the experiments but occasionally loading the network.

The tests were performed with five scenes showing the same motive, a reflecting text in front of a rectangular mirror and two spheres. The text and the rectangle consist of triangles. The scene is illuminated by two point light sources. The number of scene primitives is increased by refining the rectangle into sub-rectangles without changing the visual impression of the picture. The scene sizes are listed in Fig. 3. The pictures were calculated at a ray tracing depth of either one or four, i.e. one respective four generations of reflection and refraction.

In most cases the experimental approach was as follows. The SHADER process controlling the image synthesis is running on orion. orion also holds the data on its local disk. Hence the node with the SHADER process is not loaded by any rendering activity, and vice versa, the rendering nodes only are involved in rendering and not in administration. For the experiments, one, three, six, and nine rendering nodes were used. In all but the case of nine nodes, the rendering nodes were diskless.

The times of computation measured concern the complete image synthesis procedure. They are calculated as difference between the start time and the finishing time of the SHADER process. Sometimes, the cpu times of all processes as well as the times for system calls (I/O ...) and the real used time (global time) are shown too.

The critical parts of CARTOON are the accesses to the file system and the sequentialization by the SHADER process. Parameters of control are the size of tasks and the

<table>
computing environment nodes:

machine	diskless	server
borneo	no	–
celebes	yes	corse
corse	no	–
fidji	no	–
hawai	yes	kuba
island	yes	kuba
juist	yes	corse
kuba	no	–
orion	no	–
orkney	yes	corse
taiwan	yes	corse
timor	yes	kuba
sumba	yes	borneo
</table>

sizes of test scenes:

scene	# primitives
t3	3 792
t14	14 328
t35	34 966
t56	55 700
t235	234 877

sizes of tasks:

identifier	# view	# refl./refr.	# shadow
e10a5s7.5	10 000	5 000	7 500
e10a5s7.5	15 000	7 500	11 250
e20a10s15	20 000	10 000	15 000
e30a15s22.5	30 000	15 000	22 500
e50a25s37.5	50 000	25 000	37 500

Figure 3: Computing environment and task configurations.

number of nodes. Subject of analysis is the calculation time of CARTOON dependent on these parameters.

5.1 Influence of the task size

One parameter influencing the time of computation is the number of rays in a task. Small tasks have the advantage that more tasks have to be distributed. This allows a more flexible reaction on the current load of the participating rendering nodes. Short tasks are also favorable if a higher number of nodes is available, since then there are enough tasks to let them participate all. A natural limit of the length of the tasks is the main memory size of the rendering nodes. Big tasks may cause paging, slowing-down the calculation. The advantage of big tasks in turn is that the good asymptotic behavior of the data structures of the ray-z-buffer algorithm can only be played out with increasing size. Further the complete scene has to be read less frequently than for short tasks.

In order to measure the influence of the task size on the calculation time, jobs with different size were calculated for all five scenes with one respectively three nodes. Five configurations of different numbers of rays of view, rays of reflection and refraction, and rays of shadow were used, cf. Fig. 3. The number of rays in the different categories was chosen so that the storage requirements were similar in the three groups. The identifier in the table codes the number of rays of view (e), reflection and refraction (a), and shadow (s).

Fig. 4, left, shows the cpu time and the total time for the scene t35 for ray tracing depth 4 and one rendering node. Fig. 4, right, shows the same information in the case of three rendering nodes. The resolution of the picture was 512×512. The measurements show the total time decreasing with a growing task size. If the task size becomes larger the paging rate increases which in turn increases the time of calculation.

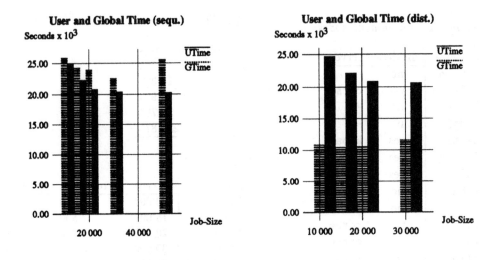

Figure 4: CPU time and total time dependent on the task size, one rendering node (left) and three rendering nodes (right).

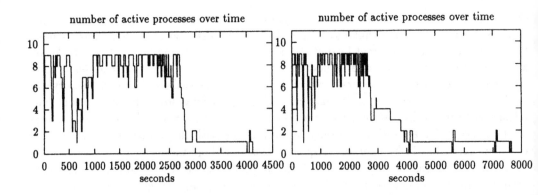

Figure 5: Number of active rendering processes over time during image synthesis with nine rendering nodes and one SHADER node, ray tracing depth 1 (left) and 4 (right).

Fig. 5 shows protocols of calculations with ray tracing depth 1 and 4. The graphics can be divided into three phases. In the first phase, the calculation of the rays of view, the number of processes varies considerably. The SHADER process initially produces a set of tasks. Since the rendering processes work faster for rays of view than the SHADER process is able to process the results, the set of tasks will be reduced soon. After some time, the SHADER process has created tasks based on the result files of the rays of view. This initializes the second phase. Since the new tasks (rays of reflection/refraction) run considerably longer than the first tasks, the SHADER process is able to process the results faster than the rendering processes can produce new results. Hence the jam of result files is dissolved. The third phase covers the flat curve at the end of image synthesis when only one task for rays of reflection and refraction and one task for rays of shadows are processed. The influence of the sequential termination grows with increasing size of the tasks. Experiments on the scenes t35 and t56 with tasks of doubled size have shown results which were 12% – 17% worse.

Consequently, for a higher number of nodes large tasks have further disadvantages. If the number of rays of reflection or refraction has become so small that only one or a few tasks are generated in one generation, the calculation can only be distributed on few machines thus diminishing the degree of parallelism. For small task sizes more tasks are generated so that more nodes can work in parallel.

A solution of this problem, however not applied here, consists in adapting the task size. In the main phase tasks of a size efficient with respect to asymptotic running time may be defined while in final phase the size of the tasks might be reduced in order to fill the nodes. In the following tasks of fixed size `e10a5s7.5` are used.

5.2   Distribution of the computation time of rendering tasks

Fig. 6 shows the total times of tasks in separate for rays of view, rays of reflection/refraction, and rays of shadow. The variance is considerable, in particular for the rays of reflection and refraction.

A reason for the different running times lies in the number of intersection test performed, and, in relation, the number of intersection points occurring between rays and primitives for a given task. In particular, for higher generation of rays it might happen that they are interreflected between primitives, and thus are guaranteed to have intersection points.

5.3   Influence of the number of nodes

In order to determine the influence of the number of machines on the calculation all scenes were calculated with one, three, six, and nine render nodes, and one additional SHADER node. Fig. 7 compiles the computing times for the ray tracing depth 1 and 4.

For parallel computations the influence of the number of nodes is usually expressed by the speed-up. The speed-up is the quotient of the times of calculation of the sequential case against the parallel case. The first number in the parentheses behind the times in Fig. 7 shows the speed-up quotients in this sense.

The speed-up quotients obtained are poor. One reason is the long sequential terminating phase already described in sect. 5.1. The better second numbers in the parentheses

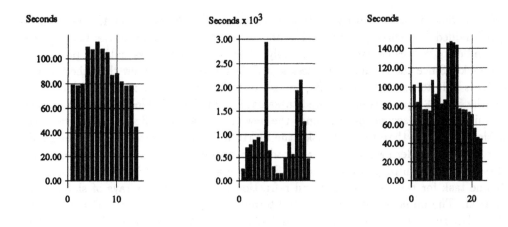

Figure 6: Total times of the tasks with rays of view (left), rays of reflection and refraction (middle) and rays of shadow (right), executed during image synthesis.

ray tracing depth 1:

	# rendering nodes			
scene	1	3	6	9
t3	5 499 (1.0/1.0)	3 388 (1.6/1.6)	2 772 (2.0/2.0)	3 062 (1.8/1.8)
t14	9 854 (1.0/1.0)	3 614 (2.7/2.7)	2 916 (3.4/3.4)	2 988 (3.3/3.6)
t35	18 350 (1.0/1.0)	6 843 (2.7/2.8)	4 380 (4.2/4.3)	4 222 (4.3/4.7)
t56	30 056 (1.0/1.0)	10 068 (3.0/3.0)	6 415 (4.7/4.7)	6 020 (5.0/5.1)
t235	92 778 (1.0/1.0)	34 175 (2.7/2.7)	20 166 (4.6/5.0)	15 770 (5.9/6.0)

ray tracing depth 4:

scene	1	3	6	9
t3	6 757 (1.0/1.0)	4 292 (1.6/1.7)	3 191 (2.1/2.2)	3 113 (2.2/2.3)
t14	11 627 (1.0/1.0)	5 032 (2.3/2.4)	4 294 (2.7/3.3)	4 054 (2.9/3.7)
t35	22 557 (1.0/1.0)	10 461 (2.5/2.7)	8 394 (3.1/4.0)	7 761 (3.3/5.6)
t56	35 553 (1.0/1.0)	17 254 (2.5/2.7)	11 731 (3.7/4.9)	11 544 (3.8/5.0)
t235	133 106 (1.0/1.0)	54 076 (2.5/2.9)	37 327 (3.6/4.9)	35 069 (3.8/5.3)

Figure 7: Times of computation in seconds and speed-up quotients (in parentheses).

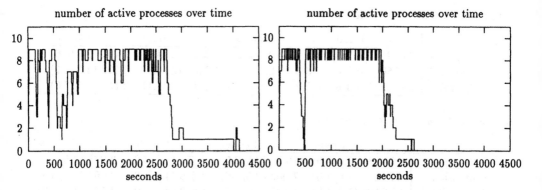

Figure 8: Number of active rendering processes over time during image synthesis with nine rendering nodes and one shader process (left) respectively four shader processes (right).

in Fig. 7 are obtained by cutting off the terminating phase. Regarding these numbers appears legal because of the remarks at the end of section 5.1. The corrected numbers give an impression of the speed-ups which might be achievable.

5.4 Influence of the number of shader processes

Another reason for the bad speed-up values is the bottleneck at the SHADER process. The SHADER process may occasionally not be able to process the results as fast as they are delivered. The bottleneck can be reduced by using more than one SHADER process. In the following multiple SHADERs are introduced by partioning the picture in several subpictures each of which is controlled by a separate SHADER process. In the experiments reported here four subimages are used. Now four SHADER processes apply for the rendering nodes. Fig. 8 shows the distribution of the processes for calculations with one respectively four SHADER processes. The effect is like expected (Fig. 9, first table, row 3). While the SHADER process is reading a result file, an other shader process uses the free rendering nodes for its tasks. Since now four processes are working on the result files, neither a jam nor a gap of tasks occur.

5.5 Influence of separate control

Up to now the shader processes and the rendering processes ran on different nodes in order to eliminate the influence of a local file system at the rendering nodes. The measurements show that the administrative nodes with the SHADER are idle for a large portion of time. Hence it is natural to use them during idle periods for rendering too. For this purpose orion was now loaded by the RIS/AD servers and one resp. four SHADER processes. A rendering process was additionally started on orion if the short-term and medium-term load factor were below a given threshold. The results are compiled in Fig. 9, second table. The load by one SHADER process and the RIS/AD servers is so low that in the sequential case a speed-up was achieved, also because of the local file system of orion. Four SHADER processes, however, load the machine so heavily that the threshold of the load factors was quickly achieved in the initial phase of the calculation.

one additional administration node:

	1 node	3 nodes	6 nodes	9 nodes
1 s/rek 4	25 896 (1.0/1.0)	10 461 (2.5/2.7)	8 394 (3.1/4.0)	7 761 (3.3/5.6)
1 s/rek 1	18 350 (1.0/1.0)	6 843 (2.7/2.8)	4 380 (4.2/4.3)	4 222 (4.3/4.7)
4 s/rek 1	16 129 (1.0/1.0)	5 805 (2.8/2.8)	3 151 (5.0/5.1)	2 653 (6.1/7.0)

no additional administration nodes:

	1 node	3 nodes	6 nodes	9 nodes
1 s-r/orion	17 684 (1.0/1.0)	7 056 (2.5/2.5)	4 753 (3.7/3.8)	3 905 (4.5/4.6)
4 s-r/orion	17 684* (1.0/1.0)	7 002 (2.5/2.6)	3 886 (4.6/4.9)	3 067 (5.8/6.6)
4 s-r/unlimit.	17 684⁻ (1.0/1.0)	6 883 (2.6/2.7)	4 623 (3.8/4.0)	3 704 (4.8/5.3)
4 s-r/2+2	17 684⁺ (1.0/1.0)	6 570 (2.7/2.8)	3 714 (4.8/5.0)	2 777 (6.4/7.2)

* measured: 26 757
⁻ measured: 22 780
⁺ impossible configuration

two additional administration nodes:

	1 node	3 nodes	6 nodes	9 nodes
4 s/2+2	16 474 (1.0/1.0)	5 621 (2.9/3.0)	3 288 (5.0/5.2)	2 224 (7.4/7.7)

Figure 9: Results for scene t35, ray tracing depth 1.

Until now at most one CPMS process was running on a rendering node. Now the restriction is abolished. Processes are now allowed to be started until the load factor exceeds 2.5. The SHADER process is running on orion. The results are displayed in Fig. 9, row 3 of the second table. They show that cutting the limits of the number of processes on a node leads to a speed-up in only one case. Often there were running three to five HERA processes on one machine, hindering one another.

5.6 Influence of secondary memory

A further bottleneck may come from the fact that up to now the input data for image synthesis lay on the same disk. In order to quantify the influence of secondary memory in this case, the scene t35 was calculated with two administration nodes, each of them having two running SHADERs. The results are shown in Fig. 9, row 4 of the second table and the third table. Fig. 10 shows the process behavior. Different from the previous plots, a very balanced behavior can be recognized.

Thus in order to unburden the file system it is useful to distribute the data on several disks attached to different nodes. The input data are accessed only in the reading mode and can be held in multiple copies. The result files of the rendering processes can be distributed on several disks which are in turn accessed by the SHADER. This reduces the number of accesses per disk. With increasing number of nodes, however, the Ethernet may become the bottleneck.

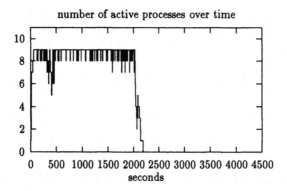

number of active processes over time

Figure 10: Process behavior for two administrating machines with separate disks and two SHADER processes on each of them.

5.7 Summary

Five aspects of image synthesis by a distributed version of breadth-first ray tracing were investigated. These are the mutual dependency of tasks, the influence of the size of tasks, the bottlenecks by the administrating SHADER process respectively the file system, and the restriction of the number of processes on a node. The results are as follows. The mutual dependency of tasks consisting of rays of different generations enforces a sequentialization of the image synthesis process if the number of rays is small. By a refined partioning of the tasks, this effect might be reduced. The size of tasks induces two opposite effects. A high number of rays in a task optimizes the query time due to the sublinear time requirements of query processing. Small tasks, in contrary, cause more jobs which can be distributed more uniformly over the rendering nodes. A single SHADER process is demanded too much, already for a small number of rendering nodes, in processing the results and in constructing new tasks. This bottleneck can be remedied by introducing more than one SHADER process, for example by partitioning the picture into subpictures each of which has its own SHADER process. A significant better efficiency is also obtained by distributing the data on more than one file. This makes particular sense for calculations with a higher number of nodes involved.

Fig. 11 gives a survey of the best speed-up quotients obtained for the different number of nodes, and the experiments for which the best speed-up was achieved.

6. Concluding remarks

In this contribution, breadth-first ray tracing was investigated as an alternative to conventional depth-first ray tracing. It could be demonstrated that this approach is not only of theoretical interest. Breadth-first ray tracing and the ray-z-buffer algorithm involved can be implemented practically, at least when simplifying the data structures somewhat, and can be used for image synthesis. Although the implementation shows the theoretically predicted asymptotic time behavior, the times of computation are high when compared with good implementations of conventional ray tracing. This property certainly depends

	1	1 + 1	2 + 1	3	1 + 3	2 + 3
t	15 660	16 129	16 474	6 570	5 805	5 621
su	1.0/1.0	1.0/1.0	1.0/1.0	2.7/2.8	2.8/2.8	2.9/3.0
pt	15 660	32 258	49 442	19 710	23 220	28 105
case	sequ.	4 s/rek 1	4 s/2+2	4 s-r/2+2	4 s/rek 1	4 s/2+2

	6	1 + 6	2 + 6	9	1 + 9	2 + 9
t	3 714	3 151	3 288	2 777	2 653	2 224
su	4.8/5.0	5.0/5.1	5.0/5.2	6.4/7.2	6.1/7.0	7.4/7.7
pt	22 284	22 057	26 307	24 999	26 530	24 464
case	4 s-r/2+2	4 s/rek 1	4 s/2+2	4 s-r/2+2	4 s/rek 1	4 s/2+2

Figure 11: Survey of the best speed-ups obtained dependent on the number of nodes (administrating+rendering) involved, including the experiment for which the best speed-up (su) was achieved. Additionaly, the processor-time product (pt) is displayed.

partially on the special C++ implementation. Nevertheless, the problem should be inspected further.

One approach for reducing the unavoidable high time requirements of ray tracing is parallelization. A main part of this contribution is the detailed investigation of the behavior of a distributed version of breadth-first ray tracing. The results are summarized in section 5.7. The hardware platform used consists of a local area network of workstations. This naturally limits the number of processors available. Investigations of breadth-first ray tracing with more processors and different architectures remains still to be done. The use of networks of workstations is of practical interest since the typical application profile of workstations show significant idle times of the processors which can be used for computationally intensive tasks.

The main advantage of breadth-first ray tracing is a requirement of working storage only dependent on the resolution of the picture to be calculated. Usually the maximum resolution of a picture is fixed by technical boundary conditions, like video resolution or the resolution of typical workstation graphics, while the storage requirements of the scene varies strongly with the application. Hence the hardware resources necessary for breadth-first ray tracing can be assumed fixed, independent of the application which has significant implications for practice. However, seen from practice, the storage requirements seem high. Because of the dramatically growing storage capacities available for example in workstations this property seems not to be severe.

References

Apollo Computer, Inc., 1987, Network Computing System (NCS) Reference, Order No. 010200 Rev. 00, 330 Billerica Road, Chelmsford, MA 01824

Birrell, A.D., B. J. Nelson, 1984, Implementing Remote Procedure Calls, ACM TOCS, 2, 39–59,

Borodin, A., J. E. Hopcroft, 1985, Routing, Merging and Sorting on Parallel Models of Computation, J. of Computer and System Science 30, 130–145,

Chazelle, B., 1985, Fast Searching in a Real Algebraic Manifold with Application to Geometric Complexity, Proceedings CAAP'85, 145–156

Dobkin, P.D., H. Edelsbrunner, 1984, Space Searching for Intersecting Objects, Proceedings 25th IEEE FOCS, 387–391

Eager, D.L., E. D. Lazowska, J. Zahorjan, 1988, The Limited Performance Benefits of Migrating Active Processes for Load Sharing, Proc. of the 1988 ACM SIGMETRICS Conference, Measurement and Modeling of Computer Systems, 63–72,

Edelsbrunner, H., E. Welzl, 1986, Halfplanar Range Search in linear Space and $O(n^{0.695})$ Query Time, Information Processing Letters 23, 289–293

Glassner, A., 1989, An Introduction to Ray Tracing, Academic Press, San Diego, CA

Haussler, D., E. Welzl, 1986, Epsilon-Nets and Simplex Range Queries, Proceedings 2nd ACM Symposium on Computational Geometry, 61–71

Kleinrock, L., 1975, Queueing Systems, Vol. I: Theory, John Wiley, New York

Lamparter, B., H. Müller, J. Winckler, 1990, The Ray-z-Buffer – An Approach for Ray Tracing Arbitrarily Large Scenes, Research Report, Institut für Informatik, Universität Freiburg

Leister, W., H. Müller, A. Stößer, B. Neidecker, 1988, "Occursus cum novo" – Computer Animation by Raytracing in a Network, New Trends in Computer Graphics, Springer-Verlag, Berlin, 83–92

Müller, H., 1988, Realistische Computergraphik – Algorithmen, Datenstukturen und Maschinen, Informatik-Fachberichte, 163, Springer-Verlag, Berlin

Müller, H., 1989, Paralleles Ray-Tracing mit günstigem Prozessor/Speicher/Zeit-Trade-Off, CAD und Computergraphik 12(5), 161–170

Overmars, M.H., 1983, The Design of Dynamic Data Structures, Springer-Verlag, Berlin

Peterson, J.W., 1987, Distributed Computation for Computer Animation, Proceedings USENIX87, 24–36

Samet, H., 1990, The Design and Analysis of Spatial Data Structures, Addison-Wesley, Reading, Mass.

Schmitt, A., H. Müller, W. Leister, 1988, Ray Tracing Algorithms – Theory and Practice, in: Theoretical Foundations of Computer Graphics and CAD, NATO ASI Series, Vol. 40, Springer-Verlag, Berlin, 997–1030

Stroustrup, B., 1986, The C++ Programming Language, Addison-Wesley, Reading, Mass.

SUN Microsystems, Inc., Mountain View, CA., 1990, Network Programming Guide

Wang, Y.-T., R. J. T. Morris, 1985, Load Sharing in Distributed Systems, IEEE Transactions on Computers C-34, 204–217

Welzl, E., 1988, Partition Trees for Triangle Counting and Other Range Search Problems, Proceedings 4th ACM Symposium on Computational Geometry, 23–33

Willard, D.E., 1982, Polygon Retrieval, SIAM J. on Comput. 11, 149–165

Yao, A.C., 1982, Space-Time-Tradeoff for Answering Range Queries, Proceedings 14th ACM STOC, 128–135

Yao, A.C., F.F. Yao, 1985, A General Approach to d-dimensional Geometric Queries, Proceedings 17th ACM STOC, 163–168

Restricted Orientation Computational Geometry[*]

Bengt J. Nilsson[††]   Thomas Ottmann[†]   Sven Schuierer[†]
Christian Icking[§]

Abstract

In this paper we survey some results in restricted orientation computational geometry. The aim is to embed our own results into a more general context. We discuss methods for making object queries, computing shortest paths, and questions on restricted orientation convexity. Furthermore, we give an optimal algorithm for computing shortest paths when three arbitrary orientations are allowed for path links and obstacle edges.

1   Introduction and Definitions

Many problems in computational geometry become easier when the number of orientations of the objects concerned is restricted. This holds, in particular, for visibility, shortest path, and query processing problems. In this paper we discuss the underlying methods for efficient storage and computation of geometric objects with a fixed number of orientations.

We now present some definitions that will be needed throughout the rest of this paper. First we deal with the definition of the direction and orientation of a line. The *direction* of a line l is defined as the (counterclockwise) angle the line forms with the x-axis and is denoted by $\Delta(l)$. The *opposite direction* $\bar{\Delta}(l)$ of $\Delta(l)$ is defined as $\Delta(l) + \pi$. We define the *orientation* of a line l as the one value in $\{\Delta(l), \bar{\Delta}(l)\}$ that is in $(-\pi/2, \pi/2]$. It is denoted by $\theta(l)$.

In the following we deal with sets of orientations which will be denoted by $\mathcal{O}$ where $\mathcal{O} \subseteq (-\pi/2, \pi/2]$. We say a line l is $\mathcal{O}$-*oriented* or an $\mathcal{O}$-*line* if $\theta(l) \in \mathcal{O}$. In this way we can talk also of $\mathcal{O}$-rays or $\mathcal{O}$-line segments. If $\mathcal{O}$ consists of only one orientation, say θ, then we also talk of a θ-*oriented* set or a θ-*set*. As for the representation of $\mathcal{O}$ we assume in the following that $\mathcal{O}$ is given as a sorted list of c orientations $\mathcal{O} = \{\theta_1, \theta_2, \ldots, \theta_c\}$ with $-\pi/2 < \theta_1 < \theta_2 < \cdots < \theta_c \leq \pi/2$. Here, c is usually some small previously defined constant. Two orientations α_1 and α_2 in $(-\pi/2, \pi/2]$ with $\alpha_1 < \alpha_2$ are called *neighbouring* if there is no orientation of $\mathcal{O}$ in the interval (α_1, α_2) or if $[\alpha_1, \alpha_2]$ completely contains $\mathcal{O}$. In particular, we assume that we can search for a given orientation in $\mathcal{O}$ in time $O(\log c)$ and, within the same time bound, report the next smaller and larger neighbours in $\mathcal{O}$

---

[*]This work was supported by the Deutsche Forschungsgemeinschaft under Grant No. Ot 64/5–4.
[†]Institut für Informatik, Universität Freiburg, Rheinstr. 10–12, W-7800 Freiburg, Germany.
[‡]Department of Computer Science, Lund University, Box 118, 221 00 Lund, Sweden.
[§]Fernuniversität Hagen, Praktische Informatik VI, Elberfelderstr. 95, W-5800 Hagen 1, Germany.

if the orientation is not in $\mathcal{O}$. We also assume that it is possible to do a clockwise or counterclockwise traversal of the orientations in $\mathcal{O}$ in time $O(c)$.

If the orientations in $\mathcal{O}$ are not referred to explicitly and only the number of orientations in $\mathcal{O}$ is of interest, we also use the following terminology. A set of segments and polygons in the plane or in space (a set of polyhedra) is called *c-oriented* if the orientations of the segments and edges of the polygons (of the polyhedra) are taken from a fixed set of c orientations. Each object in a c-oriented set is called a *c-oriented object*.

As an example consider a set of 2-oriented polygons in the plane. We may assume w.l.o.g. that the two orientations are just the horizontal and vertical direction. Thus, a 2-oriented polygon is a rectilinear polygon, and the "rectilinearly oriented geometry" is an intensively studied but special case of "c-oriented geometry".

The paper is now organized as follows. In the next section we give an overview of efficient methods for storing restricted orientation geometric objects so as to be able to make intersection queries and related operations as fast as possible. Section 3 is then concerned with a survey of the two dimensional restricted orientation shortest path problem among obstacles. In Section 4 we give an optimal algorithm to compute a three oriented shortest path among non-intersecting homothetic triangular obstacles. Finally, Section 5 deals with some results on restricted orientation convexity and visibility. In particular, we concern ourselves with the definition and efficient computation of the $\mathcal{O}$-convex hull and the $\mathcal{O}$-kernel of a polygon.

2 Query Processing for c-oriented Sets of Objects

When dealing with sets of objects in two- or three dimensional space it is natural to pose queries which take the spatial aspects of the geometric objects into account. The given set of objects and the respective query object may belong to the same or to different classes of geometric objects. An example for the first case is the *polygon intersection query*: Given a set S of simple polygons in 2-space and a simple query polygon P in 2-space; report all polygons in S which have a non-empty intersection with P. An example for the second case is the *visibility query*: Given a set of polygonal faces in 3-space and a viewing ray as query object, i.e., a point v and a viewing direction θ in 3-space; report the first face F that lies immediately below v in direction θ. It is easy to state dozens of geometric query problems of this kind. In each case, one can further distinguish between a *static* version of the query (where no insertions and deletions on the given set of objects are allowed) and a *dynamic* version (where the dictionary operations insert and delete are applicable to the set of objects).

Solving a geometric query problem requires to find a data structure for storing the set of objects such that by using the structure the respective queries can be answered efficiently. In the dynamic case it must also be possible to update the structure efficiently after an insertion or a deletion. Solutions to dynamic query problems are quite often used as the crucial building blocks in algorithms for solving important geometrical problems like the hidden-line-elimination and the hidden-surface-removal problems.

The large variety of geometric queries contrasts surprisingly with the small number and the simplicity of (dynamic) structures to store geometric objects. Segment trees, interval trees, range trees, and priority search trees are the structures of choice for storing sets of points and sets of parallel line segments in 2-space (see [PS85]). These structures are then cleverly combined to represent more complicated sets of objects in the plane and in higher dimensional space.

It was Güting [Gut83] who first introduced the notion of a c-oriented set of geometric objects and explored the technique of decomposing a geometric query for these sets such that the above mentioned standard structures became applicable.

Recall that a set of segments and polygons in the plane or in space (a set of polyhedra) is called c-*oriented* if the orientations of the segments and edges of the polygons (of the polyhedra) are taken from a fixed set of c orientations.

We will now briefly survey some results found in the literature for query processing for c-oriented sets of geometrical objects. Our aim is to exemplify the two main principles for solving these problems. The first is the technique of decomposing a query into directions and the second is the technique of building hierarchical structures from simpler ones.

As a first example we sketch the solution of the *stabbing number query* problem, cf. [Gut83]:

Object set: A set S of c-oriented simple polygons in the plane (without vertical edges and with a total number of n edges).

Query object: A point $q = (x, y)$.

Answer: The stabbing number of q in S, that is, the total number of polygons in S which enclose q.

This problem can be solved as follows: For each of the c-orientations a "slanted" segment-range tree is constructed. For a given orientation, this is a segment tree storing all edges of polygons in S which are parallel to the given orientation. Each of these edges is represented by $O(\log n)$ subintervals, each of which corresponds to a node in the tree. The subintervals stored at a given node of the segment tree (comprising the first level of the structure) are ordered according to increasing y-values and stored in a range tree. Thus, we have a hierarchical structure, a segment tree with a range tree associated to each node in the segment tree. Figure 1 shows an example of the structure storing a slanted set of five edges. The second level of the structure (i.e., the internal structure of the nodes of the segment tree) is not shown completely. Instead of visualizing the range tree structures we have just depicted the subintervals in y-order.

Furthermore, each polygon edge e has attached to it a tag which is -1 if e is a top edge of a polygon having the interior of the polygon below it and which is $+1$, otherwise. A polygon $P \in S$ contains a query point $q = (x, y)$ if the total number of bottom edges of P below q exceeds the total number of top edges of P below q by exactly 1. Therefore, a stabbing number query for a point $q = (x, y)$ can be answered by performing a search on each of the c slanted segment-range trees and determining the total sum of tags of all edges below q. In each tree, x is used as a search argument to determine the at most $O(\log n)$ nodes in the first level structure which contain subintervals stabbed by x. If we store in each inner node of the range trees on the second level the sum of all tag values of its sons, we can determine in $O(\log n)$ steps per node of the first level the sum of all tags attached to intervals below (x, y). The total sum of these numbers is the stabbing number. This shows that the stabbing number can be computed in time $O(c \cdot \log^2 n)$.

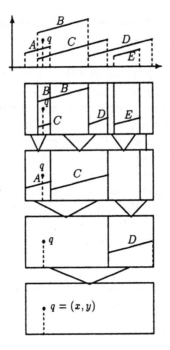

Figure 1: Example of a slanted segment-range tree.

By augmenting the segment-range tree with additional links (—a technique called "layering"—) the query time can be improved to $O(c \cdot \log n)$. The structure can be constructed in time $O(n \log n)$ and requires $O(n \log n)$ space.

It should be obvious that a slanted segment-range tree as described above can also be used to answer *intersection queries* with a vertical line segment efficiently. In order to report all line segments intersecting a given vertical query segment with end points (x, y_1) and (x, y_2), search the segment tree with the x-value and report at each node on the search path all those (slanted) line segments which fall into the range $[y_1, y_2]$ at this x-value using the range tree. This takes time $O(\log^2 n + k)$ where k is the size of the answer. Extending this observation we can immediately solve the c-oriented line segment intersection searching problem (*LSI-searching*), for short, cf. [Gut84] which is defined as follows.

Object set: A set $\mathcal{L}$ of n c-oriented line segments in the plane.

Query object: A c-oriented line l.

Answer: All line segments in $\mathcal{L}$ having a non-empty intersection with l.

We simply consider all c^2 possible pairs (ς, ς') of orientations. For each pair (ς, ς') with $\varsigma \neq \varsigma'$ we build a segment-range tree for the segments in $\mathcal{L}$ parallel to ς as before, that is, we assume w.l.o.g. that ς' is vertical. The LSI-searching problem for a line segment l in orientation ς' can now be solved by posing intersection queries to all $c-1$ segment-range trees storing the subsets of $\mathcal{L}$ with segments parallel to ς, $\varsigma \neq \varsigma'$, and, finally, by determining those line segments in $\mathcal{L}$ which are parallel to l and overlap with l.

The first $c - 1$ queries are the well-known ones discussed above; the latter one can easily be answered in time $O(\log n + t)$ and space $O(n)$, where t is the size of the answer, by using a structure which composes a binary search tree and an interval tree, see [Gut84].

The LSI-searching problem is one of the subproblems to which the *polygon intersection searching problem* can be reduced. This problem is defined as follows.

Object set: A set $\mathcal{P}$ of c-oriented simple polygons in the plane with a total number of n edges.

Query object: A c-oriented simple polygon Q.

Answer: All polygons $P \in \mathcal{P}$ such that P and Q have a non-empty intersection.

Two arbitrary polygons P and Q intersect if and only if two edges of P and Q intersect, P is completely contained in Q, or Q is completely contained in P. We know already how to report all those polygons in $\mathcal{P}$ which have a non-empty edge intersection with the query polygon Q. We solve the LSI-searching problem for each edge of Q. In order to solve the polygon intersection searching problem we have to solve the two remaining inclusion problems. For that purpose, we first represent Q by an (internal) point and report all polygons in P containing this point. This is a variant of a stabbing query. Next we represent each polygon in $\mathcal{P}$ by an (internal) point and report all points contained in the query polygon Q. This is a variant of a range query with a polygonal region as the query region. Güting [Gut84] shows how to handle both problems. We only mention the remarkable fact, that again hierarchical combinations of well known structures like interval, range, and priority search trees are sufficient for this task.

All query problems and their solutions discussed so far are static. That is, no insertions or deletions are allowed for the given set of c-oriented objects. In most cases, it is straightforward to see that the hierarchical structures to solve the static variant of a query problem can be dynamized. In any case, general techniques like global or partial rebuilding can be applied to dynamize the structures. However, in many cases, one can do better by using so-called semi-dynamic structures. In this case, the set of objects may change between queries. However, it is not possible to insert arbitrary objects but only those which belong to a prespecified global set of objects.

In order to give an example for this situation we will now discuss a special case of the hidden-line-elimination problem (HLE-problem, for short) .

Let us assume that we are given a set of c-oriented faces in 3-space such that all faces are parallel to the x-y-plane and each face has constant z-coordinate. We would like to report the parts of the input faces visible from a point at $z = \infty$. For the case $c = 2$ this special case of the HLE-problem is known as the *window rendering problem*: We assume that the set consists of isothetic rectangles which are given in front-to-back order, see Figure 2.

For lines of sight parallel to the z-axis the visible portion (from a point at $z = \infty$) is shown in Figure 3.

We assume that all faces are known in advance. The visible portion of the input scene can now be computed as follows: Because the faces are given in front-to-back order, we

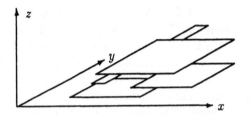

Figure 2: A special case of the HLE-problem.

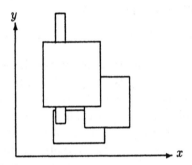

Figure 3: A view from $z = \infty$.

can deal with them one after the other in that order and maintain the visible contour of the faces dealt with so far.

In the case of rectangular faces, the visible contour is a rectilinear polygon. In general it is a c-oriented polygon. Let us assume that C is the current contour and R the next face in front-to-back order. Then, we have to compute

- all edge intersections of R and C,

- all edges of R completely inside/outside C,

- all edges of C completely inside R.

This allows us to compute the visible portions of R and to update the contour C. Figure 4 shows an example for the case that C is a rectilinear polygon and R is a rectangle. The contour C may be considered as a dynamic set of c-oriented line segments: The portions of C whose projection is covered by the projection R do not contribute to the new contour, hence, have to be removed from C; and portions of R outside C become a part of the new contour, hence, have to be inserted into C.

Note that all segments which ever belong to C during the front-to-back sweep through the input scene are segments with endpoints in a previously known discrete raster. Thus, we have a semi-dynamic case.

From the above discussion it should be clear that this special case of the HLE-elimination problem can be reduced to the *dynamic* version of the polygon intersection searching problem for c-oriented polygons.

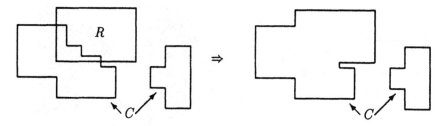

Figure 4: The contour of a set of rectangles.

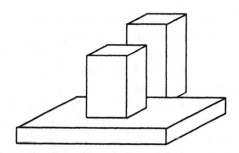

Figure 5: Hidden line elimination of c-oriented faces.

The details of this construction can be found in [GO87] where it is shown that the window rendering problem for a set of n isothetic rectangles can be solved in time $O((n + k) \log^2 n)$ where k is the size of the output. This was the first output-sensitive solution for a special case of the HLE-problem. It can easily be extended to sets of c-oriented polygonal faces given in front-to-back (depth-)order. The solution has been improved and extended many times, cf. [Ber88,Ber90,GAO90,PVY90].

Unfortunately, the dynamic contour maintenance technique cannot solve the case of arbitrary polygons and of faces with no depth-order, i.e., with cyclic overlap. Both problems, i.e., arbitrary polygonal faces and cyclic overlap, have been solved by applying new techniques and structures. In the current context we are only interested in the case where the given set of faces is c-oriented; but there may be no front-to-back (depth-)order of the faces. An example is shown in Figure 5.

A technique called *tracing visibility maps* invented by de Berg, Overmars, and Sharir [dBO90,OS89] leads to an output sensitive algorithm for solving the HLE- and the hidden surface removal problem.

For a given set $\mathcal{F}$ of non-intersecting faces in 3-space the visibility map $\mathcal{M}(\mathcal{F})$ is computed. That is, a polygonal decomposition of the projection plane into maximal regions where a single face (or no face at all) from $\mathcal{F}$ is visible. The edges of $\mathcal{M}(\mathcal{F})$ are parts of the projections of edges of faces in $\mathcal{F}$. The vertices of $\mathcal{M}(\mathcal{F})$ are either visible vertices of faces in $\mathcal{F}$ or visible intersections between projected face edges. It can now be shown that each connected component of $\mathcal{M}(\mathcal{F})$ must contain at least one visible vertex of a face in $\mathcal{F}$. Hence, $\mathcal{M}(\mathcal{F})$ can be computed in two steps: First, compute for each

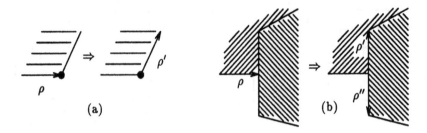

Figure 6: A step in tracing the visibility map.

component a visible vertex. Second, trace the component starting from a visible vertex.

The first step can be solved by answering a *visibility query*, for each vertex v of a face in $\mathcal{F}$: Lift v against the viewing direction to a point v' such that v' is visible and then determine the first face in $\mathcal{F}$ below v' in the viewing direction. Vertex v is visible if and only if the first face below v' in the viewing direction is the one containing v. The second step requires to answer *ray shooting queries*: When running along a visible ray ρ starting from a visible vertex we will either reach another visible vertex of a face in $\mathcal{F}$ or the edge will become hidden by some face in $\mathcal{F}$, see Figure 6 (a) and (b).

In the first case we can immediately continue tracing the visibility map by following ray ρ' starting from the next visible vertex. In the second case (and in order to distinguish between the two cases) we have to find the first intersection of the ray ρ with the projection of an edge that passes above ρ. Then, we continue tracing the visibility map by following both rays ρ' and ρ'' starting at the intersection point. From this discussion it should be clear that we have to answer the following queries efficiently: First, the *visibility query* defined as follows:

Object set: A set $\mathcal{F}$ of c-oriented faces in 3-space.

Query object: A visible query point q.

Answer: The first face in $\mathcal{F}$ that lies immediately below q in the viewing direction (or report that no face lies below q).

The second query is the *ray shooting query*:

Object set: A set $\mathcal{F}$ of c-oriented faces in 3-space.

Query object: A ray ρ in 3-space which is parallel to one of the c-orientations.

Answer: The first intersection of the projection of ρ with the projection of an edge of a face in $\mathcal{F}$ that passes above ρ.

de Berg and Overmars [dBO90] show how to build structures that can be used to answer these queries. In both cases the possibility of decomposing a query into c^2 and c^3, respectively, simpler ones is exploited. Then, appropriate variants of segment and range trees are built for each of the simpler queries. That is, again the techniques of decomposing a query into directions and of building hierarchical structures suffice.

3 Restricted Orientation Shortest Paths

*Yes, there are two paths you can go by, but in the long run
there's still time to change the road you're on.*

J. Page, R. Plant.

The problem of computing the shortest paths between points in d-space where the paths avoid given obstacles is a problem that lies in the main stream of Computational Geometry. This problem has several applications in Robotics, VLSI-design, and Geographical Information Systems. In most cases the obstacles are represented by a set of polyhedra having a total of n vertices.

There are several versions of this problem; the *one-shot problem* where we are given a point pair, s and t, and asked to find a shortest path between the two points; the *semi-query problem* where we are given one point, the target, and asked to preprocess the environment so that source point queries can be performed as fast as possible returning a shortest path between the source and the target; and finally, the *full-query problem* where we are asked to preprocess the environment so that queries for arbitrary source and target points can be made as fast as possible.

It can be shown that the general shortest path problem is NP-hard in more than two dimensions [Can87] so most results have been given for the two dimensional problem. Many algorithms that solve the one-shot problem in two dimensions involve the construction of a "critical graph". This graph maps a set of points in the plane to nodes of the graph and ensures that for each pair of points a shortest path between the points is modeled by the shortest path between the corresponding nodes of the graph. The critical graph, typically, has $\Theta(n^2)$ size and the problem, thus, being reduced to a graph searching problem can be solved by application of Dijkstra's algorithm [Dij59] or some other shortest path-finding algorithm (e.g., [FT84]) to the graph, yielding running times of $O(n^2)$.

We will in this section describe sequential algorithms that solve restricted orientation shortest path problems in the planar setting. The first question to ask is, of course, what we mean by restricted orientation shortest paths? We can restrict

1. the orientation of the shortest path links,

2. the orientation of the boundary edges of the obstacles, or

3. the orientation of both the shortest path links and the edges of the obstacles.

3.1 Definitions

In the following let $\mathcal{O}$ be a finite set of orientations $\mathcal{O} = \{\theta_1, \theta_2, \ldots, \theta_c\}$. A path $\mathcal{P} = l_1, \ldots, l_k$ consisting of line segments l_i, for $1 \leq i \leq k$ is said to be *valid* if each $\theta(l_i) \in \mathcal{O}$, for $1 \leq i \leq k$. The length of a valid path denoted $len(\mathcal{P})$ is the sum of the euclidean lengths of the line segments.

The $\mathcal{O}$-*distance* $d_{\mathcal{O}}(p, q)$ is the length of the shortest valid path $\mathcal{P}$ disregarding obstacles and connecting p and q. Widmayer, Wu, and Wong [WWW87] prove that the path realizing the distance must be monotone with respect to the orthogonals of all orientations in $\mathcal{O}$ and, therefore, the segments of the path can be taken only from the two neighbouring orientations θ_i and θ_{i+1} in $\mathcal{O}$ for which $\theta_i < \theta([p, q]) < \theta_{i+1}$, where $[p, q]$ is the line segment between p and q. If the set of orientations is rectilinear, then the $\mathcal{O}$-distance $d_{\mathcal{O}}(p, q)$ is exactly the L_1 distance between p and q.

3.2 Results Based on Critical Graphs

Larson and Li [LL81] were the first to consider restricted orientation shortest paths. They examine the one-shot problem when path links are rectilinear and the obstacles are arbitrarily oriented simple polygons. They build a version of the critical graph by constructing a node for each of the obstacle vertices together with the source/target points and an edge between two nodes when there is a *staircase* connecting the corresponding points. A staircase is a path between the points which is monotone with respect to the orthogonals of all allowed orientations (in this case the two axes). A Dijkstra type algorithm is then applied to the graph and a shortest path is produced in $O(n^2)$ time.

Clarkson, Kapoor, and Vaidya [CKV87] present an interesting version of the critical graph used to compute the one-shot version of the shortest path among arbitrarily oriented polygonal obstacles in the L_1 metric. Their result does not assume path links to be rectilinear but, as can easily be seen, any L_1 shortest path can be exchanged for a rectilinear path which has the same length although in some cases it has larger size since a rectilinear path may consist of many more segments.

They reduce the size of the graph, the *shortest path preserving graph*, by adding more nodes to it. In the standard critical graph the nodes usually represent vertices of obstacles and the source/target points. Clarkson *et al.* add Steiner points (points not originally in the input description) reducing the size of the graph in this way. This sounds like a contradiction but let us give a hint of how the algorithm works. It recursively constructs nodes and edges of the graph in the following way. For each obstacle vertex and the source and target points, from now on denoted *input points*, a node is constructed. Through the median of the x-coordinates of the input points a vertical line ℓ is placed and for each of the input points that are seen from this line (i.e., the horizontal line segment between the vertex and the line does not intersect the interior of any obstacle) a node of the graph is constructed representing the point on the line having the same y-coordinate as the input point it sees. Additionally, an edge between the node representing the obstacle vertex and the node representing the Steiner point is added. This gives us $O(n)$ Steiner points on ℓ and furthermore we construct edges between nodes corresponding to consecutive points on ℓ when they can see each other (i.e., a vertical line segment between the points does not cross any obstacles); see Figure 7. The scheme is then recursively applied to the input points lying to the left of ℓ and to those lying to the right of ℓ.

Since at each recursive step the number of obstacle vertices we look at is halved, there are $O(\log n)$ levels of the recursion and at each level we add no more than $O(n)$ Steiner points. Thus, at most $O(n \log n)$ Steiner points are constructed in total. Also, since the nodes corresponding to these points have constant degree (at most 4, one for each possible axis parallel direction) the number of edges of the resulting graph is also bounded by $O(n \log n)$. Clarkson *et al.* show how to construct the graph in $O(n \log^2 n)$ time using plane sweep and sorting as their main tools. Once the graph is constructed, Dijkstra's algorithm can be used to find the shortest path in $O(n \log^2 n)$ time.

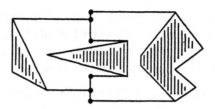

Figure 7: Steiner points and corresponding edges of the Shortest Path Preserving Graph.

Lee, Chen, and Yang [LCY90] use a similar approach to solve the rectilinear shortest path problem among weighted obstacles. In their setting it is allowed to cross the interior of an obstacle but only at additional cost. They achieve the same time and storage bounds as Clarkson *et al.*

Widmayer [Wid90] improves on the result by Clarkson *et al.* by showing how to construct the shortest path preserving graph in time $O(n \log n)$ time which is optimal given the size of the graph.

Reich [Rei91] generalizes the approach taken by Clarkson *et al.* and Widmayer to c arbitrary orientations and shows that the shortest path preserving graph has $O(cn \log n)$ size and can be computed in $O(cn \log n)$ time. The first observation made is that if only two orientations are involved, then they do not necessarily have to be orthogonal. Instead it suffices to do the split along the first orientation θ_1 and compute the "visibilities", the Steiner points that see the input points, along the second orientation θ_2. The idea then becomes to apply this construction first for orientations θ_1 and θ_2, then for θ_2 and θ_3, and so on, each time adding $O(n \log n)$ Steiner points to the graph. The final step is to perform the construction on the orientations θ_c and θ_1. This approach works since a shortest path consists of a sequence of staircases where the segments of a staircase have orientations from a pair of neighbouring orientations. Application of Dijkstra's algorithm to this graph gives the shortest path in $O(cn \log(cn) \log n)$ time.

3.3 Tree based Solutions

de Berg [dB91] looks at the case when both path links and obstacle edges are rectilinear with the further restriction that the obstacle edges form the boundary of a simple rectilinear polygon. His primary interest lies in computing the link shortest path but he shows that in this setting the path computed is also shortest in the L_1 metric. He applies a divide and conquer approach to preprocess the polygon for the full-query problem and subdivides the polygon by a rectilinear chord so that the two parts contain (roughly) the same number of vertices and he shows that only if the source and target lie in different components will the path intersect the chord. In this way de Berg builds a balanced tree with the polygon at the root, the two divided polygons being the sons of the root, and so on. The leaves are reached when the cut provides rectangular shapes. By building a point location structure on top of the rectangles [Kir83,EGS86,ST86], the rectangles containing the source and target query points can be found in $O(\log n)$ time. The nearest common ancestor of the two rectangles is found in the tree and the two paths from each rectangle to the nearest common ancestor can be glued together at the chord representing the cut at this node and thus the path is obtained in additional time proportional to its size. Since each vertex of the polygon is maintained at each level of the tree, the time and storage bounds for the preprocessing become $O(n \log n)$.

McDonald and Peters [MP89] give a linear time algorithm in this setting for the one-shot problem. Their idea is the following very simple one. From the source and target points draw lines downward until the boundary of the polygon is reached. Connect the two intersection points with the part of the boundary between them. This gives a so called starting path for which it is shown that, when certain local transformations between points on the path that are either horizontally or vertically visible are performed, the length of the path can be reduced. The transformations are simply the introduction of shortcuts in the path. When no more transformations can be performed, the resulting path is called the ending path. McDonald and Peters prove that the ending path is shortest in both the L_1 and link metric and can be computed in linear time.

Schuierer [Sch91] improves on the result by de Berg and gives an optimal linear time and storage algorithm for the full-query problem. By using mainly the same ideas as de Berg he partitions the polygon into *histograms* and constructs the *dual tree* of this partition. A histogram is a monotone rectilinear polygon where one of the monotone chains is a single line segment and the dual tree is a tree with a node representing each histogram in the partition and an edge between two nodes if the corresponding histograms share an edge. In the same way as before, a point location structure is built on top of the histograms and once the source and target points are queried, the algorithm finds in $O(\log n)$ time the histograms the two points lie in and the common ancestor in the tree is found. In more or less the same way as before the two paths are glued together at the common ancestor in additional time proportional to the size of the output.

de Berg, van Kreveld, Nilsson, and Overmars [dBvKNO90] consider shortest paths in a setting where both path links and obstacle edges are rectilinear. (Obstacles are polygonal regions.) The metric they use is a linear combination of the L_1 and the link metric, i.e., a the cost of a path is the Euclidean length of the segments it consists of plus an additional cost for each turn the path makes. Using the standard critical graph approach they are able to solve the one-shot problem in $O(n^2)$ time. The main contribution, however, is based on the observations that Dijkstra's algorithm gives the shortest path from the source point s to all the vertices (the so called *shortest path tree*) and that the second link of a shortest path from any point to s (in the metric considered, the generalization of the L_1 and link metric) touches a vertex. These observations provide the means for the construction of an additional data structure which can be attached to the shortest path tree and answers target queries in $O(\log n + k)$ time where k is the size of the reported path. The data structure, called the *slab tree*, is a variant of the segment tree and subdivides the plane into regions such that for every point in one region the second link of a shortest path to the source always passes through the same vertex. The technique of subdividing the space into regions such that for every point in one region the solution to some problem is "similar" and, hence, can be precomputed, has very general applications. This technique is called the *locus approach*.

The data structure can be computed in $O(n \log n)$ time, uses $O(n \log n)$ storage, and can be attached to the shortest path tree computed by any of the methods in Section 3.2

as long as both path links and obstacle edges are rectilinear.

3.4 Results based on Plane Sweep

In some cases efficient solutions can be developed if it can be proven that the shortest path is monotone with respect to some direction. In such cases a plane sweep can be performed along this direction, yielding the shortest path.

Lee and Preparata [LP84] consider the case when the obstacles are parallel line segments and show how to compute the euclidean shortest path between two points in $O(n \log n)$ time. They also extend the result using the locus approach so that the semi-query problem can be solved with $O(n \log n)$ time preprocessing and $O(\log n + k)$ query time where k is the size of the resulting path.

In the case of the Lee and Preparata algorithm the similarity constraint for the locus approach is such that for every point in one region the first link of the shortest path to the target point joins the same obstacle end point. Once the subdivision has been constructed, which they do with a plane sweep approach, planar point location [Kir83,EGS86,ST86] can be used with the query point and the resulting path, thus, reported.

de Rezende, Lee, and Wu [dRLW89] show that in the case when the environment consists of non-intersecting axis-parallel rectangles and the path is rectilinear, a subdivision can be constructed so that the one-shot problem can be solved in $O(n \log n)$ time. We give a fairly detailed description of their construction.

The first observation they make is that a rectilinear path starting at the source point s and that is monotone with respect to both the x- and the y-axis is a shortest path to s. That is, for any point p on the path, the subpath between s and p is a shortest path between the two points. Thus, the subdivision is made in the following way. We define the $(0, \frac{\pi}{2})$-path to be the monotone path (w.r.t., both the x- and the y-axis) starting at s such that the links of the path directed away from s have direction 0 and $\frac{\pi}{2}$ (the first one having direction 0). The path is not allowed to intersect the interior of any obstacle and it has smallest y-coordinate over all such paths. Similarly the $(0, \frac{\bar{\pi}}{2})$-path, is the monotone path starting at s such that the links of the path directed away from s have direction 0 and $\frac{\bar{\pi}}{2} = \frac{\pi}{2} + \pi$ (also with the initial segment having direction 0). The path is not allowed to intersect the interior of any obstacle and it has largest y-coordinate over all such paths. Rotating the setting three times by $\frac{\pi}{2}$ (counterclockwise) and each time applying the definition gives the $(\frac{\bar{\pi}}{2}, 0)$-path, the $(\frac{\bar{\pi}}{2}, \bar{0})$-path $(\bar{0} = 0 + \pi)$, and so on, a total of eight paths which subdivide the plane around s. Number the paths P_1 to P_8 counterclockwise starting with the $(0, \frac{\bar{\pi}}{2})$-path and let region R_i be the region bounded by the two paths P_i and P_{i+1} when $1 \le i < 8$ and let R_8 be the region bounded by the paths P_1 and P_8. Since the boundaries of the regions are shortest paths, the shortest path from s to any point in a region R_i will be contained in the region R_i. This result is used when the shortest paths are computed. Because of symmetry with respect to a rotation of $\frac{\pi}{2}$ it is only necessary to show how to find the shortest path from s to t when t lies either in R_1 or R_2. de Rezende et al. show that if t is in R_1, then the shortest path from s to t is monotone with respect to the x-axis and if t is in R_2, then the shortest path is a staircase between the two points and, therefore, monotone with respect to both the x- and the y-axis. To compute and report the shortest path a plane sweep algorithm is used. The shortest paths from s to all corners of the obstacles is computed during the sweep

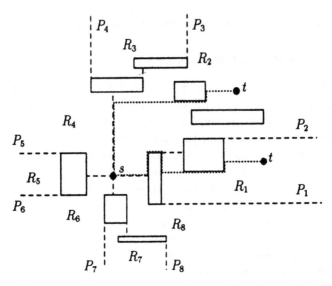

Figure 8: The subdivision around s and examples of two shortest paths.

with the help of a ray shooting data structure. Hence, the shortest path can be computed in $O(n \log n)$ time. Refer to Figure 8.

To find the correct region that t lies in binary searches on the boundary paths are performed (on the x-coordinate) which yields at most four segments having the same x-coordinate as t. Additional tests are performed to find the segments (and, hence, the paths) immediately above and immediately below t, thus, specifying which of the regions contain t in $O(\log n)$ time.

If the plane sweeps for each region are performed in a preprocessing step, then ray shooting can be used to solve the semi-query problem in $O(\log n + k)$ time where k is the size of the reported path.

In a recent paper by ElGindy and Mitra [EM91] the full-query problem is solved using the techniques we have displayed. The setting is the same as in the result by de Rezende et al., i.e., the obstacles are non-intersecting axis parallel rectangles and paths must be rectilinear. The construction is based on the critical graph approach. The graphs they construct, the *carrier graphs*, are three directed acyclic planar graphs of linear size that contain the shortest paths between all pairs of obstacle corner points. The carrier graphs can be computed by plane sweep in $O(n \log n)$ time. Using the planar separator theorem of Lipton and Tarjan [LT79], which partitions the m nodes of a planar graph into three sets V_1, V_2, and S in such a way that a node in V_1 is never adjacent to a node in V_2 and conversely a node in V_2 is never adjacent to a node in V_1, $|V_i| \leq 2m/3$, for $i = 1, 2$, and $|S| \leq \sqrt{8m}$, they build a balanced tree structure by associating the nodes in S to the root of the tree and the connected components of V_1 and V_2 to the children of the root. The separator theorem is then recursively applied to the connected components of V_1 and V_2 to build the subtrees.

For directed acyclic graphs there exists a linear time algorithm [Joh77] (in the number of nodes and edges) which computes the shortest path tree from a node. This algorithm is applied to all the nodes of the graph in S (the nodes associated to the root of the tree) and then recursively down the tree. The complete preprocessing requires $O(n^{1.5})$ time and shortest path queries on pairs of nodes in the carrier graphs can be performed in $O(\sqrt{n} + k)$ time where k is the size of the output.

To handle arbitrary points it is sufficient to note that the carrier graphs subdivide the plane into rectangular regions and, therefore, the shortest path passes through one of the four corner points of the region. This corner point corresponds to a node of a carrier graph and, hence, it is only necessary to locate the regions that the query points lie in and then perform a query in the above described data structure. To do this we apply a planar point location strategy as in [Kir83,EGS86,ST86] using $O(n \log n)$ preprocessing and $O(\log n)$ query time.

4 An Algorithm for Three Orientations

In this section we present, in detail, an algorithm combining the techniques of Lee and Preparata [LP84] and de Rezende et al. [dRLW89] to find the shortest path given three orientations, i.e., a solution to the one shot problem. Our algorithm is a clarification and correction of a previous version presented by Icking [Ick88].

We begin by making the assumption that the orientations of obstacle boundary edges are the same as the allowed orientations for shortest path links. In the case of two orientations, any staircase consists of segments from the two orientations and is monotone with respect to the orthogonals of the orientations. A subdivision of the space according to staircases as in Figure 8 therefore has boundaries that are shortest paths. When more orientations are allowed it is usually not possible to find a subdivision into regions with boundaries that are monotone with respect to the orthogonals of the orientations and, hence, such a subdivision does not necessarily have boundaries that are shortest paths. However, if the following constraint holds, it is possible to prove that a subdivision allowing a plane sweep approach to compute shortest paths can be constructed.

Constraint: *If θ is a direction with $\theta = \theta_i$ or $\theta = \bar{\theta}_i$ with $\theta_i \in \mathcal{O}$, then there is an orientation $\theta' \in \mathcal{O}$ such that the first obstacle edge hit by a ray in direction θ starting at any point always has orientation θ'. Furthermore, all obstacles are convex.*

If four or more orientations are given, then the only set of obstacles that obeys our constraint is a set of line segments all having the same orientation. In this case a plane sweep algorithm similar to the one presented by Lee and Preparata [LP84] solves the shortest path problem. In the case of two orientations a simple generalization of the algorithm by de Rezende et al. [dRLW89] does the trick.

Hence, it remains to show what happens in the three orientations case. To obey the constraint it is easy to see that obstacles must be either $n/2$ parallel line segments, in which case we can apply the technique mentioned above, or $n/3$ non-intersecting homothetic triangles with sides having their orientations in $\mathcal{O}$. We assume the latter to be the case and w.l.o.g. that $\mathcal{O} = \{-\frac{\pi}{4}, 0, \frac{\pi}{4}\}$. We denote the orientations by their index in $\mathcal{O}$, that is, $-\frac{\pi}{4}$ is orientation 1, and so on. The approach we take is to compute the shortest path tree from a fixed source point s to all obstacle vertices and a given target point t. Given this tree it is then a simple matter of following the path from t to s to get the shortest

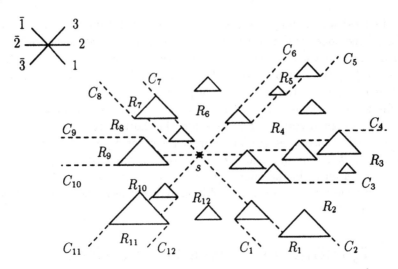

Figure 9: The subdivision into at most twelve regions around s.

path between these points. We will also show how, with some additional preprocessing, the semi-query problem can be solved in this setting.

Since a half line having any of the allowed directions intersects a boundary segment of an obstacle which always has the same orientation, we can construct a subdivision according to the following rule. From s move in direction 1 until an obstacle is reached. The boundary segment has, because of the constraint, always orientation 3. Thus, the move can continue in direction 3 or $\bar{3}$. Assume we move in direction $\bar{3}$ until the obstacle corner is reached and then we continue recursively in direction 1 as before. This gives a chain of segments having direction 1 and $\bar{3}$ which we call the $(1,\bar{3})$-chain. In the same way we can define the $(1,3)$-chain, the $(2,\bar{3})$-chain, the $(2,3)$-chain, and so on. We get a total of at most twelve chains (two for each initial direction) that subdivide the plane around s. Number the chains in counterclockwise order starting with the $(1,\bar{3})$-chain as $C_1, C_2, \ldots, C_{12}$. We denote by R_i the region bounded by the chains C_i and C_{i+1} for $1 \leq i < 12$ and by R_{12} the region bounded by C_{12} and C_1. Refer to Figure 9.

We only have to show how to compute the shortest path when t lies in $R_1, \ldots, R_4$. This is because the regions R_5 and R_9 are symmetric to R_1, R_6 and R_{10} are symmetric to R_2, R_7 and R_{11} are symmetric to R_3, and R_8 and R_{12} are symmetric to R_4. The symmetry is with respect to rotation but does not follow immediately with our choice of $\mathcal{O}$. However, if you chose $\mathcal{O} = \{-\frac{\pi}{3}, 0, \frac{\pi}{3}\}$, this symmetry is easily seen and it holds, of course, for every choice of three orientations. Furthermore, the regions R_1 and R_3 are symmetric with respect to a rotation and a mirroring operation. Thus, we only have three cases to take care of and we show how to handle each of them separately.

We will use a ray shooting structure enabling us to find the first obstacle we hit when we move from a point in one of the six allowed directions. Edelsbrunner $et~al.$ [EOS84] provide such a structure and we state their result in the following lemma.

Lemma 4.1 ([EOS84]) *The first obstacle hit from a query point in a fixed direction can*

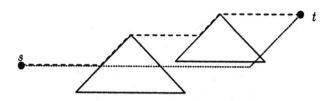

Figure 10: Example of a direct optimal path (dashed lines).

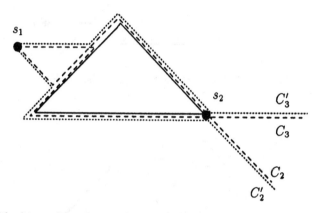

Figure 11: A blocking obstacles with corner point s_2 and incident chains C_2, C_3, C_2', and C_3'.

be found in $O(\log n)$ time with a data structure that can be computed in $O(n \log n)$ time and $O(n)$ storage.

Using this result we can build the shortest path tree from s to all the vertices (including t). We begin by showing the construction for the easiest case which arises when t lies in R_2.

4.1 The Target Lies in R_2

We show that for any point in R_2 there is a simple way to find a shortest path to s. To do this we first need the following definition.

Definition 4.1 *A direct optimal path between two points p and q is any path which has length equal to $d_O(p, q)$; see Figure 10.*

Note that not all pairs of points have a direct optimal path between them.
    Furthermore, we need the concept of a blocking obstacle.

Definition 4.2 *A blocking obstacle is an obstacle which is incident to both the chain C_2 (the $(1,3)$-chain starting at s) and C_3 (the $(2,\bar{3})$-chain starting at s).*

The two chains C_2 and C_3 cross at a corner point of a blocking obstacle. We denote this point s_i with $2 \le i \le r$ in the order in which they appear on C_2 as the chain is traversed

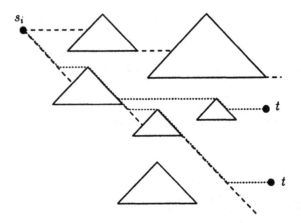

Figure 12: Shortest paths when t lies in R_2.

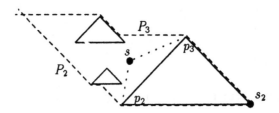

Figure 13: Illustration for the proof of Lemma 4.3.

starting from s. In addition we let $s = s_1$. Let C_2' be the lower chain when we traverse C_2 and C_3 from s and similarly let C_3' be the upper chain. These chains consist of alternating sequences of subchains from C_2 and C_3 where the switches occur at the points s_i and at the edges of blocking obstacles that have orientation 3. Refer to Figure 11 for an example.

We are now in a position to state the crucial lemma which provides the means to solve the shortest path problem when t is in R_2.

Lemma 4.2 *For a point t in R_2 there is a corner point s_i such that t can be connected to s_i with a direct optimal path.*

Proof: We construct a path consisting of segments with directions $\bar{2}$ and $\bar{1}$ from any point t to s_i.

From t move in the $\bar{2}$ direction until an obstacle or the chain C_2 is hit. Continue in the $\bar{1}$ direction until the top corner of an obstacle is reached and continue recursively until the segment of C_2 that is incident to s_i is reached. Finally, follow the segment incident to s_i of C_2 to the point s_i. The path, thus, constructed is monotone with respect to the orthogonals of all orientations in $\mathcal{O}$ and, hence, a direct optimal path from t to s_i; see Figure 12. $\qquad\square$

Next we need to show how to compute the shortest path from s to all the points s_i. We begin by proving the result for s and s_2.

Lemma 4.3 *Let B be the blocking obstacle having a corner point at s_2 and let p_2 be the corner point of B (different from s_2) that C_2' passes. Similarly, define p_3 as the corner point of B that C_3' passes. The shortest path from s to s_2 is either the shortest path from s to p_2 joined with the line segment between p_2 and s_2 or the shortest path from s to p_3 joined with the line segment between p_3 and s_2.*

Proof: It is enough to prove that the shortest path must pass through either p_2 or p_3. We give a constructive proof of this.

Construct a chain P_2 starting from s_2 in the following way. The first link is the segment between s_2 and p_2 and from p_2 move in the $\bar{1}$ direction until an obstacle is hit. By the constraint the edge touched has orientation 2. Continue in direction $\bar{2}$ until the corner point of the obstacle is found and continue from there in a recursive manner. This gives a sequence of segments from s_2 that are directed in the $\bar{2}$ and $\bar{1}$ directions. Since P_2 is monotone with respect to the orthogonals of all orientations in $\mathcal{O}$, one possible shortest path between any point on P_2 and s_2 is the subpath of P_2 between the two points. Similarly construct a chain P_3 starting at s_2, passing p_3, and consisting of links that have directions $\bar{1}$ and $\bar{2}$. By the same argument P_3 is also a shortest path. A shortest path between s and s_2 must intersect either P_2 or P_3; so let q be this intersection point. Since a subpath of a shortest path must also be a shortest path, the part between q and s_2 is either the subpath of P_2 or the subpath of P_3 between these points and therefore the shortest path passes either p_2 or p_3; see Figure 13. □

If we know the shortest path from s to both p_2 and p_3, we can easily find the shortest path to s_2. Repeated application of the lemma establishes similar results for the pairs s and s_i, when $2 < i \leq r$ and, hence, we can incrementally construct the shortest paths from s to all the points s_i for $2 \leq i \leq r$.

To compute the shortest paths from s to the corner points of blocking obstacles we can view these as belonging to the regions R_1 or R_3 respectively and we show how to compute the shortest path from s to these points in the next section. Hence, it remains to be shown how to compute the shortest path tree to all other obstacle vertices in R_2. R_2 consists of a number of disconnected regions with a point s_i, for $2 \leq i \leq r$, at the upper left corner. We construct the shortest path tree from each s_i to the vertices in the same region and in the next section we show how to fill in the parts of the tree between the pairs s_i and s_{i+1}. To build the partial tree we need the ray shooting structure of Lemma 4.1 with rays in the $\bar{2}$ direction.

The construction of the partial shortest path tree is now easy. Incrementally from s_i (using a plane sweep in the 1 direction) construct the shortest paths by shooting backwards from a vertex v in the $\bar{2}$ direction to get the first obstacle edge hit and from there move in the $\bar{1}$ direction to the corner point v' of the obstacle. Attach the shortest path to v by adding the two links made to the shortest path from s_i to the v'. This construction takes $O(n \log n)$ time using the ray shooting structure.

Shortest path queries can now be made as follows. Make a query with our query point t in the ray shooting structure to get the appropriate obstacle edge. Move from the touching point in direction $\bar{1}$ until the vertex v' is reached. The shortest path from t to

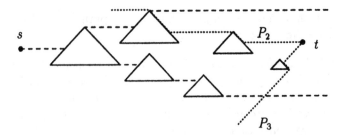

Figure 14: First links of shortest path have direction $\bar{2}$ or $\bar{3}$.

v' consists of the two links used and from v' we can follow the shortest path tree to s, in all using $O(\log n + k)$ time where k is the size of the reported path.

4.2 The Target Lies in R_1 or R_3

Because of the similarity between the regions R_1 and R_3 we only show how to solve the shortest path problem for one of them. We choose to display the algorithm when t lies in R_3. The algorithm is based on plane sweep in the spirit of [LP84]. The sweep line has orientation 1 and updates the shortest path tree at obstacle vertices. The vertices are handled in the order they occur as the sweep line moves from left to right and are stored in a priority queue. As the sweep passes an obstacle triangle it first encounters the *left corner point* and later the two *right corner points* of the triangle.

Unfortunately the points s_i, with $2 \leq i \leq r$, as they were defined in the previous section, can have shortest paths to s that lie alternatingly in the regions R_1 and R_3. Therefore the plane sweeps to compute the shortest path tree must be made simultaneously for both of these regions. By Lemma 4.3 we know that the shortest path to a point s_i is completely specified by the two other corner points of the associated blocking obstacle and, hence, when one of the sweeps reaches a point s_i it must wait until the other sweep reaches that same point before it can proceed, because we must know the shortest paths to both of the other corner points of the blocking obstacle in order to determine the shortest path to s_i.

First we show that we can assume that the paths we construct always start in one of two possible directions.

Lemma 4.4 *If t is a point in R_3, there is a shortest path from t to s that starts with a link having either direction $\bar{2}$ or direction $\bar{3}$.*

Proof: Construct the chain P_2 starting at t by moving in direction $\bar{2}$ until an obstacle is hit. By the constraint the obstacle edge has orientation 1 and we continue in direction $\bar{1}$ until the corner point is reached. Proceed with the scheme recursively to get a chain consisting of links having directions $\bar{2}$ and $\bar{1}$. Similarly construct the chain P_3 starting at t by moving in the $\bar{3}$ direction until an obstacle is hit and continuing in the 1 direction.

Now assume that the shortest path does not start with either a $\bar{2}$ or a $\bar{3}$ directed link. In that case, the shortest path intersects one of the chains P_2 or P_3 at some point q since s lies between the two chains. Since subpaths of a shortest path must also be shortest

Figure 15: The three possible types of staircases.

paths, we can follow the subpath of the constructed chain (P_2 or P_3) from t to q. Since this path is monotone with respect to the orthogonals of all orientations in $\mathcal{O}$, the new path we construct is no longer than the shortest path; see Figure 14. □

A shortest path from t to s consists of staircases between vertices that are direct optimal. Hence, within R_3 we have from the previous lemma that such staircases consist of two segments that are directed (towards s) in the $\bar{2}$ followed by the $\bar{1}$ direction, the $\bar{2}$ followed by the $\bar{3}$ direction, the $\bar{3}$ followed by the $\bar{2}$ direction, and the $\bar{3}$ followed by the 1 direction. We are going to construct shortest paths that prefer to start in the $\bar{2}$ direction from t implying that the staircases consisting of a $\bar{3}$ directed segment followed by a $\bar{2}$ directed one are not used since they can be exchanged for staircases starting in the $\bar{2}$ direction instead. We denote the staircases as type a, b, and c, respectively; see Figure 15.

Lemma 4.5 *There is a shortest path from s to t where t lies in R_3 that is monotone with respect to a line orthogonal to the 1 orientation.*

Proof: From the previous discussion we know that there is a shortest path from s to t consisting of staircases only of the types a, b, and c. These staircases are all monotone with respect to the specified orientation and furthermore so is any chain consisting of appended staircases of these types. □

We apply the locus approach to subdivide the region R_3 into a *shortest path map*, SPM for short, consisting of subregions $R_3(v)$ each having a designated vertex v such that $R_3(v)$ is the locus of the points q having a shortest path from s to q passing v with a final staircase of type a, b, or c. That is, v can be reached from q by a two-link staircase of one of the three above mentioned types. If we let $w(v)$ denote the length of the shortest path from s to a vertex v and break ties by saying that the point q belongs to $R_3(v)$ if vertex v comes after vertex v' in the order of the sweep (denoted $v \succeq v'$), we have formally

$$R_3(v) = \{q \mid w(v) + d_{\mathcal{O}}(v, q) < w(v') + d_{\mathcal{O}}(v', q)\} \bigcup$$
$$\{q \mid w(v) + d_{\mathcal{O}}(v, q) = w(v') + d_{\mathcal{O}}(v', q) \text{ if } v \succeq v'\}.$$

We subdivide each region further into three different regions $R_3^i(v)$, with $i = a$, b, or c according to the type of staircase that gives the shortest path to v. During the sweep we maintain these regions.

The boundary of a region $R_3^i(v)$ consists of sequences of *bisectors*. A bisector is the locus of the points having shortest paths of equal length via the designated vertices of adjoining regions subject to path type restrictions.

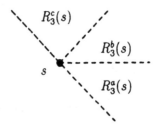

Figure 16: The regions subdividing $R_3(s)$ and their bisectors (dashed lines).

The approach we take is to maintain the set of bisectors that currently intersect the sweep line and keep them in a dictionary in the order they appear on the sweep line when this line is traversed from plus infinity to minus infinity. This allows for fast access of the bisectors and furthermore two neighbouring bisectors in the dictionary bound a region making efficient point location queries on the sweep line possible. We have to make updates of the dictionary at *event points* where topological changes occur to the region boundaries. The updates are performed when the event points are reached by the sweep line. Event points are induced by the occurrence of three different types of events.

1. An obstacle corner point, the source s, or the target t,

2. two (or, in the degenerate case, more) bisectors intersect, or

3. a bisector intersects an obstacle.

The third case need not be considered if we insert bisectors along the sides of the obstacles making these events occur under Case 2. The processing at each event point involves the deletion of old bisectors, the insertion of new bisectors, and the computation of bisector intersection points.

Consider the bisectors bounding the regions associated to the source point s. It is easy to see that the bisectors are half lines starting at s having directions 1, 2, 3, and $\bar{1}$ bounding the regions $R_3^a(s)$, $R_3^b(s)$, and $R_3^c(s)$ respectively. A point in the region to the left of the 1-oriented line passing through s cannot be contained in any of the specified regions since it is not possible to reach s using the allowed types of staircases. Refer to Figure 16.

When v and v' are different vertices with $v \succeq v'$ and the plane sweep locates v in $R_3^i(v')$ we must introduce the bisectors bounding the three regions associated to v. Since there are three different types of corner points and three different types of regions we get a total of nine cases that have to be tested for to correctly introduce the bisectors associated to v.

Let us display the construction for a left corner point v lying in region $R_3^c(v')$. A point p in the region $R_3^c(v)$ can reach v with a staircase of type c and since $v \in R_3^c(v')$, v can reach v' also with a staircase of type c. Hence, from p there is a direct optimal path to v'. We also introduce bisectors along the edges of the obstacles in order to easily detect intersections between obstacle edges and bisectors. The other eight cases are handled in a similar manner; see Figure 17.

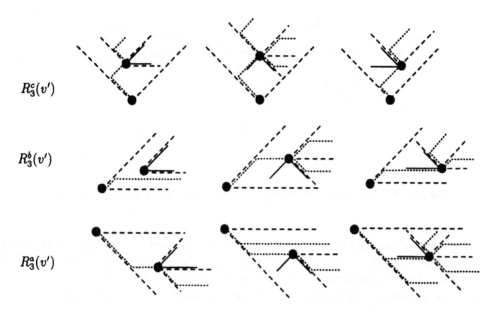

Figure 17: The nine cases of bisectors induced by a corner point v in region $R_3^i(v')$. Dashed lines denote bisectors, dotted lines denote staircases, and solid lines denote obstacle edges.

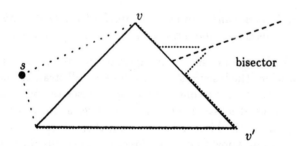

Figure 18: The bisector separating regions associated to the right corner points of an obstacle.

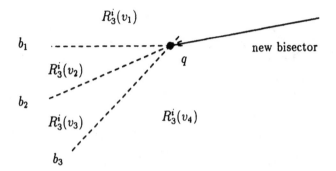

Figure 19: Bisectors intersecting at q and the bisector issuing from q.

When v and v' are the two right corner points of an obstacle a bisector separating the regions associated to these two corner points has to be introduced. This bisector is a line having orientation that bisects the orientations 2 and 3; see Figure 18.

The next question is what happens when two (or more) bisectors intersect.

Lemma 4.6 *If the bisectors $b_1, b_2, \ldots, b_r$ intersect at a point q, then there is only one bisector issuing from q.*

Proof: Assume the bisectors to be counterclockwise ordered and let $R_3^i(v_j)$ be the region directly above bisector b_j. Extend the bisectors past the point q. A point above b_1 can connect to v_1 with the correct type of staircase. Similarly this holds for points below b_r with respect to v_{r+1}. By continuity, there are points past q which are points of the bisector bounding $R_3^i(v_1)$ and $R_3^i(v_{r+1})$ and, therefore, it is the only bisector issuing from q. Refer to Figure 19. □

Finally, we prove that the *SPM* has nice properties.

Lemma 4.7 *The SPM is a planar straight line graph of size $O(n)$ with the regions $R_3^i(v)$ being monotone with respect to a line orthogonal to the 1 orientation.*

Proof: The *SPM* is planar since all the intersection points are nodes of the graph and the edges are straight since the bisectors we introduce are all straight lines. The graph has linear size since we induce at most a constant number of bisectors per obstacle and bisector intersection point removes at least one old and introduces at most one new bisector.

Associate a direction to the bisectors away from their starting point. From the construction of the bisectors we know that these directions lie in the range $[1, \bar{1}]$ implying the monotonicity of the regions. □

We can now describe the algorithm to compute the shortest path tree from s for all the vertices in R_3. Note that we have (part of) the shortest path tree for (some of) the vertices incident to R_2. Also, the shortest path tree for the vertices incident to R_4 can be precomputed if necessary since the paths follow the chain C_4 from the vertex to s. The chain is monotone with respect to the orthogonals of all orientations in $\mathcal{O}$ resulting in direct optimal paths to s for the vertices incident to R_4. The other vertices are stored in a priority queue in the order they appear on the sweep line. Starting at s we construct the

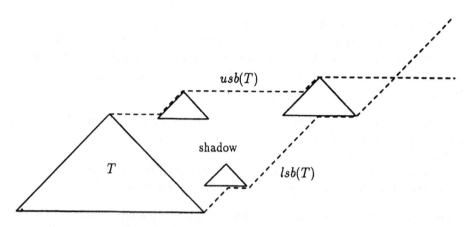

Figure 20: The chains $usb(T)$ and $lsb(T)$ bounding the shadow of obstacle T.

bisectors as in Figure 16 and store them in the dictionary. Event points are then handled in the following way as the sweep line passes them.

We locate the region $R_3^i(v^*)$ containing the event point e by performing a search in the dictionary and check of what type the event point is. If e is an obstacle corner point v, we extend the shortest path tree from v to v^* with a staircase of type i. We induce the bisectors as in Figure 17 and test if v is a right corner point (assume it to be the top one) in which case we also process the other right corner point v' (the bottom one) of that obstacle and compute the bisector separating $R_3^a(v)$ and $R_3^c(v')$ as in Figure 18.

If e is the intersection point of bisectors we simply compute the new one issuing from e. Hence, we must delete the bisectors that intersect at e from the dictionary and introduce a new bisector b starting at e. Once b is computed, it is inserted into the dictionary and we compute the intersection point of b with either the bisector above b or the one below b in the dictionary. The intersection point is then inserted in the priority queue as a new event point. It is clear, since the SPM has linear size, that we can only introduce a linear number of event points. Hence, since searches in the dictionary can be performed in $O(\log n)$ time if the dictionary is implemented as a balanced tree, the total time for the computation is $O(n \log n)$.

If the SPM is explicitly computed, we can preprocess it for point location [Kir83, EGS86,ST86] in $O(n \log n)$ time and, hence, perform shortest path queries to s in $O(\log n)$ time.

4.3　The Target Lies in R_4

This case involves a mixture of the techniques used in the two previous sections, ray shooting and the locus approach. In order to make the distinction between the correct approach to use we need the concept of a shadow.

Let T be an obstacle in R_4. From the top right corner of T move in the 2 direction until an obstacle T' is hit. Continue along the edge of T' in the 3 direction until the top right corner point of T' is reached. Apply the scheme recursively to this corner point to get a chain $usb(T)$ (the upper shadow boundary). In a similar manner we construct the chain $lsb(T)$ (the lower shadow boundary) from the bottom right corner of T by moving in the 3 direction until an obstacle is hit and continuing along this obstacle edge in the 2 direction until the bottom right corner is found. Recursive application provides the sought chain.

Definition 4.3 *The shadow of an obstacle T in region R_4 is the region bounded by the 1 oriented edge of T and the two chains $usb(T)$ and $lsb(T)$ until their first intersection point. Refer to Figure 20.*

A maximal shadow is a shadow which is not contained in any other shadow.

A maximal obstacle is an obstacle whose shadow is maximal.

Note that a pair of shadows are either disjoint or one is completely contained in the other.

We can compute the shadows of the obstacles in R_4 in the following way. Precompute the chains $usb(T)$ and $lsb(T)$ for all the obstacles T in R_4 with plane sweeps in the $\bar{2}$ and $\bar{3}$ directions. Using the ray shooting structures of Lemma 4.1 the chains can be computed in $O(n \log n)$ time. Furthermore the first intersection point between pairs of chains is computed by traversing the chain $usb(T)$ and for each segment perform a binary search over the chain $lsb(T)$ to check for the intersection point. This takes $O(n \log n)$ time for all the chains since the number of segments of all the chains is at most linear. It is now easy to explicitly construct the shadows by joining the first part of the $lsb(T)$ chain to the first part of the $usb(T)$ chain and the 1 oriented segment of T. With the planar point location scheme of [Kir83,EGS86,ST86] we can preprocess the shadows in $O(n \log n)$ time for point location queries that each take $O(\log n)$ time. Using this we can in additional $O(n \log n)$ time find the set M of maximal shadows and preprocess them for planar point location.

This allows us to state the crucial lemma providing the solution to the shortest path problem when t lies in R_4.

Lemma 4.8 *Any point in R_4 that does not lie in a (maximal) shadow has a direct optimal path to s.*

Proof: We construct the path to s. Let t be a point in R_4 not lying in a shadow. From t move in the $\bar{2}$ direction until the boundary of a shadow of some obstacle T is hit. (If no such boundary is hit we stop when the chain C_5 is reached and follow that chain to s.) Follow the chain $lsb(T)$ to the bottom right corner of T and continue recursively in the $\bar{2}$ direction as before. This gives a chain P which at some point intersects C_5 and from there continues to s along C_5. The chain P is monotone with respect to the orthogonals of all the orientations in $\mathcal{O}$ and, hence, is a direct optimal path from t to s; see Figure 21. □

The computation of a shortest path tree for corner points outside the shadows can now be done efficiently along the same lines as in Section 4.1 with a plane sweep using ray shooting and point location in the set M of maximal shadows as the main tools.

In the case that a vertex or the target point t lies in a shadow we note that all the lemmata proved for the case R_3 also hold for the shadows in R_4 and, hence, the locus approach as presented in Section 4.2 can be used. The computations take $O(n \log n)$ time in total.

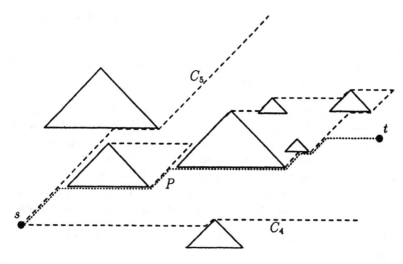

Figure 21: The shortest path from s to t when t lies outside the shadows.

As before these plane sweep operations can be performed in a preprocessing step whereafter queries for a point t can be performed in $O(\log n + k)$ time with planar point location and ray shooting.

We state our result in the following theorem.

Theorem 4.9 *If $\mathcal{O}$ is a set of three orientations and $\mathcal{T}$ is a set of $n/3$ non-intersecting homethetic triangles with sides having their orientations in $\mathcal{O}$, then the algorithm we have described solves the $\mathcal{O}$-oriented one-shot shortest path problem in $O(n \log n)$ time. If $O(n \log n)$ time for preprocessing is allowed, subsequent target queries can be performed in $O(\log n + k)$ time where k is the size of the reported path.*

5 Restricted Orientation Convexity

Another field that has received a considerable amount of interest in restricted orientation geometry is *restricted orientation convexity*, also called *$\mathcal{O}$-convexity*. In the previous sections we considered problems where the orientation of a boundary segment of the objects is restricted to a given set of orientations. We are now no longer concerned with this type of local constraints. Instead, we will investigate restrictions of the *global* shape of the objects. We base these investigations on the concept of *convexity*.

In many applications such as optimization, statistics, and combinatorics [PS85] convex sets allow fast and efficient algorithms. But the requirement of convexity is often too restrictive. As we have seen before one area of particular interest in computational geometry is given by rectilinear geometry. Therefore, several attempts have been made to adapt the definition of convexity to the rectilinear world. It took some effort starting with the work of Montuno and Fournier [MF82], Nicholl, Lee, Liao, and Wong [NLLW84], and Ottmann, Soisalon-Soininen, and Wood [OSW84] before a satisfactory definition of *ortho-*

convexity was developed by Rawlins and Wood [RW88]. They define an ortho-convex set as follows.

Definition 5.1 *A set S is* ortho-convex *if its intersection with any axis parallel line is either empty, a point, or a line segment.*

Rectilinear ortho-convex sets have been studied mostly in the context of polygon covering. We give a short overview of the results in this area. Keil [Kei86] considers the problem of covering a monotone rectilinear polygon with the minimal number of ortho-convex sets. He obtains an $O(n^2)$ algorithm. Reckhow and Culberson [RC87] show that this is indeed optimal and extend his algorithm to polygons with three "dent orientations" [Rec87] within the same time bound. A similar result is achieved by Motwani et al. [MRS88b].

The definition of ortho-convexity should be contrasted with that of a convex set.

Definition 5.2 *A set S is* convex *if its intersection with any line is either empty, a point, or a line segment.*

In the next section we show how to generalize the definitions of convexity and ortho-convexity. The major aim of the new definition is to introduce a parameter such that both of the above definitions are encompassed and the development of "generic" algorithms which treat ortho-convex and convex sets in a uniform way is possible. We start off by introducing some terminology.

5.1 Definitions

In the following we deal with sets of orientations $\mathcal{O}$ that consist of the union of closed intervals $[\alpha_1, \beta_1] \cup [\alpha_2, \beta_2] \cup \cdots \cup [\alpha_c, \beta_c]$ with $-\pi/2 < \alpha_1 \leq \beta_1 < \alpha_2 \leq \cdots < \alpha_c \leq \beta_c \leq \pi/2$. In particular, we assume that it is possible to do a clockwise or counterclockwise traversal of the intervals of $\mathcal{O}$ in time $O(c)$. For a fixed set of orientations $\mathcal{O}$, we can now define what an $\mathcal{O}$-*convex set* is.

Definition 5.3 *A set S is $\mathcal{O}$-convex if its intersection with any $\mathcal{O}$-line is either empty, a point, or a line segment.*

If we take $\mathcal{O}$ to be $(-\pi/2, \pi/2]$, then an $\mathcal{O}$-convex set is convex in the sense of Definition 5.2 and in the same way, we obtain the definition of ortho-convexity for $\mathcal{O} = \{0, \pi/2\}$. We give some examples of $\mathcal{O}$-convex sets in Figure 22.

There are a number of observations that follow immediately from the definition of an $\mathcal{O}$-convex set.

(i) $\mathcal{O}$-convex sets may be disconnected (see Figure 22b).

(ii) The family of $\mathcal{O}$-convex sets is closed under intersection, i.e., if the sets C_i, with i in some index set I, are $\mathcal{O}$-convex, then so is $\bigcap_{i \in I} C_i$.

A family of sets with the last property, is called a *convexity space*. Convexity spaces have been investigated in an abstract setting and numerous results have been obtained in this context [Deg79,Jam82,KW71,Lev51,RW89a,SRW89,Sie77]. In particular, convexity spaces give rise to the notion of a "hull" as the intersection of all sets containing a given set.

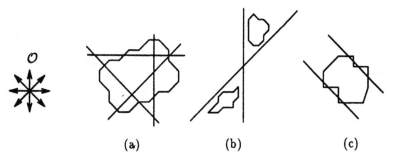

Figure 22: Examples of $\mathcal{O}$-convex sets. (a) and (b) are $\mathcal{O}$-convex, for the given $\mathcal{O}$, while (c) is not.

Definition 5.4 *The intersection of all $\mathcal{O}$-convex sets containing set S is called the $\mathcal{O}$-hull of S and denoted by $\mathcal{O}$-hull(S).*

As can be easily seen the $\mathcal{O}$-hull of a connected set is simply-connected.

In the following we treat three main aspects of $\mathcal{O}$-convexity. First we look at some of the properties of convex sets that have an analog in the theory of $\mathcal{O}$-convexity. We then describe how to compute the $\mathcal{O}$-hull of a polygon in order to illustrate the techniques used for hull computations. Finally, we take a look at a notion of visibility that is based on $\mathcal{O}$-convexity.

5.2   Convexity and $\mathcal{O}$-convexity

As we have pointed out before, $\mathcal{O}$-convexity is a generalization of the usual convexity based on line segments. A natural question that arises in this context is for which properties of convex sets there exist analogs in the theory of $\mathcal{O}$-convexity [RW88,RW89b,Raw87]. Among the numerous interesting properties of convex sets the following ones have been chosen to illustrate what kind of results can be expected for $\mathcal{O}$-convex sets.

1. **Simple connectedness:** A convex set is simply connected.

2. **Intersection:** The intersection of any family of convex sets is again convex.

3. **Halfplane intersection:** A convex set is the intersection of all halfplanes containing it.

4. **Separation:** If p is a point that does not belong to the convex set C, then there is a line that separates p and C.

5. **Visibility:** A convex set contains the line segment between any two points contained in it.

Though the first two properties have already been addressed previously, we include these in the following discussion. As we have seen it is not true that $\mathcal{O}$-convex sets are connected but the components they consists of are simply connected, that is, they do not

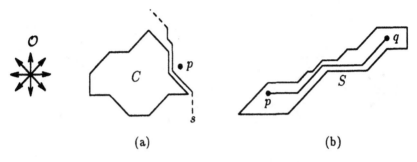

Figure 23: $\mathcal{O}$-halfplanes and $\mathcal{O}$-visibility.

contain holes since any $\mathcal{O}$-line that intersects the interior of a hole does not intersect the set in a point or a line segment. We already noted that the family of $\mathcal{O}$-convex sets form a convexity space and, hence, the second property holds.

Before we are in a position to state an analog to Property 3, we need the concept of $\mathcal{O}$-*stairhalfplanes* which can be viewed as generalizations of halfplanes. A biinfinite $\mathcal{O}$-convex curve s is called an $\mathcal{O}$-*stairline*. The curve s divides the plane into two halfspaces which are called $\mathcal{O}$-*stairhalfplanes*. With this definition we are now able to state an analog to the halfplane intersection property. Note that we have to restrict ourselves to the components of $\mathcal{O}$-convex sets in this case. For the proof of the following statements we refer to [RW89b] and [Raw87].

$\mathcal{O}$-**stairhalfplane intersection:** A connected $\mathcal{O}$-convex set is the intersection of all $\mathcal{O}$-stairhalfplanes containing it (see Figure 23a).

There are two different analogs in $\mathcal{O}$-convexity to the separation property. The first formulation is more a statement about the containment of a point in the $\mathcal{O}$-hull of a set. But if we consider $(-\pi/2, \pi/2]$-convexity, it turns out to be equivalent to the separation property. Note that we have to restrict ourselves again to connected $\mathcal{O}$-convex sets.

$\mathcal{O}$-**separation (1):** A point p belongs to the $\mathcal{O}$-hull of a connected set S if and only if there is an $\mathcal{O}$-line through p that intersects S on both sides of p.

The second statement is a direct consequence of the $\mathcal{O}$-stairhalfplane intersection property.

$\mathcal{O}$-**separation (2):** If p is a point that does not belong to the connected $\mathcal{O}$-convex set C, then there is an $\mathcal{O}$-stairline that separates p and C (see again Figure 23a).

We now turn to the visibility property. As with the separation property there are also two different ways to generalize the visibility property. The first one again involves $\mathcal{O}$-lines.

$\mathcal{O}$-**visibility (1):** If two points in an $\mathcal{O}$-convex set S lie on an $\mathcal{O}$-oriented line, then S contains the line segment between them.

For the second version we need the concept of an $\mathcal{O}$-*staircase* which is defined as a bounded $\mathcal{O}$-convex curve. $\mathcal{O}$-staircases play an important role in the theory of $\mathcal{O}$-convexity and will be investigated more closely in the section about $\mathcal{O}$-visibility. The second analog to Property 5 can now be stated as follows.

$\mathcal{O}$-visibility (2): A connected $\mathcal{O}$-convex set contains one $\mathcal{O}$-staircase between any two points in it (see Figure 23b).

5.3 The $\mathcal{O}$-hull of a Polygon

In this section we are concerned with the computation of the $\mathcal{O}$-hull of a polygon P. The algorithm we present here is based on a characterization of the boundary of an $\mathcal{O}$-convex set. In order to introduce it we need the notion of an $\mathcal{O}$-extremal point. If S is a connected closed set, a point p in S is called $\mathcal{O}$-extremal if there is an $\mathcal{O}$-line that intersects S only in p. Two $\mathcal{O}$-extremal points p and q of a polygon P are called consecutive if p is before q on a counterclockwise traversal of the boundary of P and there is no other $\mathcal{O}$-extremal point between p and q. The point q is then called the successor of p. With this definition the following theorem can be shown [Raw87].

Theorem 5.1 *A simply-connected closed set is $\mathcal{O}$-convex if and only if the parts of its boundary between any two consecutive $\mathcal{O}$-extremal points are $\mathcal{O}$-staircases.*

We now describe an algorithm that computes the $\mathcal{O}$-hull of a simple polygon. The first observation we make is that the $\mathcal{O}$-extremal points of P and $\mathcal{O}$-hull(P) coincide [RW87]. The idea of the algorithm is now to compute the set E of $\mathcal{O}$-extremal points of P and, then, to construct an $\mathcal{O}$-staircase between two consecutive points in E that is as close to the boundary of P as possible. Since the vertices of the convex hull $conv(P)$ of P are those points p of P for which there is some line l that intersects P only in p, E is a subset of the vertices of $conv(P)$. So the first step of the algorithm is to compute the convex hull of P which can be done in linear time [BG84,GY83]. In order to compute E from $conv(P)$ we proceed as follows. For each vertex v of $conv(P)$, we compute the two intervals of orientations $(\alpha_v, \beta_v) \cup (\gamma_v, \delta_v)$ of the lines that intersect P only in v where $\gamma_v = \alpha_v + \pi$ and $\delta_v = \beta_v + \pi$. This can easily be done by looking at the orientations of the neighbouring edges of v. Now, v is $\mathcal{O}$-extremal if and only if $\mathcal{O} \cap ((\alpha_v, \beta_v) \cup (\gamma_v, \delta_v)) \neq \emptyset$. Note that when proceeding from one vertex v to its successor v' on $conv(P)$ we have $\alpha_{v'} = \beta_v$. Hence, by stepping simultaneously through the vertices of $conv(P)$ and the ranges of $\mathcal{O}$ we can find the $\mathcal{O}$-extremal points of P in time $O(n + c)$ if P consists of n edges. Figure 24 illustrates the procedure.

It is now easy to construct an algorithm to step along the vertices in between each pair of consecutive extremal vertices of P and find the the vertices of P which belong to $\mathcal{O}$-hull(P) [RW87]. This is illustrated in Figure 25.

As opposed to computing the $\mathcal{O}$-convex hull of a polygon computing the $\mathcal{O}$-convex hull of a set of points in the plane can only be done for one orientation at a time. The fastest known algorithm runs in time $O(cn \log n)$ and can only process finite sets of orientations [Raw87].

5.4 $\mathcal{O}$-Visibility

$\mathcal{O}$-convexity also leads to a generalized notion of visibility. As line segments are the basis for the definition of "standard" visibility in the plane, we now look at a notion of visibility that is based on $\mathcal{O}$-staircases (see again Figure 23b).

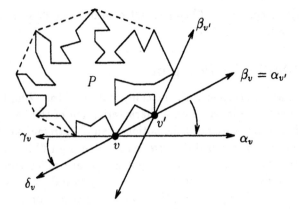

Figure 24: Computing the $\mathcal{O}$-extreme vertices of a polygon.

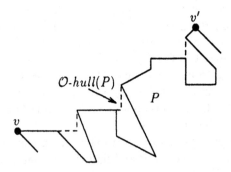

Figure 25: The computation of the $\{0, 90\}$-hull between v and v' of E.

Definition 5.5 *Two points p and q in a set S O-see each other or are O-visible from each other if there is an O-staircase in S that connects p and q.*

As in the case of $\mathcal{O}$-convexity the concept of *ortho-visibility* (i.e., $\mathcal{O} = \{0, \pi/2\}$) has received a lot of attention. Again it has been mostly studied in the context of polygon covering. Culberson and Reckhow consider the problem of covering a rectilinear horizontally monotone polygon with the minimal number ortho-starshaped polygons [CR89] and achieve a $O(n^2)$ algorithm. A polygon P is called *ortho-starshaped* if there exists a point p in P that ortho-sees all other points in P. The point p is also called an *ortho-guard* in this case. Motwani et al. [MRS88a] show that minimally ortho-guarding a simple rectilinear polygon can be done in polynomial time.

If we turn to general $\mathcal{O}$-visibility, some work has been done on computing the $\mathcal{O}$-*kernel* of a polygon [Raw87,SRW91]. The $\mathcal{O}$-kernel of a polygon is defined as follows.

Definition 5.6 *The O-kernel of a polygon P is the set of points in P which O-see all other points in P, i.e.,*

$$\mathcal{O}\text{-}kernel(P) = \{p \in P \mid p \; \mathcal{O}\text{-}sees \; all \; other \; points \; q \in P\}.$$

In the following we will restrict ourselves to simple polygons and finite $\mathcal{O}$.

$\mathcal{O}$-visibility in simple polygons between two points is fairly well understood since it can be decomposed into $\{\theta\}$-visibility between the two points, for each $\theta \in \mathcal{O}$. The following theorem states this more precisely.

Theorem 5.2 *If P is a simple polygon and p and q are two points in P, then we have that*

$$p \; \mathcal{O}\text{-}sees \; q \; if \; and \; only \; if \; p \; \{\theta\}\text{-}sees \; q, \; for \; all \; \theta \in \mathcal{O}.$$

Proof: see [SW91]. □

As an immediate consequence we have that the $\mathcal{O}$-kernel of a polygon P can be obtained as the intersection of all $\{\theta\}$-kernels of P, i.e.,

$$\mathcal{O}\text{-}kernel(P) = \bigcap_{\theta \in \mathcal{O}} \{\theta\}\text{-}kernel(P).$$

Another very interesting property of the $\mathcal{O}$-kernel illustrating the close relationship between convexity and $\mathcal{O}$-convexity is stated in the next theorem.

Theorem 5.3 *If P is a simple polygon, then we have that O-kernel(P) is a connected O-convex set.*

If we are given an algorithm to compute the $\{\theta\}$-kernel of a simple polygon, the above observation about the relationship between the $\mathcal{O}$-kernel and the $\{\theta\}$-kernels immediately yields an algorithm to compute the $\mathcal{O}$-kernel of a simple polygon, for finite $\mathcal{O}$, since the intersection of polygons can be computed efficiently.

So we only have to consider the special case that $|\mathcal{O}| = 1$. W.l.o.g. we can assume that $\mathcal{O} = \{0\}$. Given a polygon P, we wish to determine $\{0\}$-*kernel(P)*. That is, the set of all points which see every point in P via a $\{0\}$-staircase which lies in P. Note that a $\{0\}$-staircase is a curve which is monotone with respect to the y-axis as can be easily seen

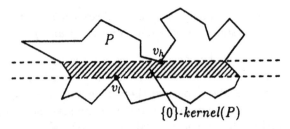

Figure 26: Computing the {0}-kernel of a polygon.

from the definition of a monotone curve [PS85]. In the following we describe an algorithm to find {0}-*kernel*(P) in linear time and space.

Consider a reflex vertex v_i in P where v_{i-1} and v_{i+1} are either both above or both below v_i. These vertices create two types of "extrema"—*reflex maxima* and *reflex minima*. Note that a horizontal edge with two reflex vertices may also form a reflex maximum or minimum. With these definitions we have the following result [SW91,Raw87].

Lemma 5.4 *Given a simple polygon P, {0}-kernel(P) is the horizontal slab of P between the lowest reflex minimum and the highest reflex maximum.*

The above lemma implies that we just have to find the lowest reflex minimum v_l and highest reflex maximum v_h and then output the left and right part of the boundary of P with a y-range in the interval $[v_h, v_l]$ in order to compute {0}-*kernel*(P). This is illustrated in Figure 26. Clearly, all of this can be done in linear time. The above considerations can be summarized in the following theorem.

Theorem 5.5 *If P is a simple polygon, then {0}-kernel(P) can be computed in time linear in the number of vertices.*

The algorithm to compute the {θ}-kernel of a polygon P allows us to construct the $\mathcal{O}$-kernel of P, for finite $\mathcal{O}$, in the following manner. For each $\theta \in \mathcal{O}$, we compute {θ}-kernel and then intersect the kernels obtained to yield $\mathcal{O}$-*kernel*(P). Since we have to apply the {0}-kernel subroutine c-times, the algorithm needs at least time $\Omega(n \cdot c)$ to compute $\mathcal{O}$-*kernel*(P) even if we do not take the time for intersecting the {θ}-kernels of P into account. It can be shown that by computing the intersection of the {θ}-kernels simultaneously in one scan of the boundary of P, the time complexity can be reduced to $O(n \log c)$ [SRW91] which is another example of an algorithm that makes very efficient use of the global restrictions of $\mathcal{O}$-convexity.

References

[Ber88]   M. Bern. Hidden surface removal for rectangles. In *Proc. 29th ACM Symposium on Theory of Computing*, pages 183–192, 1988.

[Ber90]   M. Bern. Hidden surface removal for rectangles. *Journal of Comp. Syst. Sciences*, 40:49–69, 1990.

[BG84]   B. K. Bhattachara and H. El Gindy. A new linear convex hull algorithm for simple polygons. *IEEE Transactions on Information Theory*, IT-30:85–88, 1984.

[Can87]   J.F. Canny. *The Complexity of Robot Motion Planning*. PhD thesis, MIT, 1987. Published by MIT Press in the Series: ACM Doctoral Dissertation Awards, 1987.

[CKV87]   K.L. Clarkson, S. Kapoor, and P.M. Vaidya. Rectilinear shortest paths through polygonal obstacles in $O(n \log^2 n)$ time. In *Proc. 3rd ACM Symp. on Computational Geometry*, pages 251–257, 1987.

[CR89]   J. Culberson and R. Reckhow. *A Unified Approach to Orthogonal Polygon Covering Problems via Dent Diagrams*. Technical Report TR 89-6, Department of Computing Science, University of Alberta, Edmonton, Alberta, Canada, February 1989.

[dB91]   M. de Berg. On rectilinear link distance. *Computational Geometry: Theory and Applications*, 1(1):13–34, 1991.

[dBO90]   M. de Berg and M. H. Overmars. Hidden surface removal for axis-parallel polyhedra. In *Proc. 31st IEEE Symp. on Foundations of Computer Science*, pages 252–261, 1990.

[dBvKNO90] M. de Berg, M. van Kreveld, B.J. Nilsson, and M. Overmars. Finding shortest paths in the presence of orthogonal obstacles using a combined L_1 and link metric. In *Proc. 2nd Scandinavian Workshop on Algorithm Theory*, pages 213–224, Springer Verlag, Lecture Notes in Computer Science 447, 1990.

[Deg79]   E. Degreef. Pasting and folding convexity spaces. *Bulletin de la Societé Mathematique du Belgique*, XXXI(Fasc. II-Ser. B):215–230, 1979.

[Dij59]   E.W. Dijkstra. A note on two problems in connection with graphs. *Numer. Math.*, 1:269–271, 1959.

[dRLW89]   P.J. de Rezende, D.T. Lee, and Y.F. Wu. Rectilinear shortest paths with rectangular barriers. *Journal of Discrete and Computational Geometry*, 4:41–53, 1989.

[EGS86]   H. Edelsbrunner, L.J. Guibas, and J. Stolfi. Optimal point location in a monotone subdivision. *SIAM Journal of Computing*, 15(2):317–340, 1986.

[EM91]   H. ElGindy and P. Mitra. Orthogonal shortest route queries among axes parallel rectangular obstacles. 1991. Manuscript.

[EOS84]   H. Edelsbrunner, M.H. Overmars, and R. Seidel. Some methods of computational geometry applied to computer graphics. *Computer Vision, Graphics, and Image Processing*, 28:92–108, 1984.

[FT84]   M.L. Fredman and R.E. Tarjan. Fibonacci heaps and their uses in improved network optimization algorithms. In *Proc. 25th IEEE Symp. on Foundations of Computer Science*, pages 338–346, 1984.

[GAO90]   M. T. Goodrich, M. J. Atallah, and M. H. Overmars. An input-size/output-size trade off in the time-complexity of hidden surface removal. In *Proc. 17th International Colloquium on Automata, Languages, and Programming, LNCS 443*, pages 689–702, 1990.

[GO87]   R. H. Güting and Th. Ottmann. New algorithms for special cases of the hidden line elimination problem. *Computer Vision, Graphics, and Image Processing*, 40:188–204, 1987.

[Gut83]   R. H. Güting. Stabbing c-oriented polygons. *Information Processing Letters*, 16:35–40, 1983.

[Gut84]   R. H. Güting. Dynamic c-oriented polygonal intersection searching. *Information and Control*, 63:143–163, 1984.

[GY83]   R. L. Graham and F. F. Yao. Finding the convex hull of a simple polygon. *Journal of Algorithms*, 4:324–331, 1983.

[Ick88]   C. Icking. Kürzeste Pfade mit Hindernissen bei festen Orienterungen. September 1988. Unpublished Manuscript, Presented at the Freie Universität Berlin.

[Jam82]   R. E. Jamison-Waldner. A perspective on abstract convexity: classifying alignments by varieties. In D. C. Kay and M. Breen, editors, *Convexity and Related Combinatorial Geometry, Proceedings of the 2nd University of Oklahoma Conference*, pages 113–150, Marcel Dekker, Inc., New York and Basel, 1982. Lecture Notes in Pure and Applied Mathematics 76.

[Joh77]   D.B. Johnson. Efficient algorithms for shortest paths in sparse networks. *Journal of the ACM*, 1–13, 1977.

[Kei86]   J. M. Keil. Minimally covering a horizontally convex polygon. In *Proc. 2nd ACM Symp. on Computational Geometry*, pages 43–51, 1986.

[Kir83]   D.G. Kirkpatrick. Optimal search in planar subdivision. *SIAM Journal of Computing*, 12:28–35, 1983.

[KW71]   D. C. Kay and E. W. Womble. Axiomatic convexity theory and the relationship between the Carathéodory, Helly and Radon numbers. *Pacific Journal of Mathematics*, 38:471–485, 1971.

[LCY90]   D.T. Lee, T.H. Chen, and C.D. Yang. Shortest rectilinear paths among weighted obstacles. In *Proc. 6th ACM Symp. on Computational Geometry*, pages 301–310, 1990.

[Lev51]   F. W. Levi. On Helly's theorem and the axioms of convexity. *Journal of the Indian Mathematical Society*, 15:65–76, 1951.

[LL81]   R.C. Larson and V.O. Li. Finding minimum rectilinear distance paths in the presence of barriers. *Networks*, 11:285–304, 1981.

[LP84]   D.T. Lee and F.P. Preparata. Euclidean shortest paths in the presence of rectilinear barriers. *Networks*, 14:393–410, 1984.

[LT79]   R.J. Lipton and R.E. Tarjan. A separator theorem for planar graphs. *SIAM Journal of Numerical Analysis*, 177–189, 1979.

[MF82]   D. Y. Montuno and A. Fournier. *Finding the X-Y Convex Hull of A Set of X-Y Polygons*. Technical Report CSRG-148, Univerity of Toronto, 1982.

[MP89]   K.M. McDonald and J.G. Peters. *Smallest Paths in Simple Rectilinear Polygons*. Technical Report TR 89-4, School of Computing Science, Simon Fraser University, 1989.

[MRS88a]   R. Motwani, A. Raghunathan, and H. Saran. Covering orthogonal polygons with star polygons: the perfect graph approach. In *Proc. 4th ACM Symp. on Computational Geometry*, pages 211–223, 1988.

[MRS88b]   R. Motwani, A. Raghunathan, and H. Saran. Perfect graphs and orthogonally convex covers. In *Fourth Annual SIAM Conference on Discrete Mathematics*, 1988.

[NLLW84]   T. M. Nicholl, D. T. Lee, Y. Z. Liao, and C. K. Wong. Constructing the x-y convex hull of a set of x-y polygons. *BIT*, 33:157–171, 1984.

[OS89]   M. H. Overmars and M. Sharir. Output-sensitive hidden surface removal. In *Proc. 30th IEEE Symp. on Foundations of Computer Science*, pages 19–28, 1989.

[OSW84]   Th. Ottmann, E. Soisalon-Soininen, and D. Wood. On the definition and computation of rectilinear convex hulls. *Information Sciences*, 33, 1984.

[PS85]   F.P. Preparata and M.I. Shamos. *Computational Geometry — an Introduction*. Springer Verlag, 1985.

[PVY90]   F. P. Preparata, J. S. Vitter, and M. Yvinec. Output-sensitive generation of the perspective view of isothetic parallelepipeds. In *Proc. 2nd Scandinavian Workshop on Algorithm Theory, LNCS 447*, pages 71–84, 1990.

[Raw87]   G. Rawlins. *Explorations in Restricted-Orientation Geometry*. PhD thesis, University of Waterloo, 1987.

[RC87]   R. Reckhow and J. Culberson. Covering a simple orthogonal polygon with a minimum number of orthogonally convex polygons. In *Proc. 3rd ACM Symp. on Computational Geometry*, pages 268–277, 1987.

[Rec87]   R. Reckhow. *Covering Orthogonally Convex Polygons with Three Orientations of Dents*. Technical Report TR87-17, University of Alberta, 1987.

[Rei91]   G. Reich. *Finitely-Oriented Shortest Paths in the Presence of Polygonal Obstacles*. Technical Report "Bericht 39", Institut für Informatik, Universität Freiburg, Germany, October 1991.

[RW87]   G. Rawlins and D. Wood. On the optimal computation of finitely-oriented convex hulls. *Information and Computation*, 72:150–166, 1987.

[RW88]   G. Rawlins and D. Wood. Ortho-convexity and its generalizations. In Godfried T. Toussaint, editor, *Computational Morphology*, pages 137–152, Elsevier Science Publishers B. V., (North-Holland), 1988.

[RW89a]   G. Rawlins and D. Wood. A decomposition theorem for convexity spaces. *Journal of Geometry*, 36:143–159, 1989.

[RW89b]   G. Rawlins and D. Wood. *Restricted-Oriented Convex Sets*. Research Report CS-89-01, University of Waterloo, 1989.

[Sch91]   S. Schuierer. An optimal data structure for shortest rectilinear path queries in a simple polygon. 1991. Manuscript, Institut für Informatik, Universität Freiburg, Germany.

[Sie77]   G. Sierksma. Relationships between Carathéodory, Helly, Radon and Exchange numbers of convexity spaces. *Nieuw Archief voor Wiskunde*, XXV:115–132, 1977.

[SRW89]   S. Schuierer, G. Rawlins, and D. Wood. *Visibility, Skulls, and Kernels in Convexity Spaces*. Data Structuring Group Research Report CS-89-48, University of Waterloo, Ontario, Canada, October 1989.

[SRW91]   S. Schuierer, G. Rawlins, and D. Wood. A generalization of staircase visibility. In H. Bieri, editor, *Computational Geometry—Methods, Algorithms, and Applications, LNCS 553*, pages 277–288, Springer-Verlag, 1991.

[ST86]   N. Sarnak and R.E. Tarjan. Planar point location using persistent search trees. *Communications of the ACM*, 29:669–679, 1986.

[SW91]   S. Schuierer and D. Wood. *Restricted Orientation Visibility*. Technical Report 40, Institut für Informatik, Universität Freiburg, 1991.

[Wid90]   P. Widmayer. *On Shortest Paths in VLSI design*. Technical Report "Bericht 19", Institut für Informatik, Universität Freiburg, Germany, March 1990. Also to appear in: Annals of Operations Research, 1991.

[WWW87]   P. Widmayer, Y.F. Wu, and C.K. Wong. On some distance problems in fixed orientations. *SIAM Journal of Computing*, 16:728–746, 1987.

Monotonous Bisector* Trees - a Tool for Efficient Partitioning of Complex Scenes of Geometric Objects

H. Noltemeier, K. Verbarg, C. Zirkelbach *

Abstract

We are concerned with the problem of partitioning complex scenes of geometric objects in order to support the solutions of proximity problems in general metric spaces with an efficiently computable distance function. We present a data structure called *Monotonous Bisector* Tree*, which can be regarded as a divisive hierarchical approach of centralized clustering methods (compare [3] and [12]). We analyze some structural properties showing that Monotonous Bisector* Trees are a proper tool for a general representation of proximity information in complex scenes of geometric objects.

Given a scene of n objects in d-dimensional space and some Minkowski-metric. We additionally demand a general position of the objects and that the distance between a point and an object of the scene can be computed in constant time. We show that a Monotonous Bisector* Tree with logarithmic height can be constructed in optimal $O(n \log n)$ time using $O(n)$ space. This statement still holds if we demand that the cluster radii, which appear on a path from the root down to a leaf, should generate a geometrically decreasing sequence.

We report on extensive experimental results which show that Monotonous Bisector* Trees support a large variety of proximity queries by a single data structure efficiently.

1 Introduction

The appropriate and efficient representation of proximity information in large sets of objects is a crucial problem in a wide range of applications [13]. We will not try to give an account of this field; we will mention only some examples directly related to our results. For instance consider a large scene of objects S (as points, line segments, polygons, ...) in

*Lehrstuhl für Informatik I, Universität Würzburg, Am Hubland, D - 8700 Würzburg, Fed. Rep. of Germany. This work was supported by the Deutsche Forschungsgemeinschaft (DFG) under contract (No 88/6 - 4).

the plane and a distance function d. Now, we want to move an arbitrary object o within this scene avoiding collisions with the objects of the scene. If the scene is huge, it is useful to find at first all objects which might become dangerous to o and hand them over to the motion-planning algorithm. So, we need a data structure and an algorithm to retrieve the set

$$\{s \in S \mid d(o, s) \leq MAXDIST\}$$

efficiently, where $MAXDIST$ denotes a suitable limitation of proximity.

One approach is the use of cluster centers [3]: given an arbitrary space E, a distance function $d :. E \times E \longrightarrow \mathbb{R}_+^0$ satisfying the triangle inequality and a finite set $S \subset E$ of objects. After selecting a subset $E' \subset E$ with $k \geq 2$ elements, each $s \in S$ is related to its *cluster center* i.e. its nearest neighbor in E'. Thus, the partition is carried out by the (generalized) Voronoi-diagram [14] of the cluster centers. This provides a partitioning method which is sensitive to the underlying distance function d, because any separation sheet is given by the bisector of two cluster centers. This separation scheme, of course, is more flexible than the separation by hyperplanes which are parallel to the axis, which is the concept of the k-d-tree and the Quadtree [1] [15] [11] and thus, for example, it is possible to separate natural groupings. In general, a higher degree of flexibility in choosing the separation sheet allows to carry out the separation more sensitive to the spatial position of the objects. This is also the idea of the polygon-tree [16] and the cell-tree [6], however those and related data structures don't take care of the underlying metric. With this intention, for every cluster center $e \in E'$ let

$$RADIUS(e) := \max \{d(e, s) \mid s \in S \text{ and } e \text{ is the cluster center of } s\}$$

denote the corresponding *cluster radius*. The recursive use of this partitioning method generates a k-nary tree which is suitable for representing proximity properties by means of the cluster centers and the corresponding radii [7]. For example, if we search for the objects in the neighborhood of $p \in E$ in S, the search process can prune the subtree of the actual cluster center e if

$$d(p, e) - RADIUS(e) \geq MAXDIST$$

holds. On the other hand, the whole subtree can be accepted, if

$$d(p, e) + RADIUS(e) \leq MAXDIST$$

holds. If we search for the nearest neighbor of $p \in E$ in S the search process can prune the subtree of the actual cluster center e if

$$d(p, e) - RADIUS(e) \geq DACTUAL$$

holds with $DACTUAL$ denoting the distance of p to its actual nearest neighbor in S. The first example can be regarded as an absolute neighborhood query and the latter one as a relative neighborhood query.

Here we notice, if a cluster center represents a cluster element, then the cluster radius estimates the loss of spatial information. Therefore, the generation of representative cluster centers (cluster centers with small radii) is a general goal of this clustering technique.

Early attempts date back to Kalantari and McDonald [9]. They use a data structure, called *bisector tree*, which can be regarded as a straightforward generalization of binary search trees (which support nearest neighbor search in $\mathbb{R}^1$) to normed spaces. Unfortunately, those early approaches failed in the following **two criteria** which are necessary to support proximity queries efficiently:

1. The radii of the elements stored in nodes which appear on a path from the root down to a leaf should generate a monotonously decreasing sequence. So, we do not permit *eccentric sons* i.e. successors in the tree that have larger radii than the current center.

2. The height of the tree should be $O(\log |S|)$ to achieve small subtrees.

Now, this paper is organized as follows. To overcome the disadvantages caused by eccentric sons, we present a new type of the bisector tree – the so-called *Monotonous Bisector Tree* (see [17]) – for partitioning large sets of points in section 2. Afterwards, in section 3, we generalize this approach to complex scenes of "higher" geometric objects introducing *Monotonous Bisector* Trees*. Finally, in section 4, we summarize experimental results and point out applications; to some of them we will turn our attention in near future.

2 Monotonous Bisector Trees

Let E be an arbitrary space with distance function d and $S \subset E$ a finite set of n points with $s_1 \in S$. Now, a *Monotonous Bisector Tree* $MBT(S, s_1)$ is a binary tree having the following features:

$1 \leq |S| \leq 2$: $MBT(S, s_1)$ consists of a single node containing the elements of S.

$|S| > 2$:   The root w of $MBT(S, s_1)$ contains s_1 and a point $s_2 \in S \setminus \{s_1\}$. The subtrees of w are $MBT(S_1, s_1)$ and $MBT(S_2, s_2)$ with

$$\{s \in S \mid d(s, s_i) < d(s, s_j)\} \subseteq S_i \subseteq \{s \in S \mid d(s, s_i) \leq d(s, s_j)\}$$

where $i \neq j$, $S_1 \cup S_2 = S$ and $S_1 \cap S_2 = \emptyset$.

Now the construction of the tree in its basic steps is as follows: Starting with a given element $s_1 \in S$ we recursively choose a second splitting element $s_2 \in S$. Then we relate each $s \in S$ to its cluster center s_1 or s_2, respectively, which provides a partition in the upper sense. These two cluster centers are reached down to their corresponding subtrees. So, each node (except of the root) contains exactly one redundant element – which preserves linear storage (see fig. 1 and fig. 2, which show two partitions in their first few steps under different metrics). To achieve a good start, the first cluster center should be chosen carefully, for instance in the euclidean case the nearest neighbor of the center of the smallest enclosing circle which can be computed in linear time [10].

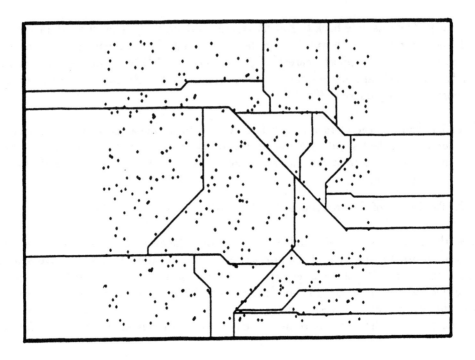

Fig. 1:   Monotonous Bisector Tree of a set of 400 points under L_1-metric
            Height: 3

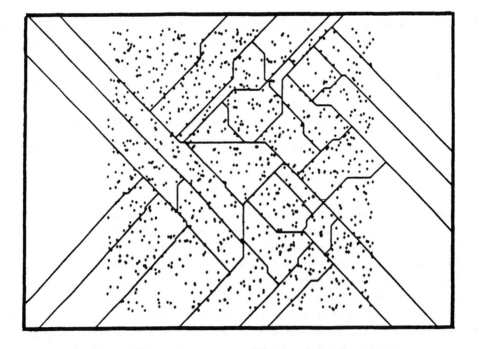

Fig. 2:   Monotonous Bisector Tree of a set of 1000 points under L_∞-metric
            Height: 4

The proposed method removes the disadvantages of bisector trees by an adaptive sequential insertion of new cluster points in those areas, where the greatest error (with respect to the two criteria demanded in the introduction) occurs. The main problem in this context is the separation of the elements in S with respect to an imaginary second splitting element. If we choose this splitting element carefully, we gain a partition of the scene which is sensitive to the spatial position of the elements in S and to the distance function d, because the partition is carried out by the bisector of the two cluster centers of a node. This is the basic idea which enables us to prove the following theorem.

Theorem 1

1. MBTs do not have eccentric sons. The radii of the elements stored in nodes which appear on a path from the root to a leaf generate a monotonously decreasing sequence (justifying the term: *monotonous* tree).

2. Let $S \subset \mathbb{R}^d$ be a finite set of n points. For any L_p-metric ($1 \leq p \leq \infty$) a MBT with logarithmic height can be constructed in optimal $O(n \log n)$ time and $O(n)$ storage.

3. Let $S \subset \mathbb{R}^2$ be a finite set of n points. For any *convex distance function* [1] a Monotonous Bisector Tree with logarithmic height can be constructed in optimal $O(n \log n)$ time using $O(n)$ storage.

The last two statements still hold if we demand that the radii of clusters, which appear on a path from the root down to a leaf, should generate a geometrically decreasing sequence.

Proof: The first statement is immediately implied by the structure of the tree. We now sketch the proof of the latter two in a sequence of lemmas. The complete proofs can be found in [17] and [18].

The goal to achieve logarithmic height using $O(n \log n)$ preprocessing time can be reduced to the following

Problem: Given a finite set S of points in $\mathbb{R}^d$. Find in $O(|S|)$ time two points $a, b \in S$ such that each of the two half-spaces defined by the bisector of a and b contains at least a constant fraction of S.

Lemma 1.1: For any given convex distance function d, all possible Voronoi regions are star-shaped.

The proof can be found in [2].

Let $\|b - a\|$ denote the euclidean distance of $a \in \mathbb{R}^d$ and $b \in \mathbb{R}^d$.
For $p \in \mathbb{R}^d$ and $\delta \in \mathbb{R}_+^0$ we denote the ball $K_\delta(p) := \{x \in \mathbb{R}^d \mid \|p - x\| \leq \delta\}$.
For $a, b \in \mathbb{R}^d$ and a convex distance function d let $H(a, b) := \{x \in M \mid d(a, x) \leq d(b, x)\}$ denote the half-space associated to the point a, given by the bisector of a and b.

---

[1]A distance function based on an expanding convex shape is called *convex distance function* and was first defined by Minkowski. Indeed, in some references it is called the *Minkowski distance function* [2].

Lemma 1.2: For every convex distance function d there exists an $\epsilon > 0$ such that for every $a, b \in \mathbb{R}^d$ $\quad K_{\epsilon \|a-b\|}(a) \subset H(a,b)$ holds.

This depends on the fact that in any convex distance function the speed has an upper and a lower non-negative bound. (If λ_1 denotes its infimum and λ_2 its supremum we can choose $\epsilon := \epsilon(d) := \frac{\lambda_1}{\lambda_1+\lambda_2}$). Let in the following denote $\alpha := \alpha(d) := \arcsin(\epsilon)$.

The combination of lemma 1.1 and lemma 1.2 implies immediately

Lemma 1.3: For every $a, b, x \in \mathbb{R}^d$ the following statement holds:

$$\{\lambda x + (1-\lambda) b \mid 0 \le \lambda \le 1\} \cap K_{\epsilon \|a-b\|}(a) \ne \emptyset \implies x \in H(a,b)$$

Let $\angle(v_1, v_2)$ denote the (positive) angle given by the two vectors $v_1 \in \mathbb{R}^d$ and $v_2 \in \mathbb{R}^d$. For $a \in \mathbb{R}^d$, $v \in \mathbb{R}^d$ ($\|v\| = 1$) and $0 \le \beta \le \pi$ we define the cone

$$W(a,v,\beta) := \{x \in \mathbb{R}^d \mid \angle(v, x-a) \le \frac{\beta}{2}\}$$

and the double-cone

$$DW(a,v,\beta) := W(a,v,\beta) \cup W(a,-v,\beta).$$

Applying lemma 1.3 (see figure 3) we gain

Lemma 1.4: Given a double-cone $DW(p,v,\alpha) \subset \mathbb{R}^d$ and two finite point sets $A, B \subset \mathbb{R}^d$ where

$$A \subset W(p,v,\alpha) \quad \text{and} \quad B \subset W(p,-v,\alpha).$$

If we choose $a_0 \in A$ and $b_0 \in B$ such that

$$\begin{aligned} a_0 v &= \min\{a v \mid a \in A\} \\ b_0 v &= \max\{b v \mid b \in B\} \end{aligned}$$

then $A \subset H(a_0, b_0)$ and $B \subset H(b_0, a_0)$ holds.

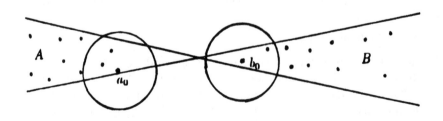

Fig. 3

In the remainder of the proof we still have to show that it is possible to construct in linear time a double-cone with angle $\leq \alpha$ where each cone contains at least a constant fraction of S. In the plane this is possible for every $0 < \alpha \leq \pi$. Up to now we solve this problem in $\mathbb{R}^d$ only for $\alpha \geq \frac{\pi}{2}$ which reduces the generality of convex distance functions to the case of L_p-metrics. We investigate at first the plane case (statement 3):

Lemma 1.5: Given a double-wedge $DW(p,v,\beta) \subset \mathbb{R}^2$ and two finite sets $A, B \subset \mathbb{R}^2$ where

$$A \subset W(p,v,\beta) \quad \text{and} \quad B \subset W(p,-v,\beta)$$

then we find in $O(|A| + |B|)$ time a double-wedge $DW(p',v',\beta/2)$ where

$$|W(p',v',\beta/2) \cap A| \geq \lceil |A|/2 \rceil \quad \text{and} \quad |W(p',-v',\beta/2) \cap B| \geq \lceil |B|/2 \rceil.$$

Let $DW(p,v,\beta)$ be given by the two lines g_1 and g_2 (see figure 4). We apply a median-cut to the set A using an oriented line g with direction v. Now the double-wedge defined by g_1 and g or the double wedge defined by g_2 and g is a solution.

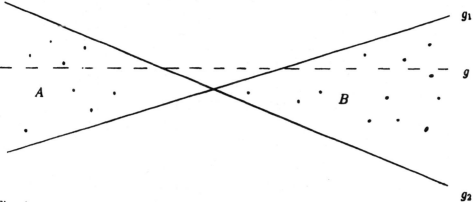

Fig. 4

In a first step we separate the set S by the vertical line which is given by the median of the first component. Thus we achieve a double-wedge with angle π. The recursive application of lemma 1.5 to the resulting double-wedges will provide a double-wedge with angle $\leq \alpha$ where each wedge contains at least a constant fraction of S. Due to the fact that the median can be found in linear time we solve this problem in $O(n) + O(\frac{n}{2}) + O(\frac{n}{4}) + \ldots = O(n)$ time. This completes the proof of the plane case (statement 3).

Now we turn our attention to the higher-dimensional case (statement 2). Let $\|b - a\|_p$ $(1 \leq p \leq \infty)$ denote the L_p-distance of $a \in \mathbb{R}^d$ and $b \in \mathbb{R}^d$. With the help of the *Binomial Formula* we can show:

Lemma 1.6: Let $a, b, c \in \mathbb{R}^d$ with $\|c - a\|_p \geq \|c - b\|_p$. Then each

$$x \in Q := \{(x_1, \ldots, x_d)^T \in \mathbb{R}^d | a_i < b_i \Longrightarrow x_i \geq c_i \quad \text{and} \quad a_i > b_i \Longrightarrow x_i \leq c_i\}$$

has the following property: $\|x - a\|_p \geq \|x - b\|_p$.

Lemma 1.7: Let $S \subset \mathbb{R}^d$ ($d \in \mathbb{N}_+$) be a set of n points. Then we can find in $O(n)$ time three points $p^1, p^2, p^3 \in \mathbb{R}^d$ and two sets of indices $I_1, I_2 \subset \{1, \ldots, d\}$, such that

$$I_1 \cup I_2 = \{1, \ldots, d\}, \quad I_1 \cap I_2 = \emptyset$$

$$p_i^1 \leq p_i^2 \leq p_i^3 \quad \text{if} \quad i \in I_1$$

$$p_j^1 \geq p_j^2 \geq p_j^3 \quad \text{if} \quad j \in I_2$$

and each set

$$
\begin{aligned}
A &:= \{x \in S \,|\, x_i \leq p_i^1 \text{ if } i \in I_1 \quad \text{and} \quad x_j \geq p_j^1 \text{ if } j \in I_2\} \\
B &:= \{x \in S \,|\, p_i^1 \leq x_i \leq p_i^2 \text{ if } i \in I_1 \quad \text{and} \quad p_j^2 \leq x_j \leq p_j^1 \text{ if } j \in I_2\} \\
C &:= \{x \in S \,|\, p_i^2 \leq x_i \leq p_i^3 \text{ if } i \in I_1 \quad \text{and} \quad p_j^3 \leq x_j \leq p_j^2 \text{ if } j \in I_2\} \\
D &:= \{x \in S \,|\, x_i \geq p_i^3 \text{ if } i \in I_1 \quad \text{and} \quad x_j \leq p_j^3 \text{ if } j \in I_2\}
\end{aligned}
$$

contains at least a constant fraction of S (see figure 5).

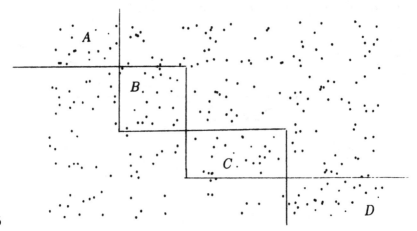

Fig. 5

For the exhaustive prove of this lemma which is an improvement of Heusinger's lemma 3.3 in [7] we refer to [17]. If we choose $a \in B$ and $b \in C$ lemma 1.6 guarantees that $A \subset H(a, b)$ and $D \subset H(b, a)$ holds, which completes the prove of the second statement.

Due to the fact that in any convex distance function the unit sphere can be covered by a constant number of equal sized smaller spheres it is possible to reduce a cluster radius by a factor $0 < q < 1$ after a constant number of k (depending on q and the dimension) splitting steps. The alternating application of balancing and reducing the cluster radii doesn't touch the complexities and provides a tree with logarithmic height and a development of the cluster radii in the sense of a geometrically decreasing sequence.

However, there are simple examples demonstrating, that it is impossible to generate balanced Monotonous Bisector Trees for a set of "higher" objects (as line segments, polygons, ...). That leads to a generalization of this data structure in the following section.

3 Monotonous Bisector* Trees

Let $S \neq \emptyset$ be a finite set of objects, $E \neq \emptyset$ a (not necessarily finite) set of *splitting elements* with $e_1 \in E$ and $d : E \times S \longrightarrow \mathrm{I\!R}^0_+$ a distance function. A *Monotonous Bisector* Tree* $MBT^*(S, e_1)$ is a binary tree having the following properties:

$1 \leq |S| \leq 2$: $MBT^*(S, e_1)$ consists of a single node containing the elements of S.

$|S| > 2$:   The root w of $MBT^*(S, e_1)$ contains e_1 and a point $e_2 \in E \setminus \{e_1\}$. The subtrees of w are $MBT^*(S_1, e_1)$ and $MBT^*(S_2, e_2)$ with

$$\{s \in S \mid d(e_i, s) < d(e_j, s)\} \subseteq S_i \subseteq \{s \in S \mid d(e_i, s) \leq d(e_j, s)\}$$

where $i \neq j$, $S_1 \neq \emptyset$, $S_2 \neq \emptyset$, $S_1 \cup S_2 = S$ and $S_1 \cap S_2 = \emptyset$.

Here, we apply our idea by reaching down the cluster centers to their corresponding subtrees. Notice, that a MBT is a Monotonous Bisector* Tree where $S = E$. Now we select the cluster centers from the set E of splitting elements and store the objects of S in the buckets of the tree (see fig. 6 for an example).

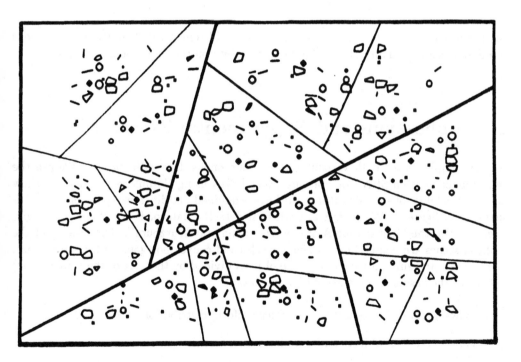

Fig. 6:   Monotonous Bisector* Tree of a set of 300 points, line segments and polygons under L_2-metric (cluster centers are marked by a ♦)
Height: 3

In addition to theorem 1, we can prove

Theorem 2

1. MBT^*s do not have eccentric sons. The radii of the elements stored in nodes which appear on a path from the root to a leaf generate a monotonously decreasing sequence.

2. Let S be a finite set of n convex objects in d-dimensional space and $E = \mathbb{R}^d$ the set of splitting elements. We demand that the distance between a point and an object of S can be computed in constant time.

   (a) For any *symmetrical convex distance function* (for instance any L_p-Metric), a MBT^* with logarithmic height and geometrically decreasing radii can be constructed in optimal $O(n \log n)$ time and $O(n)$ storage.

   (b) If we additionally demand that at most k objects of S intersect any common hyperplane, the objects of the scene S need not to be convex to hold (a).

For the proof we refer to [19]. In addition we should remark, that under the conditions of statement 2 the quality of balance doesn't depend on the dimension.

4 Applications and Experimental Research

We have implemented both variants of the Monotonous Tree with success. We ran the performance tests on SUN workstations under UNIX using C implementations. To show the practicability of our algorithms we have examined six different types of scenes illustrated in figure 7. While A-E are artificial data the data of F are of natural origin, received from the "Institut für Astronomie, Universität Würzburg". The objects of the artificial scenes are points, line segments, circles and convex polygons with bounded size. The overlap (the summarized area of the objects divided by the area of the whole scene) is 0.06. In the case of F we have only point data.

A shows a scene of disjoint objects under uniform distribution.

B shows a scene of objects under uniform distribution.

C shows a scene of objects distributed along a sinus curve.

D shows a scene of objects distributed along a diagonal line.

E shows a scene of objects distributed to seven clusters.

F shows a picture of two galaxies (10000 data points).

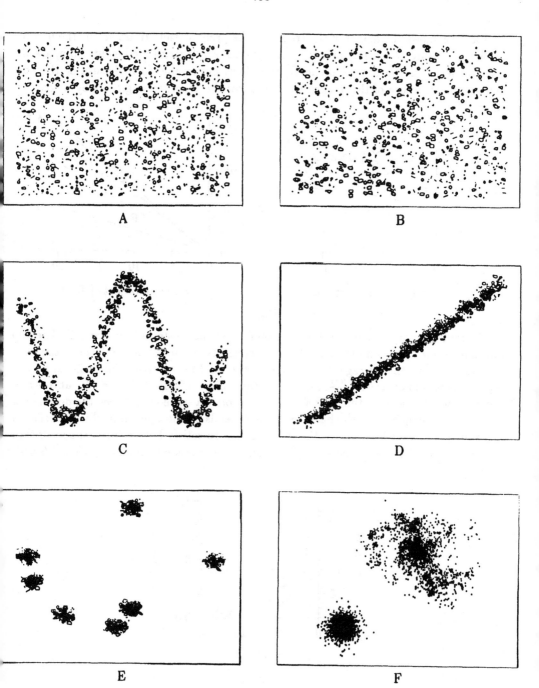

Fig. 7

Figure 8 shows the height of the trees and the preprocessing times versus the number of objects. Using $O(n \log n)$ preprocessing we achieve logarithmic height (compare the dashed lines). In the case of scene D, the algorithm is able to make use of the one-dimensional structure of this scene, which reduces the preprocessing costs by a constant factor.

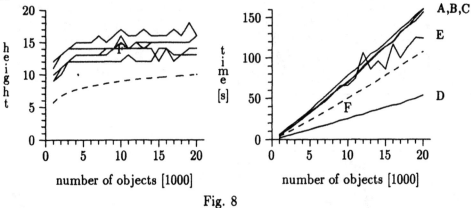

Fig. 8

Figure 9 gives an example of the development of the clusterradii in scene F. The two solid lines show the maximum and the average cluster radii versus the level in the tree. The crosses mark the average balance versus the level in the tree. The balance b for a single node is defined as $b := \frac{|l-r|}{l+r}$, where l is the number of objects in the left subtree and r the number of objects in the right subtree. We notice a trade-off between the decrease of the radii and the quality of the balance. That depends on the algorithm which satisfies in each splitting-step at least one of the two criteria. To satisfy both criteria the algorithm is forced to be adaptive to the spatial character of the scene (compare figure 1,2,6 with figure 10).

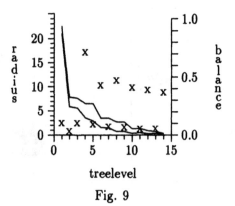

Fig. 9

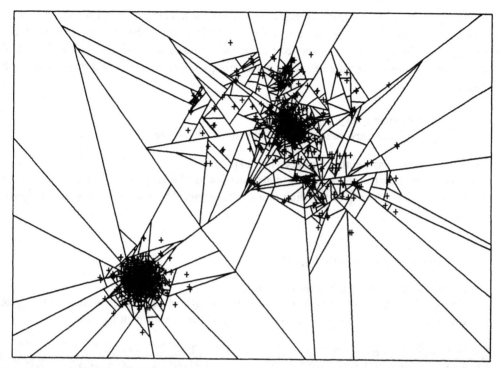

Fig. 10:   Monotonous Bisector* Tree of scene F

The general concept of information retrieval, as described in the introduction, enables us to support a large variety of proximity queries by a single data structure. Our experiments show this for:

- nearest-neighbor queries

- fixed-radius-near neighbor-queries

- ray-shooting queries

- range queries

- points/objects in polygon retrieval

- objects hitting polygon retrieval

- objects hitting curve retrieval

- hidden-line/surface queries

- special problems of motion planning

Performing the list of proximity queries we achieve an average query time of $\log n + k$ where k is the size of the output. So we found out in general that the query cost is the complexity of the output if the size of the output is large with respect to the height of the tree. We demonstrate this result by performing a constant set of 500 queries for each of the following types:

- nearest-neighbor query (fig. 13)
  The query-points are randomly distributed in the scene.

- fixed-radius-near-neighbor query (fig. 14)
  The query-points are randomly distributed and the radii are randomly chosen in the range from 0 to $\frac{1}{5}$ of the diameter of the scene. The whole query-scene is shown in fig. 11.

- visibility query (fig. 15)
  We used a set of unlimited cones.

- objects hitting curve retrieval (fig. 16)
  The curves consist of five edges, where the length of each edge is limited by $\frac{1}{10}$ of the diameter of the scene. The whole query-scene is shown in fig. 12.

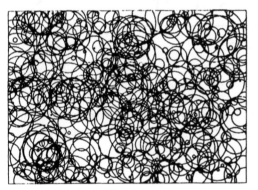
Fig. 11

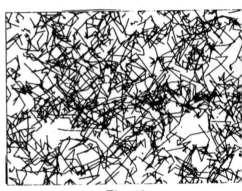
Fig. 12

The average results for each query are shown on the left series for scene A and on the right series for scene E. The solid curve reports the quotient of the running time and the number of the reported objects. To achieve a performance measure which is independent of the harware we also used the number of the touched nodes (dotted curve) and the number of the touched objects (dashed curve) instead of the running time. So we can say, roughly speaking, that the curves tell us the amortised costs of each reported object.

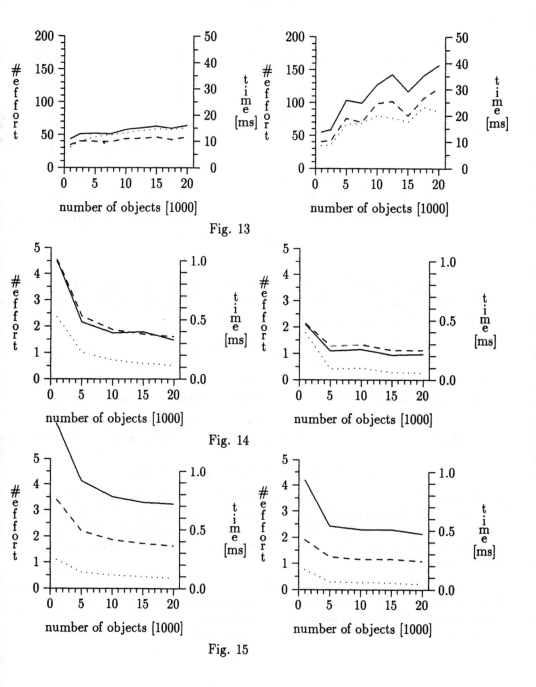

Fig. 13

Fig. 14

Fig. 15

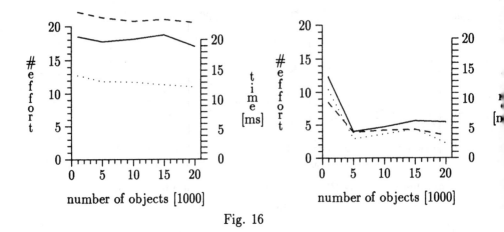

Fig. 16

In near future, we will turn our attention to further applications: imagine the position of an object not exactly fixed, but can be estimated by its limited radius of action. Our concept still works, if we define the cluster radius as follows:

$$RADIUS_\varepsilon(e) := RADIUS(e) + \varepsilon,$$

where ε denotes the maximum radius of action that occurs in the cluster. If ε is small with respect to the whole scene, this idea enables us to work efficiently under uncertainties.

Furthermore, if we are faced with a scene of continuously moving objects, there is always a linear function $\varepsilon(t)$, depending on the time t, to estimate the cluster radius as follows:

$$RADIUS(e, t) := RADIUS(e, t_0) + \varepsilon(t - t_0).$$

The linear function $\varepsilon(t)$ is given by the maximum possible speed of a cluster element. Due to the fact, that the motions are continuous, there is always a $t_{max} > 0$ which guarantees, that for each $0 \leq t \leq t_{max}$ the cluster center e is still a proper representative of the cluster elements. The calculation of t_{max} as a threshold value of local and global rebuilding is a goal of further research.

The efficiency of our data structure in a scene with a high degree of overlapping objects is still unsettled today. Performance tests in this field are one goal of experimental research. We also will set the decomposition of large problems to our work with applications in image analysis and image understanding.

References

[1] J. L. Bentley, *Multidimensional Binary Search Trees Used for Associative Searching*, Communications of the ACM, Vol. 18, No. 9, 1975

[2] L. P. Chew, R. L. Drysdale III, *Voronoi Diagrams Based on Convex Distance Functions*, 1st ACM Symposium on Computational Geometry, Baltimore, Maryland, 1985

[3] F. Dehne and H. Noltemeier, *A Computational Geometry Approach to Clustering Problems*, Proceedings of the 1st ACM Symposium on Computational Geometry, Baltimore, Maryland, 1985

[4] F.Dehne and H. Noltemeier, *Voronoi Trees and Clustering Problems*, Information Systems, Vol. 12, No. 2, Pergamon London, 1987

[5] H. Edelsbrunner, *Algorithms in Combinatorial Geometry*, EATCS Monographs in Computer Science, Vol. 10, Springer - Verlag, Berlin - Heidelberg, 1987

[6] O. Günther, *Efficient Structures for Geometric Data Management*, LNCS 337 (ed. G.Goos, J.Hartmanis), Springer, Berlin - Heidelberg, 1988

[7] H. Heusinger, *Clusterverfahren für Mengen geometrischer Objekte*, Report, Universität Würzburg, 1989

[8] H. Heusinger und H. Noltemeier, *On Separable Clusterings*, Journal of Algorithms, Vol. 10, Academic Press, 1989

[9] I. Kalantari, G. McDonald, *A Data Structure and an Algorithm for the Nearest Point Problem*, IEEE Transactions on Software Engineering, Vol. SE-9, No.5, 1983

[10] N. Megiddo, *Linear-Time Algorithms for Linear Programming in $\mathbb{R}^3$ and Related Problems*, SIAM Journal of Comput., Vol. 12, 1983

[11] F. Murtagh, *A Survey of Recent Advances in Hierarchical Clustering Algorithms*, The Computer Journal, Vol. 26, No. 4, 1983

[12] H. Noltemeier, *Voronoi Trees and Applications*, in H. Imai (ed.): "Discrete Algorithms and Complexity" (Proceedings), Fukuoka/Japan, 1989

[13] H. Noltemeier, *Layout of Flexible Manufacturing Systems - Selected Problems*, Proceedings of the Workshop on Applications of Combinatorial Optimization in Science and Technology (COST), New Brunswick, New Jersey, 1991

[14] F.P. Preparata and M.I. Shamos, *Computational Geometry – An Introduction*, Springer - Verlag, New York, 1985

[15] H. Samet, *The Quadtree and Related Hierarchical Data Structures*, ACM Computing Surveys, Vol. 16, 1984

[16] D. E. Willard, *Polygon Retrieval*, SIAM J. Comput., Vol. 11,No. 1, 1982

[17] C. Zirkelbach, *Monotonous Bisector Trees and Clustering Problems*, Techn. Report, Universität Würzburg, 1990

[18] C. Zirkelbach, *Partitionierung mit Bisektoren*, Techn. Report, Universität Würzburg, 1990

[19] C. Zirkelbach, *Monotone Bisektor* Bäume unter Minkowski-Metrik*, Techn. Report, Universität Würzburg, 1991

Learning Convex Sets
Under Uniform Distribution

Bernd Schmeltz [*][†]

Technische Hochschule Darmstadt

Abstract

In order to learn a convex set C, an algorithm is given a random sample of points and the information which of the points belong to C. From this sample a set C' is constructed which is supposed to be a good approximation of C. The algorithm may have a small probability of failing. We measure the quality of the approximation by minimizing the probability that a random test point selected under the same distribution as the sample points is classified correctly. That minimum is taken over a set of distributions associated with C.

Learnability depends on the choice of these distributions of the sample points. If we allow too many distributions, then convex sets are not learnable. We set up a model for learning from equidistributed samples. Let $1/m$ be the error probability for classifying a random test point. We show that for learning d-dimensional convex sets a sample of size $\Theta(m^{(d+1)/2})$ is sufficient and necessary. The upper bound is obtained by analysing the sample size needed for the convex hull algorithm.

1 Learnability

Various notions of machine learning have been defined. The concepts differ concerning the objects to be learnt (sets, boolean or arbitrary functions), the way of learning (different types of queries with or without a teacher), and the definition of success (the objects must be learnt exactly or approximately for various kinds of approximations).

In this paper we deal with learning subsets of a given universe $\mathcal{M}$. Since we have a geometrical scene in mind, we will call the elements of $\mathcal{M}$ points. Such a subset $T \subseteq \mathcal{M}$ is called a *concept*. Now, a subset of the power set of $\mathcal{M}$ is fixed, the *concept class* $\mathcal{T}$. The machine is said *to learn a concept class* $\mathcal{T}$ if it can identify a given concept $T \in \mathcal{T}$ (at least approximately) using some given information about T.

---

[*] Inst. f. Theoretische Informatik, Alexanderstr. 10, W-6100 Darmstadt, Germany,
e-mail: schmeltz@iti.informatik.th-darmstadt.de
[†] Research supported by DFG grant RE 672/1

Our algorithms learn by *examples*. An example is an input $x \in M$ given to the algorithm to which one information bit is added, indicating whether $x \in T$. We will distinguish between positive examples ($x \in T$) and negative ones ($x \notin T$).

We further adopt the model of *PAC-learning* (PAC = probably almost correct). In order to learn a concept $T \in \mathcal{T}$ the algorithm is given random examples. It then constructs some approximation T' of T. Two parameters ϵ and δ are used to denote the required quality of the approximation and the maximal probability of failure, respectively. We have to allow a certain probability of failure because the random examples might not yield any good approximation. In the PAC-learning model the quality of approximation is measured by the probability

$$\delta := \Pr(T \Delta T'),$$

where Δ denotes the symmetric difference of sets. This can be interpreted as the probability that a wrong answer is given to the question whether a random test point belongs to the concept class T. The same probability distribution is used for the sample and for the test point. The learning algorithm must succeed for any choice of the probability distribution [BEHW89].

There is an elegant characterisation of the concept classes which can be learnt under the PAC-model.

Definition 1.1 : *We say that a set $M \subseteq \mathcal{M}$ is* **shattered** *by the concept class $\mathcal{T}$ if the set*

$$\{T \cap M : T \in \mathcal{T}\}$$

is equal to the power set of M. The **VC-dimension** *(Vapnik-Chervonenkis-dimension) of $\mathcal{T}$ is the maximal cardinality of a set M shattered by $\mathcal{T}$.*

Theorem 1.2 : *A concept class is learnable under the PAC-model if and only if its VC-dimension is finite.*

This is a strong tool for proving that a concept class is not learnable. Forcing the learning algorithm to succed for all probability distributions turns out to be too strong for some interesting concept classes including the class of convex sets. Therefore, we change the model, retaining the use of the same distribution for the sample and the test point. However, we want to reduce the set of distributions. We also want to be able to specify the distribution set separately for each concept. Our notion of learning is formally defined as follows.

Definition 1.3 : *Given a universe $\mathcal{M}$, we say that a system $\mathcal{S} \subseteq \mathcal{P}(\mathcal{M}) \times \mathcal{F}$, where $\mathcal{P}$ denotes the power set and $\mathcal{F}$ a set of probability distributions on $\mathcal{M}$, is* **learnable** *if the following hold (we identify an algorithm with the function it computes):*

(i) $\exists$ *algorithm* $\mathcal{A}_1 : (\epsilon, \delta) \mapsto n$,

(ii) $\exists$ *algorithm* $\mathcal{A}_2 : (\epsilon, \delta, n, x_1, \ldots x_n) \mapsto T' = T'(x_1, \ldots, x_n) \subseteq \mathcal{M}$,

(iii) $\forall \epsilon > 0 \quad \forall \delta > 0 \quad \forall S = (T, F) \in \mathcal{S}$
$\quad \Pr\left[\Pr\left(T'(X_1, \ldots, X_n) \, \Delta \, T \mid X_1, \ldots, X_n\right) > \epsilon\right] \leq \delta,$

where $X_1, \ldots, X_n$ are random points chosen with respect to F and the outer probability is computed with respect to F, too. $\mathcal{S}$ is **learnable with positive examples** if the X_i are chosen according to $F|_T$ (F restricted on T). The approximation T' gives rise to two kinds of errors when testing whether a point belongs to the concept: there may be points in $T \backslash T'$, and there may be points in $T' \backslash T$. Accordingly, we say that $\mathcal{S}$ is **learnable with one-sided error** if $T' \subseteq T$.

2 Convex Sets

We show how different choices of the associated probability distributions yield different results on the learnability of convex sets. Let $\mathcal{C}$ be the set of all d-dimensional compact convex sets. We study two different systems of convex sets.

1. Let $\mathcal{F}_1$ be the set of all probability distributions on $\mathbf{R}^d$, and define $\mathcal{S}_1 = \mathcal{C} \times \mathcal{F}_1$.

2. $\mathcal{S}_2$ is defined by

$$(C, F) \in \mathcal{S}_2 \qquad \Longleftrightarrow \qquad C \in \mathcal{C} \text{ and } F|_T \text{ is the equidistribution } .$$

Theorem 2.1 : $\mathcal{S}_1$ is not learnable for $d \geq 2$.

Proof : From the definition, $\mathcal{S}_1$ is learnable according to our notion if and only if $\mathcal{C}$ is PAC-learnable. Therefore, the theorem follows from the fact that the VC-dimension of $\mathcal{C}$ is infinite [BEHW89]. Let M be the set of the vertices of a convex polyhedron, and let M' be an arbitrary subset of M. The convex hull of M' contains no other vertices of the polyhedron. We see, each subset of M results from an intersection with a convex set, which means that M is shattered by $\mathcal{C}$. Since the number of vertices of polyhedra can be arbitrarily large, the VC-dimension of $\mathcal{C}$ is infinite. ∎

Theorem 2.2 : Let $d \geq 2$, $\epsilon = 1/m$, and $\delta \geq \exp(-O(m))$; then $\mathcal{S}_2$ is learnable with $O(m^{(d+1)/2})$ positive examples and one-sided error.

From now on, as in this theorem constants depend on the dimension d. Let vol denote the volume of an object where an index may indicate the dimension of the object. For instance, surfaces of d-dimensional objects are measured using vol_{d-1}. For the proof of the theorem we need the following technical lemma about convex domains.

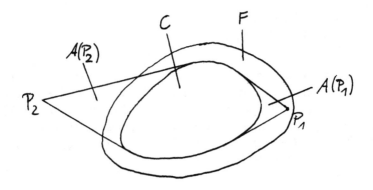

Figure 1: Two points $P_1 \in F$ and $P_2 \notin F$.

Lemma 2.3 : *Let C be a convex set in $\mathbf{R}^d$ with $\text{vol}(C) = 1$. For a point $P \in \mathbf{R}^d$ let*

$$A(P) := \text{conv}(C \cup \{P\}) \backslash C \,,$$

where conv denotes the convex hull. There are constants $c, \epsilon_0 > 0$ such that for any $\epsilon < \epsilon_0$ the set

$$F = F(C, \epsilon) := \left\{ P \notin C \,\Big|\, \text{vol}(A(P)) \leq c\,\epsilon^{\frac{d+1}{2}} \right\}$$

satisfies

$$\text{vol}(F) \leq \epsilon \,.$$

Proof : It suffices to show that $\text{vol}(F(C, \epsilon)) \leq c'\epsilon$ for some constant c'. Suppose we know that

$$\text{vol}(\tilde{F}(C, \epsilon)) \leq c'\,\epsilon \qquad \text{where}$$
$$\tilde{F} := \{ P \notin C \mid \text{vol}(A(P)) \leq \tilde{c}\,\epsilon^{(d+1)/2} \} \,.$$

Choosing

$$c := \tilde{c}\,(c')^{-(d+1)/2}$$

implies

$$\text{vol}(F(C, \epsilon)) = \text{vol}(\tilde{F}(C, \epsilon/c')) \leq \epsilon$$

which then completes the proof.

For each convex set C, there is a linear transformation L of $\mathbf{R}^d$ which preserves volumes such that the diameter of $L(C)$ is bounded by a fixed constant D. Note that $L(F(C, \epsilon)) = F(L(C), \epsilon)$. Since the lemma holds for C if and only if it holds for $L(C)$, we only have to prove the lemma for convex sets with a diameter bounded by D.

Let

$$C_a = \{ P | \text{dist}(P, C) \leq a \} \,, \qquad S_a = \text{bd}(C_a) \,, \qquad \text{and} \qquad F_a = F \cap S_a \,,$$

where dist denotes the Euclidean distance and bd the boundary or surface.

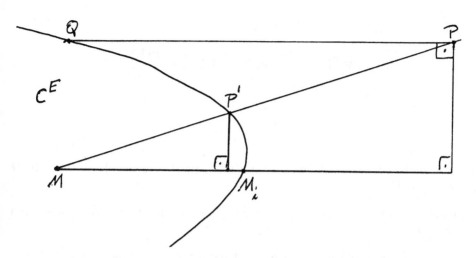

Figure 2: Construction of the point Q associated with P

As a consequence of the bound on the diameter, we have $\text{vol}_{d-1}(S_0) \le c_0$ for some fixed constant $c_0 > 0$. Also, C contains a sphere $K(M, R)$ with center M and a fixed radius R which we shall use later. The following equation holds

$$\text{vol}(F) = \int_0^{a_{\max}} \text{vol}_{d-1}(F_a) da \qquad \text{where} \quad a_{\max} = c_1 \, \epsilon^{\frac{d+1}{2d}} \, ,$$

for some constant c_1. If $a > a_{\max}$ then $A(P)$ contains a cone of height $a_{\max}$ and base $\Omega(a_{\max}^{d-1})$. This implies $F_a = \phi$ if c_1 is chosen large enough. The case $a < O(\epsilon)$ need not be considered, because

$$\bigcup_{0 < a < O(\epsilon)} F_a \subseteq \bigcup_{0 < a < O(\epsilon)} S_a \subseteq C_\epsilon \backslash C \qquad \text{where} \quad \text{vol}(C_\epsilon \backslash C) \le O(\epsilon) \, ,$$

implying

$$\text{vol}(F) \le O(\epsilon) + \int_\epsilon^{a_{\max}} \text{vol}_{d-1}(F_a) da \, .$$

We will now examine the intersections of C and F_a with the following system $\mathbf{E}$ of planes:

Cover the surface of C with small spheres $K(M_i, r)$. For each M_i choose $d - 1$ pairwise orthogonal planes through M_i and M, the center of the sphere contained in C. This way, we get a finite system $\mathbf{E}_0$ of planes. The system $\mathbf{E}$ contains all planes E parallel to some plane $E_0 \in \mathbf{E}_0$ such that $\text{dist}(E, E_0) \le R/2$.

We will show that each point $P \in S_a$, $0 < a \le a_{\max}$, is contained in $d - 1$ pairwise orthogonal planes in $\mathbf{E}$ if r is chosen small enough. Consider the straight line $\overline{PM}$ and let $P' := \overline{PM} \cap S_0$. There is some M_i with

$$\text{dist}(P', \overline{M_i M}) \le \text{dist}(P', M_i) \le r \, .$$

Since $\text{dist}(P, M) \leq a_{\max} + D \leq c_1 + D$, we have

$$
\begin{aligned}
\text{dist}(P, \overline{M_i M}) &\leq \text{dist}(P', \overline{M_i M}) \cdot \frac{\text{dist}(P, M)}{\text{dist}(P', M)} \\
&\leq r \cdot \frac{c_1 + D}{R} \\
&\leq \frac{R}{2}
\end{aligned}
$$

for r small enough. Therefore, the planes through P parallel to the planes through M and M_i belong to $\mathbf{E}$.

With each point $P \in C_a$ associate a point $Q \in S_0$ such that $\overline{PQ} \parallel \overline{MM_i}$ and $\text{dist}(P, \overline{MM_i}) \leq R/2$.

The angle α between $\overline{PQ}$ and a tangential hyperplane of C in Q is bounded away from zero because $\sin \alpha \geq R/2D$. (We define a hyperplane to be tangential if it contains points on the surface, but no inner point of C.)

For a plane $E \in \mathbf{E}$ let

$$
\mathbf{E}_E := \{ E' \in \mathbf{E} : E' \parallel E \} ,
$$

and

$$
S_a^E := S_a \cap E, \quad S^E := S \cap E, \quad C^E := C \cap E, \quad C_a^E := C_a^E \cap E .
$$

Assume that for each plane $E \in \mathbf{E}$ through P, the angle under which C^E is seen from P is at least $\pi - \varphi_a$ where

$$
\varphi_a := c_2 \, k^{\frac{2}{d-1}} \sqrt{\epsilon} \quad \text{and} \quad k := \frac{a}{\epsilon} .
$$

Then the intersection of a hyperplane through Q, E, and $A(P)$ is a line l_E of length $x_E \geq \Omega(a/\phi_a)$. Therefore, $P \notin F$ if the constant c_2 is chosen small enough, because $A(P)$ contains a cone of height $\Omega(a)$ and base $\Omega((a/\varphi_a)^{d-1})$, which has a volume $\geq c\epsilon^{(d+1)/2}$.

We define

$$
F_a^E := \{ P \in S_a^E \mid C^E \text{ is seen from } P \text{ under an angle} \leq \pi - \varphi_a , \; x_E \leq O(a/varphi_a) \} ,
$$

$$
F_a^{\mathbf{E}_E} = \bigcup_{E' \in \mathbf{E}_E} F_a^{E'} ,
$$

and

$$
f_a^E := \{ Q \in S_0^E \mid \overline{PQ} \parallel \overline{MM_i}, \text{ where } E \parallel E_0 \in \mathbf{E}_0 \text{ and } M_i \in E_0 \} .
$$

We have already seen that

$$
F_a \subseteq \bigcup_{E \in \mathbf{E}_0} F_a^{\mathbf{E}_E}
$$

which implies

$$\text{vol}_{d-1}(F_a) \leq \sum_{E \in \mathbf{E}_0} \text{vol}_{d-1}\left(F_a^{\mathbf{E}_E}\right).$$

To fix an upper bound for $\text{vol}_{d-1}\left(F_a^{\mathbf{E}_E}\right)$ we want to use f_a^E, which is a one-dimensional object. The correctness of the next formula is guaranteed by the fact that the angle between any $E \in \mathbf{E}$ and a tangential hyperplane at a point $Q \in S_0^E$ is bounded away from zero. This follows from the bound on the diameter of C and the fact that a tangential hyperplane does not intersect with $K(M, R)$ which contains a point at distance $R/2$ for each direction which is orthogonal to E.

For $E \in \mathbf{E}_0$ let $d\omega$ be the surface element of $F_a^{\mathbf{E}_E}$ and let s be the arc length along $F_a^{E+\vec{v}}$. Then for every point $P \in F_a^{\mathbf{E}_E}$ we have

$$d\omega = O(ds\, d\vec{v})$$

and therefore,

$$
\begin{aligned}
\text{vol}_{d-1}\left(F_a^{\mathbf{E}_E}\right) &\leq \int_{F_a^{\mathbf{E}_E}} d\omega \\
&\leq O\left(\int_{|\vec{v}| \leq R/2,\ \vec{v} \perp E} \int_{s=0}^{s_{\max}} ds\, d\vec{v}\right) \\
&\leq O\left(\int_{|\vec{v}| \leq R/2,\ \vec{v} \perp E} \text{vol}_1(F_a^{E+\vec{v}}) d\vec{v}\right).
\end{aligned}
$$

It suffices to bound

$$\text{vol}_1\left(F_a^{E+\vec{v}}\right) \leq \text{vol}_1\left(f_a^{E+\vec{v}}\right).$$

Now we are left with a two-dimensional problem where we have sets C^E with area and perimeter $\Theta(1)$. These properties follow from the bound on the diameter and the fact that C^E contains the circle $C^E \cap K(M, R)$ with a radius of size at least $\sqrt{3}\pi R/2$. We ask whether a point $P \in S_a^E$ belongs to F_a^E. Find the endpoints R_1, R_2 of the two arcs of length

$$b = \frac{a}{\varphi_a}$$

starting from Q, one for each direction. If $P \in F_a^E$, then by following the arcs from R_1 to R_2, a tangent is turned by an angle $\psi \geq \Omega(\varphi) \geq \Omega(\varphi_a)$. However,

$$\int_{S_0^E} \psi\, ds = O(b),$$

where s is the arc length along f_a^E, implying

$$\text{vol}_1(f_a^E) \leq \int_{\{Q: \psi > \varphi_a\}} ds \leq O\left(\frac{b}{\varphi_a}\right) = O\left(k^{-\frac{d+1}{d-1}}\right).$$

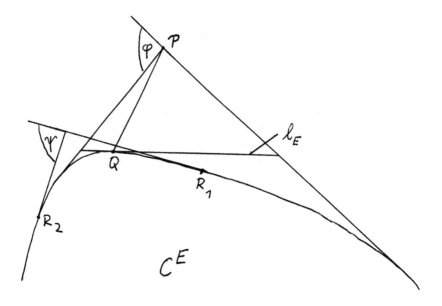

Figure 3: The points and angles associated with P and C^E

Using this and the previous inequalities we get

$$\mathrm{vol}_1(f_a^E) \leq O\left(a^{-\frac{d+1}{d-1}} \epsilon^{\frac{d+1}{d-1}}\right)$$

$$\mathrm{vol}_1(F_a^E) \leq O\left(a^{-\frac{d+1}{d-1}} \epsilon^{\frac{d+1}{d-1}}\right)$$

$$\mathrm{vol}_{d-1}(F_a) \leq O\left(a^{-\frac{d+1}{d-1}} \epsilon^{\frac{d+1}{d-1}}\right)$$

$$\mathrm{vol}_d(F) \leq O\left(\epsilon + \int_\epsilon^{a_{\max}} \left(a^{-\frac{d+1}{d-1}} \epsilon^{\frac{d+1}{d-1}}\right) da\right)$$

$$\leq O\left(\epsilon + \epsilon^{-\frac{2}{d-1}} \epsilon^{\frac{d+1}{d-1}}\right)$$

$$\leq O(\epsilon),$$

which completes the proof. ∎

Proof : (of Theorem 2.2)

W.l.o.g. we may assume $\mathrm{vol}(C) = 1$. If not, one can apply a linear transformation L such that $\mathrm{vol}(L(C)) = 1$. The transformed sample points are equidistributed in $L(C)$. As in the proof of the lemma we may assume that the diameter of C is bounded. We prove the theorem by analysing how the volume of the convex hull of the sample grows while we are successively adding new points.

We start with a sample Q_0 of size $c_3 m$. Let $C_0 = \mathrm{conv}(Q_0)$. The constant c_3 is chosen such that

$$\Pr\{\mathrm{vol}(C \backslash C_0) \leq \epsilon_0\} \geq 1 - \frac{\delta}{2}.$$

To see that this is possible, cover C with a grid. If the grid is fine enough, having a sample point in every cell which is completely contained in C will guarantee $\mathrm{vol}(C \backslash C_0) \leq \epsilon_0$. The probability that a specific cell contains none of the points is at most $(1 - c_4)^{c_3 m}$, for some constant c_4 with $0 < c_4 < 1$. The probability that there is a cell which contains none of the points, is of order $\exp(-\Omega(c_3 m)) \leq \delta/2$, for c_3 small enough.

Now, sequences C_i and ϵ_i can be defined by

$$C_i := \mathrm{conv}(C_{i-1} \cup \{P_i\})$$

and

$$\epsilon_i := \mathrm{vol}(C \backslash C_i) .$$

To determine P_i, for each i, we succesively generate samples Q_{ij} of size $|Q_{ij}| = m$ until one of the samples contains a point $P_i \notin F(C_{i-1}, \epsilon_{i-1}/2)$. Let J_i denote the index j for which this happens.

Since $\mathrm{vol}(A(P_i)) \geq \Omega(\epsilon_i^{(d+1)/2})$, we get the recurrence

$$\epsilon_i \leq \epsilon_{i-1} - \Omega\left(\epsilon_{i-1}^{\frac{d+1}{2}}\right) ,$$

which implies

$$\epsilon_i \leq O\left(i^{-\frac{2}{d-1}}\right) .$$

The process stops when $\epsilon_i \leq \epsilon$ for some i, from which follows

$$i = i_{\max} = \Omega\left(m^{\frac{d-1}{2}}\right) .$$

The total number of points is then given by $c_3 m + \sum_{i=1}^{i_{\max}} m J_i$. We estimate the probability that Q_{ij} contains the point P_i. According to Lemma 2.3, the region for possible points P_i has a volume of at least $\epsilon_{i-1}/2 \geq \epsilon/2$. Therefore, the probability p' that Q_{ij} contains no such point is bounded by $p' \leq (1 - \epsilon/2)^m \leq \sqrt{1/e} =: p$. We use p instead of p' and notice that the J_i are bounded by stochastically independent geometrically distributed random variables X_i with parameter $(1 - p)$. The probability that their sum is greater than $3 i_{\max}$ decreases exponentially with ϵ. ∎

Theorem 2.4 : *Let $d \geq 2$, $\epsilon = 1/m$, and $\delta \leq \exp(-\Omega(m))$; then learning S_2 requires $\Omega(m^{(d+1)/2})$ sample points.*

Proof : Let B be the d-dimensional sphere of volume $1 + 2\epsilon$. There are $k := \Theta((c_5 \epsilon)^{-(d-1)/2})$ disjoint spherical segments of B with height $c_5 \epsilon$ each, and volume $\Omega((c_5 \epsilon)^{(d+1)/2})$. The constant c_5 is chosen such that the total volume of all segments is 4ϵ. Consider sets C which are obtained from B by removing half of the spherical segments. Let $n := c_6(\epsilon^{-(d+1)/2})$, where the constant c_6 will be chosen later. The expected number of segments containing a sample point is $2\epsilon n \leq O(c_6 k)$. For small c_6 this is only a small fraction of all segments. The probability of having more than twice this number of segments is very small. Since any choice of the right number of segments is correct for some C, the approximation C' of the algorithm satisfies

$$\mathrm{vol}(C \vartriangle C') \geq \epsilon$$

in the worst case. ∎

3 References

[GW84] P. M. Gruber, J. M. Wills: *Convexity and its Applications*, Birkhäuser Verlag, pp. 131 ff.

[BEHW89] A. Blumer, A. Ehrenfeucht, D. Haussler, M. K. Warmuth: *Learnability and the Vapnik-Chervonenkis-Dimension*, J. ACM 36, pp. 929–965.

[V84] L. G. Valiant: *A Theory of the Learnable*, C. ACM 27, pp. 1134–1142.

[VC71] V. N. Vapnik, A. Ya. Chervonenkis: *On the Convergence of Relative Frequencies of Events to Their Probabilities*, Theoret. Probl. and Its Appl. 16, pp. 264–280.

[HW87] D. Haussler, E. Welzl: *Epsilon Nets and Simplex Range Qeries*, Disc. Comput. Geometry, pp. 127–151.

Spatial Access Structures for Geometric Databases [*]

Hans-Werner Six [†]   Peter Widmayer [‡]

Abstract

This paper surveys basic concepts of spatial access structures for geometric databases. We discuss the isolated plausibility arguments on which spatial access structure design decisions are traditionally based whenever efficiency is the primary goal, and we propose a more integrated view. This helps to explain phenomena that have been observed in experiments, and it lays the foundation for tailoring spatial access structures to the particular application requirements.

1   The setting

It is a well established fact that traditional — such as relational — database systems are inappropriate for a large class of nonstandard applications. On the one hand, modeling and querying nonstandard data may be unnatural in a traditional system, and on the other hand, the resulting inefficiency — such as a long response time to a geometric query — may render the system altogether useless. The management of geometric objects, for instance in CAD or cartography, is a prime example of an application where efficiency is the bottleneck; this bottleneck cannot be eliminated without the help of suitable access structures (see also Günther et al. 1990).

In this paper, we present the basic concepts of current geometric access structures and the efficiency arguments involved. The first part of our presentation is in the spirit of Widmayer (1991); different discussions can be found in Günther 1988, Nievergelt 1989, Seeger 1989, Henrich 1990, van Oosterom 1990, Shaffer et al. 1990, Samet 1990a, 1990b, Ooi 1990, Blankenagel 1991. Since we aim at a clear picture of the facts behind the façade, we disregard clever tricks with narrow applicability. Before presenting access structure concepts in the next section, let us now define which geometric objects and operations we consider, and how access structures are used to support operations.

---

[*]This work has been supported by the Deutsche Forschungsgemeinschaft DFG, grants Si 374/1 and Wi 810/2

[†]Praktische Informatik III, FernUniversität, Postfach 940, D-W 5800 Hagen

[‡]Institut für Informatik, Albert-Ludwigs-Universität, Rheinstr. 10-12, D-W 7800 Freiburg

1.1 Geometric objects

A geometric object is characterized by a geometric component that determines shape and position of the object in space. In CAD for VLSI, for instance, aligned rectangles of the different layers of a chip describe the physical chip layout; in cartography, a partition of space into polygons describes land uses or political entities. Objects may possess a non-geometric component, in addition to a geometric one, such as the name of a chip layer for an aligned VLSI rectangle or the name of a country in a political map. We distinguish between the geometric and the non-geometric component with respect to the defined operations: whatever is significant for geometric operations — such as distance or intersections of polygons — is considered to be geometric; anything else is considered to be non-geometric, even if it is determined by the geometry, like the area of a polygon.

Geometric objects may be complex in two ways: On the one hand, the complex geometry makes geometric algorithms complicated and slow; on the other hand, the representation of an object may be complicated and long. Since the problems resulting from geometric object complexity are not the topic of this paper, we will restrict our discussion to simple geometric objects with a short description and easy and fast geometric algorithms; these objects may serve as containers for more complex objects.

1.2 Operations

Geometric operations refer to the spatial position of objects, most often to spatial proximity. A range query asks for all objects that intersect a given query range. A nearest neighbor query asks for an object in the database that is closest to a given query point. Since the set of objects changes dynamically, insertions and deletions, and hence exact match queries, must also be supported.

1.3 Data structures

Data structures support geometric queries by realizing a fast but inaccurate filter for the response: The data structure allows to identify a superset of the set of desired objects. In a refinement step, each object returned by the data structure needs to be inspected. One reason for this approach is the complex geometry of objects that suggests the conservative approximation of each object by a simpler object of a fixed type, a container. The smallest aligned rectangle enclosing an object, the bounding box, is the most famous container: A data structure for aligned rectangles can be used to support geometric operations on arbitrary objects. For simplicity, we assume that a data item representing a geometric object is given by its geometric key; for a bounding box, the geometric key is the coordinates of the left, right, lower and upper rectangle boundary. We refrain from discussing the problems of maintaining object descriptions of variable length; for simplicity, we even assume that the description of the data item is fairly short.

Since the number of objects in an integrated geometric database easily goes into the millions (Crain 1990), we assume that the data are stored on a secondary storage medium with fixed size blocks that can be addressed directly, such as a magnetic disk. Here lies the other reason for the filtering and the refinement step: Since blocks on external storage can be accessed only as a whole, it is in general unavoidable to access objects that do not belong to the response of a query. The data structure for secondary storage supports the filtering step only, that is, the selection of all blocks to be accessed.

As a consequence, we focus on secondary storage access structures for multidimensional aligned rectangles (or, equivalently, multidimensional intervals), or even multidimensional points in special cases. In order to support range queries efficiently, these data structures should respect the spatial proximity of objects by distributing objects physically on disk according to their location in space. Therefore, it is not enough to organize a suitable extra index on the data; the geometric data structures need to be the primary data organization, with its effect on the physical clustering of objects in blocks.

1.4 The problem

Let us resume by defining the data maintenance problem more precisely as follows. Let d be the dimension of the space we consider, and let U_i be the universe in dimension i, $1 \leq i \leq d$. Let $U = U_1 \times U_2 \times \ldots \times U_d$ denote the d-dimensional universe of all geometric objects. Each geometric object g in an arbitrary set G of geometric objects is given by a d-dimensional bounding box b and other attributes that are not relevant for geometric operations. For each dimension i, $1 \leq i \leq d$, a bounding box b is the interval with left boundary l_i and right boundary r_i, $l_i, r_i \in U_i$, $l_i \leq r_i$. In total, $b = (l_1, r_1, l_2, r_2, \ldots, l_d, r_d)$ represents the d-dimensional interval $[l_1, r_1] \times \ldots \times [l_d, r_d]$. We use dot notation (as known from records in programming languages) to denote components; that is, component l_i of bounding box b is denoted by $b.l_i$, and similarly for $b.r_i$ and $g.b$. For brevity, we write $g.l_i$ or $g.r_i$ for $g.b.l_i$ or $g.b.r_i$. We are interested in a secondary storage access structure S that supports the following operations for a set G of geometric objects efficiently:

- *range query* $(w, S(G))$:
  For the query range (window) w and the set of objects G stored in S, return each object $g \in G$ whose bounding box $g.b$ intersects w. Here w is a d-dimensional interval, and the intersection of two topologically closed objects is defined as the closure of the intersection of the interior of the objects (as proposed by Tilove (1980) to avoid certain anomalies);

- *exact match query* $(b, S(G))$:
  For bounding box b and set G of geometric objects stored in S, return an object $g \in G$ with $g.b = b$;

- *insert* $(g, S(G))$:
  For the geometric object g and the set G of geometric objects stored in S, add g to G; the result is $S(G \cup \{g\})$;

- *delete* $(b, S(G))$:
  For bounding box b and set G of geometric objects stored in S, delete an object g with $g.b = b$ from G; the result is $S(G \setminus \{g\})$.

We are not interested in treating special cases explicitly, such as ambiguities in exact match queries, insertions or deletions; we will therefore assume uniqueness whenever this facilitates our discussion.

2   Basic concepts

The operations exact match, insert, and delete do not refer to the location of objects in space, in spite of the geometric key. They can be supported efficiently with traditional secondary storage access schemes, such as B-trees (Comer 1979) or dynamic hashing (Enbody et al. 1988), by simply concatenating the $2d$ key components of a d-dimensional bounding box lexicographically into a single key. Only in range queries, spatial proximity comes into the picture; we refrain from discussing other spatial queries explicitly, since range queries suffice to illustrate the basic concepts.

Since external storage access operations are far slower than main memory accesses or computation steps, usually the number of block accesses needed to answer a range query measures the complexity of that operation. Rarely, a closer look is taken towards the constituents of block access time, namely disk seek time, latency time and block transfer time (Weikum et al. 1987, Wang et al. 1987). Here, seek plus latency time exceeds transfer time by far on standard magnetic disks. If we consider the blocks on a disk to be arranged in a total linear order with relative addresses $0, 1, \ldots$, and if we assume that block $i + 1$ can be transferred immediately after the transfer of block i without any extra seek or latency time, then it is obvious that there may be an advantage to reading more than one block in a sequence. This can be achieved by defining a logical block to consist of a number of physical blocks, or even by systematically distributing data items on blocks in such a way that few sequences of blocks must be accessed in response to a range query (Hutflesz et al. 1988, 1991). In any case, a block that needs to be read should contain as many desired data as possible. For range queries, this implies that all objects stored in a block should be neighbors in space; we call this *local order preservation*. The requirement that objects in nearby blocks should be close in space, called *global order preservation*, can be achieved even less strictly in general, but may nevertheless increase efficiency for appropriate circumstances.

2.1   Associating objects with blocks

To preserve local order, geometric objects are associated with blocks according to their geometric key, the bounding box. This is achieved by means of geometric regions: With each block B_j in a set B of blocks, we uniquely associate a region $R_j \subseteq U$ in a set R of regions, $1 \leq j \leq m$, where m is the current number of blocks. Typically, a block's region is the bounding box of the objects stored in the block (Guttman 1984) or a part in a partition of the universe (Nievergelt et al. 1984). We also denote R_j by $R(B_j)$, and B_j by $B(R_j)$. A block in this context may consist of a number of logical blocks, such as overflow blocks, without further structure.

With each geometric object g, a set $R(g.b) \subseteq R$ of regions is associated uniquely via its key $g.b$. To illustrate this principle, let us look at point objects in some detail. Here we have $g.b.l_i = g.b.r_i$ for all objects $g \in G$ and all dimensions i, $1 \leq i \leq d$; we write $g.p$ (point) instead of $g.b$ and $p = (p_1, p_2, \ldots, p_d)$. In this case, usually R is chosen such that the regions partition U. With each geometric object g, we associate the region containing point $g.p$. Region boundaries are uniquely associated with one of the regions bounded.

Many popular space partitions are generalizations of well-known one-dimensional ones: *multidimensional linear hashing* (Ouksel et al. 1983, Kriegel et al. 1986, 1989, Hutflesz et al. 1988) generalizes linear hashing, the *grid file* (Nievergelt et al. 1984) and the *BANG file* (Freeston 1987, 1989a) generalize extendible hashing, and the *k-d-B-tree* (Robinson 1981) generalizes the B-tree. Except for the BANG file, all of these partitions have rectangular regions. This appears to make sense for rectangular range queries. If nothing is known beforehand about the aspect ratio of query ranges, square regions seem to suggest themselves.

The freedom of choosing regions is limited: on the one hand, regions should in some way match the objects (not a problem for point objects), and on the other hand, regions themselves need to be maintained, just like geometric objects. Qualitatively, the situation is similar to what we know from one-dimensional access structures: If regions adapt to objects in a more flexible way (such as B-trees do, as against linear hashing), the management of regions becomes a heavier burden (such as the internal nodes in a leaf-oriented B-tree, as against a counter in linear hashing), but the number of blocks needed to store the objects decreases. We distinguish between region definitions that are based only on the number of objects and not on their geometry, and those that take the geometry into account. The former allow for data structures without much overhead for region management, i.e., structures without directory, whereas the latter make a directory (of more than constant size) necessary.

2.2   Data structures without directory

For multidimensional linear hashing, the management of regions is as simple as possible: the number n of objects fully determines the partition of the universe into regions. Since the storage space capacity of a block is assumed to be a constant, say $c \in \mathbb{N}$ objects, the number m of regions is determined by a fixed, desired storage space utilization of $\alpha = n/(c \cdot m)$. This number of regions is reached by repeatedly cutting a region into two new regions, according to a fixed scheme; the initial region is the universe. For maintaining the partition of the universe into regions, it is therefore sufficient to keep track of the number of cuts that have taken place since the beginning. Hence, we do not need an extra data structure — a directory — for maintaining the partition. On the other hand, the partition cannot adapt to the *set* of objects; therefore, in general, a fixed size block will not be large enough to store all objects in its region, and hence overflow blocks will be necessary. As a result, query efficiency will be acceptable only if geometric objects are distributed rather evenly in space.

2.3 Data structures with directory

Structures that adapt the regions to the set of objects do need a directory to maintain the set of regions. At least for point objects, the region maintenance problem may be the hardest part of the data structuring problem. As in the one-dimensional case, a directory can be built on a mixture of the address computation (as in hashing) and the key comparison (as in trees) techniques. For illustration purposes, assume $U_i = [0, 1)$ for each i with $1 \leq i \leq d$. In address computation techniques, we represent a coordinate value $x \in [0, 1)$ (for p_i, l_i or r_i) by the bit sequence $b_1 b_2 b_3 \ldots$ (of conceptually infinite length) of the fractional part of the binary representation of x, i.e., $x = \sum_{j=1}^{\infty} b_j 2^{-j}, b_j \in \{0, 1\}$. Depending on our needs, we pick a finite prefix with value $x_k = \sum_{j=1}^{k} b_j 2^{-j}$; its length k is called *resolution*, the sequence itself is called a *binary radix sequence*. In dimension i with resolution k_i, a *binary radix interval* I_i is an interval that can be created from U_i by repeated cutting in halves; such an interval has a left end point x_h and a length 2^{-j}, for $0 \leq h \leq j \leq k_i$. For d binary radix intervals $I_1, \ldots, I_d$, call $I_1 \times \ldots \times I_d$ a *binary radix region*. Almost all geometric data structures based on address computation arrive at regions through set operations on binary radix regions, where a region is viewed as a point set. Mostly, the union operation is enough; sometimes, e.g. for the BANG file, set difference is used in addition. The resolution of binary radix regions is chosen only as large as necessary to avoid overflow blocks (or other undesired phenomena, such as lack of balance in the BANG file).

In contrast to address computation, key comparison based data structures allow for a free choice of region boundary positions. Hence, regions fit objects more closely, but the expected effort to maintain regions increases. Mixtures of address computation and key comparison techniques try to make use of both, good worst case behavior in trees and fast expected access by hashing. Typically, each node in the tree is an external storage block whose interior is organized by hashing; data structures of this type are sometimes called *hash trees* (Otoo 1986, Seeger 1989).

Since a directory must be designed to support range queries, we request for simplicity that for each object g associated with a region, $g.b$ intersects the region. Clearly, each object is associated with at least one and at most all of the regions intersected by its bounding box; for point objects, there is no reason to choose more than one region. Hence, to answer a range query, it suffices to access all blocks whose regions intersect the query range.

2.4 Associating rectangles with regions

Whereas it is fairly obvious how to associate point objects with regions, this is not true for rectangular objects: in a partition of the universe into regions, a rectangle need not be enclosed in any one region. In that case, the only way of handling range queries efficiently requests that the rectangle is associated with each of the regions it intersects, and hence that the object is stored in each of the corresponding blocks; this technique is known as *clipping*. In general, clipping may degrade performance substantially, since the number of objects (copies) to be stored increases, which in turn increases the number of regions, thereby again increasing the number of copies, a vicious circle (Six et al. 1986, 1988).

If we allow instead that regions may *overlap* without any restriction, we can define for each rectangle at least one region that encloses the rectangle. To answer range queries efficiently, it is then sufficient to associate a rectangle with one of the regions that enclose it. However, if the directory does not tell with which of these regions a rectangle is associated, an exact match query may become quite inefficient, since all candidate regions may have to be inspected; this is the case with the R-tree (Guttman 1984). In addition, if regions tend to overlap too much, the geometric selectivity of the access structure suffers, with a negative effect also on range query performance (Greene 1989).

As a third possibility, a rectangle may be viewed as a *point* in some parameter space. For simplicity, most often a d-dimensional rectangle $b = (l_1, r_1, \ldots, l_d, r_d)$ is viewed as a $2d$-dimensional point $p = (p_1, \ldots, p_{2d})$, with $p_{2i-1} = l_i$ and $p_{2i} = r_i$ for $1 \leq i \leq d$. A range query in the original space maps into a half-open range query in parameter space, i.e., a range query whose query region extends to half the boundaries of the parameter space. Many arguments and experiments have been made to reveal the performance that can be expected from parameter space transformations (Hinrichs 1985, Seeger et al. 1988, Henrich et al. 1989, Henrich 1990).

All known data structures for rectangles are limited to these three basic ingredients: clipping, overlapping regions, and point transformations (Six et al. 1986, 1988, Seeger et al. 1988). Therefore, data structures for points do not only cover a special case of objects, but can also be used to maintain sets of parameter points. Multidimensional point data structures can be obtained from suitable generalizations of one-dimensional structures. In a different approach, multidimensional points are mapped to one-dimensional ones and maintained in one-dimensional structures (Tropf et al. 1981, Orenstein et al. 1984, Faloutsos 1985, 1988, Manola et al. 1986, Hutflesz et al. 1988, Orenstein 1989, 1990, Faloutsos et al. 1989, Jagadish 1990b, Abel et al. 1990, van Oosterom 1990); the advantage is the fact that one-dimensional structures are conceptually simpler and have been investigated for a long time, the disavantage is the fact that the mapping into one-dimensional space does not preserve the overall geometric situation of the multidimensional space.

2.5 Different regions for different operations

Range query efficiency can be improved by distinguishing regions for inserting new objects from regions for querying: in a range query, a bounding box of the objects actually stored in a block may provide for higher geometric selectivity than the block's region. In general, for a block B we have not only one region $R(B)$, but instead we have a region $RI(B)$ for inserting elements, plus a different region $RS(B)$ for searching, i.e., exact match, range query and delete operations. In most cases, $RS(B)$ must be contained in $RI(B)$; a very simple family of data structures for rectangles, where each rectangle is associated with the region containing its center point, is the only exception to this rule. For given sets RS and RI, with each geometric object g we associate via its key $g.b$ a set $RS(g.b) \subseteq RS$ of search regions and a set $RI(g.b) \subseteq RI$ of insertion regions. The distinction between insertion regions and search regions makes point data structures more efficient (Seeger 1989, Seeger et al. 1990), and it does even more so for rectangle data structures (Hutflesz et al. 1990); in some cases, this distinction alone turns a point data structure into a rectangle data structure (Ooi 1987, Seeger et al. 1988, Ooi et al. 1989, Freeston 1989b).

2.6 Growing and shrinking

The association of regions with objects changes dynamically: Upon insertion or deletion of an object we check by means of a growth or shrinkage criterion whether the number of blocks and, hence, of regions, should increase or decrease. Growth is typically induced by reaching a prespecified storage space utilization (for structures without directory) or by a block overflow (for structures with directory). To realize growth, we select an appropriate block and split its region into two; then, we associate two blocks with the new regions (one of the two blocks may be the old one that was split, but at least one new block is added). The function that associates an object with a set of blocks tells where to store the objects in the block that was split. In case this growth step preserves the criterion for growth, we repeat it; this may be the case if a block split does not eliminate an overflow.

Shrinking the number of regions and blocks is often more complicated, but fortunately also less important, since sets of data rarely shrink in practice. Also, in many data structures shrinking is not necessary for correctness, but only for efficiency; this is not true for growing, unless overflow blocks are allowed. Essentially, shrinking reverses growing: a shrinking step, induced by a delete operation, selects two suitable blocks and merges them. Both, the two blocks and the two regions, are merged into one. Two suitable regions and blocks, however, do not always exist; in that case, shrinking is impossible. To remain efficient, data structures have to make sure that for a decreasing number of objects, eventually a sufficient number of shrinking steps is possible. In this paper, we will not be concerned with further details of shrinking steps from now on.

2.7 An algorithmic framework

To identify the basic concepts underlying most efficient data structures for geometric objects more rigorously, let us propose here a simple algorithmic framework for the considered operations:

– *range query* $(w, S(G))$:
    determine all search regions RS_j with $RS_j \cap w \neq \emptyset$;
    foreach of these RS_j **do**
        read block $B_j = B(RS_j)$;
        report all g in B_j with $g.b \cap w \neq \emptyset$;

– *exact match query* $(b, S(G))$:
    determine the set $RS(b)$;
    repeat for a search region $RS_j \in RS(b)$ not yet considered,
        read block $B_j = B(RS_j)$
    until an object g with $g.b = b$ is stored in B_j
        {successful search}

or all search regions in $RS(b)$ have been considered
{unsuccessful search};

$-$ *insert* $(g, S(G))$:
   {assume that g is not yet in G, or duplicates are allowed}
   determine the set $RI(g.b)$;
   foreach $RI_j \in RI(g.b)$ **do**
      enter g into $B_j = B(RI_j)$ {here, it can become necessary to extend
         B_j by an overflow block; depending on the growth
         criterion, this is temporary or permanent};
      while growth criterion is satisfied **do**
         select block B_S to be split;
         from $RI(B_S)$ and the objects in B_S, determine two new
            regions RI_1, RI_2 within $RI(B_S)$ according to
            the split strategy;
         distribute all objects from B_S accordingly on
            $B_1 = B(RI_1)$ and $B_2 = B(RI_2)$
            {one of both blocks can be B_S, at least the
            other must be newly allocated};
         determine $RS(B_1)$ and $RS(B_2)$ accordingly from the objects
            in B_1 and B_2;

$-$ *delete* $(b, S(G))$:
   {assume that in G, there is exactly one object g with $g.b = b$}
   determine the set $RS(b)$;
   foreach $RS_j \in RS(b)$ **do**
      remove g from $B_j = B(RS_j)$, if g occurs there;
      while shrinkage criterion is satisfied **do**
         select a pair of blocks B_1 and B_2 to be merged
            according to the merge strategy;
         store the objects of B_1 and B_2 together in B_3
            {one of the two old blocks can be B_3, at least
            the other must be deallocated};
         determine $RS(B_3)$ and $RI(B_3)$.

This algorithmic framework is too general to reveal much about spatial access structures. Nevertheless, it indicates a few places where data structuring techniques should be applied. To define a particular data structure, we obviously need to make at least the following decisions:

1. How should regions look like? What is a split strategy and what is a merge strategy to achieve this dynamically? In case block addresses must be associated with regions so as to preserve global order, which rule should be applied?

2. How should objects be associated with regions?

3. What should be the criterion for growth, what should it be for shrinking? How should blocks be selected for split and for merge operations?

4. How can we maintain regions in a way that supports all necessary operations on regions efficiently?

These questions may serve as a template for the definition of data structures; together with the algorithmic framework, answers to these questions propose a simple implementation of the desired operation.

3 Isolated efficiency arguments for spatial searching

In this section, we want to give an overview on the folklore arguments on the efficiency of spatial searching. These arguments mostly come from data structure design experiences; due to the complexity of the situation, they are sometimes fairly wishy-washy. A fundamental problem with the arguments is the fact that they are only available "ceteris paribus"; that is, even the qualitative efficiency effect of the change of one design parameter in a data structure (will the change increase or decrease efficiency?) can only be told under the assumption that nothing else changes. This assumption, however, is not only a critical one: Due to the high interdependency between design parameters, it is *never* satisfied. Nevertheless, a closer look at the folklore arguments, to be taken in this section, informs about the spectrum of possible effects of design decisions. The next section illustrates how these isolated effects can be brought together quantitatively in a way that allows to judge a design change on the basis of an objective function for the efficiency of range queries.

The efficiency of operations is considered to be determined by the number of external block accesses, or, far less frequently, by the number of disk seek operations. Spatial access structures aim at a good average case efficiency for range queries, without even clearly defining what *average* means. Stochastic geometry (Harding et al. 1974, Matheron 1975, Santalo 1976, Stoyan 1987, Mecke et al. 1990) has shown that it is by no means easy to talk about a random geometric situation in a reasonable sense; we do not expect a mathematical model of typical situations in CAD or cartography to be found in the near future. Except for some very rare cases in which analytical results are available (Regnier 1985, Flajolet et al. 1986, Devroye 1986), statements about the efficiency of operations in data structures must be based on plausibility arguments and experiments.

3.1 Measures of efficiency

At times, plausibility arguments are supported by definitions of measures of efficiency that work for a comparison of different data structures, but also for a comparison of design alternatives within one data structure, such as the split strategy. In the execution of a range query, let ex be the number of external storage accesses (overflow blocks count separately), ro the number of retrieved objects (that is, the number of objects in accessed blocks), and ao the number of objects that form the answer. The following measures of efficiency have been proposed in the literature:

- $(\frac{ao}{n})/(\frac{ex}{m})$ (Robinson 1981); this value is close to 1, if the percentage of the objects in the answer with respect to all objects is close to the percentage of the accessed blocks with respect to all blocks;

- ao/ro (Nievergelt et al. 1984, Orenstein 1990), the precision of the filter step, is ideally 1, and can be as low as 0;

- $ao/(ex \cdot c)$ (Seeger 1989, Henrich 1990), the hit ratio, is similar to the precision of the filter step, but with the storage space utilization taken into account.

All of these measures of efficiency suffer from more or less severe flaws. We only mention them to roughly illustrate the objectives in the design and the comparison of data structures; none of the data structures, however, strictly optimizes any of these measures. Instead, plausibility arguments are used to pronounce the design decisions illustrated in the previous section.

3.2 Data structure design decisions

Let us now summarize our understanding of the discussion on design decisions and their effects on efficiency. We feel that for a general setting, data structures without directory must be ruled out because of their lack of adaptivity. To focus our presentation, the criterion for growth can then be fixed to a block overflow; i.e., whenever a block overflows, it needs to be split into two blocks. Let us assume that an object is associated with one of the regions that contain its bounding box; i.e., we disregard clipping, due to its narrow range of application. Since close to all spatial access structures define regions to be (multidimensional) rectangles, let us restrict our discussion to this case. This makes us disregard partitions of the universe into convex polyhedra (as e.g. in the cell tree, Günther 1988) or into polyhedra with fixed orientations (Jagadish 1990a); however, we do not drop the BANG file from consideration, because its non-rectangular regions, formed by set difference operations starting at rectangular regions, are represented implicitly by their constituent rectangles anyway. Since maintaining regions is now similar to maintaining bounding boxes, we restrict our attention to hierarchical spatial access structures, including the extreme form of a totally flat hierarchy. In this situation, a split strategy for overfull blocks is the major remaining design decision. Let us therefore discuss split strategies for data blocks in some detail; split strategies for directory blocks are similar, but have to take the directory particularities into account.

3.3 Split strategies

For point data structures, no two data block regions share a common point; the same is true within each level of the directory hierarchy. To split a block into two, its rectangular region is partitioned into two regions at a *split hyperplane*. To define the split hyperplane, we first choose the dimension perpendicular to the hyperplane, the *split dimension*, and then the position of the hyperplane in the split dimension, the *split position*. To support range queries of unknown aspect ratio, regions of roughly equal length sides seem most appropriate. Hence, the split dimension is chosen as the dimension of one of the region's longest sides. For binary radix regions, the split position is then fixed to the center of the (multidimensional) rectangle side. This seems to be a good choice, if the aspect ratios (length of shortest side, divided by length of longest side) of both resulting regions should be as close to 1 as possible.

On the other hand, a binary radix split may distribute the geometric objects quite unevenly between the two regions: In the extreme case, all objects are associated with one of the regions; then, the split does not solve the overflow problem at all. Even if the overflow is resolved, splitting into sets of unequal sizes leads to low storage space utilization which in turn leads to poor range query performance. Here, a split at the median of the objects is better; however, maintaining arbitrary (data dependent) split positions in the directory uses more space, and for a sequence of insertions, median splitting makes regions sensitive to the sequence (as opposed to the set) of inserted objects. The conflict between the regularity and hence efficiency of binary radix splits on one hand and arbitrary (median) splits on the other is resolved to some extent in the BANG file: Here, a binary radix split of the region that contains the larger number of objects is repeated until that region contains at most half of all objects. This guarantees a balance between the numbers of objects in both resulting regions, but makes more than one binary radix split necessary to split a region into two.

Data structures for non-point objects, such as the members of the R-tree family, split a region into two according to some optimization criterion. Under the restriction of achieving at least a certain balance in the number of objects, geometric criteria like overlap of both resulting regions, sum of their areas, or sum of their perimeters, and combinations of these criteria, are minimized, most often heuristically (Beckmann et al. 1990). This is possible only if arbitrary split positions and dimensions can be selected. To gain some efficiency due to higher regularity, the R-file (Hutflesz et al. 1990) overlaps BANG file regions; this does lead to efficient but complicated operations.

In order to avoid the problems of overlapping regions, parameter point transformations have been widely investigated. Since these transformations do not preserve the spatial neighborhood of objects in the original space, and since the distribution of parameter points tends to be extremely skew, a large directory and low storage space utilization in data blocks tend to result. As a consequence, query efficiency may be quite low, except for special situations.

All of these arguments, if applied in isolation, sound rather convincing. The interaction of the factors, however, seems to be far from understood. In the next section, we shall try to point out that this interaction lies at the very heart of the data organization problem, and to shed some light onto this interaction. Especially, the interaction of factors may make any one isolated argument incorrect: For instance, overlapping block regions may be more efficient than disjoint ones, and lower space utilization may be more efficient than higher utilization.

4 An integrated view of the efficiency of spatial searching

The plausibility arguments of the previous section illustrate several single aspects of the efficiency of spatial searching, but not their interdependence. To resume, range query efficiency requests (1) economy of space, i.e., high block utilization; (2) geometric selectivity, i.e., small region overlap; (3) adaptivity of the data structure, with choices ranging from highly adaptive arbitrary splits with long representation to less adaptive binary radix splits with short representation. Let us now try to illustrate quantitatively the interdependence of these factors, starting with a very simplistic model; we feel that more work is needed to make our observations meaningful for the general case.

4.1 Efficiency as a minimization problem

For our discussion of design decisions for spatial data structures, it suffices to simply define the efficiency of a range query as the number of block accesses needed to answer the query, or, equivalently, as the number of regions (data or directory) that intersect the query range; the more complicated measures of efficiency of the previous section do not tell more than this simple one in our argumentation. For explanation purposes, let us look at two-dimensional space. A region R_j is a rectangle, say with height Y_j and width X_j. Consider a range query with a query rectangle r of fixed height y and fixed width x whose center occurs at each possible position in the bounded universe $U = U_1 \times U_2 = [0, 1) \times [0, 1)$ with equal probability. Then $X_j \cdot Y_j$ is the probability that the center of r lies in R_j, and under the assumption that R_j is far enough off the boundary of the universe, $(X_j + x) \cdot (Y_j + y)$ is the probability that r intersects R_j. Geometrically, $(X_j + x) \cdot (Y_j + y)$ is just the area of the region R_j, inflated by a frame of width $x/2$ at the left and the right and of height $y/2$ at the bottom and the top. For simplicity, let us neglect the inaccuracy that results from the situation at the boundary of the universe. Range query efficiency is now optimum if the sum of the areas of all inflated regions is minimum, under the restriction that the association of objects with regions is legal, and the block capacity restriction is satisfied: $\sum_{j=1}^{m}(X_j + x) \cdot (Y_j + y) \to \min$.

Since regions have to be defined without knowing r, and indeed query rectangles are different in different queries, let us fix — again for simplicity — the aspect ratio of a query rectangle to be 1. This seems to be appropriate unless some shape bias is known beforehand, since the expected value of the aspect ratio is 1 if all aspect ratios are equally likely. Then, for query square r with width and height q, we get the following minimization problem: $\sum_{j=1}^{m}(X_j + q) \cdot (Y_j + q) \to \min$; that is, $\sum_{j=1}^{m}(X_j Y_j + q(X_j + Y_j) + q^2) \to \min$, or, equivalently, $\sum_{j=1}^{m} X_j Y_j + q \sum_{j=1}^{m}(X_j + Y_j) + q^2 m \to \min$.

In geometric terms, this function combines the sum of all region areas, the weighted sum of all region perimeters, and the weighted number of regions. Even though it is very simple minded, this function quantitatively illustrates a number of plausibility arguments: For instance, the term $q^2 m$ tells that high data block utilization is a more important factor if query ranges are larger. Instead of discussing the terms of the formula in isolation, let us try to gain some insight on how to design an efficient data structure for spatial searching. For simplicity, let us restrict our discussion to data block regions, even though our formula includes directory block regions.

Whenever the data structure *partitions* the data space (at least on the data block level, and most often on each level of the directory tree), the $\sum_{j=1}^{m} X_j Y_j$ term equals 1, no matter how regions are chosen. For *very small query ranges*, say $q \ll X_j + Y_j$ for any region R_j, the $q^2 m$ term is negligible, and we get $\sum_{j=1}^{m}(X_j + Y_j) \to \min$, i.e., the sum of data block region perimeters is to be minimized. The fact that region perimeters may play some role in the optimization has already been observed for the R*-tree (Beckmann et al. 1990); our formula may help to explain part of this observation. For *very large query ranges*, say $q \gg X_j + Y_j$, the only significant term is $q^2 m$; i.e., the data block utilization should be maximized.

In cases where regions may *overlap*, *very small query ranges* make the $\sum_{j=1}^{m} X_j Y_j$ term dominate the others; i.e., the sum of the areas of all regions should be minimized, or, if the universe is to be covered with regions, the region overlap should be minimized. For *very large query ranges*, again $q^2 m$ dominates the rest, indicating that data block utilization is to be maximized.

Let us now try to learn from our formula how to split a data block in a spatial data structure.

4.2   Split strategies

The simplest way of deducing a split strategy consists of just applying the global optimization criteria in each local split decision. In a data structure whose data block regions partition the universe, we aim at minimizing the region perimeters and the number of regions. The former dictates the split of a rectangular region parallel to a shortest rectangle side, the latter dictates a split at the median of the objects. Since these two goals do not conflict, they can always be achieved simultaneously. For the median split, however, short term and long term optimality may be quite different: depending on the future insertions of objects, the current median may or may not happen to be a good estimate of the objects to come. Furthermore, median splits on data block level may render median splits on higher levels in a hierarchical directory impossible. Both problems are avoided with binary radix splits; in total, we feel that in many cases, binary radix splits may prove to be more efficient.

For overlapping data block regions, the optimization goals for small and large query regions conflict: little overlap and balanced distribution cannot always be achieved simultaneously. Depending on the expected size of query ranges, we may aim at directly optimizing our formula in a region split. To our knowledge, this dependence of the split strategy on the query ranges has not been made explicit so far in the literature, even though it influences the corresponding performance experiments.

A closer look at our objective function reveals more details about split strategies. For instance, the break-even point between the $\sum_{j=1}^{m} X_j Y_j$ term and the $q \sum_{j=1}^{m}(X_j + Y_j)$ term where $X_j = c_j Y_j$ for the aspect ratio c_j of region R_j lies at $q = \frac{c_j}{c_j+1} Y_j$ for each individual region R_j. Hence, for $q \geq \frac{c_j}{c_j+1} Y_j$, the perimeter term of the formula dominates. In a split operation, we may minimize the sum of both resulting perimeters only, disregarding the sum of areas completely, without being too far off the total optimum: Because $X_j Y_j < q(X_j + Y_j)$ and $q^2 > 0$, $\sum_{j=1}^{m} X_j Y_j$ contributes at most half to the value of the objective function, and therefore we are off the minimum by at most a factor of 2.

The corresponding statement is not true in the symmetric case of $q < \frac{c_j}{c_j+1} Y_j$, since pure area minimization may lead to a value of the objective function that is arbitrarily far off the optimum. In addition, this also holds for pure perimeter minimization in that case. Fortunately, for most practical cases we can safely assume $q > Y_j > \frac{c_j}{c_j+1} Y_j$ and hence primarily minimize the perimeters.

We have carried out quite a few performance experiments with several data structures, sets of data, and range queries, to experimentally support the conclusions drawn from the study of the objective function for range query efficiency. In spite of the extreme simplicity of the objective function, the experiments tend to support the conclusions; nevertheless, they do need further elaboration. However, it is already clear that some well-known choices of split positions in a data space partition, like median split, mean split and radix split, behave almost as expected. Unexpectedly, in the experiments the storage space utilization has always been close to $\ln 2$, even though median splits should tend to lead to better space utilization than radix splits. As expected, the radix split leads to shortest perimeters among the three strategies, and together with its simplicity seems the method of choice to us.

We had to make a different observation for overlapping regions. Our experiments have shown that an exact minimization of the objective function (Becker et al. 1992) for a fixed size query square (i.e., q fixed) at each split in an R-tree does not lead to higher efficiency for the intended range queries than almost any reasonable R-tree split strategy, e.g. the quadratic split of Guttman (1984). This clearly indicates that local optimization of the objective function in a split may be different from global optimization, and it points to an area of further investigations.

Acknowledgement

We gratefully acknowledge the support of the Deutsche Forschungsgemeinschaft DFG of our investigations of spatial access structures for geometric databases, and the common efforts of our team members B. Becker, S. Gschwind, A. Henrich, A. Hilbert, A. Hutflesz, T. Ohler, B.-U. Pagel, G. Thiemt, and H. Toben over the years of our DFG project, as well as helpful discussions with P. Franciosa, A. Frank, O. Günther, R. H. Güting, H.-P. Kriegel, J. Nievergelt, Th. Ottmann, H. Samet, H.-J. Schek, and B. Seeger.

References

Abel, D.J., D.M. Mark (1990): A comparative analysis of some two-dimensional orderings; International Journal of Geographical Information Systems, Vol. 4, No. 1, 21–31

Becker, B., P. Franciosa, S. Gschwind, T. Ohler, G. Thiemt, P. Widmayer (1992): Enclosing many boxes by an optimal pair of boxes; to appear in Proceedings of the 9th Symposium on Theoretical Aspects of Computer Science, Paris, 1992

Beckmann, N., H.-P. Kriegel, R. Schneider, B. Seeger (1990): The R*-tree: an efficient and robust access method for points and rectangles; Proc. ACM SIGMOD International Conference on the Management of Data, Atlantic City, New Jersey, 322–331

Blankenagel, G. (1991): Intervall-Indexstrukturen und externe Algorithmen für Nicht-Standard-Datenbanksysteme, Doctoral Dissertation, FernUniversität Hagen

Comer, D. (1979): The ubiquitous B-tree; ACM Computing Surveys, Vol. 11, No. 2, 121–138

Crain, I.K. (1990): Extremely large spatial information systems: a quantitative perspective; Proc. 4th International Symposium on Spatial Data Handling, Zürich, 632–641

Devroye L. (1986): Lecture notes on bucket algorithms; Birkhäuser, Boston

Enbody, R.J., H.C. Du (1988): Dynamic hashing schemes; ACM Computing Surveys, Vol. 20, No. 2, 85–113

Faloutsos, C. (1985): Multiattribute hashing using Gray codes; Proc. ACM SIGMOD International Conference on the Management of Data, Washington D.C., 227–238

Faloutsos, C. (1988): Gray codes for partial match and range queries; IEEE Transactions on Software Engineering, Vol. 14, 1381–1393

Faloutsos, C., S. Roseman (1989): Fractals for secondary key retrieval; Proc. 8th ACM SIGACT/SIGMOD Symposium on Principles of Database Systems, 247–252

Flajolet P., C. Puech (1986): Partial match retrieval of multidimensional data; Journal of the ACM, Vol. 33, No. 2, 371–407

Freeston, M.W. (1987): The BANG file: a new kind of grid file; Proc. ACM SIGMOD International Conference on the Management of Data, San Francisco, 260–269

Freeston, M.W. (1989a): Advances in the design of the BANG file; Proc. 3rd International Conference on Foundations of Data Organization and Algorithms, Paris, Lecture Notes in Computer Science, Vol. 367, Springer, Berlin, 322–338

Freeston, M.W. (1989b): A well-behaved file structure for the storage of spatial objects; Symposium on the Design and Implementation of Large Spatial Databases, Santa Barbara, Lecture Notes in Computer Science, Vol. 409, Springer, Berlin, 287–300

Greene, D. (1989): An implementation and performance analysis of spatial data access methods; Proc. 5th International Conference on Data Engineering, Los Angeles, 606–615

Günther, O. (1988): Efficient structures for geometric data management; Lecture Notes in Computer Science, Vol. 337, Springer, Berlin

Günther, O., A. Buchmann (1990): Research issues in spatial databases; IEEE CS Bulletin on Data Engineering, Vol. 13, No. 4, 35–42

Guttman, A. (1984): R-trees: a dynamic index structure for spatial searching; Proc. ACM SIGMOD International Conference on the Management of Data, Boston, 47–57

Harding, E.F., D.G. Kendall (1974): Stochastic Geometry; Wiley, New York

Henrich, A. (1990): Der LSD-Baum: eine mehrdimensionale Zugriffsstruktur und ihre Einsatzmöglichkeiten in Datenbanksystemen; Doctoral Dissertation, FernUniversität Hagen

Henrich, A., H.-W. Six, P. Widmayer (1989): The LSD-tree: Spatial access to multidimensional point- and non-point objects; 15th International Conference on Very Large Data Bases, Amsterdam, 45–53

Hinrichs, K.H. (1985): The grid file system: implementation and case studies of applications; Doctoral Dissertation, ETH Zürich

Hutflesz, A., H.-W. Six, P. Widmayer (1988): Globally order preserving multidimensional linear hashing; Proc. 4th International Conference on Data Engineering, Los Angeles, 572–579

Hutflesz, A., H.-W. Six, P. Widmayer (1990): The R-file: An efficient access structure for proximity queries; Proc. 6th International Conference on Data Engineering, Los Angeles, 372–379

Hutflesz, A., P. Widmayer, C. Zimmermann (1991): Global order makes spatial access faster; International Workshop on Data Base Management Systems for Geographical Applications, Springer

Jagadish, H.V. (1990a): Spatial search with polyhedra; Proc. 6th International Conference on Data Engineering, Los Angeles, 311–319

Jagadish, H.V. (1990b): Linear clustering of objects with multiple attributes; Proc. ACM SIGMOD International Conference on the Management of Data, Atlantic City, New Jersey, 332–342

Kriegel, H.-P., B. Seeger (1986): Multidimensional order preserving linear hashing with partial expansions; Proc. International Conference on Database Theory, Lecture Notes in Computer Science, Vol. 243, Springer, Berlin, 203–220

Kriegel, H.-P., B. Seeger (1989): Multidimensional quantile hashing is very efficient for non-uniform distributions; Information Sciences, Vol. 48, 99–117

Manola, F., J.A. Orenstein (1986): Toward a general spatial data model for an object-oriented DBMS; Proc. 12th International Conference on Very Large Data Bases, Kyoto, 328–335

Matheron G. (1975): Random sets and integral geometry; Wiley, New York

Mecke, J., R.G. Schneider, D. Stoyan, W.R.R. Weil (1990): Stochastische Geometrie; DMV-Seminar Vol. 16, Birkhäuser, Basel

Nievergelt, J. (1989): 7 ± 2 criteria for assessing and comparing spatial data structures; Symposium on the Design and Implementation of Large Spatial Databases, Santa Barbara, Lecture Notes in Computer Science, Vol. 409, Springer, Berlin, 3-28

Nievergelt, J., H. Hinterberger, K.C. Sevcik (1984): The grid file: an adaptable, symmetric multikey file structure; ACM Transactions on Database Systems, Vol. 9, No. 1, 38-71

Ooi, B.C. (1987): A data structure for geographic database; GI-Fachtagung Datenbanksysteme für Büro, Technik und Wissenschaft, Informatik-Fachberichte, Vol. 136, Springer, Berlin, 247-258

Ooi, B.C. (1990): Efficient query processing in geographic information systems, Lecture Notes in Computer Science, Vol. 471, Springer, Berlin

Ooi, B.C., R. Sacks-Davis, K.J. McDonell (1989): Extending a DBMS for geographic applications; Proc. 5th International Conference on Data Engineering, Los Angeles, 590-597

Orenstein, J.A. (1989): Redundancy in spatial databases; Proc. ACM SIGMOD International Conference on the Management of Data, Portland, 294-305

Orenstein, J.A. (1990): A comparison of spatial query processing techniques for native and parameter spaces; Proc. ACM SIGMOD International Conference on the Management of Data, Atlantic City, New Jersey, 343-352

Orenstein, J.A., T.H. Merrett (1984): A class of data structures for associative searching; Proc. 3rd ACM SIGACT/SIGMOD Symposium on Principles of Database Systems, Waterloo, 181-190

Otoo, E.J. (1986): Balanced multidimensional extendible hash tree; Proc. 5th ACM SIGACT-SIGMOD International Symposium on Principles of Database Systems, Cambridge, Massachusetts, 100-113

Ouksel, M., P. Scheuermann (1983): Storage mappings for multidimensional linear dynamic hashing; Proc. 2nd ACM SIGACT/SIGMOD Symposium on Principles of Database Systems, 90-105

Regnier, M. (1985): Analysis of grid file algorithms; BIT Vol. 25, 335-357

Robinson, J.T. (1981): The K-D-B-tree: a search structure for large multidimensional dynamic indexes; Proc. ACM SIGMOD International Conference on the Management of Data, Ann Arbor, 10-18

Samet, H. (1990a): The design and analysis of spatial data structures; Addison-Wesley, Reading

Samet, H. (1990b): Applications of spatial data structures; Addison-Wesley, Reading

Santaló, L.A. (1976): Integral geometry and geometric probability; Addison-Wesley, Reading

Seeger, B. (1989): Entwurf und Implementierung mehrdimensionaler Zugriffsstrukturen; Doctoral Dissertation, Universität Bremen

Seeger, B., H.-P. Kriegel (1988): Techniques for design and implementation of efficient spatial access methods; Proc. 14th International Conference on Very Large Data Bases, Los Angeles, 360–371

Seeger, B., H.-P. Kriegel (1990): The buddy-tree: an efficient and robust access method for spatial data base systems; Proc. 16th International Conference on Very Large Data Bases, Brisbane, 590–601

Shaffer, C.A., H. Samet, R.C. Nelson (1990): QUILT: a geographic information system based on quadtrees; International Journal of Geographical Information Systems, Vol. 4, No. 2, 103–131

Six H.-W., P. Widmayer (1986): Hintergrundspeicherstrukturen für ausgedehnte Objekte; 16. Jahrestagung der Gesellschaft für Informatik, Berlin, Informatik-Fachberichte, Vol. 126, Springer, Berlin, 538–552

Six H.-W., P. Widmayer (1988): Spatial searching in geometric databases; Proc. 4th International Conference on Data Engineering, Los Angeles, 496–503

Stoyan, D., W.S. Kendall, J. Mecke (1987): Stochastic geometry and its applications; Wiley, New York, 1987.

Tilove, R.B. (1980): Set membership classification: A unified approach to geometric intersection problems; IEEE Transactions on Computers, C-29, 874–883

Tropf, H., H. Herzog (1981): Multidimensional range search in dynamically balanced trees; Angewandte Informatik, Vol. 2, 71–77

van Oosterom, P. (1990): Reactive data structures for geographic information systems; Doctoral Dissertation (Proefschrift), Rijksuniversiteit Leiden

Wang, J.-H., T.-S. Yuen, D.H.-C. Du (1987): On multiple random access and physical data placement in dynamic files; IEEE Transactions on Software Engineering, Vol. 13, No. 8, 977–987

Weikum, G., B. Neumann, H.-B. Paul (1987): Konzeption und Realisierung einer mengenorientierten Seitenschnittstelle zum effizienten Zugriff auf komplexe Objekte; GI-Fachtagung Datenbanksysteme für Büro, Technik und Wissenschaft, Informatik-Fachberichte, Vol. 136, Springer, Berlin, 212–230

Widmayer, P. (1991): Datenstrukturen für Geodatenbanken; in: Entwicklungstendenzen bei Datenbank-Systemen, ed. G. Vossen, K.-U. Witt, Oldenbourg, München, 317–361

On Spanning Trees with Low Crossing Numbers[*]

Emo Welzl[¶]

Abstract

Every set S of n points in the plane has a spanning tree such that no line disjoint from S has more than $O(\sqrt{n})$ intersections with the tree (where the edges are embedded as straight line segments). We review the proof of this result (originally proved by Bernard Chazelle and the author in a more general setting), point at some methods for constructing such a tree, and describe some algorithmic and combinatorial applications.

1 Introduction

Over the recent years there has been considerable progress in the simplex range searching problem. In the planar version of this problem we are required to store a set S of n points such that the number of points in any query triangle can be determined efficiently. One of the combinatorial tools developed for this problem are spanning trees with low crossing numbers.

Let S be set of n points in the plane. For a spanning tree on S and a line h, the *crossing number of h* in the tree is defined as $c_h = a + \frac{b}{2}$, where a is the number of edges $\{p, q\}$ in the tree with p and q on opposite sides of h, and b is the number of edges with exactly one endpoint on h. h *crosses* an edge, if that edge contributes to the crossing number of h. Note that an edge completely contained in the line h does not contribute to the crossing number. The *crossing number* of the tree is the maximal crossing number of any line.

In other words, a spanning tree with crossing number c ensures that no line (disjoint from S) intersects the straight line embedding of the tree in more than c edges. It has been shown in [CW89], that every set of n points allows a spanning tree with crossing number $O(\sqrt{n})$, which is tight. In Section 2 we review the proof of this result (which is treated in [CW89] in a more general setting, for arbitrary dimension, and for set systems of finite VC-dimension, see Section 5). We derive an explicit constant for the bound on the crossing number. The proof builds on a packing lemma for a pseudodistance on points in the presence of a set of lines (where the distance between two points is the number of separating lines), and on a reweighting technique, which has been applied to several seemingly unrelated problems, see [CF88, Cla89, AM90, Mat91b, AK91].

---

[*]Supported by the Deutsche Forschungsgemeinschaft, "Schwerpunktprogramm Datenstrukturen und effiziente Algorithmen", grant We 1265/1-2.

[¶]Institut für Informatik, Freie Universität Berlin, Arnimallee 2-6, W-1000 Berlin 33, Germany, e-mail: `emo@tcs.fu-berlin.de`

Spanning trees are useful in a number of applications. The original motivation for introducing the concept in [Wel88] was the triangle range searching problem which can be solved in $O(\sqrt{n}\log n)$ query time and linear space via spanning trees. This is close to the lower bound of $\Omega(\sqrt{n})$ for linear space data structures in the so-called arithmetic model [Cha89]. Recently, this lower bound has actually been achieved in [Mat91c]. Several different algorithmic applications are described in [Aga89, EGH+89, Aga91, AvKO91, CJ91, AS91]. For example, spanning trees with low crossing numbers can be used for ray shooting among line segments in the plane (i.e., we want to preprocess line segments in the plane such that the first segment intersected by a query ray can be efficiently computed).

In Section 3 we indicate the application to triangle range searching, and we present two recent combinatorial results which can be easily derived from spanning trees with low crossing numbers [MWW91, Pac91].

Section 4 indicates some of the building blocks of algorithms for constructing spanning trees with low crossing numbers. This will lead us to a randomized Monte-Carlo algorithm; however, we did not try to present the best known time bounds for construction. Finally in Section 5, we point at the generalizations to higher dimensions.

We tried to keep the paper largely self-contained, so that in particular in Sections 2 and 3 little foreknowledge should be required. Hence we start by reviewing some basics before we plunge into the rest of the paper.

Notation and basics. Let S be a set of n points in the plane, and let G be a set of ℓ lines in the plane. We say that S is in *general position*, if no three points lie on a common line, and no two points lie on a vertical line. G is in *general position*, if no three lines contain a common point, no two lines are parallel, and no line is vertical.

We denote by H_S the set of lines containing at least two points in S; if S is in general position, then $|H_S| = \binom{n}{2}$. $\tilde{H}_S$ is a *representative set* of lines for S, if whenever a line g (disjoint from S) partitions the set S into nonempty sets S' and S'' (on the respective sides of g), then there is a line h in $\tilde{H}_S$ which induces the same partitioning. It is an easy exercise to verify, that there is always a representative set of at most $\binom{n}{2}$ lines.

The *arrangement* $\mathcal{A}(G)$ of G is the partitioning of the plane induced by G into *vertices* (intersections of lines in G), *edges* (connected components on the lines in the complement of the vertices), and *cells* (connected components of the plane in the complement of the lines). Obviously, there are at most $\binom{\ell}{2}$ vertices, at most ℓ^2 edges, and a bound of $\binom{\ell}{2}+\ell+1$ on the number of cells is also not too hard to prove; if G is in general position, then all three bounds are attained cf. [Ede87].

We will use the *point/line duality* defined by: for a point $p = (a, b)$, the dual image p^* is the nonvertical line with equation $y = ax + b$, and for a nonvertical line g with equation $y = cx + d$, the dual image g^* is the point $(-c, d)$. This mapping preserves incidences between lines and points (i.e. p lies on g if and only if g^* lies on p^*), and it preserves the relative position between a point and a line (i.e. p lies above g if and only p^* lies above g^*).

For two nonvertical lines g and h, define the *double wedge of g and h* as the two open quadrants (defined by the two lines) which are disjoint from the vertical line through the common point of g and h; if g and h are parallel, then the double wedge degenerates to the strip between the two lines. Now a line g intersects the open line segment with endpoints p and q, if and only if g^* lies in the double wedge defined by p^* and q^*.

We frequently use the inequalities $1 + x \le e^x$, for all real numbers x, and $\sum_{i=1}^{n} \frac{1}{\sqrt{i}} < 2\sqrt{n}$, for all positive integers n.

Conventions. All points and lines we consider in Sections 2, 3, and 4 are assumed to lie in the plane!

2 Proof of existence

We want to prove that every set of n points in the plane allows a spanning tree such that no line has more than $O(\sqrt{n})$ crossings with the tree. Note that it suffices to concentrate on a representative set $\tilde{H}_S$ of lines: Let T be a spanning tree on S. Clearly, by definition, every line disjoint from S has a line in $\tilde{H}_S$ with the same (number of) crossings. If h contains points from S, then we consider two parallel lines h' and h'' on both sides of h, but sufficiently close so that all points in S (except those on h) have the same position relative to h' (and to h'') as to h. Then the respective crossing numbers satisfy $c_h = \frac{c_{h'} + c_{h''}}{2}$. That is, the maximum crossing number is attained by a line disjoint from S.

The $O(\sqrt{n})$ bound is asymptotically the best we can hope for. To see this for some positive integer n, choose a set G of $\ell = \lceil \sqrt{2n} \rceil$ lines in general position, and place n points into the cells of the arrangement, no two points in the same cell (which is possible, since $\binom{\ell}{2} + \ell + 1 \ge n$). Every edge of an (arbitrary) spanning tree will be crossed by at least one of the lines in G; thus there must be a line in G with at least $\frac{n-1}{\ell} = \Theta(\sqrt{n})$ crossings.

If we start the construction of our tree, then it looks like a good idea to begin with an edge $\{p, q\}$, such that p and q are separated by as few as possible lines in a representative set. To provide a bound on this number is our next step.

A packing lemma [Cha88, CW89]. Suppose we are given a set S of $n \ge 2$ points with diameter Δ (i.e. Δ is the maximal Euclidean distance between any two points in the set). Then there are two points at distance at most $\sigma = \frac{4\Delta}{\sqrt{n}}$. This can be easily seen by the fact that the closed disks of radius $\frac{\sigma}{2}$ centered at the points in S are contained in a 'large' disk of radius $\frac{3}{2}\Delta$ centered at an arbitrary point in S (this is true if $\sigma \le \Delta$; otherwise the claim is trivial). If the small disks were pairwise disjoint, then they cover an area of $n\frac{\sigma^2\pi}{4} = 4\Delta^2\pi$ in the large disk of radius $\frac{3}{2}\Delta$, which is not possible. Hence two disks intersect, and the respective centers have distance at most σ.

We will use the same idea as just described to show that for any set S of n points, and any set G of ℓ lines there is always a pair of points separated by less than $\frac{2\ell}{\sqrt{n}}$ of the lines. To this end we introduce a *pseudodistance* δ_G for pairs of points (relative to G) by $\delta_G(p, q) = a + \frac{b}{2}$, where a is the number of lines in G which have p and q on opposite sides, and b is the number of lines which contain exactly one of the two points p and q. It is easily seen that δ_G is a pseudometric (i.e. it is symmetric and satisfies the triangle inequality).

For a point p and a real number σ, we let $D_G(p, \sigma)$ denote the set of vertices v in the arrangement of G with $\delta_G(p, v) \le \sigma$. The sets $D_G(p, \sigma)$ will play the role of disks, and the cardinality of $D_G(p, \sigma)$ will play the role of area in our proof, and so we need a lower bound on this quantity in terms of σ.

Lemma 2.1 *If G is a set of ℓ lines in general position, and σ is an integer, $0 \leq \sigma \leq \lceil \frac{\ell}{2} \rceil$, then $|D_G(p, \sigma)| \geq \binom{\sigma+1}{2}$ for all points p disjoint from G.*

Proof. Choose a line g through p which intersects the same number of lines in G on both sides of p. Such a line exists, since we can take a directed line h through p and rotate it, while observing the number of intersections on h preceding p. After rotating h by π this will be the number of intersections succeeding p; so in between we must meet a situation as required for g (note that if ℓ is odd, then g must be parallel to one of the lines in G).

Now consider the intersections $q_1, q_2, \ldots, q_{\lfloor \ell/2 \rfloor}$ on g on one side of p, enumerated in such a way that $\delta_G(p, q_i) = i - \frac{1}{2}$ (if g passes through a vertex, we may perturb g with p to make sure that all lines in G create distinct intersections). Let us first assume that $\sigma \leq \lfloor \frac{\ell}{2} \rfloor$. Then, for all $i \leq \sigma$, q_i has at least $\sigma - i + 1$ vertices on its line at distance at most $\sigma - i + \frac{1}{2}$; all these vertices have distance at most σ from p (by the triangle inequality). If we collect vertices at distance at most σ in the same way on the other side of p, we obtain $2(\sigma + \cdots + 2 + 1) = 2\binom{\sigma+1}{2}$ such vertices, each of which may be counted at most twice. This gives the claimed bound for $\sigma \leq \lfloor \frac{\ell}{2} \rfloor$.

If ℓ is odd, and $\sigma = \lceil \frac{\ell}{2} \rceil$, then the above procedure gives us a count of $2(\sigma + \cdots + 2)$ only. Now we recall that there is a line $h \in G$ parallel to g which contains at least two points at distance at most $\lceil \frac{\ell}{2} \rceil$; take the two vertices incident to the infinite edges on h. In this way we have again counted $2\binom{\sigma+1}{2}$ vertices, each vertex at most twice. The lemma is proved. □

The bound in Lemma 2.1 can be shown to be tight.

Lemma 2.2 *Let G be a set of ℓ lines, and let S be a set of $n \geq 2$ points. Then there are two distinct points p and q in S with $\delta_G(p, q) \leq \frac{2\ell}{\sqrt{n}}$.*

Proof. Choose some positive integer k with the property that

$$(\lfloor \frac{2k\ell}{\sqrt{n}} \rfloor + 1) \lfloor \frac{2k\ell}{\sqrt{n}} \rfloor > \frac{(2k\ell)^2}{n} . \tag{1}$$

Replace each line h in G by two buckets of k parallel copies each, such that the 'original' h lies between these two buckets, and the two buckets are sufficiently close to h, so that there are no points from S within a bucket, and between a bucket and its original. So the only points from S between the two buckets are those which lie on h. The resulting set G' has $\ell' = 2k\ell$ lines, no point in S lies on a line in G' and for any pair $\{p, q\}$ of points in S, $\delta_{G'}(p, q) = 2k\delta_G(p, q)$. Then perturb the lines in G' to general position such that no line moves over a point in S; this does not change the pseudodistance $\delta_{G'}$ between points in S.

For $n \leq 4$ the assertion of the lemma is trivial; so we have to consider only the case $n \geq 5$ and Lemma 2.1 applies to $\sigma = \lfloor \frac{\ell'}{\sqrt{n}} \rfloor$. We get

$$\sum_{p \in S} |D_{G'}(p, \sigma)| \geq n \binom{\sigma+1}{2} > n \frac{\ell'^2}{2n} > \binom{\ell'}{2} ,$$

(where property (1) proved to be useful). Since there are only $\binom{\ell'}{2}$ vertices, there must be two 'disks' $D_{G'}(p,\sigma)$ and $D_{G'}(q,\sigma)$, $p,q \in S$, $p \neq q$, which overlap in a vertex; by the triangle inequality their centers p and q have pseudodistance $\delta_{G'}(p,q)$ at most 2σ. Hence, $\delta_G(p,q) \leq \frac{1}{2k} 2\lfloor \frac{\ell'}{\sqrt{n}} \rfloor \leq \frac{2\ell}{\sqrt{n}}$, the bound claimed in the lemma. □

We need to extend Lemma 2.2 to sets of lines G where every line h has a positive real weight $w(h)$ associated. The pseudodistance $\delta_G(p,q)$ is now defined as $a + \frac{b}{2}$, where a is the sum of weights associated with lines separating p and q, and b is the sum of weights associated with lines which contain exactly one of the two points p and q.

Lemma 2.3 *Let G be a finite set of weighted lines with overall weight Δ, and let S be a set of $n \geq 2$ points. Then there are two distinct points p and q in S with $\delta_G(p,q) \leq \frac{2\Delta}{\sqrt{n}}$.*

Proof. Let k be some positive integer. Replace every line h in G by two buckets of $\lceil k \cdot w(h) \rceil$ unweighted lines each, in the same way as described in the previous proof. We obtain a set G' of at most $2k\Delta + 2\ell$ unweighted lines to which we can apply Lemma 2.2. It supplies us with two points p and q with $\delta_{G'}(p,q) \leq \frac{4k\Delta + 4\ell}{\sqrt{n}}$. If ℓ is the number of lines in G, then

$$\delta_G(p,q) \leq \frac{\delta_{G'}(p,q)}{2k} \leq \frac{2\Delta}{\sqrt{n}} + \frac{2\ell}{k\sqrt{n}} .$$

In other words, for every $\epsilon > 0$ we find points p and q with $\delta_G(p,q) \leq \frac{2\Delta}{\sqrt{n}} + \epsilon$. Since there are only finitely many points, this implies the lemma. □

Construction by iterative reweighting [Wel88, CW89]. Using Lemma 2.2 we can easily show that for n points S and ℓ lines G the greedy algorithm (using δ_G as weight function on edges) constructs a spanning tree on S with weight at most $\sum_{i=2}^{n} \frac{2\ell}{\sqrt{i}} \leq 4\ell\sqrt{n}$. That is, the average crossing number of a line in G is $4\sqrt{n}$. We will show that by a different construction we can guarantee this bound (up to a low order term) for all lines.

Theorem 2.4 *Every set S of n points has a spanning tree with crossing number at most $4\sqrt{n} + O(n^{1/4}\sqrt{\log n})$.*

Proof. Let G_0 be a representative set of lines, $\ell = |G_0| \leq \binom{n}{2}$, and let $S_0 = S$. We start the construction of the spanning tree by choosing two points p and q in S_0 which are separated by the smallest number of lines in G_0 (i.e. no more than $\frac{2\ell}{\sqrt{n}}$). Next we put the edge $\{p,q\}$ into the edge set of our tree and remove p from the point set which gives $S_1 = S_0 - \{p\}$.

For the rest of the construction we need some means to ensure that no line gathers too many crossings. That is lines which have already many crossings with the edges constructed so far should cross a next edge less likely. We will achieve this by assigning weights to the lines. To be precise, a line which has c crossings so far will have multiplicity $(1 + \mu)^c$ for $\mu > 0$ a parameter to be chosen later.

Hence, we continue our construction by multiplying by $1 + \mu$ the weight of all lines in G_0 which separate p and q; this gives a new set G_1 of weighted lines with overall weight $\Delta_1 \leq \ell(1 + \frac{2\mu}{\sqrt{n}})$. Then we continue the construction with G_1 and S_1: we choose two points p_1 and q_1 which are separated by lines of overall minimal weight, add edge $\{p_1, q_1\}$ to the edge set, remove p_1, and multiply the weights of separating lines by $1 + \mu$, and proceed as above.

After i steps we have a set G_i of weight

$$\Delta_i \le \Delta_{i-1}\left(1 + \frac{2\mu}{\sqrt{n-(i-1)}}\right) \le \ell \prod_{j=0}^{i-1}\left(1 + \frac{2\mu}{\sqrt{n-j}}\right)$$

and a set S_i of $n - i$ points.

Step $n - 1$ completes the construction of a spanning tree for S. What is the crossing number of this tree? Let c_h denote the number of crossings of line h in the tree. Then h is represented with weight $(1 + \mu)^{c_h}$ in G_{n-1}, that is

$$\Delta_{n-1} = \sum_{h \in G_0} (1 + \mu)^{c_h} .$$

However, we have also a bound of

$$\Delta_{n-1} \le \ell \prod_{j=2}^{n}\left(1 + \frac{2\mu}{\sqrt{j}}\right) < \ell\, e^{\sum_{j=1}^{n}(2\mu/\sqrt{j})} \le e^{4\mu\sqrt{n}+2\ln n} .$$

Hence, we may conclude that

$$c_h < \frac{1}{\ln(1+\mu)}(4\mu\sqrt{n} + 2\ln n) ,$$

for all lines h which implies $c_h < 4\sqrt{n} + O(n^{1/4}\sqrt{\log n})$ for the choice of μ which minimizes this bound (see Appendix). $\qquad\Box$

The theorem and its proof provide us with a number of immediate consequences. A spanning path is *simple*, if only line segments corresponding to consecutive edges on the path intersect.

Corollary 2.5 *Every set S of n points has a simple spanning path with crossing number at most $4\sqrt{n} + O(n^{1/4}\sqrt{\log n})$.*

Proof. The asymptotic bounds follow directly from Theorem 2.4, if we double the edges in a spanning tree of crossing number c, and consider an Eulerian walk in this graph, which has crossing number $2c$. We can now simply scan this walk and omit points which have occurred before. In this way the number of crossings with a line cannot increase. Let $p_0, p_1, \ldots, p_{n-1}$ be the resulting spanning path with crossing number at most $2c$. If two line segments $\overline{p_{i-1}p_i}$ and $\overline{p_{j-1}p_j}$, $1 \le i < j - 1 \le n - 2$ intersect then we replace the edges $\{p_{i-1}, p_i\}$ and $\{p_{j-1}, p_j\}$ by new edges $\{p_{i-1}, p_{j-1}\}$ and $\{p_i, p_j\}$ to obtain the spanning path

$$p_0, p_1, \ldots, p_{i-1}, p_{j-1}, p_{j-2}, \ldots, p_{i+1}, p_i, p_j, p_{j+1}, \ldots, p_{n-1} .$$

The crossing number of no line increases, and the *Euclidean* length decreases. Consequently, after a finite number of steps we have obtained a simple spanning path with crossing number at most $2c$.

In order to achieve the claimed constant we have to look at the proof of the theorem once more. We proceed as for the construction of a tree, except that we are more careful about the points we put into the sets S_i. We keep as an invariant, that the edges constructed so far give a set of vertex disjoint paths on S (some of which are just isolated vertices), and we let S_i contain all isolated vertices, and exactly one point of degree one from each path. In the next step, we choose two points p and q of minimal pseudodistance (with respect to the current weighted set of lines) in S_i. The addition of edge $\{p, q\}$ merges two connected components; we remove p and q from S_i, and add one of the two points of degree one in this component to the set, which gives us S_{i+1}. After the appropriate reweighting of the lines we continue the construction. The calculus of the analysis stays the same and gives the claimed bound. The constructed path can be converted into a simple one by the same procedure as described in the first paragraph of the proof. □

Corollary 2.6 *Every set S of n points has a matching of size k with crossing number at most $\frac{4k}{\sqrt{n}} + O(\sqrt{k \ln n / \sqrt{n}})$, for integers k, $\frac{1}{2}\sqrt{n} \ln n \le k \le \frac{n}{2}$, and with crossing number at most $\frac{2e \ln n}{\ln(\sqrt{n} \ln n/(2k))}$, for integers $k \le \frac{1}{2e}\sqrt{n} \ln n$.*

Proof. The construction of a matching works in the obvious way (referring to the notation in the proof of Theorem 2.4). We choose the edge of minimal pseudodistance, remove its two points from the current point set, and reweight the lines with new crossings. Now S_i has $n - 2i$ points. After k steps we have a matching of required size. Via the overall weight Δ_k of G_k we get the following bound for the number of crossings of lines in G_0:

$$\sum_{h \in G_0} (1 + \mu)^{c_h} = \Delta_k \le \ell \prod_{i=1}^{k}\left(1 + \frac{2\mu}{\sqrt{n - 2(i-1)}}\right) < \ell e^{\sqrt{2}\mu \sum_{j=0}^{k-1} \frac{1}{\sqrt{n/2-j}}}$$

$$< \ell e^{\sqrt{2}\mu 2(\sqrt{n/2} - \sqrt{n/2-k})} = \ell e^{2\mu(\sqrt{n} - \sqrt{n-2k})} < e^{4\mu k/\sqrt{n} + 2\ln n}.$$

The last inequality uses that $\sqrt{n} - \sqrt{n - x\sqrt{n}} \le x$ for all x, $0 \le x \le \sqrt{n}$.

It follows that $c_h \ln(1 + \mu) < \frac{4\mu k}{\sqrt{n}} + 2\ln n$, and we obtain the bounds claimed in the corollary by the appropriate choice of μ (see Appendix). □

It is perhaps interesting to consider explicitly the bound for some values of k. For $k = n^{1/2-\epsilon}$, the lemma gives a bound of $O(\frac{1}{\epsilon})$; for $k = \sqrt{n}$, we obtain $O(\frac{\log n}{\log \log n})$; for $k = \sqrt{n} \ln n$, the crossing number does not exceed $O(\log n)$. The bounds for $k = \Omega(\sqrt{n} \log n)$ are asymptotically tight. It remains open whether there is always a matching of size $\sqrt{n}$ with constant crossing number.

The constant. We have not presented the best possible constant. Nevertheless, we briefly indicate the best bounds known to the author. Let us first observe that a lower bound of $\sqrt{n} - 1$ for spanning trees can be obtained by a slight refinement of the lower bound construction in the beginning of the section. For a positive integer n choose a set G of $\ell = 2\lceil\sqrt{n}\rceil$ lines in general position. Then we assign colors to the cells such that no two adjacent cells (i.e. cells which share a common edge) have the same color. (Choose a fixed point o in one of the cells and color a cell red if for a point p in this cell $\delta_G(o, p)$ is odd, and color the cell blue otherwise.) We place n points in the cells of the larger color class – no two points in the same cell (which is possible since $\frac{1}{2}(\binom{\ell}{2} + \ell + 1) \ge n$). Any two of these points are separated by at least 2 lines. Hence, the overall number of crossings between the set of ℓ lines and any spanning tree is at least $2(n-1)$; hence, there is always a line with at least $\frac{2(n-1)}{\ell} \ge \sqrt{n} - 1$ crossings.

Although the bound in Lemma 2.1 is tight, the bound can be improved to $|D_G(p, \sigma)| \geq 3\binom{\sigma+1}{2}$, if p has pseudodistance at least σ to every point in an infinite cell, and if $\sigma \leq \frac{\ell}{3}$; this follows from a result on k-sets proved in [EHSS89]. With this bound we can improve the estimates in Lemmas 2.2 and 2.3 to $\frac{2\ell}{\sqrt{3n}}$ and $\frac{2\Delta}{\sqrt{3n}}$ (up to low order terms). The bound in Theorem 2.4 improves to $(\frac{4}{\sqrt{3}} + o(1))\sqrt{n}$. So the optimal constant lies in the range between 1 and 2.31.

3   Applications

We present three applications of spanning trees, paths, or matchings with low crossing numbers. The first is algorithmic, while the second and third are primarily of combinatorial interest. Nevertheless, the proofs reveal also algorithms for computing the structures whose existence we have proven.

Counting points in halfplanes [CW89].   Suppose we want to count the points below a nonvertical line from a given point set S, and we have to answer many such queries. Thus it pays off to prepare the points in a data structure.

The structure we use is a simple spanning path $p_1, p_2, \ldots, p_n$ of S with low crossing number c. The edges on the path are enumerated so that edge $\{p_i, p_{i+1}\}$ gets number i. For a nonvertical line h disjoint from S, let I^+ the set of indices of edges $\{p_i, p_{i+1}\}$ with p_i below h and p_{i+1} above h, and let I^- be the set of indices of edges $\{p_i, p_{i+1}\}$ with p_i above h and p_{i+1} below h. Then the number of points in S below h is given by $\sum_{i \in I^+} i - \sum_{i \in I^-} i$, if p_n lies above h, and $n + \sum_{i \in I^+} i - \sum_{i \in I^-} i$, if p_n lies below h. Thus, if we can determine the c_h crossings of line h with the path, then the number of points below h can be computed with c_h additions and subtractions. Here we can invoke a result from [CG89], which states that the edges of a simple path can be stored with $O(n)$ space, such that the first edge hit by a ray can be computed in $O(\log n)$ time. Clearly, this structure can be used to compute the intersections of a line with a path in $O(k \log n)$ time, where k is the number of intersections.

Theorem 3.1 *Every set S of n points can be stored in $O(n)$ space, such that the number of points in S below any query line can be computed in $O(\sqrt{n} \log n)$ time.*   ⊡

The structure can readily be used also for counting points in triangles within the same asymptotic time bounds.

Colorings with low discrepancy [MWW91].   We want to color a set of n points in the plane by red and blue, such that every halfplane contains roughly the same number of red and blue points. How well can we achieve that goal? This type of questions are investigated in the field of discrepancy ([Spe87], [BC87]).

For technical reasons we switch to colors -1 and $+1$. A coloring of a point set S is a mapping $\chi : S \to \{-1, +1\}$. The *discrepancy of* χ is defined as $\max_{h^*} |\chi(S \cap h^*)|$, where $\chi(A) = \sum_{p \in A} \chi(p)$, and the maximum is taken over all halfplanes h^*.

Theorem 3.2 *For every set S of n points there is a coloring χ with discrepancy at most $2\sqrt{2}\, n^{1/4}\sqrt{\ln n} + O(\log n)$.*

Proof. Assume that n is even (if not, we may ignore one point temporarily; the discrepancy grows at most by one by adding it back with an arbitrary color). Let M be a perfect matching on S with crossing number c. We consider the set C of all colorings χ with $\chi(p) + \chi(q) = 0$ for all $\{p, q\} \in M$. Note that every element of C has discrepancy at most c. We show that there is a better coloring in C by considering colorings randomly chosen from C. We need the well-known Chernoff bound (see e.g. [Spe87], [HR90]) in the following form: If X is the sum of k independent random $\{-1, +1\}$ variables — each variable attains -1 and $+1$ with equal probability —, then $\text{Prob}(|X| > \lambda\sqrt{k}) < 2e^{-\lambda^2/2}$.

Let h be a nonvertical line disjoint from S with c_h crossings in M, and let h^- be the halfplane below h. Set

$$B_h = \{p \in S | p \in h^- \text{ and } h \text{ crosses the edge in } M \text{ containing } p\} \ .$$

Then $|B_h| = |c_h|$, $\chi(S \cap h^-) = \chi(B_h)$, and for a random χ in C,

$$\text{Prob}(|\chi(B_h)| > \lambda\sqrt{c_h}) < 2e^{-\lambda^2/2} \tag{2}$$

If $\lambda = 2\sqrt{\ln n}$ then the bound in (2) becomes $2n^{-2}$. Let $\tilde{H}_S$ be a representative set of lines with $|\tilde{H}_S| \leq \binom{n}{2} < n^2/2$. Thus there is a coloring χ_0 in C with $\chi_0(S \cap h^-) \leq 2\sqrt{c_h \ln n} \leq 2\sqrt{c \ln n}$ for all h in $\tilde{H}_S$; this coloring χ_0 is good for all (open or closed) halfplanes below lines. We have $|\chi(A)| = |\chi(S - A)|$ for all $\chi \in C$ and all $A \subseteq S$, which takes care of halfplanes above lines. The lemma follows, since there is a perfect matching with $c = 2\sqrt{n} + O(n^{1/4}\sqrt{\log n})$, see Corollary 2.6. □

[Bec91] proves a lower bound of $\Omega(n^{1/4-\epsilon})$, for any $\epsilon > 0$, for the discrepancy of colorings for halfplanes.

Mutually avoiding segments [Pac91]. Two closed line segments are called *avoiding*, if the lines supporting the segments intersect outside both segments. The following result was first proved in [AEG+91]; the simple proof below was presented in [Pac91].

Theorem 3.3 *Every set S of n points in general position allows $\frac{1}{8}\sqrt{n} - O(n^{1/4}\sqrt{\log n})$ mutually avoiding line segments with endpoints in S.*

Proof. Let $p_0, p_1, \ldots, p_{n-1}$ be a spanning path with crossing number $c - 1$. For convenience add also the edge $\{p_{n-1}, p_0\}$ to obtain a spanning cycle with crossing number c. We show that among the n edges on this path there are $\lceil \frac{n}{2c+1} \rceil$ edges which define mutually avoiding line segments. To this end consider the graph which has the set L of line segments $\overline{p_{i-1}p_i}$, $i = 1, 2, \ldots, n-1$, and $\overline{p_{n-1}p_0}$, as vertices. Two vertices are adjacent, if their corresponding line segments are not avoiding. A line containing a line segments s in L intersects at most c of the line segments in $L - \{s\}$ (it's at most c including the adjacent segments on the cycle!). Consequently, our graph has at most cn edges. A graph with n vertices and cn edges has an independent set (i.e. a set of vertices where no two are adjacent) of cardinality $\lceil \frac{n}{2c+1} \rceil$ (the existence of a $\lceil \frac{n^2}{2m+n} \rceil$ size independent set in a graph with n vertices and m edges follows from Turan's theorem, cf. [Bol78]). But an independent set in this graph corresponds to a set of mutually avoiding line segments; the theorem follows due to the bounds on c previously derived. □

It is not known whether there are point sets which do not allow a linear number of mutually avoiding line segments.

4 Construction

The proof of existence of spanning trees with low crossing numbers in Theorem 2.4 describes an algorithm which can be implemented in polynomial time. A number of more efficient algorithms can be found in the literature [EGH+89, Aga91, Mat91d, Mat90, AS91]. We will present some of the basic ingredients of these algorithms, which will lead us to a randomized algorithm which computes in expected $O(n\sqrt{n\log n})$ time a spanning tree whose crossing number does not exceed $O(\sqrt{n\log n})$ with high probability.

The first step in making an algorithm more efficient is to reduce the number of lines which have to be considered in a construction.

Test sets. Given a set S of n points and two nonvertical lines g and h, we define $\delta_S^*(g, h) = a + \frac{b}{2}$, where a is the number of points from S in the double wedge defined by g and h, and b is the number of points from S which lie on exactly one of the lines g and h. Similar to δ on points, δ^* is a pseudometric on lines. In fact, if we denote by S^* the lines dual to the points in S, then $\delta_S^*(g, h) = \delta_{S^*}(g^*, h^*)$.

For a real number σ, we call a set H of lines a σ-test set for S, if for every line g disjoint from S, there is a line $h \in H$ with $\delta_S^*(g, h) \leq \sigma$.

Lemma 4.1 Let S be a set of n points and let H be a σ-test set for S. If the maximal crossing number of a line in H in a spanning path on S is C, then the crossing number of this path (for all lines) is at most $C + 2\sigma$.

Proof. For any two lines g and h, observe that if g crosses an edge which is not crossed by h, then one of the two endpoints of this edge has to lie in th double wedge of g and h, or on g. Since every point is incident to at most two edges on a *path*, we easily get that the respective crossing numbers c_g and c_h satisfy $|c_g - c_h| \leq 2\delta_S^*(g, h)$. The lemma is an immediate consequence of this fact. ⬜

Lemma 4.2 Let S be a set of n points and let σ be an integer with $0 \leq \sigma \leq n$. (i) There exists a σ-test set of at most $4(\frac{n}{\sigma})^2$ lines. (ii) If S is in general position, then, for every positive real λ, a set of lines obtained by connecting at least $(2 + \lambda)(\frac{n}{\sigma})^2 \ln n$ random pairs of points in S is a σ-test set with probability at least $1 - n^{-\lambda}$.

Proof. We prefer to dualize the scenario. In the dual environment statement (i) claims that for a set $G (= S^*)$ of $\ell (= n)$ lines, there exists a set Q of $4(\frac{\ell}{\sigma})^2$ points, such that every point p disjoint from G has a point $q \in Q$ with $\delta_G(p, q) \leq \sigma$. Choose Q as a maximal set of points, where any two points have pseudodistance δ_G greater than σ. Lemma 2.2 implies that Q contains at most $(\frac{2\ell}{\sigma})^2$ points, and the maximality of Q guarantees the desired property.

For a proof of (ii), we have to consider a set R of r random vertices in $\mathcal{A}(G)$, G a set of ℓ lines in general position. For any point p disjoint from G, a random vertex has pseudodistance at most σ from p with probability $|D_G(p, \sigma)|/\binom{\ell}{2} > (\frac{\sigma}{\ell})^2$ (use Lemma 2.1). Hence, the probability that all points in R have pseudodistance more than σ from p is less than

$$\left(1 - \left(\frac{\sigma}{\ell}\right)^2\right)^r \leq e^{-r\sigma^2/\ell^2}. \tag{3}$$

For $r \geq (2 + \lambda)(\frac{\ell}{\sigma})^2 \ln \ell$, the expression in (3) is bounded by $\ell^{-2-\lambda}$. Let P be a set of $m = \binom{\ell}{2} + \ell + 1$ points, one in each cell of $\mathcal{A}(G)$. Then with probability at most $m\ell^{-2-\lambda} \leq \ell^{-\lambda}$ there is a point in P which has pseudodistance more than σ from all points in R (for $\ell \geq 2$, $m \leq \ell^2$). Since every point disjoint from G has a point in P at pseudodistance 0, the lemma is proved. $\qquad\square$

The algorithm. Let G be a set of lines, and let p be a point. For a nonvertical line h (not necessarily in G), we say that h *sees* p (and p *sees* h) in $\mathcal{A}(G)$, if p lies on or above h, and the closed vertical segment connecting h and p is disjoint from all lines in $G - \{h\}$; (if p lies on h, then p sees h if and only if p lies on no line in $G - \{h\}$). Thus a point p which lies on a single line g in G sees g and no other line, and if p is contained in two or more lines in G, then p sees no line at all. Every point p sees at most one of the lines in G.

The algorithm proceeds now as follows. We assume that the set S of n points is in general position, and that $n \geq 2$. First we take a random sample T of n lines connecting points in S; this will be a σ-test set, for $\sigma \leq 2\sqrt{n \ln n}$, with probability $1 - n^{-2}$. Then we construct a set $F \subseteq T$ of $\tau \leq \sqrt{n \ln n}$ lines such that no line in $T - F$ sees more than $\kappa \leq 2e\sqrt{n \ln n}$ points from S in $\mathcal{A}(F)$ (the construction of F will be described below). We add to F a horizontal line h_0, which lies below all points in S. Each point p in S is projected vertically on a line from F directly below (or through) p; this gives a set S' of n projections. For $g \in F$, let S'_g be the points in S' which lie on g; if a point in S' lies on several lines in F, then we put it only in one set S'_g.

We add two extra vertical lines h^- and h^+ which lie to the left (right, respectively) of all points in S. On every line g connect all points in S'_g by a path along g, starting at the intersection of g with h^- and ending at the intersection of g with h^+. Connect these paths via edges on h^- and h^+ so that no line intersects more than two of these extra edges. Note that the resulting spanning path P' has crossing number $3 + \tau$ at most ('3' accounts for crossings on h_0, h^-, and h^+). Now we consider the *vertical* edges connecting the points in $S - S'$ to their projections in S'. A line $g \in T - F$ crosses such a vertical edge only if it sees the upper endpoint in $\mathcal{A}(F)$, or it contains the lower endpoint.

For a line $g \in T$, consider a line g' parallel to and below g, but sufficiently close so that no point in $(S' \cup S) - g$ changes its relative position to g' (compared to g). For all lines $g \in T$, g' crosses at most $3 + \tau$ edges in P'. If $g \in F$, then g' crosses no vertical edge, and if $g \in T - F$, then g crosses at most κ vertical edges.

In order to obtain a path on S we walk along P' with excursions along vertical edges, and we enumerate the points in S as we meet them on this walk. For any line $g \in T$, the primed version g' crosses at most $3 + \tau + 2\kappa$ edges, and since $\delta^*_S(g, g') \leq 1$ (recall that we assume S to be in general position), no line in T has crossing number exceeding $5 + \tau + 2\kappa$. Consequently, the crossing number of the path is at most $5 + \tau + 2\kappa + 2\sigma$ (by Lemma 4.1), which is at most $5 + (5 + 4e)\sqrt{n \ln n} = O(\sqrt{n \log n})$ with probability $1 - n^{-2}$.

It remains to show how a set F obscuring many visibilities is constructed.

Obscuring sets

Lemma 4.3 *Let S be a set of n points, and let G be a finite set of lines. For a random set R of r lines in G, and for a random line g in $G - R$, the expected number of points in*

S seen by g in $\mathcal{A}(R)$ is at most $\frac{n}{r+1}$.

Proof. We employ backwards analysis, cf. [Sei91]. Observe that g sees a point p in $\mathcal{A}(R)$ if and only if g sees p in $\mathcal{A}(R \cup \{g\})$. Thus the quantity we are interested in is the same as the expected number of points from S seen by a random line $g \in R'$ in $\mathcal{A}(R')$, with R' a random set of $r + 1$ lines in G. Since every point in S sees at most one line in R', this number is bounded by $\frac{n}{r+1}$. $\quad\square$

We will use the lemma to make the following conclusion: If we choose r lines R at random, then with probability at least $\frac{1}{2}$ the expected number of points seen by a line in $G - R$ is at most $\frac{2n}{r+1}$; in this case at most $\frac{|G-R|}{e}$ lines see more than $\frac{2en}{r+1}$ points (we use Markov's inequality twice).

We start the construction of F by choosing a random sample R_0 of $r = \lfloor \sqrt{\frac{n}{\ln n}} \rfloor$ lines in $H_0 = T$. We determine the set $H_1 \subseteq H_0 - R_0$ of lines which see more than $\frac{2en}{r+1} \leq 2e\sqrt{n \ln n}$ points from S in $\mathcal{A}(R_0)$. If $|H_1| > |H_0|/e$ — which happens with probability less than $\frac{1}{2}$ —, then we choose a new sample R_0 from H_0 until $|H_1| \leq |H_0|/e$ holds. In the same way we produce a set R_1 of r lines in H_1, such that the set $H_2 \subseteq H_1 - R_1$ of lines which see more than $\frac{2en}{r+1}$ points in $\mathcal{A}(R_1)$ satisfies $|H_2| \leq |H_1|/e$. If we continue like this, we have exhausted all lines in T after at most $\lceil \ln \frac{|T|}{r} + 1 \rceil \leq \ln n$ steps (at least for n large enough), and the expected number of samples we took is at most twice this number. The union F of all R_i's constitutes a set of at most $r \ln n \leq \sqrt{n \ln n}$ lines, and no line in $T - F$ sees more than $2e\sqrt{n \ln n}$ points in $\mathcal{A}(F)$. (The constants can be decreased at the cost of a larger constant in the running time.)

If we are interested in the existence of F only, then we may choose '2' as 1.

Lemma 4.4 *Let S be a set of n points and let G be a set of ℓ lines. For every positive integer $r \leq \min\{n, \ell\}$, there is a set F of $r \lceil \ln \frac{\ell}{r} + 1 \rceil$ lines in G, such that no line in $G - F$ sees more than $\frac{en}{r+1}$ points of S in $\mathcal{A}(F)$.* $\quad\square$

Time complexity. What is the time complexity of the construction of F? When we choose a random sample R of r lines then we construct the arrangement $\mathcal{A}(R)$ in $O(r^2)$ time, cf. [Ede87]. Then, for every point in S, we determine the cell the point is contained in: We simply determine the line in R directly below a point p by looking at all lines (in $O(nr)$ time for all points). Then, for each line $g \in R$, we look at the points which have this line below and determine the respective edges of the arrangement directly below these points (this works again in $O(nr)$, if every point checks all edges on 'its' line). As we have located all points in their cells, we provide a list of points in each cell sorted by x-coordinate. Now we want to compute the number of points seen by a line $h \notin R$. We determine the cells intersected by h by threading the line through the arrangement in $O(r)$, cf. [Ede87]. In each cell visited, we take the x-coordinates of the first and last point of h in the closure of this cell. h can see only points in this cell which have their x-coordinates in this range. In the sorted lists we can determine these points in $O(\log n + k')$, k' the number of points in this range. Similar to the proof of Lemma 4.3, we can show that the expected sum of all k' over all cells intersected by h is at most $\frac{2n}{r+1}$. So the expected time spent for a line h is $O(r \log n + \frac{n}{r+1})$. Altogether, if ℓ lines have to be checked, we spend time $O(nr + \ell(r \log n + \frac{n}{r+1})) = O(n\sqrt{\frac{n}{\log n}} + \ell(\sqrt{n \log n}))$. The expected number of times we have to handle such a set R is $O(\log n)$, and the number of lines to be checked decreases geometrically. Hence, the overall expected time for constructing F is $O(n\sqrt{n}\log n)$. The spanning path can easily be obtained from the arrangement $\mathcal{A}(F)$ within this time bound.

Theorem 4.5 *There is a randomized algorithm which computes for any set of n points in general position a spanning path in expected $O(n\sqrt{n}\log n)$ time, such that the crossing number does not exceed $O(\sqrt{n}\log n)$ with probability $1 - n^{-2}$.* □

With some more sophistication, the algorithm can be tuned to have close to linear running time (see [Mat91d] for some of the ideas required). Test sets are used in most efficient constructions of spanning trees with low crossing numbers [Mat91d, Mat90, Aga91]. Efficient (deterministic) constructions of test sets are described in [Mat91b]. The idea of repeated sampling on 'bad' lines for the construction of obscuring sets is taken from [CSW90].

A deterministic $O(n\sqrt{n}\log^2 n)$ algorithm which gives a spanning tree with $O(\sqrt{n})$ crossing number is described in [Mat90]. [AS91] can produce a tree with crossing number $O(n^{1/2+\epsilon})$ in time $O(n^{1+\epsilon})$ for any $\epsilon > 0$, and they describe how such a tree can be maintained under a sequence of insertions and deletions. So-called simplicial partitions ([Mat91b], see Section 5) can be used to obtain a spanning tree with crossing number $O(\sqrt{n})$ in time $O(n^{1+\epsilon})$ for any $\epsilon > 0$ (where the constant in the crossing number depends on ϵ), [Mat91a].

5 Discussion

The result on spanning trees generalizes to higher dimensions and other geometric objects: For every set of n points in d-space there is a spanning tree, such that no hyperplane intersects the straight line embedding of the tree in more than $O(n^{1-1/d})$ points, which is tight. The proof of the general result starts off by providing a higher-dimensional counterpart of Lemma 2.1, and then proceeds almost verbatim as in the planar case. Similarly, we can always find a tree which has $O(n^{1-1/d})$ crossings with any ball, if we define that a ball crosses an edge if exactly one endpoint of the edge lies in the ball.

For a set system $(X, \mathcal{R})$, $\mathcal{R} \subseteq 2^X$, we can also consider spanning trees on finite subsets A of X. We say that a set $R \in \mathcal{R}$ crosses an edge $\{x, y\}$ of the tree, if $|R \cap \{x, y\}| = 1$. Then it is possible to prove the existence of a spanning trees with crossing number $O(n^{1-1/d})$, where d is some combinatorial parameter associated with the set system (related to the VC-dimension); details can be found in [CW89].

An important extension of matchings with low crossing numbers, *simplicial partitions*, were introduced in [Mat91b]. In the planar version, for a set S of n points, such a partition consists of pairs (t_i, S_i), $i = 1, 2, \ldots, m$, where the t_i's are open triangles or line segments with $t_i \supseteq S_i$, and the S_i's form a partition of S. It is shown that for any r there is a simplicial partition such that $m = O(r)$, the cardinalities of the S_i's are roughly balanced ($|S_i| \leq \frac{2n}{m}$ for all i, to be precise), and no line intersects more than $O(\sqrt{m})$ of the t_i's. Note that perfect matchings with low crossing numbers are related to simplicial partitions with $m = \frac{n}{2}$. Simplicial partitions can be efficiently constructed, and they allow improvements in many algorithmic applications, [Mat91b].

We conclude by stating two open problems.

Problem 1 *Is there a constant C, such that every set of n points in the plane has a matching of size $\sqrt{n}$ whose straight line embedding is intersected in no more than C edges by any line disjoint from the points?*

Corollary 2.6 gives a bound of $O(\frac{\log n}{\log\log n})$ on C; a constant number of intersections can be guaranteed, if a matching of size $n^{1/2-\epsilon}$ is required, for any fixed $\epsilon > 0$.

Problem 2 *Given n points S and n nonvertical lines G in the plane, is there always a set F of $O(\sqrt{n})$ lines in G, such that no line in $G - F$ sees more than $\sqrt{n}$ points of S in $\mathcal{A}(F)$; a line $h \in G - F$ sees a point p in $\mathcal{A}(F)$ if p lies on or above h, and the closed vertical segment connecting p and h is disjoint from all lines in F?*

Lemma 4.4 gives a bound of $O(\sqrt{n}\log n)$ on the size of F.

References

[AEG+91] Boris Aronov, Paul Erdős, Wayne Goddard, Daniel Kleitman, Michael Klugerman, János Pach, and Leonard Schulman. Crossing families. In *Proc. 7th Annual ACM Symposium on Computational Geometry*, pages 351–356, 1991.

[Aga89] Pankaj Agarwal. Ray shooting and other applications of spanning trees with low stabbing number. In *Proc. 5th Annual ACM Symposium on Computational Geometry*, pages 315–325, 1989.

[Aga91] Pankaj Agarwal. *Intersection and Decomposition Algorithms for Planar Arrangements*. Cambridge University Press, 1991.

[AK91] Noga Alon and Daniel Kleitman. Piercing convex sets and the Hadwiger Debrunner (p, q)-problem. Manuscript, 1991.

[AM90] Noga Alon and Nimrod Megiddo. Parallel linear programming in fixed dimensions almost surely in constant time. In *Proc. 31st Annual IEEE Symposium on Foundations of Computer Science*, pages 574–582, 1990.

[AS91] Pankaj Agarwal and Micha Sharir. Applications of a new space partitioning technique. Manuscript, 1991.

[AvKO91] Pankaj Agarwal, Marc van Kreveld, and Mark Overmars. Intersection queries for curved objects. In *Proc. 7th Annual ACM Symposium on Computational Geometry*, pages 41–50, 1991.

[BC87] József Beck and William Chen. *Irregularities of Distributions*. Cambridge University Press, 1987.

[Bec91] József Beck. Quasi-random 2-colorings of point sets. Technical Report 91-20, DIMACS, 1991.

[Bol78] Béla Bollobás. *Extremal Graph Theory*. Academic Press, 1978.

[CF88] Bernard Chazelle and Joel Friedman. A deterministic view of random sampling and its use in geometry. In *Proc. 29th Annual IEEE Symposium on Foundations of Computer Science*, pages 539–549, 1988.

[CG89] Bernard Chazelle and Leonidas Guibas. Visibility and intersection problems in plane geometry. *Discrete Comput. Geom.*, 4:551–589, 1989.

[Cha88]   Bernard Chazelle. Tight bounds on the stabbing number of spanning trees in Euclidean space. Technical Report CS-TR-155-88, Princeton University, Department of Computer Science, 1988.

[Cha89]   Bernard Chazelle. Polytope range searching and integral geometry. *J. Amer. Math. Soc.*, 2:637–666, 1989.

[CJ91]   Siu Wing Cheng and Ravi Janardan. Space-efficient ray-shooting and intersection searching: Algorithms, dynamization, and applications. In *Proc. 2nd Annual ACM-SIAM Symposium on Discrete Algorithms*, pages 7–16, 1991.

[Cla89]   Kenneth Clarkson. Las vegas algorithms for linear and integer programming when the dimension is small. Manuscript, 1989.

[CSW90]   Bernard Chazelle, Micha Sharir, and Emo Welzl. Quasi-optimal upper bounds for simplex range searching and new zone theorems. In *Proc. 6th ACM Symp. on Comp. Geom.*, pages 23–33, 1990.

[CW89]   Bernard Chazelle and Emo Welzl. Quasi-optimal range searching in spaces of finite VC-dimension. *Discrete Comput. Geom.*, 4:467–489, 1989.

[Ede87]   Herbert Edelsbrunner. Algorithms in combinatorial geometry. *Springer-Verlag, Heidelberg, Germany*, 1987.

[EGH+89]   Herbert Edelsbrunner, Leonidas Guibas, John Herschberger, Raimund Seidel, Micha Sharir, Jack Snoeyink, and Emo Welzl. Implicitly representing arrangements of lines or segments. *Discrete Comput. Geom.*, 4:433–466, 1989.

[EHSS89]   Herbert Edelsbrunner, N. Hasan, Raimund Seidel, and X. J. Shen. Circles through two points that always enclose many points. *Geom. Dedicata*, 32:1–12, 1989.

[HR90]   Torben Hagerup and Christine Rüb. A guided tour of Chernoff bounds. *Inform. Process. Lett.*, 33:305–308, 1990.

[Mat90]   Jiří Matoušek. More on cutting arrangements and spanning trees with low crossing number. Technical Report B 90-02, Freie Universität Berlin, Fachbereich Mathematik, Institut für Informatik, 1990.

[Mat91a]   Jiří Matoušek, 1991. Private communication.

[Mat91b]   Jiří Matoušek. Efficient partition trees. In *Proc. 7th Annual ACM Symposium on Computational Geometry*, pages 1–9, 1991.

[Mat91c]   Jiří Matoušek. Range searching with efficient hierarchical cuttings. Manuscript, 1991.

[Mat91d]   Jiří Matoušek. Spanning trees with low crossing number. *RAIRO Inform. Théor. Appl.*, 6:103–123, 1991.

[MWW91]   Jiří Matoušek, Emo Welzl, and Lorenz Wernisch. Discrepancy and ϵ-approximations for bounded VC-dimension. In *Proc. 32nd Annual IEEE Symposium on Foundations of Computer Science*, pages 424–430, 1991.

[Pac91]   János Pach. Drawing graphs. Talk presented at the Dagstuhl seminar on 'Computational Geometry', 1991.

[Sei91]   Raimund Seidel.   Backwards analysis of randomized geometric algorithms. Manuscript, 1991.

[Spe87]   Joel Spencer. *Ten Lectures on the Probabilistic Method.* Society for Industrial and Applied Mathematics, 1987.

[Wel88]   Emo Welzl. Partition trees for triangle counting and other range searching problems. In *Proc. 4th Annual ACM Symposium on Computational Geometry*, pages 23–33, 1988.

Appendix: Optimal choice of reweighting factor $1 + \mu$.

We want to estimate $\min_{\mu > 0} f(\mu)$ for

$$f(\mu) = \frac{1}{\ln(1 + \mu)} (a\mu + b) , \tag{4}$$

with $a, b > 0$. The first derivative of f is

$$f'(\mu) = \frac{a \ln(1 + \mu) - (a\mu + b)(1 + \mu)^{-1}}{\ln^2(1 + \mu)} .$$

So a local extremum (which obviously has to be a minimum) is achieved when

$$a\mu + b = a(1 + \mu) \ln(1 + \mu) , \tag{5}$$

or, equivalently, when

$$e^x(1 - x) = 1 - c , \tag{6}$$

where we write x short for $\ln(1 + \mu)$, and c short for b/a. Equality (6) has exactly one solution.

Let us first consider the case $c \leq 1$. Then, for $x = \sqrt{c}$,

$$e^x(1 - x) \geq (1 + x)(1 - x) = (1 - c) ,$$

and, for $x = \sqrt{2c}$,

$$e^x(1 - x) = 1 - \sum_{i=1}^{\infty} \frac{(i - 1)x^i}{i!} < 1 - \frac{x^2}{2} = 1 - c .$$

Consequently, (6) is satisfied for some x in the range $\sqrt{c} \leq x < \sqrt{2c}$; so the optimal μ has to be chosen such that

$$\sqrt{b/a} \leq \ln(1 + \mu_{opt}) < \sqrt{2b/a}, \text{ for } b \leq a .$$

If we substitute (5) into (4), then we get for the optimal μ that $f(\mu) = a(1 + \mu)$, and so

$$min_{\mu > 0} f(\mu) < ae^{\sqrt{2b/a}} = a + O(\sqrt{ab}), \text{ for } b \leq a ,$$

since $e^y \leq 1 + (\frac{e^{\sqrt{2}} - 1}{\sqrt{2}})y$ for $0 \leq y \leq \sqrt{2}$. (For $a = b$, we get $\min_{\mu > 0} f(\mu) = ea$.)

If $c > 1$, then we rewrite (6) as

$$z(\ln z - 1) = c - 1 ,$$

where $z = \mu + 1$. We assume actually that c is sufficiently large, say, $c \geq e$. For $z = \frac{ec}{\ln c}$,

$$\frac{ec}{\ln c}(\ln ec - \ln \ln c - 1) = c(e - \frac{e \ln \ln c}{\ln c}) > c - 1 ,$$

and, for $z = \frac{c-1}{\ln c}$,

$$\frac{c - 1}{\ln c}(\ln(c - 1) - \ln \ln c - 1) < (c - 1)(1 - \frac{\ln \ln c + 1}{\ln c}) < c - 1 .$$

Therefore, μ has to be chosen such that

$$\frac{b/a - 1}{\ln(b/a)} < 1 + \mu_{opt} < \frac{eb}{a \ln(b/a)} , \quad \text{for } b \geq ea ,$$

which implies

$$\min_{\mu > 0} f(\mu) < \frac{eb}{\ln(b/a)}, \quad \text{for } b \geq ea .$$

High Performance Universal Hashing, with Applications to Shared Memory Simulations*

Martin Dietzfelbinger [†‡]   Friedhelm Meyer auf der Heide [†§]

Abstract

We describe and analyze a new high performance universal class of hash functions which can be constructed fast, evaluated in constant time, and which have properties very similar to the "ideal" hash function, namely a random function. We illustrate the capabilities of the new class by considering simple perfect hashing schemes.

We further survey recent results in a very important application area of the new hash functions, namely results on simulations of parallel shared memory machines on parallel machines that only can communicate via a distributed memory.

1   Introduction

The paper deals with design, analysis, and applications of high performance universal classes of hash functions.

The classical application of hashing lies in implementations of dictionaries, i. e., data structures that support the instructions insert, delete and lookup of data items identified by keys x from some universe U.

Besides the numerous implementations by variants of dynamic search trees (AVL-trees, 2–3-trees etc., for an overview see [18]), dynamic hashing strategies are often considered. Here a hash function h is used that maps the universe U into a hash table, i. e., to the positions of an array A whose size should be linear in the number of currently stored data items. A data item with key x is stored in $A[h(x)]$. There are several strategies known to handle collisions, i. e., cases where different keys are mapped to the same position in A, see [18].

We always identify data items with their keys. Assume that a set $S \subseteq U$ of n keys is currently stored in the dictionary. The keys of S that are mapped to the same position i of A form the *ith bucket B_i (of S under h)*.

To illustrate important features of hash functions which characterize their performance, consider the well known strategy "hashing by chaining". Here each position of A is a linked list ("chain"). In list $A[i]$, the elements from B_i are stored. For a lookup for x,

---

*Supported in part by DFG-Grant Me 872/1-4 in the Schwerpunktprogramm "Datenstrukturen und effiziente Algorithmen".

[†]Fachbereich 17 · Mathematik–Informatik and Heinz-Nixdorf-Institut, Universität-GH-Paderborn, D-W-4790 Paderborn, Germany

[‡]email: M.Dietzfelbinger@uni-paderborn.de

[§]email: fmadh@uni-paderborn.de

we have to check whether $x \in B_{h(x)}$, i. e., whether x is stored in the list $A[h(x)]$. For an update for x, we have to modify $A[h(x)]$ accordingly.

Further, as the dictionary changes its size dynamically, and as we want to use linear space only, we have to rebuild the whole structure from time to time, using a new h and a new A of different size.

Thus the performance of such a hashing strategy depends on

- **space**, i. e., size of the hash table,

- **construction time**, i. e., time needed to construct a new hash function,

- **evaluation time**, i. e., time to evaluate h,

- **bucket sizes** (see the section on high performance universal hashing below for criteria to measure bucket sizes).

A deterministic hashing strategy which uses a fixed hash function h is called a *uniform hashing strategy*.

In this case, using e. g. $h(x) = x \bmod m$, very good performance (constant amortized time, linear space) can be obtained on the *average, average taken over all instruction sequences of length n*.

The disadvantage of uniform hashing strategies is its very bad worst case performance; it may happen that each instruction needs time $\Theta(n)$ to be executed. Therefore, Carter and Wegman ([4]) introduced a randomized version of hashing strategies, called *universal hashing*.

Here one applies a probabilistic dynamic hashing strategy, where one chooses randomly a hash function h from a universal class $\mathcal{H}$ of hash functions and then executes the (deterministic) strategy from above. If $\mathcal{H}$ is a "good" universal class, then one can prove optimal bounds as above for the *worst case expected time*, i. e., for the maximum over all expected (w. r. t. the random choice of $h \in \mathcal{H}$) runtimes, maximum taken over all sequences of n instructions. For "sufficiently good" universal classes, one can even show that the worst case expected time bound is *very reliable* in the sense that the algorithm stays within this bound with probabiliy $1 - 1/p(n)$, where $p(n)$ is a polynomial in the current size n of the dictionary. In the next paragraph we describe the criteria that make up a "good" universal class of hash functions.

High performance universal hashing

We will only be interested in hash functions $h : U \to \{0, \ldots, n-1\}$ which have constant evaluation time and $O(n)$ randomized construction time.

The property "h splits S into small buckets" we will measure in several ways. We shall note how random functions, i. e. $\text{RANDOM}_n = \{h \mid h : U \to \{0, \ldots, n-1\}\}$ behave for the given measure. This is important information because RANDOM_n is the "ideal" universal class as far as bucket sizes are concerned (but they are clearly unrealistic because they need much space and high evaluation time.)

Let $\mathcal{H} \subseteq \{h \mid h : U \to \{0, \ldots, n-1\}\}$ be some class, $U = \{0, \ldots, p-1\}$. The probabilities below are defined relative to a random choice of $h \in \mathcal{H}$. Carter and Wegman [4] have introduced the notion of universality as a measure for the performance of such classes $\mathcal{H}$.

Criterion 1: Universality. $\mathcal{H}$ is k-*universal* if there is some $c > 0$ such that for each $j \leq k$, $x_1 < \cdots < x_j \in U$, $a_1, \ldots, a_j \in \{0, \ldots, n-1\}$ it holds that $\Pr(h(x_1) = a_1, \ldots, h(x_j) = a_j) \leq c/n^j$. (RANDOM$_n$ is n-universal).

The following notions describe several ways of formalizing the idea that buckets are small. Let $S \subseteq U$, $|S| = n$ be arbitrary. S is split into buckets $B_0, \ldots, B_{n-1}$ by a randomly chosen $h \in \mathcal{H}$.

Criterion 2: Individual bucket size. For each $i \in \{0, \ldots, n-1\}$, B_i should be small with high probability.

(For a randomly chosen $h \in$ RANDOM$_n$, $\Pr(|B_i| \geq n) \leq (u/e)^{-u}$.)

Criterion 3: Maximum bucket size. $\max\{|B_i|, i = 0, \ldots, n-1\}$ should be expected small, or even with high probability small.

(For $h \in$ RANDOM$_n$, $E(\max\{|B_i|, i = 1, \ldots, n\}) = \Theta(\log(n)/\log\log(n))$, and $\Pr(\max\{|B_i|, i = 0, \ldots, n-1\} \geq u) \leq u^{-u/2}$ for $u \geq c \cdot \log(n)/\log\log(n)$, for a suitable constant $c > 0$.)

Criterion 4: f-weighted bucket sizes. Consider a function $f : \mathbb{N}^n \to \mathbb{N}$, e.g., $f(b_0, \ldots, b_{n-1}) = \sum_{0 \leq i < n} (b_i)^k$ for fixed k, or $f(b_0, \ldots, b_{n-1}) = \sum_{0 \leq i < n} 2^{b_i} \cdot f(|B_0|, \ldots, |B_{n-1}|)$ should be expected linear in n, or even linear in n with high probability, for a rapidly growing function f.

(For $h \in$ RANDOM$_n$, $E(\sum_{0 \leq i < n} |B_i|^{\alpha|B_i|}) = O(n)$ and $\Pr(\sum_{0 \leq i < n} |B_i|^{\alpha|B_i|} \geq c \cdot n) \leq 2^{-\sqrt{n}}$ for a suitable $c > 0$ and sufficiently small $\alpha > 0$.)

Previous work on high performance hash functions

Polynomials of given degree d as hash functions are widely used and analyzed in [4, 19, 5]. If we demand constant evaluation time, thus take d to be constant, we get much weaker properties than mentioned above for random functions, for example, one can only prove an $O(n^{1/(d+1)})$ bound for the expected maximum bucket size.

In [20], a construction of an n^ϵ-universal hash function is given that can be evaluated in constant time and constructed in time $O(n^\epsilon)$ for arbitrary $\varepsilon \in (0, 1)$. The analysis of bucket sizes shows very similar results as for random functions. The constants in the time and space bounds for that class depend exponentially on r, where n^r is the size of the universe.

New results on high performance hash functions

In Section 2 we describe and analyze a new class of hash functions and illustrate its capabilities by using it to design a perfect hashing scheme à la FKS (after the famous scheme due to Fredman, Komlós and Szemerédi, see [10]). The use of our hash functions turns the expected linear time bound for constructing the scheme into a very reliable bound, which is guaranteed with overwhelming probability.

The analysis uses several non-trivial tail estimates, i.e., probability bounds for the event that a random experiment yields a result far away from its expectation. Beside well known bounds due to Chernoff and Hoeffding, we apply a new, very powerful consequence of a martingale tail estimate, shown independently by McDiarmid and Hagerup in [17] and [13].

Our new universal class is very similar to our class previously described in [8, 7]. Its advantage is that it is simpler and, more importantly, allows an easier analysis.

Applications to the design of dictionaries

In [8] (see also [9]) we have designed a dictionary that uses linear space and performs in real-time, i. e., it is able to accept instructions in fixed constant length time intervals. It is randomized of the Monte-Carlo type and fails to meet the real time assumption only with negligibly small probability Parallel variants, implemented on a p-processor CRCW PRAM, are presented in [6] and [9]. The latter one can perform a sequence of batches of p instructions in real time, using optimal space $O(n)$, if $n \geq p^{1+\epsilon}$ for arbitrary $\epsilon > 0$. Very recently a parallel dictionary with comparable features was presented in [11]. It already works in optimal space for $n \geq p$. On the other hand it allows less parallelism, p instructions are executed by $p/\log^*(p)$ processors in (optimal) time $O(\log^*(p))$. The construction generalizes static parallel hashing schemes as presented in [2] and [16].

Applications to shared memory simulation

Hashing is the most promising method for simulating a shared memory of an n-processor PRAM on an n-processor parallel machines where the memory is distributed among n modules (DMM). In Section 3 we deal with recent developments in this area and focus on the simulations implicitly designed and analyzed in our dictionary for DMMs from [7]. In particular we try to give some insight into the idea of our time-processor optimal shared memory simulation which simulates an $n \log(n)$-processor PRAM on an n-processor distributed memory machine, both with concurrent-read/write capabilities, with optimal expected delay $O(\log(n))$.

We note here that a more complicated simulation scheme has recently lead to a faster simulation: In [15] it is shown how to simulate an $n \log \log(n) \log^*(n)$-processor PRAM on an n-processor distributed memory machine with expected optimal delay $O(\log \log(n) \log^*(n))$.

Section 3 is a survey, it does not contain full proofs but only tries to give some insight into the basic problems and ideas connected to shared memory simulations based on hashing strategies.

2 A new class of hash functions

2.1 Preliminaries

Let us fix some basic notation.

Definition 2.1 *Let $h : U \to \{0, \ldots, s - 1\}$, and let $S \subseteq U$.*

(a) *The jth bucket is $B_j^h := \{ x \in S \mid h(x) = j \}$.*

(b) *Its size is $b_j^h := |B_j^h|$.*

(c) *The set of keys colliding with $x \in U$ is $B_x^{\text{coll},h} := \{y \in S \mid h(y) = h(x)\}$.*

(d) *The number of keys colliding with $x \in U$ is $b_x^{\text{coll},h} := |B_x^{\text{coll},h}|$.*

(e) *h is called l-perfect for S if $b_i^h \leq l$ for all $i \in \{0, \ldots, s - 1\}$.*

(f) *If h is chosen at random from some class, we write B_j for the random set B_j^h and b_j for the random variable b_j^h, analogously for B_x^{coll} and b_x^{coll}.*

Our constructions will be based on the following universal class of hash functions: Let p be prime, $U = \{0, 1, \ldots, p-1\}$ be the *universe*. Consider two parameters: $d \geq 2$, the *degree*, and $s \geq 1$, the *table size*. Define

$$\mathcal{H}_s^d := \{ h_\alpha \mid \alpha = (\alpha_0, \ldots, \alpha_{d-1}) \in U^d \},$$

where for $\alpha = (\alpha_0, \ldots, \alpha_{d-1}) \in U^d$ we let

$$h_\alpha(x) := \left(\sum_{0 \leq i < d} \alpha_i x^i \bmod p \right) \bmod s, \quad \text{for } x \in U.$$

We will have h chosen uniformly at random from $\mathcal{H}_s^d$. Here and in the following, all probabilities are with respect to the probability space resulting from choosing a hash function at random; no assumptions about the distribution of the input keys are made. We recall two useful facts concerning $\mathcal{H}_s^d$. Assume for the following that some set $S \subseteq U$ with $|S| = n$ is given.

Fact 2.2 ([5]) *Let $n \leq s$. For each d there is a constant $c_d \leq 2$ so that for all $S \subseteq U$ with $|S| = n$ and all h randomly chosen from $\mathcal{H}_s^d$ we have the following:*

(a) $\Pr\left(h \text{ is } (d-1)\text{-perfect for } S \right) \geq 1 - \dfrac{c_d}{d!} \cdot n \cdot (n/s)^{d-1}.$

(b) *For $0 \leq j < s$ arbitrary:*

$$\Pr(b_j \geq u) \leq \begin{cases} c_d \cdot (e^{u-1}/u^u) \cdot (n/s)^u, & \text{for } 1 \leq u < d; \\ c_d \cdot (e^{d-1}/u^d) \cdot (n/s)^d, & \text{for } d \leq u. \end{cases}$$

In particular, for $s \geq n$ and $u \geq d$, we have $\Pr(b_j \geq u) = O(u^{-d})$.

Next, we list some probabilistic estimates. First, we quote a classical theorem that estimates the probability for a sum of independent *bounded* random variables to deviate far from the expected value, and a theorem in the same spirit dealing with sums of independent random variables that are approximately geometrically distributed, thus *unbounded*.

Theorem 2.3 (Hoeffding [14]) *Let $X_1, \ldots, X_n$ be independent random variables with values in the interval $[0, z]$ for some $z > 0$. Let $Y := \sum_{1 \leq i \leq n} X_i$ and $m := E(Y)$. Then for all a, $0 < a < nz - m$, we have*

$$\Pr\left(Y \geq m + a \right) \leq \left[\left(\frac{m}{m+a} \right)^{m+a} \left(\frac{nz-m}{nz-m-a} \right)^{nz-m-a} \right]^{1/z} \leq \left(\frac{m}{m+a} \right)^{(m+a)/z} \cdot e^{a/z}.$$

(The second inequality holds since $(1 + \frac{x}{\alpha})^\alpha \leq e^x$ for $\alpha > 0$.) $\qquad\square$

Lemma 2.4 ([8]) *Let $m \geq 1$, $w_1, \ldots, w_m > 0$ be arbitrary. Abbreviate $\sum_{i=1}^m w_i$ by W and $\max\{w_i \mid 1 \leq i \leq m\}$ by M. Assume that $X_1, \ldots, X_m$ are independent random variables so that for $1 \leq i \leq m$ holds*

$$\Pr(X_i > L \cdot w_i) \leq 2^{-L}, \quad \text{for } L = 1, 2, 3, \ldots.$$

Then

$$\Pr\left(\sum_{i=1}^{m} X_i \geq 3 \cdot l \cdot W\right) \leq e^{-(l-1)W/M}, \quad \text{for } l = 1, 2, 3, \dots .$$

(Note that $E(\sum_{i=1}^{m} X_i) \leq 2W$.) □

The following theorem (a proof can be found in [17]; it was also noted in [13]) is extremely helpful when we need to estimate the probability that a random variable T deviates far from its mean in case T is a function of many independent variables each of which has only small influence on T. The usefulness of this theorem for analyzing hash functions and parallel dictionary algorithms has been noted before (BasHag:91p,GMV:91).

Theorem 2.5 ([17]) *Let $X_1, \dots, X_n$ be independent random variables with ranges $\Omega_1, \dots, \Omega_n$. Further, let $g: \prod_{1 \leq i \leq n} \Omega_i \to \mathbb{R}$ be an arbitrary function so that g changes by at most a constant $\vartheta > 0$ in response to a change in a single component, i. e.,*

$$\left| g(\omega_1 \dots, \omega_{i_0}, \dots, \omega_n) - g(\omega_1 \dots, \omega_{i_0}', \dots, \omega_n) \right| \leq \vartheta,$$

for $\omega_i \in \Omega_i$, $1 \leq i \leq n$, and $\omega_{i_0}' \in \Omega_{i_0}$ arbitrary. Let $T := g(X_1, \dots, X_n)$. Then for all $t \geq 0$ we have

$$\Pr\left(T \geq E(T) + t\right) \leq e^{-t^2/(2\vartheta^2 n)}.$$

□

The proof of this theorem is based on a "martingale tail estimate" ("Azuma's inequality"); this is why also arguments based on Theorem 2.5 are often referred to as "martingale estimates".

2.2 Definition and basic analysis

Definition 2.6 *Assume $r, s \geq 1$ and $d \geq 2$.*

(a) *For arbitrary $f: U \to \{0, 1, \dots, rs - 1\}$ define $f_1(x) := f(x) \text{ div } s$ and $f_2(x) := f(x) \bmod s$, for $x \in U$. (a div b means $\lfloor a/b \rfloor$.)*

(b) *For $f: U \to \{0, 1, \dots, rs - 1\}$ and $a_0, \dots, a_{r-1} \in \{0, 1, \dots, s - 1\}$ let the function $h = h(f, a_0, \dots, a_{r-1})$ be defined by*

$$h(x) := \left(f_2(x) + a_{f_1(x)} \right) \bmod s \quad, \text{ for } x \in U.$$

(c) *The class $\mathcal{R}(r, s, d)$ consists of all functions $h(f, a_0, \dots, a_{r-1})$ with $f \in \mathcal{H}_{rs}^d$ and $a_0, \dots, a_{r-1} \in \{0, \dots, s - 1\}$.*

Remark 2.7 (a) The class $\mathcal{R}(r, s, d)$ is d-universal. (The proof is a straightforward variant of the proof that $\mathcal{H}_s^d$ has this property, see [5].)

(b) Note that f and the pair (f_1, f_2) are practically the same function. It will be convenient to regard the range of (f_1, f_2) as an $r \times s$-array.

(c) If $f \in \mathcal{H}_{rs}^d$ is given as $f(x) = F(x) \bmod rs$, where

$$F(x) = \left(\sum_{0 \leq l < d} \alpha_l x^l \right) \bmod p,$$

an efficient way for evaluating $h = h(f, a_0, \ldots, a_{r-1})$ is given by the formula

$$h(x) = \Big(F(x) + a_{(F(x)\,\mathrm{div}\,s)\,\mathrm{mod}\,r}\Big) \bmod s.$$

If s and r are powers of 2, the div and mod operations have a particularly simple implementations by shift and bitwise AND operations.

(d) Obviously, a function $h \in \mathcal{R}(r, s, d)$ can be stored in $O(d+r)$ cells, can be evaluated in time $O(d)$, and can be generated in $O(d + r)$ steps. One may even assume that the setup time is constant if only f is chosen at the beginning and the offset a_i is chosen only when the first key x with $f_1(x) = i$ appears, for each $i \in \{0, \ldots, r-1\}$.

Before embarking on the rigorous analysis of the class $\mathcal{R}(r, s, d)$, let us (informally) explain the effect of such a function on the keys $x \in U$. First, the function f maps the keys into an $r \times s$-array (x is mapped into the cell in row $f_1(x)$ and column $f_2(x)$ of the array). In a second step, row i is shifted cyclically by an offset a_i, i.e., key x is moved from column $f_2(x)$ to column $(f_2(x) + a_i) \bmod s$. These shifts are independent for the different rows. The hash value $h(x)$ is given by the number of the column to which x is moved by these two steps.

For the following we assume that a set $S \subseteq U$ with $|S| = n$ is given, and that $rs > n$. The nice behaviour of the class $\mathcal{R}(r, s, d)$ rests essentially on the fact that if $n/(rs)$ is sufficiently small then with high probability f will be $(d - 1)$-perfect on S; this property implies that each row i of the array can contribute at most $d - 1$ keys to the quantity $b_j = |\{x \in S \mid h(x) = j\}|$.

Definition 2.8 *For $0 \le i < r$, let $\hat{B}_i^f := \{x \in S \mid f_1(x) = i\}$ (the elements of S mapped to the ith row of the array).*

Lemma 2.9 *We have $\Pr(f$ is $(d-1)$-perfect for $S) = 1 - O\left(n^d/(rs)^{d-1}\right)$, if f is chosen at random from $\mathcal{H}_{rs}^d$.*

Proof: This is immediate from Fact 2.2(a). □

Definition 2.10 *Let $f: U \to \{0, 1, \ldots, rs - 1\}$ be a function that is $(d-1)$-perfect on S. We fix f and consider only the random experiment of choosing $a_0, \ldots, a_{r-1}$. Formally, let*

$$\mathcal{R}_f(r, s) := \Big\{h(f, a_0, \ldots, a_{r-1}) \,\Big|\, a_0, \ldots, a_{r-1} \in \{0, \ldots, s-1\}\Big\}.$$

We write $\Pr_f(\mathcal{A})$ for $\Pr(\mathcal{A} \mid \mathcal{R}_f(r, s))$ and $E_f(X)$ for $E(X \mid \mathcal{R}_f(r, s))$, for arbitrary events $\mathcal{A}$ and random variables X.

We start with proving some fundamental, important properties of the functions from $\mathcal{R}(r, s, d)$. These properties are close to what one would get for random functions, compare the section on high performance universal hashing in the Introduction and, e.g., [12].

Theorem 2.11 *Let $S \subseteq U$ with $|S| \le n$, and assume that f is $(d-1)$-perfect. Then for h randomly chosen from $\mathcal{R}_f(r, s)$ the following holds.*

(a) $\Pr_f\left(b_j \geq u \cdot \dfrac{n}{s}\right) \leq \left(\dfrac{e^{u-1}}{u^u}\right)^{(n/s)/(d-1)}$, for $u \geq 1$, $0 \leq j < s$;

(b) $\Pr_f\left(b_x^{\text{coll}} > d + u \cdot \dfrac{n}{s}\right) \leq \left(\dfrac{e^{u-1}}{u^u}\right)^{(n/s)/(d-1)}$, for $u \geq 1$, $x \in U$.

Note the special case $n \leq s$:

(a') $\Pr_f(b_j \geq u) \leq \left(\dfrac{e^{u-1}}{u^u}\right)^{1/(d-1)}$, for $u \geq 1$, $0 \leq j < s$;

(b') $\Pr_f(b_x^{\text{coll}} > d + u) \leq \left(\dfrac{e^{u-1}}{u^u}\right)^{1/(d-1)}$, for $u \geq 1$, $x \in U$.

Corollary 2.12 *In the situation of the preceding theorem, we have:*

(a) $\Pr_f\left(\max\{b_j \mid 0 \leq j < s\} \geq u \cdot \dfrac{n}{s}\right) \leq u^{-u \cdot (n/s)/(2(d-1))}$,

  for $u \geq \max\{C, 5(d-1) \cdot (s \ln s/n)/\ln(s \ln s/n)\}$, where C is some constant.

(b) $E_f(\max\{b_j \mid 0 \leq j < s\}) = O\left(\dfrac{n}{s} + \dfrac{\log s}{\log(s \log s/n)}\right).$

The formulas simplify in the special case $n = s$:

(a') $\Pr_f\left(\max\{b_j \mid 0 \leq j < n\} \geq u\right) \leq u^{-u/(2(d-1))}$, *for $u \geq 5(d-1) \cdot \ln n/ \ln \ln n$.*

(b') $E_f\left(\max\{b_j \mid 0 \leq j < n\}\right) = O\left(\dfrac{\log n}{\log \log n}\right).$

Proof of Theorem 2.11:   Assume that $|S| = n$. (Otherwise add some dummy elements.) Fix $f: U \to \{0, \ldots, rs - 1\}$ that is $(d-1)$-perfect on S.

(a) Fix j, $0 \leq j < s$. We define random variables X_i, $0 \leq i < r$, that measure the contribution of the "f-buckets" $\hat{B}_i^f$ to B_j, as follows:

$$X_i := \left|\left\{x \in S \mid h(x) = j \text{ and } f_1(x) = i\right\}\right|, \quad \text{for } 0 \leq i < r.$$

Obviously, we have

$$b_j = \sum_{0 \leq i < r} X_i.$$

We observe that, by definition,

$$X_i = \left|\left\{x \in S \mid f_1(x) = i \text{ and } f_2(x) = (j - a_i) \bmod s\right\}\right|, \quad \text{for } 0 \leq i < r.$$

Now a_i is randomly chosen, hence $(j - a_i) \bmod s$ is a random element of $\{0, \ldots, s - 1\}$. Thus, X_i is the number of elements of S in a randomly chosen cell of the ith row of the $r \times s$-array that forms the range of f. This implies the following:

(i) $0 \leq X_i \leq d - 1$, for $0 \leq i < r$;

(ii) the X_i, $0 \le i < r$, are independent;

(iii) $E_f(X_i) = \frac{1}{s} \cdot |\{x \in S \mid f_1(x) = i\}| = \frac{1}{s} \cdot |\hat{B}_i^f|$, for $0 \le i < r$.

From (iii) we get the (obvious) expected value of b_j:

$$m := E_f(b_j) = E_f\left(\sum_{0 \le i < r} X_i\right) = \frac{1}{s} \cdot \sum_{0 \le i < r} |\hat{B}_i^f| = \frac{1}{s} \cdot |S| = \frac{n}{s}.$$

Applying Hoeffding's Theorem (Theorem 2.3) immediately yields

$$\Pr_f\left(b_j \ge u \cdot \frac{n}{s}\right) \le \Pr_f\left(\sum_{0 \le i < r} X_i \ge um\right) \le \left(\left(\frac{m}{um}\right)^{um} \cdot e^{um-m}\right)^{1/(d-1)} \le \left(\frac{e^{u-1}}{u^u}\right)^{m/(d-1)},$$

which is (a).

(b) This is proved in exactly the same way as (a), excepting that in addition to f also $a_{f_1(x)}$ is considered fixed. At most $d - 1$ elements of $B_{f_1(x)}^f$ are mapped to the same cell as x by h; the contribution of the other $\hat{B}_i^f$, $i \ne f_1(x)$, to b_x^{coll} is analyzed just as in (a). □
Proof of Corollary 2.12: This follows from Theorem 2.11(a) by calculations along standard lines, cf. [19]. We omit the details. □

Remark 2.13 (a) Note that for the (unconditional) probabilities $\Pr(b_x^{\text{coll}} \ge u)$ and $\Pr(b_j \ge u)$ tighter estimates than those given in the theorem are available if $u \le d$, cf. Remark 2.7(a) and Fact 2.2(b).

(b) For $s \ge n^{1+\epsilon}$ we have (by Fact 2.2(a)) that $\Pr(h$ is $(d - 1)$-perfect on $S) \ge 1 - O(n^{1-\epsilon(d-1)})$. Without increasing the evaluation time, the class $\mathcal{R}(r, s, d)$ offers the possibility of much increasing the probability for l-perfectness for a constant l. Namely, if f is $(d - 1)$-perfect on S then (as is not hard to show) we have

$$\Pr_f(h \text{ is } (t - 1)(d - 1)\text{-perfect on } S) \ge 1 - \frac{n^{1+\epsilon}}{t! n^{\epsilon t}}.$$

Thus, for h chosen at random from $\mathcal{R}(n, n, d)$ we have

$$\Pr(h \text{ is } (t - 1)(d - 1)\text{-perfect on } S) \ge 1 - O(n^{2-d}) - \frac{n^{1+\epsilon}}{t! n^{\epsilon t}}.$$

We do not further consider this case, and assume $s \le n$ from here on.

2.3 Refined methods

The basic properties given in the previous theorem are already very useful if the class $\mathcal{R}(r, s, d)$ is to be used in a simple hashing scheme, e. g., in chained hashing. We want to study the class a little more closely. Below, we will only consider the case $|S| = r = s = n$.

Remark 2.14 Note that if it is desirable that the space needed to store h is smaller than n, also $r = n^\delta$ for some $\delta < 1$ is a suitable choice as long as $n/(rs)$ remains sufficiently small. Also, for $n/\log n \le s \le n$ the class $\mathcal{R}(r, s, d)$ exhibits a behaviour comparable to that of random functions.

Definition 2.15 *Assume $r = s = n$. We abbreviate $\mathcal{R}(n, n, d)$ by $\mathcal{R}(d)$; if the value of d is inessential, we also write simply $\mathcal{R}$.*

We are interested in extensions of the basic property

$$E\left(\sum_{0 \le j < n} (b_j)^k\right) = O(n), \quad \text{for } 2 \le k \le d,$$

which $\mathcal{R}(d)$ shares with all other d-universal classes. We show that $\mathcal{R}(d)$ allows us to extend this property in 2 directions:

  (i) it also holds for sums of higher powers $(b_j)^k$, $k > d$, even for sums of exponentials $(b_j)^{\alpha b_j}$;

  (ii) sums of powers (or exponentials) as above are linear not only in the expected case, but even with probability $1 - O(n^{-c})$.

We start with the expected values.

Lemma 2.16 *Let $S \subseteq U$ with $|S| \le n = r = s$. Let $d \ge 2$ and $0 < \alpha < 1/(d-1)$, and assume that $f: \{0, \ldots, n^2 - 1\}$ is $(d-1)$-perfect on S. Let $h \in R_f(n, n)$ be randomly chosen. Then*

  (a) $E_f\left((b_j)^{\alpha b_j}\right) = O(1), \quad \text{for } 0 \le j < n;$

  (b) $E_f\left((b_j)^k\right) = O(1), \quad \text{for } 0 \le j < n \text{ and } k \ge 1;$

  (c) $E_f\left((b_x^{\text{coll}})^{\alpha b_x^{\text{coll}}}\right) = O(1), \quad \text{for } x \in U;$

  (d) $E_f\left((b_x^{\text{coll}})^k\right) = O(1), \quad \text{for } x \in U \text{ and } k \ge 1.$

(The constants on the right hand side depend on d, α, and k.)

Corollary 2.17 *In the situation of the preceding lemma we have*

  (a) $E_f\left(\sum_{0 \le j < n} (b_j)^{\alpha b_j}\right) = O(n);$

  (b) $E_f\left(\sum_{0 \le j < n} (b_j)^k\right) = O(n), \quad \text{for } k \ge 1.$ $\qquad\qquad\qquad\qquad\square$

Proof of Lemma 2.16: (a) By Theorem 2.11(a') we know that

$$\Pr_f(b_j = u) \le \Pr_f(b_j \ge u) \le \left(\frac{e^{u-1}}{u^u}\right)^{1/(d-1)}, \quad \text{for } u \ge 1.$$

Thus, for $0 < \alpha < 1/(d-1)$,

$$\begin{aligned}
E_f\left((b_j)^{\alpha b_j}\right) &= \sum_{u \ge 0} u^{\alpha u} \cdot \Pr_f(b_j = u) \\
&\le 1 + \sum_{u \ge 1} e^{-u \cdot ((1/(d-1) - \alpha) \cdot \ln u - 1/(d-1))} \\
&= O(1).
\end{aligned}$$

(b) As in (a), we calculate

$$E_f\left((b_j)^k\right) = \sum_{u \geq 1} u^k \cdot \Pr_f(b_j = u)$$

$$\leq \sum_{u \geq 1} e^{-u \cdot ((\ln u - 1)/(d-1) + (k \ln u)/u)}$$

$$= O(1).$$

(c) and (d) are proved similarly. □

Next we want to show that the sums estimated in Corollary 2.17 are close to their expectation with probability $1 - O(n^{-c})$. We need some more technical preparations.

Definition 2.18 *Let $S \subseteq U$ with $|S| = n$.*

(a) *We say that a function $f: U \to \{0, \ldots, n^2 - 1\}$ distributes S well if it is $(d-1)$-perfect on S and*

$$|\hat{B}_i^f| = \left|\left\{x \in S \mid f_1(x) = i\right\}\right| \leq n^{1/4}, \quad \text{for } 0 \leq i < n.$$

(b) *The subclass $\mathcal{R}_S(d)$ (or $\mathcal{R}_S$) of $\mathcal{R}(d)$ consists of all functions $h = h(f, a_0, \ldots, a_{n-1}) \in \mathcal{R}(d)$ for which f distributes S well.*

If we regard the range of f as an $n \times n$-array, as discussed above, then the subclass $\mathcal{R}_S(d)$ consists of those functions $h = h(f, a_0, \ldots, a_{n-1})$ for which f maps at most $(d-1)$ keys from S into each cell of the array and at most $n^{1/4}$ into each row. We show that $\mathcal{R}_S(d)$ contains almost all functions from $\mathcal{R}(d)$.

Lemma 2.19 *For arbitrary $c \geq 1$, if the constant d is chosen sufficiently large, the following holds: For arbitrary $S \subseteq U$ with $|S| = n$ we have*

$$\frac{|\mathcal{R}_S(d)|}{|\mathcal{R}(d)|} = 1 - O(n^{-c}).$$

Proof: We first choose the function $f \in \mathcal{H}_{n^2}^d$ at random. The function f_1 determined by this is easily seen to be d-universal, i. e., it behaves essentially the same as a function chosen at random from $\mathcal{H}_s^d$; thus, by Fact 2.2(b) f_1 satisfies

$$\Pr\left(\exists i \in \{0, \ldots, n-1\}: |f_1^{-1}(i) \cap S| \geq n^{1/4}\right) = O\left(\frac{n}{n^{d/4}}\right) = O(n^{1-d/4}).$$

Thus, in view of Fact 2.2(a), we have

$$\Pr(f \text{ distributes } f \text{ well}) \geq 1 - O(n^{2-d}) - O(n^{1-d/4}),$$

which is $1 - O(n^{-c})$ for d large enough. □

Remark 2.20 The proof of an analogous lemma for the universal classes studied in [8, 7] is much more involved; it uses deep results about $\mathcal{H}_n^d$.

Theorem 2.21 *Let $c \geq 1$ be fixed, and let $S \subseteq U$ with $|S| \leq n = r = s$. Then for $C > 0$ and $d \geq 2$ sufficiently large and $\alpha > 0$ sufficiently small the following holds for $h \in \mathcal{R}(d)$ chosen at random:*

(a) $\Pr\left(\sum_{0 \le j < n} (b_j)^{\alpha b_j} \ge C \cdot n\right) = O(n^{-c})$;

(b) $\Pr\left(\sum_{0 \le j < n} (b_j)^k \ge C \cdot n\right) = O(n^{-c})$, for $k \ge 1$.

Proof: We only consider (a); the proof of (b) is similar. Let

$$M_\alpha := \sum_{0 \le j < n} (b_j)^{\alpha b_j}.$$

In view of Corollary 2.17(a) and of Lemma 2.19 it suffices to show the following, for some fixed f that distributes S well:

(a') $\Pr_f (M_\alpha \ge E_f(M_\alpha) + n) = O(n^{-c})$.

Thus, fix such an f. For technical reasons, we define truncated versions of the bucket sizes. Note that by Corollary 2.12(a') we have

$$\Pr_f\left(b_j \le \frac{D \log n}{\log \log n} \text{ for } 0 \le j < n\right) = 1 - O(n^{-c}),$$

for a suitably large constant D. Thus, if we define

$$\hat{b}_j := \min\{b_j, (D \log n)/\log \log n\}, \text{ for } 0 \le j < n$$

and

$$\hat{M}_\alpha := \sum_{0 \le j < n} (\hat{b}_j)^{\alpha \hat{b}_j},$$

then $\Pr_f(M_\alpha \ne \hat{M}_\alpha) = O(n^{-c})$; further, it is clear that $E_f(M_\alpha) \ge E_f(\hat{M}_\alpha)$. Thus, in order to show (a'), it suffices to prove that

(a") $\Pr_f\left(\hat{M}_\alpha \ge E_f(\hat{M}_\alpha) + n\right) = O(n^{-c})$.

For fixed f, the hash function $h = h(f, a_0, \ldots, a_{n-1})$, and hence also $\hat{M}_\alpha$ is a function of the independent random variables $a_0, \ldots, a_{n-1}$. In order to apply Theorem 2.5 we must estimate the effect a change in a single one of the offsets a_i has on $\hat{M}_\alpha$. If a_i is changed, only the hash values $h(x)$ of the up to $n^{1/4}$ many keys x in $\hat{B}_i^f$ change. Thus, the total number of $\hat{b}_j$'s that can increase is bounded by $|\hat{B}_i^f| \le n^{1/4}$; similarly for the total number of $\hat{b}_j$'s that decrease. Since, by definition, all $\hat{b}_j$ are in $[0, (D \log n)/\log \log n]$, the total change of the sum $\hat{M}_\alpha$ in response to changing one a_i is bounded by

$$\vartheta := n^{1/4} \cdot \left(\frac{D \log n}{\log \log n}\right)^{\frac{\alpha D \log n}{\log \log n}} \le n^{1/4} \cdot n^{\alpha D}.$$

Applying Theorem 2.5 now yields (using the notation $\exp(y)$ for e^y, and assuming $\eta := \frac{1}{2} - 2\alpha D > 0$):

$$\Pr_f\left(\hat{M}_\alpha \ge E_f(\hat{M}_\alpha) + n\right)$$
$$\le \exp\left(-n^2 \big/ (2n \cdot (n^{1/4+\alpha D})^2)\right)$$
$$= \exp(-\Omega(n^{-\eta}))$$
$$= O(n^{-c}).$$

Remark 2.22 Several authors ([3, 11]) have proved (by a different application of the martingale tail theorem) that if h is randomly chosen from $\mathcal{R}$ then the random variables $A_u := |\{j \mid 0 \leq j < n \text{ and } b_j \geq u\}|$ (the number of buckets of size at least u) can be tightly bounded, as follows: For arbitrary $c > 0$ there is another constant C so that

$$\Pr\left(\exists u : u \geq 1 \text{ and } A_u \geq C \cdot \frac{n}{2^u}\right) = O(n^{-c}).$$

From this, some of the results of the previous theorem can also be derived. The constants obtained for the estimates of sums of powers $(b_j)^k$ are much smaller in our direct approach.

2.4 Application: Improving the performance of the FKS scheme

In this subsection, we sketch the construction of Fredman, Komlós, and Szemerédi [10] that provides a *static* dictionary with constant lookup time in the worst case, and show how a simple substitution of one hash class by another results in a probabilistic construction that takes linear time with high probability (whereas the original construction only guaranteeed linear expected time). Basically, the data structure is the following.

Assume a set $S \subseteq U$ of n keys is given. A level-1 hash function $h : U \to \{0, \dots, n-1\}$ splits S into the buckets $B_j^h = \{x \in S \mid h(x) = j\}$, for $0 \leq j < n$. For each of the buckets B_j^h there is a secondary hash table ST_j of size $2|B_j^h|^2$ and a level-2 hash function $h_j : U \to \{0, \dots, 2|B_j^h|^2 - 1\}$ that is one-to-one on B_j^h. The element $x \in S$ is stored in position $h_j(x)$ of subtable ST_j, where $j = h(x)$. Access to the subtables and to (the programs for) the functions h_j is facilitated by a primary hash table HT with n entries. For $0 \leq j < n$, entry $HT[j]$ of this table contains a pointer to ST_j and a description of h_j. In order to construct (probabilistically) such a structure that takes space $O(n) = O(|S|)$, the following procedure is used. It is exactly the algorithm proposed in [10], excepting that the level-1 hash function h is chosen from $\mathcal{R}(d)$ instead of $\mathcal{H}_n^2$.

Algorithm 2.23 (Modified FKS scheme)

1. Choose $h \in \mathcal{R}(d)$ at random.

2. If $\sum\limits_{0 \leq j < n} |B_j^h|^2 > C \cdot n$ then go to 1.

3. For $0 \leq j < n$ do

   (a) Choose $h_j \in \mathcal{H}_{2|B_j^h|^2}^2$ at random.

   (b) If h_j is not one-to-one on B_j^h then go to (a).

   (c) Enter the description of h_j in $HT[j]$, and enter x in position $h_j(x)$ of ST_j, for $x \in B_j^h$.

Proposition 2.24 *Algorithm 2.23 constructs a perfect hash table for S that uses space $O(n)$. For arbitrary $c > 0$, the probability that the running time is at most $D \cdot n$ can be made $1 - O(n^{-c})$, by choosing the constants d and D large enough.*

Proof: By Theorem 2.21(b), applied for $k = 2$, we have that (for C and d sufficiently large)

$$\Pr\left(\sum_{0 \le j < n} |B_j|^2 > C \cdot n \right) = O(n^{-c}).$$

Thus, with probability $1 - O(n^{-c})$, Steps 1 and 2 of the algorithm are executed only once and result in an h with $\sum_{0 \le j < n} |B_j|^2 \le C \cdot n$. We define random variables Y_j, $0 \le j < n$, by

$$Y_j := \text{number of steps spent in Step 3 for } B_j.$$

It follows easily from Fact 2.2(a), applied for $d = 2$, that there is a constant K so that

$$\Pr(Y_j > L \cdot K \cdot |B_j^h|^2) \le 2^{-L} , \text{ for } L = 1, 2, 3, \dots .$$

Let $W := K \cdot \sum_{0 \le j < n} |B_j^h|^2$, and let $M := \max\{K|B_j^h|^2 \mid 0 \le j < n\}$. Then $n \le W \le KCn$, and by Corollary 2.12(a') we have that $M \le K(\log n)^2$ with probability $1 - O(n^{-c})$. Further, by a straightforward application of Lemma 2.4, we get

$$\Pr\left(\sum_{0 \le j < n} Y_j \ge 3lW \mid M \le K(\log n)^2 \right) \le e^{-(l-1)W/(K \log n)^2},$$

which means that the running time of Step 3 is $O(n)$ with probability $O(n^{-c})$. $\qquad \square$

3 Shared memory simulations based on hashing strategies

3.1 The computation models

A parallel random access machine (PRAM) consists of processors $P_1, \dots, P_m$ and a shared memory with cells $U = \{1, \dots, p\}$, each capable of storing one integer. The processors work synchronously and have random access to the shared memory cells.

We distinguish PRAM models according to their capabilities of dealing with concurrent read and concurrent write, i. e., with the situation where more than one processor tries to simultaneously access the same shared memory cell for reading or writing.

We consider the following rules for dealing with memory access conflicts:

exclusive read (ER): simultaneous reading is forbidden.

concurrent read (CR): simultaneous reading is allowed.

exclusive write (EW): simultaneous writing is forbidden.

concurrent write (CW): simultaneous writing is allowed.

Resolution rules: The result of the attempt of $P_{i_1}, \dots, P_{i_s}$, $i_1 < \dots < i_s$ to write simultaneously $x_1, \dots, x_s$ to cell j is the following:

Collision: a special collision symbol appears in cell j.

Arbitrary: an arbitrary one of the values $x_1, \dots, x_s$ appears in cell j; in this non-deterministic model, all choices of values x_j, for all concurrent writes, yield the same correct result of the algorithm.

Priority: x_1 appears in cell j.

According to the combination of rules for reading or writing, we talk about EREW PRAMs, CREW PRAMs, CREW PRAMs, CRCW PRAMs. We refer to CRCW PRAM with a given resolution rule as a COLLISION-PRAM, ARBITRARY-PRAM, or PRIORITY-PRAM.

A *distributed memory machine (DMM)* consists of n processors $Q_1, \ldots, Q_n$ and n memory modules $M_1, \ldots, M_n$. Each module has a communication window where it can read from or write into. For the processors, these windows act like shared memory cells. Thus we can talk about EREW DMMs, COLLISION-DMMs, etc. in the sense described above.

We only consider step by step simulations of PRAMs on DMMs. This means that we can describe, given a computation of a PRAM of length t, in which modules each shared memory cell, together with its current content, is stored in the DMM. We can describe this "storage configuration at time t" by a bipartite graph that connects each shared memory cell j to each module where j, together with its current content, is stored.

The *delay* of a simulation is the factor by which the simulating machine is slower than the simulated machine. The *load* is the quotient $\frac{m}{n}$ of the sizes of the PRAM and the DMM. A simulation is *time-processor optimal* if its load is proportional to its delay.

In case of randomized simulations, we say that delay $O(D)$ is guaranteed with polynomially high probability if for each $c > 0$ we can design a randomized simulation algorithm that works correctly with delay $O(D)$ with probability at least $1 - O(n^{-c})$.

3.2 Shared memory simulations based on simple hashing

The easiest kind of simulation is based on the idea of defining the storage configuration at time t independently of t, at the beginning of the simulation, by choosing randomly a hash function $h : U \to \{1, \ldots, n\}$ from a universal class $\mathcal{H}$. h defines the storage configuration in the obvious way: cell x is stored in module $M_{h(x)}$.

If we want to simulate an n-processor PRAM on a DMM of the same size, the delay is determined by the **evaluation time of h** and the **maximum contention of the modules**:

If cells $S = \{x_1, \ldots, x_n\}$ are accessed for reading or writing, the contention of module M_i is the size $b_i^h = |h^{-1}(i) \cap S|$ of the ith bucket, the maximum contention is $\max\{b_i^h \mid i = 1, \ldots, n\}$, the maximum bucket size.

It is easy to check that for the simulation of a EREW or CREW PRAM, a COLLISION-DMM can be used, for a CRCW PRAM a CRCW DMM with the same write conflict rule will do.

Using the universal class $\mathcal{R}(d)$ from Section 2, Theorem 2.11 guarantees that the evaluation time is constant and the maximum contention is $O(\log(n)/\log\log(n))$ with polynomially high probability. Thus we get:

Theorem 3.1 *Using hash functions from $\mathcal{R}(d)$, a hashing based simulation of an n-processor CREW PRAM on an n-processor COLLISION-DMM or an n-processor CRCW PRAM on an n-processor CRCW PRAM with the same resolution rule can be designed. It has delay $O(\log(n)/\log\log(n))$ with polynomially high probability.*

We now want to design time-processor optimal simulations based on the above hashing approach. Consider an $n \log n$-processor PRAM and an n-processor DMM. A time-processor optimal simulation has to achieve delay $O(\log(n))$. As above we again distribute the shared memory among the processors using a randomly chosen $h \in \mathcal{R}(d)$. Each processor Q_i of the DMM now simulates $\log(n)$ processors of the PRAM, i. e., for simulating one PRAM step, it has to execute $\log(n)$ accesses to shared memory cells $x_{i,1}, \ldots, x_{i,\log(n)}$, say.

In addition to the two parameters evaluation time and contention, we now have to face a further, algorithmic problem:

Access scheduling: design a protocol which specifies how (e. g. in which order) each Q_i presents its accesses to cells $x_{i,1}, \ldots, x_{i,\log(n)}$ to the modules.

To see that access scheduling is a non-trivial problem consider the following scenario: Assume that the hash function h distributes the at most $n \log n$ keys in $X = \{x_{i,j} \mid i = 1, \ldots, n, j = 1, \ldots, \log(n)\}$ evenly among the n modules, i. e., we get maximum contention $O(\log(n))$. An obvious way to present the $x_{i,j}$'s to the modules is as follows. (Assume the ARBITRARY rule at the windows of the modules, for simplicity.) Each Q_i presents its keys $x_{i,1}, \ldots, x_{i,\log(n)}$ to modules $M_{h(x_{i,1})}, \ldots, M_{h(x_{i,\log(n)})}$, in this order. Each key $x_{i,j}$ is presented to $M_h(x_{i,j})$ until it is accepted by the module, i. e., has succeeded to arrive at the window of the module.

Now assume that the $n \times \log(n)$-matrix $X = (x_{i,j})_{\substack{1 \le i \le n \\ 1 \le j \le \log(n)}}$ is partitioned into n many $\frac{1}{2}\log(n) \times 2$-submatrices, the keys in each submatrix are mapped to the same module, and the mapping of submatrices to modules is one-to-one.

If now the (nondeterministic) ARBITRARY rule prefers $x_{i,j}$ to $x_{i',j'}$ if (i,j) is lexicographically smaller than (i',j'), it is easily seen that it takes time $\Theta(\log(n)^2)$ until all accesses are executed, i. e., we are by a factor $\Theta(\log(n))$ slower than the maximum contention bound.

On the other hand, for each $n \times \log(n)$ matrix X there is an access schedule that guarantees $O(\log(n))$ time for executing all accesses. To see this consider the bipartite graph whose vertex sets are the processors $\{Q_1, \ldots, Q_n\}$ and the modules $\{M_1, \ldots, M_n\}$, and Q_i is connected to M_l if $x_{i,j}$ for some $j \in \{1, \ldots, \log(n)\}$ is mapped to l. As this graph has degree $O(\log(n))$ it can be edge colored with $O(\log(n))$ colors. The variables $x_{i,j}$ associated to one color class can be sent to the modules in one time unit. Thus an access schedule that presents one color class after the other to the modules needs time $O(\log(n))$.

Clearly this coloring can not be computed fast enough, therefore efficient deterministic access schedules are not known.

In [1] Anderson and Miller design a randomized access schedule which needs expected time $O(\log(n))$, if all $x_{i,j}$'s are distinct, and the windows of the modules follow the collision rule, i. e., if an $n \log n$-processor EREW-PRAM is simulated on an n-processor COLLISION-PRAM.

If we use a randomly chosen hash function from $\mathcal{R}(d)$, we have constant evaluation time, maximum contention $O(\log(n))$ with polynomially high probability, see Lemma 2.12, and $O(\log(n))$ time for the access schedule.

The above construction was shown by Valiant in [21]. He used the more complicated n^ε-universal class of hash functions designed by Siegel, and only allowed a shared memory size polynomial in n. Using hash functions from $\mathcal{R}(d)$ we get:

Theorem 3.2 *Using hash functions from $\mathcal{R}(d)$ and the access schedule from [1], a time-processor optimal simulation of an $n \log n$-processor EREW PRAM on an n-processor COLLISION-DMM with expected delay $O(\log(n))$ can be designed.*

The above access schedule can not be used if duplicates appear in X, i.e., if we want to simulate a CRCW PRAM, no matter which write conflict rule is assumed for the DMM.

In [7] we have designed a distributed dictionary which can be used for a time-processor optimal simulation of an n-processor ARBITRARY- or PRIORITY-PRAM on an n-processor ARBITRARY- or PRIORITY-DMM with expected delay $O(\log(n))$. This simulation also distributes the shared memory cells among the modules using a hash function $h \in \mathcal{R}(d)$. The accesses of each processor are processed in the fixed given order — Q_i processes $x_{i,1}, x_{i,2}, \ldots x_{i,\log(n)}$, in this order. The key idea is that Q_i does not execute the access of $x_{i,j}$ until it has arrived at the module $M_{h(x_{i,j})}$, but rather gives this job to a randomly chosen "colleague".

A distributed dictionary is a data structure, implemented on an n-processor DMM, which can be fed with instructions Insert, Delete, Lookup from each processor simultaneously. The answer of a Lookup is correct for some state of the dictionary between the time the Lookup instruction is issued and the time it is answered.

Theorem 3.3 *Using hash functions from $\mathcal{R}(d)$, a distributed dictionary with the following features can be implemented on an n-processor ARBITRARY- (or PRIORITY-) DMM.*
Let $c > 0$ be arbitrary.

1) *$N \geq n^{1+\epsilon}$ instructions, $\frac{N}{n}$ per processor, can be executed in expected optimal time $O(\frac{N}{n})$.*

2) *Each processor needs space $O(\frac{N}{n})$ if N elements are currently in the dictionary (worst case).*

3) *Every lookup has expected constant response time.*

4) *n concurrently executed lookups are all answered in expected time $O(\log(n)/\log\log(n))$.*

5) *$k \geq \log(n)$ lookups from each processor are all answered after expected optimal time $O(k)$.*

In the sequel we sketch the basic ideas of this construction applied to simulating an $n \log n$-processor ARBITRARY-PRAM on an n-processor ARBITRARY-DMM with expected optimal delay $O(\log(n))$. (Note that such a simulation is implicit in Theorem 3.3(5); also note that Theorem 3.1 for CRCW-machines follows from Theorem 3.3(4).)

The simulation works in the same way as shown for Theorem 3.2, except for a new access schedule.

Assume that Q_i wants to access shared memory cells $x_{i,1}, \ldots, x_{i,\log(n)}$, and all $x_{i,j}$ are distinct. (We shall later remove this restriction.) We are in the same situation as in Theorem 3.2, i.e., we have expected maximum contention $O(\log(n))$, and constant evaluation time. We now describe a new access schedule.

Assume that we have two classes of n processor, each: $IP_1, \ldots, IP_n$, the input processors (IP's), and $WP_1, \ldots, WP_n$, the working processors (WP's). Assume further, that only read instruction are to be executed. (For writes we can proceed analogously.)

New_access_schedule

This algorithm proceeds in rounds $t = 1, 2, 3, \ldots$. At the beginning of round 1, each WP is idle.

Round t:

Step 1: job distribution

a) Each WP that is currently idle randomly choses an IP. The WP is busy (i. e., not idle) from now on; it is waiting at the IP.

b) Each IP does the following: If j many WP's are waiting at the IP, then it passes a new one of its read requests to $\min\{j, 2\}$ many of them, as long as it still has such requests.

Step 2: job execution

A WP that has a job "read x" computes $j = h(x)$ and tries to write its read request to the window of M_j. Each M_j answers D request. A WP that got an answer returns the answer to the IP_l it got the job from. For this it tries at most D' times to give the answer to IP_l via the window of M_l, until it succeeds. (D, D' will be sufficiently large constants.)

It is easily checked that each round takes constant time on an ARBITRARY-DMM. Thus we have to bound the number of rounds necessary to satisfy all read requests. For this purpose consider a fixed job $R := $ "read $x_{i,j}$", to be performed by WP_l. How long is WP_l busy with this job? It needs some time, $\text{wait}(\tau)$, to wait at IP_i for the job τ, then some time, $\text{busy}(\tau)$, to pass τ to $M_{h(x_{i,j})}$, then some time, $\text{return}(\tau)$, to return the result to IP_i.

Lemma 3.4 $\Pr(\text{wait}(\tau) + \text{return}(\tau) \geq u) \leq e^{-\alpha u}$ *for some* $\alpha > 0$. *For a proof see* [7].

In order to bound $\text{busy}(\tau)$, we observe the algorithm from the point of view of the module M_l, $l = h(x_{i,j})$. A *lifecycle* of M_l is a maximum length time interval in which M_l is permanently busy with processing requests passed to M_l by WP's. The lifecycle into which τ falls is called $L(\tau)$, its length $l(\tau)$. The following is obvious.

Lemma 3.5 $\text{busy}(\tau) \leq l(\tau)$

Thus we have to bound $l(\tau)$. This is the most involved part in [7] and is omitted here. As a result we get:

Lemma 3.6 $\Pr_f(l(\tau) \geq u) \leq e^{-\beta u}$ *for some* $\beta > 0$ *if* $f \in \mathcal{H}_{n^2}^d$ *distributes* X *well*. (For the notation see Definitions 2.10 and 2.18.) □

It is not too hard to see that the work to be done with the $n \log n$ jobs is sufficiently evenly distributed among the processors. Thus, as (by Lemmas 3.4, 3.5, 3.6) for each job, only constant time is necessary with high probability, $O(\log(n))$ expected time suffices to execute all jobs.

The reason why the jobs can be proved to be evenly distributed among the working processors is that the WPs randomly choose input processors to get jobs from. We do not know about the performance of the algorithm where each IP executes its jobs itself, in the given order.

We now turn to the simulation of an $n \log n$-processor ARBITRARY-PRAM on an n-processor ARBITRARY-DMM.

In this case the matrix $X = (x_{i,j})_{\substack{1 \le i \le n \\ 1 \le j \le \log(n)}}$ no longer consists of distinct addresses of shared memory cells, but duplicates may occur. Thus we are not allowed to present all $x_{i,j}$'s to the respective modules, because the contention now can be very large (up to $n \log n$, if all $x_{i,j}$'s are identical). Therefore we have to *eliminate duplicates* before they are presented to the modules.

It does not seem to be feasible to eliminate all duplicates, but this is also not necessary. The reason is that it suffices to make sure that no duplicates occur during a lifecycle. This is in fact all we need for the analysis of Lemma 3.6. Therefore it suffices to extend the above algorithm such that duplicates *in lifecycles* are identified.

In [7] an algorithm is presented that eliminates duplicates in lifecycles efficiently. Now it is possible to conclude:

Theorem 3.7 *Using hash functions from $\mathcal{R}(d)$, the new access schedule and the algorithm for eliminating duplicates within lifecycles, a time-processor optimal shared memory simulation of an $n \log(n)$-processor ARBITRARY-PRAM on an n-processor ARBITRARY-DMM with optimal expected delay $O(\log(n))$ can be designed.*

References

[1] R. J. Anderson and G. L. Miller. Optical communication for pointer based algorithms. Technical Report CRI 88-14, University of Southern California, Comp. Sci. Dept., 1988.

[2] H. Bast and T. Hagerup. Fast and reliable parallel hashing. In *Proc. of the 3rd Ann. ACM Symp. on Parallel Algorithms and Architectures*, pages 50–61, 1991.

[3] H. Bast and T. Hagerup. *Personal communication.* 1991.

[4] J. L. Carter and M. N. Wegman. Universal classes of hash functions. *J. Comput. Syst. Sci.*, 18:143–154, 1979.

[5] M. Dietzfelbinger, A. Karlin, K. Mehlhorn, F. Meyer auf der Heide, H. Rohnert, and R. E. Tarjan. Dynamic perfect hashing: Upper and lower bounds. Technical Report 77, Universität–GH–Paderborn, Fachbereich Mathematik/Informatik, Jan. 1991. *Revised Version* of the paper of the same title that appeared in *Proc. of the 29th IEEE Ann. Symp. on Foundations of Computer Science*, pages 524–531, 1988.

[6] M. Dietzfelbinger and F. Meyer auf der Heide. An optimal parallel dictionary. In *Proc. of the 1989 ACM Symp. on Parallel Algorithms and Architectures*, pages 360–368, 1989. (Revised version to appear in *Information and Computation*).

[7] M. Dietzfelbinger and F. Meyer auf der Heide. How to distribute a dictionary in a complete network. In *Proc. of the 22nd Ann. ACM Symp. on Theory of Computing*, pages 117–127, 1990.

[8] M. Dietzfelbinger and F. Meyer auf der Heide. A new universal class of hash functions and dynamic hashing in real time. In M. S. Paterson, editor, *Proceedings of 17th ICALP*, pages 6–19. Springer, 1990. Lecture Notes in Computer Science 443.

[9] M. Dietzfelbinger and F. Meyer auf der Heide. Dynamic hashing in real time. *To appear*, 1992.

[10] M. L. Fredman, J. Komlós, and E. Szemerédi. Storing a sparse table with $O(1)$ worst case access time. *J. Assoc. Comput. Mach.*, **31**(3):538–544, July 1984.

[11] J. Gil, Y. Matias, and U. Vishkin. Towards a theory of nearly constant time parallel algorithms. In *Proc. of the 32nd IEEE Ann. Symp. on Foundations of Computer Science*, pages 698–710, 1991.

[12] G. H. Gonnet. Expected length of the longest probe sequence in hash code searching. *J. Assoc. Comput. Mach.*, **28**(2):289–304, Apr. 1981.

[13] T. Hagerup. Constant-time parallel integer sorting. In *Proc. of the 23rd Ann. ACM Symp. on Theory of Computing*, pages 299–306, 1991.

[14] W. Hoeffding. Probability inequalites for sums of bounded random variables. *J. Am. Stat. Ass.*, **58**:13–30, 1963.

[15] R. M. Karp, M. Luby, and F. Meyer auf der Heide. Efficient PRAM simulation on a distributed memory machine. *In Preparation*, 1991.

[16] Y. Matias and U. Vishkin. Converting high probability into nearly-constant time – with applications to parallel hashing. In *Proc. of the 23rd Ann. ACM Symp. on Theory of Computing*, pages 307–316, 1991.

[17] C. McDiarmid. On the method of bounded differences. In J. Siemons, editor, *Surveys in Combinatorics, 1989*, pages 148–188. Cambridge University Press, 1989. London Math. Soc. Lecture Note Series 141.

[18] K. Mehlhorn. *Data Structures and Algorithms 1: Sorting and Searching.* Springer-Verlag, Berlin, 1984.

[19] K. Mehlhorn and U. Vishkin. Randomized and deterministic simulations of PRAMs by parallel machines with restricted granularity of parallel memories. *Acta Informatica*, **21**:339–374, 1984.

[20] A. Siegel. On universal classes of fast high performance hash functions, their time-space tradeoff, and their applications. In *Proc. of the 30th IEEE Ann. Symp. on Foundations of Computer Science*, pages 20–25, 1989. *Revised Version*.

[21] L. G. Valiant. General purpose parallel architectures. In J. van Leeuwen, editor, *Handbook of Theoretical Computer Science, Vol. A: Algorithms and Complexity*, chapter 18, pages 943–971. Elsevier, Amsterdam, 1990.

Distributed Game Tree Search on a Massively Parallel System

R.Feldmann P.Mysliwietz B.Monien

Abstract

We present our distributed $\alpha\beta$-algorithm and show how $\alpha\beta$-enhancements like iterative deepening, transposition tables, history tables etc. that are useful in the sequential game tree search can be applied to a distributed algorithm. The methods we describe are suitable even for large distributed systems. We describe an extension of the Young Brothers Wait Concept that we introduced to reduce the search overhead. For the first time experiments with bigger processor networks (up to 256 Transputers) show good results. We obtained a speedup of 126 running our algorithm with 256 processors.

There are mainly two reasons for this improvement. The first is that our algorithm has an inherent good load balancing, i.e. the workload using 256 processors is roughly 83% although one computation takes on the average only 300 seconds (with 256 processors).

The second reason for the good speedup achieved is the bounding of the search overhead by the extended Young Brothers Wait Concept and the efficient use of a distributed hash table. We give a cost and gain analysis of this hash table showing its superior behavior compared to other approaches.

The developed techniques have been incorparated in the distributed chess program Zugzwang, that serves as a tool for our experiments. Moreover Zugzwang participated with good results in some tournaments, for example winning the bronce medall in the 2nd Computer Games Olympiad 1990.

1 INTRODUCTION

The $\alpha\beta$-algorithm is the most popular algorithm to evaluate game trees. Several authors [KM75, Bau78, Pea80, CM83] have analysed its behaviour. Given the heuristic values of the leaf positions in the game tree, the $\alpha\beta$-algorithm computes the value of the root node together with the best move possible in the root position. The sequential $\alpha\beta$-algorithm as well as its parallelization gained a lot of interest through its application in computer chess and other game playing programs.

The sequential behaviour of the $\alpha\beta$-algorithm poses difficulties for the parallelization of the algorithm. Early approaches were made by [FF80, ABD80] but resulted in only poor speedups. There are mainly three difficulties one has to overcome : First, the cutoffs of the sequential algorithm may be overlooked by the distributed algorithm resulting in

---

*Department of Mathematics and Computer Science, University of Paderborn, West Germany

search overhead. Second, the problem of load balancing is very difficult. This is caused by the unpredictable size of subproblems as well as by the idle times resulting from iterative deepening. Third, the sequential $\alpha\beta$-algorithm strongly profits by several $\alpha\beta$-enhancements as iterative deepening, transposition tables, history tables, killer lists etc.. The emulation of the $\alpha\beta$-enhancements often causes a delay in the distributed algorithm. For example iterative deepening is inherent sequential and the transposition table should be accessible to all processors in the system.

The reduction of search overhead was one of the main topics in the field of parallel $\alpha\beta$-algorithms. Akl et.al. proposed the mandatory work first approach in [ABD80]. The PVS algorithm is used in [MP85, MOS86, Sch89b, New88, HSN89]. A description of this algorithm can be found in [MC82]. It evaluates right sons of game tree nodes with a minimal $\alpha\beta$-window in parallel and then re-evaluates them if necessary. Processors are assigned to subtrees along the principal variation. Alternatively, game tree nodes are evaluated in parallel only if they had acquired an $\alpha\beta$-bound before ([FK88]). In [VM87, FMMV89, FMMV90], we introduced the Young Brothers Wait Concept that prevents nodes from being evaluated in parallel which do not have an evaluated left brother. In this paper, we describe an extension to the Young Brothers Wait Concept that is inspired by [Hsu90]. Hsu presented in his thesis a parallel $\alpha\beta$-algorithm that strictly dominates the weaker form of $\alpha\beta$ with the deep cutoffs disabled. Hsu claims a lower bound for the speedup to be "something like N/c, where c is about 3 to 5", in the range possibly up to 100000 processors. However, there are no experimental results due to the fact that his algorithm reflects a special hardware environment that is not available yet.

The PVS algorithm, the approach of Ferguson and Korf, and the Young Brothers Wait Concept guarantee that the best ordered game trees are searched without any search overhead. This is very efficient, if the game trees to be searched are close to the minimal game tree, as it usually is the case for sequential chess programs. However, to keep the game trees close to the minimal game tree, the sequential chess programs use several $\alpha\beta$-enhancements. The transposition tables (a table that keeps track of the positions already evaluated) turned out to be crucial for the performance.

In [MP85], Marsland and Popowich compared local and global transposition tables. Schaeffer uses a hybrid version of these methods for his chess program Sun Phoenix ([MOS86, Sch89b]). All these approaches suffer heavily from either the communication bottleneck or the information loss. We give a cost and gain study of our distributed transposition table presented in [FMM90]. This transposition table is, virtually, a global table that is physically distributed among all the processors in the network. Access to this table is by routing requests and entries from a demanding processor to the processor responsible for the entry. We show that in the processor range available the cost to access this table by routing is much smaller than the gain resulting from the huge table size. Moreover this approach is easily scalable without introducing bottlenecks (as when using a global transposition table located at a single processor) and without the loss of valuable informations (as when using tables with local access only).

In [Sch89a] Schaeffer stated that speedups are strongly tied to the (in)efficiency of the $\alpha\beta$-search and that the use of $\alpha\beta$-enhancememts in a parallel implementation of the $\alpha\beta$-algorithm dramatically affects the performance of a parallel implementation.

Most of the algorithms have been tested experimentialy by the various researchers, although mostly with only few processors. The results are a speedup of 5.93 using 16 processors in [HSN89], 5.67 using 9 processors in [MOS86, Sch89b] and 5.03 using 8 processors in [New88]. Moreover, increasing the number of processors either decreases the speedup ([HSN89]) or at least does not increase it ([MOS86, Sch89b]). The speedup of 101 using 256 processors presented in [OF88] has been achieved by parallelizing a suboptimal version of the sequential $\alpha\beta$-algorithm. In [FMM90], we presented a speedup of 34 using a 64 processor system, improving previous results.

The distributed system we use is build up with transputers. A transputer is a processor that is designed for distributed computing. It has four communication links that are used to build up processor networks. Since each processor has a constant degree of four, not all the processors are neighbored. Therefore communication between nonneighbored processors has to be done by routing messages via the intermediate processors. However, this is supported by the transputer architecture and therefore rather efficient, if a suitable interconnection scheme is used.

In this paper we give a short introduction to game tree search and review our distributed $\alpha\beta$-algorithm as presented in [FMMV90]. In section 4 we describe our extension to the Young Brothers Wait Concept and in section 5 we compare the costs and gains of a distributed transposition table. Experimental results given in section 6 show improved speedup even for massively parallel searches with 256 processors.

2 SEQUENTIAL GAME TREE SEARCH

The task in game tree search can be described as follows. Given is a game position in a two person zero sum game with complete information (for example chess), its associated game tree (the tree that corresponds to the possible moves of each opponent) and a heuristic function that maps game positions onto their value. The task now is to compute the value of the root position together with the best possible move in the root position. There is a trival solution to this problem, which is minmaxing. Call the player that is to move in the root position MAX and its opponent MIN. The value $F(v)$ of any node v in the game tree can recursively be determined as follows :

$$F(v) = \begin{cases} \text{heuristic value of } v \text{ from MAX point of view, if } v \text{ is leaf node,} \\ max\{F(w) \mid w \text{ is a succsessor of } v\}, \text{if MAX is to move in } v \\ min\{F(w) \mid w \text{ is a succsessor of } v\}, \text{if MIN is to move in } v \end{cases}$$

The $\alpha\beta$-algorithm ([KM75]) is an extension to minmaxing that visits only those nodes that may influence the value of the root node. This is achieved by assigning a search window to each node.

In figure 2 we give an example computation of the sequential $\alpha\beta$-algorithm. First the value $F(v.1) = 20$ of the first son of a node v is computed. This gives a search window of $[20, \infty]$ for node $v.2$, i.e. only values for $v.2$ within this window may influence the value of the root node. This enables to cutoff the right sons of $v.2$ since the value of $v.2.1$ already implies that $F(v.2) \leq 10$ because $v.2$ is a MIN node. Note that a parallel algorithm that computes the values of $v.1$ and $v.2$ in parallel would not be able to make this cutoff. This demonstrates the sequential behavior of $\alpha\beta$-search.

Knuth and Moore showed that if the first successor of any node is always the best successor (i.e $F(v) = F(v.1)$), then the $\alpha\beta$-algorithm is optimal in the sense, that there

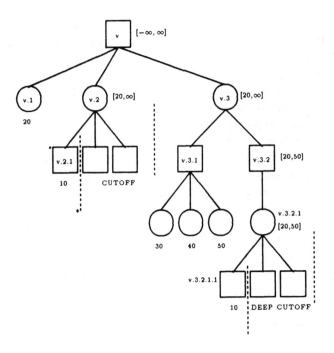

Figure 1: Example computation of the sequential $\alpha\beta$-algorithm

is no algorithm computing the value of the root node visiting less nodes. In this case of best first ordering, the $\alpha\beta$-algorithm visits $O(b^{d/2})$ leafs in a game tree of depth d and uniform branching factor b. However, in the case of the worst first ordering, $\alpha\beta$ visits all b^d leafs of the game tree. This is the same number of leafs minmaxing visits in any game tree. This shows the important role of move ordering.

Several heuristics, some dependent on the game and some not, have been studied and used to achieve a good ordering. Iterative deepening is among the heuristics common to most games. The program starts to evaluate a game tree of height 1 (i.e search depth 1) and increments the depth by one until the desired search depth is reached (or the allotted time has run out). Due to the exponential growth in complexity the first iterations do not hurt too much, but the move ordering for a search depth i can be improved by the knowledge gained during the prior iteration. For instance the best move found during an iteration is searched first during the next iteration, giving a good probability to be the best move in this iteration.

One of the most important mechanisms is the transposition table. Transposition tables store informations about positions that have already been evaluated. This information may be used, if positions are visited more than once. This may occur for two reasons : a position can be reached by several move sequences, and many positions visited during a prior iteration are also visited in the succeeding iteration.

Stored information includes the minmax value, the best move and the corresponding search depth. Before a subtree is searched, a check is done whether the transposition table can provide any useful information. This may lead to the elimination of the whole subtree or to an improved tree ordering, if the best move stored is considered first. In chess, for example, these and other heuristics lead to almost perfect move ordering.

3 OUR DISTRIBUTED $\alpha\beta$-ALGORITHM

3.1 Basic Algorithm

In this section, we recall our strategy for solving tree search problems with a distributed system. Our strategy is fully distributed and allows the use of an arbitrary number of processors. It has proven to behave well not only if applied to game tree search but also to branch and bound applications ([MV87]). A first version of a distributed $\alpha\beta$-algorithm using this strategy is described in [VM87]. A more detailed description of the distributed algorithm can be found in [FMMV90].

In our strategy every processor has the same program and all processors perform similar tasks. We do not use any kind of centralized mechanisms, because this would lead to a bottleneck if the number of processors increases.

The processors communicate with each other by sending messages via communication channels called links. These links are two-way point to point connections between two processors. Communication between processors that are not adjacent (i.e. there is no link connecting them) is done by message routing. Our distributed system is build up with transputers. These are processors that are desingned for distributed computing. Each transputer has four communication links. As an interconnection scheme for the processors we use the deBruijn graph [deB46]. The deBruijn graph has the required degree four and diameter $log_2(n)$ where n is the number of nodes. This guarantees that the average distance between two nodes is small. Therefore messages are routed only via a small number of processors to reach their target processor.

We talk of search problems in terms of nodes of the corresponding search tree. The root ϵ of a game tree represents the whole search problem to compute $F(\epsilon)$. For any non-leaf v the problem to evaluate v has the subproblems to evaluate some sons $v.i$. The subsolutions are combined (by maximization or minimization) in order to yield $F(v)$. The computation starts with the root node assigned to one of the processors, the other processors are idle. A processor, that works on a problem, splits it into subproblems. Since only one subproblem is attacked at a time, the other subproblems are stored in the local memory. Therefore, it is possible to transfer those subproblems to other processors. If there is more than one subproblem ready for transmission, then the algorithm will transmits one at the highest level in the tree.

In our scheme, idle processors must take care to get work for themselves (with the exception of the initial search problem which is assigned to one of the processors). This means that an idle processor has to ask one of the other processors for work. A processor is responsible for each problem it receives and for its solution. It can send subproblems to other processors, which then become its slaves. After its subproblem is finished, it has to respond with the solution of the problem. The processor which the root node is assigned to, will eventually finish with the solution of the whole problem.

Figure 2 shows a few snapshots of a distributed computation. Processor P_1 is working on a problem rooted at v. Currently it works on subproblems located in the subtree rooted at $v.1.1$. An idle processor P_2 sends a request for work to P_1. Therefore P_1 transmits node

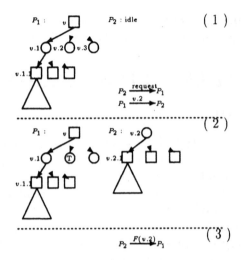

Figure 2: Example computation of the distributed algorithm

$v.2$ to P_2 which is already generated but not evaluated. P_1 labels this node as transmitted and P_2 starts to work on that problem. After P_2 has generated the successors of $v.2$ it is able to distribute this subproblems upon request, too. After P_2 finishes work on $v.2$ with or without the help of other processors, it returns the value $F(v.2)$ to P_1.

This example does not take into account $\alpha\beta$-windows and cutoffs. Since a search window has been assigned to each node by the $\alpha\beta$- algorithm, this window clearly has to be transmitted, whenever a node is sent to a requesting processor. Each processor that observes an improvement of a search window assigned to a node v has to inform all of its slaves with subproblems rooted below v. Three different actions may force the update of a search window:

(i) finishing the evaluation of a local subproblem

(ii) receiving the solution of a subproblem solved by a slave

(iii) receiving an UPDATE-message from the master

The three cases can be handled in the same way:
Decreasing a search window for a node v forces the update of all current search windows below v. If some subproblems rooted below v have been transmitted, these processors are informed by a NEWBOUND-message. Note that this rule is applied recursively. Actually a search window for a node v may not only be decreased, but can also collapse. In this case, all problems located below v are immediately finished. To reduce the number of communications, we introduce a special message CUTOFF, which is sent to all processors that got a subproblem rooted below v. This prevents them from responding their results, which are of no use now. A processor receiving a CUTOFF-message finishes the problem it is working on and sends a CUTOFF-message to all of its slaves.

Using a zero-width approach (see [CM83, MC82]), the above remains essentially true. Although, in almost every case, a NEWBOUND-message leads to an immediate cutoff. Only processors working on moves that had to be re-searched may possibly continue their work with an improved window. The processors are completely responsible for the problems they receive, If a processor determines a fail high or fail low it must re-search this problem with an open search window and must respond to its master after this re-search.

In our implementation, a random chosen processor is asked for work, regardless of its distance in the processor network. This leads to a very efficient load balancing, especially if the game trees are very irregular like those found in chess programs.

In [HSN89], Hyatt concludes that future algorithms will be more complex in order to allow for an efficient use of a large number of processors. We believe that this very simple load balancing scheme is the solution to the problem of unequal work assignment. Note that we make no restriction to the size of problems that may be distributed. Every node may be distributed, although the receiving processor will often find this node to be a leaf node. This prevents processors from performing large searches while lots of other processors may be idle.

Since the wide variation of tree sizes appears to be one of the main reasons for the often used PVS approach to fall short on achieving good speedups ([New88]), several recent approaches to distributed $\alpha\beta$-search made the way towards a more dynamic correspondence between processors and nodes of the game tree. Hyatt improved the PVS algorithm to EPVS ([HSN89]). Schaeffer improved PVS to DPVS ([MOS86] and more recently to a more dynamic version of DPVS ([Sch90]). Our solution makes the consequent step to a really dynamic processor allocation.

3.2 The Young Brothers Wait Concept

Search overhead arises if the parallel algorithm visits nodes the sequential algorithm would not visit. To prevent the algorithm from searching many superfluous nodes we have to choose subproblems for transmission carefully. We use a concept we call Young Brothers Wait Concept which is defined in [FMMV90]. This concept avoids any search overhead if working on best ordered game trees and has comparably small search overhead if working on well ordered game trees:

Assume a processor P is working on a subproblem rooted at a node v and is currently visiting a node $w = v.v_1.v_2.\cdots.v_n$. When a request for work arrives, it has to decide which subproblem (if any) it is going to transmit. The set of all subproblems ready for transmission at this moment, is the set of all right brothers of nodes $v.v_1.\cdots.v_i$ ($i \in \{1,\cdots,n\}$).

The Young Brothers Wait Concept now postulates:

> The eldest son of any node must be completely evaluated before younger brothers of that node may be transmitted.

Especially, if all subproblems ready for transmission do not yet have an evaluated left brother, then these subproblems have to wait. They can not be transmitted unless the evaluation of the first son has finished. Note that the node $v.2$ transmitted in the example computation in figure 2 may not be transmitted if the Young Brothers Wait Concept is applied.

This restriction reduces search overhead. Assume a node $v.i$ without evaluated elder brother is transmitted from a processor P_1 to a processor P_2. The search overhead will be very large, if the evaluation of $v.1$ on P_1 causes a cutoff. In this case all the work P_2 does on its subproblem is completely superfluous. Note that the probability for a cutoff after evaluation of the first son is very high, especially in game trees, which are not far away from being best ordered. Even if the evaluation of $v.1$ does not cause a cutoff, an improvement of the search window for v and thus for $v.i$ is very likely. In this case, P_2 has evaluated $v.i$ with, probably, a worse search window. Therefore, it may visit many nodes that it would not have visited in the presence of the improved window.

Although the Young Brothers Wait Concept does not prevent us from doing superfluous work in general, it leads to good behavior when searching well ordered game trees and to perfect behavior in the case of best ordered game trees.

3.3 Transposition Table Use

Transposition tables are large hash tables in which positions are stored together with the results already computed for these positions. The transposition table has two effects: First, the game tree to be searched is not really a tree but a directed acyclic graph. By simple move transposition the $\alpha\beta$-algorithm may reach a position that has been evaluated before. In this case the needed results can be obtained from the transposition table. The second effect is much more useful. The method of iterative deepening implies that many chess positions are searched several times with different search depths. For example the root of the game tree is searched with depths $1, 2, 3, \ldots, d$ in order to determine the best move. To keep the trees with larger search depth well ordered a move from the transposition table for a position v, is always tried first during the next iteration.

Since transposition tables are an important mechanism to achieve good move ordering, the parallelization of the transposition table is crucial to the overall performance of a parallel $\alpha\beta$-searcher.

Three approaches have been tried in distributed algorithms to give the transposition table the same power as in the sequential algorithm:

- global transposition table
  One special processor holds the whole hash table. Requests and stores to the transposition table must be sent to this processor. Answers are returned.

- local transposition table
  Every processor holds its own local hash table

- distributed transposition table
  The hash table is distributed among all processors. Thus every processor holds a part of the hash table

Global transposition tables have been shown to decrease the performance of a parallel game tree search algorithm (see [MP85]). All processors want to access the global transposition table placed at one processor. This leads to a bottleneck in the algorithm. Therefore, using this approach, the alternatives are to restrict the number of accesses to the transposition table or to overload the communication capabilities of the processor that holds the global transposition table. The first alternative results in a large search overhead of the parallel algorithm, the second alternative results in a delayed transposition table access.

The approach of local transposition tables where every processor can access only his own table has been shown to increase search overhead ([MP85]). Hybrid versions of these two approaches did not perform well ([Sch89b]).

The third method to hold transposition tables is to distribute the whole table among all processors. Every processor holds a part of the data structure. Requests and stores to as well as answers from the transposition table must be implemented by exchanging messages between the requesting processor and the one that holds the requested transposition entry. This approach is used by Otto and Felten in [OF88]. The first advantage of this method is that the whole knowledge accumulated in the transposition table is available to all processors. On the other side the communication delays that "destroy the programs performance" ([MP85]) can be kept very small because the communication bottleneck of a central transposition manager is avoided. The main reason for us, however, to choose the distributed transposition table approach was that the transposition table grows with the underlying distributed system. The more processors we use the more transposition table entries are accessible to all processors. In section 5 we study the costs and gains of a distributed transposition table in more detail.

We implemented the distributed transposition table as described below. Each of the processors holds an equal amount of the transposition table entries in its local memory. A hash function $h : \{chesspositions\} \rightarrow \{0, \cdots, p \cdot k - 1\}$ is used to determine the processor number $h(v) \bmod p$ and the local entry address $h(v) \; div \; p$. Here p is the number of processors used and k the number of transposition entries available at a single processor. A processor that wants to access the transposition entry for node v sends a REQUEST-message for $h(v) \; div \; p$ to processor $h(v) \bmod p$. A processor that gets a REQUEST-message for the local address x sends back the transposition entry $T(x)$ in an ANSWER-message. The transposition entry is checked at the receiver of the ANSWER-message. Whenever a processor wants to store a transposition entry for node v, it sends a PUT-message for $h(v) \; div \; p$ to processor $h(v) \bmod p$.

In section 5 we show that this is an efficient method.

4 EXTENSIONS TO THE YBWC

In this section we present an extension of the Young Brothers Wait Concept. This extension is inspired by Hsu's Delayed Branching Scheduling Strategy described in [Hsu90]. The general idea is to avoid parallelism in some parts of the tree. The nodes of the minimal game tree are searched in parallel whenever possible. Some nodes of the rest of the game tree, however, are searched in a way that no brother of a node v is searched unless the evaluation of v has finished. Hsu showed that his parallel algorithm dominates the sequential algorithm without deep cutoffs. However, his algorithm needs a very fast central host processor, which controls the evaluation of the above part of the game tree.

In order to avoid this central host processor we use a stronger version of the Young Brothers Wait Concept to reduce search overhead in our distributed system. To do so, we assign the same types to the nodes of the game tree as in [Hsu90]:

- The root of the game tree has type 1.

- The first successor position of a type 1 node has type 1, all other successors have type 2.

- The first successor position of a type 2 node has type 3, all other successors have type 2.

- All successor positions of a type 3 node have type 2.

We extend the Young Brothers Wait Concept by the following rule:

> All promising elder sons of any type 2 node must be evaluated before younger brothers of that node may be transmitted.

After these promising successors have been completely evaluated, parallelism is allowed as for any other node in the game tree. A move is called promising if it has been found in the transposition table, or if it is a nonnegative capture move, or even if it is a killer move. The idea is that if a cutoff occurs at node v then this cutoff is produced very often by one of the promising moves. This stronger version of the Young Brothers Wait Concept can be considered as a weaker version of the Delayed Branching Scheduling Strategy.

The first difference is that we restrict parallelism at a node v only if there are still some promising successor positions unevaluated. The second difference to the method of Hsu is that we allow different type 2 siblings that have a cutoff failure after the evaluation of the first successor position to be re-expanded in parallel. In the algorithm of Hsu, this is controlled by the host processor. In our distributed algorithm, processors would have to communicate in order to guarantee that the above rule is not violated.

We will show in section 6 that this reduction of parallelism results in only a slightly weaker processor load but reduces the search overhead significantly.

5 COSTS AND GAINS OF A DISTRIBUTED TRANSPOSITION TABLE

In this section, we discuss the use of a distributed transposition table. We will outline the costs in terms of communication costs and delayed transposition table access. On the other hand, we will give some insights, how much the distributed algorithm gains by the enlarged transposition table.

In the distributed version of our algorithm, we make use of a transposition table of size $p \times 16 \times 10^4$ where p is the number of processors. Logically, we look at all the local tables as one global transposition table which is distributed over the whole system. Therefore, we allow a processor remote access to the transposition table of any other processor by message routing. For almost every node in the game tree the transposition table is accessed for, three messages (read-request, read-answer, store) are routed through the network.

This communication causes two kinds of delays.

1. The read access to the transposition table is delayed by the time necessary to route the messages.

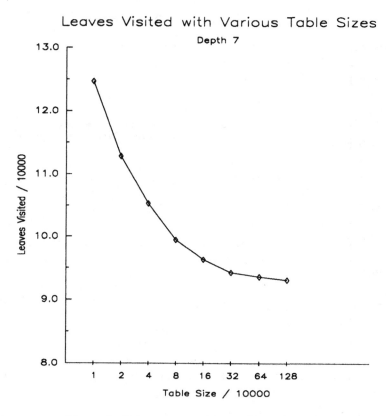

Figure 3: Using transposition tables of various size

2. The routing of messages as well as the serving of remote transposition table accesses delays the processor which holds the entry and the processors on the path between sender and receiver.

To keep the first kind of delay small, we use the method of preupdating a position. Whenever a processor p starts the evaluation of a node v and wants to read the transposition entry for node v, p updates the hash function of v. It sends a read-request for v to the processor that holds the entry for v and then updates the position v itself. After the position v is updated, p waits for the read-answer message that gives possibly some information about node v. In almost all cases, the information from the transposition table does not cause the node v to be cut off. Therefore, the update of position v would have been done anyway.

Since the maximum distance between to nodes in the deBruijn graph grows only logarithmic, messages are routed only via a small number of processors to reach their target processor. Thus, answers to read-request messages will arrive quickly and only a small number of processors is interrupted by the message. We will show in section 6 that both of these delays are kept quite small in our algorithm.

To point out the gains of the sequential algorithm using a larger transposition table, we measured the performance of the sequential algorithm for various transposition table

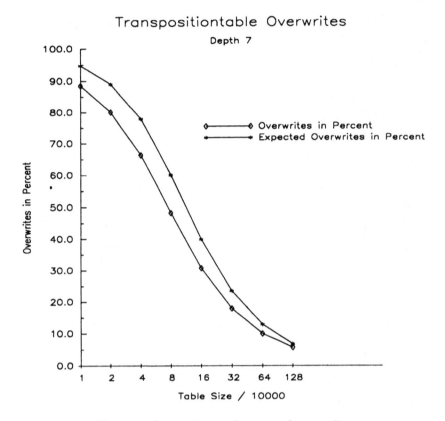

Figure 4: Overwrites and expected overwrites

sizes. Those sizes, which are larger than 16×10^4 are obtained by simulating the sequential algorithm in a distributed system. Figure 3 shows the number of leaves that are searched during a 7-ply search on the well known Bratko-Kopec set of 24 chess positions ([BK82]).

Figure 4 shows the percentage of overwrites and expected overwrites relatively to the number of all stores that happened during the search. The percentage of expected overwrites P_{ovw} can be calculated by the formula

$$P_{ovw} := 100 \cdot (\sum_{i=1}^{i=24} s_i) / (\sum_{i=1}^{i=24} p_i)$$

where s_i is the number of stores that happened during the search of the i-th problem. Here

$$p_i := s_i - m \cdot [1 - (\frac{m-1}{m})^{s_i}],$$

where m is the size of the transposition table , is the number of overwrites that are to be expected during the search of the i-th problem. We observe that the percentage of overwrites is a little bit smaller than the percentage of expected overwrites. This is due to our hash function, which is slightly better than random.

More important is the fact, that for all tests with an percentage of expected overwrites $\leq 50\%$ the number of leaves remains nearly constant. Using a 16×10^4 sized transposition table on the average roughly 18×10^4 nodes required a transposition access. In the next section, we will present speedup data for 8-ply searches. Roughly 125×10^4 nodes on the average require a transposition access during an 8-ply searches with one processor. This results in a percentage of expected overwrites of 87.2% when a 16×10^4 sized transposition table is used. Therefore, the sequential version would need a transposition table of size $\geq 78 \times 10^4$ to achieve a percentage of expected overwrites $\leq 50\%$. On the one side, this means that one has to increase the size of the transposition table by more than a factor of 4.5 per processor in order to achieve a transposition table for the sequential algorithm which guarantees good performance of an 8-ply search. This however is impossible due to hardware constraints. On the other side, it turns out that the 256 processor system has only very advantage compared to the 8 processor system, because both systems have enough transposition table entries to guarantee good performance of 8-ply searches. It was impossible for us to run all the sequential 8-ply searches for various transposition table sizes.

However, if the curves for the 8-ply searches can be compared to the curves of the 7-ply searches then this indicates that the sequential version of our algorithm could be speeded up by the use of a larger transposition table by roughly 20% if there were no hardware constraints. A sequential algorithm that is 20% faster would decrease the speedups we present in section 6 by 20%.

6   EXPERIMENTAL RESULTS

In this section we show how effective the distributed chess program *ZUGZWANG* searches game trees using the above described methods. We present results for speedup, work load, search overhead, delay of the transposition table accesses and the delay caused by routing messages. We will show, that the extension of the Young Brothers Wait Concept decreases the search overhead. The very good load balancing properties of our algorithm however guarantee that the work load remains nearly constant.

All the results we present here are obtained from an 8-ply search on the Bratko-Kopec set of test positions. The nondeterminism of the transposition access causes differences between the runtimes of the parallel algorithm for single positions of the test set. However, we observed that these effects are very small ($\leq 3\%$ for 256 processors) if the whole test set is considered.

For fixed search depth d we define the following measures for the performance of our distributed algorithm running a d-ply search: Let B_i be the i-th position from the Bratko-Kopec set of test positions, Let $T_i(p)$ be the total time, $I_i(p)$ the average idle time and $N_i(p)$ the number of nodes visited by the p processor version of our distributed algorithm for a d-ply search on B_i. Let $W_i(p)$ be the average amount of time a processor spent waiting for all answers from the transposition table during a d-ply search on B_i after it has finished the update of the position.

Then we define

$$SPE(p) := (\sum_{i=1}^{24} T_i(p))/(\sum_{i=1}^{24} T_i(1))$$

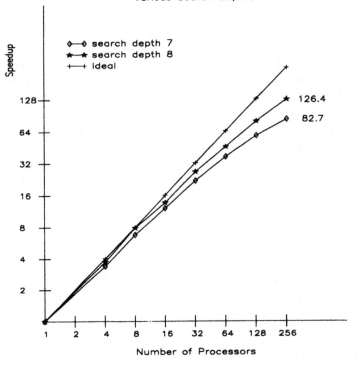

Figure 5: Speedups for 7-ply and 8-ply search

$$LD(p) := 100 \cdot [1 - (\sum_{i=1}^{24} I_i(p))/(\sum_{i=1}^{24} T_i(p))]$$

$$SO(p) := 100 \cdot [1 - (\sum_{i=1}^{24} N_i(p))/(\sum_{i=1}^{24} N_i(1))]$$

$$RD(p) := 100 \cdot [\frac{\sum_{i=1}^{24} N_i(p)}{\sum_{i=1}^{24}(T_i(p) - I_i(p))}/\frac{\sum_{i=1}^{24} N_i(1)}{\sum_{i=1}^{24} T_i(1)}]$$

$$TD(p) := 100 \cdot [(\sum_{i=1}^{24} W_i(p))/(\sum_{i=1}^{24} T_i(p))]$$

to be the speedup, work load, search overhead, delay caused by routing messages and delay caused by the transposition access of the p processor version respectively.

The curves for $SPE(p)$, $LD(p)$, $SO(p)$, $RD(p)$ and $TD(p)$ are given in the three diagrams 5, 6, 7 and 8 for an 8-ply search and processor numbers 4,8,16,32,64,128 and 256.

It is worth to note that the average runtime of the 256 processor system for an 8-ply search of a test position is 300 sec, which is tournament speed.

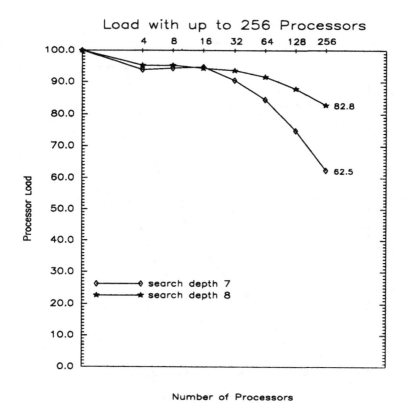

Figure 6: Processor load for 7-ply and 8-ply search

The speedup of the 256 processor system is 126.36, the work load is 82%. The search overhead is kept quite small (44.5%) by the extension of the Young Brothers Wait Concept.

The curves in figure 8 show the delay caused by message routing and delayed access to the transposition table. The delay caused by delayed transposition access is slightly increasing. However, it is negligible even for the 256 processor system (5%). The second curve shows the loss of performance that is caused by routing messages. This delay is roughly 10% for the 256 processor system.

In figure 9, we compare the results of three different versions of *ZUGZWANG* running on 256 processors: The column *YBWC+* shows the performance we mentioned above. The column *YBWC-* shows the performance of *ZUGZWANG* without the extensions of the Young Brothers Wait Concept. The reduction of parallelism in the search decreased the search overhead by 15% On the other side the excellent load balancing properties of our algorithm are the reason for the fact, that the work load of the processors is nearly the same.

The column *TR-* gives the performance of our system when the distributed transposition table has the same size as the sequential one. That is we reduced the transposition table size at every processor from 16×10^4 to 625. The speedup drops from 126 to 100. This is the same loss of speedup that we expected in section 5 in the case that the se-

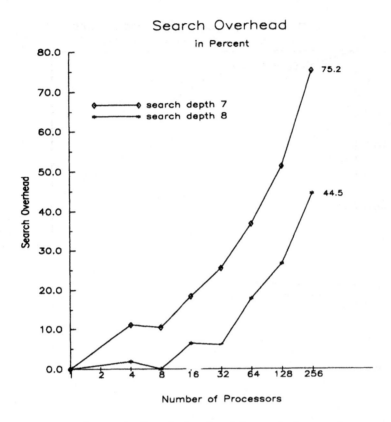

Figure 7: Search Overhead for an 8-ply search

quential algorithm would be allowed to use a transposition table of the same size as the distributed algorithm.

7 CONCLUSIONS

We presented a distributed game tree search algorithm and the implementation of this algorithm in a distributed chess program. To our knowledge, the algorithm shows the best performance that has ever been reported so far for a parallel or distributed implementation of the $\alpha\beta$-algorithm. Moreover, the algorithm uses all state-of-the-art $\alpha\beta$-enhancements in a very efficient manner. The excellent load balancing properties of our algorithm enabled us to implement Iterative Deepening as well as the Extended Young Brothers Wait Concept without a serious decrease of work load. As a result the strength of the distributed chess program is increased enormeously compared to the sequential version.

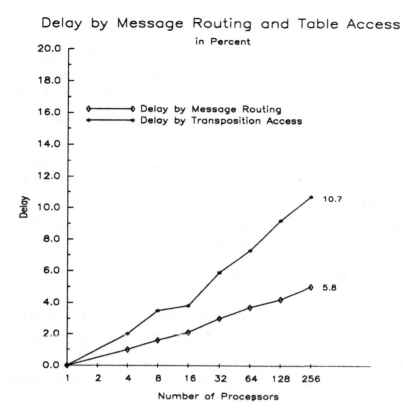

Figure 8: Processor delay during 7-ply and 8-ply search

	YBWC+	YBWC-	TR-
$SPE(p)$	126.3	118.1	99.8
$LD(p)$	82.0	84.9	84.5
$SO(p)$	44.5	60.5	89.6

Figure 9: Performance of the 256 processor system

References

[ABD80]   S.G. Akl, D.T. Barnard, and R.J. Doran. Simulation and analysis in deriving time and storage requirements for a parallel alpha-beta pruning algorithm. *IEEE International Conference on Parallel Processing*, pages 231–234, 1980.

[Bau78]   G.M. Baudet. On the branching factor of the alpha-beta pruning algorithm. *Artificial Intelligence*, (10):pp 173–199, 1978.

[BK82]   I. Bratko and D. Kopec. *A Test for Comparison of Human and Computer Performance in Chess, in Advances in Computer Chess 3, M.R.B. Clarke (editor)*, pages 31–56. Pergamon Press, 1982.

[CM83]   M.S. Campbell and T.A. Marsland. A comparison of minmax tree search algorithms. *Artificial Intelligence*, (20):pp 347–367, 1983.

[deB46]   N.G. deBruijn. A combinatorial problem. *Indagationes Math.*, 8:pp 461–467, 1946.

[FF80]   R.A. Finkel and J.P. Fishburn. Parallel alpha-beta search on arachne. *IEEE International Conference on Parallel Processing*, pages pp 235–243, 1980.

[FK88]   Ch. Ferguson and R.E. Korf. Distributed tree search and its application to alpha-beta pruning. *Proceedings AAAI-88, Seventh National Conference on Artificial Intelligence*, 2:pp 128–132, 1988.

[FMM90]   R. Feldmann, B Monien, and P. Mysliwietz. A fully distributed chess program. *Advances in Computer Chess VI (D. Beal ed.)*, pages pp 1–27, 1990.

[FMMV89] R. Feldmann, B. Monien, P. Mysliwietz, and O. Vornberger. Distributed game-tree search. *ICCA Journal*, 12(2):pp 65–73, 1989.

[FMMV90] R. Feldmann, B. Monien, P. Mysliwietz, and O. Vornberger. *Distributed Game Tree Seach, in Parallel Algorithms for Machine Intelligence and Pattern Recognition, V. Kumar, L.N. Kanal and P.S. Gopalakrishnan (editors)*. Springer Verlag, 1990.

[HSN89]   M. Hyatt, B.W. Suter, and H.L. Nelson. A parallel alpha/beta searching algorithm. *Parallel Computing*, (10):pp 299–308, 1989.

[Hsu90]   F.H. Hsu. *Large Scale Parallelization of Alpha-Beta Search: An Algorithmic Architectural Study with Computer Chess*. PhD thesis, Carnegie Mellon University, Pittsburgh, USA, 1990.

[KM75]   D.E. Knuth and R.W. Moore. An analysis of alpha - beta pruning. *Artificial Intelligence*, (6):pp 293–326, 1975.

[MC82]   T.A. Marsland and M.S. Campbell. Parallel search of strongly ordered game trees. *Computing Surveys*, 14(4):pp 533–551, 1982.

[MOS86]   T.A. Marsland, M. Olafsson, and J. Schaeffer. *Multiprocessor Tree-Search Experiments, in Advances in Computer Chess 4 D.F. Beal (editor)*, pages 37–51. Pergamon Press, 1986

[MP85]   T.A. Marsland and F. Popowich. Parallel game tree search. *IEEE Transactions on Pattern Analysis and Machine Intelligence*, 7(4):pp 442–452, 1985.

[MV87]   B. Monien and O. Vornberger. Parallel processing of combinatorial search trees. *Proceedings International Workshop on Parallel Algorithms and Architectures*, Math. Research Nr. 38, Akademie - Verlag Berlin, pages 60–69, 1987.

[New88]   M. Newborn. Unsynchronized iterative deepening parallel alpha-beta search. *IEEE Transactions on Pattern Analysis and Machine Intelligence*, pages 687–694, 1988.

[OF88]   S.W. Otto and E.W. Felten. Chess on a hypercube. Technical report, California Institute of Technology, USA, 1988.

[Pea80]   J. Pearl. Assymptotic properties of minmax trees and game searching procedures. *Artificial Intelligence*, (14):pp 113 139, 1980.

[Sch89a] J. Schaeffer. Comment on 'distributed game tree search'. *ICCA Journal*, 12(4):pp 216–217, 1989.

[Sch89b] J. Schaeffer. Distributed game-tree searching. *Journal of Parallel and Distributed Computing*, 6(2):pp 90–114, 1989.

[Sch90]   J. Schaeffer. Personal communication. 1990.

[VM87]   O. Vornberger and B. Monien. Parallel alpha-beta versus parallel sss*. *Proceedings IFIP Conference on Distributed Processing, Distributed Processing, North Holland*, pages pp 613–625, 1987.

Balanced Strategies for Routing on Meshes

Manfred Kunde*, Thomas Tensi*

Abstract

This paper analyzes three methods for packet routing on grids. The central algorithmic concept is to achieve a good performance by keeping the processor load balanced. At first, packets are considered as atomic. A balanced load is guaranteed by the algorithm itself. By using techniques like orthogonal overlapping of simple algorithms and colouring highly efficient, but complicated algorithms can be designed. In contrast, the second algorithm class presented is very simple and achieves load balance by derouting which can be considered as an hardware property. The disadvantage of this approach is its slowness in the worst case. Finally, in the third strategy class presented the packets are split up into subpackets which are routed along the network in a pipelined fashion. Here the balancing is achieved by local reservation of communication channels. For several variants of this method worst-case configurations are discussed.

1 Introduction

In this paper we discuss different approaches for data routing on grids of processors. Grids have been widely accepted as a realistic topology for the interconnection of parallel processors. In contrast to the common PRAM-model — where communication between two arbitrary processors can be done in constant time — for processor networks with sublinear node degree special algorithms are necessary to minimize the total communication time.

A $n_1 \times \ldots \times n_r$-grid is a set $grid(n_1, \ldots, n_r)$ of $N = n_1 \cdot \ldots \cdot n_r$ identical processors where each processor $P = (p_1, \ldots, p_r), 0 \leq p_i \leq n_i - 1$, is directly connected to all its nearest neighbours only. A processor $Q = (q_1, \ldots, q_r)$ is called nearest neighbour of P iff the manhattan distance between P and Q is 1 $(d(P, Q) = \sum_{i=1}^{2} |p_i - q_i|)$. The control structure of the grid of processors is assumed to be of the MIMD type (Multiple Instruction Multiple Data). That is, each processor has its own program memory, different processors can perform different instructions at the same clock period, there is a global clock, and each processor can send data only to its nearest neighbours during one clock period. Bidirectional communication can occur with all nearest neighbours in one clock cycle. Furthermore, each processor has only a limited number of registers for data (e.g. the buffer size is constant or $\log N$).

The problem of "data routing" can be informally defined as bringing the right data to the right processors at the right time. There are two principal ways to organize the routing of data. The first one (called *circuit switching*) is in the style of a telephone network. For

---

*Institut für Informatik, TU München, Arcisstr. 21, 8000 München 2

certain time slots exclusive physical connection paths are established through the network from source processors to their destinations.

In the second approach (called *packet routing* or *packet switching*) — which will be discussed in this paper — the data, organized in packets or messages, move through the net from processor to processor. Two methods are basically distinguished: *store-and-forward routing* and *message routing*.

Sections 2 and 3 consider "store-and-forward routing": a method in which the packets travel through the network without getting subdivided in any way. The fundamental time unit is the time to transport a packet from a processor to one of its nearest neighbours. During such a time unit a channel is reserved for the transport of exactly one packet. In the next step the packet can be forwarded to another processor or wait for some steps in that processor it just arrived at.

In section 3 a routing method is presented where a packet may not stay in a processor except when having reached its destination. Thus a processor has to send away all incoming packets in the next step according to some priority scheme. We call this algorithm class *pulsating algorithms*.

In the last section a variant of "message routing" [KK79] is discussed. For message routing a packet is split up into several subpackets called *flits*. The first subpacket (the header) knows the destination address and all other subpackets have to follow the first in a wormlike fashion, because they have no destination information. A prominent subcase of that is therefore called "wormhole routing" [DS87]. In this manner the transport of flits is spread over different channels forming a connected path over several processors. The last flit, the tail, informs the respective processors that the channels passed by the packet need no longer be reserved for that actual packet (see also [KT91, Nga89]). Message routing and wormhole routing were proposed as feasible routing methods for general networks.

As a prototypical problem for all those methods we will examine the permutation routing problem which has been extensively studied in the literature and is fundamental especially in the case of dense data traffic. In a *permutation routing problem* each processor in the mesh sends and finally receives one packet. Furthermore the so-called *multi-packet-problems* will be introduced as variants which are also useful for the design of algorithms for the simple permutation problem.

In this paper we present and analyze different approaches to routing on grids. All those methods presented try to keep the packets "balanced" in some sense within the network. This concept of "keeping the load balanced" has not only proved to be of interest for theory because it simplifies the understanding and analysis of some complicated algorithms but balancing algorithms are normally also more efficient. In the algorithms of this paper balancing is done in several ways: In section 2 the algorithms maintain balance by a clever exploitation of local information and derouting. They are a bit complicated but close to elementary bounds. The algorithms from section 3 achieve balance by immediately getting rid of incoming packets in the next time step regardless of whether any progress is made or not. In section 4 packets block other packets by reserving paths in the network and thus maintain a nearly equal load in the processors.

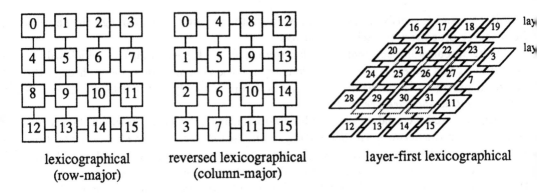

lexicographical
(row-major)

reversed lexicographical
(column-major)

layer-first lexicographical

Figure 1: Indexings

2 Multi-Packet-Routing and Related Methods

In this section we present the some fundamental methods for the design of store-and-forward algorithms on meshes. As mentioned in the introduction we focus on permutation-routing on $n \times \ldots \times n$ meshes with MIMD architecture and a small number of packets which can be buffered at each processor.

For the problem of routing permutations on $n \times n$ meshes by store-and-forward routing many algorithms have been given. Some of them are based on sorting and need only $3n + O(\text{low order})$ steps and a buffersize of 1 packet [MSS86, SS86, TK77]. Recently it was shown that sorting (and thus routing based on sorting) can be done in $2.5n + o(n)$ steps if a buffer size of two packets is available [Kun91a]. A randomized algorithm of Krizanc, Rajasekaran and Tsantilas [KRT88] solves this problem by $2n + O(\log n)$ steps with constant buffersize. The optimal deterministic approach of a $2n - 2$ algorithm with constant buffersize was proposed by Leighton, Makedon and Tollis [LMT89] which matches the lower distance bound. On r-dimensional grids for h-h routing the previous best result was by one of the authors [Kun91a] where routing takes $\lceil h/(4r) \rceil 2(r-1)n + \lceil h/(2r) \rceil n + O(\text{low order})$ transport steps with a buffer of h.

2.1 Elementary Definitions and Methods

Before coming to the algorithms some basic definitions are given. We will concentrate on grids where all sidelengths are equal, that is $n_i = n$ for all $i = 1, \ldots, r$.

In the course of the discussion we will need a notation for slices of intervals. Let $[a_i, b_i]$ denote a closed interval of integers. Then $([a_1, b_1], \ldots, [a_i, b_i], \ldots, [a_r, b_r])$ is given by the standard cartesian product of the intervals. $[x, x]$ is abbreviated by x and $[0, n-1]$ by $*$.

As special submeshes so-called *blocks* of various dimensions are frequently used. Blocks are simply non-overlapping r-dimensional cubes of sidelength $b := n/k$ for some integer k. A grid substructure of dimension s consists of k^s blocks where block $B(k_1, \ldots, k_s)$ contains the processors $([k_1 b, (k_1 + 1)b - 1], \ldots, [k_s b, (k_s + 1)b - 1])$.

Later on we will use sorting as an elementary subprocedure within some submesh. We will use two *indexings*: the *lexicographical indexing* (where the first coordinate is most significant) and its counterpart the *reversed lexicographical indexing* with the last coordinate most significant. For the multipacket case — where the internal registers are

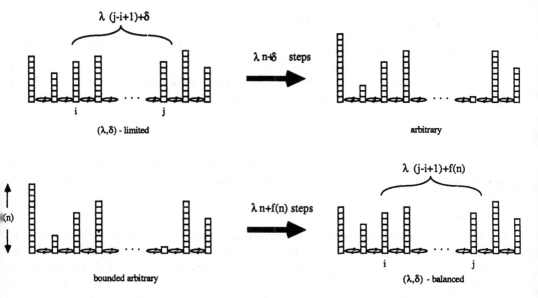

Figure 2: Linear Routing

seen as making up a new virtual coordinate – the notions of *layer-last* and *layer-first* indexing will be used with the evident meaning (see figure 1). For any index function g and processors P and Q the *interval of processors (or addresses)* lying between P and Q *with respect to indexing g* (denoted by $[P, Q]_g$) are processors with index between that of P and Q. These so-called *indexed intervals* are especially helpful for an accurate description of different types of routing problems.

We assume that during the computation each processor is able to store a limited amount of packets. For sidelength n we assume that the size of the *additional buffer* is given by $f(n)$ or $rf(n)$ where $2 \leq f(n) \leq n^{1-1/r}$. Typical buffer sizes are for example $\log n$, $n^{1/r}$ or a constant c. It turns out that even for algorithms routing partial permutations it is helpful to solve subproblems which are not partial permutation routing problems. In these cases the address function is no longer a 1-to-1 mapping as in the case of permutation routing. It may happen that there are up to $f(n)$ packets in the beginning and a similar number of packets at the end in a processor.

To classify these temporary and final packet distributions further we call an r-dimensional routing problem (λ, δ)-*balanced with respect to indexing g* if and only if for all intervals of processors $[P, Q]_g$ there are at most $\lambda(g(Q) - g(P) + 1) + \delta$ packets with destination in the interval of processors $[P, Q]_g$. A *loading* of an r-dimensional mesh at some time step t is said to be (λ_t, δ_t)-*limited* if and only if all intervals of processors $[P, Q]_g$ contain at most $\lambda_t(g(Q) - g(P) + 1) + \delta_t$ packets. In both cases λ is called the *load factor* and δ the *load deviation*. Be aware that the term "balanced" describes an inherent problem property independent from the actual processor loading, while the term "limited loading" characterizes snapshots of configurations.

As a final definition a fundamental paradigm problem will be the case where each processor sends and receives exactly h packets. We call an $(h, 0)$-balanced problem with initial $(h, 0)$-limited loading a *partial $h - h$ routing problem*, $h \geq 1$ an integer. In case of $h = 1$ it is called a *permutation problem*.

2.2 Routing on Linear Arrays

In this subsection strategies for routing on one-dimensional meshes are presented as basic operations for routing in r-dimensional arrays.

Due to the lack of space complete proofs for lemmata can be found in [KT91] or [Kun91b]. The first lemma is for routing on linear arrays, where the initial loading is limited while the final loading is arbitrary.

Lemma 1

Assume a linear array with n processors with an initial (λ, δ)-limited loading, $\lambda \geq 1$, and an arbitrary loading finally. Then the number of transport steps needed for routing is at most $\lambda n + \delta$.

Proof Sketch:

The idea of the proof is to focus on packets going in one direction (say: right) starting at some processor i. A packet once started moves on without ever getting delayed. As the number of packets travelling right via i is bounded (the problem is (λ, δ)-limited !) the lowest priority rightbound packet is guaranteed to have left i at $t = t(i) = \lfloor (i + 1)\lambda + \delta \rfloor$. The sum of that term together with the distance to the destination can be bounded by $n\lambda + \delta$. □

The next lemma shows that similar results can be obtained for balanced problems. The routing strategy in this case is to give highest priority to packets which have to travel the farthest.

Lemma 2

A (λ, δ)-balanced routing problem, $\lambda \geq 1, \delta \leq f(n)$, on a linear array of n processors with buffer size $f(n)$ can be solved by at most $\lambda n - 1 + f(n)$ transport steps. □

The initial and final situations for the two lemmata are depicted in figure 2.

For special cases even bigger improvements can be achieved. One can pipeline cyclic shifts in a linear array efficiently whenever their shift offsets $(i_1, \ldots, i_j)$ satisfy some property. Due to the lack of space we only give a simple version of the lemma (without proof):

Lemma 3 (bundle of four shifts [Kun91b])

On a linear array of n processors the four shifts $\{i, n/2 - i, n/2 + i, n - i\}$ can be routed in n transport steps.
(This lemma can be generalized to an arbitrary number of shifts for so-called *dense bundles*.) □

This lemma will come in handy for the simultaneous routing of layers in the r-dimensional multipacket problem.

2.3 1-1 Routing on Two-Dimensional Grids

The starting point of permutation routing on two-dimensional grids was the well-known *greedy algorithm*, where packets are first routed along one dimension (e.g. the row) until

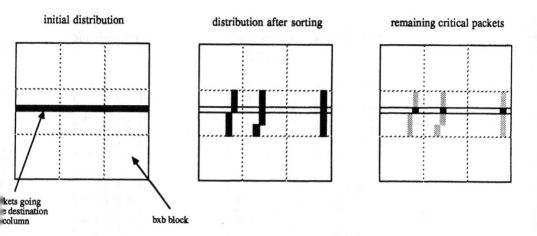

initial distribution   distribution after sorting   remaining critical packets

kets going
e destination
column   bxb block

Figure 3: Sort-And-Route-Algorithm

they have corrected one coordinate. Then they are routed along the second coordinate until they have reached their destination.

The simple greedy algorithm has one great disadvantage: If many packets in a row want to go to the same column a buffer size of $O(n)$ is needed. Leighton has shown, however, that this is unlikely in the average case where a constant buffer size is normally sufficient [Lei90].

To overcome that accumulation of packets Valiant and Brebner [VB81] as well as Rajasekaran et. al. [KRT88] have developped probabilistic algorithms which smear packets for the same destination area along some small strip thus decreasing the required buffer size and increasing the step number only slightly. A deterministic variant of this idea was found by one of the authors [Kun89]. He improved the buffer requirements of the greedy algorithm substantially by the introduction of a prephase using sorting procedures on on two-dimensional grids.

For the algorithm — called *Sort-And-Route* — the total mesh is partitioned into blocks of sidelength b. Within these blocks the packets are then sorted lexicographically according to their destinations. This has the effect of uniformly distributing packets with identical destination row into a strip of width b which guarantees a limited buffer size (see figure 3).

This algorithm is asymptotically optimal for routing problems which have a $(1, f(n))$-limited initial loading and are $(1, f(n))$-balanced with respect to the lexicographical indexing. Remember that permutation routing is included in this class of routing problems. Careful analysis gives the following result:

Theorem 4 ([Kun89])
A $(1, f(n))$-balanced routing problem, $f(n) \leq n^{1/2}$, with initial $(1, 0)$-limited loading can be solved by at most $2n + O(n/f(n))$ steps on an $n \times n$ grid. $\qquad\Box$

The previous algorithm as well as the greedy algorithm have one important property useful for the design of algorithms based on them: they are *uniaxial* [KT91]. In a *uniaxial algorithm* in one time step all processors may communicate along one coordinate axis only i.e. all communication directions are parallel. This property is shared by many other

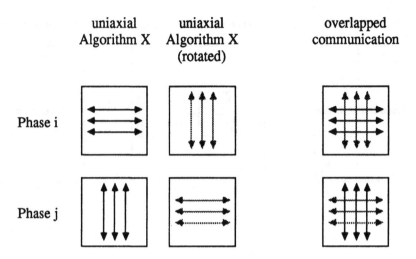

uniaxial   uniaxial   overlapped

Algorithm X   Algorithm X   communication

(rotated)

Figure 4: Overlapping uniaxial algorithms

algorithms. Note, however, that the best algorithm for permutation routing by Leighton et al. [LMT89] does not have this property.

2.4 h-h Routing

For the problem of routing a $h - h$ routing problem where the initial and final loading of a processor is exactly h packets one central idea exploited in the following subsections will be the *orthogonal overlapping of uniaxial algorithms*. By uniaxiality we can independently let data streams flow along orthogonal axes (see figure 4). As an algorithmic base we will use the uniaxial *Sort-and-Route*. For the *overlapped Sort-and-Route* the total mesh is again partitioned into blocks. Within these blocks the packets are then sorted according to their addresses. The orthogonal phases will need different index schemes for the sorting, namely lexicographical and reversed lexicographical indexing. That means we have to use different linear orderings of packets placed in different layers.

Algorithm 5 (overlapped Sort-And-Route)

- in parallel: route all packets in even layers along the rows to their destination columns and route all packets in odd layers along the columns to their destination rows;
- in parallel: route all packets in even layers along the columns and all packets in odd layers along the rows to their destination processors;

Note that both parts are completely orthogonal and thus no interference of packets can occur. By bounding the number of packets in a row going for a certain column (and vice versa) the following theorem can be obtained.

Theorem 6 ([KT91])

Partial *h-h* routing on an $n \times n$ mesh can be done in $\frac{3}{2}hn + O(n/f(n))$ transport steps with a buffer size of $O(hf(n))$.

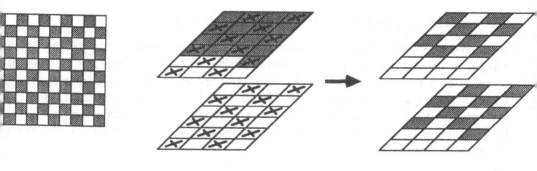

Colouring of the processors   Sorting and Exchanging Every Other Packet

Figure 5: Colouring and exchanging packets in layers

A further improvement is possible, if the $h - h$ problem consists of a *sequence of h permutation problems*. Then we know from the beginning that packets placed in an arbitrary layer initially form a permutation problem.

Corollary 7

A sequence of h permutation problems can be routed within $hn + O(n/f(n))$ transport steps on a mesh without wrap-arounds.   □

As seen in the previous part there is some gap between h-h routing and h permutation routing which is caused by a possible concentration of packets for a destination column in even layers (or analogously for a row within odd layers). It would be advantageous to exchange some packets in even and odd layers to at least approximate the situation given by h permutation routing.

This is indeed possible by some prephase.

An underlying idea for this prephase is to partition the addresses into classes (called *colours* and given as the remainder of the sum of the destination coordinates modulo 2) such that about half the number of processors of an arbitrary rectangle is in each class. By sorting with respect to these colors and by a subsequent distribution of every other packet into odd resp. even layers the desired separation of packets is achieved.

In the prephase in each $b \times b$ block packets are sorted in mixed order with respect to layer-first row-major indexing. *Mixed order* means that a packets colour is most significant in the sorting order. The indexing makes packets with small addresses go into layer 1 and those ones with large addresses into layer h.) Then, in all processors P with $colour(P) = 0$ interchange packets of layer $2i - 1$ and $2i$ for $i = 1, ..., h/2$. (For the general idea see figure 5.)

By that prephase the number of packets in a row heading for a certain destination column can be bounded by about $3hr/4$ which gives the following theorem.

Theorem 8 ([KT91])

Partial h-h routing on an $n \times n$ mesh can be done in $\frac{5}{4}hn + O(hn/f(n))$ transport steps with a buffer size of $O(hf(n))$, where $f(n) \leq n^{1/3}$.   □

2.5 Time Analysis for h Packet Splitting

Until now we considered packets as atomic units. The time needed for a transport step was just a unit, in our case just 1. However, if the packets have a size of s bits then it seems to be a realistic assumption that the transport of a packet needs $\rho s + t_{set}$ time, where ρ is a *transfer rate* (depending on the technical abilities of the channels) and t_{set} is a constant *set-up time* needed by the processor to prepare a packet for the transfer. If the splitting of packets into smaller subpackets is allowed then we obtain the following theorem.

Theorem 9
If packet splitting is allowed, then the permutation routing problem with packets of size s only needs transportation time $ns\rho + 2nt_{set} + o(n)$ on an $n \times n$ mesh.

Proof:
Packet splitting routing is a special case of permutation routing in each layer. In each layer the same permutation takes place. Split up the packets into 2 subpackets. Then by corollary 7 and for $h = 2$ the total number of transportation steps is $2n + o(n)$. Since the packet size is only $s/2$ the transport time for a single step reduces to $\rho \cdot s/2 + t_{set}$. $\qquad\square$

That means that for large packet size where the overhead t_{set} can be neglected a time speed up of factor almost 2 is achieved. This improvement even holds when we compare the splitting approach with the optimal non-splitting algorithm of Leighton et al. [LMT89] needing time $(2n - 2)(s\rho + t_{set})$. The disadvantage of our algorithm over that algorithm is the adaptive buffersize which is a function of n, while Leighton et al. use constant sized buffers.

A new result by one of the authors [Kun91b] based on $h - h$ sorting beats this result with $\rho sn/2 + O(\text{low order})$ for arbitrary dimensional grids.

2.6 Generalization to r dimensions

The techniques presented above can also be used for the r-dimensional case. The idea is to rearrange packets along dimension axes r to 3 such that after this phase in all two-dimensional planes $(*, *, p_3, \ldots, p_r)$ the problem is balanced. This overlapped rearrangement is done by sorting the packets in blocks according to their destination addresses and then distributing them along the appropriate dimension axis.

One of the authors recently [Kun91b] gave a further improvement of the above method by guaranteeing that the prephase exploits the connections very efficiently.

By using the properties of *dense bundles of shifts* (see lemma 3) and an additional pipelining of the rearrange and correction phases the total time needed can be substantially reduced:

Theorem 10 ([Kun91b])
Consider a $h - h$ routing problem, $h \geq r$ and $h \geq 9$ on an r-dimensional cube with sidelength n and buffersize of $hf(n)$ packets, $f(n) \leq n^{r/(r+1)}$. It can non-uniaxially be solved in

$$\lfloor 5(h - 1)/4 \rfloor + 2r - 2n + O(\text{low order}) \text{ transport steps.} \qquad\square$$

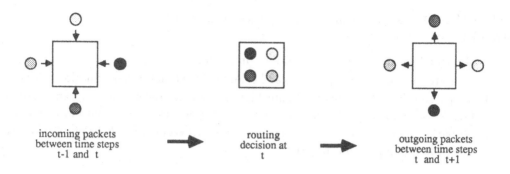

incoming packets
between time steps
t-1 and t

routing
decision at
t

outgoing packets
between time steps
t and t+1

Figure 6: Pulsating algorithm step in one processor

3 Pulsating Routing

In the previous section the advantage of keeping the packet load balanced within the network was demonstrated. This idea is realized here by using an algorithm which tries to maintain this balance locally.

One can accomplish this when each processor always sends away any packets (not destined for itself) in the next cycle regardless of whether they are making any progress or not. The idea is depicted in figure 6. We call this type of algorithm *pulsating algorithm* because the processors act as pulsators that always keep undelivered packets moving.

It seems that this algorithmic idea was first reported in [BH85]. The evident advantages of this kind of algorithm is that a processor only needs a buffer of the initial load size or the number of incoming edges (whatever is larger). Surprisingly enough no theoretical results (apart from empirical in [Nga89]) have been published so far. A general strategy where the number of packets misrouted in a processor is minimized has been explored by several researchers without success and thus seems to be very hard to analyze even for the two-dimensional case.

As nearly nothing has been published on that method in this section we will have a closer look at those kinds of algorithm. Here we concentrate on a variant of the general strategy on a two-dimensional grid similar to the greedy algorithm where packets first try to correct one coordinate and then the other. Such strategies are easier to handle, but we hope to gain some insight for more complicated strategies.

In the variant discussed a packet is in one of two phases: *row-phase* or *column-phase*. A packet in the row-phase stays in its row until it reaches its destination column. There it competes for entering the column and either enters the column or is rejected. If it is in its destination column, it is in the column-phase. Any misrouting will take place in the column unless there are more than two packets in a processor which want to go into the same column. Here we focus on to variants: the *strictly dimension-oriented strategy* where packets which have already been in the column phase are not kicked out by packets entering the column phase and the *priority respecting strategy* where low priority column-phase packets may get rejected into the row-phase. In the priority respecting variant it might happen that a packet switches between row- and column phase quite often.

Algorithm 11 (row-column-pulsating algorithm step)
For each processor do

1. absorb all packets destined for current processor;
2. separate packets according to row- and column phase (packet in destination column);
3. for packets in column phase: route highest priority packet correctly and second highest in remaining column direction; other packets are rejected into row phase;
4. for packets in row phase: route high priority packet correctly and the eventual other packet in remaining row direction; □

There are some remarks to be made: Firstly, within a processor there are at most two packets in the row phase; thus step 4 is well-defined. Secondly, there is some imprecision in step 4 because if there only are packets in the row-phase which have already reached their destination column, it is not clear where they should go. We just define that whenever a packet is misrouted, it is misrouted towards the closer margin of the grid. The idea behind that design decision is that whenever a packet has reached the margin no further contention can take place so that packet is guaranteed to make progress soon.

Note that this algorithm class is very similar to the greedy-algorithm whenever additional buffer for low-priority packets is allowed in the processors. With buffer of size 4 the greedy algorithm performs optimally in the average case for permutation routing as was shown by Leighton [Lei90]. This can also be applied to our algorithm.

3.1 Upper Bounds for Arrays With a Small Number of Rows

In this subsection we will discuss some variant of the priority respecting row-column pulsating algorithm where the misrouting of packets switching from column- to row-phase is clearly defined. For this variant an upper bound is given for arrays with a small number of rows. The presentation is very sketchy here as the details are somewhat involved. A complete version of this section can be found in an upcoming paper.

For the rest of this subsection we will assume a permutation problem on a $m \times n$ array of processors (with even n). The *class* of a packet is given by the distance of its destination to the upper and lower margin (whichever is smaller). Priorization is first done on class (the smaller the higher) and then on remaining projected distance in the current travelling direction (the larger the higher).

The central idea to get an upper bound is to observe the flow of packets across an arbitrary cut in a processor row. We assume the cut between processors j and $j + 1$ in some row (where wlog. $j \leq n/2$). It can be shown that for a small number of classes (and thus rows) misrouted packets will only pass the cut until time $n - j$. After that time packets behind the cut travel on without further delay within the row.

Careful analysis shows that only some packets can be repelled past the cut. We call those packets *critical packets*. One could think that by some bad configuration the critical packets might be close to the margin and still have to travel a long way. The next lemma shows that this is not the case by giving a gathering property for critical packets, because they gather directly behind the cut with high priority packets closer to the cut:

Lemma 12 (Critical packets gather at cut sorted)
Assume that a time $t' \geq t + j$ has passed. Focus on processor $k \in A_j$ where processor k

Two Cords of Packets Blocking a Third One   Two Stage Blockade

Figure 7: Worst Case Configuration for Strictly Dimension-Oriented Row-Column
Pulsating Routing

contains a critical packet and k is a minimum. Then any processor $k' > k$ with contains
a critical packet. Additionally the maximum priority packet of all critical packets still in
A_j is in the maximum processor $k \in A_j$.   □

This means that after some time packets behind the cut which want to leave the interval
become sorted according to their priority. Thus we know that for arbitrary j after time
$n - j$ no delay in the row phase occurs. The critical packets in A_j are packed behind the
cut and their number can be bounded by $\lfloor j - 1 \rfloor$. By the previous lemma at each time
step a critical packet leaves the interval and after n steps all are gone. This leads to the
following theorem:

Theorem 13
For an $m \times n$ grid ($m \leq 5$) all packets have arrived in their destination columns at time
n and will not be delayed any further. Thus all packets reach their destination after at
most $n + m - 1$ steps (which is optimal).   □

3.2 Lower Bound for the Strictly Dimension-Oriented Strategy

To show that the strictly dimension-oriented strategy is worse than linear we construct a
worst case example for the $n \times n$ case.

Call packets subsequent in a row a *cord*. The central idea now is to block the header
packet of one cord by two cords from other rows which want to go to the same destination
column as the aforementioned header. Note that in the strictly dimension-oriented strategy whenever both column edges are used even a high priority packet for that column is
repelled (see figure 7).

If we initialize the mesh rows with cords of packets of decreasing priority and assign
the destination rows appropriately a recursive cascade of blockades can be constructed
(see figure 7). As always two cords block another one the blockade dependency graph is
a binary tree.

Analysis shows that $\log \log n$ successive blockades are possible and that each blockade
delays the cords of the next by $\Omega(n)$ steps. Thus the following theorem holds:

Theorem 14

The lower bound for row-column pulsating routing on an $n \times n$ mesh takes at least $\Omega(n \cdot \log \log n)$ steps. □

It is not yet clear if this bound is also valid for the priority respecting strategy or even for the general pulsating algorithm where the number of packets misrouted is minimized.

4 Oblivious Restricted Message Routing

In contrast to the previous sections message routing assumes that the packets are split up into non-independent parts called *flits*. These flits are routed through the network in a pipelined fashion.

The idea of balancing which was central to the other sections is implemented here by packets blocking each other such that no accumulation of packets can occur in one processor. We will come to that later on.

Note that algorithms of this class have mostly been empirically analyzed for their behaviour. In this section we will recall methods and results previously presented in [KT90] where to our knowledge a first complexity-theoretic analysis of a variant of message routing has been done.

Since there are different understandings of message routing we will first of all give a more detailed description of our model as given in [KT90].

Definition 15 (Message routing)

In a message routing strategy each packet is split up into h linearly-ordered equal size subpackets (*flits*). These flits are routed in a store and forward manner (e.g. at most one flit may travel across an edge in one time step) with the following restrictions:

1. As soon as the first flit (so-called *header flit*) has travelled across an edge, this edge is reserved for use by flits from this packet only.
2. An edge is used by flits with increasing index.
3. As soon as the last flit (so-called *tail flit*) has travelled across an edge, the reservation for this edge is cancelled.
4. After each routing step adjacent flits are either in the same or in adjacent processors (the flit sequence is consecutive). □

Unfortunately strictly dimension oriented variants of message routing in this sense may behave like store-and-forward routing in row-column manner with respect to buffer size. Imagine the case where all packets in a row want to go to a certain column; now a buffer size of $O(n)$ is needed.

A good idea is to somehow report back the nonavailability of the buffer for another packet. This was done with the wormhole-routing concept by Dally and Seitz [DS87]. The important idea here is that the packets or packet flits are stored along a path and no buffer overflow can occur. It should be mentioned that the idea is not without problems because some transitive ripple-through effects may occur where the blocking information has to be distributed globally in one time step.

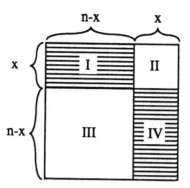

Figure 8: General structure of worst-case example

In [KT90] the wormhole approach in order to avoid buffer overflow was modified towards a more restricted model of message routing where balancing is still maintained by the blocking of edges:

Definition 16 (Restricted message routing)
A restricted message routing strategy is a message routing strategy where the following additional restrictions are met:

- The number of processors the flits of a packet reside in (so-called *extension* [MS90]) is always greater than one, except at the beginning and the end of the transmission, i.e. header and tail flit are in between in different processors.
- Whenever a flit can follow the header flit, it does.

$\square$

Note that by this definition packets travelling in that fashion cannot overtake another one going in the same direction.

Two further restrictions seem to be practical: The local routing direction should be simple to compute. Using the same idea as in section 3 the packets first travel along one dimension and then the other one. The method falls in the class of *oblivious* strategies. Those are very easy to implement. E.g. Flaig [Fla87] proposed a clever form of prefix encoding which is only possible for a simple row-column strategy. We assume additionally that our algorithms are *pure*, i.e. if a packet can leave a processor, it will at once.

The aim is to find out how fast routing can take place when conflicts between competing packets are resolved by different priority schemes (e.g. only looking at some static parameter like the distance between actual and destination processor for each packet involved).

4.1   Worst-Case Configuration for Permutations

To simplify the presentation we will concentrate on the case where we only have two flits per packet. Note that all results presented here can also be shown for the h-flit case (see [KT90]). In the two flit case the position of a packet is thought to be in the processor where its tail flit resides. The position of the header flit can easily be deduced.

In order to get lower bounds worst case examples were constructed in [KT90] which behave badly for a given strategy. Although we only concentrate on the packets in a

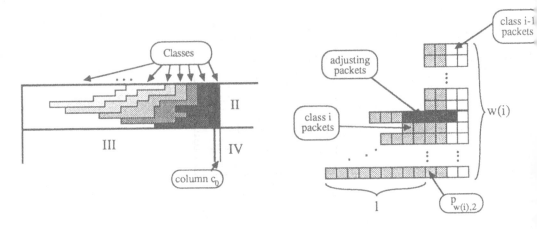

Figure 9: Generic worst-case example

small part of the grid (mainly an $x \times (n - x)$ strip (I) in the upper left part routed to a $(n - x) \times x$ strip (IV) in the lower right part; see figure 8), the construction of a complete permutation is easy. We just let packets in the other area II and III stay in place (so these packets do not block other packets) and route packets in (IV) into (I) (so they do not block packets in (I), because they first travel along the rows into (III) and then vertically into (I)).

The central idea of the worst-case examples is to block low priority packets by high priority ones. It is quite straightforward to construct such a configuration for the case of statically assigned priorities where packets of a class form a consecutive queue in their destination column thus blocking the leading blocking packets in subsequent rows (which are of the same class, but have less priority). The messages behind the leading row packet want to cross the stream of packets but cannot, because they are blocked by the initial packet (note that packets may not overtake another one). As soon as this initial packet joins the queue of packets moving vertically the whole row moves one column right. By a cascade of packets with decreasing priorities a low priority packet can get blocked for about $\Omega(n^2)$ time.

This means that we do not get far with just static priorities.

A very natural idea is to take the local waiting time into account. Thus a packet with low static priority will eventually win against other ones with a higher static priority. This is a kind of fairness to overcome possible worst case behaviour of a too simple static priority decision.

The local waiting time of a packet is defined as the number of steps the packet header is at the current processor. Based on that in [KT90] four variants of priority are considered: 1. compete by static priority only (forget the waiting time); 2. a packet waiting longer is preferred; 3. if a packet waits longer than v it is preferred over packets waiting shorter than v; 4. same as (3) but packets with the longest waiting time larger than v have highest priority. In case of equality in the waiting time component the unique static priority decides.

A single worst-case example for case (2) — with some small modifications — turns out bad for all the other cases as well.

The worst-case example for the case where packets waiting longer are preferred is shown in figure 9a. We have several classes of packets constituting incarnations where each incarnation blocks the next one for some time. A zoomed view of an incarnation can be seen in figure 9b. Let w denote the height of the incarnation, l the length of the last row of each class.

Now we focus on the behaviour of one incarnation say i. Let packets of class i go to column $c_0 + i$. Additionally we assume the packets have increasing priority from top to bottom and packets of class i in row r are denoted by $p_{r,j}$ where $p_{r,1}$ is the rightmost packet. Let $w(i) := w - i$ denote the last row of incarnation i.

Eventually those rows of packets from class i have arrived at their destination column with their first packets. Now conflicts occur only for the down edge of processor $(s, c_0 + i)$ as soon as it becomes available. Both $p_{s,2}$ and $p_{s-1,1}$ want to go down. This conflict is resolved in favour of the element coming in horizontally (higher static priority). But now the whole row moves one processor right; thus each packet in the row resets its local waiting time to 0. Whenever the down edge becomes available for the next time, the packet from above is preferred, as it has waited longer than the packet which has just moved in.

Extending this argumentation inductively at each processor $(r, c_0 + i)$ with $r = 1, \ldots,$ $w(i)$ the preferred input direction is switched between horizontal and vertical each time forwarding takes place. The edges between the processing elements have capacity one and the internal input selectors change their input preference each time the processor's output edge becomes free.

It is easy to see, that the flow rate of the rows grows by a factor of two when going down one row. Thus — to achieve a corresponding initial situation for the next incarnation — the length of the rows has also to increase by a factor of two.

Unfortunately there are technical problems with this naive approach. The blockade breaks prematurely at the first row with only two packets of class i. But these can be overcome by introducing adjustment packets.

By analysis of the structure of the worst-case example and selection of appropriate values for x, l, w and the number of incarnations the following theorem can be obtained:

Theorem 17
The worst case time for pure 2-flit row-column message routing with priorisation on local waiting time is $\Omega(n^2)$. □

4.2 Lower Bounds for Common Priorizations

As mentioned before the worst-case example above serves as a generic one for the other strategies.

The main idea is to assign the static priorities for the packets of one incarnation by using the sequence of packets which leave the lower right processor $(w(i), c_0 + i)$. The packet leaving first is assigned the highest static priority, the packet leaving last the smallest.

It can quite straightforwardly be shown that using this priority assignment the conflict resolution for this specific example in each of the 3 remaining strategies is the same as in strategy 2. This ensures that the configurations change identically to case 2 and thus also take time $\Omega(n^2)$.

Note that the worst-case example above can be extended to the h-flit case and also to r dimension [KT90]. This leads to the following result:

Theorem 18
The worst case time for h-flit row-column message routing on an r-dimensional grid ($r \geq 2$) with any of the four priorisations is $\Omega(hn^{\lceil \frac{r+1}{2} \rceil})$. □

Hence restricted message routing might behave very badly in certain circumstances. But note that the configurations are very fragile with respect to slight modifications or delays. Thus it seems not very likely that such bad cases occur very often. A definite answer to that could only be given by a precise average case analysis.

4.3 Upper Bounds

To find out how well the technique presented here performs an upper bound can be given. This upper bound is tight for the 2-dimensional-case, but there is a significant gap in the r-dimensional case.

Theorem 19 ([KT90])
The h-flit strictly dimension-oriented restricted message routing on an r-dimensional grid with any pure priorisation takes at most $O((h+r)n^r)$ steps.

Proof:
Consider the n ($r-1$)-dimensional hyperplanes $(*,\ldots,*,i)$ for $i \in [0, n-1])$. Pick one of them and call it $\mathcal{HP}$. Pick an arbitrary packet q in $\mathcal{HP}$. Now assume q is travelling in dimension j. It can be shown that at least one packet travelling in the same linear subarray as q leaves dimension j for $j+1$ after at most n steps. Inductively after at most $O(rn)$ steps a packet q' wants to leave dimension $r-1$ for dimension r — i.e. the hyperplane itself — in the next time step. Now the action in $\mathcal{HP}$ might come to a standstill because q' can get blocked by other packets (from other hyperplanes), which also enter the same tower of processors, say $(p_1, \ldots, p_{r-1}, *)$. Now in a linear array of length n after at most $O(nh)$ steps after injection any packet has proceeded by at least one position (which means also that each packet in its destination column arrives after at most $O(n^2h)$ steps at its destination). Thus q' will have left its plane and reached its destination after $O(nh)$ steps. Note that now the same argumentation can be applied to the packets remaining in $\mathcal{HP}$. Thus it takes $O(n(r+h))$ steps to get rid of at least one packet in the plane, so it takes at most $O((h+r)n \cdot n^{r-1})$ steps to get rid of all. Thus after $O((h+r) \cdot n^r)$ all packets have left their hyperplanes and are absorbed after at most $O(n^2h)$ additional steps. □

5 Conclusion

In this paper three methods for packet routing on grids have been presented: overlapped store-and-forward routing with prephases, pulsating store-and-forward routing and oblivious restricted message routing. The central algorithmic concept was to achieve a good performance by keeping the processor load balanced.

It is very hard to make a fair comparison between the strategies presented. For large packet sizes a store-and-forward approach is normally not very practical when large distances between source and destination are involved. Whenever the traffic in the network is low a split-packet or message routing approach is more appropriate. But note that even a split-up into independent packets may be questionable due to the fact, that the data itself is split, but that each subpacket has to carry the destination address information additionally. For small flit sizes as used in implementations (normally a very small number of bits) this is impractical.

When taking simplicity of implementation as a criterion the highly phase-oriented algorithms of section 2 seem to be too complicated. Additionally it should be recalled that in our models the internal computation time could be neglected with respect to the communication time. For store-and-forward routing with large packet sizes this seems to be a realistic assumption. Note, however, that when processors are located physically very close (e.g. on a wafer) and the packet sizes are small more primitive strategies like wormhole routing are to be preferred.

As we have chosen permutation routing as the paradigm problem in this paper we necessarily neglected the handling of dynamic problems. It is not clear whether the algorithms in section 2, which assume a time where all routing starts, could be modified for such a situation. In contrast e.g. the pulsating algorithm can handle dynamic problems easily.

In spite of the points against the overlapped store-and-forward algorithms (mostly because they have to do a complex packet administration internally) it should be recalled that they behave nearly optimally in dense traffic situations. In those situations row-column message-routing and variants of pulsating routing fail by using long runtimes.

As a final remark let us point out that it is still open whether there are algorithms which are simple to implement but nevertheless have a good run time and a low buffer consumption. It may turn out that on grids these requirements are impossible to fulfill simultaneously.

References

[BH85]   A. Borodin and J. E. Hopcroft. Routing, merging and sorting on parallel models of computation. *Journal of Computer and System Sciences*, 30:130–145, 1985.

[DS87]   William J. Dally and Charles L. Seitz. Deadlock-free message routing in multiprocessor interconnection networks. *IEEE Transactions on Computers*, C-36(5):547–553, May 1987.

[Fla87] Charles M. Flaig. VLSI mesh routing systems. Technical Report 5241-TR-87, California Institute of Technology, Computer Science Departement, 1987.

[KK79]   Parviz Kermani and Leonard Kleinrock. Virtual cut-through: A new computer communication switching technique. *Computer Networks*, 3:267–286, 1979.

[KRT88] D. Krizanc, S. Rajasekaran, and T. Tsantilas. Optimal routing algorithms for mesh-connected processor arrays. In Reif [Rei88], pages 411–422.

[KT90]   Manfred Kunde and Thomas Tensi. Bounds for oblivious restricted message routing on grids. In Gottfried Wolf, Tamás Legendi, and Udo Schendel, editors, *Parcella '90, Proceedings of V. International Workshop on Parallel Processing by Cellular Automata and Arrays, Berlin*, pages 227–238, Berlin, 1990. Akademie-Verlag.

[KT91]   Manfred Kunde and Thomas Tensi. $(k - k)$-routing on multidimensional mesh connected arrays. *Journal of Parallel and Distributed Computing*, 11:146–155, 1991.

[Kun89]   Manfred Kunde. Packet routing on grids of processors. In H. Djidjev, editor, *Optimal Algorithms*, volume 401 of *Lecture Notes in Computer Science*, pages 254–265. Springer-Verlag, New York, Berlin, Heidelberg, London, Paris, Tokyo, 1989.

[Kun91a]   Manfred Kunde. Concentrated regular data streams on grids: Sorting and routing near to the bisection bound. In *Proceedings FOCS'91*, pages 141–150, 1991.

[Kun91b]   Manfred Kunde. *Routing and Sorting on Grids*. Habilitation thesis, Technische Universität München, 1991.

[Lei90]   Tom Leighton. Average case analysis of greedy routing algorithms on arrays. In *Proceedings of the 1990 ACM Symposium on Parallel Algorithms and Architectures, Crete, Greece*, pages 2–10. ACM, 1990.

[LMT89]   Tom Leighton, Fillia Makedon, and Ioannis Tollis. A $2n-2$ step algorithms for routing in an $n \times n$ array with constant size queues. In *Proceedings of the 1989 ACM Symposium on Parallel Algorithms and Architectures, Santa Fe*, pages 328–335. ACM, 1989.

[MS90]   Filia Makedon and Adonis Simvonis. On bit-serial packet routing for the mesh and the torus. In *Proceedings of the 3rd Symposium of Frontiers of Massively Parallel Computation, Maryland*, 1990.

[MSS86]   Y. Ma, S. Sen, and I.D. Scherson. The distance bound for sorting on mesh-connected processor arrays is tight. In *Proceedings FOCS*, pages 255–263, 1986.

[Nga89]   John Y. Ngai. *A Framework for Adaptive Routing in Multicomputer Networks*. PhD thesis, California Institute of Technology, Computer Science Department, 1989. Caltech-CS-TR-89-09.

[Rei88]   J.H. Reif, editor. *VLSI Algorithms and Architectures, Proceedings of the 3rd Aegean Workshop on Computing AWOC, Korfu*, number 319 in Lecture Notes in Computer Science. Springer-Verlag, New York, Berlin, Heidelberg, London, Paris, Tokyo, July 1988.

[SS86]   C.P. Schnorr and A. Shamir. An optimal sorting algorithm for mesh-connected computers. In *Proceedings STOC, Berkley*, pages 255–263, 1986.

[TK77]   C.D. Thompson and H.T. Kung. Sorting on a mesh-connected parallel computer. *Communications of the ACM*, 20:263–270, 1977.

[VB81]   L. G. Valiant and G. J. Brebner. Universal schemes for parallel communication. In *Proceedings STOC*, pages 263–277, 1981.

Complexity of Boolean Functions on PRAMs
– Lower Bound Techniques[*]

Mirosław Kutyłowski[†]

Abstract

Determining time necessary for computing important functions on parallel machines is one of the most important problems in complexity theory for parallel algorithms. Recently, a substantial progress has been made in this area. In this survey paper, we discuss the results that have been obtained for three types of parallel random access machines (PRAMs): CREW, ROBUST and EREW.

1   Introduction

Parallel random access machine (PRAM) is a most abstract model of parallel computers, where interprocessor communication is realized using a shared memory. Each processor of a PRAM can access any cell of a shared memory in one computation step. This is certainly an unrealistic assumption, but it makes the analysis of the parallel algorithms much easier, and we can can concentrate ourselves on inherent complexity of a given problem. This is a reason, why most parallel algorithms have been described in terms of PRAMs.

Each PRAM consists of a collection of processors and common memory cells. Each computation consists of several computation steps. At each step, the processors perform in parallel the following: a processor can read from at most one memory cell; then it does some internal computing (which is deterministic unless otherwise specified); and finally, it has the possibility to write into a chosen memory cell. The first question that comes to mind is how the memory access conflicts are resolved. Many solutions are possible and they lead to a number of different types of PRAMs. If any number of processors can read from a given memory cell simultaneously, then we call it Concurrent-Read PRAM. The PRAMs that forbid concurrent reads are called Exclusive-Read PRAMs. Similarly, Concurrent-Write PRAM is a PRAM that allows many processors to write into a given memory cell during one computation step. Exclusive-Write PRAMs forbid concurrent write into the same cell during one step. Usually, it requires a very careful design of the algorithm to insure that the concurrent reads or writes do not occur. If during computation of an Exclusive-Read (Exclusive-Write) PRAM a read (write) conflict occurs then the computation is interrupted in an emergency state. There are three

---

[*]Supported by DFG Grant ME 872/1–4

[†]Fachbereich Mathematik-Informatik, Universität-GH Paderborn, Postfach 1621, D-W-4790 Paderborn, Germany. Email: mirekk@uni-paderborn.de

main types of PRAMs considered: Exclusive-Read Exclusive-Write (EREW) PRAMs, Concurrent-Read Exclusive-Write (CREW) PRAMs, and Concurrent-Read Concurrent-Write (CRCW) PRAMs. In a case of a CRCW PRAM, one must define value that is written if more than one processor attempts to write into the same cell at the same time. Therefore, many different types of CRCW PRAMs have been defined (COMMON, TOLERANT, COLLISION, ARBITRARY, PRIORITY, ...).

If a PRAM M computes a function f of n arguments, then the arguments are stored initially in the first n memory cells (one argument per cell). The result is given at the last moment of the computation in some specially chosen memory cell.

We investigate time necessary for computing functions on PRAMs. For the sake of simplicity we consider Boolean functions. Each Boolean function f is a function over a finite domain $\{0,1\}^n$ for some $n \in I\!N$, $f: \{0,1\}^n \to \{0,1\}$. We say that time complexity of a function f within a family of PRAMs $\mathcal{A}$ is at most t if there is a PRAM $R \in \mathcal{A}$ that computes f and R performs at most t steps for every input string. Since we consider each finite function separately, the time bounds that we consider are called nonuniform.

The overall strategy of determining lower bounds for Boolean functions on PRAMs is the following: First a complexity measure m for Boolean functions is defined. We require that $m(f)$ should be relatively easy to compute for each Boolean function f. Then the time complexity of f in a given class of PRAMs is expressed in terms of $m(f)$. Of course, such a connection between a complexity measure and time complexities on PRAMs is sometimes difficult to find. Nevertheless, most results that are known are based on this idea.

2 Concurrent-Read Exclusive-Write PRAMs

The first impression is that functions like $OR_n(x_1, \ldots, x_n) = x_1 \vee \ldots \vee x_n$ cannot be computed in less than $\log n$[†] steps. However, it is not true as shown by Cook, Dwork and Reischuk [4]:

Algorithm 2.1 *There is an n-processor CREW PRAM that computes OR_n in approximately $0.72 \log n$ steps.*

The basic observation is that it is possible to compute OR_2 by a single write operation. Suppose that processor P knows a value $x \in \{0,1\}$ and a cell C stores a value $y \in \{0,1\}$. Then P writes into C if and only if $x = 1$, and the value written is 1. It is easy to see that after writing C always contains $x \vee y$. The algorithm of Cook, Dwork and Reischuk runs so that the processors compute the logical OR for larger and larger groups of the input arguments. Coalescing such groups is done through reading (a processor knowing the OR of one group reads a cell that stores the value of the OR of an other group, and computes the OR of the union of both groups) and through writing (a processor knowing that the value of the OR for a group is equal to 1 writes 1 into a cell storing the value of the OR of another group, and thereby computes the OR for the union of both groups even if it does not write). Applying this mechanism, it is possible to organize the algorithm so that, after step t, each processor knows the value of the OR for a group of F_{2t} input arguments,

---

[†]throughout the paper, log stands for log to the base 2

and each cell stores the value of the OR of a group of F_{2t+1} arguments, where F_j denotes a Fibonacci number: $F_0 = 0$, $F_1 = 1$ and $F_{j+2} = F_{j+1} + F_j$, for $j \geq 0$. Therefore the above algorithm requires $\phi(n) := \min\{t : F_{2t+1} \geq n\}$ steps to compute OR_n.

2.1 Lower bounds for Boolean functions

2.1.1 Critical complexity lower bounds

The first complexity measure relating Boolean functions with their time complexities on CREW PRAMs was *critical complexity* used by Cook, Dwork and Reischuk [4]. It was later generalized by Nisan [19] to *block-critical complexity*. If f is a function of n arguments then the block-critical complexity of f, denoted $bc(f)$, is the maximum of the numbers

$$\max\{l \mid \exists S_1, \ldots, S_l \subseteq \{1, \ldots, n\} \text{ disjoint s. t. } f(\vec{a}^{S_j}) \neq f(\vec{a}), \text{ for } 1 \leq j \leq l\}$$

taken over all inputs $\vec{a}$, where $\vec{a}^S$ is obtained from $\vec{a}$ by flipping all bits in positions $i \in S$. If each S_i is to contain exactly one element then we get a definition of $c(f)$, *critical complexity* of f. Cook, Dwork and Reischuk [4] prove the following lower bound (the formulation in terms of $bc(f)$ is due to Nisan, the constants presented are due to Parberry and Yan [20]):

Theorem 2.1 *Let f be a Boolean function. Every CREW PRAM computing f makes at least $0.5 \log(bc(f))$ steps.*

Interestingly, there is a tight upper bound shown by Nisan [19]:

Theorem 2.2 *Every Boolean function f can be computed by a CREW PRAM running in time $\approx 2.88 \log(bc(f))$.*

Now we sketch the most important ideas of the proof of Theorem 2.1. We consider an input $\vec{a_0}$ and a set $I \subseteq \{1, \ldots n\}$ such that for every $i \in I$, $f(\vec{a_0}) \neq f(\vec{a_0}(i))$ where $\vec{a_0}(i)$ is the string obtained from $\vec{a_0}$ by flipping the ith bit (so we work with $c(f)$ instead of $bc(f)$). Now let us consider a machine computing f. We say that index i *influences* a processor P at step t on input $\vec{a}$ if the state of P at step t on input $\vec{a}$ differs from the state of P at step t on input $\vec{a}(i)$. Similarly we define indexes influencing the cells. Let $K(P, t, \vec{a})$ and $L(M, t, \vec{a})$ be the set of indexes influencing processor P and cell M respectively, at step t on input $\vec{a}$. The proof estimates cardinalities of the sets $K(P, t, \vec{a})$ and $L(M, t, \vec{a})$ as a function of t. Since the output cell C after the last step T on input $\vec{a_0}$ is influenced by at least $|I|$ indexes, we get immediately a bound on T. Let K_t be the maximal cardinality of the set $K(P, t, \vec{a})$ over all inputs $\vec{a}$ and processors P. Similarly we define L_t. Cook, Dwork and Reischuk show by induction on t that the sizes of K_t and L_t grow at most exponentially with t. It is quite easy to see that $K_{t+1} \leq K_t + L_t$. The difficult part is to express L_{t+1} in terms of K_{t+1} and L_t. The problem is to estimate the number of indexes influencing a cell M if *no processor writes* into M at step $t+1$ on input $\vec{a}$. The indexes influencing M are these indexes that influence M at step t on $\vec{a}$ (at most L_t indexes), and these indexes u that make a processor write into M at step $t+1$ on $\vec{a}(u)$. Let $U = \{u_1, \ldots, u_r\}$ be the set of the later indexes. For $u \in U$, by P_{z_u} we denote the processor that writes into M at step $t+1$ on $\vec{a}(u)$. Let e be the number of pairs (i, j) such that $i, j \in U$ and $P_{z_i} \neq P_{z_j}$.

First we prove that $e \leq r \cdot K_{t+1}$. Consider $i, j \in U$ such that $P_{z_i} \neq P_{z_j}$. If $j \notin K(P_{z_i}, t+1, \vec{a}(i))$ then P_{z_i} writes into M at step $t+1$ on $\vec{a}(i)(j)$. Similarly, if $i \notin K(P_{z_j}, t+1, \vec{a}(j))$ then P_{z_j} writes into M at step $t+1$ on $\vec{a}(j)(i) = \vec{a}(i)(j)$. It follows that either $j \in K(P_{z_i}, t+1, \vec{a}(i))$ or $i \in K(P_{z_j}, t+1, \vec{a}(j))$ since no write conflict may occur. The number of pairs (i, j) such that $i \in K(P_{z_j}, t+1, \vec{a}(j))$ is at most $r \cdot K_{t+1}$, hence $e \leq r \cdot K_{t+1}$.

Now we show that $e \geq r(r - K_{t+1})/2$. Clearly for each $j \in U$, index j influences P_{z_j} on input $\vec{a}$. We take an $i \in U$. If $P_{z_j} = P_{z_i}$, then j influences P_{z_i}. There are at most K_{t+1} indexes j influencing P_{z_i}. Hence there are at least $r - K_{t+1}$ indexes j such that $P_{z_i} \neq P_{z_j}$. Summing up over all i, and dividing by two, since each pair has been considered twice, gives $e \geq r(r - K_{t+1})/2$. By the inequalities obtained, we get $r \cdot K_{t+1} \geq r(r - K_{t+1})/2$, that is, $3K_{t+1} \geq r$. Hence $L_{t+1} \leq L_t + 3K_{t+1}$.

2.1.2 Degree complexity lower bounds

The second important complexity measure, after critical complexity, used for lower bound results is the notion of degree. It provides easier and in most cases more precise lower bounds. The results presented in this section originate from the papers [5, 6] by Dietzfelbinger, Kutyłowski and Reischuk and [17] by Kutyłowski.

Each Boolean function of n arguments can be represented by a polynomial with n variables over an arbitrary field $\mathbb{F}$. Indeed, one can represent a Boolean function by a Boolean formula with the operators $\wedge$ and $\neg$. Then we replace each expression $L \wedge M$ by $L \cdot M$, and $\neg L$ by $(1 - L)$. Obviously, the polynomial resulting gives value 1 (respectively 0) for an input $\vec{x} \in \{0, 1\}^n$ if and only if the Boolean function has value 1 (respectively 0) on $\vec{x}$. One can easily prove that for a given Boolean function there is exactly one such polynomial, provided that it contains no terms of the form x^j for $j > 1$. By the degree of a polynomial p we mean the size of the biggest monomial occurring in p. For instance, degree of the polynomial $x_1 - x_1 x_2 x_7 + 2x_3 x_2$ is 3, because of the monomial $x_1 x_2 x_7$ consisting of 3 variables. Throughout this section, we shall consider only polynomials over $\mathbb{Q}$ (polynomials over finite fields are investigated in section 5). For a Boolean function f, let $\deg(f)$ denote the degree of the polynomial over $\mathbb{Q}$ representing f.

Theorem 2.3 *If a Boolean function f is computed by a CREW PRAM in T steps, then $T \geq \phi(\deg(f)) \approx 0.72 \log(\deg(f))$.*

We sketch the proof of this theorem. Each state q of a processor (a cell) P after step t can be characterized by a Boolean function $f_{P,q,t}$ such that for every input $\vec{x}$, $f_{P,q,t}(\vec{x}) = 1$ if and only if processor (cell) P is in state q after step t in the computation on input $\vec{x}$. The crucial observation is that one can estimate the maximal degree of the functions $f_{P,q,t}$ in terms of t. Each processor has a fixed initial state, so $f_{P,q,0}$ is a constant function 0 or 1, for each q and P. These functions have degree 0. If C_i is one of the input cells, then two initial contents of C_i are possible. If x_i is the variable denoting the ith input bit, then these states of C_i are represented by the polynomials x_i and $1 - x_i$ of degree 1. Other contents are not possible and therefore are represented by the constant polynomial 0. We may assume that the processors do not forget information. In this case, each processor state is determined one to one by a sequence of the symbols already read. It follows that if a processor P in state q at step t reads from a cell C that contains a symbol s, then the state of P changes to the state that corresponds to the polynomial $f_{P,q,t-1} \cdot f_{C,s,t-1}$. The degree of this polynomial is at most the sum of the degrees of $f_{P,q,t-1}$ and $f_{C,s,t-1}$. Now we inspect what happens in the case of a write operation. The important and usually difficult case is when no processor writes at step t into a cell C containing a symbol s. This happens if and only if $f_{C,s,t-1} = 1$ and $f_{P_i,q_i,t} = 0$, for each P_i, q_i such that processor P_i writes in state q_i into C at step t. No concurrent write can ever occur, hence the polynomial $f_{P_1,q_1,t} + f_{P_2,q_2,t} + \ldots + f_{P_i,q_i,t}$ correctly represents the situation "somebody writes into C at step t". So the polynomial $f_{C,s,t}$ is equal to $f_{C,s,t-1} \cdot (1 - (f_{P_1,q_1,t} + f_{P_2,q_2,t} + \ldots + f_{P_i,q_i,t}))$. The degree of $f_{C,s,t}$ is therefore at most the degree of $f_{C,s,t-1}$ plus the maximum of the degrees of $f_{P_1,q_1,t}, f_{P_2,q_2,t}, \ldots, f_{P_i,q_i,t}$.

Summarizing our observations, if p_t denotes the maximal degree of the polynomials $f_{P,q,t}$ over all processors P and states q, and c_t denotes the maximal degree of the polynomials $f_{C,s,t}$ over all cells C and symbols s, then the following holds:

$$p_0 = 0, \quad c_0 = 1 \ ;$$
$$p_{i+1} \le p_i + c_i, \quad c_{i+1} \le p_{i+1} + c_i \quad \text{for } i \ge 0.$$

It follows that $p_t \le F_{2t}$ and $c_t \le F_{2t+1}$. If a CREW PRAM computes a function f in T steps, then after step T the output cell C stores the value of f. Hence $f(\vec{x}) = 1$ if and only if $f_{C,1,T}(\vec{x}) = 1$, that is, $f = f_{C,1,T}$. So $\deg(f) \le F_{2T+1}$, and $T \ge \phi(\deg(f))$. This completes the proof of Theorem 2.3.

In many cases, determining the degree of a Boolean function is not difficult. We can make the things even easier as shown by the following theorems:

Theorem 2.4 *If f is a Boolean function of n arguments and $|f^{-1}(1)| = 2^i \cdot u$ for u odd, then each CREW PRAM computing f makes at least $\phi(n - i) \approx 0.72 \log(n - i)$ steps.*

Let $\text{PARITY}_n(x_1, \ldots, x_n) = \sum x_i \pmod 2$.

Theorem 2.5 *If f is a Boolean function of n arguments and*

$$\left| \left\{ \vec{a} \mid f(\vec{a}) = 1 \wedge \text{PARITY}_n(\vec{a}) = 0 \right\} \right| \neq \left| \left\{ \vec{a} \mid f(\vec{a}) = 1 \wedge \text{PARITY}_n(\vec{a}) = 1 \right\} \right|,$$

then each CREW PRAM computing f makes at least $\phi(n) \approx 0.72 \log(n)$ steps.

For the first theorem, one can show that if $|f^{-1}(1)| = 2^i \cdot u$ for u odd, then $\deg(f) \le n - i$. The second theorem follows from the fact that the coefficient of the monomial $x_1 x_2 \cdots x_n$ in the polynomial representing f is equal to $\pm \sum_{\vec{a} \in f^{-1}(1)} (-1)^{PARITY_n(\vec{a})}$.

2.1.3 Matching upper bounds

Since most Boolean functions of n arguments have degree n [6], $\phi(n) \approx 0.72 \log n$ is the lower bound for most Boolean functions. On the other hand, each Boolean function of n arguments can be computed in time $\phi(n) + 1$ by a CREW PRAM with $n \cdot 2^n$ processors. This can be done as follows (for a precise description see [17]): for each possible string $s = [s_1, \ldots, s_n]$ of n bits, there is a group of n processors G_s that in one step copies the input string into cells $C_{s,1}, \ldots, C_{s,n}$. Then for each $s_i = 1$, the content of the cell $C_{s,i}$ is changed from 1 to 0 or from 0 to 1. Next, G_s computes the OR_n of the bits stored in $C_{s,1}, \ldots, C_{s,n}$. This is 0 if and only if the input string is equal to s. Hence for an input string s, only the group G_s gets 0 as the result. Then the first processor of G_s writes the value of the function on s into the output cell.

It is interesting to see that for many important functions, the computation time $\phi(n)$ can be almost achieved with only n processors, as shown by Dietzfelbinger, Kutyłowski and Reischuk [7]:

Theorem 2.6 *The following can be performed by n-processor CREW PRAMs in time* $\phi(n) + o(\log n)$:

- *evaluating Boolean formulas of size n and depth $\log n$,*

- *computing symmetric functions of n bits,*

- *computing parallel prefix for a product of n arguments for each associative operation over a k-valued domain for $k = o(\sqrt{\log n})$ (hence for instance, adding two n-bit binary numbers),*

- *sorting strings of n bits.*

There is a rich variety of techniques used by the above algorithms. We sketch only one method that is quite frequently used. Consider for example the function PARITY_n. The CREW PRAM computation that we describe consists of several stages. With the beginning of each stage i we associate values $y_{i,1}, \ldots, y_{i,s(i)}$ such that $\mathrm{PARITY}_{s(i)}(y_{i,1}, \ldots, y_{i,s(i)})$ is equal to the PARITY of the input string. The number $s(i)$ is getting smaller after each stage, until finally $s(i) = 1$ after the last stage. Let $k = k(i) = \max\{j \mid n/s(i) \geq 2^j\}$. Hence each variable $y_{i,j}$ corresponds to at least 2^k processors. The stage i is performed in the following way: Divide the values $y_{i,1}, \ldots, y_{i,s(i)}$ into disjoint groups of k elements, each group corresponding to $k \cdot 2^k$ processors. Then compute the PARITY of each group using the time optimal algorithm described above. The results are taken as the values $y_{i+1,1}, \ldots, y_{i+1,s(i+1)}$ used by the next stage. Hence $s(i + 1) = s(i)/k(i)$. Note that $n/s(i + 1)$ is bigger than $n/s(i)$ and therefore the groups considered for stage $i + 1$ are bigger than these of stage i. Such dynamic incrementing the size of the groups leads to $L = O(\log(n)/\log\log(n))$ stages of the above algorithm. For each stage, few extra steps are necessary, hence together the algorithm runs in time

$$\sum_{i=1}^{L}(\phi(k(i)) + 1 + c) \approx \sum_{i=1}^{L} 0.72 \log(k(i)) + O(L) = 0.72 \log(\prod k(i)) + O(L)$$

$$= 0.72 \log(n) + O(L) = 0.72 \log(n) + O(\log(n)/\log\log(n)).$$

2.2 CREW PRAMs working on restricted domains

So far we have considered Boolean functions on domains $\{0,1\}^n$, $n \in I\!N$. The situation might be quite different if a domain is only a subset of $\{0,1\}^n$. We discuss it on the example of the k-compaction problem. The inputs for k-compaction problem are strings containing at most k ones and otherwise 0's. The output is a set of all positions in the input string where the 1's are stored. Hagerup and Nowak [14] show tight bounds for solving k-compaction problem:

Theorem 2.7 *When no restrictions are placed on the number of processors, k-compaction problem for strings of length n can be solved by a CREW PRAM in time $O(\min\{k, \log n\})$, and at least $\Omega(\min\{k, \log n\})$ steps are necessary.*

The upper bound is straightforward. The proof of the lower bound uses similar technique as introduced in section 2.1.1. On the other hand, a direct application of the methods based on degree complexity yields only a lower bound $\Omega(\log k)$.

Note that 2-compaction problem for strings of length n can be solved in a constant time by an n^2-processor CREW PRAM, and in $O(\log \log n)$ steps by an n-processor CREW PRAM.

For the first algorithm, for every pair of input bits there is a processor testing if they are different from 0. The single processor that encounters two values different from 0 may write the result into the output cell without causing a write conflict. If no processor writes, then there is at most one 1 in the input string. Then for each $i \leq n$, processor P_i reads the ith bit and if it is not equal to 0, then P_i writes i into the output cell. For the second algorithm, divide the input into $\sqrt{n}$ substrings of length $\sqrt{n}$ and solve 2-compaction problem for each substring using $\sqrt{n}$ processors. There are $\sqrt{n}$ results, with at most 2 of them nonempty. Applying the first algorithm, one can find these nonempty results in a constant number of steps with $(\sqrt{n})^2 = n$ processors.

Fich and Ragde [9] prove that this algorithm is optimal.

Theorem 2.8 *Solving 2-compaction problem for strings of length n requires more than $(\log \log n - \log \log(5p/n))/2$ steps of a CREW PRAM with $p \geq n$ processors.*

The idea of the proof is the following. For each step t, a set V_t of input variables is constructed with $|V_t| \geq n^{2^{2t}}/(5p)^{2^{2t}-1}$. The input strings with all variables outside V_t set to 0 have the property that after step t a state of each processor and memory cell depends on at most one variable of V_t. During the next step, a processor knowing one variable of V_t may read a cell knowing another variable of V_t. After reading, the processor state depends on both variables. A similar effect may occur after writing. To find V_{t+1} we define a graph over V_t with an edge between each x_i and x_j such that a processor knowing x_i reads from (writes into) a cell knowing x_j. V_{t+1} is chosen as an independent subset of V_t of the maximal size. By a theorem of Turan, this set is big enough to get the required approximation of $|V_{t+1}|$. Clearly, if a computation terminates after T steps, then $|V_T| = 1$. Hence, $1 \geq n^{2^{2T}}/(5p)^{2^{2T}-1}$ and Theorem 2.8 follows.

2.3 Open problems for CREW PRAMs

The lower bounds yield by critical complexity and degree are independent from the number of processors used by a PRAM. More precise methods, taking the number of processors into account, are still not known. Few upper bounds for the bounded number of processors have been presented in section 2.1.3.

The following versions of CREW PRAMs may be considered:

Oblivious: for each step t and cell C, either no processor ever writes into C at step t or some fixed processor P writes into C at step t, for every input string.

Always writing: for each step t and cell C, either no processor ever writes into C at step t or for each input string there is a processor that writes into C at step t.

Owner write: each cell has its "owner", the only processor that might write into this cell.

Nonoblivious: the model without any restrictions.

Nisan shows that for CREW PRAMs with an unbounded number of processors and cells, these models are equivalent [19]. More precisely, he proves that for each Boolean function the computation times in these models differ by only a constant factor (sometimes they really differ by a constant factor). It is not known whether it is true for CREW PRAMs with a bounded number of processors. A positive answer might simplify the search for lower bounds for CREW PRAMs with a bounded number of processors.

The next important step to make CREW PRAMs more realistic is to assume that memory cells can store binary words of a fixed size that is called *wordsize*. Restricting simultaneously the wordsize and the number of processors may lead to a dramatical increase of computation time, as shown by Bellantoni [3]. Namely, computing most Boolean functions of n arguments takes at least $\frac{n}{w} - 2\log p - 9$ steps on CRCW PRAMs with p processors and wordsize w. This result follows from a counting argument and says nothing about the functions that are difficult to compute on such PRAMs.

3 Nondeterministic CREW PRAMs

At each step, a processor of a nondeterministic CREW PRAM may have different alternatives how to proceed, but no matter how the individual processors behave, no write conflicts are allowed to occur. A function f is computed by such a machine if for all inputs $\vec{a}$ with $f(\vec{a}) = 1$ there is at least one computation that yields the output 1, and for $\vec{a}$ with $f(\vec{a}) = 0$ there is no such computation. Note that the OR can be computed in a constant time in this model. So, the bounds of section 2.1.1 and 2.1.2 do not apply to nondeterministic CREW PRAMs. Quite easily, one can show the following lemma:

> If a Boolean function f can be computed by a nondeterministic CREW PRAM
> in time T, then $f = \bigvee_{g \in \Gamma} g$ for a set Γ of Boolean functions where each $g \in \Gamma$
> can be computed by a CREW PRAM (deterministic) in time T.

Suppose that f is a Boolean function such that for each function g, $0 \neq g \leq f$, computing g on a CREW PRAM requires at least T steps. Then, by the above lemma, each nondeterministic CREW PRAM computing f runs in time at least T. There are many functions having this property. For example, if $0 \neq g \leq \text{PARITY}_n$, then by Theorem 2.5, computing g takes at least $\phi(n)$ CREW PRAM steps. Similarly, if f is a function of n arguments and $|f^{-1}(1)| \leq 2^k$, then for each g, $0 \neq g \leq f$, we get $|g^{-1}(1)| \leq 2^k$, and by Theorem 2.4, computing g takes at least $\phi(n-k)$ steps of a CREW PRAM. Therefore, we obtain the following theorem due to Dietzfelbinger, Kutyłowski and Reischuk [5, 6]:

Theorem 3.1 *(a) If $0 \neq f \leq \text{PARITY}_n$, then every nondeterministic CREW PRAM computing f makes at least $\phi(n) \approx 0.72 \log n$ steps.*

(b) If $0 \neq f$ is a Boolean function of n arguments and $k = \lfloor \log |f^{-1}(1)| \rfloor$, then every nondeterministic CREW PRAM computing f makes at least $\phi(n-k) \approx 0.72 \log(n-k)$ steps.

4 Probabilistic CREW PRAMs

At each step, a processor of a probabilistic CREW PRAM decides by means of a random experiment what computation path to follow. The probability of a write conflict has to be zero. The machine must yield the correct results with probability greater than $\frac{1}{2}$ (unbounded error case) after a given number of steps. We consider also a bounded-error model, where the correct result must be given with probability at least $\frac{1}{2} + \epsilon$ for a fixed ϵ.

4.1 Unbounded-error probabilistic CREW PRAMs

One can easily define a probabilistic CREW PRAM that computes OR_n in one step with probability greater than $\frac{1}{2}$. Simply, a processor chooses randomly $i \leq n$ and examines the ith input bit. If it is 1, then the answer is 1. If it is 0, then the machine answers 0 with probability $\frac{2n-1}{4(n-1)} > \frac{1}{2}$, and 1 otherwise. It is easy to see that if the input string contains a 1, then the machine answers 1 with probability at least $\frac{1}{n} + \frac{n-1}{n} \cdot \frac{2n-3}{4(n-1)} = \frac{2n+1}{4n} > \frac{1}{2}$.

Surprisingly, Dietzfelbinger, Kutyłowski and Reischuk [5, 6] show that $PARITY_n$ cannot be computed by a probabilistic CREW PRAM with unbounded error faster than by deterministic CREW PRAMs.

Theorem 4.1 *If a probabilistic CREW PRAM computes* $PARITY_n$ *in* T *steps (with unbounded error), then* $T \geq \phi(n) \approx 0.72 \log(n)$.

We briefly sketch the proof. For each probabilistic CREW PRAM there is a probabilistic CREW PRAM that makes only one random guess (from a finite domain) at the beginning of the computation and yields the results with the same probabilities after the same number of steps. Each of these guesses defines a deterministic CREW PRAM, and therefore a Boolean function computed by this machine. Let M be such a probabilistic CREW PRAM computing $PARITY_n$ in T steps, and Γ be the family of functions defined by the random guesses for M. For $g \in \Gamma$, let p_g be the probability that M chooses a machine computing g. Define a real-valued function $h = \sum_{g \in \Gamma} p_g \cdot g$. It can be easily checked that for all $\vec{a} \in \{0,1\}^n$:

$$\text{Prob}(M \text{ outputs } 1 - PARITY_n(\vec{a}) \text{ on input } \vec{a}) = |h(\vec{a}) - PARITY_n(\vec{a})|.$$

Hence $h(\vec{a}) < \frac{1}{2}$ for all $\vec{a}$ of even parity and $h(\vec{a}) > \frac{1}{2}$ for all $\vec{a}$ of odd parity.

Since each $g \in \Gamma$ can be computed in T steps, $\deg(g) \leq F_{2T+1}$. Hence $\deg(h) \leq F_{2T+1}$, too. On the other hand, one may show that the coefficient of the monomial $x_1 x_2 \cdots x_n$ in the polynomial defining h is equal to:

$$\pm \sum_{\vec{a} \in \{0,1\}^n} h(\vec{a}) \cdot (-1)^{PARITY_n(\vec{a})} = \pm \left(\sum_{\vec{a} \in PARITY_n^{-1}(0)} h(\vec{a}) - \sum_{\vec{a} \in PARITY_n^{-1}(1)} h(\vec{a}) \right).$$

The first sum is greater than $\frac{1}{2} \cdot 2^{n-1}$, the second sum is smaller than $\frac{1}{2} \cdot 2^{n-1}$. Hence their difference cannot be equal to 0. So $\deg(h) = n$ and therefore $T = \phi(n)$.

4.2   Bounded-error probabilistic CREW PRAMs

Using a result of Szegedy [21], Dietzfelbinger, Kutyłowski and Reischuk [5, 6] show that in the case of the bounded-error model, probabilistic CREW PRAMs are not significantly faster than deterministic CREW PRAMs (this result follows also from the paper of Nisan [19], however this yields a constant factor bigger than 8).

Theorem 4.2 *The probabilistic CREW PRAM time complexity of a Boolean function in the bounded-error model differs from the deterministic CREW PRAM time complexity at most by a factor of 8 and an additive term depending on the error ϵ.*

The key lemma leading to this result is the following:

> *If a Boolean function f is computed by a probabilistic CREW PRAM in T steps with bounded error ϵ, then $T \geq \phi(\sqrt{\epsilon \cdot bc(f)})$.*

5   ROBUST PRAMs

So far, we have not considered PRAMs that allow concurrent writes (so called CRCW PRAMs). It is easy to see that concurrent write capability adds much to computational power of a PRAM. For instance, OR_n can be computed in one step by a CRCW PRAM: First, the input bits are read in parallel by n processors. Then the processors that have read 1 write 1 into the output cell. This is a correct algorithm for COMMON CRCW PRAMs where in a case of a write conflict all processors must attempt to write the same symbol and the symbol actually written coincides with the symbol that the processors attempt to write. The speed-up against CREW PRAMs is dramatic: from $\Theta(\log n)$ to 1 step. However, we are in a typical annoying situation. In order to construct a correct algorithm, we have had to determine precisely how the machine behaves in a case of a write conflict. There are many reasonable ways of resolving write conflicts leading to many different types of CRCW PRAMs. Hagerup and Radzik [15] proposed the most general model of CRCW PRAMs, which they call a ROBUST PRAM. They assume that in a case of a write conflict the symbol actually written is chosen nondeterministically from the set of **all** symbols that are used by the machine. However, an algorithm must compute the correct answer no matter what values appear when write conflicts occur. By this assumption, such an algorithm is working correctly on any CRCW PRAM, in other words, it is *robust* against machine type. This is a nice property, but, as we shall see in the next subsection, the price that we have to pay is unacceptable. Namely, computation times on ROBUST PRAMs are almost the same as in the case of CREW PRAMs. This means that ROBUST PRAMs are significantly slower than other CRCW PRAMs.

5.1   Degree complexity for computations on ROBUST PRAMs

In this subsection we sketch the results obtained by Fich, Impagliazzo, Kapron and King [8] and Kutyłowski [18]. In order to show a lower time bound T for computing a function f on ROBUST PRAMs it suffices to prove that some CRCW PRAMs with specially chosen way of resolving write conflicts require at least T steps for computing f. This will be our overall strategy.

We start with machines of wordsize 1, where each memory cell may store only one bit. Consider the following way of resolving write conflicts. If a cell C contains $h \in \{0,1\}$ and during a given step n_0 processors attempt to write 0 into C and n_1 processors attempt to write 1 into C, then the value written into C is

$$h + (0 - h) \cdot n_0 + (1 - h) \cdot n_1 \pmod{2}.$$

It is easy to see that this definition is consistent with the case when at most one processor writes. The states of the processors and memory cells of the resulting machine can be described by Boolean functions, as in the case of the CREW PRAM. Each Boolean function can be represented by a polynomial over the field $\mathbb{F}_2 = \{0,1\}$. This representation is well suited for these machines because of the way of concurrent writing (summation modulo 2 corresponds to addition in $\mathbb{F}_2$).

We have to estimate complexity of polynomials over $\mathbb{F}_2$ representing states of processors and memory cells after a given number of steps. As complexity measure we take degree, denoted now by $\deg_2$ to indicate that we consider polynomials over $\mathbb{F}_2$. We check that degrees of the polynomials representing cell states approximately double during one step. The important case is again the case of writing. The polynomial describing the state of cell C in which it contains 1 after step t is

$$H(\vec{x}) = h(\vec{x}) + (0 - h(\vec{x})) \cdot \big(f_0(\vec{x}) + \ldots + f_l(\vec{x})\big) + (1 - h(\vec{x})) \cdot \big(g_0(\vec{x}) + \ldots + g_m(\vec{x})\big) \quad \text{(over } \mathbb{F}_2),$$

where polynomial h represents the state in which C contains 1 after step $t - 1$, $f_0, \ldots, f_l$ and $g_0, \ldots, g_m$ represent the states of processors that cause writing 0, respectively 1, into C at step t. Then $\deg_2(H)$ is bounded by $\deg_2(h) + \max\{\deg_2(w) \mid w \in \{f_0, \ldots, f_l\} \cup \{g_0, \ldots, g_m\}\}$. The polynomial representing the state of C after step t in which C contains 0 is $1 - H(\vec{x})$, that is, of the same degree as $H(\vec{x})$. More elaborate counting shows that after step t degrees of the polynomials representing states of memory cells do not exceed F_{2t+1}.

If such a machine computing function f halts after step T, then the output cell contains 1 if and only if f has value 1 on the given input. Therefore $\deg(f) \leq F_{2T+1}$. Let $\text{ROBUST}_w(f)$ denote the number of steps necessary to compute a Boolean function f on ROBUST PRAMs of wordsize w. Thus we have obtained the following theorem:

Theorem 5.1 *For every Boolean function f,*

$$\text{ROBUST}_1(f) \geq \phi(\deg_2(f)) \approx 0.72 \log(\deg_2(f)).$$

In particular, $\text{ROBUST}_1(\text{OR}_n) \geq \phi(n)$.

It is astonishing that, by the above result, computing OR_n requires exactly the same number of steps of a ROBUST PRAM of wordsize 1 as of a CREW PRAM.

In Theorem 5.1, one can replace $\mathbb{F}_2$ by any finite field $\mathbb{F}_p$. Then the time bound is $c \cdot \log(\deg_p(f))$ where $c \approx \frac{1}{\log(2p-1)}$. Thereby, we get lower bounds $\Omega(\log(n))$ for such functions as PARITY_n (it is easy to see that $\deg_2(\text{PARITY}_n) = 1$ but $\deg_3(\text{PARITY}_n) = n$).

The lower bound of Theorem 5.1 holds for an arbitrary number of processors but only for the machines of wordsize 1. However, since one can simulate one step of a ROBUST PRAM of wordsize w by $\log(w)$ steps of a ROBUST PRAM of wordsize 1, we get the following lower bound:

Theorem 5.2 *For every Boolean function f and a prime number q,*

$$\text{ROBUST}_w(f) \geq \Omega\left(\frac{\log(\deg_q(f))}{\log w}\right).$$

We describe the idea of the simulation mentioned above. Each memory cell C of wordsize w is coded by a group G_C of w cells of wordsize 1 so that each bit of a word stored by C is placed in a separate cell of G_C. We describe how to read these w cells in $\log(w)$ steps without using memory cells of wordsize greater than 1 (this is the key point of the simulation). It requires a preprocessing for which we use 2^w groups of w processors each. Each group P_s, named by a binary string s of length w, checks whether the cells of G_C store string s. It can be done in $\log(w)$ steps, for instance by the algorithm of Cook, Dwork and Reischuk [4]. Exactly one group P_s gets a positive answer. Then P_s encodes the content of C in a different way. 2^w cells containing initially 0's are used. The first processor of P_s writes 1 into one of these cells, namely the cell with the index s. Then we are ready for simulation of reading from C. For each processor R of the original machine we have a large set of processors that simulate R. If R reads from C, then these processors read in parallel all 2^w cells that code the content of C. The processors that read the cell storing 1 get full information about the content of C and can further perform the simulation. The other processors fail and are not used anymore.

Theorem 5.2 provides good lower bounds for reasonable wordsizes such as $\log(n)$. There is a lower bound that holds for every wordsize provided that the number of processors is "realistic":

Theorem 5.3 *Let f be a Boolean function. If an n-processor ROBUST PRAM (of an arbitrary wordsize) computes f in T steps, and $\log(\deg_2(f)) \geq (\log \log n)^2$, then*

$$T = \Omega(\sqrt{\log(\deg_2(f))}).$$

The proof is based on the observation that during t steps an n-processor ROBUST PRAM really uses only about n^{2^t} symbols in the common memory. It corresponds to wordsize $\log(n) \cdot 2^t$ and can be simulated with a delay $\log \log(n) + t$ by a ROBUST PRAM of wordsize 1. Hence, if f is computed in T steps by an n-processor ROBUST PRAM, then there is a ROBUST PRAM of wordsize 1 that computes f in $T \cdot (\log \log(n) + T)$ steps. So

$$T \cdot (\log \log(n) + T) \geq \Omega(\log(\deg_2(f)))$$

and Theorem 5.3 follows.

We say that a CRCW PRAM is deterministic, if the result of a concurrent-write operation is uniquely determined by the state of the machine immediately before writing. All lower bounds obtained so far for ROBUST PRAMs were in fact lower bounds for some special deterministic CRCW PRAMs. The lower bounds of Theorems 5.2 and 5.3 do not cover one case: when a ROBUST PRAM uses a lot of processors and the memory cells have a big wordsize. This has a deep reason. Fich, Impagliazzo, Kapron and King [8] show that each deterministic CRCW PRAM with 2^n processors and one memory cell of wordsize n can compute OR_n in two steps. We sketch their construction. They consider the following situation: each processor in a given set W attempts to write its number into a fixed cell. The outcome of this operation, denoted by $v(W)$, depends on the set W. By a set theoretical argument, they show that the set of 2^n processors can be partitioned into sets A, N, D with $|D| = n$ such that the following holds:

$$\exists_{S \subseteq D} \forall_{S' \subseteq D} \ (S' \neq S \Rightarrow v(A \cup S) \neq v(A \cup S')).$$

Using this property, OR_n can be computed as follows: Let each input bit be read by one processor in D. Then during the write phase, processors attempt to write their numbers into a fixed cell: processors in A always attempt to write, processors in N never attempt to write, a processor in S attempts to write if it reads 0 from the input, a processor in $D \setminus S$ attempts to write if it reads 1 from the input. It is easy to see that $OR_n(\vec{x}) = 0$ if and only if the result of writing is $v(A \cup S)$.

5.2   ROBUST PRAMs working on restricted domains

In this section, we show that ROBUST PRAMs may be useful for functions defined over restricted domains. As in section 2.2, we consider the compaction problem. For small k, the k-compaction problem can be solved in $O(\log k)$ time by a ROBUST PRAM with n processors. This is much faster than is possible for CREW PRAMs.

We start with a simple algorithm for the 2-compaction problem. First, we arrange n input cells in a square of size $\sqrt{n} \times \sqrt{n}$. Additionally, we use memory cells $Z_1, \ldots, Z_{\sqrt{n}}$ and $S_1, \ldots, S_{\sqrt{n}}$. Each input cell is read by a processor, and if the cell stores 1, then its name is written into 2 cells. Namely, the processor that reads the input cell lying in the row i and the column j writes (i, j) into Z_i and S_j. Then two 2-compaction problems are considered: one for $Z_1, \ldots, Z_{\sqrt{n}}$ and one for $S_1, \ldots, S_{\sqrt{n}}$, in order to find places where these cells contain symbols different from 0. It can be done in 3 steps by a CREW PRAM with $n = (\sqrt{n})^2$ processors. Note that if the input cells containing 1's do not lie in the same row of the input tableau, then there is no write conflict while writing into $Z_1, \ldots, Z_{\sqrt{n}}$, and $Z_1, \ldots, Z_{\sqrt{n}}$ contain the correct addresses of the input cells that store 1's. Similarly, if these input cells do not lie in the same column, then $S_1, \ldots, S_{\sqrt{n}}$ contain the correct addresses of the input cells that store 1's. It cannot happen that two different cells lie in the same row **and** in the same column, hence at least one of the solutions given by $S_1, \ldots, S_{\sqrt{n}}$ and $Z_1, \ldots, Z_{\sqrt{n}}$ is correct. It is easy to find which one.

The second algorithm, due to Hagerup [12], solves the k-compaction problem for an arbitrary k:

Algorithm 5.1 Let $k \in I\!N$. The k-compaction problem for inputs of length n can be solved in $O(\log k)$ time by a ROBUST PRAM with $\sum_{i=1}^{k} \binom{n}{k}$ processors.

The algorithm uses auxiliary memory cells $A(1), A(2), \ldots, A(k)$ initially containing 0's. For each subset S of the input cells of cardinality at most k, there is a corresponding set of $|S|$ processors. In $O(\log(|S|)) = O(\log k)$ steps, these processors check whether each cell of S contains 1. If it is found true, then the first processor corresponding to S writes the tuple of $|S|$ addresses of the cells of S into cell $A(|S|)$. If there are exactly l input cells that contain 1's, then after the write step: the cells $A(l+1), \ldots, A(k)$ still contain 0's; the cell $A(l)$ contains the tuple of all l addresses of the input cells that store 1's; the cells $A(1), \ldots, A(l-1)$ have unpredictable contents caused by write conflicts. In $O(\log k)$ steps, the last cell $A(i)$ with a content different from 0 is determined. Then the content of $A(i)$ is copied into the output cell.

Now, we sketch the idea of a ROBUST PRAM algorithm for the k-compaction problem due to Kowaluk and Loryś [16]:

Algorithm 5.2 *Let $k \leq O(\sqrt{\log n})$. The k-compaction problem for inputs of length n can be solved by an n-processor ROBUST PRAM running in $O(\log k)$ time.*

(The authors claim that the algorithm still works for larger k's.) We describe only the most important features of the algorithm. The general idea is to write the addresses of the input cells that store 1's into a relatively small tableau of cells. It should be written so that each address of an input cell storing 1 occurs at least once in the tableau (which is difficult) and the tableau contains no garbage (which is easy). Then the addresses stored in the tableau are collected. This is possible, since the size of the tableau is small relative to the size of the input string n, and we can use n processors.

Let $l = 2k \cdot (k-1)$. By a classical result from number theory, one can show that in the interval $[n^{\frac{1}{2k}}, 2 \cdot n^{\frac{1}{2k}}]$ there are at least l prime numbers. We fix l different prime numbers from this interval, and call them $p_1, \ldots, p_l$. The following key property holds:

If $a_1, \ldots, a_k \in \mathbb{N} \cap [1, n]$ are all different, then

$$\forall_{1 \leq j \leq k} \, \exists_{1 \leq i \leq l} \, \forall_{r \neq j} \quad a_j \not\equiv a_r \bmod p_i.$$

The proof is quite easy: For a moment we fix j, $j \leq k$. Let $Z_{jr} = \{p_i \mid i \leq l \text{ and } a_j \equiv a_r \bmod p_i\}$. Clearly, $|Z_{jr}| < 2k$, since $|a_j - a_r| < n$. Hence $|\bigcup_{r \neq j} Z_{jr}| < 2k \cdot (k-1)$, for each j. So, there is $p_i \notin \bigcup_{r \neq j} Z_{jr}$. Then $a_j \not\equiv a_r \bmod p_i$, for each $r \neq j$.

The algorithm uses a tableau with l rows, row i consisting of p_i memory cells $S_i(0), \ldots, S_i(p_i - 1)$. During the first phase of the algorithm, for each input cell j that stores 1, and each $i \leq l$, a processor attempts to write j into cell $S_i(j \bmod p_i)$. (Performing this in $\log(k)$ steps with n processors is not straightforward, but we do not specify more details.) Write conflicts may occur at many places, producing unpredictable results, but by the property shown above, for each cell j storing 1, there is i such that the processor writing j into the cell $S_i(j \bmod p_i)$ is the only processor accessing this cell.

After writing, some cells might be affected by write conflicts. To eliminate any garbage, for each cell C of the tableau storing an $i \neq 0$, it is checked if the ith input cell stores 1. If not, then 0 is written into C.

Now the addresses stored in the tableau are collected. Note that each row contains at most k addresses. The addresses stored in each row are found by Algorithm 5.1. The number of the processors used is at most

$$l \cdot \sum_{i=1}^{k} \binom{2 \cdot n^{\frac{1}{2k}}}{i} \leq l \cdot (2 \cdot n^{\frac{1}{2k}})^k \leq n.$$

Concatenating the sets of addresses from l rows can be done in a straightforward way in $O(\log l) = O(\log k)$ steps.

5.3 Probabilistic ROBUST PRAMs

By the results of section 5.1, ROBUST PRAMs have almost the same computational power as CREW PRAMs. This is no longer true for probabilistic ROBUST PRAMs, as shown by Hagerup and Radzik [15]. They prove that even such powerful CRCW PRAMs like PRIORITY PRAMs can be efficiently simulated by probabilistic ROBUST PRAMs:

Theorem 5.4 *Let $\epsilon, \beta \in I\!R$ be fixed. One step of an n-processor PRIORITY PRAM can be simulated with probability at least $1 - n^{-(\log n)^{\beta}}$ by $\log\log(n)$ steps of a probabilistic ROBUST PRAM that uses at most $n(\log n)^{1+\epsilon}$ processors .*

We sketch the technique leading to a similar simulation for ARBITRARY PRAMs. An ARBITRARY PRAM, in a case of a write conflict, allows one processor (which can be arbitrary) to write what it wants. To perform a simulation of an ARBITRARY by a probabilistic ROBUST PRAM, for each memory cell C where a write conflict occurs, we must randomly choose a single processor that attempts to write into C. Moreover, the probability of the success must be high. For a cell C, we consider an array U_C of $\log(n)$ rows, each row consisting of $e \cdot \log(n)$ cells (e is a constant required for technical reasons). If a processor P wants to write into C, then, during the simulation, P chooses i, for $i = 1, \ldots, \log(n)$, being chosen with probability 2^{-i} (with probability $2^{-\log(n)}$, the processor chooses no row and remains inactive). Then P chooses a number j from the uniform distribution over $\{1, \ldots, \log(n)\}$. Finally, P attempts to write its name into the jth cell in row i of U_C. We say that P is successful if, after writing, the name stored in this cell is the name of P. Because of a possible write conflict, it may happen that this cell stores something that is not the name of a processor that has attempted to write its name there. However, if exactly one processors writes into a cell, then this processor is successful. (The opposite may not be true.)

One can prove that if m processors of the original ARBITRARY PRAM attempt to write into cell C and

$$c \cdot 2^{i-1} \cdot \log(n) \le m \le c \cdot 2^i \cdot \log(n)$$

($c \in I\!N$), then the number of the simulating processors that write into row i of U_C is $d \cdot \Theta(\log(n))$ with probability $1 - n^{d \cdot \Omega(1)}$. Moreover, at least half of these processors will be successful with probability $1 - n^{-d \cdot \Omega(1)}$, if the constants are appropriately chosen. It is easy to mark the names of successful processors written into U_C. Then, for each successful processor, it is checked if its name is stored in the first marked cell of U_C. Since U_C contains $e \cdot (\log(n))^2$ cells, this can be done by a CREW PRAM in $\Omega(\log\log(n))$ time.

6 Exclusive-Read Exclusive-Write PRAMs

In this section, we consider the EREW PRAM, the most restrictive PRAM. There are relatively few results on the EREW PRAM, and there is no deep understanding of the nature of the exclusive read restriction. The results that we present give only some insight into the problem.

In section 2, we have proved lower bounds for computing Boolean functions on CREW PRAMs. Clearly, these bounds hold for the EREW PRAM, too. In the case of the OR_n, we have obtained an exact bound, since Algorithm 2.1 is an EREW algorithm. I memory cells of wordsize n can be used, then each Boolean function of n arguments can be computed by an EREW PRAM in $\lceil \log n \rceil + 1$ steps. No method is known to achieve the computation time matching the bound $\approx 0.72 \log n$, which is the lower bound for most Boolean functions of n arguments. (Recall that it is possible for CREW PRAMs with exponentially many processors.) For some functions, it is possible to achieve computation time $c \cdot \log n$ for a constant c, $c < 1$. We discuss such an algorithm for the PARITY$_n$ with running time $\approx 0.86 \log n$ [5, 7].

The algorithm computes PARITY for larger and larger groups of the input cells. When the computation terminates, there is exactly one group consisting of all input arguments. If a processor P knowing PARITY(A), for a subset of input arguments A, reads a cell that stores PARITY(B), for some subset B of the input arguments, and $A \cap B = \emptyset$, then processor P can add these values modulo 2 to compute PARITY$(A \cup B)$. If forming larger groups, with computing their parities, is confined to reading phases of the computation steps, then it is easy to see that the algorithm takes at least $\lceil \log n \rceil + 1$ steps. The key to a faster computation is to achieve forming larger groups during write phases. As for the OR$_n$, at first it seems to be impossible, since by writing, the old content of a cell is always overwritten. However, we can apply the following trick. Suppose that there are a processor P knowing a number $x \in \{0, 1\}$ and cells C_0, C_1, each storing a number $y \in \{0, 1\}$. Processor P writes symbol '$*$' into cell C_x. Then the cell C_{1-x} still stores y that is different from '$*$'. So if, after the writing, a cell C_i, for $i \in \{0, 1\}$, stores a symbol $j \neq *$, then we can conclude that $x = 1 - i$ and $y = j$. In that sense, the cell C_i codes both values x and y. This effect of appending information instead of overwriting combined with broadcasting techniques described in the next subsection (broadcasting is required since we need two copies of each cell before "appending" information) is the key to computing PARITY of 5 bits in two steps. Applying it as a subprocedure leads to an algorithm with computation time approximately $0.86 \log n$:

Algorithm 6.1 *For each n, there is an n-processor EREW PRAM that computes PARITY$_n$ in $2 + \lceil \log_5(n/2) \rceil$ steps.*

6.1 Algorithms and lower bounds for chosen problems

To get a deeper insight into EREW PRAMs, we consider three problems, for which tight upper and lower bounds are known.

6.1.1 Range searching

Snir [22] defines a range searching problem of size n: For an input consisting of $n + 1$ numbers $x_1, \ldots, x_n$ and y such that $x_1 < x_2 < \ldots < x_n$, find the index i such that $x_i < y \leq x_{i+1}$ (by definition, $x_0 = -\infty$ and $x_{n+1} = \infty$). There is an algorithm that solves the range searching problem of size n in $O(\sqrt{\log n})$ time [22]. Snir shows a matching lower bound:

Theorem 6.1 *An EREW PRAM that solves the range searching problem of size n makes at least $\sqrt{\log n}$ steps.*

For the above theorem, we assume that the input numbers $x_1, \ldots, x_n, y$ are quite arbitrary; more precisely, they can be chosen from a fairly large set. The size of this set depending on

n and the number of processors and cell of an EREW PRAM is chosen so that Ramsey's theorem can be applied.

6.1.2 Broadcasting

The most crucial difference between EREW and CREW PRAMs is that, in the case of an EREW PRAM, broadcasting information from one cell to many processors cannot be done by a concurrent-write operation and requires a large number of steps. Beame, Kik and Kutyłowski [2] show that making m copies of a single cell requires $\Theta(\log m)$ steps:

Theorem 6.2 *Let $m \in \mathbb{N}$.*

- *Generating m copies of a single memory cell takes at least $\approx 0.53 \log m$ steps on every EREW PRAM (the exact value is known and denoted by $\kappa(m)$).*

- *Assume that $k \in \mathbb{N}$ and a cell C may store only the numbers $1, 2, \ldots, k$. There is an EREW PRAM that makes m copies of cell C in $\kappa(m) + O(\log \log k)$ steps.*

First we sketch the proof of the lower bound. Suppose that a cell C may contain only 0 or 1. Then the content of C can be described by a single Boolean variable x. Since this is the only input to the algorithm, each processor state or content of a memory cell during broadcasting is represented by a Boolean formula in variable x. There are only 3 such satisfiable formulas: $1, x, \neg x$. Recall that if s_1, s_2 are different states of a processor (cell) after step t, and f_1, f_2 are formulas representing s_1, s_2, then $f_1 \wedge f_2$ cannot be satisfied. It follows that, at each moment of the computation, a processor (a cell) can reach either only one state, represented by 1, or exactly two states, represented by x and $\neg x$. In the later case, we get a processor (cell) knowing the value of x. Let p_t (c_t) be the number of processors (cells) knowing the value of x after step t. We show that $p_{t+1} \leq p_t + c_t$, and $c_{t+1} \leq c_t + 2p_{t+1}$, for each t. The first inequality is obvious. The new processors knowing the value of x at step $t+1$ are these that read the cells knowing the value of x. There are c_t such cells, hence $p_{t+1} \leq p_t + c_t$. During the write phase, only the processors knowing the value of x can generate new cells knowing the value of x. Each such processor may reach only two different states, in each state can write into at most one memory cell. Hence the number of cells that a processor may affect at one step is at most two. At this moment, there are p_{t+1} processors knowing the value of x, hence $c_{t+1} \leq c_t + 2p_{t+1}$.

It follows from the proved inequalities that $c_t \approx (3.73)^t$. Hence to make m copies at least $\approx 0.53 \log m$ steps are necessary.

In order to get a matching upper bound, we show that one processor P that knows the value of $x \in \{0, 1\}$ can pass this information into 2 cells at one step. Take cells C_i, for $i = 0, 1$, each C_i storing initially number i. If $x = 0$, then P writes 0 into C_1. If $x = 1$, then P writes 1 into C_0. It is easy to see that, after writing, both C_0 and C_1 store number x. This trick leads to the optimal algorithm making c_t copies of a cell storing $x \in \{0, 1\}$ in t steps, where $c_t \approx (3.73)^t$ is defined by:

$$p_0 = 0, \quad c_0 = 1 \ ;$$
$$p_{i+1} = p_i + c_i, \quad c_{i+1} = 2p_{i+1} + c_i \quad \text{for } i \geq 0.$$

Hence to create m copies, approximately $0.53 \log m$ steps suffice. For $x \in \{0, 1, \ldots, k-1\}$, constructing a time optimal algorithm is also possible: First we create $\lceil \log k \rceil + 1$ copies of cell C. Applying a straightforward algorithm, it takes $O(\log \log k)$ steps. Then in one step, we create the binary representation of x, each bit stored in a separate cell. Next, applying the optimal algorithm for broadcasting single bits, m copies of each bit of the binary representation of x are made. Thereby, m copies of the binary representation of x are created. In $O(\log \log k)$ steps, we decode x from each binary representation, getting m cells storing x. The total computation time is $\approx 0.53 \log m + O(\log \log k)$. One can even reduce the number of processors (cells) to $3m$, if the above algorithm is carefully designed.

6.1.3 Merging sorted strings

We consider the following merging problem: Given two sorted strings X and Y of n numbers each. Compute the sorted string of length $2n$ consisting of the elements of X and Y, each element occurring as many times as in X and Y together. We consider two versions of this problem: for the first one, the numbers occurring inside the input strings are 0's and 1's, only. For the second version, these elements belong to a big but still reasonable set of numbers, for instance $\{1, \ldots, n\}$. It is easy to construct CREW PRAMs solving these merging problems in a constant time. As an example, we consider merging of bit strings. If for each bit in X there is a processor that inspects this bit and the bit following it, exactly one processor, detecting the change from 0 to 1 in X, will know the number of 0's in X. This processor writes this number into a fixed memory cell without a write conflict. The number of 0's in Y can be determined in the same way, and the sum of these two numbers can be computed and written into a fixed cell. Then $2n$ processors read from this cell, and each of them produces one output bit. Note that this algorithm cannot be converted to a fast EREW algorithm, because of the concurrent-read operation during the last step that requires $\Omega(\log n)$ simulation steps. In this section, we discuss the results of Hagerup and Kutyłowski [13] concerning complexity of merging on EREW PRAMs.

We start with a simple argument showing that the second problem requires $\Omega(\log n)$ steps. We reduce the broadcasting problem to merging. Let us consider the following strings of length n: $w = <1, 2, \ldots, n>$, $v_1 = <n, n, \ldots, n>$, and $v_2 = <1, n, n, \ldots, n>$. Merging w with v_1 and w with v_2 give results that differ on positions $2, 3, \ldots, n$. Hence, in order to broadcast x, for $x \in \{1, n\}$, it suffices to merge string w with the string $<x, n, \ldots, n>$. By examining any of the numbers on positions $2, 3, \ldots, n$ in the output string, it is possible to determine x. Since broadcasting x into $n - 1$ locations must take $\Omega(\log n)$ steps, merging these strings takes $\Omega(\log n)$ steps, too. One might expect that the same bound holds for the first merging problem. However:

Algorithm 6.2 *Two sorted bit strings of length n can be merged in $O(\log \log n)$ time by an EREW PRAM.*

The algorithm is too technical to be sketched here, and we confine ourselves to few hints. Consider a rectangular tableau with $\sqrt{n}$ rows and $2n/\sqrt{n}$ columns, with column-major order, i.e., the first $\sqrt{n}$ elements of the tableau are the elements of the first column, ordered from the top to bottom, the next $\sqrt{n}$ elements make the second column, etc.. The initial step is to store input strings X, Y in such a tableau, X followed by the reverse of Y. Then each row of the tableau is sorted recursively (it is possible since to sort a row we need only to merge the first half of the row with the reverse of the second half). It is not difficult to see that this yields the correct output string with the exception of at most one column. This "critical" column is the only column that contains both 0's and 1's in the output string. The critical column can be approximately located at an early stage of the computation. Consider a row i. Before sorting the rows, one can easily find the last 0 in X and the first 0 in Y lying in row i. Hence the number of 0's in row i, denoted by z_i, can be easily determined. Then the critical column after sorting the rows is the column z_i or z_{i+1}. Exact locating the critical column is not possible (a "broadcasting" argument can be applied). So the algorithm has to correct the values in the critical column without knowing where the critical column is. The solution is to write correct values into a small area that *surrounds* the critical column. Generating these values and their addresses is the most difficult part of the algorithm that we are not able to expose here.

A close relative of the merging problem can be considered, which is called rank-merging: Given two sorted sequences X and Y of length n each, mark each input number with an element of the set $\{1, \ldots, 2n\}$, called its *rank*, such that distinct input numbers receive distinct ranks, and such that if some input value is smaller than another value, then its rank is also smaller (the ranks should represent a correctly sorted output sequence). Intuitively, the rank of an input number is its position in the output sequence. Adding the restriction that each element of X or Y should receive a larger rank than the element preceding it in X or Y, if any (i.e., the relative order of the elements in X and Y is to be preserved), we obtain the problem of *stable rank-merging*. Hagerup and Kutyłowski [13] show that stable rank-merging requires $\Omega(\log n)$ EREW steps for inputs of length n, whereas unstable rank-merging can be performed by an EREW PRAM that runs in $O(\log \log n)$ time for bit strings of length n.

6.2   Open problems for EREW PRAMs

The crucial difference between the CREW and the EREW PRAM is that in the case of the EREW PRAM information is processed locally, with the "neighborhoods" defined dynamically through read and write operations. It seems obvious that such "local" computations should be slower than CREW computations, where an instantaneous broadcasting of a message to all processors is possible through a concurrent-write operation. There are examples proving this true, but only for restricted domains or functions over large domains [11]. Fich and Wigderson [10] present Boolean functions that can be computed quickly by CREW PRAMs and that require a long time to solve on EROW PRAMs. (Recall that the EROW PRAM is an EREW PRAM for which every cell has its owner, the only processor that may write into it.) They consider Boolean decision tree evaluation problems $D_{m,h}$. An input for $D_{m,h}$ is a string determining queries placed in the binary tree of height h, each query named by a binary string of length m, and a string of 2^m bits defining the values of 2^m possible queries. A standard CREW PRAM procedure computes $D_{m,h}$ in $O(\log m + \log h)$ steps. Using probabilistic methods, Fich and Wigderson show a much higher lower bound for the EROW PRAM:

Theorem 6.3 *Every (probabilistic) EROW PRAM computing $D_{3T,6T^2}$ requires at least $T/2$ steps.*

Because of a complicated information flow in the case of the EREW PRAM, it is not known how to generalize this result for EREW PRAMs.

For the CREW PRAM, time complexity of a Boolean function can be determined (up to a constant factor) in terms of block sensitivity. The lower bound holds for the EREW case, but the tight upper bound shown by Nisan apply only to the CREW PRAMs. For the EREW PRAM, no upper bound except the trivial $\lceil \log n \rceil + 1$ is known. So for functions with block sensitivity $o(n)$, there is a large gap between known lower and upper bounds. To close this gap, presumably new complexity measures (more related to information flow) should be discovered.

Specially interesting seems investigating EREW PRAMs of a small wordsize. For such machines, the information transfer is severely restricted. Determining lower time bounds for this case would say something substantial about communication complexity of Boolean functions.

References

[1] P. Beame and J. Hastad. Optimal bounds for decision problems on the CRCW PRAM. *J. ACM*, 36 (1989), 643–670.

[2] P. Beame, M. Kik and M. Kutyłowski. Information broadcasting by Exclusive Read PRAMs. *Submitted.*

[3] S. J. Bellantoni. Parallel random access machines with bounded memory wordsize. *Inform. and Comput.*, 91 (1991), 259–273.

[4] S. Cook, C. Dwork, and R. Reischuk. Upper and lower time bounds for parallel random access machines without simultaneous writes. *SIAM J. Comput.*, 15 (1986), 87–97.

[5] * M. Dietzfelbinger, M. Kutyłowski and R. Reischuk. Exact time bounds for computing Boolean functions on PRAMs without simultaneous writes. In *Proc. 2nd ACM Symposium on Parallel Algorithms and Architectures* (Heraklion), Association for Computing Machinery, 1990, 125–135.

[6] * M. Dietzfelbinger, M. Kutyłowski and R. Reischuk. Exact lower bounds for computing Boolean functions on CREW PRAMs. A journal version of the first part of [5], *submitted.*

[7] * M. Dietzfelbinger, M. Kutyłowski and R. Reischuk. Realistic time-optimal algorithms for Boolean functions on Exclusive-Write PRAMs. A journal version of the second part of [5].

[8] F. E. Fich, R. Impagliazzo, B. Kapron and V. King. Limits on the power of parallel random access machines with weak forms of write conflict resolution. *Preliminary draft*, 1991.

[9] F. E. Fich, and P. Ragde. *Personal communication.*

*the papers supported by DFG-Schwerpunktprogramm "Datenstrukturen und effiziente Algorithmen" are marked with *

[10] F. E. Fich and A. Wigderson. Towards understanding exclusive write. In *Proc. 1st ACM Symposium on Parallel Algorithms and Architectures* (Santa Fe), Association for Computing Machinery, 1989, 76–82.

[11] E. Gafni, J. Naor and P. Ragde. On separating the EREW and CROW models. *To appear in Theoret. Comput. Sci..*

[12] T. Hagerup. *Personal communication* .

[13] * T. Hagerup and M. Kutyłowski. Fast merging on the EREW PRAM. *Submitted.*

[14] T. Hagerup and M. Nowak. Parallel retrieval of scattered information. In *Pr c. International Congress on Automata Languages and Programming* (Stresa), European Association for Theoretical Computer Science, 1989, 439–450.

[15] T. Hagerup and T. Radzik. Every ROBUST CRCW PRAM can efficiently simulate a PRIORITY PRAM. In *Proc. 2nd ACM Symposium on Parallel Algorithms and Architectures* (Crete), Association for Computing Machinery, 1990, 125–135.

[16] M. Kowaluk and K. Loryś. *Personal communication* .

[17] M. Kutyłowski. Time complexity of Boolean functions on CREW PRAMs. *SIAM J. Comput.* 20 (1991).

[18] * M. Kutyłowski. Lower time bounds for computing Boolean functions on ROBUST PRAMs. *Preliminary draft* , 1991.

[19] N. Nisan. CREW PRAMs and decision trees. In *Proc. 21st ACM Symposium on Theory of Computing* (Seattle), Association for Computing Machinery, 1989, pp. 327–335.

[20] I. Parberry and P. Y. Yan. Improved upper and lower time bounds for parallel random access machines without simultaneous writes. *SIAM J. Comput.*, 20 (1991), 88–99.

[21] M. Szegedy. Algebraic methods in lower bounds for computational models with limited communication. Ph. D. dissertation, University of Chicago, Chicago, Illinois, 1989.

[22] M. Snir. On parallel searching. *SIAM J. Comput.*, 14 (1985), 688–708.

Enumerative vs. Genetic Optimization
Two Parallel Algorithms for the Bin Packing Problem

Berthold Kröger, Oliver Vornberger
Department of Mathematics and Computer Science, University of Osnabrück
Albrechtstraße 28, 4500 Osnabrück, Germany

Two parallel, problem-specific algorithms to compute a certain optimization problem, the two-dimensional Bin Packing Problem, are set against. A parallel branch–&–bound procedure which guarantees to find the optimal solution is compard to a heuristic genetic algorithm which successively improves a set of solutions. Both algorithms were implemented on a local memory multiprocessor system of 32 transputers. Empirical results indicate that - due to the problem's complexity - sophisticated heuristics are the only mean to get reasonable solutions for larger problem sizes.

1. Introduction

Combinatorial optimization means the task of finding an integer solution vector v, which minimizes / maximizes a criterion function $f(v)$ subject to a set of constraints $R(v)$. Since the range for v is discrete and limited, only a finite number of feasible solutions exist, which have to be examined in order to get the solution v we are looking for. Representatives of combinatorial problems are the Traveling Salesman Problem [9,15,19] and the Vertex Cover Problem [18,21,22]. Most of these optimization problems stem from the area of operations research.

Solving an optimization problem to optimality (i.e. to find the best solution) requires a systematic search through the whole solution space containing all integer vectors which accomplish the given task and fulfill the constraints.

Exactly this integer restriction for the components of a solution vector complicates the algorithmic solution of an optimization task. As a consequence most of these problems have the (for the user unpleasant) feature that algorithms for solving them are extremely time- and/or place-intensive (NP-complete, [6]). In contrast to this time- and/or space-consuming behaviour, most users are interested in getting a solution after having waited a "reasonable" amount of time. The arising conflict can be solved in two ways:
The first possibility to reduce the runtime is to prevent to do an exhaustive search within the solution space in any case. Instead, the search procedure is guided into those regions which promise to find optimal solutions and skips regions which are of no use. Following the second possibility, the demand for calculating the global best solution is renounced and convergency towards suboptimal solutions (local maxima/minima) is also accepted. Efficient approaches for strategies of this kind are sophisticated heuristics like simulated annealing, tabu search, neural computing or evolutionary strategies.
In addition, both strategies can be speeded up by parallelization, i.e. by the use of processor networks. Refering to the first approach mentioned above, parallelization means to spread the computational work onto several processors. For an even distribution of the workload over all processors a load-balancing strategy must be integrated into these algorithms. Parallelization of heuristics like neural computing or evolutionary strategies is straight forward as their concepts are inherent parallel.

In the present paper both alternatives are applied to solve a certain optimization problem, the two-dimensional Bin Packing Problem. A branch–&–bound algorithm as a representative for an enumerative search procedure which systematically examines the whole solution space is formulated and subsequently parallelized to make it run on a multiprocessor network. A genetic algorithm, on the other hand, represents a sophisticated, randomized (**not** random), heuristic search strategy which tries to find optimal solutions by provoking an adaptive behaviour of a set of feasible solutions. Genetic algorithms are inherent parallel, which makes their multiprocessor implementation quite natural.

The abilities and efficiencies of both strategies are contrasted in this paper, for which both algorithms were implemented on a local memory multiprocessor system of 32 transputers.

The *two-dimensional Bin Packing Problem* is a special kind of a combinatorial optimization problem. Given a set $R := \{(l_i, w_i) \mid i=1, ..., m ; l_i$ is the length, w_i the width of rectangle $i\}$ of non oriented "smaller" rectangles and a two-dimensional bin B, the task is to generate a pattern how to place the elements of R into B. Packing is intended to be *orthogonal* i.e. each rectangle has to be placed with one of its borders in parallel to a border of B. Suppose B to have a theoretically unbounded height and a given width w, what we are looking for is the packing scheme whose maximal vertical expansion in B is minimal.

A typical input for the regarded Packing Problem where six rectangles have to be packed into B is presented in figure 1 along with an optimal solution (packing scheme).

Figure 1: The two-dimensional Packing Problem; typical input (left), output (right)

The special feature of the regarded problem consists in the enormous size of its solution space. To make the amount of possible solutions finite, only those packing schemes are considered, where none of the rectangles can be moved left- or downwards (these layouts are called BL-schemes in the following). This request means no restriction to the solution of the Bin Packing Problem, because a simple proof [10] indicates that for each non BL-scheme there exists a pattern which fulfils this demand with a decreased or unchanged value of the criterion function. The intuitive arguement of this proof is that the compression of a packing scheme left- and downwards in B (to result in a BL-scheme) might lead to a reduction of its vertical expansion, but will never enlarge it. Even when requesting the BL-condition, the solution space contains at least $m! * 2^m$ different packing schemes (including m rectangles), since already $m!$ different sequences of putting the rectangles into B exist which still do not determine their orientations. In addition, each of these sequences might lead to an exponential number of different packing schemes when trying all orientation combinations. The amount of *optimal* solutions is quite large, too, since each BL-scheme can be duplicated thrice by symmetrical schemes.

The outline of the rest of this paper is as follows:
In the following two sections the branch-&-bound and the genetic algorithm for solving the Bin Packing Problem are proposed. The parallelization of both algorithms is described in some detail. Section 4 contains some empirical results for the parallel implementations of the two algorithms being presented. Concluding remarks will finish this paper.

2. A Parallel Branch–&–Bound Approach for the Bin Packing Problem

A straight-forward strategy to solve the Bin Packing Problem is to generate all possible packing schemes, which obviously ensures to find the one whose vertical expansion is minimum. But due to a "combinatorial explosion" this enumerative strategy will lead to an unacceptable amount of computing time even for modest values of the input size m (i.e. the cardinality of the set of rectangles R).

A classical and efficient approach to work on optimization problems in general is the branch-&-bound technique. The exhaustive search within the solution space is guided by a branch-&-bound algorithm into its most promising parts, with the hope to find a solution which might prove that certain parts of the solution space remain of no use for finding the optimum and can be ignored. A *parallel* branch-&-bound strategy spreads the computational work onto several processors, providing that each processor analyzes distinct parts of the solution space.

To be more precise, a branch-&-bound algorithm can be characterized as follows:

A set of so called *subproblems* is generated and expanded. Each subproblem refers to a partial solution with a subset of R (the smaller rectangles) already being packed into B.

A lower bound is appointed to each subproblem P estimating the quality of the solution that still can be gained out of P. This bound predicts the expected minimum value of the criterion function when further expanding P.

Subproblems are stored in a priority queue according to their bounds, with the subproblem whose bound is lowest at the front. In every iteration step the cheapest subproblem (the one which seems to yield the cheapest solution) is removed from the front of the queue and expanded by the use of a so-called *branching step*. Refering to the Bin Packing Problem expansion of a subproblem in general is done by additionally packing one of the not yet considered rectangles of R.

Of course, a subproblem Q whose lower bound $g(Q)$ exceeds the best solution found so far is not considered any longer. Since these not paying subsolutions are not extended by a branch-&-bound algorithm, a dramatical decrease of the part of the solution space being analyzed by the algorithm can be reached (cutoffs can be made in the solution tree), however without preventing the optimal solution to be found. Thus, the exponential runtime which has to be spent for investigating the whole solution space can be reduced. But in the worst case it is still exponential in the problemsize.

A parallel branch-&-bound approach is used in [17,21] to solve the Vertex Cover Problem very efficiently on a multiprocessor network. Anomalies like a superlinear or a sublinear speedup which can arise by parallelizing branch-&-bound algorithms are examined in [16,22] in more detail. General considerations of branch-&-bound methods can be found in [15] for the sequential and in [16,18] for the distributed case.

Our aim is to parallelize a sequential branch-&-bound algorithm being formulated to solve the regarded Bin Packing Problem. The resulting parallel algorithm works asynchronous, that means, all processors are performing the same task on individual data (on individual, local priority queues) and no processor has to wait for some specific data from a neighbor at any time.

Since hardly any branch-&-bound algorithm is known up to now for solving the Bin Packing Problem and since the sequential branch-&-bound algorithm is a main component of the parallel one, the next section briefly introduces our sequential branch-&-bound algorithm for solving the two-dimensional Bin Packing Problem.

2.1. Subproblems

Each branch-&-bound algorithm works on subproblems. Referring to the Bin Packing Problem a subproblem consists of a subset $S \subseteq R$ of rectangles already being packed, defining a complementary subset $R - S$ of rectangles which still are to be packed. Since lots of totally different schemes might result from packing a set S of rectangles into B, a subproblem which merely specifies its corresponding set S, fails to uniquely describe a (partial) packing scheme. As a consequence, the shape of the occupied area of B has to be specified, too, in order to get a unique representation of a packing scheme by a subproblem. The shape can be encoded e.g. by fixing the locations at which the elements of S are placed in B.

Furthermore, a list of coordinates (called "blocked points") is related to each subproblem, indicating locations at which the subproblem must not be expanded, since this was already previously tried. The number of items in the list grows linear with the number of rectangles being packed; its knowledge is obligatory to avoid the generation of identical packing schemes (cp. 2.3).

The downmost, not blocked upper-left or lower-right corner of an already packed rectangle is called *starting point*. This point suggests a location where one of the remaining rectangles from $R - S$ can be added to the scheme by (temporarily) placing the lower-left corner of the rectangle at the starting point. Obviously, a starting point p need not be identical to the definite point in B at which a rectangle is placed, since a placement at the starting point might not necessarily lead to a bottom-left-justified packing scheme (see figure 5). But each starting point p already has to fix at least one coordinate of the definite position of the lower-left corner for each newly added rectangle. For efficiency reasons, the starting point p is also included into the encoding of a subproblem.

Given a starting point p, the definite placement point $\hat{p}$ (i.e. the point at which a rectangle of $R - S$ is placed with its lower-left corner) can be calculated by the following algorithm:

First the chosen rectangle is temporary placed at p, then it is moved -starting at p- left- or downwards as far as possible (depending on which coordinate is fixed by p) to $\hat{p} \in B$, if such movement is possible. (Otherwise $p = \hat{p}$ holds.) See figure 5 for an example.

The corresponding point $\hat{p}$ has to be computed seperately for each rectangle of $R - S$, since the distance for which the starting point is moved left- or downward to $\hat{p}$ might depend on the lateral length of the considered rectangle.

2.2. Sequential Algorithm

The abstract algorithm listed below gives an idea of how the sequential branch-&-bound strategy for solving the Bin Packing Problem works.

Let C denote an arbitrary packing scheme of some rectangles from R suggesting a starting point p and let b be the corresponding lower bound. Then $P = (C, b)$ forms a subproblem. Let $P_0 = (C_0, b_0)$ be an arbitrary initial solution with all rectangles from R being placed and let the packing scheme C_0 reach the (not necessary optimal) vertical expansion b_0. Such initial solutions can be found by the use of a greedy strategy, they serve as an initial upper bound that decides whether a generated subproblem is worth to be expanded.

Subproblems whose lower bound b predict an improved solution (compared to P_0; i.e. $b < b_0$) and which should be expanded are called *reasonable* subproblems in the following. The sequential branch-&-bound algorithm iterates as long as the priority queue contains reasonable subproblems.

Initialization of the priority queue is done by inserting the "empty bin" where none of the rectangles is already placed together with the lower-left corner of B as a starting point and the obvious lower bound $\lceil (\sum_{i=1}^{n} l_i * w_i) / w \rceil$. Then the algorithm looks as follows:

Initialization:

```
Compute an initial temporary solution P₀ = (C₀,b₀)
Put the empty bin with bound ⌈(∑ lᵢ*wᵢ) / w⌉ into the queue
                                i=1
```

Processing:

```
WHILE the queue contains reasonable subproblems DO
    Remove the cheapest subproblem P = (C,b) from the queue
    Create j new subproblems C₁, ..., Cⱼ (for a j ≥ 1)
    FOR i=1 TO j
        IF Cᵢ contains all elements of R
            THEN        {Cᵢ is solution}
                IF vertical_expansion (Cᵢ) < vertical_expansion (C₀)
                    THEN replace P₀ by (Cᵢ, vertical_expansion (Cᵢ))
            ELSE        {Cᵢ is not a solution}
                compute the corresponding lower bound bᵢ for Cᵢ
                IF bᵢ < b₀
                    THEN insert (Cᵢ, bᵢ) into the queue
```

After termination of this algorithm P_0 contains the optimal solution, i.e. C_0 is the cut whose vertical expansion of value b_0 is minimal.

For a complete understanding of the algorithm listed above, the following topics still have to be explained:

- How does the expansion of a subproblem C to the new subproblems $C_1, ..., C_j$ proceed? (or: How does the branching step work ?)

- How is the lower bound refering to a subproblem C computed ?

2.3. Branching Step

Besides its most important requirement to generate all valid orthogonal, bottom-left-justified packing schemes, the *branching step* should be efficiently applicable within a parallel algorithm, too.

De Cani [2] assigns an unique identity $\in \{r_1, ..., r_m\}$ to each member of R to be able to generate all permutations $(r_{i_1}, ..., r_{i_m})$ which is a mean to verify the creation of all possible packing schemes. In a precomputation phase the currently considered permutation is analyzed whether it leads to a packing scheme which has already been generated before. If not, the permutation is worked out towards a complete packing scheme in the following way: As determined by their sequence in the considered permutation, the rectangle r_{i_j} successively is placed in the current scheme (formed by having placed $r_{i_1}, ..., r_{i_{j-1}}$) at all locations where it leads to an allowable BL-scheme. Having sucessfully included the rectangle r_{i_j} at least in one of its possible orientations into the scheme, the previous procedure is applied to rectangle $r_{i_{j+1}}$, else it is applied to the rectangle r_{i_j} again at a modified location.

Application of De Cani's branching rule within a parallel algorithm seems to be less efficient, as – besides the partial packing schemes which are distributed among processors – the corresponding permutation of the identities has to be exchanged as well.

The branching step we have developed follows a different strategy: Here, the location (i.e. the starting point $p \in B$) is fixed and *all remaining* rectangles of $R - S$ are to be placed in both orientations at a point $\hat{p} \in B$ resulting from p. Again, each addition of a rectangle must preserve the BL-condition and then forces to generate a new subproblem. Packing an element r_i of R –

S is omitted at a point $\hat{p}$ if it would cause r_i to overlap with another rectangle of S. In difference to De Cani, our strategy makes no use of a predefined sequence according to which the rectangles are to be placed and it avoids the formation of large "holes" in the packing scheme since new rectangles are always placed at the border of the current scheme.

To describe the branching step used in our algorithm in more detail, the following definitions are needed:

Each pair $p_1 = (x_1, y_1), p_2 = (x_2, y_2)$ of points from B can be arranged by the following irreflexive partial order:

$$p_1 <_S p_2 :\Leftrightarrow (y_1 < y_2) \text{ or } (y_1 = y_2 \text{ and } x_1 < x_2)$$

Let (C, b) denote the subproblem which is to be expanded, where C describes a (not complete) packing scheme for a subset $S \subset R$ of already positioned rectangles and where $p = (x, y) \in B$ is chosen as a starting point.

A point $\tilde{p} = (\tilde{x}, \tilde{y})$ in B is called *successor* of a starting point $p = (x, y)$, iff

  i) $\tilde{p}$ is a lower-right or upper-left corner of some rectangle r_1 of S

  ii) $\tilde{p}$ is not an element of the left or lower border of some rectangle $r_2 \neq r_1$, besides as a cornerpoint.

  iii) $p <_S \tilde{p}$ and no $\hat{p} \in B$ exists with: $p <_S \hat{p} <_S \tilde{p}$ ($\tilde{p}$ is the "smallest" successor).

In an analogous way $\bar{p}$ is defined as a *predecessor* of p, when iii) is replaced by $\bar{p} <_S p$. Referring to figure 4, $\tilde{p}$ is the successor of p and p is the predecessor of $\tilde{p}$.

Expansion of a packing scheme C is done in two successive steps:

In the first part of the branching step several new subproblems may be generated. All rectangles of $R - S$ which fit into the width at the starting point p (see Figure 5) are consecutively placed at their definite starting point $\hat{p}$ generating a new subproblem for each of this placements. Remind that each non square element of $R - S$ may be rotated for 90° before doing this test, since no orientation of the rectangles has to be respected. As a consequence, at most two expanded subproblems are generated for each non square element of $R - S$. Since identical packing schemes should not be generated twice, moving a rectangle towards its definite placement point must not end with $\hat{p}$ being identical to a point in B which was blocked (see below!) in a previous branching step. Having found a valid point $\hat{p}$, the enlarged subproblem is generated by orthogonally placing the considered rectangle of $R - S$ with its lower-left corner at $\hat{p}$. Calculation of the successor of $\hat{p}$ brings the generation of a new subproblem to an end.

At most one additional subproblem is generated in the second part of the branching step. Now, none of the rectangles of $R - S$ is placed with its lower-left corner at the starting point p, but p is blocked for placing any rectangle. As a consequence there is left some waste at p. Without having enlarged the packing scheme, the successor $\tilde{p}$ of p is immediately calculated by examining all upper-left and lower-right corners of the rectangles in the pattern (see figure 4). If no successor of p can be found, the branching step terminates.

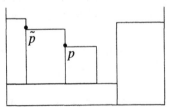
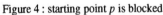

Figure 4 : starting point p is blocked

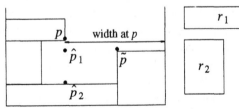

Figure 5 : moving the starting point p to $\hat{p}_i$ for $r_i \in R - S$

The intention to introduce the successor notation is to ensure the placement of rectangles as downmost and as leftmost in B as possible(see figures 4 & 5). However, in order to generate all (and consequently for certain instances the optimal packing schemes), it might be useful not to place a rectangle at the current point p, but to leave a hole at p. Instead the expansion of a subproblem is continued with a successor $\tilde{p}$ of p as a starting point. The necessity for the second part of the branching step is motivated best by the following example:

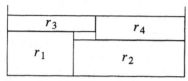

Figure 6 : optimal layout for 4 rectangles

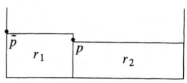

Figure 7 : generated subproblem

Figure 6 shows an optimal layout of the four rectangles r_1, r_2, r_3 and r_4. The subproblem with the rectangles r_1 and r_2 already placed as it would be generated by our branching step is illustrated in figure 7. Let p denote the starting point. Merely placing the rectangles r_3 and r_4 at p without blocking p will never lead to an optimal packing scheme, since this requires to skip p and to put the next rectangle at a successor $\tilde{p}$ of p.

As a consequence, blocked starting points can be characterized by the fact that they must not be used as starting points to find definite placement points. This implies a "hole" in the packing scheme. Each blocked point has to be a predecessor of the current starting point. But, not all predecessors of a starting point must be blocked, since the placement of rectangles at some of the predecessors might have failed due to the small height over these points.

As mentioned above (cp. figure 5), several different placement points can be appointed to a starting point p when moving (different) rectangles downwards. But, moving different rectangles leftwards towards their definite placement point, our branching step ensures that this movement will always result in an unique placement point.

Another difficulty occurs when moving rectangles downwards towards their definite placement points. For an example consider figure 5. Suppose $\tilde{p}$ has been blocked, resulting in the packing scheme presented in figure 5. Temporary packing rectangle r_2 at the starting point p and moving r_2 downwards into its definite placement point $\hat{p}_2$ causes a situation in which the lower-right corner of r_2 becomes a predecessor of the previously blocked point $\tilde{p}$. According to our branching step, $\tilde{p}$ would be selected for a starting point in a forthcoming branching step. Since $\tilde{p}$ is still blocked, no rectangle can be placed at this point. For this reason, $\tilde{p}$ is unblocked in order to not prevent some solutions to be generated.

2.4. Lower Bound

For computing the *lower bound* which estimates the quality of a subproblem P we have invented a collection of heuristics, each of which works for certain specific schemata of packing schemes. A straight-forward lower bound is calculated by simply adding the areas of the elements of $R - S$ to the area overflowing the starting point $p = (x, y)$ and then dividing this sum by the width w of B and adding the resulting value (rounded off) to x. Unfortunately, the quality of this bound is poor. For some packing schemes however, more precise predictions are currently not possible. Further implemented heuristics, in general, try to get a more precise prediction of the expected vertical expansion by looking in detail at the current subproblem. Then, specific features of the considered subproblem (like too small widths at the starting point) are examined as well as specific features of some elements of $R - S$ (like maximal length / width of a rectangle from $R - S$). All these heuristics can be computed very efficiently, but some work still has to be done in order to improve the quality of this bound, i.e. to improve the ability to predict the value of the criterion function as early as possible.

In contrast to the general branch-&-bound strategy which was proposed in the previous section, not only the bound determines the position at which a subproblem is inserted into the queue (which influences the selection rule of the branch-&-bound algorithm). Caused by the difficulties to calculate a sharp lower bound, further heuristics had to be implemented to indicate the quality of a subproblem. As a consequence, subproblems are stored according to a key which is computed by concatenating the lower bound with a second value. Either this second key equals the cardinality of the corresponding set $R - S$ or a number which indicates the density (i.e. the percentual amount of the area which is covered by rectangles to the rectangular area which is spent for this packing scheme) of the present scheme. Thus, if two subproblems have the same lower bound, the subproblem whose value of the second key is smaller is inserted at a higher priority position in the queue. Choosing the second key according to the first variant mentioned above, a depth-first search is supported, since almost "complete" subproblems are favoured as long as the bound remains the same. The experiments we made pointed out that this strategy does not lead to satisfying results, so that we applied the density-heuristic to support the evaluation of subproblems.

2.5. Parallel Branch-&-Bound

In order to reduce the exponential runtime (exponential in the cardinality of R) needed by the sequential branch-&-bound algorithm we have developed a scheme which modifies these algorithms to make them run on a transputer network. The resulting distributed algorithm works asynchronously with each transputer performing an identical algorithm, working on its local memory and communicating with other processors only by sending messages.

2.5.1. Necessity for Load Balancing

The lack of a global memory in a transputer network forces to emulate the single priority queue which was implemented in the sequential algorithm. In our distributed version each processor maintains its individual, local priority queue to store the subproblems it generates. Thus, the content of the single, sequential queue is spread in the distributed algorithm over several processors in the network.

Consider an implementation where each processor is only allowed to exclusively work on its local priority queue and each processor refrains from sending / receiving of subproblems to / from a neighbor. Then, the following effects will occur:

First, some processor's priority queue might run empty, i.e. might not contain any reasonable subproblems promising a better solution than the current one, whilst other processors are working on their hugely filled queues. The affected processors become idle. This phenomenon results from the fact that some subproblems are in a way "easier" to solve, they need only very few further branching steps either to get a solution or to increase the bound to a value which is unacceptable high. Especially when this effect occurs in an early stage of the branch-&-bound algorithm and the affected processors remain idle for the major part of the distributed runtime, the efficiency of the whole algorithm is heavily reduced.

Second, it is not advisable to let a processor work on subproblems regardless of the quality of their corresponding lower bounds. Too "expensive" subproblems will probably not lead to the optimal solution and therefore it is useful to provide each processor with subproblems that are of minimal cost within the whole network.

Third, it may happen that some processors generate and work on subproblems that can be proven to be of no use for solving the problem, whilst other processors have lots of promising subproblems in their queues. This effect occurs, if some processors do not get knowledge about the quality of the best solutions being found by remote processors. Then, these processors might consider subproblems as reasonable (worth to be expanded), although the corresponding lower bound value exceeds the vertical expansion of the current best solution found elsewhere in the network.

A main design strategy for our parallelization scheme therefore is to prevent the occurence of the described effects and to enable each processor to work on reasonable subproblems almost for the whole run of the distributed algorithm. To achieve this, we had to implement strategies which support the exchange of subproblems and the distribution of solutions over the whole network, i.e. we had to do some kind of *load balancing*.

2.5.2. Scheme of the Distributed Algorithm

For each transputer the distributed branch-&-bound algorithm schematically looks as follows:

PAR

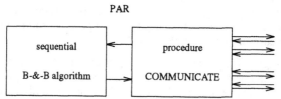

Figure 8 : scheme of the distributed branch-&-bound algorithm for one processor

Essentially on each processor in the network two processes are running in parallel:

On the one hand a sequential branch-&-bound algorithm is implemented which is very similar to one previously described. Differences are caused by the individual initialization of each queue and the location of the queues, which was chosen to be in the parallel communication process. Initializing each queue individually is obligatory to effect that no two processors are working on identical subproblems.

For initializing the queues, each processor calculates according to its processor_id i ($i \in \{0, ..,31\}$) the ith leaf in a fragment of the sequential solution tree, whose leftmost nodes on depth 1 are expanded in order to get at least as many subproblems as the number of processors in the network. (For reasonable sizes of R only some nodes on depth 1 have to be expanded.) In the *sequential solution tree* the subproblems being generated by the branching step serve as the nodes which are connected by directed edges. An edge (P_i, P_j) from subproblem P_i to subproblem P_j exists, iff P_j results from expanding subproblem P_i, i.e when applying the branching step to P_i. The root of this tree is the "empty cut" where none of the rectangles is already placed (cp. sections 2.2. & 2.3.).

Calculation of its initial subproblems is done by each processor straight-forward merely on the basis of the knowledge how the sequential solution tree looks like and makes **no** use of the branch-&-bound algorithm.

2.5.3. Load Balancing

In parallel to the sequential branch-&-bound algorithm the procedure COMMUNICATE is running. The task of this procedure is the organization of the ingoing and outgoing links. Here, the algorithms for doing the load balancing and for controlling the local priority queue are hosted. Load balancing is done similar to [17]:

Each processor assigns a value *queue_weight* to its local queue that represents its quality. Let s be the total number of subproblems in the queue promising a better solution than the temporary solution $P_0 = (C_0, b_0)$, i.e. the queue consists of subproblems $P_1, ..., P_s$ which are reasonable. Let $bound(P_i)$ denote the value of the lower bound assigned to subproblem P_i, then

$$queue\_weight := \sum_{i=1}^{s}(b_0 - bound(P_i))^2$$

Thus, the quality (of the solution which still is achievable) determines the portion each subproblem P_i contributes to the queue-weight, since "cheap", more promising subproblems increase the value of the weight more heavily than less promising. By squaring the difference between the lower bound values and the value of the current best solution the impact of cheap subproblems is respected over-proportionally. Thus, a heap containing 100 subproblems promising to improve the current best solution by 1 is appointed the same weight as the queue containing only one subproblem which improves the current best solution by 10.

In order to do the load balancing as described above and to keep the workload of all processors fairly equal, it is useful to balance the local queues with respect to their weights.

For this reason each processor performs a load balancing step (i.e. initiates certain communications) if either its queue-weight decreases or increases in contrast to the weights of its neighbors. As a consequence, there is the need for each processor to be continuously informed abouts its neighbor's current queue-weights.

If the local queue-weight of a processor P *increases* at least for a fixed percental amount, P calculates the average queue-weight of its neighbors. Should the weight of P's queue exceed (for a certain threshold) the average weight of the neighbors, P sends some of its best subproblems to those neighbors, whose queue-weights are lowest. The amount of subproblems being sent by P depends on the quality of P's queue, but it must not exceed a fixed amount (MAX.SP) of its best subproblems, in order to keep the queue-weights balanced. Following these communications, P recalculates its own heapweight and informs all of its neighbors.

If the local queue-weight of P *decreases* at least for a fixed percental amount, P sends its new weight to all of its neighbors. A neighbor Q of P receiving this weight again is forced (under certain conditions) to calculate the average weight of all its neighbors. But in contrast to the case of an increasing weight, the receiving processor Q may send its most promising subproblems to the neighbor (here : P) which causes this actions by having sent its queue-weight. Again, the neighbor P only gets subproblems from Q if the weight of P's queue is below the average weight being calculated by Q.

This load balancing strategy combines two generally accepted strategies for distributing work load in a processor network which lacks global memory. Most of the distributed algorithms for these networks up to now either use a "send-on-request" approach, where a processor asks for work (subproblems) when its local queue is empty, or a "send-*without*-request" approach, where processors spontaneously and undemanded send subproblems in certain intervals to their neighbors. The strategy we use includes the demanded exchange of subproblems when on decreasing queue-weight the distribution of this weight forces some neighbors to react, as well as the unrequested sending of work when processors submit subproblems because of their increasing queue-weight.

Let queue_weight.old be the value of the queue-weight which was sent last to all neighbors (initially queue_weight.old = 0), let WEIGHT.UP, WEIGHT.DOWN, MAX.SP and TOLER-ANCE be some parameters whose values are experimentally determined in order to optimize the algorithm, let "degree" denote a processor's degree refering to the communication graph and let the "minimal neighbor" be the neighbor, whose most recently sent queue-weight is the lowest compared to the most recently sent queue-weights of the other neighbors. Then, the communication procedure looks as follows (the parts which provide the computational process with work is skipped as well as the protocol for the distributed termination detection) :

```
PROC communicate ()

  WHILE active DO
    on receipt of a subproblem(C,b) from computing process do :
      IF b is smaller than the local smallest upper bound
        THEN   insert(C,b) into the queue
               modify queue_weight

    on receipt of a subproblem(C,b) from a neighbor i do :
      IF b is smaller than the local smallest upper bound
        THEN
          IF computing process is waiting
            THEN send(C,b) to computing process
            ELSE insert(C,b) into the queue
                 modify queue_weight
          modify neighborweight[i]

    on receipt of a new solution(C,b) do :
      IF b is smaller than the local smallest upper bound
        THEN (C₀,b₀):=(C,b)
             send(C,b) to all neighbors
             queue_weight:= calculate new queue-weight
             send queue_weight to all neighbors

    on receipt of a queue-weight w from a neighbor i do :
      IF (w < neighborweight[i]) OR (w = 0)
        THEN
          neighborweight[i]:= w
          average:= average queue-weight of the neighbors
          IF queue_weight > (1 + TOLERANCE) * average
            THEN
              min_neighbor:= i
              FOR j=0 TO (degree-1)
                IF queue_weight is still large enough
                  THEN
                    send_sp:= 0
                    target:= (min_neighbor +j) MOD degree
                    WHILE (neighborweight[target] < average)
                      AND (send_sp < MAX.SP) DO
                        send a subproblem(C,b) to target
                        send_sp:= send_sp + 1
                        modify neighborweight[target]
                    modify queue_weight
```

```
on queue_weight < (1 - WEIGHT.DOWN)*queue_weight.old do :
   send queue_weight to all neighbors

on queue_weight > (1 + WEIGHT.UP)*queue_weight.old do :
   average:= average queue-weight of the neighbors
   IF queue_weight > (1 + TOLERANCE) * average
      THEN
         min_neighbor:= search "minimal neighbor"
         FOR j=0 TO (degree-1)
            IF queue_weight is still large enough
               THEN
                  send_sp:= 0
                  target:= (min_neighbor +j) MOD degree
                  WHILE (neighborweight[target] < average)
                    AND (send_sp < MAX.SP) DO
                       send a subproblem(C,b) to target
                       send_sp:= send_sp + 1
                       modify neighborweight[target]
               modify queue_weight
```

2.5.4. Termination Detection

For detecting the termination of all processes in a network of processors it is not sufficient to examine whether all local queues are empty and none of the computing processes is still working. It might happen that all "active"-subproblems (subproblems which have been generated and are worth to be expanded) are resident neither in a priority queue nor in a computing process, since some subproblems might be in transmisson to a neighboring processor when the test for idlenesss is made. That's why each termination detection that merely checks the current state of the queues and of the computing processes must fail and more sophisticated termination detection schemes are necessary.

Termination of our distributed algorithm is detected by a "two-wave"-algorithm similar to [5]. The protocol used in our algorithm makes heavily use of of a hamiltonian cycle which is included in our network topology and which assigns to each processor an unique *ring neighbor*. The implemented termination detection protocol looks as follows:

Each processor is in one of the states {*white, black, colorless*} and its initial state is *colorless*. Being in one of the states {*white, black*}, a processor returns to the state *colorless* when receiving a reasonable subproblem from a neighbor.

If the transputer whose processor_id i equals 0 gets idle, its state is changed to *white* and a *white*-token is passed to its ring neighbor. On receiving this message, a processor whose id $i \neq 0$ changes its state to *white* if it is idle, otherwise it keeps the token and forwards it the next time the processor becomes idle.

When processor 0 receives the *white*-token and still is in the *white_state*, it changes its state to *black* and forwards a *black*-token to its ring neighbor. Being in state *colorless* when receiving the *white*-token, processor 0 starts a new *white*-token the next time it becomes idle.

On receiving a *black*-token each processor (exception: processor 0) forwards this message when being in a state $\neq$ *colorless*, otherwise the color of the token is changed to white and forwarded the next time this processor becomes idle.

Termination is detected if processor 0 receives a *black*-token.

3. A Parallel Genetic Algorithm for the Bin Packing Problem

Along with the rise of parallel computers in the 80s, the demand for adequate distributed software (which can efficiently solve cpu-intensive tasks) was increasing, too. For simplicity reasons, these demands were satisfied first by modifying former sequential algorithms in order to make them run on processor networks. More elegant approaches to implement parallel problem solvers on a parallel architecture make use of inherent parallel algorithms. Their method of working very often is borrowed from nature, as neural networks model the brain's way of working and genetic algorithms model the biological evolutionary process.

Genetic algorithms are one of the most promising approaches to apply concepts from nature as an example how to solve certain problems. By the use of genetic operators as mutation, selection and crossover a population of candidate solutions is continously improved until either all individuals of the population stagnate in not necessary global extremes or a fixed number of generations is completed. As in nature, the genetic operators do not work on the individuals as they appear "in real life", but on their chromosomal representation. The individuals are encoded to enable certain modifications on a genetic level. Different to nature is that the size of the population is fixed and that the quality of evolution can be measured in terms of a fitness function which should be similar to the criterion function to be optimized. New trials are generated from the genetic material of a population by selecting individuals whose genes either are randomly mutated or combined with the genetic material of other individuals from the population. These trials (offsprings) are evaluated for their ability to optimize the criterion function and eventually integrated into the population.

As genetic algorithms stand for a randomized search procedure, they do not guarantee that the optimal solution is found. However, several difficult optimization problems have been efficiently and successfully tackled by genetic algorithms.

When implementing genetic algorithms on a transputer network its sparse communication graph means no disadvantage (as it is if highly connected neural networks are implemented), instead it supports the simulation of certain evolutionary strategies (limited neighborhoods) in a natural way.

Applications of genetic algorithms to combinatorial optimization have mainly concentrated for the last five years on the Traveling Salesman Problem [8,9,19]. But the approach was also applied to other representatives from this class of problems (Job Shop Scheduling in [4], Placement Problem in [20]), whose computations are known to be space and time intensive.

3.1. Genetic Encoding

The most obvious genetic representation of a packing scheme results from a directed graph, where each node represents a rectangle in the scheme (together with its orientation). There are two kind of edges, called t-edges and r-edges. A directed t-/r-edge leading from rectangle r_i to a rectangle r_j determines r_j to be an immediate neighbor to the top or to the right of r_i. Thus, caused by the BL-condition each node v_j whose appointed rectangle does not touch the bottom- or left-border of B in the scheme has two incoming edges. These two edges fix the location at which the lower-left corner of the rectangle which corresponds to v_j is placed. Due to the orthogonality of the scheme, it is sufficient to fix the lower-left corner of a rectangle in order to uniquely represent the position of a rectangle except its orientation.

Unfortunately, even small changes in the packing scheme (like turning a rectangle for 90°) might force the modification of almost the complete graph, since some of the relative positions which are valid before moving the rectangle may not be valid after the movement in order to fulfill the BL-condition. For this reason we did not choose the directed graph to encode instances of the Packing Problem, but a directed binary tree. This tree is yield by deleting several edges from the graph described above.

Then, either a t-edge or a r-edge is allowed to enter a node representing the rectangle r_j (exception: root). Consequently, this single edge only fixes one dimension of the location at which the corresponding lower-left corner of r_j is placed. The second (still open) dimension results from packing r_j as a valid BL-scheme. Although each node r_i may have at most one outgoing t-edge and one outgoing r-edge, r_i might determine one coordinate of the lower-left corners of *several* rectangles $r_{j_1}, ..., r_{j_l}$. (Several rectangles are placed immediately above or right to r_i). In this case the $r_{j_1}, ..., r_{j_l}$ have to be recorded in the tree by a sequence of r-edges resp. t-edges starting from the leftmost to the rightmost resp. from the downmost to the upmost of these rectangles.

Transformation of a genetic encoding (genotype) into its outer appearance as a packing scheme (phenotype) is done by successively placing the rectangle whose predecessor in the tree is already included in the scheme, starting with the root node to be packed first. Due to the removal of edges, certain conflicts occur as in general each expansion of a packing scheme brings out two new rectangles which meet the requirements to be placed next. In order to generate an unique packing scheme from a genetic representation, each node is additionally assigned an unique number called *priority*. If a conflict arises, the rectangle of highest priority is placed next.

Figure 9 presents two genotypes which only differ in the priorities (marked as indices to the nodes) and their corresponding phenotype representations as a packing scheme. For transferring the genotype representation into its phenotype the rectangles are placed in the sequence r_1, r_2, r_6, r_5 at their corresponding locations. After having placed r_5, the left hand side example demands to add r_3 to the scheme next, as its priority exceeds the one of r_4. Rectangle r_3 has to be placed right to r_6, but it has to be moved downwards due to the BL-condition. In the right hand side example the priority of r_4 is largest after having packed r_5 so that r_4 is placed prior to r_3.

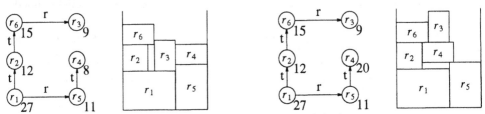

Figure 9: two slightly different genotypes and their phenotypes

The introduction of priorities ensures the uniqueness in mapping a genetic representation onto a phenotype. Of course, the inversion is not true, as each packing scheme owns several encodings. As illustrated in figure 9, even small changes of the priorities may have strong effects on the corresponding phenotypes, which are not predictable when merely analyzing the individual on genotype level.

Summing up, each individual is encoded by a quadrupel $G = (V, E, o, p)$ with $V = \{r_1, ..., r_n\}$ and E generated as described above. o and p denote two functions with $o : V \rightarrow \{turned, not turned\}$ determining the orientation for each rectangle and $p : V \rightarrow \mathbb{Z}$ its priority.

The most problematic feature of this encoding mechanism is its lack to reveal the admissibility and the quality of the packing scheme it represents. For example, checking whether no rectangle overlaps the borders of B cannot be done on genotype level but always demands to construct the phenotype.

3.2. Genetic Operators

Each evolutionary algorithm for solving combinatorial optimization problems aims at generating individuals, whose value of the criterion function is optimal (whose fitness is best).

To do so, it is not intended to make an exhaustive search over the whole solution space, but to examine only its most promising parts. For this reason, a genetic algorithm in general will not discover the global best solution within a solution space (or will not be able to verify the optimality of a solution), but end in a suboptimal solution of a local extreme.

However, in order to generate as good individuals as possible, an evolutionary strategy submits the individuals to the operators *evaluation, mutation, recombination* and *selection*.

The adaption of these operators to the Packing Problem with respect to its genetic encoding is described in the following subsections. Let $\Phi = (V, E, o, p)$ be an individual out of a population $\Pi = \{\Phi_1,..., \Phi_n\}$.

3.2.1. Evaluation

By means of the evaluation function ε the adaption of individuals to their environment (also called their *fitness*) is measured. For solving an optimization problem it is intended to create an offspring whose fitness is maximal which corresponds to a minimal vertical expansion of the instances of the Bin Packing Problem. However, merely applying the vertical expansion to calculate the fitness of an individual Φ can not lead to satisfactory results: This is caused first by the small bandwidth of reasonable criterion function values, and second by the merely one-dimensional analysis which this criterion function applies to the scheme and which is not able to immediately indicate two-dimensional aspects like the density of the layout.

Let h and w denote the height resp. width of the smallest bounding box covering all $r_i \in V$ in the scheme which is described by Φ and let s_h and s_w be the sum of all lateral lengths of rectangles which cover the top resp. the right border of the bounding box (cp. figure 10).

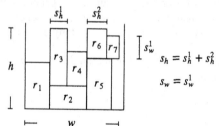

Figure 10: height and width of the bounding box, lateral lengths s_h, s_w

Let *scale* denote a scaling factor which is fixed to $10^{\lceil \log_{10} w \rceil}$, then the fitness of individual Φ is alternatively measured by one of the following evaluation functions ε_i:

$$\varepsilon_1(\Phi) = \frac{scale^2}{(((h * scale) + w) * scale) + s_h} \quad , \quad \varepsilon_2(\Phi) = \frac{scale}{(h * scale) + s_h}$$

$$\varepsilon_3(\Phi) = \frac{scale}{(h * scale) + (s_h + (h - s_w))}$$

Evaluation function ε_1 is based on three characteristic values h, w and s_h of an individual Φ. On identical values of h, the smaller value of w determines which out of two individuals is appointed the higher fitness, otherwise the smaller value of h counts. If two individuals yield equal values for h and w, the individual whose value of s_h is smaller gets the better fitness. A small value of s_h indicates a dense packing scheme below the "elevation" which causes s_h, i.e.

a scheme whose value of h is very likely to be reducable.

Unfortunately, on some instances ε_1 tends to stagnate in solutions which do not use the bin's whole width w, leaving small but high holes which cannot be filled by any rectangle. That's why ε_2 no longer makes use of the width w. Motivated by the good experiences when introducing s_h for fitness evaluation, one can argue that an almost maximal value of s_w must lead to a good individual, too. This strategy is followed by the fitness function ε_3.

Section 4.3.1. proposes several experiments to indicate which of these evaluation functions works best.

3.2.2. Mutation

With the mutation operator $\mu(\Phi)$ a random change of genes (gene = components of a chromosome) is intended. The purpose of mutation is to create new genetic information and it is applied to ensure a certain variance within the population. Refering to the solution of optimization problems, the mutation operator is used to randomly generate new points in the solution space, thus supporting to overcome local extremes. By adjusting the mutation frequency and the kind of the mutation operator its effect can be influenced. In general, the mutation frequency is low which makes mutation quite unlikely to occur.

With respect to the Packing Problem, the following operations are offered to mutate the genes of a single individual:

i) variation of the set of edges E by an operator μ_E to find a new position for one of the rectangles r_j or to exchange the positions of two rectangles r_i and r_j.

ii) variation of the function o by an operator μ_o to alter the orientation of a rectangle r_j (i.e. to turn r_j for 90˚).

iii) variation of the priority function p by an operator μ_p to modify the priority of rectangle r_j.

Application of the operators described in i) and ii) in general demand the replacement of further rectangles in order to ensure a non-overlapping BL-scheme after each mutation. For this reason, the subtree T_s whose root is one of the rectangles to be "mutated" is deleted from the graph (V, E) describing Φ. Then, r_j (and if necessary r_i, too) is (are) placed at its (their) new position(s) and subsequently all remaining rectangles from T_s are reinserted by keeping their sequence, orientations and priorities.

3.2.3. Recombination and Crossover

The recombination operator is used to model the sexual propagation of individuals. Two individuals $\Phi_f = (V, E_f, o_f, p_f)$ and $\Phi_m = (V, E_m, o_m, p_m)$ of the current population are combined to create an offspring Ω which inherits certain genetic information of its parents.

Normally, recombination consists of projecting each chromosome (the carrier of the genotype in cells) of one of the parents to the offspring. As the genetic encoding of the Packing Problems represents each individual only by one chromosome (one tree), the only possibility to make recombination is to do it on gene level. This recombination is called *crossover*.

The crossover operator consequently provokes that genes of the parents are inherited by the offspring. Refering to the Packing Problem it is not possible simply to transmit all genes of one parent each, because this could cause an invalid solution to be generated (some rectangles overlap the borders of B).

Recombination is done in our algorithm between two individuals Φ_f and Φ_m resulting in one offspring $\Omega = (V, E_\Omega, o_\Omega, p_\Omega)$. To do recombination, a subtree $T_s = (V_s, E_s)$, $V_s \subseteq V$, $E_s \subseteq E_f$ of the parent Φ_f is determined which includes at least *min* and at most *max* nodes (*min* and *max* are user-definable parameters). It is demanded, too, that merely packing the rectangles as described by T_s into the bin B, leads to a valid scheme without overlapping the borders of the bin. After having found such a subtree T_s (for an example see the subtree of figure 11 within the circle) the complete subtree is implanted into the offspring, i.e. E_Ω is set to E_s. Then, the offspring has to be enlarged to a complete scheme by adding the remaining rectangles from V − V_s (i.e. the rectangles not included in the subtree T_s).

For this, the second parent Φ_m is traversed in the same sequence as it would be traversed when generating Φ_m's phenotype (cp. section 3.1.). If the current node is from V_s (i.e. it is already included in the offspring) it is skipped, otherwise it is added to the offspring Ω at the downmost location where it leads to a valid BL-scheme. To find these locations, one simply considers all still uncomplete nodes of Ω (i.e. all nodes whose outdegree is less than 2) and determines the node whose upper-left corner or lower-right corner is downmost and able to incorporate the current node as a top resp. right neighbor in a valid BL-scheme. Then, E_Ω has to be enlarged in accordance.

The value of $o_\Omega(r)$ is set to $o_f(r)$ for all $r \in V_s$ and to $o_m(r)$ for all $r \in V − V_s$, thus maintaining the orientation of the parent they are copied from. The function p_Ω is modified in the following way:

$p_\Omega(r)$ is set to $p_f(r)$ for all $r \in V_s$ which means that together with the subtree T_s the corresponding priorities are copied to the offspring. For each $r \in V − V_s$, $p_\Omega(r)$ has to be smaller than each $p_f(\tilde{r})$, $\tilde{r} \in V_s$, but its priority has to be bigger than each $p_f(\tilde{r})$, $\tilde{r} \in V − V_s$ which is added subsequent to the insertion of r into the offspring. This strategy ensures to keep the desired sequence of insertions.

Figures 11 and 12 illustrate the recombination process: Two parents Φ_f and Φ_m (represented by their genotypes (a) and (b) in figure 11) are selected; T_s is chosen to include all nodes and edges within the bolded ellipse. The remaining nodes from $V − V_s$ (i.e. the non-crossed nodes of (b) in figure 11) have to be inserted into the offspring in the sequence and orientation which is determined by Φ_m.

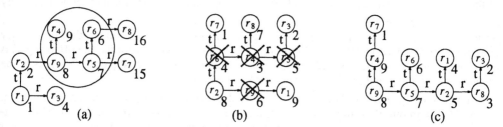

Figure 11 : Recombination of genotypes; two parents Φ_f (a) and Φ_m (b); one offspring (c)

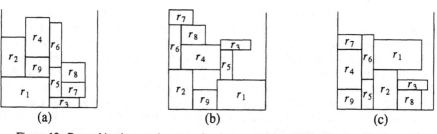

Figure 12 : Recombination on phenotype level; parents (a) and (b); offspring (c)

The crossover operator seems to over-proportionally support the inheritance of the genotype of one parent to the offspring, but this effect can be diminished by means of the parameters *min* and *max*. It is important to note, that each crossover creates a valid offspring which can be directly used to continue the evolutionary process.

3.2.4. Selection

Selection is incorporated into a genetic algorithm to guide the search towards the more promising parts of the solution space. Individuals of higher fitness should be selected more frequent to recombine with others in order to inherit their good features more often to the off-springs. However, a too frequent selection of the same individual will cause the whole population to be interspersed with its characteristics, which results in a loss of genetic manifold. The population will stagnate in local extremes.

For doing recombination, in our algorithm two individuals are selected from the population Π = $\{\Phi_1,..., \Phi_n\}$. This choice can be done according to different strategies, but in general, the following procedures are proposed in literature [7]:

random choice: individuals are randomly selected from the population to recombine, with a uniform distribution over the whole population.

best choice: the individual of highest fitness is selected.

proportional choice: an individual is selected with a probability which is proportional to its fitness. Thus, fitter individuals are more frequently selected.

ranking choice: to avoid the effect that the fittest individuals dominiate the preceding strategy, this rule selects an individual with a probability which is proportional to the rank (and not the absolute value) of its fitness within the population.

In our algorithm the second parent Φ_m is always randomly selected from Π. The choice of Φ_m is unproblematic since its influence on the offspring remains quite small (cp. 3.2.3). The effect of the four selection strategies on the quality of the algorithm are discussed in section 4.3.3. by some experimental results.

Again two strategies are applicable in our algorithm to determine the integration of a newly generated offspring Ω into the population Π. Following the first possibility, the offspring Ω is taken over into Π if its fitness $\varepsilon(\Omega)$ exceeds the fitness $\varepsilon(\Phi_f)$ of its first parent, whereas in the second strategy the population is renewed by Ω on no account.

In order to keep the size of Π constant, the individual whose fitness is worst is removed from the population in our algorithm, if a new offspring Ω has to be incorporated into Π. This strategy models a *survival of the fittest* philosophy, as individuals of higher fitness have a greater chance to survive several generations.

Merely accepting offsprings whose fitness exceeds the corresponding value of its parent Φ_f certainly forces the overall fitness of the population to converge very fast at the beginning, but it will cause a stagnation of the population's fitness if the number of generations increases. As a consequence, the algorithm will terminate with its best individual being equivalent merely to a local maximum. This effect is stressed, if parent Φ_f is chosen to be the individual whose fitness is best among Π. When running our experiments the following surprising observation could be made: When selecting the individual of highest fitness as parent Φ_f and thus directly guiding the search, the results were worse compared to the random selection of both parents. Although convergency was achieved with lower speed, at any time the population provides sufficient genetic material to make progress in search.

3.3. Parallelization of the Genetic Algorithm

Parallelization of genetic algorithms differs from the one applied to the branch–&–bound algorithm. Instead of the distribution of workload among processors, now genetic material is to be submitted. The parallelization of genetic algorithms means a conceptual extension whose ideas again are motivated by their appearance in nature.

For the parallel genetic algorithm 32 Holland-like [11] sequential genetic algorithms are running asychronously on a transputer network of the corresponding size. The parallel algorithm follows Darwin's "island"-approach. On each island (processor) a local population is resident, which evolves independently of the populations on the other islands. An exchange of individuals only happens in irregular intervals, when individuals are island-overlappingly selected for recombination. Thus, each of the sequential (island) algorithms works on an internal population Π_{int} of a fixed size n. In order to enable each algorithm a limited access to non-local individuals, each internal population is enlarged by a set Π_{ext} containing the best individuals being found by neighboring processors. The term "neighborhood" is used in this sense as a logical neighborhood, it does not refer to the topological neighborhood which is determined by the network connecting the processors, but it describes those processors which exchange individuals. In general (cp. section 4.3.2.), the cardinality of Π_{ext} is limited by a value far below the number of processors. The cardinality of Π_{ext} as well as the composition of each neighborhood are parameterized. Again, the concept of the limited neighborhood is borrowed from nature. Most creatures select their partners out of small surroundings, which is intended to be simulated by this strategy.

Then, the distributed genetic algorithm on each processor schematically looks as follows:

```
local.best := Ø
ε(local.best) := 0
generation := 0
initialize local population Π := Πint ∪ Πext = {Φ1, ..., Φn} ∪ Ø
WHILE generation < max.generations
  generation := generation + 1
  select individuals Φf and Φm out of Π
  recombine Φf and Φm to the offspring Ω
  IF random(0,100) < mutation.frequency
    THEN mutate offspring with Ω := μ(Ω)
  IF ε(Ω) > ε(local.best)
    THEN
      select individual from Πint and eliminate it
      Πint := Πint ∪ {Ω}
      local.best := Ω
      send local.best to all neighboring processors
    ELSE IF Ω is selected to be included into Π
      THEN
        select individual from Πint and eliminate it
        Πint := Πint ∪ {Ω}
  IF neighbor i has sent new individual Φi
    THEN
      remove last individual sent by i from Πext
      Πext := Πext ∪ {Φi}
```

To update the sets Π_{ext} on the different processors, the genetic algorithm has to get some additional components:

Each processor keeps the individual of highest fitness which was locally generated (stored as `local.best`). If this individual has to be updated with a new offspring Ω, this offspring is delivered to all processors whose neighborhood contains the sending processor. On receipt of an (improved) individual Φ being created by neighbor i, each processor modifies its set Π_{ext}, as it replaces the former best individual of processor i by Φ.

On each processor, its initial local population is created by the use of a simple heuristic, which places the rectangles in the sequence and orientation to be defined previously. Variation of the sequences and orientations ensures the generation of sufficient initial individuals, whose qualities cover a large bandwidth of vertical expansions. The `mutation.frequency` is a parameter from the intervall $(0,100)$ whose enlargement makes mutation more likely if the random numbers are uniformly distributed in the interval $(0,100)$.

4. Experimental Results

For an empirical analysis, the distributed branch-&-bound and the distributed genetic algorithm which were introduced in the previous sections were implemented in OCCAM on a transputer network of 32 INMOS processors T800.

4.1. Experimental Environment

Each T800 transputer integrates a very fast CPU (sometimes supported by a floating point unit), local memory, a memory interface and four communication links on a single chip [12]. These communication links are the main improvement of the transputer technology. By them an arbitrary number of transputers can be connected to a processor network which offers an enormous computing power at reasonable costs.

Using these links the transmisson of data between two processors is enabled, removing the bottleneck of conventional von-Neumann architectures which have to communicate via a shared bus. Communication over the links does not effect the performance of the CPU, since the autonomous link-interfaces have DMA (direct memory access) capabilities.

Here are some technical data of the T800 transputer type we use:

processor	:	32-bit RISC architecture; 1.5 MFLOPS sustained (scalar) operations
memory	:	4 Kbytes static on-chip RAM; 50 ns memory cycle; 80 Mbytes/sec. data rate
interface	:	32-bit wide multiplexed bus allows direct access of up to 4 Gbytes external memory; data rate 26,6 Mbytes/sec.
links	:	4 full duplex serial links with DMA block transfer; transfer rate 20 Mbits/sec.; on each link two OCCAM channels can be placed in opposite directions

The transputer does not only allow a 1:1 mapping of processes to processors (transputers); it is able to run in a multitasking mode, too. As a consequence, on each transputer several processes may run in parallel (logically !), scheduled by a hardware scheduler.

With regard to the restriction of the number of available links, the topolgies of transputer networks are limited to graphs with a maximal degree of 4. Figure 13 shows the topology of our transputer network consisting of $n = 32$ transputer. The topolgy includes a hamiltonian cycle which is needed for intitializing and controlling the system. Processor i is always connected to processor $(i + 1) \mod n$ and to $(i - 1) \mod n$ which results in a hamiltonian cycle. In addition, for i being odd, processor i is connected to the processors $(i + 14) \mod n$ and $(i - 14) \mod n$ and for i being even (exception $i \in \{0, 6\}$), processor i is connected to the processors $(i + 6) \mod n$ and $(i - 6) \mod n$. Note, that processor 0 only has three of its four links available, since one link is needed for a connection to the I / O - system. The proposed topology has diameter 4 (i.e. the maximum of all shortest paths between each pair of processors has length 4) and an average distance of 2.41 between each pair of processors. Reaching a small diameter of a network is mainly desireable to accelerate the overall distribution of information or work among the processors.

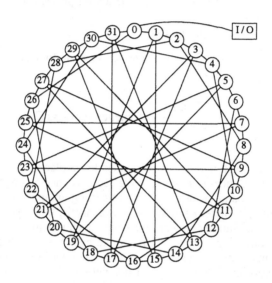

Figure 13: network with $n = 32$ transputers, diameter 4, average distance 2.41

The I/O - System which is connected to our transputer network consists of a transputer board being plugged into a SUN 3/260. Using this hardware configuration an on-line visualization of how our distributed algorithms work is possible. For this reason, data being calculated somewhere in the network can be routed to the transputer which is hosted in the SUN 3/260. This transputer passes the data via a VME-bus to the SUN-processor on which some graphic routines are running. Figure 14 schematically shows the configuration which enables an on-line visualization.

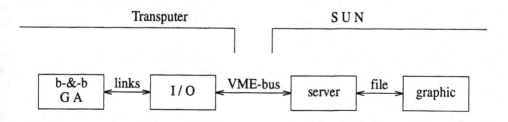

Figure 14: schematical configuration for an on-line visualization

4.2. Results for the Parallel Branch–&–Bound Algorithm

For analyzing the performance of a distributed algorithm one is generally interested in the *speedup* and the *efficiency*. Let $T_k(P)$ denote the execution time needed for computing problem P from a set C of instances using k processors, then the following definitions are valid:

$$S_n(P) \quad := \quad \frac{T_k(P)}{T_{n*k}(P)} \quad \text{speedup for problem } P,$$

$$E_n(P) \quad := \quad \frac{S_n(P)}{n} \quad \text{efficiency for problem } P,$$

$$AS_n(C) \quad := \quad \frac{\sum\limits_{P \in C} T_k(P)}{\sum\limits_{P \in C} T_{n*k}(P)} \text{average speedup for class } C$$

$$E_n(C) \quad := \quad \frac{AS_n(C)}{n} \quad \text{efficiency for class } C$$

Each instance contains a fixed number of rectangles to be placed. The determination of the speedup for each of the instances requires to solve each instance on one hand on a k-processor network and on the other hand on the network containing an amount of processors which is equal to an integer multiple (here: n) of k. For our analysis, the larger network was fixed to contain 32 transputers. The smaller network we have not chosen to include merely one processor, since the memory on a single transputer is limited by 4 Mbytes which was not enough for most of our experiments. Thus, we used a 8-processor network to compute the effiency and the speedup of our algorithm. The topology of this network is similar to the one of the larger network, as it also contains a hamiltonian cycle and includes some chords which are of length 2 (instead of length 5 in the 32-processor network).

Table 1 presents some results we got when testing the performance of our algorithm. The set C of instances we used for these experiments consisted of 10 sets each containing $m = 10$ randomly generated rectangles. The choice of m is problematic, it depends on the amount of memory which is available for the implementation of the priority queue. Using a branch-&-bound strategy each increase of the problem size m leads to a dramatic increase of the number of subproblems to be stored and probably forces to enlarge the size of the queue. It was not possible for us to further enlarge the problemsize m, due to the memory limitations mentioned above.

The width of the bin B was set to 30. The parameter values of the distributed algorithm were fixed to WEIGHT.UP = 0.6, WEIGHT.DOWN = 0.3, MAX.SP = 1 and TOLERANCE = 0.5. These values were found experimentally.

The implemented load balancing strategy provokes a certain undeterministic behaviour of the algorithm, as the distribution of the most promising subproblems is time-crucial. For this reason, each of the generated testpattern was run ten times. The average value of the corresponding results are included in table 1.

As stated in table 1, an average speedup of nearly 4.2, being equivalent to an efficiency of more then 104% is reached when using 32 processors. But, this average value is some kind of misleading, since some of the individual values for the speedup and the efficiency strongly differ.

instance no.	32 processors		8 processors		8 versus 32	
	time	iterat.	time	iterat.	speedup	efficiency
0	18.22	16438	30.13	6641	1.653	0.413
1	20.96	16925	69.89	14322	3.334	0.834
2	23.04	17696	185.83	38640	8.065	2.016
3	7.22	5494	10.67	2156	1.479	0.370
4	75.91	67696	592.21	140662	7.801	1.950
5	10.70	8394	43.25	9112	4.041	1.010
6	5.36	4093	6.06	1164	1.129	0.282
7	35.59	28794	156.41	32310	4.395	1.099
8	106.16	81997	170.75	32645	1.608	0.402
9	5.90	4429	23.65	4796	4.012	1.003
Average	30.906	25196	128.88	28245	4.170	1.043

Table 1: Average execution times in seconds and number of iterations
for 10 packing schemes on 8 and 32 transputers; individual and average speedup

The main question arising from table 1 is why these enormous differences of the individual efficiency values occur. We believe that the deviation is caused by the heuristic which influences the insertion of subproblems into the priority queue (cp. section 2.4.). As the lower bound fails to indicate the value of the criterion function when only few rectangles are placed, the same lower bound value is appointed to many subproblems. Thus, merely the density-heuristic determines the position at which these subproblems are inserted in the queue. This heuristic equals a saw-tooth function; its values first increase when inserting additional rectangles without enlarging the height of the scheme, but but the values suddenly drop when the placement of a new rectangle leads to a strong enlargement of the rectangular shape needed to enclose the packing scheme.

Due to this feature, subproblems which are erroneously evaluated as "good" subproblems may keep this quality during their next iteration steps. As a consequence, the choice of the most promising subproblem equals a game of chance whose winner (32-processor version of the algorithm or 8-processor version) may vary. In our experiences, the 32-processor version in the average had the better chance since an average speedup of slightly more than 4 is reached when enlarging the number of processors by a factor of 4. The algorithm on the larger network, however, does have the small advantage that most of its priority queues are initialized with a subproblem which is on depth 2 in the sequential solution tree, whereas all processors in the smaller network are initialized by subproblems of depth 1.

Having a closer look at table 1, a great difference between the average runtimes (listed in seconds) required to solve randomly generated instances comes to light. Instance no. 6 merely consumes a 1/20 fraction of the runtime needed for instance no. 8, although in both cases 10 rectangles are to be placed. Again, this phenomena is caused by the lack of the lower bound procedure to differentiate between promising and non-promising subproblems and it is stressed by the heuristic we apply to insert the subproblems into the queue. Due to the weakness of the lower bound, in an early stage of the algorithm the density heuristic exclusively determines which subproblems are to be expanded and which remain uninspected in the queue. Having expanded a subproblem, those subproblems which keep their lower bound, but which get a decreased value of the density heuristic are inserted at low positions in the queue. However, those subproblems which increase or only slightly decrease their packing density are very likely to keep their high priority positions. So it might happen that subproblems leading to the optimal solution have to wait patiently in the queue until they get expanded.

In the average, no *search-overhead* appears since the amount of iterations needed in the 32-processor network is less compared to the number of iterations needed on the 8-processor system. This indicates that in the average case the load balancing strategy works well. Again, some of the individual results behave totally different.

Table 2 offers some detailed statistical information gained from running instance no. 8.

Proc. Id.	wait	total	in	out	in_w	out_w	iter	queue
0	7.57	106.79	84	58	222	69	2541	945
1	8.38	106.79	100	56	305	68	2591	1705
2	8.08	106.79	68	98	283	78	2581	1118
3	7.75	106.79	76	62	294	69	2409	1782
4	8.08	106.79	66	72	285	71	2484	2219
5	8.25	106.79	78	64	312	73	2576	1424
6	8.21	106.79	60	62	212	71	2605	1540
7	8.64	106.79	108	60	311	71	2695	1410
8	7.73	106.79	94	96	315	76	2513	943
9	7.55	106.79	94	57	308	69	2709	544
10	8.37	106.79	62	55	280	68	2659	1417
11	7.89	106.79	92	62	295	83	2512	1626
12	7.34	106.80	60	56	283	68	2518	1426
13	8.32	106.80	158	192	330	71	2534	1483
14	7.33	106.80	70	51	287	97	2505	790
15	7.16	106.80	114	62	301	69	2626	720
16	6.76	106.80	64	64	280	67	2514	376
17	7.93	106.80	86	61	286	71	2666	762
18	8.92	106.80	96	140	297	68	2643	1597
19	7.77	106.80	60	64	280	89	2479	1288
20	8.40	106.80	88	68	332	71	2571	1826
21	8.52	106.80	64	70	283	74	2578	1799
22	9.26	106.80	74	128	292	72	2670	2260
23	7.59	106.80	60	60	283	81	2493	1344
24	8.79	106.80	122	170	314	69	2576	2209
25	8.64	106.80	58	74	285	90	2621	2150
26	9.17	106.80	72	124	313	72	2761	1812
27	8.41	106.80	66	64	282	83	2640	1489
28	8.10	106.80	96	64	302	70	2522	1978
29	8.01	106.80	68	88	287	69	2448	1858
30	7.61	106.80	70	136	291	75	2411	937
31	7.27	106.80	70	60	286	82	2562	641
average	8.06	106.80	81	81	292	73	2569	1419

Table 2 : Statistical data for solving instance no. 8 on 32 transputers.

wait	sum of all idle times (in seconds)
total	total time (in seconds) (including computation, communication & waiting)
iter	number of iterations, i.e. number of explored subproblems
in	number of subproblems received from neighbors
out	number of subproblems sent to neighbors
in_w	number of queue-weights received from neighbors
out_w	number of queue-weights sent to neighbors
queue	maximum number of subproblems stored in the queue

As the number of iterations is fairly equal on each of the processors, the load balancing strategy is able to distribute the workload uniformly over the whole network. The average time each processor remains idle sums up to 7.5% of the processors runtime. It is interesting to notice that those processors whose number of iterations is below the average value obviously do not skip iterations due to a lack of reasonable subproblems to work on. When looking at the waiting time of these processors, in general, this value is below the average, too. This means no contradiction, because when moving rectangles leftwards in the branching step certain situations may arise which require some additional time in order to unblock previously blocked starting points.

4.3. Results for the Parallel Genetic Algorithm

The limited logical neighborhood on which our algorithm is working (see section 3.3.) is also physically existent when using a transputer network. Due to the small amount of available links, each transputer is physically neighbored to at most four processors. But, this limitation means no disadvantage for implementing parallel genetic algorithms. Quite on the contrary it supports the algorithmical modelling of our concepts of neighborhood.

We have tested our algorithm on 10 randomly generated instances including between $m = 25$ and $m = 65$ rectangles. The width of B was fixed to 100. Each instance was solved ten times.

Due to the limited space being available here, experimental results will be presented merely to the following topics.

- Which evaluation function works best ?
- What are the effects when modifying the neighborhood (i.e. when modifying Π_{ext}) ?
- Which way of choosing the individuals to recombine (cp. 3.2.4.) is to be preferred ?

All other parameters mentioned in the preceding sections remain fixed to the following values:

- $|\Pi_{int}| = n = 10$
- mutation: turning the rectangles for $90°$
- mutation.frequency $= 10$
- acceptance of offsprings: always
- $min = \dfrac{1}{12} * m \ \rightarrow \ \dfrac{1}{3} * m$, depending on the current number of generations
- $max = \dfrac{1}{2} * m \ \rightarrow \ \dfrac{4}{5} * m$, depending on the current number of generations

4.3.1. Variation of the Evaluation Function

Due to the small amount of reasonable criterion function values (i.e vertical expansions of packing schemes in the bin) there inevitably exist same valued, different looking layouts. But, which of these schemes is to be preferred by appointing a higher fitness? Some heuristic approaches to help out of this dilemma were presented in 3.1. These functions shall now be analyzed empirically for their suitability to indicate "good" packing schemes. Here, we claim the evaluation function to work best, which on the average yields the best (lowest) packing schemes in the bin.

For the results of table 3 we have fixed the size of Π_{ext} to 10 and chosen the *ranking* selection strategy. These choices are uncrucial, as different sizes of Π_{ext} and different selection strategies led to similar results.

No.	rects.	bound	known	by eval.1	by eval.2	by eval.3
0	25	>=107	<=109	110.9	111.0	111.4
1	25	>=103	<=105	106.2	106.0	106.0
2	25	>=102	<=105	107.2	107.1	107.6
3	35	>=151	<=153	155.6	155.7	155.3
4	35	>=122	<=125	126.3	126.6	126.5
5	35	>=123	<=126	127.7	127.2	127.7
6	45	>=194	<=198	200.4	199.6	200.4
7	45	>=163	<=166	167.7	167.9	168.1
8	45	>=133	<=136	137.9	137.6	138.6
9	65	= 68	= 68	68.3	68.1	68.0
sum		>=1266	<=1291	1308.2	1306.8	1309.6

Table 3 : criterion function value of the best individual after 5000 generations

Table 3 presents for each instance seperately the cardinality of R, a theoretical lower bound for the optimal solution, a present best solution and the vertical expansion of the best individual being generated (on the average of 10 runs) when evaluating all individuals by one of the three evaluation functions (eval.i refers to function ε_i).

The total area needed by all rectangles is $\sum l_i * w_i$. Together with the width w of B this leads to a lower bound of $bound := (\sum_{i=1,...,m} l_i * w_i) / w$.

Note, that this value may not be equal to the vertical expansion of an optimal packing scheme, but in no case the optimal vertical expansion can undercut the lower bound. We do not expect that the optimal packing schemes do reach these bounds (indicated by the ">" sign in front of the bound), but we currently are not able to calculate all minimal packing schemes. The best current known solution our algorithm has found in any of our (not necessarily presented) experiments is referred to by the *known*-column in the table. As a consequence, a valuation of the absolute solution qualities of the genetic algorithm can only be speculatively done without having any knowledge of the optimal solutions. However, a relative comparison of the solutions gained by different evaluation functions is feasible.

As stated in table 3, on the average function ε_2 yields the best solutions of the Packing Problem after 5000 generations, although the individual differences are not very significant. As a consequence, the algorithm is more frequently misleaded when incorporating the actual width w of the packing scheme into the evaluation function. This effect especially is evident for instance no. 6, which contains hardly any rectangles whose lateral length is of one or two units. A similar effect occurs when integrating the length s_w into the evaluation function ε_3. Then the results are even worse compared to those of ε_1. This is caused since evaluating the schemes via ε_3 forces to fill the whole width of the bin which leads to an dispered packing scheme and contradicts the efforts of ε_2 to favour dense layouts.

It is interesting, too, that none of the strategies leads to improved/deteriorated solutions independent of the problem instance, but there seems to be a strong relationship between the quality of an evaluation function and the condition of the problem instance. For the following experiments function ε_2 was exclusively used to determine the quality of individuals.

4.3.2. Variation of the Neighborhood

Let $N_k(i)$ denote the neighborhood of processor i, $|N_k(i)| = k$, which includes all those processors being reachable by processor i via a network path of sufficient length.

Changing the neighborhood of processors has an effect upon the population Π in two ways: Each enlargement of the neighborhood enlarges the set Π_{ext} of individuals and consequently the whole population, too. The selection of individuals becomes richer. Caused by the special properties of the elements in Π_{ext} the ratio of "good" individuals in the local population is increased, which should promise a faster convergency and an improved quality of the solutions.

But, it has to be noticed, too, that each enlargement of Π_{ext} will cause the global population (i.e. the union of all local populations) to loose diversity, as large neighborhoods will hardly be distinct.

Variation of the size of the neighborhoods effects the parallel genetic algorithm in a more technical manner, too:

Choosing an enlarged neighborhood means the need for additional communications to distribute the local best individuals over the whole neighborhood. This communication overhead naturally consumes cpu-time, which could be used to calculate the following generation.

In our parallel genetic algorithm the distribution of each improved local best solution is done to *all* processors (independent of the neighborhood's size) in the network. Thus, the communication overhead is leveled, as all processors which are not included in the logical neighborhood of the transmitting process ignore this information. One may argue that this strategy is not the most effective way of exchanging messages, but it makes the results of our algorithm comparable.

No.	rects.	bound	neighborhood = 2		neighborhood = 10		neighborhood = 20	
			expans.	t/gen.	expans.	t/gen.	expans.	t/gen.
0	25	>=107	111.3	0.162	111.0	0.164	110.9	0.164
1	25	>=103	106.5	0.169	106.0	0.167	105.9	0.171
2	25	>=102	107.3	0.193	107.1	0.196	107.1	0.200
3	35	>=151	156.0	0.453	155.7	0.452	155.2	0.450
4	35	>=122	127.0	0.410	126.6	0.413	127.0	0.410
5	35	>=123	127.7	0.426	127.2	0.434	127.6	0.429
6	45	>=194	200.8	0.918	199.6	0.924	199.9	0.913
7	45	>=163	168.8	0.834	167.9	0.828	168.0	0.852
8	45	>=133	138.2	0.774	137.6	0.749	138.0	0.768
9	65	= 68	68.3	2.296	68.1	2.315	68.2	2.309
sum		>=1266	1314.6		1306.8		1307.8	

Table 4 : statistical information for each instance seperately

Figures 15 and 16 and table 4 summarize the results of our experiments when the first parent Φ_f is selected by the *ranking* strategy for recombination, Φ_m is randomly chosen and the size of the neighborhood is set to 2, 10 and 20. In table 4 for each of the instances the vertical expansion of the best individual being generated (on the average of 10 runs) and the time needed to compute a generation (on the average of 10 runs; in seconds) are listed for each size of the neighborhood.

The quite long run times (listed in seconds in the *t/gen* column) to compute a generation are caused to ensure the creation of valid packing schemes after each mutation or crossover. In these cases, subsequent to each replacement of a rectangle it has to be checked whether any overlapping has occured. This is the reason why on increasing problem sizes m the time needed to compute a generation increases, too. As stated in table 4, on each instance, the time needed to calculate a new generation is not influenced by the size of the neighborhood, which proves the above statement about the communication overhead.

Comparing the results of table 4, it can be stated that on the average the cardinality 10 of Π_{ext} has led to the best results. Obviously, a reduction of Π_{ext}'s cardinality effects the quality of the solutions more heavily as an enlargement does. Similar to 4.3.1., there exist some instances for which the enlarged neighborhood produces the best individuals (within the three sizes of Π_{ext}), but for none of the instances the smallest neighborhood fits best.

In figures 15 and 16 instance no. 8 is examined in more detail; these figures contain for all cardinalities of Π_{ext} the value of the vertical expansion of the best individual (on the average of 10 runs) and the average vertical expansion of the global population (on the average of 10 runs) dependent on the current number of the generation. Having a closer look at figure 15, up to generation 2000 the course of convergency is fairly equal for each size of Π_{ext}. Having passed generation 2000, the speed of convergency for the small size of Π_{ext} slows down, although after 5000 generations the smallest and largest size of the neighborhood terminate in almost identical average solutions. The medium sized Π_{ext} brings out improved average qualities after 3500 generations and saves its small advantage up to generation 5000.

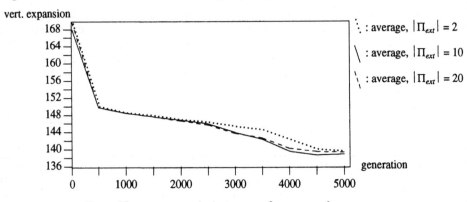

Figure 15 : convergency for instance no. 8, average values

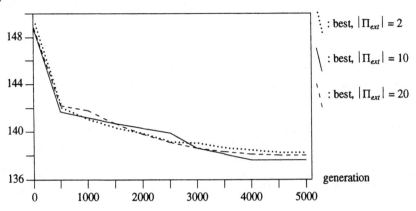

Figure 16 : convergency for instance no. 8, best values

When looking at the speed of convergency of the best individual from a population in figure 16, there is no significant difference evident between the small and the large size of Π_{ext}. For the medium sized neighborhood, however, although convergency is slowest between generation 500 and 2500, there appear some strong improvements in the following 1500 generations. These improvements guarantee the creation of the individual with the lowest value of the criterion function for instance no. 8 after 5000 generations.

4.3.3. Variation of the Choice of Parents

In section 3.2.4. a brief discussion on the effects of the different selection strategies for choosing parents to recombine is included. The presumptions made in that section are now to be supported by some experimental results. For this reason, we have compared four selection strategies for electing Φ_f out of Π. In each experiment the size of Π_{ext} was fixed to 10 and the second parent Φ_m was always randomly selected. The implemented selection strategies are:

- random choice of Φ_f out of Π (referred to as *RAN* in the following)
- choice of the "best" individual from Π (*BEST*)
- selection frequency proportional to fitness (*PROP*)
- selection frequency proportional to rank (*RANK*)

When working on large neighborhoods (large Π_{ext}), the *BEST* strategy provokes situations in which on many processors the same individual is selected for recombination (if $|\Pi_{ext}| = 10$, about 1/3 of the processors are selecting the current global best individual !). If this choice remains ineffective for several generations (i.e. no improved individual is found) the danger of getting stuck in local extremes arises. To avoid this effect selection of the "best" individual is done in *BEST* according to a *selection value*. In general, the *selection value* of each individual is equal to its fitness; but after each ineffective choice for recombination, it is decremented. Then, the "best" individual is the one, whose *selection value* is highest. Having successfully recombined an offspring, the *selection values* of its parents are reinitialized to their fitness.

In figures 17 and 18 and table 5 the results of our experiments are summarized; again, figures 17 and 18 are exclusively dealing with instance no. 8. Table 5 provides some similiar information as described in section 4.3.1.

No.	rects.	bound	known	RAN	BEST	PROP	RANK
0	25	>=107	<=109	111.0	111.2	111.0	111.0
1	25	>=103	<=105	106.0	106.3	106.3	106.0
2	25	>=102	<=105	107.5	107.5	106.9	107.1
3	35	>=151	<=153	155.5	155.9	155.6	155.7
4	35	>=122	<=125	126.2	126.7	126.3	126.6
5	35	>=123	<=126	127.7	128.0	127.3	127.2
6	45	>=194	<=198	199.7	200.7	200.0	199.6
7	45	>=163	<=166	167.9	168.6	168.9	167.9
8	45	>=133	<=136	138.0	138.6	138.4	137.6
9	65	= 68	= 68	68.0	68.3	68.0	68.1
sum		>=1266	<=1291	1307.5	1311.8	1308.7	1306.8

Table 5 : statistical information for each instance seperately

The results of table 5 indicate that on the average of all instances the *RANK* selection strategy provides the individuals whose criterion function is lowest. Furthermore, the random choice of the parent Φ_f is superior to a selection whose frequency is proportional to the fitness of the individuals. All this indicates, that the fittest individuals dominate the *PROP* selection process; an effect which is suppressed by the *RANK* and by the *RAN* selection rule. But again, the differences are not very significant.

The strategy which drastically deteriorates the qualities is the *BEST* selection approach. For none of the instances the *BEST* strategy is able to produce the individual of highest fitness (within the four selection rules), whereas some instances are most effectively treated by the *RAN* as well as by the *PROP* strategy. As a consequence, the choice of the best suited selection rule again might depend on the quality of the instance to be calculated with some average advantages for the *RANK* strategy.

Analyzing the course of convergency in figure 17 there is hardly any difference between the four selection rules to be noticed up to generation 2500. Then, the *RANK* strategy progresses with a strong improvement of the average vertical expansion. Similar observations can be made at figure 18. Here, the *BEST* strategy creates superior individuals between generation 500 and 2000, but then the population looses diversity as no remarkable improvements appear later on. Improvements of the best individual from a population actually are achieved by the *RANK* selection rule between generation 2500 and 4000. In addition, these improvements are not purchased with a decreasing speed of convergency as it was noticed by other authors, but the *RANK* selection rule enables the population to create improved offsprings by preserving the population's diversity even in progressive generations.

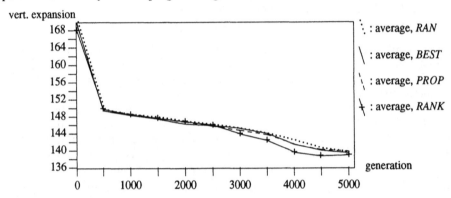

Figure 17 : convergency for instance no. 8, average values

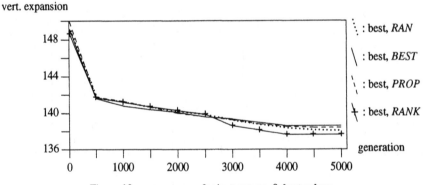

Figure 18 : convergency for instance no. 8, best values

4.3.4. Comparison to Deterministic Heuristics

After having made so much efforts to tune our parallel genetic algorithm, some cynics may argue whether the results gained by our algorithm justify these efforts or whether simple, deterministic heuristics will not do an even good job, too.

For this reason, the best results of the previous subsections are now compared to two sequential, deterministic algorithms for the Packing Problem. The *Bottom-Left* strategy of [1] as well as the *Level-Oriented* strategy of [3] are well known, efficient, but sequential heuristics, which are able to calculate reasonable solutions in a very short time. Table 6 presents the result of this somewhat "unfair" comparison, but the results are merely intended to justify the use of more sophisticated heuristics to solve the problem. The below table lists the best results being calculated by the parallel genetic algorithm on the average of 10 runs (referred to as GA in the table) together with the best values of the criterion function for the layouts which are calculated either by the Bottom-Left (BL) or by the Level-Oriented (LO) heuristic.

No.	rects.	bound	known	LO	BL	GA
0	25	>=107	<=109	119	119	111.0
1	25	>=103	<=105	113	112	106.0
2	25	>=102	<=105	111	113	107.1
3	35	>=151	<=153	159	157	155.7
4	35	>=122	<=125	128	128	126.6
5	35	>=123	<=126	131	134	127.2
6	45	>=194	<=198	204	206	199.6
7	45	>=163	<=166	171	174	167.9
8	45	>=133	<=136	138	143	137.6
9	65	= 68	= 68	69	69	68.1
sum		>=1266	<=1291	1343	1355	1306.8

Table 6 : comparison of different heustics

4.3.5. Comparison to the Branch-&-Bound Algorithm

To compare the parallel genetic algorithm with the parallel branch-&-bound algorithm, the 10 randomly generated instances of cardinality 10 which were used in section 4.2. to analyze the branch-&-bound approach had to be solved by the genetic algorithm, too.

The parallel genetic algorithm was run 10 times for each of the ten instances on the 32 processor network. So, the values in the *generations* and the *time* column (listed in seconds) are average values over these runs. The values in the *opt.* column of table denote the number of times the genetic algorithm was able to reach the global best solution. The parameter settings for the genetic algorithm were chosen in accordance to the best results which were yield in the previous sections.

instance no.	branch-&-bound		genetic algorithm		
	time	iterat.	opt.	generations	time
0	18.2	16438	10	351.6	8.5
1	21.0	16925	10	1098.4	23.4
2	23.0	17696	10	841.3	19.9
3	7.2	5494	10	2109.4	47.5
4	75.9	67696	10	2692.9	60.9
5	10.7	8394	10	710.2	17.8
6	5.4	4093	10	2515.3	59.0
7	35.6	28794	10	1037.7	24.0
8	106.2	81997	10	1254.0	28.5
9	5.9	4429	10	475.4	14.5
Average	30.9	25196	10	1308.6	30.4

Table 7 : comparison of branch-&-bound and genetic approach

As stated in table 7, on the average genetic algorithm and branch-&-bound approach are able to produce packing schemes of identical quality in almost the same (average) time. For these small-sized instances, the genetic algorithm is able to produce optimal solution in every case, although this computation sometimes is quite time-consuming. As the cardinalty of 10 rectangles to be packed means an almost "upper bound" for the size of the instances to be solved by branch-&-bound but a "lower bound" for the size of the instances which can be solved by a genetic algorithm, it is merely the genetic algorithm which may be applied to solve larger problem instances, although a guarantee to find the global optimum can not be maintained.

5. Conclusions

In this paper two parallel algorithms to solve a "difficult" optimization problem, the two-dimensional Packing Problem, are introduced. A sequential branch–&–bound procedure which guarantees to find the optimal solution was formulated. By means of an efficient load balancing strategy this algorithm was parallelized keeping in mind that the most promising subproblems are evenly distributed over all processors. The distribution of workload due to a function which qualifies the content of the local queues, allows to recognize unbalanced workload before a processor is running out of work. An observed variation of neighbored queue-weights can be eliminated by an exchange of subproblems. Furthermore, frequent communications between processors seem to be the right approach in a network of transputers since communication is supported by its architecture.

Unfortunately, due to the lack of the lower bound to predict at an early stage of the expansion of a subproblem the best value which still is achievable, only small instances could be solved by the branch–&–bound approach. The quality of the lower bound enables only very small cutoffs in the solution tree. In the literature several branch–&–bound algorithms are formulated [15,17,18] which have successfully tackled difficult optimization problems. But as a result of this work one probably can state that this approach applied to solve the Bin Packing Problem has reached its limit, at least if the amount of memory being available is restricted. Although the total memory available for the distributed algorithm is 32 Mbytes (32 times 1 Mbytes) we had some trouble in running our experiments. Without implementing some additional tricks it was almost impossible to run the sequential algorithm on a one-processor network with a 4 Mbytes memory. Again, this effect is stressed by the quality of the currently implemented lower bound. An improved lower bound might recognize those subproblems which are not worth to be expanded very early after their generation and thus reduce the amount of subproblems to be stored. Some additional work will be done in the future concerning this topic.

Sophisticated heuristics like genetic algorithms seem to be a real alternative to help out of the dilemma discribed above. The genetic algorithm being proposed in this paper to solve the Bin Packing Problem is based on a new graph-theoretical model to encode the packing schemes. Adaption of several parameters results in an algorithm which is able to compute packing schemes for large problem sizes in reasonable time. Experimental results indicate that a medium sized neighborhood is suited best to ensure convergency into nearly optimal solutions.

To still improve our genetic algorithm the encoding of packing schemes should be modified so that the calculation of the fitness of individuals as well as the verification of their admissibility are supported. This would lead to a reduction of the time needed to mutate and recombine individuals.

Our further research on genetic algorithms will concentrate on a more complicated Packing Problem. A new restriction is added which demands that all lines subdividing B (or a part of B) have to run from one side of the piece to the opposite one. Currently we believe that the addition of this *guillotine* restriction must not inevitably lead to a complicated genetic algorithm, but might enable the repair of some of the difficulties mentioned above.

References

[1] B.F. Baker, E.G. Coffman, R.L. Rivest, *Orthogonal Packing in Two Dimensions*, SIAM Journal on Computing, Vol. 9, No. 4, Nov. 1980, pp. 846 - 855.

[2] P. De Cani, *Packing Problems in Theory and Practice*, Ph. D. Thesis, University of D. Thesis, University of Birmingham, Department of Engineering Production, March 1979.

[3] E.G. Coffman, M.R. Garey, D.S. Johnson, R.E. Tarjan, *Performance Bounds for Level-Oriented two-dimensional Packing Algorithms*, SIAM Journal on Computing, Vol. 9, No. 4, Nov. 1980, pp. 808 - 826.

[4] L. Davis, *Job Shop Scheduling with Genetic Algorithms*, in: J.J. Grefenstette, Proc. of an Intern. Conf. on Genetic Algorithms and Their Application, Pittsburgh P.A., 1985, pp. 136 - 140.

[5] E.W, Dijkstra, W.H.J. Feijen, A.J.M. van Gasteren, *Derivation of a termination detection algorithm for distributed computations*, Inf. Proc. Letters 16 (1983), pp. 217 - 219.

[6] M.R. Garey, D.S. Johnson, *Computers and Intractability: A Guide to the Theory of NP-Completeness (1979)*, Freeman, San Francisco, California.

[7] D.E. Goldberg, *Genetic Algorithms in Search, Optimization and Machine Learning*, Addison-Wesley, 1989.

[8] J.J. Grefenstette, *Incorporating Problem Specific Knowledge into Genetic Algorithms*, in: J. Davis, Genetic Algorithms and Simulated Annealing, Morgan Kaufman Publ., Los Altos, 1987, pp. 42 - 60.

[9] M. Grötschel, O. Holland, *Solution of Large-Scale Symmetric Traveling Salesman Problems*, OR Report, University of Bonn, 1988.

[10] J.C. Herz, *Recursive Computational Procedure for Two-dimensional Stock Cutting*, in: IBM J. Res. Develop. 16 (1972) 5, pp. 462 - 469.

[11] J.H. Holland, *Adaption in Natural and Artificial Systems*, University of Michigan Press, Ann Arbor, MI, 1975.

[12] INMOS LTD, *The Transputer Family - Product Information*, March 1986.

[13] B. Kröger, O. Vornberger, *Solving a Cutting Stock Problem on a Transputer Network*, Proceedings of the 2nd North American Transputer Users Group Meeting, Oct. 1989, Durham, USA, pp. 393 - 404.

[14] T.H. Lai, S. Sahni, *Anomalies in Parallel Branch-and-Bound Algorithms*, Communications of the ACM, Vol. 27, No. 6, June 1984, pp. 594 - 602.

[15] E.L. Lawler, D.E. Wood, *Branch-and-Bound Methods: A Survey*, Operations Research 14 (1966), pp. 699 - 719.

[16] G. Li, B.W. Wah, *Computational Efficiency of Parallel Approximate Branch-and-Bound Algorithms*, Proc. of the 1984 International Conference on Parallel Processing, pp. 473 - 480.

[17] R. Lüling, B. Monien, *Two Strategies for Solving the Vertex Cover Problem on a Transputer Network*, Proceedings of the 3rd International Conference on Distributed Algorithms, Nice, Sep. 1989, pp. 160 - 170.

[18] B. Monien, O. Vornberger, *Parallel Processing of Combinatorial Search Trees*, Proc. of the International Workshop on Parallel Algorithms and Architectures, Suhl (GDR), May 1987, Akademie-Verlag Berlin.

[19] H. Mühlenbein, M. Gorges-Schleuter, O. Krämer, *Evolution Algorithms in Combinatorial Optimization*, Parallel Computing 7, 1988, pp. 65 - 85.

[20] D. Smith, *Binpacking with Adaptive Search*, in: J.J. Grefenstette, Proc. of an Intern. Conf. on Genetic Algorithms and Their Application, Pittsburgh P.A., 1985, pp. 202 - 206.

[21] O. Vornberger, *Transputer Networks for Operations Research Problems*, Journal of Microcomputer Applications, Special Issue on Transputer Applications, Vol. 13 (1990), pp. 69 - 79.

[22] B.W. Wah, G. Li, Ch.F. Yu, *Multiprocessing of Combinatorial Search Problems*, Computer, June 1985, pp. 93 - 108.

Area Efficient Methods to Increase
the Reliability of Circuits[*]

Rüdiger Reischuk
Bernd Schmeltz[†]
Technische Hochschule Darmstadt[‡]

Abstract

We consider the problem to construct reliable combinatorial and clocked circuits from unreliable basic elements. The main concern in this paper is the question how such fault-tolerance increases the circuit layout. In general it requires at least a logarithmic factor increase of the number of gates. We design area efficient codes for the information transfer within a Boolean circuit. Using such a code two constructions are presented to make circuits reliable without increasing the area by a square of the redundancy overhead for their sizes. The first method splits the circuit into clusters and connects the clusters reliably by groups of wires. As an alternative, a recursive layout stratey for circuits is described which uses special graph separator properties. Under certain conditions it achieves only a constant blowup of the area compared to circuits built from completely reliable elements.

At the end we apply these methods to several well studied Boolean functions. Both constructions achieve constant area redundancy for these examples.

[*] A preliminary version was presented at 6. STACS, 1989
[†] supported by Deutsche Forschungsgemeinschaft Re672/1
[‡] Institut für Theoretische Informatik, 6100 Darmstadt

1 Introduction

1.1 The Model

A circuit can be considered as a directed graphs consisting of two sorts of *elements*: nodes, in the following called *gates,* and edges, called *wires*. The Boolean basis $\mathcal{B}$, from which the type of each gate has to be chosen, has bounded fanin and bounded fanout and should be *complete*, that means every Boolean function should be computable using only these kinds of gates. For simplicity it is assumed that the total number of wires entering or leaving a gate is bounded by 4. Then a 2-dimensional layout of gates as squares or rectangles can make the connection to each wire at a different side.

If an ouput of some gate is needed as an input for many other gates it has to be duplicated. For that purpose a special (passive) *id*-gate of fanin 1 and fanout 2 is used. By a combination of such gates one can produce arbitrary many copies of a Boolean value. Special nodes of fanin 0, called *external inputs,* receive Boolean values from the outside. In addition some gates are marked as *external output gates,* their values define the output of the circuit.

We consider *combinatorial* and *clocked* (VLSI) circuits. In the first case each element of the Boolean circuit is used only once. The underlying graph has to be acyclic. For clocked circuits we assume a synchronous model, gates and wires both work with a fixed constant delay on the signal.

2-dimensional layouts of circuits use rectangular grids with a fixed internal distance between adjacent parallel grid edges. For the following considerations the numerical value of the disctance is not important, therefore we may assume it equals 1. The gates of a circuit are placed on the vertices of the grid. Wires run along the edges of the grid. On each grid vertex at most one gate, on each grid edge at most one wire can be placed . At grid vertices that are not occupied by gates a pair of wires may overlap (forming a crossing or knock-knees).

Circuit complexity theory usually assumes reliable elements. Here we consider *noisy circuits* in which elements may fail, i.e. generate a wrong value, independently with bounded probability. Then one has to face the problem for arbitrary Boolean functions f to construct circuits from unreliable elements that still compute f correctly except with a small error probability δ.

Definition 1.1 *Let f be a Boolean function and ϵ an upper bound for the error probability of circuit elements. We assume that elements fail independently with probability at most ϵ. A circuit $\tilde{C}$ computes f (ϵ, δ)--reliably if it generates the correct output vector with probability at least $1 - \delta$.*

it has been observed that the maximal allowable failure probability ϵ_{max}, such that arbitrary Boolean functions can still be computed reliably, depends on the basis $\mathcal{B}$ from which the gates have to be chosen. The maximal achievable reliability $1 - \delta$ depends on

ϵ and $\mathcal{B}$. In [P89] Pippenger discusses failure models in which the independence condition for errors is relaxed. In order to keep the analysis simple we will assume complete independence in this paper although all results below also hold for Pippenger's *majorized failure model*.

Definition 1.2 *Given ϵ and δ and a noiseless circuit C we say that a circuit $\tilde{C}$ is* **equivalent** *to C if $\tilde{C}$ (ϵ, δ)-reliably computes the same function as C does. A function f is said to be* **computable by fault-tolerant circuits** *of complexity $O(S)$ if for all small ϵ there exist a circuit of complexity $c_\epsilon S$ that $(\epsilon, O(\epsilon))$-reliably computes f. Here c_ϵ is a universal constant that only depends on ϵ and $\mathcal{B}$.*

Since the reliability decreases exponentially with the number of external output bits functions with many outputs can only be computed reliably by coding the output vector. In this case correctness is defined with respect to such a coding procedure fixed in advance: the output vector generated by the circuit has to be in the decoding set of the correct output.

The following models how random faults are distributed within a circuit and its layout seem to be the most important:

a1) errors only occur at active gates, passive id-gates and wires are fault-free;

a2) all elements of the circuit are subject to faults; the distortion of each element v happens with a fixed, possibly unknown probability $\epsilon_v \leq \epsilon$;

If errors occur at wires and passive gates the whole input vector has to be given in a redundant or coded form for the same reason as for multiple outputs. The best property one can guarantee in this situation is an error probability of at most $O(\epsilon)$ for each external input bit. In order to achieve this reliability for an external input bit that is needed at many places error correction has to be performed within larger sets of id-gates that produce the copies of this bit.

Another important distinction is whether faults are only temporary caused by noise or elements can also be subject to permanent faults. In the first case each time the circuit is used there will be a different random fault pattern. Therefore the most one could require is that for each input vector x the probability that $\tilde{C}$ given x does not output $f(x)$ is at most δ. If permanent faults occur at random we would like the circuit still to compute exactly the function f with high probability, i.e. be correct for all input vectors simultaneously. We therefore define the variants

b1) temporary faults only with the requirement: $\forall x \quad \text{Prob}[\varphi_{\tilde{C}}(x) \neq f(x)] \leq \delta$,

b2) permanent faults, too, requiring: $\text{Prob}[\varphi_{\tilde{C}} \neq f] \leq \delta$.

Here $\varphi_{\tilde{C}}(x)$ is a random variable describing the value of the output vector of $\tilde{C}$ on input x. $\varphi_{\tilde{C}}$ denotes the random function computed by $\tilde{C}$. Observe that the second case is much more restrictive. A noisy circuit $\tilde{C}$ may be highly fault-tolerant for each individual input vector, but the probability of all those fault patterns that let $\tilde{C}$ err on at least one input vector may be close to one.

For clocked circuits that reuse its elements these two kinds of faults make another difference. If only permanent faults are assumed then a fault-tolerant circuit, that happens to compute the desired function correctly, will compute reliably arbitrarily long. On the other hand assuming random noise, one has to consider the total number of bit operations. In that case an exponentially long computation cannot be performed reliably using only small hardware redundancy. Therefore, in the following we assume that the number of computation steps is polynomially bounded in the size of the clocked circuit.

1.2 Fault-Tolerant Computations

The investigation of reliable computation in the presence of noise has a long history which goes back to early work of von Neumann [N56]. He and more formally Dobrushin and Ortyukov [DO77b] showed that given an arbitrary error free circuit logarithmic redundancy with respect to the circuit size suffices to construct an equivalent fault-tolerant circuit. Here and in the following by *redundancy* with respect to a complexity measure we mean the ratio between the necessary amount in the noisy case and the case without faults. Pippenger presented an explicit construction based on these ideas in [P85]. His result says that using logarithmic redundancy with respect to the circuit size an error probability $\delta \leq O(\epsilon)$ for each output bit can be achieved for error model a1).

Since this method serves as a basis for the following let us briefly sketch it. Each wire e of a noiseless circuit is replaced by a *cable* $\tilde{e}$ consisting of r wires each of these wires carrying the same signal as e. For each gate v a *module* $\tilde{v}$, that are r gates of the same type as v, is used. The **redundancy factor** r will be chosen suitably. For every wire e serving as an input to a gate v each gate in $\tilde{v}$ takes as input exactly one distinct wire of the cable $\tilde{e}$. In addition a *correcting unit* consisting of r majority elements is attached to each module. Each such element takes a majority vote of a constant number of well chosen gates of the modul. These r majority values define the value of a cable leaving $\tilde{v}$. Using explicit constructions of expander graphs Pippenger showed how to build a design that with high probability reduces the number of faulty wires in a cable by some appropriate constant factor assuming a random distribution of faults within the cables and modules. In [P85] the following is basically shown for small ϵ:

Lemma 1.3 *For arbitrary $b \in \mathbb{N}$ there exist correcting units with r inputs, r outputs and $O(r)$ internal gates guaranteeing the following property with high probability for all γ with $3\epsilon \leq \gamma \leq 1/(8b^2)$: if at most $b\gamma r$ of the inputs have an incorrect value then at most γr of the outputs will have an incorrect value.*

Pippenger considered explicitly the case $\epsilon \leq 1/512$, $\gamma = 1/512$ and $b = 8$.

Definition 1.4 *Let γ be a fixed small fraction (for example $\gamma = 3\epsilon$). We say that a cable is **correct** if at most a portion γ of its wires do not carry the value they would* *have in an error free environment, otherwise the cable is called* **faulty**. *A module behaves correctly if its output cables are correct.*

The following result was proved in [P85].

Lemma 1.5 *If each gate and wire has error probability at most ϵ and redundancy r is used then given correct input cables a module behaves correctly with probability at least $1 - \epsilon^{cr}$ for a fixed constant $c > 0$.*

To keep the total error probability low the redundancy r has to be chosen logarithmically in the size of the circuit. Using redundancy r the error probability of a single cable or module is bounded by $\zeta \leq \exp -cr$. To achieve a total probability of at most δ for a circuit of size S is suffices to choose ζ or order δ/S, that means $r \leq O(\log S/\delta)$. Concerning circuit depth this construction generates only a constant factor overhead.

The logarithmic redundancy with respect to the number of gates cannot be improved in general since the parity function

$$\text{PARITY}_n := x_1 \oplus x_2 \oplus \ldots \oplus x_n$$

has linear size noiseless circuits, but requires size $\Omega(n \log n)$ in case of nonzero failure probability. A proof for this lower bound, which turned out to be not correct, has been published in [DO77a]. For a correct proof and generalizations of the lower bound see [PST91], [G91] and [RS91].

On the other hand, Pippenger showed in [P85] that all n-input Boolean functions with circuit size $2^n/n$ – the complexity bound which holds for almost all of these functions – have fault-tolerant circuits with constant redundancy in size. Pippenger's result has been improved by Uhlig who showed that redundancy arbitrarily close to 1 can be achieved [U87]. In contrast to the method described above these constructions only works for the error model b1). We do not know whether for the stronger model b2) a similar relation can be obtained. Let us already mention here that the fault-tolerance techniques presented in this paper apply to both error models.

The results above only consider the combinatorial aspects of circuits. The general problem to design fault-tolerant circuits with efficient geometrical layouts has not been studied so far. For networks of automata reliability questions have been investigated by Toom [T74], Gacs [G86], Gacs and Reif [GR88] and Berman and Simon [BS88]. They consider d-dimensional grids for $d \leq 3$ and other symmetric networks. Here the situation is much more restricted since a fault tolerant network has to be of the same regular topology, but may be of larger size or dimension. Given a fault-free network G of size S and a time bound T one has to find a fault-tolerant one $\tilde{G}$ of the same topology which simulates G correctly for T steps with high probability. Performance measures in this case are the time loss of the simulation and the increase of the size. Bounds on the redundancy achieved so far are realtime simulations with an $O(\log^2 S \cdot T)$ increase of the hardware [BS88] and constant hardware redundancy with logarithmic time loss [G88].

1.3 New Results

In this paper we consider Boolean circuits and their embeddings into a 2-dimensional grid. It is not difficult to see that given a layout of a noiseless circuit one can apply Pippenger's modifications and get a logarithmic expansion factor in both dimensions. Let A be the area required by the original circuit G. Each module and correcting unit consists of $O(r)$ elements. One can embed them into a square grid of side length $O(r)$. Since a wire is replaced by a cable of width r and wires may run in horizontal and vertical directions blowing up the grid by a factor $O(r)$ in both dimensions the fault-tolerant circuit $\tilde{C}$ can be embedded into the enlarged grid in a topological equivalent way. The area increases to

$$O(Ar^2) \leq O(A \log^2 S) \leq O(A \log^2 A).$$

The r^2 area redundancy for the gates cannot be improved, since to embed an expander, which is contained in every correction unit, area $\Omega(r^2)$ is necessary. In contrast we will show that the redundancy for the wire area can be kept smaller. More specific, constant redundancy can be achieved under certain conditions, for example if the wire area is proportional to the square of the circuit size. Such a relation holds for many Boolean functions with large internal information flow.

The general idea is to use two different codes for the circuit: a simple repetition code with a decreasing rate to perform computations similar to the construction described above. This requires a logarithmic increase in the number of gates. A different code, this one of positive rate, serves for the information flow in the wires, thus we only get a constant increase in the number of wires. The wire code must have specific properties. Most important, encoding and decoding should be possible in small area. Extending a construction of Kuznetsov [K73] we will show that such codes exist.

The paper is organised as follows. We start with the design of a special code to perform information transfer within a Boolean circuit. Sections 3 and 4 describe area efficient constructions and embeddings of fault-tolerant circuits. Finally, we apply these methods to the layout of specific functions and show how constant redundancy is achieved.

2 A Code to Design Fault-Tolerant Layouts

For the construction of an area efficient reliable circuit we construct a code of positive rate which is easy to encode and to decode. To make a given circuit C fault-tolerant one might try the following: take an efficient code to code blocks of internal bits generated by C and perform computation and information transfer on the codewords. But computing with the codewords instead of the original bits may heavily increase the circuit size. We do not know good upper bounds for this blowup which hold in general. Therefore two different codes will be used:

- for the gates a simple repetition code with a logarithmically decreasing rate to perform the computation – this increases the number of gates by a logarithmic factor;

- for the information flow in the wires a special code of bounded rate which gives rise to only a constant factor increase in the number of wires.

Although each information bit is coded by the gate code independently we have to take blocks of bits for the wire code. In the following *encoding* means a transformation from the gate code to the wire code and *decoding* the converse operation. The only difference to standard encoding is that for a block of information bits each single bit is given in many copies and the majority of them defines the value of the original bit.

Definition 2.1 *Let* θ, γ *be constants between 0 and 1 and* Z *be a code word of the repetition code. A vector* Z' *has* **small distortion** *from* Z *if for each information bit a portion of at most* θ *of its copies in* Z' *does not have the value as in* Z. *For the wire code we use the standard definition with the help of the hamming distance: if a vector* Y' *differs from a code word* Y *in at most* $\frac{7}{2}|Y|$ *positions, then its distortion is considered to be small.*

Let k denote the number of information bits of the wire code and l the length of a code word. A code word is distorted by independent random experiments that may switch a bit with probability at most ϵ. One may think of passing the code through a binary symmetric channel where each time the crossover error probability is at most ϵ. Let δ_{code} be the worst case probability that a distorted code word cannot be decoded correctly. For arbitrary constants d_1, d_2 we would like to achieve the following properties:

1) $l \leq \rho \cdot k$ for some constant ρ independent of k,

2) $\delta_{code} \leq 2^{-d_1 k}$,

3) there exist circuits of area $D \leq O(k^4)$ that perform the encoding, resp. decoding with failure probability at most $\delta_{cir} \leq 2^{-d_2 k}$ if the basic elements have error probability at most ϵ.

More precisely, the last condition means the following: let Z be a code word of the gate code and Y the corresponding code word of the wire code. If a vector Z' with small distortion from Z is given as input to the noisy coding circuit, then with probability at least $1 - \delta_{cir}$ the circuit outputs a vector $Y' \in \{0,1\}^l$ with hamming distance at most $\frac{7}{2}l$ from Y. The noisy decoding circuit gets a vector Y' with distance at most γl from Y and has to yield a small distorted vector of Z.

Kuznetsov describes a class of codes to design fault-tolerant memories in [K73]. We will extend this construction to yield a code suitable for our purpose here. To prove the existence of such a code consider the following ensemble of $(m \times l)$–check matrices (rows × columns) for a linear (k, l)–code ($m = l - k$). Let $\zeta_{col}, \zeta_{row} \in \mathbb{N}$ be constants, appropriate values will follow from the estimations below. We start with a matrix of all "0"s and insert ζ_{col} "1"s in each column. The positions for the insertions are chosen independently with equal probability. A matrix that has more than ζ_{row} "1"s in one of the rows or two "1"s in the same position is rejected. In that case we repeat the experiment

Thus the probability that a specific row is chosen to fill in the next "1" depends on the previous insertions and is either zero (for at most $\lfloor \zeta_{col} l / \zeta_{row} \rfloor$ entries) or $1/m \leq p \leq 1/m'$ where $m' = m - \lfloor \zeta_{col} l / \zeta_{row} \rfloor$. ζ_{col} and ζ_{row} should be chosen such that

$$\left\lfloor l \frac{\zeta_{col}}{\zeta_{row}} \right\rfloor \leq \frac{m}{2} .$$

Let C be a column of an $(m \times \gamma l)$–submatrix of such a random matrix M. Call C **good** if more than $\zeta_{col}/2$ of the "1"s are in rows that contain no other "1"s within the submatrix. We consider a column of an $(m \times (1 - \gamma)l)$–submatrix to be **bad** if less than $\zeta_{col}/2$ of the entries are in rows that contain no "1"s outside the matrix. Let q_1, q_2 be constants such that

$$q_i > 4/\zeta_{col} \qquad \text{and} \qquad q := q_1 + q_2 \leq \frac{1}{3} .$$

For a random M consider the following properties:

A1) Any $(m \times \gamma l)$–submatrix has at least $(1 - q_1) \gamma l$ good columns.

A2) Any $(m \times (1 - \gamma)l)$–submatrix has at most $q_2 \gamma l$ bad columns.

If bits of a code word get distorted we perform a correction to set them back to their original values. This is done as follows: for each code bit all check sums are computed and the bit is switched if the majority of them, that are more than $\zeta_{col}/2$, are different from zero. Then properties A1) and A2) imply:

B1) Let Y be a code word and switch arbitrary γl bits of Y. Then the correcting unit will correct at least $(1 - q_1) \gamma l$ of them.

B2) At most $q_2 \gamma l$ unswitched bits of Y are falsely "corrected".

Note that this implies that after passing a distorted code word through a single correcting unit the hamming distance decreases to at most $q_1 \gamma l + q_2 \gamma l = q \gamma l \leq \gamma l/3$. To prove B1) imagine that the submatrices comprise all columns corresponding to changed bits, for B2) that they comprise only correct bits.

Lemma 2.2 For alle $\gamma \leq \gamma_0$, where $\gamma_0 < 1$ is some fixed bound, holds: the probabilities P_1, P_2 that the properties A1, resp. A2 are not satisfied is bounded by

$$P_1 \leq O(l^{-1}) \qquad \text{and} \qquad P_2 \leq O(l^{-1/2}) .$$

Proof : To establish these bounds we need the following technical result.

Lemma 2.3 Let H' be an $(m \times \gamma l)$–submatrix, $r(i)$ the number of "1"s in its i-th row and $c(j)$ the number of "1" in its j-th column that are in rows with $r(i) = 1$. Let zcol be the number of good columns, that means columns with $c(j) > \zeta_{col}/2$, and let arow be the number of nonempty rows. Then we have the following implications

$$\text{nrow} > u_0 := \lfloor (1 - q_1 4) \zeta_{col} \gamma l \rfloor \qquad \Longrightarrow \qquad \text{gcol} > (1 - q_1) \gamma l .$$

Proof : The following inequalities can easily be verified

$$\sum_{i,r(i)>1} 1 \;\leq\; \sum_{i,r(i)>1} (r(i)-1) \;=\; \zeta_{col}\gamma l - \mathtt{nrow} \;<\; \frac{q_1}{4}\zeta_{col}\gamma l \;,$$

$$\sum_{i,r(i)=1} r(i) \;=\; \;=\; \zeta_{col}\gamma l - \sum_{i,r(i)>1}(r(i)-1) - \sum_{i,r(i)>1} 1 \;>\; \zeta_{col}\gamma l - \frac{q_1}{2}\zeta_{col}\gamma l$$

$$=\; (1-\frac{q_2}{2})\zeta_{col}\gamma l \;,$$

$$\sum_{i,r(i)=1} r(i) \;=\; \sum_{j,c(j)\leq\zeta_{col}/2} c(j) + \sum_{j,c(j)>\zeta_{col}/2} c(j) \;\leq\; \frac{\zeta_{col}}{2}(\gamma l - \mathtt{gcol}) + \zeta_{col}\,\mathtt{gcol}$$

$$=\; \frac{\zeta_{col}}{2}\,\mathtt{gcol} + \frac{\zeta_{col}}{2}\,\gamma l \;.$$

This implies

$$\mathtt{gcol} \;\geq\; \left((1-\frac{q_1}{2})\zeta_{col}\gamma l - \frac{\zeta_{col}}{2}\gamma l\right) / \left(\frac{\zeta_{col}}{2}\right) \;=\; (1-q_1)\gamma l\;.$$

■

We are now ready to prove the first lemma. Let P_3 be the probability that A1) does not hold for a fixed choice for columns of a submatrix. Then

$$P_1 \;\leq\; \binom{l}{\gamma l} P_3 \;.$$

If P_4 denotes the probability that the condition of the previous lemma is not satisfied then

$$P_3 \;\leq\; \binom{m}{u_0} P_4 \qquad\text{and}\qquad P_4 \;\leq\; \left(\frac{u_0}{m'}\right)^{\zeta_{col}\gamma l}\;.$$

Putting everything together yields

$$P_1 \;\leq\; \binom{l}{\gamma l}\binom{m}{u_0}\left(\frac{u_0}{m'}\right)^{\zeta_{col}\gamma l}\;.$$

Using

$$\binom{x}{y} \;\leq\; c\cdot\exp(y\log\frac{x}{ey})$$

for a fixed constant c we get

$$P_1 \;\leq\; c\cdot\exp\left(\gamma l\log\frac{\epsilon}{\gamma} + \xi\zeta_{col}\gamma l\log\frac{em}{\xi\zeta_{col}\gamma l} - \zeta_{col}\gamma l\log\frac{m'}{\xi\zeta_{col}\gamma l}\right)$$

$$=\; c\cdot\exp\left(\gamma l\left[\log\frac{e}{\gamma} + \zeta_{col}\log\frac{em}{m'} - \frac{q_1\zeta_{col}}{4}\log\frac{em}{\xi\zeta_{col}l}\right]\right)$$

where $\xi = 1 - q_1/4$. We can arrange that the last term in the exponent dominates the others by choosing ζ_{col} large and γ small enough, so that we get

$$P_1 \;\leq\; 2^{-2\gamma k}\;.$$

To bound P_2 again first fix the columns of the submatrix and denote the probability by P_5. Then

$$P_2 \leq \binom{l}{(1-\gamma)l} P_5 = \binom{l}{\gamma l} P_5$$

If the entries of the complementary $(m \times \gamma l)$–submatrix H'' are specified then the probability that a given column is bad is bounded by

$$P_6 \leq \binom{\zeta_{col}}{\zeta_{col}/2} \left(\frac{\zeta_{col}\gamma l}{m'} \right)^{\zeta_{col}/2}$$

since the number of nonempty rows in H'' is at most $\zeta_{col}\gamma l$. This implies

$$P_5 \leq \binom{(1-\gamma)l}{q_2\gamma l} P_6{}^{q_2\gamma l}$$

and

$$
\begin{aligned}
P_2 &\leq \binom{l}{\gamma l}\binom{(1-\gamma l)}{q_2\gamma l} P_6{}^{q_2\gamma l} \\
&\leq c \cdot \exp\left(\gamma l \log\frac{e}{\gamma} + q_2\gamma l \log\frac{e(1-\gamma)}{q_2\gamma} + q_2\gamma l\left(\frac{\zeta_{col}}{2}\log e - \frac{\zeta_{col}}{2}\log\frac{m'}{\zeta_{col}\gamma l} \right) \right) \\
&= c \cdot \exp\left(\gamma l \left[\log\frac{e}{\gamma} + q_2\log\frac{e(1-\gamma)}{q_2\gamma} - q_2\frac{\zeta_{col}}{2}\log\frac{m'}{e\zeta_{col}\gamma l} \right] \right) .
\end{aligned}
$$

Again the exponent is dominated by the last term if ζ_{col} is large and γ is small implying

$$P_2 \leq 2^{-2\gamma l} .$$

Condition A1) and A2) should hold simultaneously for all $\gamma = \gamma_i := \gamma_0 (2q)^i$, $i = 0, 1, \ldots, \lambda$. Here λ denotes the smallest i with $\gamma_i < 1/l$, thus $\lambda \leq O(\log l)$. Since the sum of all these probabilities is less than 1 for large l there exists a code which satisfies all constraints.

A correcting unit corrects a code bit if the majority of its check sums are 1. The values of the check sums are computed separately for the correction of each code bit. Since the check matrix has only $\zeta_{col} l$ "1"s this computation can be performed by a circuit with $S_{cu} \leq O(l)$ gates. If we require that

$$\xi < q\gamma\, l/S_{cu}$$

a portion ξ of faulty gates affects at most a portion $q\gamma$ of the code bits. The probability of ξS_{cu} failures decreases exponentially with S_{cu}. Thus an appropriate choice of the constants guarantees a failure probability less than δ/A^2 for the correcting unit. In the error model a2), in which passive gates are unreliable, too, errors occurring during the initial splitting are attributed to the previous active gate (outside the correcting unit) by saying that values are unpredictable if one of the splitting gates fails. Thus the situation is similar to error case a1) if we use $\epsilon' = \zeta_{row}\zeta_{col}\epsilon$.

The encoding can be performed in logarithmic circuit depth. First, to each nonzero information bit (which is given in many copies by the repetition code) we associate the corresponding unit vector and represent this vector by the code word of the wire code. Then these vectors are added by a binary tree where each addition is followed by a correcting unit. The area needed is bounded by $O(l^2 \times l \log l) \leq O(l^4)$.

To decode we use λ stages of correcting units. The gates of an error free circuit are replaced by modules and wires by cables. In a correcting stage new errors may occur at gates. A noisy correcting unit is considered to *work properly* if this number of errors is not greater than the maximum number of faulty bits remaining, that can be guaranteed by a reliable correcting unit. We will choose the number of wires per cable for each correcting stage such that with probability at least $1 - \delta_{cir}\lambda^{-1}$ this condition holds.

Lemma 2.4 *If at the beginning there are at most $\gamma_0 l$ faulty bits and all correcting stages work properly then after passing the i-th stage the number of faulty bits will have decreased below $\gamma_{i+1} l$.*

Proof : The claim holds for $i = 0$. For $i \geq 0$ after passing the $(i+1)$-st stage and assuming that no new faulty bits occur one would end up with less than $q\gamma_i l$ errors. The correcting unit is allowed to change additional $q\gamma_i l$ bits yielding a number of $2q\gamma_i \leq \gamma_{i+1}$ faulty bits. ∎

If λ is chosen minimal such that $\gamma_\lambda l < 1$ then all errors are corrected because the number of wrong bits will be less than 1. Observe that this happens with probability at least $1 - \delta_{cir}$. Next let us calculate how many wires per cable will be required to guarantee the assumed performance within each correcting unit. These units are built in such a way that any error in one of its gates affects only one of the code bits. The i-th correcting unit consists of at most S_{cu} gates and at most $q\gamma_{i+1} l$ of them may fail. Let p_i be the failure probability of a module in the i-th correcting unit then we require

$$\binom{S_{cu}}{q\gamma_{i+1} l} p_i^{q\gamma_{i+1} l} \leq \delta_{cir}\lambda^{-1} .$$

Since $\delta_{cir} = 2^{-d_2 k}$ it can easily be seen that for a suitable constant c_2 the relation $\log(1/p_i) \geq c_2/\gamma_{i+1}$ is a sufficient condition for the inequality above to hold. This is because the left hand side is bounded by $O(2^{S_{cu}-c_2 l})$. Hence to achieve error probability p_i the number of wires per cable can be bounded by $r_i \leq O(\log(1/p_i))$. The total area required is at most

$$D \leq O\left(\sum_{i=0}^{\lambda-1} (r_i l)^2\right) \leq O\left(\sum_{i=0}^{\lambda-1} \left(\frac{l}{\gamma_{i+1}}\right)^2\right) \leq O\left(\left(\frac{l}{\gamma_\lambda}\right)^2\right)$$

$$\leq O(l^4) \leq O(k^4) .$$

This proves

Theorem 2.5 *For any constants d_1, d_2 and all $k \in \mathbb{N}$ large enough there exists a (k, l, d_1, d_2)–code for binary vectors of length k and rate k/l bounded from below by some constant $\rho > 0$ (depending only on d_1, d_2). For any code word generated by a noisy circuit holds: if independently with probability at most ϵ each bit is switched then correct decoding is still possible with probability at least $1 - 2^{-d_1 k}$. The code can be encoded and decoded by a noisy circuit with failure probability at most $2^{-d_2 k}$. This circuit has depth logarithmic in k and can be layed out in area $O(k^4)$.*

3 Bytewise Computation

In the previous chapter we have shown that for information transfer – in contrast to computation – constant redundancy suffices. If one can arrange that in a circuit layout many bits run the same way, then using a code of positive rate yields only constant overhead for the wire area. Encoding and decoding asymptotically increase the size of the circuit, but not necessarily the area of the layout.

We will describe techniques how to convert a noiseless circuit C of size $|C|$ into a fault-tolerant one $\tilde{C}$ such that the area to embed $\tilde{C}$ is not much larger than that for C. Let $\mathbf{area}(C)$ denote the minimal area of a rectangular grid to embed C. The methods to be shown in many cases significantly improve the area redundancy bound $O(r^2) = O(\log^2 |C|) = O(\log^2 \mathbf{area}(C))$ obtained by embedding Pippenger's construction with logarithmic size redundancy r.

A necessary condition is that $\mathbf{area}(C)$ is at least $\Omega(|C| \log^2 |C|)$. It has been shown by information flow arguments that this condition is not very restrictive. Wires of a circuit in general require much more space than gates. For many functions their area grows quadratic in the number of gates (compare [U84],[T89]).

To extend a given ordinary error free circuit C to an (ϵ, δ)–reliable one $\tilde{C}$ our general strategy will be to partition the circuit in a suitable way. The first construction locally merges the circuit elements into larger units, whereas the second one, given in the next chapter, works recursively top down. Our aim is to derive a "supercircuit" from C, the elements of which are subcircuits of C. To make these ideas precise we start with the following

Definition 3.1 *H is called a w–clustergraph of C if it can be obtained from C by the following procedure. Partition the gates into subsets, called clusters, such that the gates of each cluster and the wires between these gates, the internal wires, can be embedded into a $(w \times w)$–grid. The remaining external wires connect different clusters. Up to w of them all starting at the same cluster g and all ending at another cluster g' are grouped together to form a cable.*

We require that the maximal number of cables a cluster is connected to is bounded by a constant. This implies that each cluster can have at most $O(w)$ external wires. For combinatorial circuits the clustergraph in addition has to be acyclic. Such a w-clustergraph H is said to perform a **bytewise computation of width** w.

Given a w–clustergraph H we first try to place the clusters and their connecting cables on a grid of smaller area A_1. Each vertex of this grid represents a square of area

$$B_1 = w^2$$

and each edge a channel of width w. A modul can completely be mapped to a single grid vertex and a cable can be routed over a single grid edge. We say that the grid has **cluster capacity** 1 and **cable capacity** 1. For an optimal embedding of a clustergraph H it should hold

$$A_1 \leq O(\text{area}(C)/B_1) .$$

If an efficient layout of C is known that routes many wires in groups of size about w this last condition can be achieved as follows: Partition the area into $w \times w$–subsquares, these will be the vertices of the new grid. Groups of wires running in parallel form a cable. If a subsquare holds part of such a cable or a crossing of two such groups then the grid will also route cables at the corresponding place, otherwise the corresponding grid-point is considered to form a cluster.

Let $A := \text{area}(C)$. In the second step each cluster is replaced by a fault-tolerant version that guarantees an error probability of at most δ/A. This can be achieved by duplicating each element of a cluster

$$r = \Theta(\log A/\delta)$$

many times. This means we use moduls with redundancy r as described in section 1.2. A cable of width up to w is divided into chunks of k wires each; their k bits are coded by the (k, l, d_1, d_2)–wire code described in the previous section. Encoders and decoders are added at the ports where cables leave and enter. k is chosen minimal such that the code satisfies the reliablity constraints

$$2^{-d_i k} \leq \frac{\delta}{3A} ,$$

that means k is also of order $\log A/\delta$. This implies that the total error probability of a chunk from the encoding where it starts to the decoding at its end is bounded by δ/A. The fault-tolerant circuit is then reorganized by placing the reliable versions of the clusters on a second grid of area A_2 where each grid vertex represents a square of area

$$B_2 = B_1 r^2 .$$

This area is sufficient to place the r copies of each gate within a cluster and to route the copies of internal wires. Constructing the fault-tolerant versions the clusters grow by the redundancy r in each dimension whereas the coding of the cables only requires the constant factor l/k. Hence, for this new grid one can allow a channel width

$$w_2 = w \cdot r \cdot \frac{k}{l} = \Theta(w \cdot r) .$$

This implies that all coded chunks of $\lfloor r\,k/l \rfloor \geq \Omega(r)$ cables can be routed simultaneously over a single grid edge. Therefore for circuits layouts, in which wires require most of the area, a value A_2 smaller than A_1 may be achievable by compacting the layout of the clustergraph. This gives the following general result.

Theorem 3.2 *Let C be a combinatorial circuit with a w-clustergraph H, where $w \geq \Omega(\log |C|)$, that can be embedded into a grid of area*

$$A_2 \leq O\left(\frac{\text{area}(C)}{w^2 \log^2 \text{area}(C)}\right)$$

of cluster capacity 1 and cable capacity $\log \text{area}(C)$. Then assuming error model a2)–b2) there exists an equivalent fault-tolerant circuit $\tilde{C}$ with $\text{area}(\tilde{C}) \leq O(\text{area}(C))$.

Proof : The area of the fault-tolerant equivalent $\tilde{C}$ can be bounded as follows: The clustergraph has at most A_2 nodes. The reliable substitute of a cluster can be embedded into a grid of area B_2. In addition, $O(k^4)$ area is necessary to code and decode a chunk of k bits. Since each cluster has only a constant number of incident cables the total additional area for a cluster is bounded by $O(w/k) \, O(k^4) = O(w \, k^3)$. This gives

$$\begin{aligned}
\text{area}(\tilde{C}) &\leq A_2 \cdot (B_2 + O(w \, k^3)) \leq O\left(\frac{\text{area}(C)}{w^2 \cdot \log^2 \text{area}(C)} \, (w^2 \, r^2 + w \, k^3)\right) \\
&\leq O(\text{area}(C)) \,,
\end{aligned}$$

since $k \leq O(\log \text{area}(C))$ and $\Theta(\log \text{area}(C)) = \Theta(r) \leq O(w)$. Each element of the clustergraph is replaced by a reliable substitute of error probability at most δ/A, thus the overall probability is bounded by δ. ∎

Let us remark that the depth of the fault-tolerant circuit $\tilde{C}$ may be larger up to a factor $O(\log k) \leq O(\log\log A)$ because the coding and decoding subcircuits have logarithmic depth in the number $\Theta(k)$ of their inputs.

Next we will establish the corresponding result for clocked circuits.

Definition 3.3 *The **computation time** of a clocked circuit is the number of synchronous steps starting when the first external input bit is read till the last external output bit is computed. Let us call the ratio between the computation time of a fault-tolerant circuit and the original one the **time delay**.*

A clocked circuit may be feed with new input vectors before the computation for the first input vector has been finished. At certain time steps, which not necessarily have to be spaced equally, such a new computation may start. The **average period** of a clocked circuit is defined as the average number of steps one has to wait before the computation on the next input vector can proceed. Correspondingly a **period delay** may occur if a clocked circuit is made fault-tolerant.

As already discussed in the introduction we assume that the computation time T of a clocked circuit is polynomially bounded in its size S, that means for the total number of bit operations $T \cdot S$: $\Theta(\log T \cdot S) = \Theta(\log S) = \Theta(\log A)$.

Theorem 3.4 *Let C be a clocked circuit with a layout of area A and a w–clustergraph, $w \geq \Omega(\log A)$, that can be embedded into a grid of area $O\left(A/w^2 \log^2 A\right)$ assuming a cable capacity $\log A$. Then for the error model a2)–b2) there exists an equivalent fault-tolerant clocked circuit $\tilde{C}$ that can be embedded in area $O(A)$. The time delay is at most $O(\log\log A)$ whereas the average period does not increase.*

Proof : The construction is similar to that for combinatorial circuits. In this case the clustergraph is not required to be acyclic. The delay factor for the time is due to encoding and decoding the wire code. This delay causes a synchronisation problem between the two different kinds of wires. External wires are slowed down by a factor of $\Theta(\log\log A)$ while internal wires are subject to a constant time loss only. The internal wires are artificially delayed by inserting series of id-gates. We therefore assume that each cluster enlarged by these additional gates can still be embedded into a grid of area $O(w^2)$.

These modifications uniformaly slow down the computation time by a factor $\tau \leq O(\log\log$ The average period, however, can be kept the same since the length of every cycle in C is multiplied exactly by τ and no additional cycles are created in $\tilde{C}$. Hence, whenever a new computation starts in C in each of the corresponding τ steps of $\tilde{C}$ a new input vector can be given to the fault-tolerant equivalent. ∎

We will now consider conditions for a w-cluster graph H of a circuit C with $\mathbf{area}(C) = A$ and its layout on a grid of area $A_1 \leq O(\mathbf{area}(C)/w^2)$ such that a compaction to a grid of larger cable-capacity is possible. Let the layout of H be denoted by $\mathcal{L}$.

Theorem 3.5 *For a given circuit C the layout $\mathcal{L}$ of its clustergraph H can be compacted to a grid of area*

$$A_2 \leq O\left(\frac{\mathbf{area}(C)}{w^2 \cdot \log^2 \mathbf{area}(C)}\right)$$

if one can find parameters n_{clust} and n_{edge} with $n_{\mathrm{edge}} \geq \max\{n_{\mathrm{clust}}, \log^2 \mathbf{area}(C)\}$ and a partition $\mathcal{P}$ of the grid points of $\mathcal{L}$ into disjoint subsets $T_1, T_2, \ldots$ with the following properties:

1) *For all T_i the number of clusters mapped to its grid points is at most n_{clust}.*

2) *Count the number of grid edges, which have one endpoint in T_i and the other outside that set and onto which a cable of H is embedded. This number does not exceed n_{edge}.*

3) *Let $\tilde{H} = (\mathcal{P}, E(\tilde{H}))$ be the graph consisting of all edges (T_i, T_j) such that for some $t' \in T_i, t'' \in T_j$ there is a cable connecting t' and t''. Then $\tilde{H}$ can be embedded into a grid of area $O(A_1/n_{\mathrm{edge}})$.*

Before giving the proof let us motivate these conditions. A set $T_i \in \mathcal{P}$ denotes a part o the grid on which H is embedded. Condition 1 means that each T_i should not contain too many clusters. Condition 2 restricts the number of neighbours for such a set. The last condition, for example, is satisfied if all the sets are subgrids of the same shape. In such a case $\tilde{H}$ can be chosen as a grid. While this would be too restrictive, condition 3 is also satisfied if the subgrids have different shapes, but the picture is still similar to a grid. This property can be achieved if there is a quite uniform distribution of the clusters in the layout. Condition 3 is weak if the number $|\mathcal{P}|$ of sets is small. But then n_{edge} must be large and the following inequalities show that this implies the number of clusters of the circuit to be small:

$$|H| \leq n_{clust} \cdot |\mathcal{P}| \leq n_{clust} \cdot O\left(\frac{A_1}{n_{edge}^2}\right) \leq O\left(\frac{\text{area}(C)}{w^2 \log^2 \text{area}(C)}\right).$$

In fact, if $|H| = \Theta(\sqrt{A_1})$ then we can choose $|\mathcal{P}| = 1$ and $n_{edge} = n_{clust} = |H|$ and this condition becomes trivial.

Proof : It suffices to explain how the reliable version of a subcircuit corresponding to a set T_i of the partition is embedded into a square of area $O(w\,n_{edge} \times w\,n_{edge})$. If $n_{edge} = \gamma \log^2 A$ for some constant γ then place reliable versions of the clusters on a $\gamma \log A \times \gamma \log A$ square implementing the interconnecting cables with at most one change of direction. This results in at most $O(\log A)$ cables per grid line. The routing of the $O(\log^2 A)$ cables that are connected to clusters of other subsets can be done according to property 3) because each edge has a capacity of $\log A$ cables. If n_{edge} is larger then we build $n_{edge}/\log^2 A$ such squares and place them on the diagonal of a large $(n_{edge}/\log^2 A) \times (n_{edge}/\log^2 A)$ square. ∎

Observe that bytewise computations naturally arise in circuits performing integer arithmetic. In the last chapter we will give examples of such fault-tolerant circuits for some well known functions: sorting bit strings, multiplying two integers and cyclic shift.

4　The Separator Construction

If the original circuit cannot easily be partitioned bytewise or the clustergraph cannot be layed out nicely, one can try a recursive strategy to construct a reliabe version with small redundancy in area: Split the graph of the circuit by appropriate separators, embed reliable equivalents of the different parts individually and finally install reliable conncections between these parts.

Definition 4.1 *A triple (V, M, E) is a **marked graph** if (V, E) is a graph and $M \subseteq V$. M is called the set of the **marked vertices**. Let $G = (V, E)$ be a graph with n vertices. We say G satisfies a **marking separator theorem** with separators of size $f(m)$ if there is a system $\mathcal{G}$ of marked subgraphs G' of G and constants α, β with $1 \leq \beta \leq \alpha^{-1/2}$ such that $(G, \{\}, E) \in \mathcal{G}$ and any $G' = (V', M', E') \in \mathcal{G}$ of size larger than some constant can be partitioned into two marked subgraphs $G_1 = (V_1, M_1, E_1)$, $G_2 = (V_2, M_2, E_2)$ with the following properties:*

1) $V' = V_1 \dot{\cup} V_2$,

2) $E_i = V_i^2 \cap E'$ for $i = 1, 2$,

3) $\alpha |V'| \geq |V_i|$ for $i = 1, 2$,

4) $|E' \backslash (E_1 \cup E_2)| \leq f(|V'|)$,

5) $M_i = (M' \cap V_i) \cup X_i$ for $i = 1, 2$, where X_i denotes the vertices in V_i incident to some edge in $E' \backslash E_i$.

6) $|M' \cap V_i| / |M'| \leq \beta |V_i| / |V'|$ for $i = 1, 2$.

7) for all $(v_1, w_1), (v_2, w_2) \in E' \backslash (E_1 \cup E_2)$ there is no directed path in G from w_1 to v_2.

Conditions 1)–4) correspond to the standard definition of a separator property. The marking of vertices serves the following purpose. Splitting the graph there remains connections between the different parts that havwe to be established. To keep track of such edges the incident vertices are marked. When splitting a graph at least a fraction $1/\beta$ of such vertices should be left in each half.

Condition 7 can be dropped in case of clocked circuits because there acyclicity is not necessary. Leiserson has shown in [L80] that a noiseless circuit with an (ordinary) f–separator can be embedded in area $O(f^2(|C|))$. We will prove that a fault-tolerant layout using asymptotically the same amount of area is also possible.

Theorem 4.2 Let C be a Boolean circuit with $\mathbf{area}(C) = \Theta(f^2(|C|))$ such that its underlying graph satisfies a marking separator theorem with separators of size $f(m) = \Theta(m^{\xi+1/2} \log^s m)$ for some $\xi > 0$ and $s \in \mathbb{R}$. Then for the failure model a2)–b2) one can construct an equivalent fault-tolerant circuit $\tilde{C}$ with $\mathbf{area}(\tilde{C}) \leq O(\mathbf{area}(C))$.

Proof : We extend Leiserson's technique to marked graphs. If one wants to construct a reliable version things get more complicated. Edges cannot be routed independently and additional space for partitioning and coding is needed. Subcircuits corresponding to the subgraphs in $\mathcal{G}$ are embedded recursively; all wires entering or leaving such a subgraph form a **thick cable**. To embed $G' \in \mathcal{G}$, embed the subgraphs G_1, G_2, connect the wires from one subgraph to the other, and let the rest of the wires form the thick cable emerging from G'.

For the reliable version let the thick cables be ensembles of cables with a logarithmic number of wires that use the code described above for information transfer. Since cables split twice for each level in the separating hierarchie, one has to decode and encode in between in order to recombine the information bits for new cables. We shall manage to do that with a constant number of "byte operations" for each new cable.

Let μ be a large constant. Split each cable according to the subgraph in which the connected vertices lie, and fill the unused bits with zeroes. Then these parts are split into

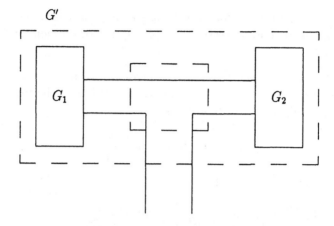

Figure 1: Decomposition of a subgraph G' for the separator construction. In the small dashed box a rearrangement of the codebits is performed due to the splitting of cables.

subcables of k/μ used bits each. Since that requires decoding, and it is known from the design which bits are used, we can arrange that for each original cable we get at most one small cable with unused bits. Now we combine μ such subcables to form a new cable. Assume that in the thick cable emerging from G' at most half of the bits do not get used. Let it consist of x cables. Then the part connected to G_1 carries at least $(1 - \alpha\beta)xk/2$ information bits and at most kx/μ unused bits. Thus in the thick cable emerging from G_1 at most half of the bits do not get used if

$$\frac{1/\mu}{(1 - \alpha\beta)/2 + 1/\mu} \leq \frac{1}{2} \,,$$

which can be achieved by choosing μ large enough, since $1 - \alpha\beta > 0$.

One can show that the area required for the transformation of x cables is bounded by $O(x^2)$ if $x \geq \Omega(\log^2 A)$: Place the clusters on the diagonal of the super grid and choose the sets $T \in \mathcal{P}$ required by theorem 3.5 as $\log A \times \log A$ subgrids.

It remains to bound the necessary area for the entire construction. Let $g(m)$ be the number of wires that have to leave a subgraph with m vertices. Then

$$g(|C|) = 0 \quad \text{and} \quad g(m) \leq \max_{1-\alpha \leq \gamma \leq \alpha} f\left(\frac{m}{\gamma}\right) + \gamma\beta\, g\left(\frac{m}{\gamma}\right) \,.$$

This implies

$$g(\alpha_1 \cdots \alpha_i\, |C|) \leq \sum_{j=0}^{i-1} f(\alpha_1 \cdots \alpha_j\, |C|)\, \beta^{i-j}\, \alpha_{j+1} \cdots \alpha_i \,,$$

where $1 - \alpha \leq \alpha_1,\ldots,\alpha_i \leq \alpha$ are determined by the decomposition. The right side is maximized if $\alpha_j = \alpha$ for all j. Therefore the following calculations use these values.

Like in the ordinary construction for embedding graphs with separators of size $f(m)$ the area for the subgraphs is now increased by $O(g(m))$ in both dimensions when they are connected.

Define $A(m)$ as the area necessary to embed a subgraph with m nodes that has an $f(m)$-separator. Let $\nu := \lceil \log |C| / \log(1/\alpha) \rceil$. Leiserson considered the function $B(m) := \sqrt{A(m)/m}$ and proved the recursion formula

$$B(m) \;\leq\; B(\alpha\, m) + \frac{f(m)}{\sqrt{m}} \ .$$

Solving this recursion for C one gets

$$B(|C|) \;\leq\; B(1) + \sum_{i=0}^{\nu} \frac{f(\alpha^i |C|)}{\sqrt{\alpha^i |C|}} \ .$$

Let $\tilde{A}(m)$ and $\tilde{B}(m) = \sqrt{\tilde{A}(m)/m}$ be the corresponding values for this construction here. If we stop the partitioning process when $m \leq \sqrt{|C|}$ then

$$
\begin{aligned}
\tilde{B}(|C|) \;\leq\;& \tilde{B}(\sqrt{|C|}) + \sum_{i=0}^{\nu/2} \frac{g(\alpha^i |C|)}{\sqrt{\alpha^i |C|}} \\
\leq\;& \tilde{B}(\sqrt{|C|}) + \sum_{i=0}^{\nu} \sum_{j=1}^{i} \frac{f(\alpha^{j-1} |C|)(\alpha\beta)^{i-j}}{\sqrt{\alpha^i |C|}} \\
=\;& \tilde{B}(\sqrt{|C|}) + \sum_{j=1}^{\nu} \left(\sum_{i=j}^{\nu} \frac{f(\alpha^{j-1} |C|)}{\sqrt{\alpha^{j-1} |C|}} \alpha^{(i-j-1)/2} \beta^{i-j} \right) \\
\leq\;& \tilde{B}(\sqrt{|C|}) + \frac{1}{(1 - \sqrt{\alpha}\beta)\sqrt{\alpha}} \sum_{j=0}^{\nu} \frac{f(\alpha^i |C|)}{\sqrt{\alpha^i |C|}} \\
\leq\;& \tilde{B}(\sqrt{|C|}) + \frac{1}{(1 - \sqrt{\alpha}\beta)\sqrt{\alpha}} B(|C|) \ .
\end{aligned}
$$

Therefore one can achieve constant redundancy if

$$\tilde{B}(\sqrt{|C|}) \;=\; \sqrt{\frac{\tilde{A}(\sqrt{|C|})}{\sqrt{|C|}}} \;\leq\; O(B(|C|)) \;=\; O\!\left(\sqrt{\frac{A(|C|)}{|C|}} \right) ,$$

that means

$$\tilde{A}(\sqrt{|C|}) \;\leq\; O\!\left(\frac{A(|C|)}{\sqrt{|C|}} \right) .$$

Using Pippenger's construction with a logarithmic redundancy it follows

$$\tilde{A}\left(\sqrt{|C|} \right) \;\leq\; O\!\left(A(\sqrt{|C|}) \log^2 |C| \right) \;\leq\; O\!\left(\frac{A(|C|)}{\sqrt{|C|}} \right) ,$$

since $A(m) = \Theta(f^2(m)) = \Theta(m^{1+2\xi} \log^{2s} m)$.

Corollary 4.3 *Let C be a clocked circuit with* $\text{area}(C) = \Theta(f^2(|C|))$ *that satisfies a marking separator theorem as above. Then assuming error model a2)-b2) one can construct an equivalent fault-tolerant circuit $\tilde{C}$ with* $\text{area}(\tilde{C}) \leq O(\text{area}(C))$. *The time delay is bounded by* $O(\log \text{area}(C) \cdot \log\log \text{area}(C))$, *whereas the average period remains unchanged.*

If H is a w–clustergraph of C with $w \geq \Omega(\log \text{area}(C))$ that satisfies a separator theorem with separators of size $f(m)$ and the area needed to embed this graph is of order $\Theta(f^2(|H|))$ then the time delay can be reduced to $O(\log\log \text{area}(C))$.

Proof : Let $A = \text{area}(C)$ and $\lambda = \log \text{area}(C)$. The equivalent for a single original wire may pass through up to $O(\lambda)$ stages of encoding and decoding which increases the length to $L \leq O(\lambda \log \lambda)$. To keep a correct timing wires that do not cross a cut have to be delayed appropriately. We achieve the delay by inserting series of id-gates to such wires after the recursive splitting up to size $\sqrt{|C|}$ has been finished. This operation increases the area by at most L^2. Therefore we get

$$\tilde{A}\left(\sqrt{|C|}\right) \leq O\left(A(\sqrt{|C|}) \cdot \lambda^2 \cdot L^2\right) \leq O\left(A(|C|)/\sqrt{|C|}\right).$$

If the clustergraph H exists then one does not have to split cables. In this case the time delay is bounded by $O(\log\log A)$. ∎

Let us take a look at the special case $f(m) = \Theta(m)$. This gives $\text{area}(C) \leq O(|C|^2)$. In this case no restrictions are necessary and we get the following

Theorem 4.4 *Let C be a combinatorial circuit with* $\text{area}(C) := A \geq \Omega(|C|^2)$. *Then for error model a2) one can construct an eqivalent reliable circuit of area $\tilde{A} \leq O(A)$.*

Proof : The graph associated with C trivially satisfies a separator theorem with $f(m) = 2m$ because of the bounded degree. Also, since the number $g(m)$ of edges leaving a subgraph H with m vertices is bounded by $g(m) = 4m \leq O(f(m))$ anyway, we don't have to take care that they are evenly divided when separating the vertices of H. Thus the conclusion of theorem 4.2 hold. ∎

5 Examples of Area Efficient Reliable Circuits

For many n-input Boolean functions with linear or almost linear circuit size it can be shown by information flow arguments that an internal transfer of $\Omega(n)$ bits has to take place no matter how the circuit is embedded into a 2-dimensional grid. This property implies an $\Omega(n^2)$ lower bound on the area of which the gates occupy only a small portion [U84]. Examples of such functions are

- multiplication of two n-bit integers (using the finite Fourier transform FFT),

- sorting n integers each of size polynomial in n

- cyclic shift of n bits.

For these functions both methods can be used to construct a reliable circuit with constant redundancy for the area. In the examples following clustergraphs are derived performing

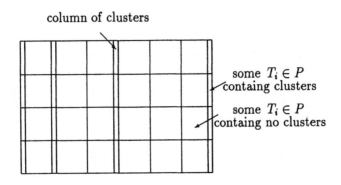

column of clusters

some $T_i \in P$ containg clusters

some $T_i \in P$ containg no clusters

Figure 2: Partition of the clusters

bytewise computations of width $k = \Theta(\log|C|) = \Theta(\log n)$. The clusters are arranged in a small number of vertical columns. The partition $\mathcal{P}$ defined in section 3 can be chosen as follows: Most subsets T_i do not contain grid points onto which clusters are mapped. In the layout such sets look like frames of size $\log^2 A \times \log^2 A$ between the columns of occupied grid points where A denotes the area of an optimal noiseless layout. The other sets contain only $\log^2 A$ clusters from one of the columns. For this partition we can choose both parameters n_{edge} and n_{clust} of order $\log^2 A$. The graph $\tilde{C}$ can be layed out as an $O(A/n_{\text{edge}}) \times O(A/n_{\text{edge}})$-grid as long as the number of columns is at most $O(\sqrt{A}/\log^2 A)$. In the examples below we can achieve a much smaller number.

5.1 Multiplication of Two Integers

According to [BK81] the layout of a Boolean circuit for the multiplication of two n-bit integers requires $\Omega(n^2)$ area. This bound can also be achieved by fault-tolerant circuits. One can compute the product with a small number of gates using the Finite Fourier transform. We may assume that $n = 2^{2t}$ for some $t \in \mathbb{N}$. Each number is subdivided into $(m/2) = 2^{t+1}$ groups of length $(k/4) = 2^{t-1}$ to form vectors in $[GF(2^k + 1)]^m$. The first $m/2$ components are set to zero. Now the FFT is computed using the primitive root $\omega = 2$ for both input integers. The FFT of the product is given by the componentwise product of the FFT of the two numbers. Using the inverse transformation we get the convolution of the two vectors. We get the components y_i of the convolution exactly (not only modulo $2^k + 1$) because

$$0 \leq y_i \leq 2^{k/4} \cdot 2^{k/4} \cdot m = 2^{2^t + t + 2} \leq 2^{2^{t+1}} = 2^k$$

for $t \geq 2$. Bytewise computation is used for the different steps of the FFT and its inverse. Each cluster has to perform one of the following tasks: multiplication of two k-bit integers, reduction modulo $2^k + 1$ of a $2k$-bit integer or addition of two k-bit integers. Each of these operations can be executed in area $O(k^2)$. For the layout of the circuit see figure 3. Cables running diagonally are routed along horizonzal and vertical grid edges.

The number of columns is at most $3 \log n$. Applying the results of section 3 we get

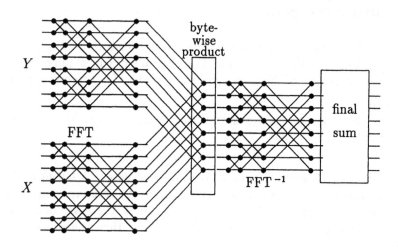

Figure 3: Switching circuit for multiplication with column structured clusters; nodes represent clusters

Theorem 5.1 *The product of two n-bit integers can be computed by a fault-tolerant circuit with a layout of area $O(n^2)$. Therefore the necessary area redundancy is bounded by a constant.*

The separator construction gives a similar result. One can apply the partitioning of theorem 4.2 in such a way that clusters are not split. Looking at the part of the circuit where the FFT is computed one notices that a horizorintal cut in the middle affects n/k cables. A similar cut for one of the two sugraphs affects $n/2k$ cables and so on. Thus the j-th recursive splitting generates subgraphs with $m_j = (n/k) \log(n/k)/2^j$ vertices for this part of the circuit, where $f(m) = n/2^j k = m/\log(n/k) < m/\log m$. The situation here is much easier than in general because each split generates subgraphs with an equal number of cluster and each contains exactly half the marked vertices. This implies the area bound

$$\tilde{A} \leq O(k^2 f^2(m_0)) \leq O(k^2 (n/k)^2) \leq O(n^2).$$

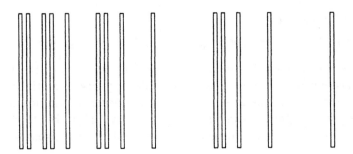

Figure 4: Column structure of the clusters in the sorting circuit

5.2 Sorting Integers

It has been shown that sorting n numbers, each of logarithmic length, requires an information exchange of $\Omega(n \log n)$ bits. Therefore any circuit requires area $\Omega(n^2 \log^2 n)$ and this amount is also sufficient. It can be achieved by fault-tolerant circuits, too.

Theorem 5.2 *n integers of logarithmic length can be sorted by a fault-tolerant circuit of area $O(n^2 \log^2 n)$.*

Proof : The sorted algorithm is based on odd-even merge. A layout is sketched in figure 5. Each cluster compares the two numbers from the entering cables and outputs the smaller one on the upper cable and the larger one on the lower one. The number of columns containing clusters is bounded by $O(\log^2 n)$. Hence theorem 3.2 and 4.2 can be applied.

We can also use the separator construction. By recursive horizontal cuts, in the j-iteration the clustergraph is split into pieces of size $m_j = \Theta\left((n/2^j) \log n)\right)$ by a separator of size

$$f(m_j) \le O((j+1)n/2^j) \le O((j+1)m_j/\log^2 m) .$$

Although this recurrence is not exactly of the form considered in theorem 4.2 direct calculations shows that the result also hold for such a function f. Therefore for a fault-tolerant circuit one can achieve the area bound

$$\tilde{A} \le O(k^2 f(m_0)) \le O(n^2 \log^2 n) .$$

5.3 Cyclic Shift

The cyclic shift problem is defined as follows. Given an input of n bits $x_1, \ldots, x_n$ and a binary number $0 \le t < n$, output $y_1, \ldots, y_n$ so that $y_i = x_{i+t}$ where indices are taken

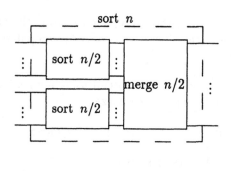

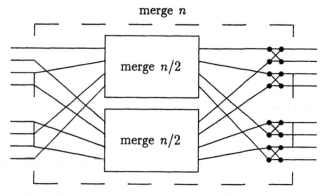

Figure 5: Switching circuit for sorting; nodes represent clusters

modulo n. Alternatively, one may consider the 1-output function

$$\texttt{shift}(x_1,\ldots,x_n,t_{\log n-1},\ldots,t_0,z_1,\ldots,z_n) := \bigvee_{i=1}^{n} x_{i+t} \wedge z_i$$

where $z_1,z_2,\ldots,z_n$ are n additional inputs. One can show that every Boolean circuit for f requires area $\Omega(n^2)$. Again we can meet this bound by a fault-tolerant layout.

Theorem 5.3 *The function* $\texttt{shift}$ *can be computed by a fault-tolerant circuit of area* $O(n^2)$.

Proof : To construct such a reliable circuit every $k = \log n$ subsequent bits of the x_i and the z_i are gathered to form a "byte". Each of the bits of the number t forms one byte by itself. For each bit of t there is one column of n/k clusters (for simplicity assume that k divides n). Thus we can index the clusters as M_{ij} where $1 \leq i \leq n/k$ and $0 \leq j \leq \lfloor \log n \rfloor$. The clusters M_{ij} get as inputs the outputs of $M_{i,j-1}, M_{i+\lfloor 2^j/k \rfloor,j-1}$, and $M_{i+\lfloor 2^j/k \rfloor,j-1}$, and the j-th bit of t. For $j = 0$ the inputs are the appropriate input bytes of the circuit. The first index is taken modulo n. Each cluster forwards what comes from $M_{i,j-1}$ if t_j is 0, and the appropiate bits from the other two clusters if t_j is 1. Finally the disjunction of the $y_i \wedge z_i$ can easily be computed. Again, clusters appear in only $O(\log n)$ columns.

Applying the separator embedding to the circuit using horizontal cuts we get subcircuits of size $m_j = \Theta(n \log n / 2^j)$ by separators of size

$$f(m_j) \leq O(n/2^j) \leq O(m_j / \log m_j) \ .$$

Therefore we get a reliable layout with area

$$\tilde{A} \leq O(f^2(m_0)) \leq O(n^2) \ .$$

∎

6 Conclusion

We have shown for combinatorial and clocked circuits that under certain topological conditions reliable computation is possible with constant or almost constant redundancy of the circuit layout area. This holds for many functions with noiseless circuits of area superlinear in the circuit size. If the area grows only linear, as it is the case for the *parity*-function or the *or*-function, then the necessary logarithmic redundancy for the circuit size trivially implies the same bound for the area. It remains an open problem to prove nonconstant area redundancy bounds for functions with larger layout area.

To achieve these area efficient fault-tolerant layouts we use a special code to transmit information between gates. Since the constants evolving from these contructions are not very small the results so far are more of theoretical interest. It would be of practical importance to find simpler codes for this purpose, or even codes for which computation and information transfer can both be performed efficiently (compare [BGW88]). This would save a lot of overhead for coding and decoding between clusters and cables.

References

[A84]   R. Ahlswede, *Improvements of Winograd's Result on Computation in the Presence of Noise*, IEEE Tr. on Information Theory 30, 1984, pp. 872–877.

[BGW88] M. Ben-Or, S. Goldwasser, A. Wigderson, *Complexity Theory for Noncryptographic Fault-Tolerant Distributed Computations*, Proc. 20th STOC, 1988, pp. 1-10.

[BK81]   R. Brent, H. Kung *The Chip Complexity of Binary Arithmetic*, J. ACM 28, 1981, pp. 521-534.

[BS88]   P. Berman, J. Simon, *Investigations of Fault-Tolerant Networks of Computers*, Proc. 20th STOC, 1988, pp. 66–77.

[DO77a]   R. Dobrushin, S. Ortyukov, *Lower Bound for the Redundancy of Self-Correcting Arrangements of Unreliable Functional Elements*, Prob. Inf. Trans. 13, 1977, pp. 59-65.

[DO77b]   R. Dobrushin, S. Ortyukov, *Upper Bound for the Redundancy of Self-Correcting Arrangements of Unreliable Functional Elements*, Prob. Inf. Trans. 13, 1977, pp. 203-218.

[G86]   P. Gács, *Reliable Computation with Cellular Automata*, J. Comp. System Sciences 32, 1986, pp. 15–78.

[G88]   P. Gács, private communication, 1988.

[G91]   A. Gál, *Lower Bounds for the Complexity of Reliable Boolean Circuits with Noisy Gates*, Proc. 32. FoCS, 1991, pp. 594-601.

[GR88]   P. Gács, J. Reif, *A Simple 3-Dimensional Real-Time Reliable Cellular Array*, J. Comp. System Sciences 36, 1988, pp. 125–147.

[LT80]   R. Lipton, *Application of a Planar Separator Theorem*, SIAM Comp. 9, 1980, pp. 615–627.

[K73]   A. Kuznetsov, *Information Storage in a Memory Assembled from Unreliable Components*, Prob. Inf. Trans. 9, 1973, pp. 254-264.

[N56]   J. von Neumann, *Probabilistic Logics and the Synthesis of Reliable Organisms from Unreliable Components*, in C. Shannon, J. McCarthy (Ed.), Automata Studies, Princeton University Press, 1956, pp. 43-98.

[P85]   N. Pippenger, *On Networks of Noisy Gates*, Proc. 26th FoCS, 1985, pp. 30–38.

[P89]   N. Pippenger, *Invariance of Complexity Measures for Networks with Unreliable Gates*, J. ACM 36, 1989, pp. 531–539.

[PST91] N. Pippenger, G. Stamoulis, J. Tsitsiklis, *On a Lower Bound for the Redundancy of Reliable Networks with Noisy Gates*, IEEE Trans. Infor. Theory 37, 1991, pp. 639-643.

[RS89]   R. Reischuk, B. Schmeltz, *Area Efficient Methods to Increase the Reliability of Circuits*, Proc. 6th STACS, 1989, pp. 314–326.

[RS91]   R. Reischuk, B. Schmeltz, *Reliable Computation with Noisy Circuits and Decision Trees – A General $n \log n$ Lower Bound*, Proc. 32. FoCS, 1991, pp. 602-611.

[T74]   A. Toom, *Nonergodic Multidimensional Systems of Automata*, Prob. Inf. Trans. 10, 1974, pp. 239–246.

[T89]   G. Turán *Lower Bounds for Synchronous and Planar Circuits*, Inform. Proc. Letters 30, 1989 pp. 37–40.

[U84]   J. Ullman, *Computational Aspects of VLSI*, Computer Science Press, 1984.

[U87]   D. Uhlig, *On Reliable Networks from Unreliable Gates*, Proc. 6. FCT Conference, 1987, pp. 462–469.

[V81]   L. Valiant, *Universality Considerations in VLSI Circuits*, IEEE Tr. on Computers 30, 1981, pp. 135–140.

[W62]   S. Winograd, *Coding for Logical Operations*, IBM J. Res. Delelop. 6, 1962, pp. 430–436.

Lecture Notes in Computer Science

For information about Vols. 1–515
please contact your bookseller or Springer-Verlag